DAVE   886-3499

Susan Brown
Phil 100
Abbott
(416) 444-7015
at Waterloo 884-5878.

THIRD EDITION

The Problems of Philosophy

Edited by

William P. Alston
University of Illinois

Richard B. Brandt
The University of Michigan

ALLYN AND BACON, INC.
Boston   London   Sydney   Toronto

Library of Congress Cataloging in Publication Data

Alston, William P   comp.
  The problems of philosophy.

  Bibliography: p.
  Includes index.
          1. Philosophy—Collected works. I. Brandt,
Richard B. II. Title.
B21.A45 1978   108   77–28886
ISBN 0-205-96110-9

Contents

C. Personal Identity

PART VI The Structure of Knowledge 601

A. Skepticism and the Foundations of Knowledge

B. Is There Knowledge Not Based on Observation?

C. Types of Inductive Inference and Their Justification

D. Knowledge of Other Minds

PART VII Perceiving the Material World 703

Preface

This book is designed to bring together under one cover a wide variety of readings that (a) are philosophically important, (b) treat those parts of philosophy with which an educated person should be familiar, and (c) are sufficiently clear and well-written to be understandable and interesting to the average college student. We have not included all the problems, much less all the readings, we would have liked to include. Those readings we have selected seem to us to be both important and suitable as a doorway into the subject.

The third edition, like the first two, is primarily concerned with the major traditional problems of philosophy. We do not share the view, currently held by some of our colleagues, that the average college student cannot understand these problems or will not be interested in them. Our experience is to the contrary. It is true, however, that many important philosophers do not excel in literary style. In this edition, we have made a number of replacements that make the major points more lucidly and simply, without loss of content. We believe beginners in philosophy will make better headway if they need not struggle with confusions, unnecessary complications, or a ponderous style. Fortunately, this policy has not entailed the elimination of the greatest figures in the history of philosophy, most of whom knew how to write: Plato, Aristotle, Anselm, Aquinas, Descartes, Hobbes, Locke, Berkeley, Hume, Kant, Mill, Nietzsche, and, more recently, James and Russell. Readings from the twentieth century are still in the majority; this stems not from a preference for the contemporary as such, but from our aim to choose the selection that best presents an important point of view, irrespective of the date of authorship.

The most extensive change in the present edition is the introduction of a new section on concrete moral problems. This section includes two conflicting points of view on abortion and a similar contrast on suicide. The inclusion of this material is not inconsistent with our earlier affirmation that the book focuses on the major traditional problems of philosophy. That focus by no means excludes considering the application of basic principles, in this case ethical principles, to concrete problems of daily life. On the contrary, the fact that the philosophical principles have such a bearing is one reason for the perennial significance of philosophy.

The introductions to the various parts have been rewritten. These introductions are intended to explain what the problems are and to provide a wider context within which the student can see the main points made by the selections, as well as their interconnections. Where an important position or argument could not be represented in the readings, we have made some reference to it in our introduction; hence, the student can hope to gain a reasonably adequate view of the problem as a whole.

The bibliographies at the end of each part have been updated in this edition. Our aim in compiling these bibliographies has been to provide lists of readings that the beginning student will find helpful in preparing papers— often the most valuable educational experience in a course in philosophy. The bibliographies are organized around topics that seem to us suitable for student papers. Presumably, every student will be interested in at least some of them, and every student will find a few topics of a level of difficulty suitable to his/her background and abilities. We have had particularly in mind the problems of students in large classes at institutions with limited library facilities. We have, therefore, as far as possible, listed readings that are available in anthologies, especially paperbacks, with the thought that the instructor can order an adequate quantity of these for the library. At the end of the book is a list of anthologies to which reference is made in the lists of readings at the end of each part. The contemporary proliferation of anthologies provides such overwhelming riches that we must apologize for the omission of those that have escaped our notice.

It is impossible to cover all the readings in this book in a one-semester course. We have provided a surplus in order to make possible different selections in accordance with the predilections of students and instructors. We feel the instructor *must* ignore certain readings and even whole sections, else the student will be overwhelmed. There is also room for choice in the order in which the parts are covered; each part has been prepared as an independent unit, though there are cross-references in the introductions. The order of presentation in the book is one that many instructors will like, but we feel that an equally sound course could be constructed beginning with the free-will problem, with ethics, or with epistemology. Whichever order is used, an instructor may wish to have students read the introduction to Part VI at the outset, since certain crucial distinctions that recur throughout the book (analytic-synthetic, a priori-a posteriori) are introduced there.

This work is a joint product. The choice of selections has been the result of lengthy discussion, and we have both had a hand in all the introductions. However, William Alston has the primary responsibility for Parts I, IV, and V, and Richard Brandt for Parts II, III, VI, and VII.

We wish to express gratitude to our students at the University of Michigan and Swarthmore College for giving us the benefit of their reactions to our introductory classes over the years: their complaints, their enthusiasms, their puzzled queries, even their occasional boredom. These all have helped us to make this a more useful book than it otherwise would have been.

William P. Alston
Richard B. Brandt

Introduction

This volume is designed to introduce the reader to philosophy by presenting some of the best discussion of some of its major problems. When the reader has mastered these discussions, he will have an accurate conception of what philosophy is; he will have first-hand acquaintance with philosophical problems and with the kinds of reasoning by which philosophers try to solve these problems.

At the outset, the student may find it useful to have a rough conception of the territory into which she is about to move; we shall now attempt to provide this. It should not be expected that this initial characterization of philosophy will be fully intelligible to the student before she has studied any actual examples of philosophizing. The best plan is for the student to read this introduction at the outset, for whatever impressions she can glean, and then return to it after having completed a study of the book. On this later reading, the student will have a vivid and concrete understanding of the various points made here concerning the nature of philosophy because of the many examples of philosophy she will have in mind.

DEFINITION OF PHILOSOPHY

Philosophy cannot be given the simple, straightforward definition in terms of subject matter that is possible for some subjects. Sociology can be defined as the study of society and zoology as the study of animals. Philosophy has no distinctive subject matter; it is about everything. What is distinctive of philosophy is the *questions* it raises. The questions are not all of one kind, although they have a kind of unity, in the sense that very often we cannot arrive at an answer to one question without also answering several others. Nevertheless, they fall into a few major types. We may define philosophy, in terms of its questions, as follows: Philosophy is an attempt to arrive at reasoned answers to *important* questions that fall outside the scope of any particular science, either because they are *normative,* or especially general, or more *fundamental* than the questions the sciences raise, or because they are about the *universe* as a *whole*. First, let us consider some examples of typical philosophical problems, and then we shall say something about the various parts of this rough definition.

TYPICAL PHILOSOPHICAL QUESTIONS

Here is a representative list of philosophical questions that are considered in this book:

I. Religious Belief
1. What is meant by the word "God"? Is there a God in this sense?
2. Do mystics really have a direct experience of God?
3. Do religious statements have meaning, and are they verifiable, in the same way as statements in the sciences?

II. Value and Obligation
4. What kinds of things (events, experiences) are worthwhile or desirable in themselves?
5. What makes actions morally right or wrong?
6. What is it for something to be desirable or right? In other words, what do the words "desirable" and "right" mean, or what should they mean?
7. How, if at all, can ethical beliefs be supported by evidence and argument? Is this anything like the way in which theories in science are supported?

III. Some Social and Personal Moral Problems
8. What may a government legitimately require its citizens to do, or not to do?
9. What principles imply that it is wrong (right) to have an abortion or to commit suicide?

IV. Free Will and Determinism
10. Do human beings ever have a free choice? In what sense of "free"?
11. Are all events, including human actions, causally determined?
12. Under what conditions are people rightfully held responsible for their actions?

V. Mind and Body
13. What is consciousness, and what is its relation to the body?
14. Can persons survive the death of their bodies?
15. Under what conditions does someone remain the *same* person through time?

VI. The Foundations of Knowledge
16. What is it to know something?
17. Can we establish generalizations (and justify predictions of future events) on the basis of observations carried out on a limited sample in the past? (The "problem of induction.")
18. Is it possible (and if so, how) to have knowledge, e.g., in mathematics

and logic, that is not based on observation. (The problem of a *priori* knowledge.)

VII. Perceiving the Material World

    19. What is it to perceive something?
    20. In what way, if at all, is perception a source of knowledge?
    21. In what sense of "material world" do we have reason for thinking that there is a material world?

IMPORTANCE

Our definition of philosophy restricts its purview to important questions. Part of what this means is that the questions are usually questions of *principle,* ones that will be of interest to everybody, at any time or place. You will undoubtedly agree, on reviewing this list, that the questions are all *large* ones, and mostly matters of principle; but you may feel that some questions are lacking in "relevance" and are not of much serious interest to anybody, let alone everybody. It may be worthwhile, then, to show how one is inevitably led into these questions from reflecting on issues that obviously are of universal and vital human concern.

    Let's begin with practical problems of choice, problems with which everyone is faced at one time or another. If you are trying to decide whether to go to graduate school or into business—an issue crucial enough for your future to require a review of what you are basically looking for in life —you can hardly avoid wondering about what makes something worthwhile in itself (question 4). Again, if you are trying to decide whether to join in a demonstration against the construction of a nuclear plant or in favor of gay liberation, and if you reflect deeply about the issue, you are bound to wonder what makes one or another line of action right or wrong (question 5). But once you have begun to consider these questions, it obviously is relevant to ask yourself whether questions of value and obligation can really be given objectively valid answers—and if so, how; or, whether, on the other hand, one person's opinion is just as good as another's (question 7). Now in considering that question, one thing that is crucial is how judgments of value and judgments of obligation are properly interpreted (question 6). For, obviously, what it takes to establish such a judgment depends on just what it says. Again, answers to question 7 differ sharply on whether ethical judgments can be tested by anything like the methods of observation and inductive reasoning used in science. In order to take an intelligent position on that issue, one must consider the nature and justification of the methods of empirical science; and that involves considering such questions as 16, 17, and 20. And so it goes. Starting from matters of universal and inescapable human concern, we see how reflection leads one into ever more abstract and abstruse problems, problems that initially may have seemed remote from any "relevance" to life.

    Let's consider another brief example of the same phenomenon. If we begin with social concerns over whether, for example, victims of social injustice should be punished for their retaliatory actions (such as looting), or whether people who, because of their early home life, have not developed a normal conscience should be held criminally liable or subject to moral disapproval for their misdeeds, one is quickly led into the general question of the nature and conditions of responsibility (question 12). From there it is a short step to thinking about whether the actions of human beings are causally determined, and in what sense persons may be said to have a free choice about what they do, and the bearing of these issues on responsibility (questions 10 and 11).

Among the questions on our list, 21 and its companion 19 are most remote from common concerns. In fact, one caricature of the philosopher is the man who persists in asking, "Do we really know that there is a chair in the corner?" when it is perfectly obvious to everyone else that there is. Nevertheless the authors have hardly ever known a student who did not find such questions important and intriguing, once they saw what the questions were and why philosophers get involved in them.

Of course, many important and vital questions are not within the province of philosophy; for instance, political questions as to how to conduct our foreign policy and medical questions about the causes of various diseases. What distinguishes philosophical questions from other important questions? In our initial definition, we specified various characteristic features of important questions that are distinctively philosophical. We shall now proceed to explain and illustrate these features.

Before doing this, however, it may be helpful to set the matter in an historical context. The roots of modern science and philosophy lie in ancient Greece, at the time of Plato and Aristotle when various forms of intellectual inquiry were going on. Specialists whom we would now classify as scientists or mathematicians were studying astronomy, geometry, and medicine. The people who then, and now, were called philosophers were working on everything else: practical philosophy (how people and society *ought* to be), logic, metaphysics (see below), and "natural philosophy," which included theorizing about the origin of the world, elementary physics, biology, psychology, and similar matters. With advances in technology (such as the invention of the telescope and the microscope) and in experimental method, many parts of "natural philosophy" have become separate provinces and are now studied by empirical scientists. But this separation and specialization did not, and could not, affect all matters investigated by the ancient Greek philosophers. In particular, it did not affect questions of the sort mentioned in our definition of philosophy. This is because, by the very character of these questions, they are not amenable to treatment by mathematics or the empirical sciences. What these questions require is reflection on all relevant considerations and an attempt to arrive at a rational judgment in the light of those considerations. This is the distinctive philosophical method, and philosophy deals with questions that are most appropriately tackled in this manner. Let's apply this point to the various types of questions mentioned in our definition.

NORMATIVE QUESTIONS

We have already indicated that philosophers are concerned with general questions of what it is right or wrong for individuals to do, of what is worthwhile in life, and of when the institutions of a society are morally just. We call these questions *normative,* because they concern how it would be *good* for things to be (how they *ought* to be) rather than how things *actually are.* These questions are about *standards* or *norms.* These are not the only normative questions. Others include, for example, questions of aesthetics, such as what makes a painting or musical composition great.

When we think of these questions as a group, we can see why they are not amenable to experimental investigation, at least in any simple way. The empirical sciences start from observation and experiment; from these data, they seek to establish generalizations and laws that cover the observed facts. At a higher level, they develop theories to explain why the laws are constituted as they are. On the basis of these laws and theories, the sciences predict the future, reconstruct the past, and discover things that are otherwise inaccessible to us, such as the interior of the sun and the structure of the atom. It seems clear that from such a descriptive and law-seeking enterprise one is not going to arrive at any conclusions concerning how man and society *ought* to be, or about what is *worthwhile.*

It is true, however, that scientists sometimes do comment on such matters. Economists make pronouncements as to what is the best economic system, and psychologists make judgments as to what is the best system of education. But if we look carefully, we can see that these normative conclusions follow from their scientific discoveries only if certain broad normative principles are assumed. For example, when dealing with education, social scientists typically assume the normative principle that one thing education ought to do is to develop the intellectual potentialities of the students.

But scientists do not investigate these basic normative principles. What they do, rather, is to use scientific results to apply such principles to specific problems. They use the results of learning theory and other parts of psychology to determine what specific sort of educational system will best develop the potentialities of certain kinds of students. It is the philosopher who takes it upon himself to make a rational judgment concerning basic normative principles themselves. This task requires broadly based critical reflection.

SOME VERY GENERAL QUESTIONS

If we look again at the subjects actively explored in the time of Aristotle that have not been absorbed into modern mathematics and the experimental sciences, we notice metaphysics and some very general problems in the area of natural philosophy. Aristotle thought of metaphysics as at least partly an inquiry about "first principles," about what is true about absolutely everything, irrespective of whether it is inorganic, animate, or human. Many philosophers today are concerned with the descendants of his questions—problems about the nature and logical relations of events, substances, qualities, relations, numbers, space, and time. Here is one such problem. The number nine could not lose some properties, such as being divisible by three, and still be the number nine; but it could lose other properties without this result, such as being the number of the known planets. Now, are some properties essential in this same way to things or persons? For instance, is it essential in this way for *you* to be human? Could *you* be changed into a frog, and still be *you?*—or is this change impossible in the same way it is impossible for nine to cease to be divisible by three? This (possible) distinction between essential and inessential properties intrigues many persons; we concede it is not very relevant to daily living! We think you will agree, however, that it is a problem to be solved by reflection and not by use of experimental methods.

Problems that are this general are not represented in our readings, but two other problems that are nearly as general are found there.

The first, an issue traditionally regarded as "metaphysical," is whether there are two fundamentally different types of substance or occurrence in the world. That is, are there physical things and also mental things (minds), or are minds and bodies essentially the same kind of thing? Alternatively, we can ask: Are there physical events (occurrences like a flash of lightning, or a metal being heated) *and* also mental events (a thought, a daydream); or are all these events really of the same kind?

The second problem, which is in the tradition of "natural philosophy," may also be called a "metaphysical" problem. It is the question of determinism: whether everything that happens is caused to happen in just the way it does. We are not asking what causes some specific type of occurrence, like tides or tornadoes. We are asking whether everything that happens will have *some* determining cause or other.

Why these two questions cannot be handled by experimental method will not be as obvious as in the case of normative questions. But consider the question of determinism. Let us agree that scientists can establish a large number of particular causal laws; for example, that copper expands when heated. How will this enable scientists to find out whether *every* event, of *every* kind, is law-governed? We know that many types of events are instances of laws, such as the motions of the planets. Can we infer from this that *all* events are law-governed? What would justify such an inference? Again, suppose it is shown that a previously accepted law does not in fact govern a certain sort of event. For example, let us say that at one time it was believed that arthritis is caused by exposure to the night air; and then, by carefully controlling experimental conditions, we show that this is not the case. Does this show that arthritis has *no* cause, that it is an example of *no* law? Clearly not; it only shows that we have not yet found the law. (This problem has plagued physicists who have said that quantum phenomena are governed only by statistical laws; their colleagues who are unconvinced can always say: "It's just that we have not yet found the deterministic laws that govern these phenomena.") Thus, it seems that the question of determinism is not a question for experiment; again, it requires *reflection* on a variety of considerations, some from within and some from outside science.

Experimental methods are also not suited to determine whether there is only one fundamental type of substance or event; at a later point we shall see why.

THE PROBLEM OF "FOUNDATIONS"

We come now to a type of problem that is the contemporary descendant of
what in Aristotle's day would have been considered a branch of logic.
This problem concerns the "foundations" of both science and everyday
beliefs and has two aspects. Let us begin with science and see the two ways
in which philosophers are concerned about foundations.

In the first place, just by engaging in scientific research, the scientist
presupposes or assumes that certain principles are true. A philosopher
who then explores the justification for believing these principles is thereby
attempting to provide a *foundation* for the sciences. Question 17 is an
obvious example. Science starts by generalizing from observed regularities.
A chemist, say, notes that all the samples of copper he has observed
have melted at 327 degrees F., and he infers that *all* samples of (pure) copper will probably melt at that temperature (given similar conditions). When
he proceeds in this way, the scientist is using the "method of induction."
A very rough statement of the inductive method is: "Infer that all members of a class will exhibit the regularities exhibited by a properly chosen
sample of that class." In using this method, the scientist is assuming that it
is a valid method of inference. It is this assumption that is under scrutiny in
the philosophical problem of induction. The philosopher asks whether
the inference is valid, and if so, what makes it valid. That is, the philosopher's
concern is to examine critically an assumption that the scientist makes,
and, in fact, has to make if she is to do experimental science, but that is not
part of her special job to investigate. We can see this kind of relationship
in many spheres. Induction is, in a sense, a tool the scientist uses. Just
as the auto mechanic or the carpenter depends on other specialists to produce tools and keep them in good working order, so the scientist does
not take it to be her job as a scientist to shape, or critically examine, the
logical and mathematical tools she uses in making her inferences.

Other questions on our list that are related to scientific activity in much
the same way are questions 18, 20, and 21. The scientist assumes that
the physical world exists and that one can discover things about it through
sense perception. If the scientist did not make these assumptions, she
would not be raising questions about the structure of the physical world and
trying to answer them by observation. Since (physical) science is *defined*
as the empirical investigation of the physical world, these assumptions are
not ones the physical scientist tries to appraise, for a negative appraisal
would imply that physical science cannot exist. If there is no physical world,
there can be no investigation of it; and if one cannot gain knowledge of it
through sense perception, it would not be sensible to investigate it by
observation.

There is a second way in which philosophers are concerned with the
foundations of science. Philosophy is concerned with *making clear* the
basic concepts of science—concepts used by all the sciences and the
special province of none. The concepts of knowledge, theory, explanation,
law, and causal connection are freely used in all the sciences. It is the
job of a physicist to *produce* knowledge and *discover* causal connections,

but not to explain what knowledge or causality *is*. (How would he use a cyclotron to do *that*?) The task of elucidating such concepts is a philosophical one.

So far we have concentrated on the philosopher's concerns with the foundations of the sciences because we wanted to make clear the distinctive business of philosophy, in contrast to the sciences. If we stopped here, one might conclude that philosophy is concerned *only* with the foundations of the *sciences.* Such an inference would be mistaken; philosophy is equally concerned with the foundations of common-sense thinking. Assumptions about what it is to perceive something (question 19) and about the way in which perception can be a source of knowledge (question 20) are present in our ordinary unsystematic perceptual commerce with the world as well as in the methodology of the sciences. Again, in the everyday conduct of life, just as much as in science, we assume that inductive inferences are justifiable. And, as we have already brought out, philosophy is concerned with the foundations of common-sense ethical thinking.

Furthermore, just as philosophers are concerned with clarifying the basic concepts of science, so are they concerned with making clear some basic concepts of ordinary thought: the concepts of a material object, of a person, of causation, of responsibility, of the right and the good, and so on.

THE UNIVERSE AS A WHOLE

Even primitive peoples speculated about the nature and origin of the universe. Virtually every religion embodies some creed about the universe as a whole. One of the earliest forms of philosophy in ancient Greece was the rational criticism of traditional religious myths and doctrines. Thus, from its origin, philosophy has been concerned with this cluster of problems: *Does the universe stem from the creative act of a personal deity, or does it have some other (or no) source? Is there any overall meaning or purpose for the universe? How does man fit into the total picture? Can any religious doctrines on these matters lay claim to truth?* These questions fall outside the purview of science. Science is concerned with exploring the "internal structure" of the physical universe. But the problems we are now considering have to do with the physical universe as a whole and its relations (or nonrelations) with a source that transcends it. Again, this is a matter for *reflection,* taking into account scientific evidence along with whatever else is relevant.

THE METHODS OF PHILOSOPHICAL INQUIRY

We have stressed the point that the method of philosophy basically consists of *reflection* on a variety of considerations relevant to a given issue. This means that the philosopher's activity is of an "armchair" variety. In cheerfully admitting this fact, which is sometimes employed as a reproach against philosophy, we are not implying that philosophy pays no attention to the results of science or to other relevant empirical facts. On the contrary, the philosopher has always felt an obligation to consider any facts that might conceivably be relevant to the problem under consideration. It is, rather, that the distinctively philosophical task begins after the fact-gathering stage of the investigation is complete. The distinctively philosophical role is to gather together whatever might be relevant to the problem, carefully consider the relations of the various pieces of evidence to each other and to the problem, and then arrive at the resolution that best takes all this into account.

We have already observed that the philosopher takes account of considerations drawn from highly disparate quarters. This is such a salient feature of philosophical inquiry that it will bear further elaboration. Scientific investigation generally is carried out within the confines of a methodology that severely limits what can be considered. A psychologist who is conducting an empirical investigation into, for example, the physiology of perception, will consider only the data that can be gathered by careful observation under carefully controlled conditions. However, a philosopher who raises questions about the nature of consciousness, or about whether conscious states are physical in nature (are identical with neural states of the brain), considers not only empirical data of the above sort but also common-sense beliefs, the supposed phenomena of parapsychology, and religious arguments designed to prove the immortality of the soul. This is not to say that a given philosopher will take all these sources of evidence equally seriously. He may even reject some supposedly pertinent considerations as worthless. But still the philosopher is not working within a set of rules that automatically excludes certain kinds of considerations as irrelevant. Just as the empirical scientist is professionally committed *not* to take certain kinds of consideration into account, so the philosopher is professionally committed not to *reject* any consideration without first examining its credentials. If someone comes to a philosopher with a point that he claims to be relevant, the philosopher is duty bound not to dismiss it without a hearing. He must either accept it as relevant or show why it is irrelevant. Philosophy is an attempt to "see the whole picture," to arrive at a resolution of its problems in the light of anything relevant, from whatever province of human experience it comes. Philosophy is the attempt to "get it all together."

It cannot be denied that, in the interest of throwing into relief the distinctive character of philosophy vis-à-vis the specialized sciences, we have overstressed the differences and played down the continuities. In particular, we have slighted the fact that scientists engage in philosophical thinking as part of their scientific activity. A scientist is sometimes forced to examine basic concepts, especially when working in a new area or developing a new type of theory. Dramatic revolutions in science, such as Einstein's Theory of Relativity, force scientists to question basic assumptions, such as the absoluteness of space and time, that they previously had taken for granted. Thus, a more subtle treatment would exhibit philosophical thinking as an aspect of any intellectual inquiry, an aspect that, in professional philosophy, occupies the center of the stage.

THE IMAGE OF THE PHILOSOPHER

There have been two seemingly disparate popular images of the philosopher: the gadfly ("fundamental" questions) and the sage (normative questions and questions about the universe as a whole). The gadfly is the skeptic, the person who questions basic assumptions and concepts. She goes around asking people what they *mean* by "good" or "know." She challenges comfortable common-sense assumptions: that chairs continue to exist when no one sees them, that perception is a source of knowledge, that conventional morality has a rational justification, that human beings have a free choice between alternatives. This is the clever reasoner, the person with a sharp eye for distinctions and a quick wit for objections. She is more adept at tearing down than at building up and delights in reducing interlocutors to confusion. The sage is the person of wisdom, who by dint of long reflection and deep experience has attained a synoptic view of things, a profound understanding of the universe and of the good for man. Which of these is the true picture of the philosopher? Both, and neither. As our brief characterization suggests, they are both deeply imbedded in the philosophical enterprise. A given philosopher usually will exhibit one aspect more than the other, sometimes one to the exclusion of the other. But the greatest philosophers always have exemplified both to a high degree. It is one of the striking features of Plato's picture of Socrates in his *Dialogues,* that Socrates appears both as the supreme gadfly, troubling his fellow Athenians with his persistent questioning until they put him to death, and, at the same time, as the most inspired of sages, with a comprehensive vision of man in the universe.

You may find some of the readings that follow not easy to understand. You doubtless will not be surprised by this, in view of the foregoing characterization of philosophy. Any important enterprise is likely to be difficult, especially one as fundamental and as wide-ranging as philosophy. Philosophy has been the work of people who find dealing in abstractions relatively easy. Its problems have engaged the energies of many of the most brilliant people in human history. There is no other discipline that can number such a succession of intellectual giants; perhaps you will bear with them when the going is heavy.

PART I

Religious Belief

Introduction

In the sphere of religion, as elsewhere, philosophy is concerned with both clarifying and criticizing fundamental beliefs. Of course, a religion is much more than a set of beliefs. It is a complex organization of individual and social activities, involving ritual, prayer, and moral effort, as well as theological beliefs. Philosophers, in attempting to understand religion, have paid some attention to all its aspects. Nevertheless, in line with the aim of rational criticism, they have concentrated on religious *beliefs,* since, they have generally supposed, it is only if these are justified that there can be any justification for the rest of the religion. One is justified in praying to the Virgin only if one is justified in believing that the Virgin exists and might be moved by one's prayers.

The religious beliefs on which a philosopher concentrates will be determined by the character of the religious tradition out of which he philosophizes. If this book had been compiled in the context of (East) Indian religion, the focus of this part would have been quite different; our selections would have been much concerned with the beliefs that the spatio-temporal world is illusory and that the only reality is an ineffable feature-less one. However, in our religious tradition, the Judaeo-Christian, the fundamental beliefs are the existence of an omnipotent, supremely good personal creator of the world (God)[1] and the immortality of man. The other distinctive beliefs rest on these two, for they all have to do with the nature, plans, and activities of God, especially as concerns man, and with the conditions of one rather than another sort of life after death. Some consideration of the question of immortality will be found in Part IV. This first section focuses on the belief in the existence of God, hereinafter termed *theism.*

Most prominent European philosophers from Plato onward have attempted to provide a rational justification for theism. Most of these attempts have involved using one or another of the classic triad of arguments—the Ontological Argument, the Cosmological Argument, and the Teleological

---

1. According to orthodox Christian theology the creator is *three* persons in one substance, rather than strictly a single person, but we shall have to ignore that refinement.

Argument. The latter two have the form of hypothetical arguments. (See Reading 58) They start with some pervasive fact about the world and argue that God is required for an adequate explanation of this fact. The Ontological Argument, by contrast, is purely *a priori;* it employs no factual premise. Its contention is that just by reflecting on the concept of God one can see that God exists.

THE ONTOLOGICAL ARGUMENT

In Reading 1, St. Anselm argues as follows: Try to deny the proposition to be proved (the existence of God) and one falls into a contradiction. For the concept of God is the concept of an absolutely perfect being ("that than which nothing greater can be conceived"). And among the things that make one being more perfect than another is existence; it is better to exist than not to exist. Hence, if we were to deny that God exists we would be asserting that the most perfect being lacks a perfection; in Anselm's words, we would be supposing that one can conceive something greater than *that than which nothing greater can be conceived.* And this is a contradiction. Hence, there is no consistent alternative to admitting that God exists.

The late Alfred North Whitehead once said that the greatest accomplishment in philosophy is to be refuted afresh in each century. By this standard, St. Anselm deserves highest honors. Most of his successors have been convinced that the argument is invalid; surely, proving the existence of God could not be that easy. Many of them have had a shot at specifying what is wrong with it. But no one is quite satisfied with the refutations of others, and so the issue remains a live one. In the process, philosophers have been stimulated to dig deeply into the logic of existential statements. The most common criticism, first made prominent by Immanuel Kant, is that it is a mistake to regard existence as a property, and hence a mistake to think of it as one of the properties that something must have if it is to be perfect. This criticism is set forth in Reading 8 and foreshadowed by the contention of Cleanthes in Hume's *Dialogues* (Reading 4) that "there is no being whose nonexistence implies a contradiction," since "Whatever we conceive as existent, we can also conceive as nonexistent."

THE COSMOLOGICAL ARGUMENT

The first three of Aquinas' five arguments (Reading 2) are variant forms of what has come to be called the "Cosmological Argument," the argument from the existence of the "cosmos," the physical universe. Aquinas's exposition is difficult for the novice to follow, both because of its compression and because it employs modes of thought that are unfamiliar today. The contemporary explanation by Copleston in Reading 3 should help the student follow Aquinas's argument.

It also will be helpful to have a restatement that presents the essentials of the Thomistic arguments in more contemporary terms. The underlying

thought of the first two arguments can be explained as follows. First, a
a crucial distinction between:

    1. A being that is brought into existence and conserved by the activity
of other things, as an animal is generated by its parents and conserved by
the food it eats. Call such a being "contingent."

    2. A being that does *not* depend on anything outside itself for its exist-
ence, but simply exists by the necessity of its own nature. Call such a being
"necessary."

    Aquinas contends that the things that make up the physical world are
all contingent. Hence, to explain any one of them, A, we must specify one or
more other things, B, that brought A into existence or conserves it. Now
what about B? If it is a necessary being, the explanation ends. We have
reached an ultimate source of other things that does not itself depend on
anything further for *its* existence. But if B in turn is contingent it, in turn,
depends for its existence on C, which in turn. . . . An infinite regress of
causes is impossible. Therefore, if we begin tracing a causal chain back from
a contingent being, sooner or later we will come to a necessary being.
There cannot be any contingent beings unless there is at least one necessary
being.

    The crucial assumption of this argument is the impossibility of an infinite
regress of causes, and most criticism has focused on this point. However,
it is important for the critic to make sure that he has understood just what
Aquinas is claiming. Nagel, in Reading 8, invokes the mathematics of infinity
to support the claim that an infinite regress of causes is quite conceivable;
but even if there are infinite series in pure mathematics, this does not show
that an infinite series of *causes* is possible. Even after we realize that Aquinas
is talking specifically about *causes,* we may suppose that what he claims to
be impossible is an infinite temporal series of causes, in which each cause
precedes its effect in time. If that were his meaning, he would have to
maintain that the physical universe cannot be temporally infinite, that it must
have had a beginning in time. But elsewhere Aquinas argues that we cannot
establish that conclusion by rational argument. As Copleston points out,
what Aquinas had in mind is a series of contemporaneous causes, arranged
in a hierarchy, with each cause sustaining the activity of the cause next lower
down. Thus, when I am writing, we might think of my hand continuously
keeping the pen active, my brain keeping my hand going. . . . But this idea
of a nontemporal, hierarchically arranged series of causes within the physical
world is so unfamiliar to contemporary thought that Copleston has difficulty
in finding plausible illustrations. We therefore are led to wonder whether
the essential line of argument might not be freed from its dependence on
the thought world of medieval physics. We can do this, and we can avoid any
assumptions at all about the details of the physical universe, by taking as
our starting point (for causal explanation) not some particular thing within
the universe but the universe as a whole. So transformed, the argument
will run as follows:

1. The physical universe is temporally either finite or infinite.
2. If it is finite, the beginning of its existence must have been due to some
   cause.
3. If it is infinite, there must be some cause, A, the action of which is re-

sponsible for the fact that this universe exists rather than some other, and rather than none at all.
4. If A owes its existence to some other cause B in a similar manner, the same question arises for B.
5. An infinite regress of causes is impossible.
6. Therefore, at some point we will encounter a necessary being.

This formulation clearly brings out the essential claim of the Cosmological Argument, that the physical universe is not self-sufficient but ultimately depends for its existence on a being that is self-sufficient. And it brings out that claim without presupposing any particular conception of the internal structure of the universe.

However, we are still confronted with the question of why one should suppose an infinite regress of causes to be impossible. It must be admitted that Aquinas' argument for this in his first two "ways" is blatantly circular. In the first way he writes: "But this cannot go on to infinity, because then there would be no first mover, and consequently, no other mover, seeing that subsequent movers move only inasmuch as they are moved by the first mover." Of course, *if* subsequent movers move only inasmuch as they are moved by the first mover, then we can't have any movers unless we have a first mover! But that is the whole question. Why suppose that subsequent movers move only inasmuch as they are moved by the first mover? But despite the vacuity of the explicit argument, Aquinas does strike deep roots in common modes of thought. It is difficult to think of existence or motion being passed along from one link to another in a causal chain without having originated somewhere. Whether there are more solid reasons behind this intuition is something we shall have to leave unresolved.

Even if we admit that there is a necessary being, we may still ask whether such a being will have the characteristics traditionally ascribed to God. Must we think of a necessary being as an omnipotent benevolent personal deity? Why shouldn't the physical universe be a necessary being? Must there be only one? (The second of these queries is posed by Nagel in Reading 8.) All of these doubts would be stilled by a demonstration that a necessary being will have all the features we expect in God, including uniqueness. That is precisely what Aquinas attempts in the section of the *Summa Theologica* following the five arguments. Thus, that section represents his attempt to justify phrases such as "this all men speak of as God," with which he ends each of the arguments. The reader is referred to the *Summa* for details.

THE TELEOLOGICAL ARGUMENT

The Teleological Argument begins from more specific facts about the world, and thereby aims at a more specific conception of the creator. The sort of fact cited is, as Aquinas puts it in his "fifth way," that "things which lack knowledge, act for an end, and this is evident from their acting always, or nearly always, . . . so as to obtain the best result." In the Middle Ages, this argument was propounded in the context of a teleological physics, in which one thinks of all natural processes as goal directed; for example, it was believed that solid bodies move downward when unimpeded because they are seeking their "proper place," the center of the earth. With the development of a mechanistic physics in the sixteenth and seventeenth centuries, the sphere of teleology was restricted to the organic realm. Thus, a more up-to-date formulation would be this: We quite often find that the constitution of animals is such as to fit them for survival and well-being in the conditions in which they live. For example, the ears of rabbits are formed so as to focus sounds coming from the rear, which is normally the direction of greatest danger for them. (Rabbits get chased.) Again, animals engage in very complicated forms of instinctive behavior that is conducive to the survival of the individual and/or species. Certain insects will deposit their eggs on a certain tree at such a time of year that the eggs will hatch just when new leaves are emerging in the spring, thus affording the new larvae an abundant food supply.[2] (Since these phenomena are as if *designed* for the preservation of the species and *adapted* for that purpose, they often are spoken of as cases of "design" or "adaptation," and the argument referred to as the "argument from design.") Now, as Aquinas says, these animals are "without knowledge," or at least without sufficient knowledge (and power) to have planned these matters. A given rabbit did not design his ears with this end in view; nor do the insects in question deposit their eggs at that particular time with the foresight that the hatching will coincide with the emergence of new leaves. Hence, we can explain such cases of adaptation only by supposing that there is a designer "behind the scenes" that has, by conscious foresight, set things up to come out this way.

The argument is sometimes, as in Hume's *Dialogues* (Reading 4), cast in the form of an argument from analogy. An artifact, such as a house or ship, is produced by an intelligent designer to serve certain purposes. Since the universe is like an artifact, in that it exhibits design, we can conclude that it probably was produced by a similar cause.

The elaborate critique of the argument by Philo in Hume's *Dialogues* makes three fundamental points:

1. The analogy between the physical universe and a house or ship is not strong enough to bear the weight of the argument.
2. There are equally plausible alternative explanations for the presence of design, e.g., the idea, based on the analogy between the universe and an organism, that the universe was generated from parent universes. (A more up-to-date version of this criticism would present the Darwinian theory of evolution as an alternative explanation for the adaptation we find in organisms.)
3. Even if the argument is valid, the most it proves is that each case of design is due to some intelligent being. It does not show that all the design in the universe is due to one being, or, if it is, that this one being is onmipotent or perfectly good. (This objection is analogous to the question raised above, as to whether the Cosmological Argument can establish the existence of God, even if it does succeed in establishing the existence of a necessary being.)

---

2. Some versions of the Teleological Argument stress quite different sorts of "design," such as the beauty of the natural world and its intelligibility for the human mind. See the suggested readings at the end of Part I.

RELIGIOUS EXPERIENCE

All the arguments we have been considering seek to provide *indirect* evidence for the existence of God; they are designed to show that we must *suppose* God to exist if we are to set our intellectual house in order. Many believers have felt no need of such indirect evidence because they have supposed themselves to have had a direct experience of the presence of God, at least as direct and unmistakable as our normal sensory experience of physical objects. (Let us call such persons "mystics.") One might take footprints in the snow as an *indication* that someone had been prowling around one's house the night before, but if one had *seen* the prowler one would not need to rely on such indirect indications. The mystic supposes himself to be in the second kind of position with respect to the existence of God.

In Reading 5, James presents a wealth of concrete detail, to illustrate the variety of mystical experiences. He then raises questions about the trustworthiness of such experiences. Though he is sympathetic with the claims of mystics, he arrives at no definite judgment. In Reading 7, Huston Smith examines, in a Jamesian spirit, the idea that psychedelic drugs can trigger off genuine religious experiences of some deeper reality; and he suggests a hypothesis as to how they might have such an effect. In Reading 6, Russell takes the negative side and argues that mystical experiences provide no knowledge.

If one tries to find rational grounds for deciding whether mystical experiences do involve a direct awareness of an objectively existing deity, there are two directions to take. On the one hand, he can look to the testimony of others for confirmation or disconfirmation. On the other hand, he can look at facts about the state of the experiencer that might throw light on the trustworthiness of the experience. Both kinds of considerations have their analogues in the critical examination of sense perception. Thus, if a man claims to have seen a Russian plane flying over Detroit, and we are trying to check up on him, we could determine whether anyone else in the vicinity at that time had seen it, or we could determine whether the man is sane, whether he is emotionally disturbed, and whether he had generally been a trustworthy reporter.

All three writers make use of both approaches. As for the first, all allude to what James calls a "pretty distinct theoretic drift" in the reports mystics make on the basis of their experiences. At widely separated times and places men have claimed to have experiencd an all-encompassing, blissful, unified reality. Smith emphasizes the point that drug-induced experiences can be indistinguishable in this respect from more conventional mystical experiences. However, James admits that he can find this unanimity only by restricting himself to mysticism of the "classical" type, and that when we admit other varieties the mutual confirmation becomes weaker. Some mystics think themselves to be in contact with a personal deity, others with an impersonal absolute unity.

The most common argument along the second line is the negative one presented by Russell. Since mystical experiences spring from abnormal conditions, we cannot expect them to be in correspondence with objective reality. It has been maintained that a person will have mystical experiences only if suffering from some psychotic or neurotic condition, but there is not sufficient evidence for such an extreme position. A more plausible claim would be that mystical experience involves a temporary abnormal state of consciousness and/or the nervous system. But whatever the abnormality alleged, the argument is subject to the retort made by James elsewhere in *The Varieties of Religious Experience:* "If there were such a thing as inspiration from a higher realm, it might well be that the neurotic temperament would furnish the chief condition of the requisite receptivity." Along similar lines, Smith speculates that certain drugs may act on the brain in such a way as to render the individual sensitive to aspects of reality normally closed off to him. In other words, the standards of normality and abnormality that we frame on the basis of what is conducive to success in dealing with the physical environment may not be applicable when dealing with a "supernatural environment." Where the environment is radically different, the conditions of effective and veridical contact with it may be quite different. Sunglasses aid accurate observation in the Arizona desert, but not in the fogbound Aleutians.

THE PROBLEM OF EVIL

Thus far, we have been considering reasons for believing in God. Now it is time to give the atheist his innings and examine grounds for disbelief. Although atheists and agnostics have been in the minority throughout the history of philosophy, they have provided some bases for disbelief, in addition to criticizing arguments on the other side. By far the strongest and best known of these is the problem of evil. Since human beings and other sentient creatures undergo suffering, deprivation, and frustration, how can we suppose that the world is the work of an omnipotent, perfectly good deity? Such a being would not wish to create a world with undesirable features, and, being omnipotent, could create whatever sort of world He preferred. In Reading 9, John Hick, a contemporary Christian thinker, seeks to show how the evildoing and suffering we find in the world might be necessary for the fulfillment of God's purpose to provide an environment in which people can develop morally.

IS THEISM INTELLIGIBLE?

In recent times, antitheistic philosophers have tended to brand theism as meaningless, rather than false.[3] There have always been problems about

---

3. Hence, the use of the term "antitheistic," rather than "atheist." If an atheist is one who holds that it is *false* that God exists, then one who holds the theistic position to be meaningless is not an atheist; a proposition must be intelligible in order to be either true or false. "The slithy toves did gyre and gimble in the wabe" is neither true nor false. It has not gotten so far as to be capable of falsity.

the intelligibility of theism. In Chapters VI–VIII of Reading 1, Anselm struggles to reconcile some apparently discrepant divine attributes, such as being omnipotent *and* incapable of lying, being compassionate *and* not subject to passion. In Reading 4, Demea maintains that terms such as "thought," "love," and "pity" when applied to God cannot mean what they mean in application to human beings. Hence, since we get whatever understanding we have of these terms from our experience of the human qualities so denominated, their meaning as applied to God is "totally incomprehensible, and the infirmities of our nature do not permit us to reach any ideas which in the least correspond to the ineffable sublimity of the Divine attributes." Demea does not explain how, in this case, he can claim not to be speaking gibberish when he affirms belief in a loving God.

This problem becomes more intractable as one's concept of God removes Him more from any similarity to human beings. In less sophisticated religions, where the gods are thought of (at least half-seriously) as existing in a bodily form, it is clear what can be meant by speaking of them as commanding, expressing anger, and forgiving. But in classical Christian theology, God is understood to be not only immaterial and so not existing in space, but as not existing in time either. There is no succession of movements in the divine existence; He exists in an "eternal now." All this poses severe difficulties for interpreting terms that imply temporal succession, such as "think" or "decide," and even greater difficulties for terms that imply bodily movement, such as "punish" or "command." Some theologians, including Aquinas, make things even worse for themselves by insisting that God is absolutely simple and without parts or aspects, so that such activities as deciding and forgiving cannot be really distinct in God. In the face of such difficulties, theists have tried to show that there is enough of the ordinary meaning of the term left to enable us to give some sense to theological statements, while their opponents have argued that there is nothing left, or at least not enough to yield statements with any religious significance.

Today the charge of meaninglessness is most often leveled in the name of the Verifiability Principle. This principle, brought to the fore in the work of the "Vienna Circle," holds that a person is making a genuine assertion only if what he says is capable of empirical confirmation or disconfirmation; that is, only if the truth of what one is saying would make a difference to the future course of our sense experience. This is the point of the parable of the gardener, presented in Reading 10. To take another example, if I assert that a particular object, such as my watch, was brought into existence at a certain time, there are established procedures for testing this. But consider the "hypothesis" that the entire universe came into existence five minutes ago, complete with human beings who seem to remember various things, records of all sorts, architectural ruins, fossils, geological strata, and so on—in short, with all the features our world actually exhibits. In that case, there *could* be no evidence that would provide a basis for choosing between this "hypothesis" and the currently accepted view that the universe has been in existence for billions of years. For any memories, records, or remains that might be adduced as evidence for a longer "career" have already been provided for by the new "hypothesis." Hence, it may be doubted that one who asserted this "hypothesis" is making a serious assertion. Isn't he just playing with words?

There is no doubt that religious beliefs, as held by unreflective believers, have the kind of implications for experience that make empirical test possible (at least in principle). Thus, the theology of a given tribe may be taken to imply that if the rain dance is gone through properly, rain will ensue; and many Christians hold that if one addresses requests to the saints or to the Virgin in certain ways, these requests will be granted. (Believers may be slow to recognize empirical refutations, but that is another matter.) However, as theology becomes more sophisticated, it becomes increasingly difficult to test. One no longer professes to know what God will do under any given conditions, the final consummation is pushed off into the indefinite future, and it looks as if God's love is taken to be compatible with any observable state of affairs whatever. Hence, the suggestion by Flew that "God loves His creatures" has been emptied of any assertive force.

One may respond to this challenge by attacking the Verifiability Principle and arguing that empirical testability is not necessary for one's utterance to constitute a genuine assertion. But none of our authors take that tack. In the responses to Flew included in Reading 10, Hare argues that religious beliefs, though not "assertions," are still fundamental assumptions about the way things are, and are correspondingly important for human life. Mitchell, on the other hand, takes the intermediate position that the believer does allow facts to count against "God loves His creatures" but, being faithful, does not allow anything to count decisively against it. In Reading 11, Hick takes a still different line. He argues that Christian theology is susceptible of an empirical test—not in the present life but after death. Of course, this consideration can show the meaningfulness of theology only if it makes sense to talk about a person's carrying on such a verification after death. Hick's attempt to demonstrate the meaningfulness of this supposition leads him into problems about personal identity, problems concerning the conditions under which we have the *same* person at different times. We shall encounter this issue again in Part IV.

1. St. Anselm

St. Anselm (1033–1109) was Archbishop of Canterbury and the most important philosopher of the eleventh century.

The Inconceivability of God's Nonexistence

Chapter II

Truly there is a God, although the fool hath said in his heart, There is no God.

And so, Lord, do thou, who dost give understanding to faith, give me, so far as thou knowest it to be profitable, to understand that thou art as we believe; and that thou art that which we believe. And, indeed, we believe that thou art a being than which nothing greater can be conceived. Or is there no such nature, since the fool hath said in his heart, there is no God? (Psalms xiv. i). But, at any rate, this very fool, when he hears of this being of which I speak—a being than which nothing greater can be conceived—understands what he hears, and what he understands is in his understanding; although he does not understand it to exist.

For, it is one thing for an object to be in the understanding, and another to understand that the object exists. When a painter first conceives of what he will afterwards perform, he has it in his understanding, but he does not yet understand it to be, because he has not yet performed it. But after he has made the painting, he both has it in his understanding, and he understands that it exists, because he has made it.

Chapters II through VIII of *Proslogium*, tr. by S. N. Deane, Open Court Publishing Company, 1903.

Hence, even the fool is convinced that something exists in the under-standing, at least, than which nothing greater can be conceived. For, when he hears of this, he understands it. And whatever is understood, exists in the understanding. And assuredly that, than which nothing greater can be conceived, cannot exist in the understanding alone. For, suppose it exists in the understanding alone: then it can be conceived to exist in reality; which is greater.

Therefore, if that, than which nothing greater can be conceived, exists in the understanding alone, the very being, than which nothing greater can be conceived, is one, than which a greater can be conceived. But obviously this is impossible. Hence, there is no doubt that there exists a being, than which nothing greater can be conceived, and it exists both in the understanding and in reality.

Chapter III

God cannot be conceived not to exist.—God is that, than which nothing greater can be conceived.—That which can be con-ceived not to exist is not God.

And it assuredly exists so truly, that it cannot be conceived not to exist. For, it is possible to conceive of a being which cannot be conceived not to exist; and this is greater than one which can be conceived not to exist. Hence, if that, than which nothing greater can be conceived, can be con-ceived not to exist, it is not that, than which nothing greater can be con-ceived. But this is an irreconcilable contradiction. There is, then, so truly a being than which nothing greater can be conceived to exist, that it cannot even be conceived not to exist; and this being thou art, O Lord, our God.

So truly, therefore, dost thou exist, O Lord, my God, that thou canst not be conceived not to exist; and rightly. For, if a mind could conceive of a being better than thee, the creature would rise above the Creator; and this is most absurd. And, indeed, whatever else there is, except thee alone, can be conceived not to exist. To thee alone, therefore, it belongs to exist more truly than all other beings, and hence in a higher degree than all others. For, whatever else exists does not exist so truly, and hence in a less degree it belongs to it to exist. Why, then, has the fool said in his heart, there is no God (Psalms xiv. 1), since it is so evident, to a rational mind, that thou dost exist in the highest degree of all? Why, except that he is dull and a fool?

Chapter IV

How the fool has said in his heart what cannot be conceived. —A thing may be conceived in two ways: (1) when the word signifying it is conceived; (2) when the thing itself is under-stood. As far as the word goes, God can be conceived not to exist; in reality he cannot.

But how has the fool said in his heart what he could not conceive; or how is it that he could not conceive what he said in his heart? since it is the same to say in the heart, and to conceive.

But, if really, nay, since really, he both conceived, because he said in his heart; and did not say in his heart, because he could not conceive; there is more than one way in which a thing is said in the heart or conceived. For, in one sense, an object is conceived, when the word signifying it is conceived; and in another, when the very entity, which the object is, is understood.

In the former sense, then, God can be conceived not to exist; but in the latter, not at all. For no one who understands what fire and water are can conceive fire to be water, in accordance with the nature of the facts themselves, although this is possible according to the words. So, then, no one who understands what God is can conceive that God does not exist; although he says these words in his heart, either without any, or with some foreign signification. For, God is that than which a greater cannot be conceived. And he who thoroughly understands this, assuredly understands that this being so truly exists, that not even in concept can it be nonexistent. Therefore, he who understands that God so exists, cannot conceive that he does not exist.

I thank thee, gracious Lord, I thank thee; because what I formerly believed by thy bounty, I now so understand by thine illumination, that if I were unwilling to believe that thou dost exist, I should not be able not to understand this to be true.

Chapter V

God is whatever it is better to be than not to be; and he, as the only self-existent being, creates all things from nothing.

What art thou, then, Lord God, than whom nothing greater can be conceived? But what art thou, except that which, as the highest of all beings, alone exists through itself, and creates all other things from nothing? For, whatever is not this is less than a thing which can be conceived of. But this cannot be conceived of thee. What good, therefore, does the supreme Good lack, through which every good is? Therefore, thou art just, truthful, blessed, and whatever it is better to be than not to be. For it is better to be just than not just; better to be blessed than not blessed.

Chapter VI

**How God is sensible (sensibilis) although he is not a body.—
God is sensible, omnipotent, compassionate, passionless; for
it is better to be these than not be. He who in any way
knows, is not improperly said in some sort to feel.**

But, although it is better for thee to be sensible, omnipotent, compassionate, passionless, than not to be these things; how art thou sensible, if thou art not a body; or omnipotent, if thou hast not all powers; or at once compassionate and passionless? For, if only corporeal things are sensible, since the senses encompass a body and are in a body, how art thou sensible, although thou art not a body, but a supreme Spirit, who is superior to body? But, if feeling is only cognition, or for the sake of cognition—for he who feels obtains knowledge in accordance with the proper functions of his senses; as through sight, of colors; through taste, of flavors,—whatever in any way cognises is not inappropriately said, in some sort, to feel.

Therefore, O Lord, although thou art not a body, yet thou art truly sensible in the highest degree in respect of this, that thou dost cognise all things in the highest degree; and not as an animal cognises, through a corporeal sense.

Chapter VII

How he is omnipotent, although there are many things of which he is not capable—To be capable of being corrupted, or of lying, is not power, but impotence. God can do nothing by virtue of impotence, and nothing has power against him.

But how art thou omnipotent, if thou art not capable of all things? Or, if thou canst not be corrupted, and canst not lie, nor make what is true, false—as, for example, if thou shouldst make what has been done not to have been done, and the like—how art thou capable of all things? Or else to be capable of these things is not power, but impotence, For, he who is capable of these things is capable of what is not for his good, and of what he ought not to do; and the more capable of them he is, the more power have adversity and perversity against him; and the less has he himself against these.

He, then, who is thus capable is so not by power, but by impotence. For, he is not said to be able because he is able of himself, but because his impotence gives something else power over him. Or, by a figure of speech, just as many words are improperly applied, as when we use "to be" for "not to be," and "to do" for what is really "not to do," or "to do nothing." For, often we say to a man who denies the existence of something: "It is as you say it to be," though it might seem more proper to say, "It is not, as you say it is not." In the same way, we say: "This man sits just as that man does," or, "This man rests just as that man does"; although to sit is not to do anything, and to rest is to do nothing.

So, then, when one is said to have the power of doing or experiencing what is not for his good, or what he ought not to do, impotence is understood in the word power. For, the more he possesses this power, the more powerful are adversity and perversity against him, and the more powerless is he against them.

Therefore, O Lord, our God, the more truly art thou omnipotent, since thou art capable of nothing through impotence, and nothing has power against thee.

Chapter VIII

How he is compassionate and passionless. God is compassionate, in terms of our experience, because we experience the effect of compassion. God is not compassionate, in terms of his own being, because he does not experience the feeling (affectus) of compassion.

But how art thou compassionate, and, at the same time, passionless? For, if thou art passionless, thou dost not feel sympathy; and if thou dost not feel sympathy, thy heart is not wretched from sympathy for the wretched; but this is to be compassionate. But if thou art not compassionate, whence cometh so great consolation to the wretched? How, then, art thou compassionate and not compassionate, O Lord, unless because thou art compassionate in terms of our experience, and not compassionate in terms of thy being.

Truly, thou art so in terms of our experience, but thou art not so in terms of thine own. For, when thou beholdest us in our wretchedness, we experience the effect of compassion, but thou dost not experience the feeling. Therefore, thou art both compassionate, because thou dost save the wretched, and spare those who sin against thee; and not compassionate, because thou art affected by no sympathy for wretchedness.

2. St. Thomas Aquinas

St. Thomas Aquinas (1225–1274) is the most famous of the
medieval Christian philosophers and has become something
like the official philosopher of the Roman Catholic Church.

From Nature to God

The existence of God can be proved in five ways.

The first and more manifest way is the argument from motion. It is
certain, and evident to our senses, that in the world some things are in
motion. Now whatever is moved is moved by another, for nothing can be
moved except it is in potentiality to that towards which it is moved;
whereas a thing moves inasmuch as it is in act. For motion is nothing
else than the reduction of something from potentiality to actuality. But
nothing can be reduced from potentiality to actuality, except by something in a state of actuality. Thus that which is actually hot, as fire,
makes wood, which is potentially hot, to be actually hot, and thereby
moves and changes it. Now it is not possible that the same thing should
be at once in actuality and potentiality in the same respect, but only in
different respects. For what is actually hot cannot simultaneously be
potentially hot; but it is simultaneously potentially cold. It is therefore
impossible that in the same respect and in the same way a thing should
be both mover and moved, *i.e.*, that it should move itself. Therefore,
whatever is moved must be moved by another. If that by which it is
moved be itself moved, then this also must needs be moved by another,
and that by another again. But this cannot go on to infinity, because then

This selection comprises the "Reply" of Part I, Question 2, Article 3, of the *Summa
Theologica*. From THE BASIC WRITINGS OF ST. THOMAS AQUINAS, edited by
A. C. Pegis. Copyright 1945 and renewed 1973 by Random House, Inc. Reprinted by
permission of the publisher.

there would be no first mover, and, consequently, no other mover, seeing that subsequent movers move only inasmuch as they are moved by the first mover; as the staff moves only because it is moved by the hand. Therefore it is necessary to arrive at a first mover, moved by no other; and this everyone understands to be God.

The second way is from the nature of efficient cause. In the world of sensible things we find there is an order of efficient causes. There is no case known (neither is it, indeed, possible) in which a thing is found to be the efficient cause of itself; for so it would be prior to itself, which is impossible. Now in efficient causes it is not possible to go on to infinity, because in all efficient causes following in order, the first is the cause of the intermediate cause, and the intermediate is the cause of the ultimate cause, whether the intermediate cause be several, or one only. Now to take away the cause is to take away the effect. Therefore, if there be no first cause among efficient causes, there will be no ultimate, nor any intermediate, cause. But if in efficient causes it is possible to go on to infinity, there will be no first efficient cause, neither will there be an ultimate effect, nor any intermediate efficient causes; all of which is plainly false. Therefore it is necessary to admit a first efficient cause, to which everyone gives the name of God.

The third way is taken from possibility and necessity, and runs thus. We find in nature things that are possible to be and not to be, since they are found to be generated, and to be corrupted, and consequently, it is possible for them to be and not to be. But it is impossible for these always to exist, for that which can not-be at some time is not. Therefore, if everything can not-be, then at one time there was nothing in existence. Now if this were true, even now there would be nothing in existence, because that which does not exist begins to exist only through something already existing. Therefore, if at one time nothing was in existence, it would have been impossible for anything to have begun to exist; and thus even now nothing would be in existence—which is absurd. Therefore, not all beings are merely possible, but there must exist something the existence of which is necessary. But every necessary thing either has its necessity caused by another, or not. Now it is impossible to go on to infinity in necessary things which have their necessity caused by another, as has been already proved in regard to efficient causes. Therefore we cannot but admit the existence of some being having of itself its own necessity, and not receiving it from another, but rather causing in others their necessity. This all men speak of as God.

The fourth way is taken from the gradation to be found in things. Among beings there are some more and some less good, true, noble, and the like. But more and less are predicated of different things according as they resemble in their different ways something which is the maximum, as a thing is said to be hotter according as it more nearly resembles that which is hottest; so that there is something which is truest, something best, something noblest, and, consequently, something which is most being, for those things that are greatest in truth are greatest in being, as it is written in Metaph. ii. Now the maximum in any genus is the cause of all in that genus, as fire, which is the maximum of heat, is the cause of all hot things, as is said in the same book. Therefore there must also be something which is to all beings the cause of their being, goodness, and every other perfection; and this we call God.

The fifth way is taken from the governance of the world. We see that things which lack knowledge, such as natural bodies, act for an end, and this is evident from their acting always, or nearly always, in the same way, so as to obtain the best result. Hence it is plain that they achieve their end, not fortuitously, but designedly. Now whatever lacks knowledge cannot move towards an end, unless it be directed by some being endowed with knowledge and intelligence; as the arrow is directed by the archer. Therefore some intelligent being exists by whom all natural things are directed to their end; and this being we call God.

3. F. C. Copleston

F. C. Copleston (b. 1907), a member of the Society of Jesus,
is one of the most distinguished contemporary historians of
philosophy.

A Commentary on Aquinas'
Five Arguments

What, then, are the familiar facts which for Aquinas imply the existence
of God? Mention of them can be found in the famous 'five ways' of proving God's existence, which are outlined in the *Summa Theologica* (Ia,
2, 3). In the first way Aquinas begins by saying that 'it is certain, and it
is clear from sense-experience, that some things in this world are moved.'
It must be remembered that he, like Aristotle, understands the term
'motion' in the broad sense of change, reduction from a state of potentiality to one of act; he does not refer exclusively to local motion. In the
second way he starts with the remark that 'we find in material things an
order of efficient causes.' In other words, in our experience of things and
of their relations to one another we are aware of efficient causality. Thus
while in the first way he begins with the fact that some things are acted
upon and changed by other things, the second way is based upon the fact
that some things act upon other things, as efficient causes. In the third
way he starts by stating that 'we find among things some which are
capable of existing or not existing, since we find that some things come
into being and pass away.' In other words, we perceive that some things

are corruptible or perishable. In the fourth proof he observes that 'we find in things that some are more or less good and true and noble and so on (than others).' Finally in the fifth way he says: 'we see that some things which lack knowledge, namely natural bodies, act for an end, which is clear from the fact that they always or in most cases act in the same way, in order to attain what is best.'

There is, I think, little difficulty in accepting as empirical facts the starting-points of the first three ways. For nobody really doubts that some things are acted upon and changed or 'moved,' that some things act on others, and that some things are perishable. Each of us is aware, for example, that he is acted upon and changed, that he sometimes acts as an efficient cause, and that he is perishable. Even if anyone were to cavil at the assertion that he is aware that he himself was born and will die, he knows very well that some other people were born and have died. But the starting-points of the two final arguments may cause some difficulty. The proposition that there are different grades of perfections in things stands in need of a much more thorough analysis than Aquinas accords it in his brief outline of the fourth way. For the schematic outlining of the five proofs was designed, not to satisfy the critical minds of mature philosophers, but as introductory material for 'novices' in the study of theology. And in any case Aquinas could naturally take for granted in the thirteenth century ideas which were familiar to his contemporaries and which had not yet been subjected to the radical criticism to which they were later subjected. At the same time there is not very much difficulty in understanding the sort of thing which was meant. We are all accustomed to think and speak as though, for example, there were different degrees of intelligence and intellectual capacity. In order to estimate the different degrees we need, it is true, standards or fixed points of reference; but, given these points of reference, we are all accustomed to make statements which imply different grades of perfections. And though these statements stand in need of close analysis, they refer to something which falls within ordinary experience and finds expression in ordinary language. As for the fifth way, the modern reader may find great difficulty in seeing what is meant if he confines his attention to the relevant passage in the *Summa Theologica*. But if he looks at the *Summa contra Gentiles* (1, 13) he will find Aquinas saying that we see things of different natures co-operating in the production and maintenance of a relatively stable order or system. When Aquinas says that we see purely material things acting for an end, he does not mean to say that they act in a manner analogous to that in which human beings consciously act for definite purposes. Indeed, the point of the argument is that they do not do so. He means that different kinds of things, like fire and water, the behaviour of which is determined by their several 'forms,' co-operate, not consciously but as a matter of fact, in such a way that there is a relatively stable order or system. And here again, though much more would need to be said in a full discussion of the matter, the basic idea is nothing particularly extraordinary nor is it contrary to our ordinary experience and expectations.

It is to be noted also that Aquinas speaks with considerable restraint: he avoids sweeping generalizations. Thus in the first argument he does not say that all material things are 'moved' but that we see that some things in this world are moved or changed. In the third argument he does not state that all finite things are contingent but that we are aware that some things come into being and pass away. And in the fifth argument he does not say that there is an invariable world-order or system but that we see natural bodies acting always or in most cases in the same ways. The difficulty, therefore, which may be experienced in regard to Aquinas' proofs of God's existence concerns not so much the empirical facts or alleged empirical facts with which he starts as in seeing that these facts imply God's existence.

Perhaps a word should be said at once about this idea of 'implication.' As a matter of fact Aquinas does not use the word when talking about the five ways: he speaks of 'proof' and of 'demonstration.' And by 'demonstration' he means in this context what he calls *demonstratio quia* (*S.T.*, Ia, 2, 2), namely a causal proof of God's existence, proceeding from the affirmation of some empirical fact, for example that there are things which change, to the affirmation of a transcendent cause. It is, indeed, his second proof which is strictly the causal argument, in the sense that it deals explicitly with the order of efficient causality; but in every proof the idea of ontological dependence on a transcendent cause appears in some form or other. Aquinas' conviction was that a full understanding of the empirical facts which are selected for consideration in the five ways involves seeing the dependence of these facts on a transcendent cause. The existence of things which change, for instance, is, in his opinion, not self-explanatory: it can be rendered intelligible only if seen as dependent on a transcendent cause, a cause, that is to say, which does not itself belong to the order of changing things.

This may suggest to the modern reader that Aquinas was concerned with causal explanation in the sense that he was concerned with framing an empirical hypothesis to explain certain facts. But he did not regard the proposition affirming God's existence as a causal hypothesis in the sense of being in principle revisable, as a hypothesis, that is to say, which might conceivably have to be revised in the light of fresh empirical data or which might be supplanted by a more economical hypothesis. This point can perhaps be seen most clearly in the case of his third argument, which is based on the fact that there are things which come into being and pass away. In Aquinas' opinion no fresh scientific knowledge about the physical constitution of such things could affect the validity of the argument. He did not look on a 'demonstration' of God's existence as an empirical hypothesis in the sense in which the electronic theory, for example, is said to be an empirical hypothesis. It is, of course, open to anyone to say that in his own opinion cosmological arguments in favour of God's existence are in fact analogous to the empirical hypotheses of the sciences and that they have a predictive function; but it does not follow that this interpretation can legitimately be ascribed to Aquinas. We should not be misled by the illustrations which he sometimes offers from contemporary scientific theory. For these are mere illustrations to elucidate a point in terms easily understandable by his readers: they are not meant to indicate that the proofs of God's existence were for him empirical hypotheses in the modern sense of the term.

· ·

It is worth emphasizing perhaps that it does not necessarily follow from Aquinas' view that a metaphysical approach to God's existence is an easy matter. It is true that he was confident of the power of the human reason to attain knowledge of God's existence; and he did not regard his arguments as standing in need of support from rhetoric or emotional appeal. And in the *Summa Theologica*, where he is writing for 'novices' in theology, he states the arguments in a bald and perhaps disconcertingly impersonal manner. But we cannot legitimately conclude that he thought it easy for a man to come to the knowledge of God's existence by philosophic reflection alone. Indeed, he makes an explicit statement to the opposite effect. He was well aware that in human life other factors besides metaphysical reflection exercise a great influence. Moreover, he would obviously agree that it is always possible to stop the process of reflection at a particular point. For Aquinas every being, in so far as it is or has being, is intelligible. But we can consider things from different points of view or under different aspects. For example, I might consider coming-into-being and passing-away simply in regard to definite instances and from a subjective point of view. It grieves me to think that someone I love will probably die before me and leave, as we say, a gap in my life. Or it grieves me to think that I shall die and be unable to complete the work which I have undertaken. Or I might consider coming-into-being and passing-away from some scientific point of view. What are the finite phenomenal causes of organic decay or of the generation of an organism? But I can also consider coming-into-being and passing-away purely as such and objectively, adopting a metaphysical point of view and directing my attention to the sort of being, considered as such, which is capable of coming into being and passing away. Nobody can compel me to adopt this point of view. If I am determined to remain on the level of, say, some particular science, I remain there; and that is that. Metaphysical reflections will have no meaning for me. But the metaphysical point of view is a possible point of view, and metaphysical reflection belongs to a full understanding of things so far as this is possible for a finite mind. And if I do adopt this point of view and maintain it in sustained reflection, an existential relation of dependence, Aquinas was convinced, should become clear to me which will not become clear to me if I remain on a different level of reflection. But just as extraneous factors (such as the influence of the general outlook promoted by a technical civilization) may help to produce my decision to remain on a nonmetaphysical level of reflection, so also can extraneous factors influence my reflection on the metaphysical level. It seems to me quite wrong to suggest that Aquinas did not regard metaphysical reflection as a possible way of becoming aware of God's existence and that he looked on it, as some writers have suggested, as being simply a rational justification of an assurance which is necessarily attained in some other way. For if it constitutes a rational justification at all, it must, I think, be a possible way of becoming aware of God's existence. But it does not necessarily follow, of course, that it is an easy way or a common way.

After these general remarks I turn to Aquinas' five proofs of the existence of God. In the first proof he argues that 'motion' or change means the reduction of a thing from a state of potentiality to one of act, and that a thing cannot be reduced from potentiality to act except under the influence of an agent already in act. In this sense 'everything which is moved must be moved by another.' He argues finally that in order to avoid an infinite regress in the chain of movers, the existence of a first unmoved mover must be admitted. 'And all understand that this is God.'

A statement like 'all understand that this is God' or 'all call this (being) God' occurs at the end of each proof, and I postpone consideration of it for the moment. As for the ruling out of an infinite regress, I shall explain what Aquinas means to reject after outlining the second proof, which is similar in structure to the first.

Whereas in the first proof Aquinas considers things as being acted upon, as being changed or 'moved,' in the second he considers them as active agents, as efficient causes. He argues that there is a hierarchy of efficient causes, a subordinate cause being dependent on the cause above it in the hierarchy. He then proceeds, after excluding the hypothesis of an infinite regress, to draw the conclusion that there must be a first efficient cause, 'which all call God.'

Now, it is obviously impossible to discuss these arguments profitably unless they are first understood. And misunderstanding of them is only too easy, since the terms and phrases used are either unfamiliar or liable to be taken in a sense other than the sense intended. In the first place it is essential to understand that in the first argument Aquinas supposes that movement or change is dependent on a 'mover' acting here and now, and that in the second argument he supposes that there are efficient causes in the world which even in their causal activity are here and now dependent on the causal activity of other causes. That is why I have spoken of a 'hierarchy' rather than of a 'series.' What he is thinking of can be illustrated in this way. A son is dependent on his father, in the sense that he would not have existed except for the causal activity of his father. But when the son acts for himself, he is not dependent here and now on his father. But he is dependent here and now on other factors. Without the activity of the air, for instance, he could not himself act, and the life-preserving activity of the air is itself dependent here and now on other factors, and they in turn on other factors. I do not say that this illustration is in all respects adequate for the purpose; but it at least illustrates the fact that when Aquinas talks about an 'order' of efficient causes he is not thinking of a series stretching back into the past, but of a hierarchy of causes, in which a subordinate member is here and now dependent on the causal activity of a higher member. If I wind up my watch at night, it then proceeds to work without further interference on my part. But the activity of the pen tracing these words on the page is here and now dependent on the activity of my hand, which in turn is here and now dependent on other factors.

The meaning of the rejection of an infinite regress should now be clear. Aquinas is not rejecting the possibility of an infinite series as such. We have already seen that he did not think that anyone had ever succeeded in showing the impossibility of an infinite series of events stretching back into the past. Therefore he does not mean to rule out the possibility of an infinite series of causes and effects, in which a given member depended on the preceding member, say X on Y, but does not, once it exists, depend here and now on the present causal activity of the preceding member. We have to imagine, not a lineal or horizontal series, so to speak, but a vertical hierarchy, in which a lower member depends here and now on the present causal activity of the member above it. It is the latter type of series, if prolonged to infinity, which Aquinas rejects. And he rejects it on the ground that unless there is a 'first' member, a mover which is not itself moved or a cause which does not itself depend on the causal activity of a higher cause, it is not possible to explain the 'motion' or the causal activity of the lowest member. His point of view is this. Suppress the first unmoved mover and there is no motion or change here and now. Suppress the first efficient cause and there is no causal activity here and now. If therefore we find that some things in the world are changed, there must be a first unmoved mover. And if there are efficient causes in the world, there must be a first efficient, and completely nondependent cause. The word 'first' does not mean first in the temporal order, but supreme or first in the ontological order.

· ·

In the third proof Aquinas starts from the fact that some things come into being and perish, and he concludes from this that it is possible for them to exist or not to exist: they do not exist 'necessarily.' He then argues that it is impossible for things which are of this kind to exist always; for 'that which is capable of not existing, at some time does not exist.' If all things were of this kind, at some time there would be nothing. Aquinas is clearly supposing for the sake of argument the hypothesis of infinite time, and his proof is designed to cover this hypothesis. He does not say that infinite time is impossible: what he says is that if time is infinite and if all things are capable of not existing, this potentiality would inevitably be fulfilled in infinite time. There would then be nothing. And if there had ever been nothing, nothing would now exist. For no thing can bring itself into existence. But it is clear as a matter of fact that there are things. Therefore it can never have been true to say that there was literally no thing. Therefore it is impossible that all things should be capable of existing or not existing. There must, then, be some necessary being. But perhaps it is necessary in the sense that it must exist if something else exists; that is to say, its necessity may be hypothetical. We cannot, however, proceed to infinity in the series or hierarchy of necessary beings. If we do so, we do not explain the presence here and now of beings capable of existing or not existing. Therefore we must affirm the existence of a being which is absolutely necessary (*per se necessarium*) and completely independent. 'And all call this being *God*.'

This argument may appear to be quite unnecessarily complicated and obscure. But it has to be seen in its historical context. As already mentioned, Aquinas designed his argument in such a way as to be independent of the question whether or not the world existed from eternity. He wanted to show that on either hypothesis there must be a necessary being. As for the introduction of hypothetical necessary beings, he wanted to show that even if there are such beings, perhaps within the universe, which are not corruptible in the sense in which a flower is corruptible, there must still be an absolutely independent being. Finally, in regard to terminology, Aquinas uses the common medieval expression 'necessary being.' He does not actually use the term 'contingent being' in the argument and talks instead about 'possible' beings; but it comes to the same thing. And though the words 'contingent' and 'necessary' are now applied to propositions rather than to beings, I have retained Aquinas' mode of speaking. Whether one accepts the argument or not, I do not think that there is any insuperable difficulty in understanding the line of thought.

The fourth argument is admittedly difficult to grasp. Aquinas argues that there are degrees of perfections in things. Different kinds of finite things possess different perfections in diverse limited degrees. He then argues not only that if there are different degrees of a perfection like goodness there is a supreme good to which other good things approximate but also that all limited degrees of goodness are caused by the supreme good. And since goodness is a convertible term with being, a thing being good in so far as it has being, the supreme good is the supreme being and the cause of being in all other things. 'Therefore there is something which is the cause of the being and goodness and of every perfection in all other things; and this we call *God*.'

. . . .

Finally, the fifth proof, if we take its statement in the *Summa Theologica* together with that in the *Summa contra Gentiles*, can be expressed more or less as follows. The activity and behaviour of each thing is determined by its form. But we observe material things of very different types co-operating in such a way as to produce and maintain a relatively stable world-order or system. They achieve an 'end,' the production and maintenance of a cosmic order. But nonintelligent material things certainly do not co-operate consciously in view of a purpose. If it is said that they co-operate in the realization of an end or purpose, this does not mean that they intend the realization of this order in a manner analogous to that in which a man can act consciously with a view to the achievement of a purpose. Nor, when Aquinas talks about operating 'for an end' in this connexion, is he thinking of the utility of certain things to the human race. He is not saying, for example, that grass grows to feed the sheep and that sheep exist in order that human beings should have food and clothing. It is of the unconscious co-operation of different kinds of material things in the production and maintenance of a relatively stable cosmic system that he is thinking, not of the benefits accruing to us from our use of certain objects. And his argument is that this co-operation on the part of heterogeneous material things clearly points to the existence of an extrinsic intelligent author of this co-operation, who operates with an end in view. If Aquinas had lived in the days of the evolutionary hypothesis, he would doubtless have argued that this hypothesis supports rather than invalidates the conclusion of the argument.

4. David Hume

David Hume (1711–1776) was perhaps the greatest of the British empiricist philosophers of the seventeenth and eighteenth centuries.

A Critique of the Argument from Design

Not to lose any time in circumlocutions, said CLEANTHES, addressing himself to Demea, much less in replying to the pious declamations of Philo, I shall briefly explain how I conceive that matter. Look around the world, contemplate the whole and every part of it: you will find it to be nothing but one great machine, subdivided into an infinite number of lesser machines, which again admit of subdivisions to a degree beyond what human senses and faculties can trace and explain. All these various machines, and even their most minute parts, are adjusted to each other with an accuracy which ravishes into admiration all men who have ever contemplated them. The curious adapting of means to ends throughout all nature resembles exactly, though it much exceeds, the productions of human contrivance, of human design, thought, wisdom, and intelligence. Since therefore the effects resemble each other, we are led to infer, by all the rules of analogy, that the causes also resemble, and that the Author of Nature is somewhat similar to the mind of man, though pos-

From Parts II–IX of the *Dialogues Concerning Natural Religion,* a work published posthumously. Subheadings added by the editors. It is a matter of controversy as to the extent to which the various participants in the *Dialogues* represent Hume's own views, but he is usually identified with Philo.

sessed of much larger faculties, proportioned to the grandeur of the work which he has executed. By this argument *a posteriori*, and by this argument alone, do we prove at once the existence of a Deity and his similarity to human mind and intelligence.

. . . .

How Strong Is the Analogy?

PHILO, after a short pause, proceeded in the following manner.

That all inferences, Cleanthes, concerning fact are founded on experience, and that all experimental reasonings are founded on the supposition that similar causes prove similar effects, and similar effects similar causes, I shall not at present much dispute with you. But observe, I entreat you, with what extreme caution all just reasoners proceed in the transferring of experiments to similar cases. Unless the cases be exactly similar, they repose no perfect confidence in applying their past observation to any particular phenomenon. Every alteration of circumstances occasions a doubt concerning the event, and it requires new experiments to prove certainly that the circumstances are of no moment or importance. A change in bulk, situation, arrangement, age, disposition of the air, or surrounding bodies, any of these particulars may be attended with the most unexpected consequences. And unless the objects be quite familiar to us, it is the highest temerity to expect with assurance, after any of these changes, an event similar to that which before fell under our observation. The slow and deliberate steps of philosophers here, if anywhere, are distinguished from the precipitate march of the vulgar, who, hurried on by the smallest similitude, are incapable of all discernment or consideration.

But can you think, Cleanthes, that your usual phlegm and philosophy have been preserved in so wide a step as you have taken when you compared to the universe, houses, ships, furniture, machines, and from their similarity in some circumstances inferred a similarity in their causes? Thought, design, intelligence, such as we discover in men and other animals, is no more than one of the springs and principles of the universe, as well as heat or cold, attraction or repulsion, and a hundred others which fall under daily observation. It is an active cause by which some particular parts of nature, we find, produce alterations on other parts. But can a conclusion, with any propriety, be transferred from parts to the whole? Does not the great disproportion bar all comparison and inference? From observing the growth of a hair, can we learn anything concerning the generation of a man? Would the manner of a leaf's blowing, even though perfectly known, afford us any instruction concerning the vegetation of a tree?

But allowing that we were to take the *operations* of one part of nature upon another for the foundation of our judgment concerning the *origin* of the whole (which never can be admitted), yet why select so minute, so weak, so bounded a principle as the reason and design of animals is found to be upon this planet? What peculiar privilege has this little agitation of the brain which we call *thought,* that we must thus make it the model of the whole universe? Our partiality in our own favor does indeed present it on all occasions, but sound philosophy ought carefully to guard against so natural an illusion.

So far from admitting, continued PHILO, that the operations of a part can afford us any just conclusion concerning the origin of the whole, I will not allow any one part to form a rule for another part if the latter be very remote from the former. Is there any reasonable ground to con-clude that the inhabitants of other planets possess thought, intelligence, reason, or anything similar to these faculties in men? When nature has so extremely diversified her manner of operation in this small globe, can we imagine that she incessantly copies herself throughout so immense a universe? And if thought, as we may well suppose, be confined merely to this narrow corner and has even there so limited a sphere of action, with what propriety can we assign it for the original cause of all things? The narrow views of a peasant who makes this domestic economy the rule for the government of kingdoms is in comparison a pardonable sophism.

But were we ever so much assured that a thought and reason resem-bling the human were to be found throughout the whole universe, and were its activity elsewhere vastly greater and more commanding than it appears in this globe, yet I cannot see why the operations of a world constituted, arranged, adjusted, can with any propriety be extended to a world which is in its embryo state, and is advancing toward that con-stitution and arrangement. By observation we know somewhat of the economy, action, and nourishment of a finished animal, but we must transfer with great caution that observation to the growth of a fetus in the womb, and still more to the formation of an animalcule in the loins of its male parent. Nature, we find, even from our limited experience, possesses an infinite number of springs and principles which incessantly discover themselves on every change of her position and situation. And what new and unknown principles would actuate her in so new and unknown a situation as that of the formation of a universe, we cannot, without the utmost temerity, pretend to determine.

A very small part of this great system, during a very short time, is very imperfectly discovered to us; and do we thence pronounce decisively concerning the origin of the whole?

Admirable conclusion! Stone, wood, brick, iron, brass, have not, at this time, in this minute globe of earth, an order or arrangement without human art and contrivance; therefore, the universe could not originally attain its order and arrangement without something similar to human art. But is a part of nature a rule for another part very wide of the former? Is it a rule for the whole? Is a very small part a rule for the universe? Is nature in one situation a certain rule for nature in another situation vastly different from the former?

. . . .

How the most absurd argument, replied CLEANTHES, in the hands of a man of ingenuity and invention, may acquire an air of probability! Are you not aware, Philo, that it became necessary for Copernicus and his first disciples to prove the similarity of the terrestrial and celestial matter because several philosophers, blinded by old systems and supported by some sensible appearances, had denied this similarity? But that it is by no means necessary that theists should prove the similarity of the works of nature to those of art because this similarity is self-evident and un-deniable? The same matter, a like form; what more is requisite to show an analogy between their causes and to ascertain the origin of all things from a divine purpose and intention? Your objections, I must freely tell you, are no better than the abstruse cavils of those philosophers who denied motion, and ought to be refuted in the same manner, by illustra-tions, examples, and instances rather than by serious argument and philosophy.

Suppose, therefore, that an articulate voice were heard in the clouds much louder and more melodious than any which human art could ever reach; suppose that this voice were extended in the same instant over all nations and spoke to each nation in its own language and dialect; sup-pose that the words delivered not only contain a just sense and meaning, but convey some instruction altogether worthy of a benevolent Being superior to mankind. Could you possibly hesitate a moment concerning the cause of this voice, and must you not instantly ascribe it to some design or purpose? Yet I cannot see but all the same objections (if they merit that appellation) which lie against the system of theism may also be produced against this inference.

Might you not say that all conclusions concerning fact were founded on experience; that when we hear an articulate voice in the dark and thence infer a man, it is only the resemblance of the effect which leads us to conclude that there is a like resemblance in the cause; but that this extraordinary voice, by its loudness, extent, and flexibility to all languages, bears so little analogy to any human voice that we have no reason to suppose any analogy in their causes; and consequently that a rational, wise, coherent speech proceeded, you knew not whence, from some accidental whistling of the winds, not from any divine reason or intelligence? You see clearly your own objections in these cavils, and I hope too you see clearly that they cannot possibly have more force in the one case than in the other.

But to bring the case still nearer the present one of the universe, I shall make two suppositions which imply not any absurdity, or impos-sibility. Suppose that there is a natural, universal, invariable language, common to every individual of human race, and that books are natural productions which perpetuate themselves in the same manner with ani-mals and vegetables, by descent and propagation. Several expressions of our passions contain a universal language: all brute animals have a natural speech, which, however limited, is very intelligible to their own species. And as there are infinitely fewer parts and less contrivance in the finest composition of eloquence than in the coarsest organized body, the propagation of an *Iliad* or *Aeneid* is an easier supposition than that of any plant or animal.

Suppose, therefore, that you enter into your library thus peopled by natural volumes containing the most refined reason and most exquisite beauty; could you possibly open one of them and doubt that its original cause bore the strongest analogy to mind and intelligence? When it reasons and discourses; when it expostulates, argues, and enforces its views and topics; when it applies sometimes to the pure intellect, sometimes to the affections; when it collects, disposes, and adorns every consideration suited to the subject; could you persist in asserting that all this, at the bottom, had really no meaning, and that the first formation of this volume in the loins of its original parent proceeded not from thought and design? Your obstinacy, I know, reaches not that degree of firmness; even your skeptical play and wantonness would be abashed at so glaring an absurdity.

But if there be any difference, Philo, between this supposed case and the real one of the universe, it is all to the advantage of the latter. The anatomy of an animal affords many stronger instances of design than the perusal of Livy or Tacitus; and any objection which you start in the former case, by carrying me back to so unusual and extraordinary a scene as the first formation of worlds, the same objection has place on the supposition of our vegetating library. Choose then your party, Philo, without ambiguity or evasion; assert either that a rational volume is no proof of a rational cause or admit of a similar cause to all the works of nature.

· ·

It sometimes happens, I own, that the religious arguments have not their due influence on an ignorant savage and barbarian, not because they are obscure and difficult, but because he never asks himself any question with regard to them. Whence arises the curious structure of an animal? From the copulation of its parents. And these whence? From *their* parents? A few removes set the objects at such a distance that to him they are lost in darkness and confusion; nor is he actuated by any curiosity to trace them further. But this is neither dogmatism nor skepticism, but stupidity, a state of mind very different from your sifting, inquisitive disposition, my ingenious friend. You can trace causes from effects; you can compare the most distant and remote objects; and your greatest errors proceed not from barrenness of thought and invention but from too luxuriant a fertility, which suppresses your natural good sense by a profusion of unnecessary scruples and objections.

Is the Divine Nature Intelligibile to Man?

Here I could observe, Hermippus, that Philo was a little embarrassed and confounded; but while he hesitated in delivering an answer, luckily for him, DEMEA broke in upon the discourse and saved his countenance.

Your instance, Cleanthes, said he, drawn from books and language, being familiar, has, I confess, so much more force on that account; but is there not some danger too in this very circumstance, and may it not render us presumptuous by making us imagine we comprehend the Deity and have some adequate idea of his nature and attributes? When I read a volume, I enter into the mind and intention of the author; I become him, in a manner, for the instant, and have an immediate feeling and conception of those ideas which revolved in his imagination while employed in that composition. But so near an approach we never surely can make to the Deity. His ways are not our ways. His attributes are perfect but incomprehensible. And this volume of nature contains a great and inexplicable riddle, more than any intelligible discourse or reasoning.

The ancient Platonists, you know, were the most religious and devout of all the pagan philosophers, yet many of them, particularly Plotinus, expressly declare that intellect or understanding is not to be ascribed to the Deity, and that our most perfect worship of him consists, not in acts of veneration, reverence, gratitude, or love, but in a certain mysterious self-annihilation of all our faculties. These ideas are, perhaps, too far stretched, but still it must be acknowledged that, by representing the Deity as so intelligible and comprehensible and so similar to a human mind, we are guilty of the grossest and most narrow partiality, and make ourselves the model of the whole universe.

All the *sentiments* of the human mind—gratitude, resentment, love, friendship, approbation, blame, pity, emulation, envy—have a plain reference to the state and situation of man, and are calculated for preserving the existence and promoting the activity of such a being in such circumstances. It seems therefore unreasonable to transfer such sentiments to a supreme existence or to suppose him actuated by them; and the phenomena, besides, of the universe will not support us in such a theory. All our *ideas* derived from the senses are confessedly false and illusive, and cannot therefore be supposed to have place in a supreme intelligence. And as the ideas of internal sentiment, added to those of the external senses, compose the whole furniture of human understanding, we may conclude that none of the *materials* of thought are in any respect similar in the human and in the divine intelligence. Now as to the *manner* of thinking, how can we make any comparison between them or suppose them anywise resembling? Our thought is fluctuating, uncertain, fleeting, successive, and compounded; and were we to remove these circumstances we absolutely annihilate its essence, and it would in such a case be an abuse of terms to apply to it the name of thought or reason. At least, if it appear more pious and respectful (as it really is) still to retain these terms when we mention the Supreme Being, we ought to acknowledge that their meaning, in that case, is totally incomprehensible, and that the infirmities of our nature do not permit us to reach any ideas which in the least correspond to the ineffable sublimity of the divine attributes.

. . . .

It seems strange to me, said CLEANTHES, that you, Demea, who are so sincere in the cause of religion, should still maintain the mysterious, incomprehensible nature of the Deity, and should insist so strenuously that he has no manner of likeness or resemblance to human creatures. The Deity, I can readily allow, possesses many powers and attributes of which we can have no comprehension. But if our ideas, so far as they go, be not just and adequate and correspondent to his real nature, I know not what there is in this subject worth insisting on. Is the name, without any meaning, of such mighty importance? Or how do you mystics, who maintain the absolute incomprehensibility of the Deity, differ from skeptics or atheists, who assert that the first cause of all is unknown and unintelligible? Their temerity must be very great if, after rejecting the production by a mind—I mean a mind resembling the human (for I know of no other)—they pretend to assign, with certainty, any other specific intelligible cause; and their conscience must be very scrupulous indeed if they refuse to call the universal unknown cause a God or Deity, and to bestow on him as many sublime eulogies and unmeaning epithets as you shall please to require of them.

Who could imagine, replied DEMEA, that Cleanthes, the calm, philosophical Cleanthes, would attempt to refute his antagonists by affixing a nickname to them, and, like the common bigots and inquisitors of the age, have recourse to invective and declamation instead of reasoning? Or does he not perceive that these topics are easily retorted, and that *anthropomorphite* is an appellation as invidious and implies as dangerous consequences as the epithet of *mystic* with which he has honored us? In reality, Cleanthes, consider what it is you assert when you represent the Deity as similar to a human mind and understanding. What is the soul of man? A composition of various faculties, passions, sentiments, ideas, united, indeed, into one self or person, but still distinct from each other. When it reasons, the ideas which are the parts of its discourse arrange themselves in a certain form or order which is not preserved entire for a moment, but immediately gives place to another arrangement. New opinions, new passions, new affections, new feelings arise which continually diversify the mental scene and produce in it the greatest variety and most rapid succession imaginable. How is this compatible with that perfect immutability and simplicity which all true theists ascribe to the Deity? By the same act, say they, he sees past, present, and future; his love and hatred, his mercy and justice, are one individual operation; he is entire in every point of space and complete in every instant of duration. No succession, no change, no acquisition, no diminution. What he is implies not in it any shadow of distinction or diversity. And what he is this moment he ever has been and ever will be, without any new judgment, sentiment, or operation. He stands fixed in one simple, perfect state; nor can you ever say, with any propriety, that this act of his is different from that other, or that this judgment or idea has been lately formed and will give place, by succession, to any different judgment or idea.

I can readily allow, said CLEANTHES, that those who maintain the perfect simplicity of the Supreme Being, to the extent in which you have explained it, are complete mystics, and chargeable with all the consequences which I have drawn from their opinion. They are, in a word, atheists without knowing it. For though it be allowed that the Deity possesses attributes of which we have no comprehension, yet ought we never to ascribe to him any attributes which are absolutely incompatible with that intelligent nature essential to him. A mind whose acts and sentiments and ideas are not distinct and successive, one that is wholly simple and totally immutable, is a mind which has no thought, no reason, no will, no sentiment, no love, no hatred, or, in a word, is no mind at all. It is an abuse of terms to give it that appellation, and we may as well speak of limited extension without figure, or of number without composition.

Pray consider, said PHILO, whom you are at present inveighing against. You are honoring with the appellation of *atheist* all the sound, orthodox divines, almost, who have treated of this subject; and you will at last be yourself found, according to your reckoning, the only sound theist in the world. But if idolaters be atheists, as I think may justly be asserted, and Christian theologians the same, what becomes of the argument, so much celebrated, derived from the universal consent of mankind?

Does the World-Designer Have to Be Explained?

But because I know you are not much swayed by names and authorities, I shall endeavor to show you a little more distinctly the inconveniences of that anthropomorphism which you have embraced, and shall prove that there is no ground to suppose a plan of the world to be formed in the divine mind, consisting of distinct ideas differently arranged, in the same manner as an architect forms in his head the plan of a house which he intends to execute.

It is not easy, I own, to see what is gained by this supposition, whether we judge of the matter by *reason* or by *experience*. We are still obliged to mount higher in order to find the cause of this cause which you have assigned as satisfactory and conclusive.

If *reason* (I mean abstract reason, derived from inquiries *a priori*) be not alike mute with regard to all questions concerning cause and effect, this sentence at least it will venture to pronounce: that a mental world or universe of ideas requires a cause as much as does a material world or universe of objects, and, if similar in its arrangement, must require a similar cause. For what is there in this subject which should occasion a different conclusion or inference? In an abstract view they are entirely alike, and no difficulty attends the one supposition which is not common to both of them.

Again, when we will needs force *experience* to pronounce some sentence, even on these subjects which lie beyond her sphere, neither can she perceive any material difference in this particular between these two kinds of worlds, but finds them to be governed by similar principles, and to depend upon an equal variety of causes in their operations. We have specimens in miniature of both of them. Our own mind resembles the one, a vegetable or animal body the other. Let experience, therefore, judge from these samples. Nothing seems more delicate, with regard to its causes, than thought; and as these causes never operate in two persons after the same manner, so we never find two persons who think exactly alike. Nor indeed does the same person think exactly alike at any two different periods of time. A difference of age, of the disposition of his body, of weather, of food, of company, of books, of passions, any of these particulars, or others more minute, are sufficient to alter the curious machinery of thought and communicate to it very different movements and operations. As far as we can judge, vegetables and animal bodies are not more delicate in their motions, nor depend upon a greater variety or more curious adjustment of springs and principles.

How therefore shall we satisfy ourselves concerning the cause of that Being whom you suppose the Author of Nature, or, according to your system of anthropomorphism, the ideal world into which you trace the material? Have we not the same reason to trace that ideal world into another ideal world or new intelligent principle? But if we stop and go no further, why go so far? Why not stop at the material world? How can we satisfy ourselves without going on *in infinitum?* And after all, what satisfaction is there in that infinite progression? Let us remember the story of the Indian philosopher and his elephant. It was never more applicable than to the present subject. If the material world rests upon a similar ideal world, this ideal world must rest upon some other, and so on without end. It were better, therefore, never to look beyond the present material world. By supposing it to contain the principle of its order within itself, we really assert it to be God, and the sooner we arrive at that divine Being, so much the better. When you go one step beyond the mundane system, you only excite an inquisitive humor which it is impossible ever to satisfy.

· ·

You have displayed this argument with great emphasis, replied CLEANTHES. You seem not sensible how easy it is to answer it. Even in common life, if I assign a cause for any event, is it any objection, Philo, that I cannot assign the cause of that cause, and answer every new question which may incessantly be started? And what philosophers could possibly submit to so rigid a rule, philosophers who confess ultimate causes to be totally unknown, and are sensible that the most refined principles into which they trace the phenomena are still to them as inexplicable as these phenomena themselves are to the vulgar? The order and arrangement of nature, the curious adjustment of final causes, the plain use and intention of every part and organ, all these bespeak in the clearest language an intelligent cause or author. The heavens and the earth join in the same testimony; the whole chorus of nature raises one hymn to the praises of its Creator. You alone, or almost alone, disturb this general harmony. You start abstruse doubts, cavils, and objections; you ask me what is the cause of this cause? I know not, I care not, that concerns not me. I have found a Deity, and here I stop my inquiry. Let those go further who are wiser or more enterprising.

I pretend to be neither, replied PHILO; and for that very reason I should never, perhaps, have attempted to go so far, especially when I am sensible that I must at last be contented to sit down with the same answer which, without further trouble, might have satisfied me from the beginning. If I am still to remain in utter ignorance of causes and can absolutely give an explication of nothing, I shall never esteem it any advantage to shove off for a moment a difficulty which you acknowledge must immediately, in its full force, recur upon me. Naturalists indeed very justly explain particular effects by more general causes though these general causes themselves should remain in the end totally inexplicable, but they never surely thought it satisfactory to explain a particular effect by a particular cause which was no more to be accounted for than the effect itself. An ideal system, arranged of itself, without a precedent design, is not a whit more explicable than a material one which attains its order in a like manner; nor is there any more difficulty in the latter supposition than in the former.

The Argument Does Not Establish the Existence of an Infinite Deity

But to show you still more inconveniences, continued PHILO, in your anthropomorphism, please to take a new survey of your principles. *Like effects prove like causes.* This is the experimental argument; and this, you say too, is the sole theological argument. Now it is certain that the liker the effects are which are seen and the liker the causes which are inferred, the stronger is the argument. Every departure on either side diminishes the probability and renders the experiment less conclusive. You cannot doubt of the principle; neither ought you to reject its consequences.

. . . .

Now, Cleanthes, said PHILO, with an air of alacrity and triumph, mark the consequences, *First*, by this method of reasoning you renounce all claim to infinity in any of the attributes of the Deity. For as the cause ought only to be proportioned to the effect, and the effect, so far as it falls under our cognizance, is not infinite, what pretensions have we, upon your suppositions, to ascribe that attribute to the divine Being? You will still insist that, by removing him so much from all similarity to human creatures, we give in to the most arbitrary hypothesis, and at the same time weaken all proofs of his existence.

Secondly, you have no reason, on your theory, for ascribing perfection to the Deity, even in his finite capacity, or for supposing him free from every error, mistake, or incoherence in his undertakings. There are many inexplicable difficulties in the works of nature which, if we allow a perfect author to be proved *a priori*, are easily solved, and become only seeming difficulties from the narrow capacity of man, who cannot trace infinite relations. But according to your method of reasoning, these difficulties become all real, and perhaps will be insisted on as new instances of likeness to human art and contrivance. At least you must acknowledge that it is impossible for us to tell, from our limited views, whether this system contains any great faults or deserves any considerable praise if compared to other possible and even real systems. Could a peasant, if the *Aeneid* were read to him, pronounce that poem to be absolutely faultless, or even assign to it its proper rank among the productions of human wit, he who had never seen any other production?

But were this world ever so perfect a production, it must still remain uncertain whether all the excellences of the work can justly be ascribed to the workman. If we survey a ship, what an exalted idea must we form of the ingenuity of the carpenter who framed so complicated, useful, and beautiful a machine? And what surprise must we feel when we find him a stupid mechanic who imitated others, and copied an art which, through a long succession of ages, after multiplied trials, mistakes, corrections, deliberations, and controversies, had been gradually improving? Many worlds might have been botched and bungled, throughout an eternity, ere this system was struck out; much labor lost, many fruitless trials made, and a slow but continued improvement carried on during infinite ages in the art of world-making. In such subjects, who can determine where the truth, nay, who can conjecture where the probability lies, amidst a great number of hypotheses which may be proposed, and a still greater which may be imagined?

And what shadow of an argument, continued PHILO, can you produce from your hypothesis to prove the unity of the Deity? A great number of men join in building a house or ship, in rearing a city, in framing a commonwealth; why may not several deities combine in contriving and framing a world? This is only so much greater similarity to human affairs. By sharing the work among several, we may so much further limit the attributes of each, and get rid of that extensive power and knowledge which must be supposed in one deity and which, according to you, can only serve to weaken the proof of his existence. And if such foolish, such vicious creatures as man can yet often unite in framing and executing one plan, how much more those deities or demons, whom we may suppose several degrees more perfect?

To multiply causes without necessity is indeed contrary to true philosophy, but this principle applies not to the present case. Were one deity antecedently proved by your theory, who were possessed of every attribute requisite to the production of the universe, it would be needless, I own (though not absurd), to suppose any other deity existent. But while it is still a question whether all these attributes are united in one subject or dispersed among several independent beings, by what phenomena in nature can we pretend to decide the controversy? Where we see a body raised in a scale, we are sure that there is in the opposite scale, however concealed from sight, some counterpoising weight equal to it; but it is still allowed to doubt whether that weight be an aggregate of several distinct bodies or one uniform united mass. And if the weight requisite very much exceeds anything which we have ever seen conjoined in any single body, the former supposition becomes still more probable and natural. An intelligent being of such vast power and capacity as is necessary to produce the universe, or, to speak in the language of ancient philosophy, so prodigious an animal, exceeds all analogy and even comprehension.

But further, Cleanthes, men are mortal, and renew their species by generation, and this is common to all living creatures. The two great sexes of male and female, says Milton, animate the world. Why must this circumstance, so universal, so essential, be excluded from those numerous and limited deities? Behold, then, the theogeny of ancient times brought back upon us.

And why not become a perfect anthropomorphite? Why not assert the deity or deities to be corporeal, and have eyes, a nose, mouth, ears, etc.? Epicurus maintained that no man had ever seen reason but in a human figure, therefore the gods must have a human figure. And this argument, which is deservedly so much ridiculed by Cicero, becomes, according to you, solid and philosophical.

In a word, Cleanthes, a man who follows your hypothesis is able, perhaps, to assert or conjecture that the universe sometime arose from something like design, but beyond that position he cannot ascertain one single circumstance, and is left afterwards to fix every point of his theology by the utmost license of fancy and hypothesis. This world, for aught he knows, is very faulty and imperfect, compared to a superior standard, and was only the first rude essay of some infant deity who afterwards abandoned it, ashamed of his lame performance. It is the work only of some dependent, inferior deity, and is the object of derision to his superiors. It is the production of old age and dotage in some super-annuated deity, and ever since his death has run on at adventures, from the first impulse and active force which it received from him. You justly give signs of horror, Demea, at these strange suppositions, but these, and a thousand more of the same kind, are Cleanthes' suppositions, not mine. From the moment the attributes of the Deity are supposed finite, all these have place. And I cannot, for my part, think that so wild and unsettled a system of theology is, in any respect, preferable to none at all.

These suppositions I absolutely disown, cried CLEANTHES; they strike me, however, with no horror, especially when proposed in that rambling way in which they drop from you. On the contrary, they give me pleasure when I see that, by the utmost indulgence of your imagination, you never get rid of the hypothesis of design in the universe, but are obliged at every turn to have recourse to it. To this concession I adhere steadily, and this I regard as a sufficient foundation for religion.

. . . .

It must be a slight fabric indeed, said DEMEA, which can be erected on so tottering a foundation. While we are uncertain whether there is one deity or many, whether the deity or deities to whom we owe our exist-ence be perfect or imperfect, subordinate or supreme, dead or alive, what trust or confidence can we repose in them? What devotion or worship address to them? What veneration or obedience pay them? To all the purposes of life the theory of religion becomes altogether useless, and even with regard to speculative consequences its uncertainty, according to you, must render it totally precarious and unsatisfactory.

Other Explanations of the Existence of the Universe

To render it still more unsatisfactory, said PHILO, there occurs to me another hypothesis which must acquire an air of probability from the method of reasoning so much insisted on by Cleanthes. That like effects arise from like causes: this principle he supposes the foundation of all religion. But there is another principle of the same kind, no less certain and derived from the same source of experience, that where several known circumstances are observed to be similar, the unknown will also be found similar. Thus, if we see the limbs of a human body, we conclude that it is also attended with a human head, though hid from us. Thus, if we see, through a chink in a wall, a small part of the sun, we conclude that were the wall removed we should see the whole body. In short, this method of reasoning is so obvious and familiar that no scruple can ever be made with regard to its solidity.

Now if we survey the universe, so far as it falls under our knowledge, it bears a great resemblance to an animal or organized body, and seems actuated with a like principle of life and motion. A continual circulation of matter in it produces no disorder, a continual waste in every part is incessantly repaired, the closest sympathy is perceived through the entire system, and each part or member, in performing its proper offices, operates both to its own preservation and to that of the whole. The world therefore, I infer, is an animal, and the Deity is the *soul* of the world, actuating it, and actuated by it.

You have too much learning, Cleanthes, to be at all surprised at this opinion, which, you know, was maintained by almost all the theists of antiquity, and chiefly prevails in their discourses and reasonings. For though sometimes the ancient philosophers reason from final causes, as if they thought the world the workmanship of God, yet it appears rather their favorite notion to consider it as his body, whose organization renders it subservient to him. And it must be confessed that, as the universe resembles more a human body than it does the works of human art and contrivance, if our limited analogy could ever, with any propriety, be extended to the whole of nature, the inference seems juster in favor of the ancient than the modern theory.

There are many other advantages, too, in the former theory which recommended it to the ancient theologians. Nothing more repugnant to all their notions, because nothing more repugnant to common experience, than mind without body, a mere spiritual substance which fell not under their senses nor comprehension, and of which they had not observed one single instance throughout all nature. Mind and body they knew because they felt both; an order, arrangement, organization, or internal machinery in both they likewise knew, after the same manner, and it could not but seem reasonable to transfer this experience to the universe, and to suppose the divine mind and body to be also coeval and to have, both of them, order and arrangement naturally inherent in them and inseparable from them.

. . . .

But here, continued PHILO, in examining the ancient system of the soul of the world, there strikes me, all of a sudden, a new idea which, if just, must go near to subvert all your reasoning, and destroy even your first inferences on which you repose such confidence. If the universe bears a greater likeness to animal bodies and to vegetables than to the works of human art, it is more probable that its cause resembles the cause of the former than that of the latter, and its origin ought rather to be ascribed to generation or vegetation than to reason or design. Your conclusion, even according to your own principles, is therefore lame and defective.

Pray open up this argument a little further, said DEMEA, for I do not rightly apprehend it in that concise manner in which you have expressed it.

Our friend Cleanthes, replied PHILO, as you have heard, asserts that since no question of fact can be proved otherwise than by experience, the existence of a Deity admits not of proof from any other medium. The world, says he, resembles the works of human contrivance; therefore its cause must also resemble that of the other. Here we may remark that the operation of one very small part of nature, to wit, man, upon another very small part, to wit, that inanimate matter lying within his reach, is the rule by which Cleanthes judges of the origin of the whole; and he measures objects, so widely disproportioned by the same individual standard. But to waive all objections drawn from this topic, I affirm that there are other parts of the universe (besides the machines of human invention) which bear still a greater resemblance to the fabric of the world, and which therefore afford a better conjecture concerning the universal origin of this system. These parts are animals and vegetables. The world plainly resembles more an animal or a vegetable than it does a watch or a knitting-loom. Its cause, therefore, it is more probable, resembles the cause of the former. The cause of the former is generation or vegetation. The cause, therefore, of the world we may infer to be something similar or analogous to generation or vegetation.

But how is it conceivable, said DEMEA, that the world can arise from anything similar to vegetation or generation?

Very easily, replied PHILO. In like manner as a tree sheds its seed into the neighboring fields and produces other trees, so the great vegetable, the world, or this planetary system, produces within itself certain seeds which, being scattered into the surrounding chaos, vegetate into new worlds. A comet, for instance, is the seed of a world, and after it has been fully ripened by passing from sun to sun and star to star, it is at last tossed into the unformed elements which everywhere surround this universe, and immediately sprouts up into a new system.

Or if, for the sake of variety (for I see no other advantage), we should suppose this world to be an animal, a comet is the egg of this animal, and in like manner as an ostrich lays its egg in the sand, which, without further care, hatches the egg and produces a new animal, so . . . I understand you, says DEMEA. But what wild, arbitrary suppositions are these? What *data* have you for such extraordinary conclusions? And is the slight, imaginary resemblance of the world to a vegetable or an animal sufficient to establish the same inference with regard to both? Objects which are in general so widely different—ought they to be a standard for each other?

Right, cries PHILO. This is the topic on which I have all along insisted. I have still asserted that we have no *data* to establish any system of cosmogony. Our experience, so imperfect in itself and so limited both in extent and duration, can afford us no probable conjecture concerning the whole of things. But if we must needs fix on some hypothesis, by what rule, pray, ought we to determine our choice? Is there any other rule than the greater similarity of the objects compared? And does not a plant or an animal, which springs from vegetation or generation, bear a stronger resemblance to the world than does any artificial machine, which arises from reason and design?

• •

The First-Cause Argument

But if so many difficulties attend the argument *a posteriori*, said DEMEA, had we not better adhere to that simple and sublime argument *a priori* which, by offering to us infallible demonstration, cuts off at once all doubt and difficulty? By this argument, too, we may prove the *infinity* of the divine attributes, which, I am afraid, can never be ascertained with certainty from any other topic. For how can an effect which either is finite or, for aught we know, may be so, how can such an effect, I say, prove an infinite cause? The unity too of the Divine Nature it is very difficult if not absolutely impossible to deduce merely from contemplating the works of nature; nor will the uniformity alone of the plan, even were it allowed, give us any assurance of that attribute. Whereas the argument *a priori* . . .

You seem to reason, Demea, interposed CLEANTHES, as if those advantages and conveniences in the abstract argument were full proofs of its solidity. But it is first proper, in my opinion, to determine what argument of this nature you choose to insist on; and we shall afterwards, from itself better than from its *useful* consequences, endeavor to determine what value we ought to put upon it.

The argument, replied DEMEA, which I would insist on is the common one. Whatever exists must have a cause or reason of its existence, it being absolutely impossible for anything to produce itself or be the cause of its own existence. In mounting up, therefore, from effects to causes, we must either go on in tracing an infinite succession without any ultimate cause at all, or must at last have recourse to some ultimate cause that is *necessarily* existent. Now that the first supposition is absurd may be thus proved. In the infinite chain or succession of causes and effects, each single effect is determined to exist by the power and efficacy of that cause which immediately preceded; but the whole eternal chain or succession, taken together, is not determined or caused by anything; and yet it is evident that it requires a cause or reason, as much as any particular object which begins to exist in time. The question is still reasonable, why this particular succession of causes existed from eternity, and not any other succession or no succession at all. If there be no necessarily existent being, any supposition which can be formed is equally possible; nor is there any more absurdity in nothing's having existed from eternity than there is in that succession of causes which constitutes the universe. What was it, then, which determined something to exist rather than nothing, and bestowed being on a particular possibility, exclusive of the rest? *External causes* there are supposed to be none. *Chance* is a word without a meaning. Was it *nothing?* But that can never produce anything. We must, therefore, have recourse to a necessarily existent Being, who carries the *reason* of his existence in himself, and who cannot be supposed not to exist without an express contradiction. There is consequently such a Being; that is, there is a Deity.

I shall not leave it to Philo, said CLEANTHES (though I know that starting objections is his chief delight), to point out the weakness of this metaphysical reasoning. It seems to me so obviously ill-grounded, and at the same time of so little consequence to the cause of true piety and religion, that I shall myself venture to show the fallacy of it. .

I shall begin with observing that there is an evident absurdity in pretending to demonstrate a matter of fact, or to prove it by any arguments *a priori*. Nothing is demonstrable unless the contrary implies a contradiction. Nothing that is distinctly conceivable implies a contradiction. Whatever we conceive as existent, we can also conceive as nonexistent. There is no being, therefore, whose nonexistence implies a contradiction. Consequently there is no being whose existence is demonstrable. I propose this argument as entirely decisive, and am willing to rest the whole controversy upon it.

It is pretended that the Deity is a necessarily existent being; and this necessity of his existence is attempted to be explained by asserting that if we knew his whole essence or nature we should perceive it to be as impossible for him not to exist as for twice two not to be four. But it is evident that this can never happen, while our faculties remain the same as at present. It will still be possible for us, at any time, to conceive the nonexistence of what we formerly conceived to exist; nor can the mind ever lie under a necessity of supposing any object to remain always in being, in the same manner as we lie under a necessity of always conceiving twice two to be four. The words, therefore, *necessary existence*, have no meaning, or, which is the same thing, none that is consistent.

But further, why may not the material universe be the necessarily existent Being, according to this pretended explication of necessity? We dare not affirm that we know all the qualities of matter; and for aught we can determine, it may contain some qualities which, were they known, would make its nonexistence appear as great a contradiction as twice two is five. I find only one argument employed to prove that the material world is not the necessarily existent Being; and this argument is derived from the contingency both of the matter and the form of the world. "Any particle of matter," it is said,[1] "may be *conceived* to be annihilated, and any form may be *conceived* to be altered. Such an annihilation or alteration, therefore, is not impossible." But it seems a great partiality not to perceive that the same argument extends equally to the Deity, so far as we have any conception of him, and that the mind can at least imagine him to be nonexistent or his attributes to be altered. It must be some unknown, inconceivable qualities which can make his nonexistence appear impossible or his attributes unalterable; and no reason can be assigned why these qualities may not belong to matter. As they are altogether unknown and inconceivable, they can never be proved incompatible with it.

Add to this that in tracing an eternal succession of objects it seems

1. Dr. Clarke.

absurd to inquire for a general cause or first author. How can anything that exists from eternity have a cause, since that relation implies a priority in time and a beginning of existence?

In such a chain too, or succession of objects, each part is caused by that which preceded it, and causes that which succeeds it. Where then is the difficulty? But the *whole*, you say, wants a cause. I answer that the uniting of these parts into a whole, like the uniting of several distinct counties into one kingdom, or several distinct members into one body, is performed merely by an arbitrary act of the mind, and has no influence on the nature of things. Did I show you the particular causes of each individual in a collection of twenty particles of matter, I should think it very unreasonable should you afterwards ask me what was the cause of the whole twenty. This is sufficiently explained in explaining the cause of the parts.

Though the reasonings which you have urged, Cleanthes, may well excuse me, said PHILO, from starting any further difficulties, yet I cannot forbear insisting still upon another topic. It is observed by arithmeticians that the products of 9 compose always either 9 or some lesser product of 9 if you add together all the characters of which any of the former products is composed. Thus, of 18, 27, 36, which are products of 9, you make 9 by adding 1 to 8, 2 to 7, 3 to 6. Thus, 369 is a product also of 9; and if you add 3, 6, and 9, you make 18, a lesser product of 9.[2] To a superficial observer so wonderful a regularity may be admired as the effect either of chance or design; but a skillful algebraist immediately concludes it to be the work of necessity, and demonstrates that it must forever result from the nature of these numbers. Is it not probable, I ask, that the whole economy of the universe is conducted by a like necessity, though no human algebra can furnish a key which solves the difficulty? And instead of admiring the order of natural beings, may it not happen that, could we penetrate into the intimate nature of bodies, we should clearly see why it was absolutely impossible they could ever admit of any other disposition? So dangerous is it to introduce this idea of necessity into the present question! And so naturally does it afford an inference directly opposite to the religious hypothesis!

But dropping all these abstractions, continued PHILO, and confining ourselves to more familiar topics, I shall venture to add an observation, that the argument *a priori* has seldom been found very convincing, except to people of a metaphysical head who have accustomed themselves to abstract reasoning, and who, finding from mathematics that the understanding frequently leads to truth through obscurity and contrary to first appearances, have transferred the same habit of thinking to subjects where it ought not to have place. Other people, even of good sense and the best inclined to religion, feel always some deficiency in such arguments, though they are not perhaps able to explain distinctly where it lies. A certain proof that men ever did and ever will derive their religion from other sources than from this species of reasoning.

2. *Repùblique des Lettres*, Aug. 1685.

5. William James

William James (1842–1910), a member of a distinguished family that included Henry James, the novelist, was equally renown as a psychologist and as a philosopher.

Are Men Ever Directly Aware of God?

The Nature of Mystical Experience

Over and over again in these lectures I have raised points and left them open and unfinished until we should have come to the subject of Mysticism. Some of you, I fear, may have smiled as you noted my reiterated postponements. But now the hour has come when mysticism must be faced in good earnest, and those broken threads wound up together. One may say truly, I think, that personal religious experience has its root and centre in mystical states of consciousness; so for us, who in these lectures are treating personal experience as the exclusive subject of our study, such states of consciousness ought to form the vital chapter from which the other chapters get their light. Whether my treatment of mystical states will shed more light or darkness, I do not know, for my own constitution shuts me out from their enjoyment almost entirely, and I can speak of them only at second hand. But though forced to look upon the subject so externally, I will be as objective and receptive as I can; and I

From Lectures XVI & XVII, "Mysticism," of *The Varieties of Religious Experience* (1902). Subheadings added by the editors.

think I shall at least succeed in convincing you of the reality of the states in question, and of the paramount importance of their function.

First of all, then, I ask, What does the expression "mystical states of consciousness" mean? How do we part off mystical states from other states?

The words "mysticism" and "mystical" are often used as terms of mere reproach, to throw at any opinion which we regard as vague and vast and sentimental, and without a base in either facts or logic. For some writers a "mystic" is any person who believes in thought-transference, or spirit-return. Employed in this way the word has little value: there are too many less ambiguous synonyms. So, to keep it useful by restricting it, I will do what I did in the case of the word "religion," and simply propose to you four marks which, when an experience has them, may justify us in calling it mystical for the purpose of the present lectures. In this way we shall save verbal disputation, and the recriminations that generally go therewith.

1. *Ineffability*

The handiest of the marks by which I classify a state of mind as mystical is negative. The subject of it immediately says that it defies expression, that no adequate report of its contents can be given in words. It follows from this that its quality must be directly experienced; it cannot be imparted or transferred to others. In this peculiarity mystical states are more like states of feeling than like states of intellect. No one can make clear to another who has never had a certain feeling, in what the quality or worth of it consists. One must have musical ears to know the value of a symphony; one must have been in love one's self to understand a lover's state of mind. Lacking the heart or ear, we cannot interpret the musician or the lover justly, and are even likely to consider him weak-minded or absurd. The mystic finds that most of us accord to his experiences an equally incompetent treatment.

2. *Noetic quality*

Although so similar to states of feeling, mystical states seem to those who experience them to be also states of knowledge. They are states of insight into depths of truth unplumbed by the discursive intellect. They are illuminations, revelations, full of significance and importance, all inarticulate though they remain; and as a rule they carry with them a curious sense of authority for aftertime.

These two characters will entitle any state to be called mystical, in the sense in which I use the word. Two other qualities are less sharply marked, but are usually found. These are:

3. *Transiency*

Mystical states cannot be sustained for long. Except in rare instances, half an hour, or at most an hour or two, seems to be the limit beyond

56

which they fade into the light of common day. Often, when faded, their quality can but imperfectly be reproduced in memory; but when they recur it is recognized; and from one recurrence to another it is susceptible of continuous development in what is felt as inner richness and importance.

4. Passivity

Although the oncoming of mystical states may be facilitated by preliminary voluntary operations, as by fixing the attention, or going through certain bodily performances, or in other ways which manuals of mysticism prescribe; yet when the characteristic sort of consciousness once has set in, the mystic feels as if his own will were in abeyance, and indeed sometimes as if he were grasped and held by a superior power. This latter peculiarity connects mystical states with certain definite phenomena of secondary or alternative personality, such as prophetic speech, automatic writing, or the mediumistic trance. When these latter conditions are well pronounced, however, there may be no recollection whatever of the phenomenon, and it may have no significance for the subject's usual inner life, to which, as it were, it makes a mere interruption. Mystical states, strictly so-called, are never merely interruptive. Some memory of their content always remains, and a profound sense of their importance. They modify the inner life of the subject between the times of their recurrence. Sharp divisions in this region are, however, difficult to make, and we find all sorts of gradations and mixtures.

These four characteristics are sufficient to mark out a group of states of consciousness peculiar enough to deserve a special name and to call for careful study. Let it then be called the mystical group.

Analogues of Mystical Experience

Our next step should be to gain acquaintance with some typical examples. Professional mystics at the height of their development have often elaborately organized experiences and a philosophy based thereupon. But you remember what I said in my first lecture: phenomena are best understood when placed within their series, studied in their germ and in their overripe decay, and compared with their exaggerated and degenerated kindred. The range of mystical experience is very wide, much too wide for us to cover in the time at our disposal. Yet the method of serial study is so essential for interpretation that if we really wish to reach conclusions we must use it. I will begin, therefore, with phenomena which claim no special religious significance, and end with those of which the religious pretensions are extreme.

The simplest rudiment of mystical experience would seem to be that deepened sense of the significance of a maxim or formula which occasionally sweeps over one. "I've heard that said all my life," we exclaim, "but I never realized its full meaning until now." "When a fellow monk," said Luther, "one day repeated the words of the Creed: 'I believe in the forgiveness of sins,' I saw the Scripture in an entirely new light; and straightway I felt as if I were born anew. It was as if I had found the door of paradise thrown wide open." This sense of deeper significance is not confined to rational propositions. Single words, and conjunctions of words, effects of light on land and sea, odors and musical sounds, all bring it when the mind is tuned aright. Most of us can remember the strangely moving power of passages in certain poems read when we were young, irrational doorways as they were through which the mystery of fact, the wildness and the pang of life, stole into our hearts and thrilled them. The words have now perhaps become mere polished surfaces for us; but lyric poetry and music are alive and significant only in proportion as they fetch these vague vistas of a life continuous with our own, beckoning and inviting, yet ever eluding our pursuit. We are alive or dead to the eternal inner message of the arts according as we have kept or lost this mystical susceptibility.

A more pronounced step forward on the mystical ladder is found in an extremely frequent phenomenon, that sudden feeling, namely, which sometimes sweeps over us, of having "been here before," as if at some indefinite past time, in just this place, with just these people, we were already saying just these things. As Tennyson writes:

> Moreover, something is or seems
> That touches me with mystic gleams,
> Like glimpses of forgotten dreams—
>
> Of something felt, like something here;
> Of something done, I know not where;
> Such as no language may declare.

Somewhat deeper plunges into mystical consciousness are met with in yet other dreamy states. Such feelings as these which Charles Kingsley describes are surely far from being uncommon, especially in youth:

> When I walk the fields, I am oppressed now and then with an innate feeling that everything I see has a meaning, if I could but understand it. And this feeling of being surrounded with truths which I cannot grasp amounts to indescribable awe sometimes. . . . Have you not felt that your real soul was imperceptible to your mental vision, except in a few hallowed moments?

The next step into mystical states carries us into a realm that public opinion and ethical philosophy have long since branded as pathological, though private practice and certain lyric strains of poetry seem still to bear witness to its ideality. I refer to the consciousness produced by intoxicants and anaesthetics, especially by alcohol. The sway of alcohol over mankind is unquestionably due to its power to stimulate the mystical faculties of human nature, usually crushed to earth by the cold facts and dry criticisms of the sober hour. Sobriety diminishes, discriminates, and says no; drunkenness expands, unites, and says yes. It is in fact the great exciter of the *Yes* function in man. It brings its votary from the chill periphery of things to the radiant core. It makes him for the moment one with truth. Not through mere perversity do men run after it. To the poor and the unlettered it stands in the place of symphony concerts and of literature; and it is part of the deeper mystery and tragedy of life that whiffs and gleams of something that we immediately recognize as excellent should be vouchsafed to so many of us only in the fleeting earlier phases of what in its totality is so degrading a poisoning. The drunken consciousness is one bit of the mystic consciousness, and our total opinion of it must find its place in our opinion of that larger whole.

Nitrous oxide and ether, especially nitrous oxide, when sufficiently diluted with air, stimulate the mystical consciousness in an extraordinary degree. Depth beyond depth of truth seems revealed to the inhaler. This truth fades out, however, or escapes, at the moment of coming to; and if any words remain over in which it seemed to clothe itself, they prove to be the veriest nonsense. Nevertheless, the sense of a profound meaning having been there persists; and I know more than one person who is persuaded that in the nitrous oxide trance we have a genuine metaphysical revelation.

Some years ago I myself made some observations on this aspect of nitrous oxide intoxication, and reported them in print. One conclusion was forced upon my mind at that time, and my impression of its truth has ever since remained unshaken. It is that our normal waking consciousness, rational consciousness as we call it, is but one special type of consciousness, whilst all about it, parted from it by the filmiest of screens, there lie potential forms of consciousness entirely different. We may go through life without suspecting their existence; but apply the requisite stimulus, and at a touch they are there in all their completeness, definite types of mentality which probably somewhere have their field of application and adaptation. No account of the universe in its totality can be final which leaves these other forms of consciousness quite disregarded. How to regard them is the question—for they are so discontinuous with ordinary consciousness. Yet they may determine attitudes though they cannot furnish formulas, and open a region though they fail to give a map. At any rate, they forbid a premature closing of our accounts with reality. Looking back on my own experiences, they all converge towards a kind of insight to which I cannot help ascribing some metaphysical significance. The keynote of it is invariably a reconciliation. It is as if the opposites of the world, whose contradictoriness and conflict make all our difficulties and troubles, were melted into unity. Not only do they, as contrasted species, belong to one and the same genus, but *one of the species*, the nobler and better one, *is itself the genus, and so soaks up and absorbs its opposite into itself*. This is a dark saying, I know, when thus expressed in terms of common logic, but I cannot wholly escape from its authority. I feel as if it must mean something, something like what the Hegelian philosophy means, if one could only lay hold of it more clearly. Those who have ears to hear, let them hear; to me the living sense of its reality only comes in the artificial mystic state of mind.

I just now spoke of friends who believe in the anaesthetic revelation.

For them too it is a monistic insight, in which the *other* in its various forms appears absorbed into the One.

"Into this pervading genius," writes one of them, "we pass, forgetting and forgotten, and thenceforth each is all, in God. There is no higher, no deeper, no other, than the life in which we are founded. 'The One remains, the many change and pass;' and each and every one of us *is* the One that remains. . . . This is the ultimatum. . . . As sure as being—whence is all our care—so sure is content, beyond duplexity, antithesis, or trouble, where I have triumphed in a solitude that God is not above."

. . . .

Certain aspects of nature seem to have a peculiar power of awakening such mystical moods.

. . . .

Here is a record from the memoirs of that interesting German idealist, Malwida von Meysenburg:

I was alone upon the seashore as all these thoughts flowed over me, liberating and reconciling; and now again, as once before in distant days in the Alps of Dauphiné, I was impelled to kneel down, this time before the illimitable ocean, symbol of the Infinite. I felt that I prayed as I had never prayed before, and knew now what prayer really is: to return from the solitude of individuation into the consciousness of unity with all that is, to kneel down as one that passes away, and to rise up as one imperishable. Earth, heaven, and sea resounded as in one vast world-encircling harmony. It was as if the chorus of all the great who had ever lived were about me. I felt myself one with them, and it appeared as if I heard their greeting: "Thou too belongest to the company of those who overcome."

. . . .

Mystical Experience in Religion

We have now seen enough of this cosmic or mystic consciousness, as it comes sporadically. We must next pass to its methodical cultivation as an element of the religious life. Hindus, Buddhists, Mohammedans, and Christians all have cultivated it methodically.

In India, training in mystical insight has been known from time immemorial under the name of yoga. Yoga means the experimental union of the individual with the divine. It is based on persevering exercise; and the diet, posture, breathing, intellectual concentration, and moral discipline vary slightly in the different systems which teach it. The yogi, or disciple, who has by these means overcome the obscurations of his lower nature sufficiently, enters into the conditions termed *samâdhi*, "and comes face to face with facts which no instinct or reason can ever know." He learns

That the mind itself has a higher state of existence, beyond reason, a superconscious state, and that when the mind gets to that higher state, then this knowledge beyond reasoning comes. . . . All the different steps in yoga are intended to bring us scientifically to the superconscious state or Samâdhi. . . . Just as unconscious work is beneath consciousness, so there is another work which is above consciousness, and which, also, is not accompanied with the feeling of egoism. . . . There is no feeling of *I*, and yet the mind works, desireless, free from restlessness, objectless, bodiless. Then the Truth shines in its full effulgence, and we know ourselves—for Samâdhi lies potential in us all—for what we truly are, free, immortal, omnipotent, loosed from the finite, and its contrasts of good and evil together, and identical with the Atman or Universal Soul.

The Vedantists say that one may stumble into superconsciousness sporadically, without the previous discipline, but it is then impure. Their test of its purity, like our test of religion's value, is empirical: its fruits must be good for life. When a man comes out of Samâdhi, they assure us that he remains "enlightened, a sage, a prophet, a saint, his whole character changed, his life changed, illumined."

The Buddhists used the word "samâdhi" as well as the Hindus; but "dhyâna" is their special word for higher states of contemplation. There seem to be four stages recognized in dhyâna. The first stage comes through concentration of the mind upon one point. It excludes desire, but not discernment or judgment: it is still intellectual. In the second stage the intellectual functions drop off, and the satisfied sense of unity remains. In the third stage the satisfaction departs, and indifference begins, along with memory and self-consciousness. In the fourth stage the indifference, memory, and self-consciousness are perfected. [Just what "memory" and "self-consciousness" mean in this connection is doubtful. They cannot be the faculties familiar to us in the lower life.] Higher stages still of contemplation are mentioned—a region where there exists nothing, and where the mediator says: "There exists absolutely nothing," and stops. Then he reaches another region where he says: "There are neither ideas nor absence of ideas," and stops again. Then another region where, "having reached the end of both idea and perception, he stops finally." This would seem to be, not yet Nirvâna, but as close an approach to it as this life affords.

 . . . .

In the Christian church there have always been mystics. Although many of them have been viewed with suspicion, some have gained favor in the eyes of the authorities. The experiences of these have been treated as precedents, and a codified system of mystical theology has been based upon them, in which everything legitimate finds its place. The basis of the system is "orison" or meditation, the methodical elevation of the soul towards God. Through the practice of orison the higher levels of mystical experience may be attained. It is odd that Protestantism, especially evangelical Protestantism, should seemingly have abandoned everything methodical in this line. Apart from what prayer may lead to, Protestant mystical experience appears to have been almost exclusively sporadic. It has been left to our mind-curers to reintroduce methodical meditation into our religious life.

The first thing to be aimed at in orison is the mind's detachment from outer sensations, for these interfere with its concentration upon ideal things. Such manuals as Saint Ignatius's Spiritual Exercises recommend the disciple to expel sensation by a graduated series of efforts to imagine holy scenes. The acme of this kind of discipline would be a semi-hallucinatory monoideism—an imaginary figure of Christ, for example, coming fully to occupy the mind. Sensorial images of this sort, whether literal or symbolic, play an enormous part in mysticism. But in certain cases imagery may fall away entirely, and in the very highest raptures it tends to do so. The state of consciousness becomes then insusceptible of any verbal description. Mystical teachers are unanimous as to this. Saint John of the Cross, for instance, one of the best of them, thus describes the condition called the "union of love," which, he says, is reached by "dark contemplation." In this the Deity compenetrates the soul, but in such a hidden way that the soul

> finds no terms, no means, no comparison whereby to render the sublimity of the wisdom and the delicacy of the spiritual feeling with which she is filled. . . . We receive this mystical knowledge of God clothed in none of the kinds of images, in none of the sensible representations, which our mind makes use of in other circumstances. Accordingly in this knowledge, since the senses and the imagination are not employed, we get neither form nor impression, nor can we give any account or furnish any likeness, although the mysterious and sweet-tasting wisdom comes home so clearly to the inmost parts of our soul. Fancy a man seeing a certain kind of thing for the first time in his life. He can understand it, use and enjoy it, but he cannot apply a name to it, nor communicate any idea of it, even though all the while it be a mere thing of sense. How much greater will be his powerlessness when it goes beyond the senses! This is the peculiarity of the divine language. The more infused, intimate, spiritual, and supersensible it is, the more does it exceed the senses, both inner and outer, and impose silence upon them. . . . The soul then feels as if placed in a vast and profound solitude, to which no created thing has access, in an immense and boundless desert, desert the more delicious the more solitary it is. There, in this abyss of wisdom, the soul grows by what it drinks in from the well-springs of the comprehension of love, . . . and recognizes, however sublime and learned may be the terms we employ, how utterly vile, insignificant, and improper they are, when we seek to discourse of divine things by their means.

I cannot pretend to detail to you the sundry stages of the Christian mystical life. Our time would not suffice, for one thing; and moreover, I confess that the subdivisions and names which we find in the Catholic books seem to me to represent nothing objectively distinct. So many men, so many minds: I imagine that these experiences can be as infinitely varied as are the idiosyncrasies of individuals.

The cognitive aspects of them, their value in the way of revelation, is what we are directly concerned with, and it is easy to show by citation how strong an impression they leave of being revelations of new depths of truth. Saint Teresa is the expert of experts in describing such conditions, so I will turn immediately to what she says of one of the highest of them, the "orison of union."

"In the orison of union," says Saint Teresa, "the soul is fully awake as regards God, but wholly asleep as regards things of this world and in respect of herself. During the short time the union lasts, she is as it were deprived of every feeling, and even if she would, she could not think of any single thing. Thus she needs to employ no artifice in order to arrest the use of her understanding: it remains so stricken with inactivity that she neither knows what she loves, nor in what manner she loves, nor what she wills. In short, she is utterly dead to the things of the world and lives solely in God. . . . I do not even know whether in this state she has enough life left to breathe. It seems to me she has not; or at least that if she does breathe, she is unaware of it. Her intellect would fain understand something of what is going on within her, but it has so little force now that it can act in no way whatsoever. So a person who falls into a deep faint appears as if dead. . . .

"Thus does God, when he raises a soul to union with himself, suspend the natural action of all her faculties. She neither sees, hears, nor understands, so long as she is united with God. But this time is always short, and it seems even shorter than it is. God establishes himself in the interior of this soul in such a way, that when she returns to herself, it is wholly impossible for her to doubt that she has been in God, and God in her. This truth remains so strongly impressed on her that, even though many years should pass without the condition returning, she can neither forget the favor she received, nor doubt of its reality. If you, nevertheless, ask how it is possible that the soul can see and understand that she has been in God, since during the union she has neither sight nor understanding, I reply that she does not see it then, but that she sees it clearly later, after she has returned to herself, not by any vision, but by a certitude which abides with her and which God alone can give her. I knew a person who was ignorant of the truth that God's mode of being in everything must be either by presence, by power, or by essence, but who, after having received the grace of which I am speaking, believed this truth in the most unshakable manner. So much so that, having consulted a half-learned man who was as ignorant on this point as she had been before she was enlightened, when he replied that God is in us only by 'grace,' she disbelieved his reply, so sure she was of the true answer; and when she came to ask wiser doctors, they confirmed her in her belief, which much consoled her. . . .

"But how, you will repeat, *can* one have such certainty in respect to what one does not see? This question, I am powerless to answer. These are secrets of God's omnipotence which it does not appertain to me to penetrate. All that I know is that I tell the truth; and I shall never believe that any soul who does not possess the certainty has ever been really united to God."

. . . .

The deliciousness of some of these states seems to be beyond anything known in ordinary consciousness. It evidently involves organic sensibilities, for it is spoken of as something too extreme to be borne, and as verging on bodily pain. But it is too subtle and piercing a delight for ordinary words to denote. God's touches, the wounds of his spear, references to ebriety and to nuptial union have to figure in the phraseology by which it is shadowed forth. Intellect and senses both swoon away in these highest states of ecstasy. "If our understanding comprehends," says Saint Teresa, "it is in a mode which remains unknown to it, and it can understand nothing of what it comprehends. For my own part, I do not believe that it does comprehend, because, as I said, it does not understand itself to do so. I confess that it is all a mystery in which I am lost." In the condition called *raptus* or ravishment by theologians, breathing and circulation are so depressed that it is a question among the doctors whether the soul be or be not temporarily dissevered from the body. One must read Saint Teresa's descriptions and the very exact distinctions which she makes, to persuade one's self that one is dealing, not with imaginary experiences, but with phenomena which, however rare, follow perfectly definite psychological types.

To the medical mind these ecstasies signify nothing but suggested and imitated hypnoid states, on an intellectual basis of superstition, and a corporeal one of degeneration and hysteria. Undoubtedly these pathological conditions have existed in many and possibly in all the cases, but that fact tells us nothing about the value for knowledge of the consciousness which they induce. To pass a spiritual judgment upon these states, we must not content ourselves with superficial medical talk, but inquire into their fruits for life.

Their fruits appear to have been various. Stupefaction, for one thing, seems not to have been altogether absent as a result. You may remember the helplessness in the kitchen and schoolroom of poor Margaret Mary Alacoque. Many other ecstatics would have perished but for the care taken of them by admiring followers. The "other-worldliness" encouraged by the mystical consciousness makes this over-abstraction from practical life peculiarly liable to befall mystics in whom the character is naturally passive and the intellect feeble; but in natively strong minds and characters we find quite opposite results. The great Spanish mystics, who carried the habit of ecstasy as far as it has often been carried, appear for the most part to have shown indomitable spirit and energy, and all the more so for the trances in which they indulged.

Saint Ignatius was a mystic, but his mysticism made him assuredly one of the most powerfully practical human engines that ever lived. Saint John of the Cross, writing of the intuitions and "touches" by which God reaches the substance of the soul, tells us that

> They enrich it marvelously. A single one of them may be sufficient to abolish at a stroke certain imperfections of which the soul during its whole life had vainly tried to rid itself, and to leave it adorned with virtues and loaded with supernatural gifts. A single one of these intoxicating consolations may reward it for all the labors undergone in its life—even were they numberless. Invested with an invincible courage, filled with an impassioned desire to suffer for its God, the soul then is seized with a strange torment—that of not being allowed to suffer enough.

. . . .

The Intellectual Content of Mysticism

Mystical conditions may, therefore, render the soul more energetic in the lines which their inspiration favors. But this could be reckoned an advantage only in case the inspiration were a true one. If the inspiration were erroneous, the energy would be all the more mistaken and misbegotten. So we stand once more before that problem of truth which confronted us at the end of the lectures on saintliness. You will remember that we turned to mysticism precisely to get some light on truth. Do mystical states establish the truth of those theological affections in which the saintly life has its root?

In spite of their repudiation of articulate self-description, mystical states in general assert a pretty distinct theoretic drift. It is possible to give the outcome of the majority of them in terms that point in definite philosophical directions. One of these directions is optimism, and the other is monism. We pass into mystical states from out of ordinary consciousness as from a less into a more, as from a smallness into a vastness, and at the same time as from an unrest to a rest. We feel them as reconciling, unifying states. They appeal to the yes-function more than to the no-function in us. In them the unlimited absorbs the limits and peacefully closes the account. Their very denial of every adjective you may propose as applicable to the ultimate truth—He, the Self, the Atman, is to be described by "No! no!" only, say the Upanishads—though it seems on the surface to be a no-function, is a denial made on behalf of a deeper yes. Whoso calls the Absolute anything in particular, or says that it is *this*, seems implicitly to shut it off from being *that*—it is as if he lessened it. So we deny the "this," negating the negation which it seems to us to imply, in the interests of the higher affirmative attitude by which we are possessed. The fountain-head of Christian mysticism is Dionysius the Areopagite. He describes the absolute truth by negatives exclusively.

> The cause of all things is neither soul nor intellect; nor has it imagination, opinion, or reason, or intelligence; nor is it reason or intelligence; nor is it spoken or thought. It is neither number, nor order, nor magnitude, nor littleness, nor equality, nor inequality, nor similarity, nor dissimilarity. It neither stands, nor moves, nor rests. . . . It is neither essence, nor eternity, nor time. Even intellectual contact does not belong to it. It is neither science nor truth. It is not even royalty or wisdom; not one; not unity; not divinity or goodness; nor even spirit as we know it, etc., *ad libitum.*

But these qualifications are denied by Dionysius, not because the truth falls short of them, but because it so infinitely excels them. It is above them. It is *super*-lucent, *super*-splendent, *super*-essential, *super*-sublime, *super everything* that can be named.

. . . .

Thus come the paradoxical expressions that so abound in mystical writings. As when Eckhart tells of the still desert of the Godhead, "where never was seen difference, neither Father, Son, nor Holy Ghost, where there is no one at home, yet where the spark of the soul is more at peace than in itself."

To this dialectical use, by the intellect, of negation as a mode of passage towards a higher kind of affirmation, there is correlated the subtlest of moral counterparts in the sphere of the personal will. Since denial of the finite self and its wants, since asceticism of some sort, is found in religious experience to be the only doorway to the larger and more blessed life, this moral mystery intertwines and combines with the intellectual mystery in all mystical writings.

"Love," continues Behmen, is Nothing, for "when thou art gone forth wholly from the Creature and from that which is visible, and art become Nothing to all that is Nature and Creature, then thou art in that eternal One, which is God himself, and then thou shalt feel within thee the highest virtue of Love. . . . The treasure of treasures for the soul is where she goeth out of the Somewhat into that Nothing out of which all things may be made. The soul here saith, *I have nothing,* for I am utterly stripped and naked; *I can do nothing,* for I have no manner of power, but am as water poured out; *I am nothing,* for all that I am is no more than an image of Being, and only God is to me I AM; and so, sitting down in my own Nothingness, I give glory to the eternal Being, and *will nothing* of myself, that so God may will all in me, being unto me my God and all things."

In Paul's language, I live, yet not I, but Christ liveth in me. Only when I become as nothing can God enter in and no difference between his life and mine remain outstanding.

. . . .

I have now sketched with extreme brevity and insufficiency, but as fairly as I am able in the time allowed, the general traits of the mystic range of consciousness. *It is on the whole pantheistic and optimistic, or at least the opposite of pessimistic. It is anti-naturalistic, and harmonizes best with twice-bornness and so-called otherworldly states of mind.*

Is Mystical Experience Veridical?

My next task is to inquire whether we can invoke it as authoritative. Does it furnish any *warrant for the truth* of the twice-bornness and super-naturality and pantheism which it favors? I must give my answer to this question as concisely as I can.

In brief my answer is this—and I will divide it into three parts:

1. Mystical states, when well developed, usually are, and have the right to be, absolutely authoritative over the individuals to whom they come.
2. No authority emanates from them which should make it a duty for those who stand outside of them to accept their revelations uncritically.
3. They break down the authority of the nonmystical or rationalistic consciousness, based upon the understanding and the senses alone. They show it to be only one kind of consciousness. They open out the possibility of other orders of truth, in which, so far as anything in us vitally responds to them, we may freely continue to have faith.

I will take up these points one by one.

1.

As a matter of psychological fact, mystical states of a well-pronounced and emphatic sort *are* usually authoritative over those who have them.

They have been "there," and know. It is vain for rationalism to grumble about this. If the mystical truth that comes to a man proves to be a force that he can live by, what mandate have we of the majority to order him to live in another way? We can throw him into a prison or a madhouse, but we cannot change his mind—we commonly attach it only the more stubbornly to its beliefs. It mocks our utmost efforts, as a matter of fact, and in point of logic it absolutely escapes our jurisdiction. Our own more "rational" beliefs are based on evidence exactly similar in nature to that which mystics quote for theirs. Our senses, namely, have assured us of certain states of fact; but mystical experiences are as direct perceptions of fact for those who have them as any sensations ever were for us. The records show that even though the five senses be in abeyance in them, they are absolutely sensational in their epistemological quality, if I may be pardoned the barbarous expression—that is, they are face to face presentations of what seems immediately to exist.

The mystic is, in short, *invulnerable,* and must be left whether we relish it or not, in undisturbed enjoyment of his creed. Faith, says Tolstoy, is that by which men live. And faith-state and mystic state are practically convertible terms.

2.

But I now proceed to add that mystics have no right to claim that we ought to accept the deliverance of their peculiar experiences, if we are ourselves outsiders and feel no private call thereto. The utmost they can ever ask of us in this life is to admit that they establish a presumption. They form a consensus and have an unequivocal outcome; and it would be odd, mystics might say, if such a unanimous type of experience should prove to be altogether wrong. At bottom, however, this would only be an appeal to numbers, like the appeal of rationalism the other way; and the appeal to numbers has no logical force. If we acknowledge it, it is for "suggestive," not for logical reasons: we follow the majority because to do so suits our life.

But even this presumption from the unanimity of mystics is far from being strong. In characterizing mystic states as pantheistic, optimistic, etc., I am afraid I over-simplified the truth. I did so for expository reasons, and to keep the closer to the classic mystical tradition. The classic religious mysticism, it now must be confessed, is only a "privileged case." It is an *extract*, kept true to type by the selection of the fittest specimens and their preservation in "schools." It is carved out from a much larger mass; and if we take the larger mass as seriously as religious mysticism has historically taken itself, we find that the supposed unanimity largely disappears. To begin with, even religious mysticism itself, the kind that accumulates traditions and makes schools, is much less unanimous than I have allowed. It has been both ascetic and antinomianly self-indulgent within the Christian church. It is dualistic in Sankhya, and monistic in Vedanta philosophy. I called it pantheistic; but the great Spanish mystics are anything but pantheists. They are with few exceptions nonmetaphysical minds, for whom "the category of personality" is absolute. The "union" of man with God is for them much more like an occasional miracle than like an original identity. How different again, apart from the happiness common to all, is the mysticism of Walt Whitman, Edward Carpenter, Richard Jeffries, and other naturalistic pantheists, from the more distinctively Christian sort. The fact is that the mystical feeling of enlargement, union, and emancipation has no specific intellectual content whatever of its own. It is capable of forming matrimonial alliances with material furnished by the most diverse philosophies and theologies, provided only they can find a place in their framework for its peculiar emotional mood. We have no right, therefore, to invoke its prestige as distinctively in favor of any special belief, such as that in the absolute idealism, or in the absolute monistic identity, or in the absolute goodness, of the world. It is only relatively in favor of all these things—it passes out of common human consciousness in the direction in which they lie.

So much for religious mysticism proper. But more remains to be told, for religious mysticism is only one half of mysticism. The other half has no accumulated traditions except those which the text-books on insanity supply. Open any one of these, and you will find abundant cases in which mystical ideas are cited as characteristic symptoms of enfeebled or deluded states of mind. In delusional insanity, paranoia, as they sometimes call it, we may have a *diabolical* mysticism, a sort of religious mysticism turned upside down. The same sense of ineffable importance in the smallest events, the same texts and words coming with new meanings, the same voices and visions and leadings and missions, the same controlling by extraneous powers; only this time the emotion is pessimistic: instead of consolations we have desolations; the meanings are dreadful; and the powers are enemies to life. It is evident that from the point of view of their psychological mechanism, the classic mysticism and these lower mysticisms spring from the same mental level, from that great subliminal or transmarginal region of which science is beginning to admit the existence, but of which so little is really known. That region contains every kind of matter: "seraph and snake" abide there side by side. To come from thence is no infallible credential. What comes must be sifted and tested, and run the gauntlet of confrontation with the total context of experience, just like what comes from the outer world of sense. Its value must be ascertained by empirical methods, so long as we are not mystics ourselves.

Once more, then, I repeat that nonmystics are under no obligation to acknowledge in mystical states a superior authority conferred on them by their intrinsic nature.

3.

Yet, I repeat once more, the existence of mystical states absolutely overthrows the pretension of nonmystical states to be the sole and ultimate dictators of what we may believe. As a rule, mystical states merely add a supersensuous meaning to the ordinary outward data of consciousness.

They are excitements like the emotions of love or ambition, gifts to our spirit by means of which facts already objectively before us fall into a new expressiveness and make a new connection with our active life. They do not contradict these facts as such, or deny anything that our senses have immediately seized. It is the rationalistic critic rather who plays the part of denier in the controversy, and his denials have no strength, for there never can be a state of facts to which new meaning may not truthfully be added, provided the mind ascend to a more enveloping point of view. It must always remain an open question whether mystical states may not possibly be such superior points of view, windows through which the mind looks out upon a more extensive and inclusive world. The difference of the views seen from the different mystical windows need not prevent us from entertaining this supposition. The wider world would in that case prove to have a mixed constitution like that of this world, that is all. It would have its celestial and its infernal regions, its tempting and its saving moments, its valid experiences and its counterfeit ones, just as our world has them; and it would be a wider world all the same. We should have to use its experiences by selecting and subordinating and substituting just as is our custom in this ordinary naturalistic world; we should be liable to error just as we are now; yet the counting in of that wider world of meanings, and the serious dealing with it, might, in spite of all the perplexity, be indispensable stages in our approach to the final fullness of the truth.

In this shape, I think, we have to leave the subject. Mystical states indeed wield no authority due simply to their being mystical states. But the higher ones among them point in directions to which the religious sentiments even of nonmystical men incline. They tell of the supremacy of the ideal, of vastness, of union, of safety, and of rest. They offer us *hypotheses*, hypotheses which we may voluntarily ignore, but which as thinkers we cannot possibly upset. The supernaturalism and optimism to which they would persuade us may, interpreted in one way or another, be after all the truest of insights into the meaning of this life.

6. Bertrand Russell

Bertrand Russell (1872–1970) was one of the most prominent philosophers of the twentieth century, having left his mark on virtually every branch of philosophy.

A Skeptical View of Mysticism

Ought we to admit that there is available, in support of religion, a source of knowledge which lies outside science and may properly be described as "revelation"? This is a difficult question to argue, because those who believe that truths have been revealed to them profess the same kind of certainty in regard to them that we have in regard to objects of sense. We believe the man who has seen things through the telescope that we have never seen; why, then, they ask, should we not believe them when they report things that are to them equally unquestionable?

It is, perhaps, useless to attempt an argument such as will appeal to the man who has himself enjoyed mystic illumination. But something can be said as to whether we others should accept this testimony. In the first place, it is not subject to the ordinary tests. When a man of science tells us the result of an experiment, he also tells us how the experiment was performed; others can repeat it, and if the result is not confirmed it is not accepted as true; but many men might put themselves into the situation in which the mystic's vision occurred without obtaining the same revelation. To this it may be answered that a man must use the appropriate sense: a telescope is useless to a man who keeps his eyes shut. The argument as to the credibility of the mystic's testimony may be prolonged almost indefinitely. Science should be neutral, since the

Bertrand Russell, *Religion and Science* (1935). Reprinted by permission of the Oxford University Press. From Chapter VII, "Mysticism."

argument is a scientific one, to be conducted exactly as an argument would be conducted about an uncertain experiment. Science depends upon perception and inference; its credibility is due to the fact that the perceptions are such as any observer can test. The mystic himself may be certain that he *knows*, and has no need of scientific tests; but those who are asked to accept his testimony will subject it to the same kind of scientific tests as those applied to men who say they have been to the North Pole. Science, as such, should have no expectation, positive or negative, as to the result.

The chief argument in favour of the mystics is their agreement with each other. "I know nothing more remarkable," says Dean Inge, "than the unanimity of the mystics, ancient, mediaeval, and modern, Protestant, Catholic, and even Buddhist or Mohammedan, though the Christian mystics are the most trustworthy." I do not wish to underrate the force of this argument, which I acknowledged long ago in a book called *Mysticism and Logic*. The mystics vary greatly in their capacity for giving verbal expression to their experiences, but I think we may take it that those who succeeded best all maintain: 1) that all division and separateness is unreal, and that the universe is a single indivisible unity; 2) that evil is illusory, and that the illusion arises through falsely regarding a part as self-subsistent; 3) that time is unreal, and that reality is eternal, not in the sense of being everlasting, but in the sense of being wholly outside time. I do not pretend that this is a complete account of the matters on which all mystics concur, but the three propositions that I have mentioned may serve as representatives of the whole. Let us now imagine ourselves a jury in a law-court, whose business it is to decide on the credibility of the witnesses who make these three somewhat surprising assertions.

We shall find, in the first place, that, while the witnesses agree up to a point, they disagree totally when that point is passed, although they are just as certain as when they agree. Catholics, but not Protestants, may have visions in which the Virgin appears; Christians and Mohammedans, but not Buddhists, may have great truths revealed to them by the Archangel Gabriel; the Chinese mystics of the Tao tell us, as a direct result of their central doctrine, that all government is bad, whereas most European and Mohammedan mystics, with equal confidence, urge submission to constituted authority. As regards the points where they differ, each group will argue that the other groups are untrustworthy; we might, therefore, if we were content with a mere forensic triumph, point out that most mystics think most other mystics mistaken on most points. They might, however, make this only half a triumph by agreeing on the greater importance of the matters about which they are at one, as compared with those as to which their opinions differ. We will, in any case, assume that they have composed their differences, and concentrated the defence at these three points—namely, the unity of the world, the illusory nature of evil, and the unreality of time. What test can we, as impartial outsiders, apply to their unanimous evidence?

As men of scientific temper, we shall naturally first ask whether there is any way by which we can ourselves obtain the same evidence at first hand. To this we shall receive various answers. We may be told that we are obviously not in a receptive frame of mind, and that we lack the requisite humility; or that fasting and religious meditation are necessary; or (if our witness is Indian or Chinese) that the essential prerequisite is a course of breathing exercises. I think we shall find that the weight of experimental evidence is in favour of this last view, though fasting also has been frequently found effective. As a matter of fact, there is a definite physical discipline, called yoga, which is practised in order to produce the mystic's certainty, and which is recommended with much confidence by those who have tried it.[1] Breathing exercises are its most essential feature, and for our purposes we may ignore the rest.

In order to see how we could test the assertion that yoga gives insight, let us artificially simplify this assertion. Let us suppose that a number of people assure us that if, *for a certain time*, we breathe in a certain way, we shall become convinced that time is unreal. Let us go further, and suppose that, having tried their recipe, we have ourselves experienced a state of mind such as they describe. But now, having returned to our normal mode of respiration, we are not quite sure whether the vision was to be believed. How shall we investigate this question?

First of all, what can be meant by saying that time is unreal? If we really mean what we say, we must mean that such statements as "this is before that" are mere empty noise, like "twas brillig." If we suppose anything less than this—as, for example, that there is a relation between events which puts them in the same order as the relation of earlier and later, but that it is a different relation—we shall not have made any assertion that makes any real change in our outlook. It will be merely like supposing that the *Iliad* was not written by Homer, but by another man of the same name. We have to suppose that there are no "events" at all; there must be only the one vast whole of the universe, embracing whatever is real in the misleading appearance of a temporal procession. There must be nothing in reality corresponding to the apparent distinction between earlier and later events. To say that we are born, and then grow, and then die, must be just as false as to say that we die, then grow small, and finally are born. The truth of what seems an individual life is merely the illusory isolation of one element in the timeless and indivisible being of the universe. There is no distinction between improvement and deterioration, no difference between sorrows that end in happiness and happiness that ends in sorrow. If you find a corpse with a dagger in it, it makes no difference whether the man died of the wound or the dagger was plunged in after death. Such a view, if true, puts an end, not only to science, but to prudence, hope, and effort; it is incompatible with worldly wisdom, and—what is more important to religion—with morality.

Most mystics, of course, do not accept these conclusions in their

1. As regards yoga in China, see Waley, *The Way and Its Power*, pp. 117-18.

entirety, but they urge doctrines from which these conclusions inevitably follow. Thus Dean Inge rejects the kind of religion that appeals to evolution, because it lays too much stress upon a temporal process. "There is no law of progress, and there is no universal progress," he says. And again: "The doctrine of automatic and universal progress, the lay religion of many Victorians, labours under the disadvantage of being almost the only philosophical theory which can be definitely disproved." On this matter, which I shall discuss at a later stage, I find myself in agreement with the Dean, for whom, on many grounds, I have a very high respect. But he naturally does not draw from his premises all the inferences which seem to me to be warranted.

It is important not to caricature the doctrine of mysticism, in which there is, I think, a core of wisdom. Let us see how it seeks to avoid the extreme consequences which seem to follow from the denial of time.

The philosophy based upon mysticism has a great tradition, from Parmenides to Hegel. Parmenides says: "What is, is uncreated and indestructible; for it is complete, immovable, and without end. Nor was it ever, nor will it be; for now *it is*, all at once, a continuous one."[2] He introduced into metaphysics the distinction between reality and appearance, or the way of truth and the way of opinion, as he calls them. It is clear that whoever denies the reality of time must introduce some such distinction, since obviously the world *appears* to be in time. It is also clear that, if everyday experience is not to be *wholly* illusory, there must be some relation between appearance and the reality behind it. It is at this point, however, that the greatest difficulties arise: if the relation between appearance and reality is made too intimate, all the unpleasant features of appearance will have their unpleasant counterparts in reality, while if the relation is made too remote, we shall be unable to make inferences from the character of appearance to that of reality, and reality will be left a vague Unknowable, as with Herbert Spencer. For Christians, there is the related difficulty of avoiding pantheism: if the world is *only* apparent, God created nothing, and the reality corresponding to the world is a part of God; but if the world is in any degree real and distinct from God, we abandon the wholeness of everything, which is an essential doctrine of mysticism, and we are compelled to suppose that, in so far as the world is real, the evil which it contains is also real. Such difficulties make thoroughgoing mysticism very difficult for an orthodox Christian. As the Bishop of Birmingham says: "All forms of pantheism . . . as it seems to me, must be rejected because, if man is actually a part of God, the evil in man is also in God."

All this time I have been supposing that we are a jury, listening to the testimony of the mystics, and trying to decide whether to accept or reject it. If, when they deny the reality of the world of sense, we took them to mean "reality" in the ordinary sense of the law-courts, we should have no hesitation in rejecting what they say, since we should find that it runs counter to all other testimony, and even to their own in their mundane moments. We must therefore look for some other sense. I

2. Quoted from Burnet's *Early Greek Philosophy*, p. 199.

believe that, when the mystics contrast "reality" with "appearance," the word "reality" has not a logical, but an emotional, significance: it means what is, in some sense, important. When it is said that time is "unreal," what should be said is that, in some sense and on some occasions, it is important to conceive the universe as a whole, as the Creator, if He existed, must have conceived it in deciding to create it. When so conceived, all process is within one completed whole; past, present, and future, all exist, in some sense, together, and the present does not have that pre-eminent reality which it has to our usual ways of apprehending the world. If this interpretation is accepted, mysticism expresses an emotion, not a fact; it does not assert anything, and therefore can be neither confirmed nor contradicted by science. The fact that mystics do make assertions is owing to their inability to separate emotional importance from scientific validity. It is, of course, not to be expected that they will accept this view, but it is the only one, so far as I can see, which while admitting something of their claim, is not repugnant to the scientific intelligence.

The certainty and partial unanimity of mystics is no conclusive reason for accepting their testimony on a matter of fact. The man of science, when he wishes others to see what he has seen, arranges his microscope or telescope; that is to say, he makes changes in the external world, but demands of the observer only normal eyesight. The mystic, on the other hand, demands changes in the observer, by fasting, by breathing exercises, and by a careful abstention from external observation. (Some object to such discipline, and think that the mystic illumination cannot be artificially achieved; from a scientific point of view, this makes their case more difficult to test than that of those who rely on yoga. But nearly all agree that fasting and an ascetic life are helpful.) We all know that opium, hashish, and alcohol produce certain effects on the observer, but as we do not think these effects admirable we take no account of them in our theory of the universe. They may even, sometimes, reveal fragments of truth; but we do not regard them as sources of general wisdom. The drunkard who sees snakes does not imagine, afterwards, that he has had a revelation of a reality hidden from others, though some not wholly dissimilar belief must have given rise to the worship of Bacchus. In our own day, as William James related,[3] there have been people who considered that the intoxication produced by laughing-gas revealed truths which are hidden at normal times. From a scientific point of view, we can make no distinction between the man who eats little and sees heaven and the man who drinks much and sees snakes. Each is in an abnormal physical condition, and therefore has abnormal perceptions. Normal perceptions, since they have to be useful in the struggle for life, must have some correspondence with fact; but in abnormal perceptions there is no reason to expect such correspondence, and their testimony, therefore, cannot outweigh that of normal perception.

The mystic emotion, if it is freed from unwarranted beliefs, and not so overwhelming as to remove a man wholly from the ordinary

3. See his *Varieties of Religious Experience.* [Above, p. 58.]

busines of life, may give something of very great value—the same kind of thing, though in a heightened form, that is given by contemplation. Breadth and calm and profundity may all have their source in this emotion, in which, for the moment, all self-centered desire is dead, and the mind becomes a mirror for the vastness of the universe. Those who have had this experience, and believe it to be bound up unavoidably with assertions about the nature of the universe, naturally cling to these assertions. I believe myself that the assertions are inessential, and that there is no reason to believe them true. I cannot admit any method of arriving at truth except that of science, but in the realm of the emotions I do not deny the value of the experiences which have given rise to religion. Through association with false beliefs, they have led to much evil as well as good; freed from this association, it may be hoped that the good alone will remain.

7. Huston Smith

Huston Smith is Professor of Philosophy at Syracuse University.

Drugs and Religious Experience

1. Drugs and Religion Viewed Historically

In his trial-and-error life explorations man almost everywhere has stum-
bled upon connections between vegetables (eaten or brewed) and actions
(yogi breathing exercises, whirling-dervish dances, flagellations) that alter
states of consciousness. From the psychopharmacological standpoint we
now understand these states to be the products of changes in brain
chemistry. From the sociological perspective we see that they tend to be
connected in some way with religion. If we discount the wine used in
Christian communion services, the instances closest to us in time and
space are the peyote of The Native American [Indian] Church and
Mexico's 2000-year-old "sacred mushrooms," the latter rendered in Aztec
as "God's Flesh"—striking parallel to "the body of our Lord" in the
Christian eucharist. Beyond these neighboring instances lie the *soma* of
the Hindus, the *haoma* and hemp of the Zoroastrians, the Dionysus of the
Greeks who "everywhere . . . taught men the culture of the vine and
the mysteries of his worship and everywhere [was] accepted as a god,"[1]
the *benzoin* of Southeast Asia, Zen's tea whose fifth cup purifies and
whose sixth "calls to the realm of the immortals,"[2] the *pituri* of the

From "Do Drugs Have Religious Import?" originally published in the *Journal of
Philosophy*, LXI (1964), pp. 517–530. Reprinted by permission of the author and editor.

1. Edith Hamilton, *Mythology* (New York: Mentor, 1953), p. 55.
2. Quoted in Alan Watts, *The Spirit of Zen* (New York: Grove Press, 1958), p. 110.

Australian aborigines, and probably the mystic *kykeon* that was eaten and drunk at the climactic close of the sixth day of the Eleusinian mysteries.[3] There is no need to extend the list, as a reasonably complete account is available in Philippe de Félice's comprehensive study of the subject, *Poisons sacrés, ivresses divines.*

More interesting than the fact that consciousness-changing devices have been linked with religion is the possibility that they actually initiated many of the religious perspectives which, taking root in history, continued after their psychedelic origins were forgotten. Bergson saw the first movement of Hindus and Greeks toward "dynamic religion" as associated with the "divine rapture" found in intoxicating beverages;[4] more recently Robert Graves, Gordon Wasson, and Alan Watts have suggested that most religions arose from such chemically induced theophanies. Mary Barnard is the most explicit proponent of this thesis. "Which . . . was more likely to happen first," she asks,[5] "the spontaneously generated idea of an afterlife in which the disembodied soul, liberated from the restrictions of time and space, experiences eternal bliss, or the accidental discovery of hallucinogenic plants that give a sense of euphoria, dislocate the center of consciousness, and distort time and space, making them balloon outward in greatly expanded vistas?" Her own answer is that "the [latter] experience might have had . . . an almost explosive effect on the largely dormant minds of men, causing them to think of things they had never thought of before. This, if you like, is direct revelation." Her use of the subjunctive "might" renders this formulation of her answer equivocal, but she concludes her essay on a note that is completely unequivocal: "Looking at the matter coldly, unintoxicated and unentranced, I am willing to prophesy that fifty theobotanists working for fifty years would make the current theories concerning the origins of much mythology and theology as out-of-date as pre-Copernican astronomy."

2. Drugs and Religion Viewed Phenomenologically

Phenomenology attempts a careful description of human experience. The question the drugs pose for the phenomenology of religion, therefore, is whether the experiences they induce differ from religious experiences reached naturally, and if so how.

Even the Bible notes that chemically induced psychic states bear *some* resemblance to religious ones. Peter had to appeal to a circumstantial criterion—the early hour of the day—to defend those who were caught up in the Pentecostal experience against the charge that they were merely drunk: "These men are not drunk, as you suppose, since it is only the third hour of the day" (Acts 2:15); and Paul initiates the com-

3. George Mylonas, *Eleusis and the Eleusinian Mysteries* (Princeton, N.J.: Princeton Univ. Press, 1961), p. 284.
4. *Two Sources of Morality and Religion* (New York: Holt, 1935), pp. 206–212.
5. "The God in the Flowerpot," *The American Scholar* 32, 4 (Autumn, 1963): 584, 586.

parison when he admonishes the Ephesians not to "get drunk with wine . . . but [to] be filled with the spirit" (Ephesian 5:18). Are such comparisons, paralleled in the accounts of virtually every religion, superficial? How far can they be pushed?

Not all the way, students of religion have thus far insisted. With respect to the new drugs, Prof. R. C. Zaehner has drawn the line emphatically. "The importance of Huxley's *Doors of Perception*," he writes, "is that in it the author clearly makes the claim that what he experienced under the influence of mescalin is closely comparable to a genuine mystical experience. If he is right, . . . the conclusions . . . are alarming."[6] Zaehner thinks that Huxley is not right, but I fear that it is Zaehner who is mistaken.

There are, of course, innumerable drug experiences that have no religious feature; they can be sensual as readily as spiritual, trivial as readily as transforming, capricious as readily as sacramental. If there is one point about which every student of the drugs agrees, it is that there is no such thing as the drug experience *per se*—no experience that the drugs, as it were, merely secrete. Every experience is a mix of three ingredients: drug, set (the psychological make-up of the individual), and setting (the social and physical environment in which it is taken). But given the right set and setting, the drugs can induce religious experiences indistinguishable from experiences that occur spontaneously. Nor need set and setting be exceptional. The way the statistics are currently running, it looks as if from one-fourth to one-third of the general population will have religious experiences if they take the drugs under naturalistic conditions, meaning by this conditions in which the researcher supports the subject but does not try to influence the direction his experience will take. Among subjects who have strong religious inclinations to begin with, the proportion of those having religious experiences jumps to three-fourths. If they take the drugs in settings that are religious too, the ratio soars to nine in ten.

· ·

In the absence of a) a single definition of religious experience acceptable to psychologists of religion generally and b) foolproof ways of ascertaining whether actual experiences exemplify any definition, I am not sure there is any better way of telling whether the experiences of the 333 men and women involved in the above studies were religious than by noting whether they seemed so to them. But if more rigorous methods are preferred, they exist; they have been utilized, and they confirm the conviction of the man in the street that drug experiences can indeed be religious. In his doctoral study at Harvard University, Walter Pahnke worked out a typology of religious experience (in this instance of the mystical variety) based on the classic cases of mystical experiences as summarized in Walter Stace's *Mysticism and Philosophy*. He then administered psilocybin to ten theology students and professors in the setting of a Good Friday service. The drug was given "double-

6. *Mysticism, Sacred and Profane* (New York: Oxford, 1961), p. 12.

78

blind," meaning that neither Dr. Pahnke nor his subjects knew which ten were getting psilocybin and which ten placebos to constitute a control group. Subsequently the reports the subjects wrote of their experiences were laid successively before three college-graduate housewives who, without being informed about the nature of the study, were asked to rate each statement as to the degree (strong, moderate, slight, or none) to which it exemplified each of the nine traits of mystical experience enumerated in the typology of mysticism worked out in advance. When the test of significance was applied to their statistics, it showed that "those subjects who received psilocybin experienced phenomena which were indistinguishable from, if not identical with . . . the categories defined by our typology of mysticism."[7]

With the thought that the reader might like to test his own powers of discernment on the question being considered, I insert here a simple test I gave to a group of Princeton students following a recent discussion sponsored by the Woodrow Wilson Society:

Below are accounts of two religious experiences. One occurred under the influence of drugs, one without their influence. Check the one you think was drug-induced.

I

Suddenly I burst into a vast, new, indescribably wonderful universe. Although I am writing this over a year later, the thrill of the surprise and amazement, the awesomeness of the revelation, the engulfment in an overwhelming feeling-wave of gratitude and blessed wonderment, are as fresh, and the memory of the experience is as vivid, as if it had happened five minutes ago. And yet to concoct anything by way of description that would even hint at the magnitude, the sense of ultimate reality . . . this seems such an impossible task. The knowledge which has infused and affected every aspect of my life came instantaneously and with such complete force of certainty that it was impossible, then or since, to doubt its validity.

II

All at once, without warning of any kind, I found myself wrapped in a flame-colored cloud. For an instant I thought of fire . . . the next, I knew that the fire was within myself. Directly afterward there came upon me a sense of exultation, of immense joyousness accompanied or immediately followed by an intellectual illumination impossible to describe. Among other things, I did not merely come to believe, but I saw that the universe is not composed of dead matter, but is, on the contrary, a living Presense; I became conscious in myself of eternal life. . . . I saw that all men are immortal: that the cosmic order is such that without any preadventure all things work together for the good of each and all; that the foundation principle of the world . . . is what we call love, and that the happiness of each and all is in the long run absolutely certain.

7. "Drugs and Mysticism: An Analysis of the Relationship between Psychedelic Drugs and the Mystical Consciousness," a thesis presented to the Committee on Higher Degrees in History and Philosophy of Religion, Harvard University, June 1963.

On the occasion referred to, twice as many students (46) answered incorrectly as answered correctly (23). I bury the correct answer in a footnote to preserve the reader's opportunity to test himself.[8]

Why, in the face of this considerable evidence, does Zaehner hold that drug experiences cannot be authentically religious? There appear to be three reasons:

1. His own experience was "utterly trivial." This of course proves that not all drug experiences are religious; it does not prove that no drug experiences are religious.

2. He thinks the experiences of others that appear religious to them are not truly so. Zaehner distinguishes three kinds of mysticism: nature mysticism, in which the soul is united with the natural world; monistic mysticism, in which the soul merges with an impersonal absolute; and theism, in which the soul confronts the living, personal God. He concedes that drugs can induce the first two species of mysticism, but not its supreme instance, the theistic. As proof, he analyzes Huxley's experience as recounted in *The Doors of Perception* to show that it produced at best a blend of nature and monistic mysticism. Even if we were to accept Zaehner's evaluation of the three forms of mysticism, Huxley's case, and indeed Zaehner's entire book, would prove only that not every mystical experience induced by the drugs is theistic. Insofar as Zaehner goes beyond this to imply that drugs do not and cannot induce theistic mysticism, he not only goes beyond the evidence but proceeds in the face of it. James Slotkin reports that the peyote Indians "see visions, which may be of Christ Himself. Sometimes they hear the voice of the Great Spirit. Sometimes they become aware of the presence of God and of those personal shortcomings which must be corrected if they are to do His will."[9] And G. M. Carstairs, reporting on the use of psychedelic *bhang* in India, quotes a Brahmin as saying, "It gives good bhakti. . . . You get a very good bhatki with bhang," *bhakti* being precisely Hinduism's theistic variant.[10]

3. There is a third reason why Zaehner might doubt that drugs can induce genuinely mystical experiences. Zaehner is a Roman Catholic, and Roman Catholic doctrine teaches that mystical rapture is a gift of grace and as such can never be reduced to man's control. This may be true; certainly the empirical evidence cited does not preclude the possibility of a genuine ontological or theological difference between natural and drug-induced religious experiences. At this point, however, we are considering phenomenology rather than ontology, description rather than interpretation, and on this level there is no difference. Descriptively, drug experiences cannot be distinguished from their natural religious counterpart. When the current philosophical authority on mysticism, W. T. Stace, was

8. The first account is quoted anonymously in "The Issue of the Consciousness-expanding Drugs," *Main Currents in Modern Thought*, 20, 1 (September–October, 1963): 10–11. The second experience was that of Dr. R. M. Bucke, the author of *Cosmic Consciousness*, as quoted in William James, *The Varieties of Religious Experience* (New York: Modern Library, 1902), pp. 390–391. The former experience occurred under the influence of drugs; the latter did not.

9. James. S. Slotkin, *Peyote Religion* (New York: Free Press of Glencoe, 1956).

10. "Daru and Bhang," *Quarterly Journal of the Study of Alcohol*, 15 (1954): 229.

asked whether the drug experience is similar to the mystical experience, he answered, "It's not a matter of its being *similar* to mystical experience; it *is* mystical experience."

What we seem to be witnessing in Zaehner's *Mysticism Sacred and Profane* is a reenactment of the age-old pattern in the conflict between science and religion. Whenever a new controversy arises, religion's first impulse is to deny the disturbing evidence science has produced. Seen in perspective, Zaehner's refusal to admit that drugs can induce experiences descriptively indistinguishable from those which are spontaneously religious is the current counterpart of the seventeenth-century theologians' refusal to look through Galileo's telescope or, when they did, their persistence on dismissing what they saw as machinations of the devil. When the fact that drugs can trigger religious experiences becomes incontrovertible, discussion will move to the more difficult question of how this new fact is to be interpreted. The latter question leads beyond phenomenology into philosophy.

3. Drugs and Religion Viewed Philosophically

Why do people reject evidence? Because they find it threatening, we may suppose. Theologians are not the only professionals to utilize this mode of defense. In his *Personal Knowledge*,[11] Michael Polanyi recounts the way the medical profession ignored such palpable facts as the painless amputation of human limbs, performed before their own eyes in hundreds of succesive cases, concluding that the subjects were imposters who were either deluding their physicians or colluding with them. One physician, Esdaile, carried out about 300 major operations painlessly under mesmeric trance in India, but neither in India nor in Great Britain could he get medical journals to print accounts of his work. Polanyi attributes this closed-mindedness to "lack of a conceptual framework in which their discoveries could be separated from specious and untenable admixtures."

The "untenable admixture" in the fact that psychotomimetic drugs can induce religious experience is its apparent implicate: that religious disclosures are no more veridical than psychotic ones. For religious skeptics, this conclusion is obviously not untenable at all; it fits in beautifully with their thesis that *all* religion is at heart an escape from reality. Psychotics avoid reality by retiring into dream worlds of make-believe; what better evidence that religious visionaries do the same than the fact that identical changes in brain chemistry produce both states of mind? Had not Marx already warned us that religion is the "opiate" of the people?—apparently he was more literally accurate than he supposed. Freud was likewise too mild. He "never doubted that religious phenomena are to be understood only on the model of the neurotic symptoms of the individual."[12] He should have said "psychotic symptoms."

11. Chicago: Univ. of Chicago Press, 1958.
12. *Totem and Taboo* (New York: Modern Library, 1938).

So the religious skeptic is likely to reason. What about the religious believer? Convinced that religious experiences are not fundamentally delusory, can he admit that psychotomimetic drugs can occasion them? To do so he needs (to return to Polanyi's words) "a conceptual framework in which [the discoveries can] be separated from specious and untenable admixtures," the "untenable admixture" being in this case the conclusion that religious experiences are in general delusory.

One way to effect the separation would be to argue that, despite phenomenological similarities between natural and drug-induced religious experiences, they are separated by a crucial *ontological* difference. Such an argument would follow the pattern of theologians who argue for the "real presence" of Christ's body and blood in the bread and wine of the Eucharist despite their admission that chemical analysis, confined as it is to the level of "accidents" rather than "essences," would not disclose this presence. But this distinction will not appeal to many today, for it turns on an essence-accident metaphysics which is not widely accepted. Instead of fighting a rear-guard action by insisting that if drug and nondrug religious experiences cannot be distinguished empirically there must be some transempirical factor that distinguishes them and renders the drug experience profane, I wish to explain the possibility of accepting drug-induced experiences as religious without relinquishing confidence in the truth-claims of religious experience generally.

. . . Drug experiences that assume a religious cast tend to have fearful and/or beatific features, and each of my hypotheses relates to one of these aspects of the experience.

Beginning with the ominous, "fear of the Lord," awe-ful features, Gordon Wasson, the New York banker-turned-mycologist, describes these as he encountered them in his psilocybin experience as follows: "Ecstasy! In common parlance . . . ecstasy is fun. . . . But ecstasy is not fun. Your very soul is seized and shaken until it tingles. After all, who will choose to feel undiluted awe? . . . The unknowing vulgar abuse the word; we must recapture its full and terrifying sense."[13] Emotionally the drug experience can be like having forty-foot waves crash over you for several hours while you cling desperately to a life-raft which may be swept from under you at any minute. It seems quite possible that such an ordeal, like any experience of a close call, could awaken rather fundamental sentiments respecting life and death and destiny and trigger the "no atheists in foxholes" effect. Similarly, as the subject emerges from the trauma and realizes that he is not going to be insane as he had feared, there may come over him an intensified appreciation like that frequently reported by patients recovering from critical illness. "It happened on the day when my bed was pushed out of doors to the open gallery of the hospital," reads one such report:

> I cannot now recall whether the revelation came suddenly or gradually;
> I only remember finding myself in the very midst of those wonderful

13. "The Hallucinogenic Fungi of Mexico: An Inquiry into the Origins of the Religious Idea among Primitive Peoples," *Harvard Botanical Museum Leaflets*, 19, 7 (1961).

moments, beholding life for the first time in all its young intoxication of loveliness, in its unspeakable joy, beauty, and importance. I cannot say exactly what the mysterious change was. I saw no new thing, but I saw all the usual things in a miraculous new light—in what I believe is their true light. I saw for the first time how wildly beautiful and joyous, beyond any words of mine to describe, is the whole of life. Every human being moving across that porch, every sparrow that flew, every branch tossing in the wind, was caught in and was a part of the whole mad ecstasy of loveliness, of joy, of importance, of intoxication of life.[14]

If we do not discount religious intuitions because they are prompted by battlefields and *physical* crises; if we regard the latter as "calling us to our senses" more often than they seduce us into delusions, need comparable intuitions be discounted simply because the crises that trigger them are of an inner, *psychic* variety?

Turning from the hellish to the heavenly aspects of the drug experience, *some* of the latter may be explainable by the hypothesis just stated; that is, they may be occasioned by the relief that attends the sense of escape from high danger. But this hypothesis cannot possibly account for *all* the beatific episodes, for the simple reason that the positive episodes often come first, or to persons who experience no negative episodes whatever. Dr. Sanford Unger of the National Institute of Mental Health reports that among his subjects "50 to 60% will not manifest any real disturbance worthy of discussion," yet "around 75% will have at least one episode in which exaltation, rapture, and joy are the key descriptions."[15] How are we to account for the drug's capacity to induce peak experiences, such as the following, which are *not* preceded by fear?

A feeling of great peace and contentment seemed to flow through my entire body. All sound ceased and I seemed to be floating in a great, very very still void or hemisphere. It is impossible to describe the overpowering feeling of peace, contentment, and being a part of goodness itself that I felt. I could feel my body dissolving and actually becoming a part of the goodness and peace that was all around me. Words can't describe this. I feel an awe and wonder that such a feeling could have occurred to me.[16]

Consider the following line of argument. Like every other form of life, man's nature has become distinctive through specialization. Man has specialized in developing a cerebral cortex. The analytic powers of this instrument are a standing wonder, but the instrument seems less able to provide man with the sense that he is meaningfully related to his environment: to life, the world, and history in their wholeness. As Albert Camus describes the situation, "If I were . . . a cat among animals, this life would have a meaning, or rather this problem would not

14. Margaret Prescott Montague, *Twenty Minutes of Reality* (St. Paul, Minn.: Macalester Park, 1947), pp. 15, 17.
15. "The Current Scientific Status of Psychedelic Drug Research," read at the Conference on Methods in Philosophy and the Sciences, New School for Social Research, May 3, 1964, and scheduled for publication in David Solomon, ed., *The Conscious Expanders* (New York: Putnam, fall of 1964).
16. Quoted by Dr. Unger in the paper just mentioned.

arise, for I should belong to this world. I would *be* this world to which I am now opposed by my whole consciousness."[17] Note that it is Camus' consciousness that opposes him to his world. The drugs do not knock this consciousness out, but while they leave it operative they also activate areas of the brain that normally lie below its threshold of awareness. One of the clearest objective signs that the drugs are taking effect is the dilation they produce in the pupils of the eyes, and one of the most predictable subjective signs is the intensification of visual perception. Both of these responses are controlled by portions of the brain that lie deep, further to the rear than the mechanisms that govern consciousness. Meanwhile we know that the human organism is inter-laced with its world in innumerable ways it normally cannot sense— through gravitational fields, body respiration, and the like: the list could be multiplied until man's skin began to seem more like a thoroughfare than a boundary. Perhaps the deeper regions of the brain which evolved earlier and are more like those of the lower animals—"If I were . . . a cat . . . I should belong to this world"—can sense this relatedness better than can the cerebral cortex which now dominates our awareness. If so, when the drugs rearrange the neurohumors that chemically transmit impulses across synapses between neurons, man's consciousness and his submerged, intuitive, ecological awareness might for a spell become inter-laced. This is, of course, no more than a hypothesis, but how else are we to account for the extraordinary incidence under the drugs of that kind of insight the keynote of which James described as "invariably a recon-ciliation"? "It is as if the opposites of the world, whose contradictoriness and conflict make all our difficulties and troubles, were melted into one and the same genus, but *one of the species,* the nobler and better one, *is itself the genus, and so soaks up and absorbs its opposites into itself"* (*op. cit.,* 379).

17. *The Myth of Sisyphus* (New York: Vintage, 1955), p. 38.

8. Ernest Nagel

Ernest Nagel, a prominent American philosopher of science, is John Dewey Professor of Philosophy at Columbia University.

The Case for Atheism

The essays in this book are devoted in the main to the exposition of the major religious creeds of humanity. It is a natural expectation that this final paper, even though its theme is so radically different from nearly all of the others, will show how atheism belongs to the great tradition of religious thought. Needless to say, this expectation is difficult to satisfy, and did anyone succeed in doing so he would indeed be performing the neatest conjuring trick of the week. But the expectation nevertheless does cause me some embarrassment, which is only slightly relieved by an anecdote Bertrand Russell reports in his recent book, *Portraits from Memory*. Russell was imprisoned during the First World War for pacifistic activities. On entering the prison he was asked a number of customary questions about himself for the prison records. One question was about his religion. Russell explained that he was an agnostic. "Never heard of it," the warden declared. "How do you spell it?" When Russell told him, the warden observed "Well, there are many religions, but I suppose they all worship the same God." Russell adds that this remark kept him cheerful for about a week. Perhaps philosophical atheism also is a religion.

The whole of the essay "Philosophical Concepts of Atheism," which originally appeared in *Basic Beliefs*, ed. Johnson E. Fairchild, and published by Sheridan House, Inc. Reprinted by permission of the author and publisher.

1.

I must begin by stating what sense I am attaching to the word "atheism," and how I am construing the theme of this paper. I shall understand by "atheism" a critique and a denial of the major claims of all varieties of theism. And by theism I shall mean the view which holds, as one writer has expressed it, "that the heavens and the earth and all that they contain owe their existence and continuance in existence to the wisdom and will of a supreme, self-consistent, omnipotent, omniscient, righteous, and benevolent being, who is distinct from, and independent of, what he has created." Several things immediately follow from these definitions.

In the first place, atheism is not necessarily an irreligious concept, for theism is just one among many views concerning the nature and origin of the world. The denial of theism is logically compatible with a religious outlook upon life, and is in fact characteristic of some of the great historical religions. For as readers of this volume will know, early Buddhism is a religion which does not subscribe to any doctrine about a god; and there are pantheistic religions and philosophies which, because they deny that God is a being separate from and independent of the world, are not theistic in the sense of the word explained above.

The second point to note is that atheism is not to be identified with sheer unbelief, or with disbelief in some particular creed of a religious group. Thus, a child who has received no religious instruction and has never heard about God, is not an atheist—for he is not denying any theistic claims. Similarly in the case of an adult who, if he has withdrawn from the faith of his fathers without reflection or because of frank indifference to any theological issue, is also not an atheist—for such an adult is not challenging theism and is not professing any views on the subject. Moreover, though the term "atheist" has been used historically as an abusive label for those who do not subscribe to some regnant orthodoxy (for example, the ancient Romans called the early Christians atheists, because the latter denied the Roman divinities), or for those who engage in conduct regarded as immoral it is not in this sense that I am discussing atheism.

One final word of preliminary explanation. I propose to examine some *philosophic* concepts of atheism, and I am not interested in the slightest in the many considerations atheists have advanced against the evidences for some particular religious and theological doctrine—for example, against the truth of the Christian story. What I mean by "philosophical" in the present context is that the views I shall consider are directed against any form of theism, and have their origin and basis in a logical analysis of the theistic position, and in a comprehensive account of the world believed to be wholly intelligible without the adoption of a theistic hypothesis.

Theism as I conceive it is a theological proposition, not a statement of a position that belongs primarily to religion. On my view, religion as a historical and social phenomenon is primarily an institutionalized *cultus* or practice, which possesses identifiable social functions and which expresses certain attitudes men take toward their world. Although it is doubtful whether men ever engage in religious practices or assume religious attitudes without some more or less explicit interpretation of their ritual or some rationale for their attitude, it is still the case that it is possible to distinguish religion as a social and personal phenomenon from the theological doctrines which may be developed as justifications for religious practices. Indeed, in some of the great religions of the world the profession of a creed plays a relatively minor role. In short, religion is a form of social communion, a participation in certain kinds of ritual (whether it be a dance, worship, prayer, or the like), and a form of experience (sometimes, though not invariably, directed to a personal confrontation with divine and holy things). Theology is an articulated and, at its best, a rational attempt at understanding these feelings and practices, in the light of their relation to other parts of human experience, and in terms of some hypothesis concerning the nature of things entire.

2.

As I see it, atheistic philosophies fall into two major groups: 1) those which hold that the theistic doctrine is meaningful, but reject it either on the ground that, (a) the positive evidence for it is insufficient, or (b) the negative evidence is quite overwhelming; and 2) those who hold that the theistic thesis is not even meaningful, and reject it (a) as just nonsense or (b) as literally meaningless but interpreting it as a symbolic rendering of human ideals, thus reading the theistic thesis in a sense that most believers in theism would disavow. It will not be possible in the limited space at my disposal to discuss the second category of atheistic critiques; and in any event, most of the traditional atheistic critiques of theism belong to the first group.

But before turning to the philosophical examination of the major classical arguments for theism, it is well to note that such philosophical critiques do not quite convey the passion with which atheists have often carried on their analyses of theistic views. For historically, atheism has been, and indeed continues to be, a form of social and political protest, directed as much against institutionalized religion as against theistic doctrine. Atheism has been, in effect, a moral revulsion against the undoubted abuses of the secular power exercised by religious leaders and religious institutions.

Religious authorities have opposed the correction of glaring injustices, and encouraged politically and socially reactionary policies. Religious institutions have been havens of obscurantist thought and centers for the dissemination of intolerance. Religious creeds have been used to set limits to free inquiry, to perpetuate inhumane treatment of the ill and the underprivileged, and to support moral doctrines insensitive to human suffering.

These indictments may not tell the whole story about the historical significance of religion; but they are at least an important part of the story. The refutation of theism has thus seemed to many as an indispensable step not only towards liberating men's minds from superstition, but also towards achieving a more equitable reordering of society. And no account of even the more philosophical aspects of atheistic thought is adequate, which does not give proper recognition to the powerful social motives that actuate many atheistic arguments.

But however this may be, I want now to discuss three classical arguments for the existence of God, arguments which have constituted at least a partial basis for theistic commitments. As long as theism is defended simply as dogma, asserted as a matter of direct revelation or as the deliverance of authority, belief in the dogma is impregnable to rational argument. In fact, however, reasons are frequently advanced in support of the theistic creed, and these reasons have been the subject of acute philosophical critiques.

One of the oldest intellectual defenses of theism is the cosmological argument, also known as the argument from a first cause. Briefly put, the argument runs as follows. Every event must have a cause. Hence an event A must have as cause some event B, which in turn must have a cause C, and so on. But if there is no end to this backward progression of causes, the progression will be infinite; and in the opinion of those who use this argument, an infinite series of actual events is unintelligible and absurd. Hence there must be a first cause, and this first cause is God, the initiator of all change in the universe.

The argument is an ancient one, and is especially effective when stated within the framework of assumptions of Aristotelian physics; and it has impressed many generations of exceptionally keen minds. The argument is nonetheless a weak reed on which to rest the theistic thesis. Let us waive any question concerning the validity of the principle that every event has a cause, for though the question is important its discussion would lead us far afield. However, if the principle is assumed, it is surely incongruous to postulate a first cause as a way of escaping from the coils of an infinite series. For if everything must have a cause, why does not God require one for His own existence? The standard answer is that He does not need any, because He is self-caused. But if God can be self-caused, why cannot the world be self-caused? Why do we require a God transcending the world to bring the world into existence and to initiate changes in it? On the other hand, the supposed inconceivability and absurdity of an infinite series of regressive causes will be admitted by no one who has competent familiarity with the modern mathematical analysis of infinity. The cosmological argument does not stand up under scrutiny.

The second "proof" of God's existence is usually called the ontological argument. It too has a long history going back to early Christian days, though it acquired great prominence only in medieval times. The argument can be stated in several ways, one of which is the following. Since God is conceived to be omnipotent, he is a perfect being. A perfect being is defined as one whose essence or nature lacks no attributes (or properties) whatsoever, one whose nature is complete in every respect. But it is evident that we have an idea of a perfect being, for we have just defined the idea; and since this is so, the argument continues, God who is the perfect being must exist. Why must he? Because his existence follows from his defined nature. For if God lacked the attribute of existence, he would be lacking at least one attribute, and would therefore not be perfect. To sum up, since we have an idea of God as a perfect being, God must exist.

There are several ways of approaching this argument, but I shall consider only one. The argument was exploded by the 18th century philosopher Immanuel Kant. The substance of Kant's criticism is that it is just a confusion to say that existence is an attribute, and that though the *word* "existence" may occur as the grammatical predicate in a sentence no attribute is being predicated of a thing when we say that the thing exists or has existence. Thus, to use Kant's example, when we think of $100 we are thinking of the nature of this sum of money; but the nature of $100 remains the same whether we have $100 in our pockets or not. Accordingly, we are confounding grammar with logic if we suppose that some characteristic is being attributed to the nature of $100 when we say that a hundred dollar bill exists in someone's pocket.

To make the point clearer, consider another example. When we say that a lion has a tawny color, we are predicating a certain attribute of the animal, and similarly when we say that the lion is fierce or is hungry. But when we say the lion exists, all that we are saying is that something is (or has the nature of) a lion; we are not specifying an attribute which belongs to the nature of anything that is a lion. In short, the word "existence" does not signify any attribute, and in consequence no attribute that belongs to the nature of anything. Accordingly, it does not follow from the assumption that we have an idea of a perfect being that such a being exists. For the idea of a perfect being does not involve the attribute of existence as a constituent of that idea, since there is no such attribute. The ontological argument thus has a serious leak, and it can hold no water.

3.

The two arguments discussed thus far are purely dialectical, and attempt to establish God's existence without any appeal to empirical data. The next argument, called the argument from design, is different in character, for it is based on what purports to be empirical evidence. I wish to examine two forms of this argument.

One variant of it calls attention to the remarkable way in which different things and processes in the world are integrated with each other, and concludes that this mutual "fitness" of things can be explained only by the assumption of a divine architect who planned the world and everything in it. For example, living organisms can maintain themselves in a variety of environments, and do so in virtue of their delicate mechanisms which adapt the organisms to all sorts of environmental changes. There is thus an intricate pattern of means and ends throughout the animate world. But the existence of this pattern is unintelligible, so the argument runs, except on the hypothesis that the pattern has been deliberately instituted by a Supreme Designer. If we find a watch in some deserted spot, we do not think it came into existence by chance, and we do not hesitate to conclude that an intelligent creature designed and made it. But the world and all its contents exhibit mechanisms and mutual adjustments that are far more complicated and subtle than are those of a watch. Must we not therefore conclude that these things too have a Creator?

The conclusion of this argument is based on an inference from analogy: the watch and the world are alike in possessing a congruence of parts and an adjustment of means to ends; the watch has a watch-maker; hence the world has a world-maker. But is the analogy a good one? Let us once more waive some important issues, in particular the issue whether the universe is the unified system such as the watch admittedly is. And let us concentrate on the question what is the ground for our assurance that watches do not come into existence except through the operations of intelligent manufacturers. The answer is plain. We have never run across a watch which has not been deliberately made by someone. But the situation is nothing like this in the case of the innumerable animate and inanimate systems with which we are familiar. Even in the case of living organisms, though they are generated by their parent organisms, the parents do not "make" their progeny in the same sense in which watch-makers make watches. And once this point is clear, the inference from the existence of living organisms to the existence of a supreme designer no longer appears credible.

Moreover, the argument loses all its force if the facts which the hypothesis of a divine designer is supposed to explain can be understood on the basis of a better supported assumption. And indeed, such an alternative explanation is one of the achievements of Darwinian biology. For Darwin showed that one can account for the variety of biological species, as well as for their adaptations to their environments, without invoking a divine creator and acts of special creation. The Darwinian theory explains the diversity of biological species in terms of chance variations in the structure of organisms, and of a mechanism of selection which retains those variant forms that possess some advantages for survival. The evidence for these assumptions is considerable; and developments subsequent to Darwin have only strengthened the case for a thoroughly naturalistic explanation of the facts of biological adaptation. In any event, this version of the argument from design has nothing to recommend it.

A second form of this argument has been recently revived in the speculations of some modern physicists. No one who is familiar with the facts, can fail to be impressed by the success with which the use of mathematical methods has enabled us to obtain intellectual mastery of many parts of nature. But some thinkers have therefore concluded that since the book of nature is ostensibly written in mathematical language, nature must be the creation of a divine mathematician. However, the argument is most dubious. For it rests, among other things, on the assumption that mathematical tools can be successfully used only if the events of nature exhibit some *special* kind of order, and on the further assumption that if the structure of things were different from what they are mathematical language would be inadequate for describing such structure. But it can be shown that no matter what the world were like —even if it impressed us as being utterly chaotic—it would still possess some order, and would in principle be amenable to a mathematical description. In point of fact, it makes no sense to say that there is absolutely *no* pattern in any conceivable subject matter. To be sure, there are differences in complexities of structure, and if the patterns of events were sufficiently complex we might not be able to unravel them. But however that may be, the success of mathematical physics in giving us some understanding of the world around us does not yield the conclusion that only a mathematician could have devised the patterns of order we have discovered in nature.

4.

The inconclusiveness of the three classical arguments for the existence of God was already made evident by Kant, in a manner substantially not different from the above discussion. There are, however, other types of arguments for theism that have been influential in the history of thought, two of which I wish to consider, even if only briefly.

Indeed, though Kant destroyed the classical intellectual foundations for theism, he himself invented a fresh argument for it. Kant's attempted proof is not intended to be a purely theoretical demonstration, and is based on the supposed facts of our moral nature. It has exerted an enormous influence on subsequent theological speculation. In barest outline the argument is as follows. According to Kant, we are subject not only to physical laws like the rest of nature, but also to moral ones. These moral laws are categorical imperatives, which we must heed not because of their utilitarian consequences, but simply because as autonomous moral agents it is our duty to accept them as binding. However, Kant was keenly aware that though virtue may be its reward, the virtuous man (that is, the man who acts out of a sense of duty and in conformity with the moral law) does not always receive his just desserts in this world; nor did he shut his eyes to the fact that evil men frequently enjoy the best things this world has to offer. In short, virtue does not always reap happiness. Nevertheless, the highest human good is the realization of happiness commensurate with one's virtues; and Kant believed that it is a practical postulate of the moral life to promote this good. But what can guarantee that the highest good is realizable? Such a guarantee can be found only in God, who must therefore exist if the highest good is not to be a fatuous ideal. The existence of an omnipotent, omniscient, and omnibenevolent God is thus postulated as a necessary condition for the possibility of a moral life.

Despite the prestige this argument has acquired, it is difficult to grant it any force. It is easy enough to postulate God's existence. But as Bertrand Russell observed in another connection, postulation has all the advantages of theft over honest toil. No postulation carries with it any assurance that what is postulated is actually the case. And though we may postulate God's existence as a means to guaranteeing the possibility of realizing happiness together with virtue, the postulation establishes neither the actual realizability of this ideal nor the fact of his existence. Moreover, the argument is not made more cogent when we recognize that it is based squarely on the highly dubious conception that considerations of utility and human happiness must not enter into the determination of what is morally obligatory. Having built his moral theory on a radical separation of means from ends, Kant was driven to the desperate postulation of God's existence in order to relate them again. The argument is thus at best a *tour de force*, contrived to remedy a fatal flaw in Kant's initial moral assumptions. It carries no conviction to anyone who does not commit Kant's initial blunder.

One further type of argument, pervasive in much Protestant theological literature, deserves brief mention. Arguments of this type take their point of departure from the psychology of religious and mystical experience. Those who have undergone such experiences, often report that during the experience they feel themselves to be in the presence of the divine and holy, that they lose their sense of self-identity and become merged with some fundamental reality, or that they enjoy a feeling of total dependence upon some ultimate power. The overwhelming sense of transcending one's finitude which characterizes such vivid periods of life, and of coalescing with some ultimate source of all existence, is then taken to be compelling evidence for the existence of a supreme being. In a variant form of this argument, other theologians have identified God as the object which satisfies the commonly experienced need for integrating one's scattered and conflicting impulses into a coherent unity, or as the subject which is of ultimate concern to us. In short, a proof of God's existence is found in the occurrence of certain distinctive experiences.

It would be flying in the face of well-attested facts were one to deny that such experiences frequently occur. But do these facts constitute evidence for the conclusion based on them? Does the fact, for example, that an individual experiences a profound sense of direct contact with an alleged transcendent ground of all reality, constitute competent evidence for the claim that there is such a ground and that it is the immediate cause of the experience? If well-established canons for evaluating evidence are accepted, the answer is surely negative. No one will dispute that many men do have vivid experiences in which such things as ghosts or pink elephants appear before them; but only the hopelessly credulous will without further ado count such experiences as establishing the existence of ghosts and pink elephants. To establish the existence of such things, evidence is required that is obtained under controlled conditions and that can be confirmed by independent inquirers. Again, though a man's report that he is suffering pain may be taken at face value, one cannot take at face value the claim, were he to make it, that it is the food he ate which is the cause (or a contributory cause) of his felt pain —not even if the man were to report a vivid feeling of abdominal disturbance. And similarly, an overwhelming feeling of being in the presence of the Divine is evidence enough for admitting the genuineness of such feeling; it is no evidence for the claim that a supreme being with a substantial existence independent of the experience is the cause of the experience.

5.

Thus far the discussion has been concerned with noting inadequacies in various arguments widely used to support theism. However, much atheistic criticism is also directed toward exposing incoherencies in the very thesis of theism. I want therefore to consider this aspect of the atheistic critique, though I will restrict myself to the central difficulty in the theistic position which arises from the simultaneous attribution of omnipotence, omniscience, and omnibenevolence to the Deity. The difficulty is that of reconciling these attributes with the occurrence of evil in the world. Accordingly, the question to which I now turn is whether, despite the existence of evil, it is possible to construct a theodicy which will justify the ways of an infinitely powerful and just God to man.

Two main types of solutions have been proposed for this problem. One way that is frequently used is to maintain that what is commonly called evil is only an illusion, or at worst only the "privation" or absence of good. Accordingly, evil is not "really real," it is only the "negative" side of God's beneficence, it is only the product of our limited intelligence which fails to plumb the true character of God's creative bounty. A sufficient comment on this proposed solution is that facts are not altered or abolished by rebaptizing them. Evil may indeed be only an appearance and not genuine. But this does not eliminate from the realm of appearance the tragedies, the sufferings, and the iniquities which men so frequently endure. And it raises once more, though on another level, the problem of reconciling the fact that there is evil in the realm of appearance with God's alleged omnibenevolence. In any event, it is small comfort to anyone suffering a cruel misfortune for which he is in no way responsible, to be told that what he is undergoing is only the absence of good. It is a gratuitous insult to mankind, a symptom of insensitivity and indifference to human suffering, to be assured that all the miseries and agonies men experience are only illusory.

Another gambit often played in attempting to justify the ways of God to man is to argue that the things called evil are evil only because they are viewed in isolation; they are not evil when viewed in proper perspective and in relation to the rest of creation. Thus, if one attends to but a single instrument in an orchestra, the sounds issuing from it may indeed be harsh and discordant. But if one is placed at a proper distance from the whole orchestra, the sounds of that single instrument will mingle with the sounds issuing from the other players to produce a marvellous bit of symphonic music. Analogously, experiences we call painful undoubtedly occur and are real enough. But the pain is judged to be an evil only because it is experienced in a limited perspective—the pain is there for the sake of a more inclusive good, whose reality eludes us because our intelligences are too weak to apprehend things in their entirety.

It is an appropriate retort to this argument that of course we judge things to be evil in a human perspective, but that since we are not God this is the only proper perspective in which to judge them. It may indeed be the case that what is evil for us is not evil for some other part of creation. However, we are not this other part of creation, and it is irrelevant to argue that were we something other than what we are, our evaluations of what is good and bad would be different. Moreover, the worthlessness of the argument becomes even more evident if we remind ourselves that it is unsupported speculation to suppose that whatever is evil in a finite perspective is good from the purported perspective of the totality of things. For the argument can be turned around: what we judge to be a good is a good only because it is viewed in isolation; when it is viewed in proper perspective, and in relation to the entire scheme of things, it is an evil. This is in fact a standard form of the argument for a universal pessimism. Is it any worse than the similar argument for a universal optimism? The very raising of this question is a *reductio ad absurdum* of the proposed solution to the ancient problem of evil.

I do not believe it is possible to reconcile the alleged omnipotence and omnibenevolence of God with the unvarnished facts of human existence. In point of fact, many theologians have concurred in this conclusion; for in order to escape from the difficulty which the traditional attributes of God present, they have assumed that God is not all powerful, and that there are limits as to what He can do in his effort to establish a righteous order in the universe. But whether such a modified theology is better off, is doubtful; and in any event, the question still remains whether the facts of human life support the claim that an omnibenevolent Deity, though limited in power, is revealed in the ordering of human history. It is pertinent to note in this connection that though there have been many historians who have made the effort, no historian has yet succeeded in showing to the satisfaction of his professional colleagues that the hypothesis of a Divine Providence is capable of explaining anything which cannot be explained just as well without this hypothesis.

6.

This last remark naturally leads to the question whether, apart from their polemics against theism, philosophical atheists have not shared a common set of positive views, a common set of philosophical convictions which set them off from other groups of thinkers. In one very clear sense of this query the answer is indubitably negative. For there never has been what one might call a "school of atheism," in the way in which there has been a Platonic school or even a Kantian school. In point of fact, atheistic critics of theism can be found among many of the conventional groupings of philosophical thinkers—even, I venture to add, among professional theologians in recent years who in effect preach atheism in the guise of language taken bodily from the Christian tradition.

Nevertheless, despite the variety of philosophic positions to which at one time or another in the history of thought atheists have subscribed, it seems to me that atheism is not simply a negative standpoint. At any rate, there is a certain quality of intellectual temper that has characterized, and continues to characterize, many philosophical atheists. (I am excluding from consideration the so-called "village atheist," whose primary concern is to twit and ridicule those who accept some form of theism, or for that matter those who have any religious convictions.) Moreover, their rejection of theism is based not only on the inadequacies they have found in the arguments for theism, but often also on the positive ground that atheism is a corollary to a better supported general outlook upon the nature of things. I want therefore to conclude this discussion with a brief enumeration of some points of positive doctrine to which by and large philosophical atheists seem to me to subscribe. These points fall into three major groups.

In the first place, philosophical atheists reject the assumption that there are disembodied spirits, or that incorporeal entities of any sort can exercise a causal agency. On the contrary, atheists are generally agreed that if we wish to achieve any understanding of what takes place in the universe, we must look to the operations of organized bodies. Accordingly, the various processes taking place in nature, whether animate or inanimate, are to be explained in terms of the properties and structures of identifiable and spatio-temporally located objects. Moreover, the present variety of systems and activities found in the universe is to be accounted for on the basis of the transformations things undergo when they enter into different relations with one another—transformations which often result in the emergence of novel kinds of objects. On the other hand, though things are in flux and undergo alteration, there is no all-encompassing unitary pattern of change. Nature is ineradicably plural, both in respect to the individuals occurring in it as well as in respect to the processes in which things become involved. Accordingly, the human scene and the human perspective are not illusory; and man and his works are no less and no more "real" than are other parts or phases of the cosmos. At the risk of using a possibly misleading characterization, all of this can be summarized by saying that an atheistic view of things is a form of materialism.

In the second place, atheists generally manifest a marked empirical temper, and often take as their ideal the intellectual methods employed in the contemporaneous empirical sciences. Philosophical atheists differ considerably on important points of detail in their account of how responsible claims to knowledge are to be established. But there is substantial agreement among them that controlled sensory observation is the court of final appeal in issues concerning matters of fact. It is indeed this commitment to the use of an empirical method which is the final basis of the atheistic critique of theism. For at bottom this critique seeks to show that we can understand whatever a theistic assumption is alleged to explain, through the use of the proved methods of the positive sciences and without the introduction of empirically unsupported *ad hoc* hypotheses about a Deity. It is pertinent in this connection to recall a familiar legend about the French mathematical physicist Laplace. According to the story, Laplace made a personal presentation of a copy of his now famous book on celestial mechanics to Napoleon. Napoleon glanced through the volume, and finding no reference to the Deity asked Laplace whether God's existence played any role in the analysis. "Sire, I have no need for that hypothesis," Laplace is reported to have replied. The dismissal of sterile hypotheses characterizes not only the work of Laplace; it is the uniform rule in scientific inquiry. The sterility of the theistic assumption is one of the main burdens of the literature of atheism both ancient and modern.

And finally, atheistic thinkers have generally accepted a utilitarian basis for judging moral issues, and they have exhibited a libertarian attitude toward human needs and impulses. The conceptions of the human good they have advocated are conceptions which are commensurate with the actual capacities of mortal men, so that it is the satisfaction of the complex needs of the human creature which is the final standard for evaluating the validity of a moral ideal or moral prescription.

In consequence, the emphasis of atheistic moral reflection has been this-worldly rather than other-worldly, individualistic rather than authoritarian. The stress upon a good life that must be consummated in this world, has made atheists vigorous opponents of moral codes which seek to repress human impulses in the name of some unrealizable other-wordly ideal. The individualism that is so pronounced a strain in many philosophical atheists has made them tolerant of human limitations and sensitive to the plurality of legitimate moral goals. On the other hand, this individualism has certainly not prevented many of them from recognizing the crucial role which institutional arrangements can play in achieving desirable patterns of human living. In consequence, atheists have made important contributions to the development of a climate of opinion favorable to pursuing the values of a liberal civilization and they have played effective roles in attempts to rectify social injustices.

Atheists cannot build their moral outlook on foundations upon which so many men conduct their lives. In particular, atheism cannot offer the incentives to conduct and the consolations for misfortune which theistic religions supply to their adherents. It can offer no hope of personal immortality, no threats of Divine chastisement, no promise of eventual recompense for injustices suffered, no blueprints to sure salvation. For on its view of the place of man in nature, human excellence and human dignity must be achieved within a finite life-span, or not at all, so that the rewards of moral endeavor must come from the quality of civilized living, and not from some source of disbursement that dwells outside of time. Accordingly, atheistic moral reflection at its best does not culminate in a quiescent ideal of human perfection, but is a vigorous call to intelligent activity—activity for the sake of realizing human potentialities and for eliminating whatever stands in the way of such realization. Nevertheless, though slavish resignation to remediable ills is not characteristic of atheistic thought, responsible atheists have never pretended that human effort can invariably achieve the heart's every legitimate desire. A tragic view of life is thus an uneliminable ingredient in atheistic thought. This ingredient does not invite or generally produce lugubrious lamentation. But it does touch the atheist's view of man and his place in nature with an emotion that makes the philosophical atheist a kindred spirit to those who, within the framework of various religious traditions, have developed a serenely resigned attitude toward the inevitable trage-dies of the human estate.

9. **John Hick**

John Hick is Professor of Theology at the University of
Birmingham.

A Christian View of the Problem of Evil

To many, the most powerful positive objection to belief in God is the fact
of evil. Probably for most agnostics it is the appalling depth and extent
of human suffering, more than anything else, that makes the idea of a
loving Creator seem so implausible and disposes them toward one or
another of the various naturalistic theories of religion.

As a challenge to theism, the problem of evil has traditionally been
posed in the form of a dilemma: if God is perfectly loving, he must wish
to abolish evil; and if he is all-powerful, he must be able to abolish evil.
But evil exists; therefore God cannot be both omnipotent and perfectly
loving.

Certain solutions, which at once suggest themselves, have to be ruled
out so far as the Judaic-Christian faith is concerned.

To say, for example (with contemporary Christian Science), that evil
is an illusion of the human mind, is impossible within a religion based
upon the stark realism of the Bible. Its pages faithfully reflect the characteristic mixture of good and evil in human experience. They record
every kind of sorrow and suffering, every mode of man's inhumanity to
man and of his painfully insecure existence in the world. There is no
attempt to regard evil as anything but dark, menacingly ugly, heart-

John Hick, PHILOSOPHY OF RELIGION, © 1963. Reprinted by permission of
Prentice-Hall, Inc., Englewood Cliffs, New Jersey. From Chapter III.

rending, and crushing. In the Christian scriptures, the climax of this history of evil is the crucifixion of Jesus, which is presented not only as a case of utterly unjust suffering, but as the violent and murderous rejection of God's Messiah. There can be no doubt, then, that for biblical faith, evil is unambiguously evil, and stands in direct opposition to God's will.

Again, to solve the problem of evil by means of the theory (sponsored, for example, by the Boston "Personalist" School)[1] of a finite deity who does the best he can with a material, intractable and co-eternal with himself, is to have abandoned the basic premise of Hebrew-Christian monotheism; for the theory amounts to rejecting belief in the infinity and sovereignty of God.

Indeed, any theory which would avoid the problem of the origin of evil by depicting it as an ultimate constituent of the universe, coordinate with good, has been repudiated in advance by the classic Christian teaching, first developed by Augustine, that evil represents the going wrong of something which in itself is good.[2] Augustine holds firmly to the Hebrew-Christian conviction that the universe is *good*—that is to say, it is the creation of a good God for a good purpose. He completely rejects the ancient prejudice, widespread in his day, that matter is evil. There are, according to Augustine, higher and lower, greater and lesser goods in immense abundance and variety; but everything which has being is good in its own way and degree, except in so far as it may have become spoiled or corrupted. Evil—whether it be an evil will, an instance of pain, or some disorder or decay in nature—has not been set there by God, but represents the distortion of something that is inherently valuable. Whatever exists is, as such, and in its proper place, good; evil is essentially parasitic upon good, being disorder and perversion in a fundamentally good creation. This understanding of evil as something negative means that it is not willed and created by God; but it does not mean (as some have supposed) that evil is unreal and can be disregarded. Clearly, the first effect of this doctrine is to accentuate even more the question of the origin of evil.

Theodicy,[3] as many modern Christian thinkers see it, is a modest enterprise, negative rather than positive in its conclusions. It does not claim to explain, nor to explain away, every instance of evil in human experience, but only to point to certain considerations which prevent the fact of evil (largely incomprehensible though it remains) from constituting a final and insuperable bar to rational belief in God.

In indicating these considerations it will be useful to follow the traditional division of the subject. There is the problem of *moral evil* or wickedness: why does an all-good and all-powerful God permit this? And there is the problem of the *nonmoral evil* of suffering or pain, both

1. Edgar Brightman's *A Philosophy of Religion* (Englewood Cliffs, N.J.: Prentice-Hall, Inc., 1940), chaps. 8–10, is a classic exposition of one form of this view.

2. See Augustine's *Confessions*, Book VII, chap. 12; *City of God*, Book XII, chap. 3; *Enchiridion*, chap. 4.

3. The word "theodicy," from the Greek *theos* (God) and *dike* (righteous), means the justification of God's goodness in the face of the fact of evil.

physical and mental: why has an all-good and all-powerful God created a world in which this occurs?

Christian thought has always considered moral evil in its relation to human freedom and responsibility. To be a person is to be a finite center of freedom, a (relatively) free and self-directing agent responsible for one's own decisions. This involves being free to act wrongly as well as to act rightly. The idea of a person who can be infallibly guaranteed always to act rightly is self-contradictory. There can be no guarantee in advance that a genuinely free moral agent will never choose amiss. Consequently, the possibility of wrongdoing or sin is logically inseparable from the creation of finite persons, and to say that God should not have created beings who might sin amounts to saying that he should not have created people.

. . . .

An objector might raise the question of whether or not we deny God's omnipotence if we admit that he is unable to create persons who are free from the risks inherent in personal freedom. The answer that has always been given is that to create such beings is logically impossible. It is no limitation upon God's power that he cannot accomplish the logically impossible, since there is nothing here to accomplish, but only a meaningless conjunction of words[4]—in this case "person who is not a person." God is able to create beings of any and every conceivable kind; but creatures who lack moral freedom, however superior they might be to human beings in other respects, would not be what we mean by persons. They would constitute a different form of life which God might have brought into existence instead of persons. When we ask why God did not create such beings in place of persons, the traditional answer is that only persons could, in any meaningful sense, become "children of God," capable of entering into a personal relationship with their Creator by a free and uncompelled response to his love.

. . . .

The necessary connection between moral freedom and the possibility, now actualized, of sin throws light upon a great deal of the suffering which afflicts mankind. For an enormous amount of human pain arises either from the inhumanity or the culpable incompetence of mankind. This includes such major scourges as poverty, oppression and persecution, war, and all the injustice, indignity, and inequity which occur even in the most advanced societies. These evils are manifestations of human sin. Even disease is fostered to an extent, the limits of which have not yet been determined by psychosomatic medicine, by moral and emotional factors seated both in the individual and in his social environment. To the extent that all of these evils stem from human failures and wrong decisions, their possibility is inherent in the creation of free persons inhabiting a world which presents them with real choices which are followed by real consequences.

We may now turn more directly to the problem of suffering. Even though the major bulk of actual human pain is traceable to man's mis-

---

4. As Aquinas said, ". . . nothing that implies a contradiction falls under the scope of God's omnipotence." *Summa Theologica*, Part I, Question 25, article 4.

used freedom as a sole or part cause, there remain other sources of pain which are entirely independent of the human will, for example, earthquake, hurricane, storm, flood, drought, and blight. In practice, it is often impossible to trace a boundary between the suffering which results from human wickedness and folly and that which falls upon mankind from without. Both kinds of suffering are inextricably mingled together in human experience. For our present purpose, however, it is important to note that the latter category does exist and that it seems to be built into the very structure of our world. In response to it, theodicy, if it is wisely conducted, follows a negative path. It is not possible to show positively that each item of human pain serves the divine purpose of good; but, on the other hand, it does seem possible to show that the divine purpose as it is understood in Judaism and Christianity could not be forwarded in a world which was designed as a permanent hedonistic paradise.[5]

An essential premise of this argument concerns the nature of the divine purpose in creating the world. The skeptic's assumption is that man is to be viewed as a completed creation and that God's purpose in making the world was to provide a suitable dwelling-place for this fully-formed creature. Since God is good and loving, the environment which he has created for human life to inhabit is naturally as pleasant and comfortable as possible. The problem is essentially similar to that of a man who builds a cage for some pet animal. Since our world, in fact, contains sources of hardship, inconvenience, and danger of innumerable kinds, the conclusion follows that this world cannot have been created by a perfectly benevolent and all-powerful deity.[6]

Christianity, however, has never supposed that God's purpose in the creation of the world was to construct a paradise whose inhabitants would experience a maximum of pleasure and a minimum of pain. The world is seen, instead, as a place of "soul-making" in which free beings, grappling with the tasks and challenges of their existence in a common environment, may become "children of God" and "heirs of eternal life." A way of thinking theologically of God's continuing creative purpose for man was suggested by some of the early Hellenistic Fathers of the Christian Church, especially Irenaeus. Following hints from St. Paul, Irenaeus taught that man has been made as a person in the image of God but has not yet been brought as a free and responsible agent into the finite likeness of God, which is revealed in Christ.[7] Our world, with all its rough edges, is the sphere in which this second and harder stage of the creative process is taking place.

This conception of the world (whether or not set in Irenaeus' theological framework) can be supported by the method of negative theodicy. Suppose, contrary to fact, this this world were a paradise from which all possibility of pain and suffering were excluded. The consequences would be very far-reaching. For example, no one could ever injure anyone else: the murderer's knife would turn to paper or his bullets to thin air; the bank safe, robbed of a million dollars, would miraculously become filled

5. From the Greek *hedone*, pleasure.
6. This is the nature of David Hume's argument in his discussion of the problem of evil in his *Dialogues*, Part XI.
7. See Irenaeus' *Against Heresies*, Book IV, chaps. 37 and 38.

with another million dollars (without this device, on however large a scale, proving inflationary); fraud, deceit, conspiracy, and treason would somehow always leave the fabric of society undamaged. Again, no one would ever be injured by accident: the mountain-climber, steeplejack, or playing child falling from a height would float unharmed to the ground; the reckless driver would never meet with disaster. There would be no need to work, since no harm could result from avoiding work; there would be no call to be concerned for others in time of need or danger, for in such a world there could be no real needs or dangers.

To make possible this continual series of individual adjustments, nature would have to work by "special providences" instead of running according to general laws which men must learn to respect on penalty of pain or death. The laws of nature would have to be extremely flexible: sometimes gravity would operate, sometimes not; sometimes an object would be hard and solid, sometimes soft. There could be no sciences, for there would be no enduring world structure to investigate. In eliminating the problems and hardships of an objective environment, with its own laws, life would become like a dream in which, delightfully but aimlessly, we would float and drift at ease.[8]

One can at least begin to imagine such a world. It is evident that our present ethical concepts would have no meaning in it. If, for example, the notion of harming someone is an essential element in the concept of a wrong action, in our hedonistic paradise there could be no wrong actions—nor any right actions in distinction from wrong. Courage and fortitude would have no point in an environment in which there is, by definition, no danger or difficulty. Generosity, kindness, the *agape* aspect of love, prudence, unselfishness, and all other ethical notions which presuppose life in a stable environment, could not even be formed. Consequently, such a world, however well it might promote pleasure, would be very ill adapted for the development of the moral qualities of human personality. In relation to this purpose it would be the worst of all possible worlds.

It would seem, then, that an environment intended to make possible the growth in free beings of the finest characteristics of personal life, must have a good deal in common with our present world. It must operate according to general and dependable laws; and it must involve real dangers, difficulties, problems, obstacles, and possibilities of pain, failure, sorrow, frustration, and defeat. If it did not contain the particular trials and perils which—subtracting man's own very considerable contribution—our world contains, it would have to contain others instead.

To realize this is not, by any means, to be in possession of a detailed theodicy. It is to understand that this world, with all its "heartaches and the thousand natural shocks that flesh is heir to," an environment so manifestly not designed for the maximization of human pleasure and the minimization of human pain, may be rather well adapted to the quite different purpose of "soul-making."

---

8. Tennyson's poem, *The Lotus-Eaters*, well expresses the desire (analyzed by Freud as a wish to return to the peace of the womb) for such "dreamful ease."

10. Antony Flew, R. M. Hare, and Basil Mitchell

Antony Flew is Professor of Philosophy at the University of
Reading in England. R. M. Hare is White's Professor of Moral
Philosophy in the University of Oxford. Basil Mitchell is
a fellow of Oriel College, Oxford.

Is the Existence of God a Factual Question?

Antony Flew

Let us begin with a parable. It is a parable developed from a tale told by
John Wisdom in his haunting and revelatory article 'God.'[1] Once upon a
time two explorers came upon a clearing in the jungle. In the clearing
were growing many flowers and many weeds. One explorer says, 'Some
gardener must tend this plot.' The other disagrees, 'There is no gardener.'
So they pitch their tents and set a watch. No gardener is ever seen. 'But
perhaps he is an invisible gardener.' So they set up a barbed-wire fence.
They electrify it. They patrol with bloodhounds. (For they remember how
H. G. Well's *The Invisible Man* could be both smelt and touched though
he could not be seen.) But no shrieks ever suggest that some intruder has
received a shock. No movement of the wire ever betrays an invisible
climber. The bloodhounds never give cry. Yet still the Believer is not

Reprinted with permission of Macmillan Publishing Co., Inc. from a symposium,
"Theology and Falsification," in *New Essays in Philosophical Theology*, Antony Flew
and Alasdair MacIntyre, editors. Published in the United States by the Macmillan
Publishing Co., Inc., 1955. Also reprinted with permission of SCM Press, Ltd., London.

1. Proceedings of the Aristotelian Society, 1944–45, reprinted as Ch. X of *Logic and
Language*, Vol. I (Blackwell, 1951), and in his *Philosophy and Psychoanalysis* (Blackwell, 1953).

convinced. 'But there is a gardener, invisible, intangible, insensible to electric shocks, a gardener who has no scent and makes no sound, a gardener who comes secretly to look after the garden which he loves.' At last the Sceptic despairs, 'But what remains of your original assertion? Just how does what you call an invisible, intangible, eternally elusive gardener differ from an imaginary gardener or even from no gardener at all?'

In this parable we can see how what starts as an assertion, that something exists or that there is some analogy between certain complexes of phenomena, may be reduced step by step to an altogether different status, to an expression perhaps of a 'picture preference.' The Sceptic says there is no gardener. The Believer says there is a gardener (but invisible, etc.). One man talks about sexual behaviour. Another man prefers to talk of Aphrodite (but knows that there is not really a super-human person additional to, and somehow responsible for, all sexual phenomena). The process of qualification may be checked at any point before the original assertion is completely withdrawn and something of that first assertion will remain (Tautology). Mr. Wells's invisible man could not, admittedly, be seen, but in all other respects he was a man like the rest of us. But though the process of qualification may be, and of course usually is, checked in time, it is not always judiciously so halted. Someone may dissipate his assertion completely without noticing that he has done so. A fine brash hypothesis may thus be killed by inches, the death by a thousand qualifications.

And in this, it seems to me, lies the peculiar danger, the endemic evil, of theological utterance. Take such utterances as 'God has a plan,' 'God created the world,' 'God loves us as a father loves his children.' They look at first sight very much like assertions, vast cosmological assertions. Of course, this is no sure sign that they either are, or are intended to be, assertions. But let us confine ourselves to the cases where those who utter such sentences intend them to express assertions. (Merely remarking parenthetically that those who intend or interpret such utterances as crypto-commands, expressions of wishes, disguised ejaculations, concealed ethics, or as anything else but assertions, are unlikely to succeed in making them either properly orthodox or practically effective.)

Now to assert that such and such is the case is necessarily equivalent to denying that such and such is not the case. Suppose then that we are in doubt as to what someone who gives vent to an utterance is asserting, or suppose that, more radically, we are sceptical as to whether he is really asserting anything at all, one way of trying to understand (or perhaps it will be to expose) his utterance is to attempt to find what he would regard as counting against, or as being incompatible with, its truth. For if the utterance is indeed an assertion, it will necessarily be equivalent to a denial of the negation of that assertion. And anything which would count against the assertion, or which would induce the speaker to withdraw it and to admit that it had been mistaken, must be part of (or the whole of) the meaning of the negation of that assertion. And to know the meaning of the negation of an assertion, is as near as makes no matter, to know the meaning of that assertion. And if there is nothing which a putative assertion denies then there is nothing which it asserts either: and so it is not really an assertion. When the Sceptic in the parable asked the Believer, 'Just how does what you call an invisible, intangible, eternally elusive gardener differ from an imaginary gardener or even from no gardener at all?' he was suggesting that the Believer's earlier statement had been so eroded by qualification that it was no longer an assertion at all.

Now it often seems to people who are not religious as if there was no conceivable event or series of events the occurrence of which would be admitted by sophisticated religious people to be a sufficient reason for conceding 'There wasn't a God after all' or 'God does not really love us then.' Someone tells us that God loves us as a father loves his children. We are reassured. But then we see a child dying of inoperable cancer of the throat. His earthly father is driven frantic in his efforts to help, but his Heavenly Father reveals no obvious sign of concern. Some qualification is made—God's love is 'not a merely human love' or it is 'an inscrutable love,' perhaps—and we realize that such sufferings are quite compatible with the truth of the assertion that 'God loves us as a father (but, of course . . .).' We are reassured again. But then perhaps we ask: what is this assurance of God's (appropriately qualified) love worth, what is this apparent guarantee really a guarantee against? Just what would have to happen not merely (morally and wrongly) to tempt but also (logically and rightly) to entitle us to say 'God does not love us' or even 'God does not exist'? I therefore put the simple central question, 'What would have to occur or to have occurred to constitute for you a disproof of the love of, or of the existence of, God?'

R. M. Hare

I wish to make it clear that I shall not try to defend Christianity in particular, but religion in general—not because I do not believe in Christianity, but because you cannot understand what Christianity is, until you have understood what religion is.

I must begin by confessing that, on the ground marked out by Flew, he seems to me to be completely victorious. I therefore shift my ground by relating another parable. A certain lunatic is convinced that all dons want to murder him. His friends introduce him to all the mildest and most respectable dons that they can find, and after each of them has retired, they say, 'You see, he doesn't really want to murder you; he spoke to you in a most cordial manner; surely you are convinced now?' But the lunatic replies 'Yes, but that was only his diabolical cunning; he's really plotting against me the whole time, like the rest of them; I know it I tell you.' However many kindly dons are produced, the reaction is still the same.

Now we say that such a person is deluded. But what is he deluded about? About the truth or falsity of an assertion? Let us apply Flew's test to him. There is no behaviour of dons that can be enacted which he will accept as counting against his theory; and therefore his theory, on this test, asserts nothing. But it does not follow that there is no difference between what he thinks about dons and what most of us think about them—otherwise we should not call him a lunatic and ourselves sane, and dons would have no reason to feel uneasy about his presence in Oxford.

Let us call that in which we differ from this lunatic, our respective *bliks*. He has an insane *blik* about dons; we have a sane one. It is important to realize that we have a sane one, not no *blik* at all; for there must be two sides to any argument—if he has a wrong *blik*, then those who are right about dons must have a right one. Flew has shown that a *blik* does not consist in an assertion or system of them; but nevertheless it is very important to have the right *blik*.

Let us try to imagine what it would be like to have different *bliks* about other things than dons. When I am driving my car, it sometimes occurs to me to wonder whether my movements of the steering-wheel will always continue to be followed by corresponding alterations in the direction of the car. I have never had a steering failure, though I have had skids, which must be similar. Moreover, I know enough about how the steering of my car is made, to know the sort of thing that would have to go wrong for the steering to fail—steel joints would have to part, or steel rods break, or something—but how do I know that this won't happen? The truth is, I don't know; I just have a *blik* about steel and its properties, so that normally I trust the steering of my car; but I find it not at all difficult to imagine what it would be like to lose this *blik* and acquire the opposite one. People would say I was silly about steel; but there would be no mistaking the reality of the difference between our respective *bliks*—for example, I should never go in a motor-car. Yet I should hesitate to say that the difference between us was the difference between contradictory assertions. No amount of safe arrivals or bench-tests will remove my *blik* and restore the normal one; for my *blik* is compatible with any finite number of such tests.

It was Hume who taught us that our whole commerce with the world depends upon our *blik* about the world; and that differences between *bliks* about the world cannot be settled by observation of what happens in the world. That was why, having performed the interesting experiment of doubting the ordinary man's *blik* about the world, and showing that no proof could be given to make us adopt one *blik* rather than another, he turned to backgammon to take his mind off the problem. It seems, indeed, to be impossible even to formulate as an assertion the normal *blik* about the world which makes me put my confidence in the future reliability of steel joints, in the continued ability of the road to support my car, and not gape beneath it revealing nothing below; in the general non-homicidal tendencies of dons; in my own continued well-being (in some sense of that word that I may not now fully understand) if I continue to do what is right according to my lights; in the general likelihood of people like Hitler coming to a bad end. But perhaps a formulation less inadequate than most is to be found in the Psalms: 'The earth is weak and the inhabiters thereof: I bear up the pillars of it.'

The mistake of the position which Flew selects for attack is to regard this kind of talk as some sort of *explanation*, as scientists are accustomed to use the word. As such, it would obviously be ludicrous. We no longer believe in God as an Atlas—*nous n'avons pas besoin de cette hypothèse.* But it is nevertheless true to say that, as Hume saw, without a *blik* there can be no explanation; for it is by our *bliks* that we decide what is and what is not an explanation. Suppose we believed that everything that happened, happened by pure chance. This would not of course be an assertion; for it is compatible with anything happening or not happening, and so, incidentally, is its contradictory. But if we had this belief, we should not be able to explain or predict or plan anything. Thus, although we should not be *asserting* anything different from those of a more normal belief, there would be a great difference between us; and this is the sort of difference that there is between those who really believe in God and those who really disbelieve in him.

The word 'really' is important, and may excite suspicion. I put it in, because when people have had a good Christian upbringing, as have most of those who now profess not to believe in any sort of religion, it is very hard to discover what they really believe. The reason why they find it so easy to think that they are not religious, is that they have never got into the frame of mind of one who suffers from the doubts to which religion is the answer. Not for them the terrors of the primitive jungle. Having abandoned some of the more picturesque fringes of religion, they think that they have abandoned the whole thing—whereas in fact they still have got, and could not live without, a religion of a comfortably substantial, albeit highly sophisticated, kind, which differs from that of many 'religious people' in little more than this, that 'religious people' like to sing Psalms about theirs—a very natural and proper thing to do. But nevertheless there may be a big difference lying behind—the difference between two people who, though side by side, are walking in different directions. I do not know in what direction Flew is walking; perhaps he does not know either. But we have had some examples recently of various ways in which one can walk away from Christianity, and there are any number of possibilities. After all, man has not changed biologically since primitive times; it is his religion that has changed, and it can easily change again. And if you do not think such changes make a difference, get acquainted with some Sikhs and some Mussulmans of the same Punjabi stock; you will find them quite different sorts of people.

There is an important difference between Flew's parable and my own which we have not yet noticed. The explorers do not *mind* about their garden; they discuss it with interest, but not with concern. But my lunatic, poor fellow, minds about dons; and I mind about the steering of my car; it often has people in it that I care for. It is because I mind very much about what goes on in the garden in which I find myself, that I am unable to share the explorers' detachment.

107

Basil Mitchell

Flew's article is searching and perceptive, but there is, I think, something odd about his conduct of the theologian's case. The theologian surely would not deny that the fact of pain counts against the assertion that God loves men. This very incompatibility generates the most intractable of theological problems—the problem of evil. So the theologian *does* recognize the fact of pain as counting against Christian doctrine. But it is true that he will not allow it—or anything—to count decisively against it; for he is committed by his faith to trust in God. His attitude is not that of the detached observer, but of the believer.

Perhaps this can be brought out by yet another parable. In time of war in an occupied country, a member of the resistance meets one night a stranger who deeply impresses him. They spend that night together in conversation. The Stranger tells the partisan that he himself is on the side of the resistance—indeed that he is in command of it, and urges the partisan to have faith in him no matter what happens. The partisan is utterly convinced at that meeting of the Stranger's sincerity and constancy and undertakes to trust him.

They never meet in conditions of intimacy again. But sometimes the Stranger is seen helping members of the resistance, and the partisan is grateful and says to his friends, 'He is on our side.'

Sometimes he is seen in the uniform of the police handing over patriots to the occupying power. On these occasions his friends murmur against him: but the partisan still says, 'He is on our side.' He still believes that, in spite of appearances, the Stranger did not deceive him. Sometimes he asks the Stranger for help and receives it. He is then thankful. Sometimes he asks and does not receive it. Then he says, 'The Stranger knows best.' Sometimes his friends, in exasperation, say 'Well, what *would* he have to do for you to admit that you were wrong and that he is not on our side?' But the partisan refuses to answer. He will not consent to put the Stranger to the test. And sometimes his friends complain, 'Well, if *that's* what you mean by his being on our side, the sooner he goes over to the other side the better.'

The partisan of the parable does not allow anything to count decisively against the proposition 'The Stranger is on our side.' This is because he has committed himself to trust the Stranger. But he of course recognizes that the Stranger's ambiguous behaviour *does* count against what he believes about him. It is precisely this situation which constitutes the trial of his faith.

When the partisan asks for help and doesn't get it, what can he do? He can (*a*) conclude that the stranger is not on our side or; (*b*) maintain that he is on our side, but that he has reasons for withholding help.

The first he will refuse to do. How long can he uphold the second position without its becoming just silly?

I don't think one can say in advance. It will depend on the nature of the impression created by the Stranger in the first place. It will depend, too, on the manner in which he takes the Stranger's behaviour. If he blandly dismisses it as of no consequence, as having no bearing upon his belief, it will be assumed that he is thoughtless or insane. And it quite obviously won't do for him to say easily, 'Oh, when used of the Stranger the phrase "is on our side" *means* ambiguous behaviour of this sort.' In that case he would be like the religious man who says blandly of a terrible disaster 'It is God's will.' No, he will only be regarded as sane and reasonable in his belief, if he experiences in himself the full force of the conflict.

It is here that my parable differs from Hare's. The partisan admits that many things may and do count against his belief: whereas Hare's lunatic who has a *blik* about dons doesn't admit that anything counts against his *blik*. Nothing *can* count against *bliks*. Also the partisan has a reason for having in the first instance committed himself, viz. the character of the Stranger; whereas the lunatic has no reason for his *blik* about dons—because, of course, you can't have reasons for *bliks*.

This means that I agree with Flew that theological utterances must be assertions. The partisan is making an assertion when he says, 'The Stranger is on our side.'

Do I want to say that the partisan's belief about the Stranger is, in any sense, an explanation? I think I do. It explains and makes sense of the Stranger's behaviour: it helps to explain also the resistance movement in the context of which he appears. In each case it differs from the interpretation which the others put upon the same facts.

'God loves men' resembles 'the Stranger is on our side' (and many other significant statements, e.g. historical ones) in not being conclusively falsifiable. They can both be treated in at least three different ways: (1) As provisional hypotheses to be discarded if experience tells against them; (2) As significant articles of faith; (3) As vacuous formulae (expressing, perhaps, a desire for reassurance) to which experience makes no difference and which make no difference to life.

The Christian, once he has committed himself, is precluded by his faith from taking up the first attitude: 'Thou shalt not tempt the Lord thy God.' He is in constant danger, as Flew has observed, of slipping into the third. But he need not; and, if he does, it is a failure in faith as well as in logic.

11. John Hick

John Hick is Professor of Theology at the University of
Birmingham.

The Verification of Belief in
God

To ask "Is the existence of God verifiable?" is to pose a question which is
too imprecise to be capable of being answered.[1] There are many different
concepts of God, and it may be that statements employing some of them
are open to verification or falsification while statements employing others of them are not. Again, the notion of verifying is itself by no means
perfectly clear and fixed; and it may be that on some views of the nature
of verification the existence of God is verifiable, whereas on other views
it is not.

Instead of seeking to compile a list of the various different concepts
of God and the various possible senses of "verify," I wish to argue with

From "Theology and Verification," originally published in the journal, *Theology
Today*, 1960. Pp. 12–31. Reprinted by permission of the author and editor.

1. In this paper I assume that an indicative sentence expresses a factual assertion
if and only if the state in which the universe would be if the putative assertion could
correctly be said to be true differs in some experienceable way from the state in which
the universe would be if the putative assertion could correctly be said to be false,
all aspects of the universe other than that referred to in the putative assertion being
the same in either case. This criterion acknowledges the important core of truth in the
logical positivist verification principle. "Experienceable" in the above formulation
means, in the case of alleged subjective or private facts (e.g., pains, dreams, after-
images, etc.), "experienceable by the subject in question" and, in the case of alleged
objective or public facts, "capable in principle of being experienced by anyone." My
contention is going to be that "God exists" asserts a matter of objective fact.

regard to one particular concept of deity, namely the Christian concept, that divine existence is in principle verifiable; and as the first stage of this argument I must indicate what I mean by "verifiable."

I

The central core of the concept of verification, I suggest, is the removal of ignorance or uncertainty concerning the truth of some proposition. That p is verified (whether p embodies a theory, hypothesis, prediction, or straightforward assertion) means that something happens which makes it clear that p is true. A question is settled so that there is no longer room for rational doubt concerning it. The way in which grounds for rational doubt are excluded varies, of course, with the subject matter. But the general feature common to all cases of verification is the ascertaining of truth by the removal of grounds for rational doubt. Where such grounds are removed, we rightly speak of verification having taken place.

To characterize verification in this way is to raise the question whether the notion of verification is purely logical or is both logical and psychological. Is the statement that p is verified simply the statement that a certain state of affairs exists (or has existed) or is it the statement also that someone is aware that this state of affairs exists (or has existed) and notes that its existence establishes the truth of p? A geologist predicts that the earth's surface will be covered with ice in 15 million years time. Suppose that in 15 million years time the earth's surface *is* covered with ice, but that in the meantime the human race has perished, so that no one is left to observe the event or to draw any conclusion concerning the accuracy of the geologist's prediction. Do we now wish to say that his prediction has been verified, or shall we deny that it has been verified, on the ground that there is no one left to do the verifying?

The range of "verify" and its cognates is sufficiently wide to permit us to speak in either way. But the only sort of verification of theological propositions which is likely to interest us is one in which human beings participate. We may therefore, for our present purpose, treat verification as a logico-psychological rather than as a purely logical concept. I suggest, then, that "verify" be construed as a verb which has its primary uses in the active voice: I verify, you verify, we verify, they verify, or have verified. The impersonal passive, it is verified, now becomes logically secondary. To say that p has been verified is to say (at least) someone has verified it, often with the implication that his or their report to this effect is generally accepted. But it is impossible, on this usage, for p to have been verified without someone having verified it. "Verification" is thus primarily the name for an event which takes place in human consciousness.[2] It refers to an experience, the experience of ascertaining that

2. This suggestion is closely related to Carnap's insistence that, in contrast to "true," "confirmed" is time-dependent. To say that a statement is confirmed, or verified, is to say that it has been confirmed at a particular time—and, I would add, by a particular person. See Rudolf Carnap, "Truth and Confirmation," Feigl and Sellars, *Readings in Philosophical Analysis*, 1949, p. 119 f.

a given proposition or set of propositions is true. To this extent verification is a psychological notion. But of course it is also a logical notion. For needless to say, not *any* experience is rightly called an experience of verifying *p*. Both logical and psychological conditions must be fulfilled in order for verification to have taken place. In this respect, "verify" is like "know." Knowing is an experience which someone has or undergoes, or perhaps a dispositional state in which someone is, and it cannot take place without someone having or undergoing it or being in it; but not by any means every experience which people have, or every dispositional state in which they are, is rightly called knowing.

With regard to this logico-psychological concept of verification, such questions as the following arise. When *A*, but nobody else, has ascertained that *p* is true, can *p* be said to have been verified; or is it required that others also have undergone the same ascertainment? How public, in other words, must verification be? Is it necessary that *p* could in principle be verified by anyone, without restriction, even though perhaps only *A* has in fact verified it? If so, what is meant here by "in principle"; does it signify, for example, that *p* must be verifiable by anyone who performs a certain operation; and does it imply that to do this is within everyone's power?

These questions cannot, I believe, be given any general answer applicable to all instances of the exclusion of rational doubt. The answers must be derived in each case from an investigation of the particular subject matter. It will be the object of subsequent sections of this article to undertake such an investigation concerning the Christian concept of God.

Verification is often construed as the verification of a prediction. However, verification, as the exclusion of grounds for rational doubt, does not necessarily consist in the proving correct of a prediction; a verifying experience does not always need to have been predicted in order to have the effect of excluding rational doubt. But when we are interested in the verifiability of propositions as the criterion for their factual meaning, the notion of prediction becomes central. If a proposition contains or entails predictions which can be verified or falsified, its character as an assertion (though not of course its character as a true assertion) is thereby guaranteed.

Such predictions may be and often are conditional. For example, statements about the features of the dark side of the moon are rendered meaningful by the conditional predictions which they entail to the effect that if an observer comes to be in such a position in space, he will make such-and-such observations. It would in fact be more accurate to say that the prediction is always conditional, but that sometimes the conditions are so obvious and so likely to be fulfilled in any case that they require no special mention, while sometimes they require for their fulfillment some unusual expedition or operation. A prediction, for example, that the sun will rise within twenty-four hours is intended unconditionally, at least as concerns conditions to be fulfilled by the observer; he is not required by the terms of the prediction to perform any special operation. Even in this case, however, there is an implied negative condition that he shall not put himself in a situation (such as immuring himself in the depths of a coal mine) from which a sunrise would not be perceptible. Other predictions, however, are explicitly conditional. In these cases it is true for any particular individual that in order to verify the statement in question he must go through some specified course of action. The prediction is to the effect that if you conduct such an experiment you will obtain such a result; for example, if you go into the next room you will have such-and-such visual experiences, and if you then touch the table which you see you will have such-and-such tactual experiences, and so on. The content of the "if" clause is of course always determined by the particular subject matter. The logic of "table" determines what you must do to verify statements about tables; the logic of "molecule" determines what you must do to verify statements about molecules; and the logic of "God" determines what you must do to verify statements about God.

In those cases in which the individual who is to verify a proposition must himself first perform some operation, it clearly cannot follow from the circumstances that the proposition is true that everybody has in fact verified it, or that everybody will at some future time verify it. For whether or not any particular person performs the requisite operation is a contingent matter.

II

What is the relation between verification and falsification? We are all familiar today with the phrase, "theology and falsification." A. G. N. Flew and others,[3] taking their cue from John Wisdom,[4] have raised instead of the question, "What possible experiences would verify 'God exists'?" the matching question, "What possible experiences would falsify 'God exists'? What conceivable state of affairs would be incompatible with the existence of God?" In posing the question in this way it was apparently assumed that verification and falsification are symmetrically related, and that the latter is apt to be the more accessible of the two.

In the most common cases, certainly, verification and falsification are symmetrically related. The logically simplest case of verification is provided by the crucial instance. Here it is integral to a given hypothesis that if, in specified circumstances, A occurs, the hypothesis is thereby shown to be true, whereas if B occurs the hypothesis is thereby shown to be false. Verification and falsification are also symmetrically related in the testing of such a proposition as "There is a table in the next room." The verifying experiences in this case are experiences of seeing and touching, predictions of which are entailed by the proposition in question, under the proviso that one goes into the next room; and the absence of such experiences in those circumstances serves to falsify the proposition.

3. A. G. N. Flew, editor, *New Essays in Philosophical Theology*, 1955, Chapter VI. (See above, p. 103.)
4. "Gods," *Proceedings of the Aristotelian Society*, 1944–45. Reprinted in A. G. N. Flew, editor, *Logic and Language*, First Series, 1951, and in John Wisdom, *Philosophy and Psycho-Analysis*, 1953.

But it would be rash to assume, on this basis, that verification and falsification must always be related in this symmetrical fashion. They do not necessarily stand to one another as do the two sides of a coin, so that once the coin is spun it must fall on one side or the other. There are cases in which verification and falsification each correspond to a side on a different coin, so that one can fail to verify without this failure constituting falsification.

Consider, for example, the proposition that "there are three successive sevens in the decimal determination of π." So far as the value of π has been worked out, it does not contain a series of three sevens, but it will always be true that such a series may occur at a point not yet reached in anyone's calculations. Accordingly, the proposition may one day be verified, if it is true, but can never be falsified, if it is false.

The hypothesis of continued conscious existence after bodily death provides an instance of a different kind of such asymmetry, and one which has a direct bearing upon the theistic problem. This hypothesis has built into it a prediction that one will after the date of one's bodily death have conscious experiences, including the experience of remembering that death. This is a prediction which will be verified in one's own experience if it is true, but which cannot be falsified if it is false. That is to say, it can be false, but *that* it is false can never be a fact which anyone has experientially verified. But this circumstance does not determine the meaningfulness of the hypothesis, since it is also such that if it be true, it will be known to be true.

It is important to remember that we do not speak of verifying logically necessary truths, but only propositions concerning matters of fact. Accordingly verification is not to be identified with the concept of logical certification or proof. The exclusion of rational doubt concerning some matter of fact is not equivalent to the exclusion of the logical possibility of error or illusion. For truths concerning fact are not logically necessary. Their contrary is never self-contradictory. But at the same time the bare logical possibility of error does not constitute ground for rational doubt as to the veracity of our experience. If it did, no empirical proposition could ever be verified, and indeed the notion of empirical verification would be without use and therefore without sense. What we rightly seek, when we desire the verification of a factual proposition, is not a demonstration of the logical impossibility of the proposition being false (for this would be a self-contradictory demand), but such weight of evidence as suffices, in the type of case in question, to exclude rational doubt.

III

These features of the concept of verification—that verification consists in the exclusion of grounds for rational doubt concerning the truth of some proposition; that this means its exclusion from particular minds; that the nature of the experience which serves to exclude grounds for rational doubt depends upon the particular subject matter; that verification is often related to predictions and that such predictions are often conditional; that verification and falsification may be asymmetrically related; and finally, that the verification of a factual proposition is not equivalent to logical certification—are all relevant to the verification of the central religious claim, "God exists." I wish now to apply these discriminations to the notion of eschatological verification, which has been briefly employed by Ian Crombie in his contribution to *New Essays in Philosophical Theology*,[5] and by myself in *Faith and Knowledge*.[6] This suggestion has on each occasion been greeted with disapproval by both philosophers and theologians. I am, however, still of the opinion that the notion of eschatological verification is sound; and further, that no viable alternative to it has been offered to establish the factual character of theism.

The strength of the notion of eschatological verification is that it is not an *ad hoc* invention but is based upon an actually operative religious concept of God. In the language of Christian faith, the word "God" stands as the center of a system of terms, such as Spirit, grace, Logos, incarnation, Kingdom of God, and many more; and the distinctly Christian conception of God can only be fully grasped in its connection with these related terms.[7] It belongs to a complex of notions which together constitute a picture of the universe in which we live, of man's place therein, of a comprehensive divine purpose interacting with human purposes, and of the general nature of the eventual fulfillment of that divine purpose. This Christian picture of the universe, entailing as it does certain distinctive expectations concerning the future, is a very different picture from any that can be accepted by one who does not believe that the God of the New Testament exists. Further, these differences are such as to show themselves in human experience. The possibility of experimental confirmation is thus built into the Christian concept of God; and the notion of eschatological verification seeks to relate this fact to the logical problem of meaning.

Let me first give a general indication of this suggestion, by repeating a parable which I have related elsewhere,[8] and then try to make it more precise and eligible for discussion. Here, first, is the parable.

Two men are traveling together along a road. One of them believes that it leads to a Celestial City, the other that it leads nowhere; but since this is the only road there is, both must travel it. Neither has been this way before, and therefore neither is able to say what they will find around each next corner. During their journey they meet both with moments of refreshment and delight, and with moments of hardship and danger. All the time one of them thinks of his journey as a pilgrimage to the Celestial City and interprets the pleasant parts as encouragements

5. *Op. cit.*, p. 126.
6. Cornell University Press, 1957, pp. 150–62.
7. Its clear recognition of this fact, with regard not only to Christianity but to any religion, is one of the valuable features of Ninian Smart's *Reasons and Faiths* (1958). He remarks, for example, that "the claim that God exists can only be understood by reference to many, if not all, other propositions in the doctrinal scheme from which it is extrapolated" (p. 12).
8. *Faith and Knowledge*, p. 150 f.

and the obstacles as trials of his purpose and lessons in endurance, prepared by the king of that city and designed to make of him a worthy
citizen of the place when at last he arrives there. The other, however,
believes none of this and sees their journey as an unavoidable and aim-
less ramble. Since he has no choice in the matter, he enjoys the good
and endures the bad. But for him there is no Celestial City to be reached,
no all-encompassing purpose ordaining their journey; only the road itself
and the luck of the road in good weather and in bad.

During the course of the journey the issue between them is not an
experimental one. They do not entertain different expectations about the
coming details of the road, but only about its ultimate destination. And
yet when they do turn the last corner it will be apparent that one of them
has been right all the time and the other wrong. Thus although the issue
between them has not been experimental, it has nevertheless from the
start been a real issue. They have not merely felt differently about the
road; for one was feeling appropriately and the other inappropriately in
relation to the actual state of affairs. Their opposed interpretations of
the road constituted genuinely rival assertions, though assertions whose
assertion-status has the peculiar characteristic of being guaranteed retro-
spectively by a future crux.

This parable has of course (like all parables) strict limitations. It is
designed to make only one point: that Christian doctrine postulates an
ultimate unambiguous state of existence *in patria* as well as our present
ambiguous existence *in via*. There is a state of having arrived as well as
a state of journeying, an eternal heavenly life as well as an earthly pilgrimage. The alleged future experience of this state cannot, of course, be
appealed to as evidence for theism as a present interpretation of our
experience; but it does suffice to render the choice between theism and
atheism a real and not a merely empty or verbal choice. And although
this does not affect the logic of the situation, it should be added that the
alternative interpretations are more than theoretical, for they render
different practical plans and policies appropriate now.

The universe as envisaged by the theist, then, differs as a totality
from the universe as envisaged by the atheist. This differences does not,
however, from our present standpoint within the universe, involve a
difference in the objective content of each or even any of its passing
moments. The theist and the atheist do not (or need not) expect different
events to occur in the successive details of the temporal process. They do
not (or need not) entertain divergent expectations of the course of history viewed from within. But the theist does and the atheist does not
expect that when history is completed it will be seen to have led to a
particular end-state and to have fulfilled a specific purpose, namely that
of creating "children of God."

The idea of an eschatological verification of theism can make sense,
however, only if the logically prior idea of continued personal existence
after death is intelligible. A desultory debate on this topic has been going
on for several years in some of the philosophical periodicals. C. I. Lewis
has contended that the hypothesis of immortality "is an hypothesis about
our own future experience. And our understanding of what would verify

it has no lack of clarity."[9] And Morris Schlick agreed, adding, "We must conclude that immortality, in the sense defined [i.e. 'survival after death,' rather than 'never-ending life'], should not be regarded as a 'metaphysical problem,' but is an empirical hypothesis, because it possesses logical verifiability. It could be verified by following the prescription: 'Wait until you die!' "[10] However, others have challenged this conclusion, either on the ground that the phrase "surviving death" is self-contradictory in ordinary language or, more substantially, on the ground that the traditional distinction between soul and body cannot be sustained.[11] I should like to address myself to this latter view. The only self of which we know, it is said, is the empirical self, the walking, talking, acting, sleeping individual who lives, it may be, for some sixty to eighty years and then dies. Mental events and mental characteristics are analyzed into the modes of behavior and behavioral dispositions of this empirical self. The human being is described as an organism capable of acting in the "high-level" ways which we characterize as intelligent, thoughtful, humorous, calculating, and the like. The concept of mind or soul is thus not the concept of a "ghost in the machine" (to use Gilbert Ryle's loaded phrase[12]), but of the more flexible and sophisticated ways in which human beings behave and have it in them to behave. On this view there is no room for the notion of soul in distinction from body; and if there is no soul in distinction from body, there can be no question of the soul surviving the death of the body. Against this philosophical background the specifically Christian (and also Jewish) belief in the resurrection of the flesh, or body, in contrast to the Hellenic notion of the survival of a disembodied soul, might be expected to have attracted more attention than it has. For it is consonant with the conception of man as an indissoluble psycho-physical unity, and yet it also offers the possibility of an empirical meaning for the idea of "life after death."

Paul is the chief Biblical expositor of the idea of the resurrection of the body.[13] His view, as I understand it, is this. When someone has died he is, apart from any special divine action, extinct. A human being is by nature mortal and subject to annihilation by death. But in fact God, by an act of sovereign power, either sometimes or always resurrects or (better) reconstitutes or recreates him—not, however, as the identical physical organism that he was before death, but as a *soma pneumatikon* ("spiritual body") embodying the dispositional characteristics and memory traces of the deceased physical organism, and inhabiting an environment with which the *soma pneumatikon* is continuous as the *ante-mortem* body was continuous with our present world. In discussing this notion we may well abandon the word "spiritual," as lacking today any precise

9. "Experience and Meaning," *Philosophical Review*, 1934, reprinted in Feigl and Sellars, *Readings in Philosophical Analysis*, 1949, p. 142.
10. "Meaning and Verification," *Philosophical Review*, 1936, reprinted in Feigl and Sellars, *op. cit.*, p. 160.
11. E.g. A. G N. Flew, "Death," *New Essays in Philosophical Theology;* "Can a Man Witness His Own Funeral?" *Hibbert Journal*, 1956.
12. *The Concept of Mind*, 1949, which contains an important exposition of the interpretation of "mental" qualities as characteristics of behavior.
13. I Cor. 15.

established usage, and speak of "resurrection bodies" and of "the resurrection world." The principal questions to be asked concern the relation between the physical world and the resurrection world, and the criteria of personal identity which are operating when it is alleged that a certain inhabitant of the resurrection world is the same person as an individual who once inhabited this world. The first of these questions turns out on investigation to be the more difficult of the two, and I shall take the easier one first.

Let me sketch a very odd possibility (concerning which, however, I wish to emphasize not so much its oddness as its possibility!), and then see how far it can be stretched in the direction of the notion of the resurrection body. In the process of stretching it will become even more odd than it was before; but my aim will be to show that, however odd, it remains within the bounds of the logically possible. This progression will be presented in three pictures, arranged in a self-explanatory order.

First picture: Suppose that at some learned gathering in this country one of the company were suddenly and inexplicably to disappear, and that at the same moment an exact replica of him were suddenly and inexplicably to appear at some comparable meeting in Australia. The person who appears in Australia is exactly similar, as to both bodily and mental characteristics, with the person who disappears in America. There is continuity of memory, complete similarity of bodily features, including even fingerprints, hair and eye coloration and stomach contents, and also of beliefs, habits, and mental propensities. In fact there is everything that would lead us to identify the one who appeared with the one who disappeared, except continuity of occupancy of space. We may suppose, for example, that a deputation of the colleagues of the man who disappeared fly to Australia to interview the replica of him which is reported there, and find that he is in all respects but one exactly as though he had travelled from say, Princeton to Melbourne, by conventional means. The only difference is that he describes how, as he was sitting listening to Dr. Z reading a paper, on blinking his eyes he suddenly found himself sitting in a different room listening to a different paper by an Australian scholar. He asks his colleagues how the meeting had gone after he ceased to be there, and what they had made of his disappearance, and so on. He clearly thinks of himself as the one who was present with them at their meeting in the United States. I suggest that faced with all these circumstances his colleagues would soon, if not immediately, find themselves thinking of him and treating him as the individual who had so inexplicably disappeared from their midst. We should be extending our normal use of "same person" in a way which the postulated facts would both demand and justify if we said that the one who appears in Australia is the same person as the one who disappears in America. The factors inclining us to identify them would far outweigh the factors disinclining us to do this. We should have no reasonable alternative but to extend our usage of "the same person" to cover the strange new case.

Second picture: Now let us suppose that the event in America is not a sudden and inexplicable disappearance, and indeed not a disappearance at all, but sudden death. Only, at the moment when the individual dies, a replica of him as he was at the moment before his death, complete with memory up to that instant, appears in Australia. Even with the corpse on our hands, it would still, I suggest, be an extension of "same person" required and warranted by the postulated facts, to say that the same person who died has been miraculously recreated in Australia. The case would be considerably odder than in the previous picture, because of the existence of the corpse in America contemporaneously with the existence of the living person in Australia. But I submit that, although the oddness of this circumstance may be stated as strongly as you please, and can indeed hardly be overstated, yet it does not exceed the bounds of the logically possible. Once again we must imagine some of the deceased's colleagues going to Australia to interview the person who has suddenly appeared there. He would perfectly remember them and their meeting, be interested in what had happened, and be as amazed and dumbfounded about it as anyone else; and he would perhaps be worried about the possible legal complications if he should return to America to claim his property; and so on. Once again, I believe, they would soon find themselves thinking of him and treating him as the same person as the dead Princetonian. Once again the factors inclining us to say that the one who died and the one who appeared are the same person would outweigh the factors inclining us to say that they are different people. Once again we should have to extend our usage of "the same person" to cover this new case.

Third picture: My third supposal is that the replica, complete with memory, etc. appears, not in Australia, but as a resurrection replica in a different world altogether, a resurrection world inhabited by resurrected persons. This world occupies its own space, distinct from the space with which we are now familiar. That is to say, an object in the resurrection world is not situated at any distance or in any direction from an object in our present world, although each object in either world is spatially related to each other object in the same world.

Mr. X, then, dies. A Mr. X replica, complete with the set of memory traces which Mr. X had at the last moment before his death, comes into existence. It is composed of other material than physical matter, and is located in a resurrection world which does not stand in any spatial relationship with the physical world. Let us leave out of consideration St. Paul's hint that the resurrection body may be as unlike the physical body as is a full grain of wheat from the wheat seed, and consider the simpler picture in which the resurrection body has the same shape as the physical body.[14]

In these circumstances, how does Mr. X know that he has been resurrected or recreated? He remembers dying; or rather he remembers being on what he took to be his death-bed, and becoming progressively weaker until, presumably, he lost consciousness. But how does he know that (to put it Irishly) his "dying" proved fatal; and that he did not, after losing consciousness, begin to recover strength, and has now simply waked up?

14. As would seem to be assumed, for example, by Irenaeus (*Adversus Haereses,* Bk. II, Ch. 34, Sec. 1).

The picture is readily enough elaborated to answer this question. Mr. X meets and recognizes a number of relatives and friends and historical personages whom he knows to have died; and from the fact of their presence, and also from their testimony that he has only just now appeared in their world, he is convinced that he has died. Evidences of this kind could mount up to the point at which they are quite as strong as the evidence which, in pictures one and two, convince the individual in question that he has been miraculously translated to Australia. Resurrected persons would be individually no more in doubt about their own identity than we are now, and would be able to identify one another in the same kinds of ways, and with a like degree of assurance, as we do now.

If it be granted that resurrected persons might be able to arrive at a rationally founded conviction that their existence is *post-mortem*, how could they know that the world in which they find themselves is in a different space from that in which their physical bodies were? How could such a one know that he is not in a like situation with the person in picture number two, who dies in America and appears as a full-blooded replica in Australia, leaving his corpse in the U.S.A.—except that now the replica is situated, not in Australia, but on a planet of some other star?

It is of course conceivable that the space of the resurrection world should have properties which are manifestly incompatible with its being a region of physical space. But on the other hand, it is not of the essence of the notion of a resurrection world that its space should have properties different from those of physical space. And supposing it not to have different properties, it is not evident that a resurrected individual could learn from any direct observations that he was not on a planet of some sun which is at so great a distance from our own sun that the stellar scenery visible from it is quite unlike that which we can now see. The grounds that a resurrected person would have for believing that he is in a different space from physical space (supposing there to be no discernible difference in spatial properties) would be the same as the grounds that any of us may have now for believing this concerning resurrected individuals. These grounds are indirect and consist in all those considerations (*e.g.*, Luke 16:26) which lead most of those who consider the question to reject as aburd the possibility of, for example, radio communication or rocket travel between earth and heaven.

V

In the present context my only concern is to claim that this doctrine of the divine creation of bodies, composed of a material other than that of physical matter, which bodies are endowed with sufficient correspondence of characteristics with our present bodies, and sufficient continuity of memory with our present consciousness, for us to speak of the same person being raised up again to life in a new environment, is not self-contradictory. If, then, it cannot be ruled out *ab initio* as meaningless, we may go on to consider whether and how it is related to the possible verification of Christian theism.

So far I have argued that a survival prediction such as is contained in the *corpus* of Christian belief is in principal subject to future verification. But this does not take the argument by any means as far as it must go to succeed. For survival, simply as such, would not serve to verify theism. It would not necessarily be a state of affairs which is manifestly incompatible with the nonexistence of God. It might be taken just as a surprising natural fact. The atheist, in his resurrection body, and able to remember his life on earth, might say that the universe has turned out to be more complex, and perhaps more to be approved of, than he had realized. But the mere fact of survival, with a new body in a new environment, would not demonstrate to him that there is a God. It is fully compatible with the notion of survival that the life to come be, so far as the theistic problem is concerned, essentially a continuation of the present life, and religiously no less ambiguous. And in this event, survival after bodily death would not in the least constitute a final verification of theistic faith.

I shall not spend time in trying to draw a picture of resurrection existence which would merely prolong the religious ambiguity of our present life. The important question, for our purpose, is not whether one can conceive of after-life experiences which would *not* verify theism (and in point of fact one can fairly easily conceive them), but whether one can conceive of after-life experiences which *would* serve to verify theism.

I think that we can. In trying to do so I shall not appeal to the traditional doctrine, which figures especially in Catholic and mystical theology, of the Beatific Vision of God. The difficulty presented by this doctrine is not so much that of deciding whether there are grounds for believing it, as of deciding what it means. I shall not, however, elaborate this difficulty, but pass directly to the investigation of a different and, as it seems to me, more intelligible possibility. This is the possibility not of a direct vision of God, whatever that might mean, but of a *situation* which points unambiguously to the existence of a loving God. This would be a situation which, so far as its religious significance is concerned, contrasts in a certain important respect with our present situation. Our present situation is one which in some ways seems to confirm and in other ways to contradict the truth of theism. Some events around us suggest the presence of an unseen benevolent intelligence and others suggest that no such intelligence is at work. Our situation is religiously ambiguous. But in order for us to be aware of this fact we must already have some idea, however vague, of what it would be for our situation to be not ambiguous, but on the contrary wholly evidential of God. I therefore want to try to make clearer this presupposed concept of a religiously unambiguous situation.

There are, I suggest, two possible developments of our experience such that, if they occurred in conjunction with one another (whether in this life or in another life to come), they would assure us beyond rational doubt of the reality of God, as conceived in the Christian faith. These are, *first*, an experience of the fulfillment of God's purpose for ourselves, as this has been disclosed in the Christian relevation; in conjunction, *second*, with an experience of communion with God as he has revealed himself in the person of Christ.

The divine purpose for human life, as this is depicted in the New Testament documents, is the bringing of the human person, in society with his fellows, to enjoy a certain valuable quality of personal life, the content of which is given in the character of Christ—which quality of life (i.e., life in relationship with God, described in the Fourth Gospel as eternal life) is said to be the proper destiny of human nature and the source of man's final self-fulfillment and happiness. The verification situation with regard to such a fulfillment is asymmetrical. On the one hand, so long as the divine purpose remains unfulfilled, we cannot know that it never will be fulfilled in the future, hence no final falsification is possible of the claim that this fulfillment will occur—unless, of course, the prediction contains a specific time clause which, in Christian teaching, it does not. But on the other hand, if and when the divine purpose *is* fulfilled in our own experience, we must be able to recognize and rejoice in that fulfillment. For the fulfillment would not be for us the promised fulfillment without our own conscious participation in it.

It is important to note that one can say this much without being cognizant in advance of the concrete form which such fulfillment will take. The before-and-after situation is analogous to that of a small child looking forward to adult life and then, having grown to adulthood, looking back upon childhood. The child possesses and can use correctly in various contexts the concept of "being grown-up," although he does not know, concretely, what it is like to be grown-up. But when he reaches adulthood he is nevertheless able to know that he has reached it; he is able to recognize the experience of living a grown-up life even though he did not know in advance just what to expect. For his understanding of adult maturity grows as he himself matures. Something similar may be supposed to happen in the case of the fulfillment of the divine purpose for human life. That fulfillment may be as far removed from our present condition as is mature adulthood from the mind of a little child; nevertheless, we possess already a comparatively vague notion of this final fulfillment, and as we move towards it our concept will itself become more adequate; and if and when we finally reach that fulfillment, the problem of recognizing it will have disappeared in the process.

The other feature that must, I suggest, be present in a state of affairs that would verify theism, is that the fulfillment of God's purpose be apprehended *as* the fulfillment of God's purpose and not simply as a natural state of affairs. To this end it must be accompanied by an experience of communion with God as he has made himself known to men in Christ.

The specifically Christian clause, "as he has made himself known to men in Christ," is essential, for it provides a solution to the problem of recognition in the awareness of God. Several writers have pointed out the logical difficulty involved in any claim to have encountered God.[15] How could one know that it was *God* whom one had encountered? God is described in Christian theology in terms of various absolute qualities, such as omnipotence, omnipresence, perfect goodness, infinite love, etc., which cannot as such be observed by us, as can their finite analogues,

15. For example, R. W. Hepburn, *Christianity and Paradox*, 1958, p. 56 f.

limited power, local presence, finite goodness, and human love. One can recognize that a being whom one "encounters" has a given finite degree of power, but how does one recognize that he has *unlimited* power? How does one observe that an encountered being is *omni*present? How does one perceive that his goodness and love, which one can perhaps see to exceed any human goodness and love, are actually infinite? Such qualities cannot be given in human experience. One might claim, then, to have encountered a Being whom one presumes, or trusts, or hopes to be God; but one cannot claim to have encountered a Being whom one recognized to be the infinite almighty, eternal Creator.

This difficulty is met in Christianity by the doctrine of the Incarnation—although this was not among the considerations which led to the formulation of that doctrine. The idea of incarnation provides answers to the two related questions: "How do we know that God has certain absolute qualities which, by their very nature, transcend human experience?" and "How can there be an eschatological verification of theism which is based upon a recognition of the presence of God in his Kingdom?"

In Christianity God is known as "the God and Father of our Lord Jesus Christ."[16] God is the Being about whom Jesus taught; the Being in relation to whom Jesus lived, and into a relationship with whom he brought his disciples; the Being whose *agape* toward men was seen on earth in the life of Jesus. In short, God is the transcendent Creator who has revealed himself in Christ. Now Jesus' teaching about the Father is a part of that self-disclosure, and it is from this teaching (together with that of the prophets who preceded him) that the Christian knowledge of God's transcendent being is derived. Only God himself knows his own infinite nature; and our human belief about that nature is based upon his self-revelation to men in Christ. As Karl Barth expresses it, "Jesus Christ is the knowability of God."[17] Our beliefs about God's infinite being are not capable of observational verification, being beyond the scope of human experience, but they are susceptible of indirect verification by the removal of rational doubt concerning the authority of Christ. An experience of the reign of the Son in the Kingdom of the Father would confirm that authority, and therewith, indirectly, the validity of Jesus' teaching concerning the character of God in his infinite transcendent nature.

The further question as to how an eschatological experience of the Kingdom of God could be known to be such has already been answered by implication. It is God's union with man in Christ that makes possible ma ı's recognition of the fulfillment of God's purpose for man as being indeed the fulfillment of *God's* purpose for him. The presence of Christ in his Kingdom marks this as being beyond doubt the Kingdom of the God and Father of the Lord Jesus Christ.

It is true that even the experience of the realization of the promised Kingdom of God, with Christ reigning as Lord of the New Aeon, would not constitute a logical certification of his claim nor, accordingly, of the

16. II Cor. 11:31.
17. *Church Dogmatics*, Vol. II, Pt. I, p. 150.

reality of God. But this will not seem remarkable to any philosopher in the empiricist tradition, who knows that it is only a confusion to demand that a factual proposition be an analytic truth. A set of expectations based upon faith in the historic Jesus as the incarnation of God, and in his teaching as being divinely authoritative, could be so fully confirmed in *post-mortem* experience as to leave no ground for rational doubt as to the validity of that faith.

SUGGESTED READINGS

Religious Belief

The Ontological Argument

Descartes, René. *Meditations,* Part V [in Edwards-Pap, Smart].
Hartshorne, Charles. *The Logic of Perfection.* La Salle, Ill.: Open Court, 1963.
Plantinga, Alvin (ed.). *The Ontological Argument.* Garden City, N.Y.: Doubleday & Company, Inc., 1965. [A comprehensive collection of writings on
the argument, pro and con.]

The Cosmological Argument

Gilson, Etienne. *The Philosophy of St. Thomas Aquinas,* trans. Edward
Bullough. Cambridge, England: W. Heffer, 1925. Chaps. 7, 9 [partly in
Mandelbaum-Gramlich-Anderson].
Hawkins, D. J. B. *The Essentials of Theism.* New York: Sheed & Ward, 1949.
Chap. 4.
Joyce, G. H. *The Principles of Natural Theology.* New York: Longmans,
Green, 1951. Chap. 3.
Rowe, W. *The Cosmological Argument.* Princeton: Princeton Univ. Press,
1975.

The Argument from Design

Du Nouy, Lecomte. *Human Destiny.* New York: New American Library
(Signet Books), 1949.
Paley, William. *Evidences of the Existence and Attributes of the Deity,* 1802
[partly in Edwards-Pap].
Plantinga, Alvin. *God and Other Minds.* Ithaca, N.Y.: Cornell Univ. Press,
1967.
Russell, Bertrand. *Religion and Science.* London: Oxford Univ. Press, 1935.
Taylor, A. E. *Does God Exist?* London: Macmillan, 1947. Sec. IV.
Tennant, F. R. *Philosophical Theology.* London: Cambridge Univ. Press,
1928–30. Vol. II, Chapter 4 [in Alston, Hick].

Religious Experience

Baillie, John. *Our Knowledge of God.* New York: Scribner's, 1939.
Broad, C. D. *Religion, Philosophy, and Psychical Research.* New York:
Harcourt, 1953, pp. 190–201 [in Alston].
Leuba, J. H. *The Psychology of Religious Mysticism.* New York: Harcourt,
1925.
Martin, C. B. *Religious Belief.* Ithaca, N.Y.: Cornell Univ. Press, 1959. Chap. 5
[in Alston].
Otto, Rudolf. *The Idea of the Holy,* trans. J. W. Harvey. London: Oxford
Univ. Press, 1923 [partly in Alston].
Pratt, James B. *The Religious Consciousness.* New York: Macmillan, 1920.

Stace, W. T. *Mysticism and Philosophy*. Philadelphia: Lippincott, 1960 [partly in Tillman-Berofsky-O'Connor].
——————— (ed.). *The Teachings of the Mystics*. New York: New American Library (Mentor Books), 1960.
———————. *Time and Eternity*. Princeton, N.J.: Princeton Univ. Press, 1952.
Underhill, Evelyn. *Mysticism*. New York: Dutton, 1930.

Criticisms of Arguments for the Existence of God

Broad, C. D. "Arguments for the Existence of God," in *Religion, Philosophy, and Psychical Research*. New York: Harcourt, 1953.
Flew, A. *God and Philosophy*. London: Hutchinson & Co., Ltd., 1966.
Kant, Immanuel. *Critique of Pure Reason,* Book II. Chap. 3 [partly in Alston, Margolis].
Laird, John. *Theism and Cosmology*. London: Allen & Unwin, 1940.
Matson, W. I. *The Existence of God*. Ithaca, N.Y.: Cornell Univ. Press, 1965.
McTaggard, J. M. E. *Some Dogmas of Religion*. London: Arnold, 1906.
Russell, Bertrand. *Why I Am Not a Christian and Other Essays*. New York: Simon & Schuster, 1957. Chaps. 1, 13.

Anti-Supernaturalistic Interpretations of Religion

Comte, Auguste. *A General View of Positivism,* trans. J. H. Bridges. London: Routledge & Kegan Paul, 1880. Chap. 6 [partly in Alston].
Dewey, John. *A Common Faith*. New Haven, Conn.: Yale Univ. Press, 1934 [partly in Bronstein-Krikorian-Wiener, 3rd ed., Mandelbaum-Gramlich-Anderson, Jarrett-McMurrin].
Feuerbach, Ludwig. *The Essence of Christianity,* trans. George Eliot. New York: Harper & Row, 1957.
Fromm, Erich. *Psychoanalysis and Religion*. London: Victor Gollancz, 1951 [partly in Abernethy-Langford, Bronstein-Schulweis].
Huxley, Julian. *Religion Without Revelation*. New York: New American Library, 1958 [partly in Alston].
Santayana, George. *Reason in Religion*. New York: Scribner's, 1905 [partly in Alston, Mandelbaum-Gramlich-Anderson, Bronstein-Krikorian-Wiener, Jarrett-McMurrin].
Wieman, H. N. *The Source of Human Good*. Chicago: Univ. of Chicago Press, 1946 [partly in Alston].

The Problem of Evil

Leibniz, G. W. *On the Ultimate Origination of Things* [partly in Sprague-Taylor].
Lewis, C. S. *The Problem of Pain*. New York: Macmillan, 1950.
Mill, J. S. "Nature," in *Three Essays on Religion* [partly in Bronstein-Schulweis, Randall-Buchler-Shirk].
Pike, Nelson (ed.). *God and Evil*. Englewood Cliffs, N.J.: Prentice-Hall, 1964. [A collection of writings on the subject.]

Royce, Josiah. *The Religious Aspect of Philosophy.* New York: Harper & Row, 1958. Chap. 12.

St. Augustine, *Confessions,* Bk. VIII [partly in Bronstein-Schulweis].

—————————. "On Free Will" [partly in Sprague-Taylor].

—————————. *The Enchiridion,* Chaps. 10–16 [partly in Hick].

Tennant, F. R. *Philosophical Theology.* London: Cambridge Univ. Press, 1930. Vol. II, Chap. 7 [partly in Abernethy-Langford, Alston, Bronstein-Schulweis, Hick].

Religious Language

Ayer, A. J. *Language, Truth, and Logic,* 2nd ed. London: Victor Gollancz, 1946. Chap. 6.

Braithwaite, R. B. *An Empiricist's View of the Nature of Religious Belief.* Cambridge: Cambridge University Press, 1955.

Demos, Raphael, and Ducasse, C. J. "Are Religious Dogmas Cognitive and Meaningful?" in Morton White (ed.), *Academic Freedom, Logic, and Religion.* Philadelphia: Univ. of Pennsylvania Press, 1953.

Flew, Antony, and MacIntyre, Alasdair (eds.). *New Essays in Philosophical Theology.* London: Student Christian Movement, 1955.

Hook, Sidney (ed.) *Religious Experience and Truth.* New York: New York Univ. Press, 1961. Pts. I, III.

MacIntyre, Alasdair. "The Logical Status of Religious Belief," in *Metaphysical Beliefs.* London: Student Christian Movement, 1957.

Mascall, E. L. *Existence and Analogy.* London: Longmans, Green, 1949.

Mitchell, Basil (ed.). *Faith and Logic.* London: George Allen & Unwin, Ltd., 1957.

Ramsey, I. T. *Religious Language.* London: SCM Press, Ltd. 1957.

St. Thomas Aquinas. *Summa contra Gentiles,* Bk. I. Chaps. 28–34 [in Hick].

—————————. *Summa Theologica,* Pt. I, Q. 1, Q. 12.

Talk of God, Royal Institute of Philosophy Lectures. New York: St. Martin's Press, 1969.

Tillich, Paul. "Religious Symbols and Our Knowledge of God," *Christian Scholar,* Vol. 38 (1955).

PART II

Value and Obligation

Introduction

Another set of beliefs, the rational appraisal of which is of great interest, is *ethical* beliefs; that is, beliefs about what is morally right or wrong, about what one's moral obligations are, about what things are good or desirable (bad or undesirable). In order to see how the philosopher's attempt to provide a rational appraisal of ethical beliefs arises out of basic concerns of human life, let us begin by considering a serious moral dilemma.

Consider a young unmarried woman who finds herself pregnant. She is, of course, confronted with the necessity of a decision. Should she marry the father (let us assume that he is willing to marry)? Should she bear the child out of wedlock? Should she have an abortion? In thinking about this problem a host of questions arise. What are the chances of her having a happy and stable marriage with this young man, considering the fact that she would otherwise not have chosen to cast her lot with him? How will marriage under these circumstances affect his future attitude toward her? Suppose that after a year or so of marriage she decides that it was a big mistake. Would there be anything wrong in getting out at that time? Does one have an obligation to stick with one's spouse no matter what? And how much of a wrench would a divorce be to those concerned? How will her family and friends react to her as an unmarried mother? How unhappy would this make her parents? And how much would she herself suffer from their reactions? As for the abortion, is it really morally wrong to kill a fetus? Do the unborn have inalienable rights, as some writers now suggest? What are the chances of damage to her own health from an abortion? And how would *this* affect her family?

It is clear that in attempting to make an important decision, one is forced to consider questions about whether certain courses of action are morally permitted, forbidden, or obligatory, and questions about the positive or negative value of the likely consequences of various possible courses of action, consequences both for the agent and for other persons affected by his/her behavior. The branch of philosophy known as "Ethics" is basically concerned with investigating the grounds or bases for answering such questions. Of course, the philosopher as such does not typically try to

131

provide answers for questions about particular situations, such as the one described above—although hopefully he/she will make use of personal philosophical insights when, as a human being, thinking about his own moral dilemmas and those of friends. The philosopher's job is rather to find some defensible *general principles* that can be applied to any particular situations that arise, general principles that will indicate what we need to determine about the particular situation in order to answer the specific questions that arise there. That is, the philosopher attempts to determine, in general, the conditions under which an action is morally permitted, forbidden, or obligatory; and he seeks to discover what it is that gives a state of affairs more or less positive or negative value (makes it more or less desirable or undesirable). The results of this investigation will consist of general ethical principles, such as, "The only thing in life that is really desirable for itself is pleasure," and, "It is never right to treat another human being only as a means to one's own ends." We shall find the philosophers in our selections supporting and attacking a number of such principles. This research for defensible general principles we may call "normative" ethics, since it seeks to establish basic norms, for action or for aspiration.

Philosophers make other inquiries about the good and the right. The most important of these usually is called "meta-ethics," which is an inquiry into the proper *interpretation* of ethical words or statements, and into the *methodology* of normative ethics—the methods by which ethical principles or beliefs can be rationally appraised or shown to be true (if they can be). In a way, meta-ethics is more fundamental than normative ethics; for we can do normative ethics intelligently only if we have, at least implicitly, some view about how ethical language is to be understood, and only if we have, at least implicitly, some view as to how ethical beliefs can be assessed rationally. But in another way, normative ethics is more fundamental; for only after some normative ethics has been done, in a relatively unself-conscious manner, do the questions of meta-ethics arise. Our first selections, from Benedict through Ayer, are primarily concerned with meta-ethics; the middle group, from Aristotle through Sartre, with normative ethics, although some of the readings give some attention to both. The final two selections, as we shall see, belong to a still different category.

META-ETHICS

Ethical Skepticism and Ethical Relativism

It is widely believed among nonphilosophers that ethical beliefs are not subject to objective test, or to confirmation by appeal to observation and experiment, in the ways beliefs about the physical world are; it is thought that a person is entitled to his own "value judgments" and that it is presumptuous of a person to think he knows that the value judgments of another are mistaken. This view is shared by quite a few philosophers. One form of it may be called "ethical skepticism": the view that a person is never rationally better justified in believing an ethical statement than he is in believing its contradictory. Why do people embrace ethical skepticism?

One very important contemporary source of this view, at least among nonphilosophers, is the findings of anthropologists, particularly their finding that moral standards and conceptions of what is fundamentally worthwhile vary to a considerable extent among the peoples of the world. Actually it was well known by Plato, more than two thousand years ago, that the values and ethical norms of the Persians and Phoenicians were different from those accepted in Athens; but Plato did not draw any skeptical inferences from the fact. In the present century, however, anthropology has had a good press and, for better or worse, the general public has been influenced by the facts anthropologists have emphasized, and has, along with many anthropologists, taken these facts to support skepticism in ethics.

Some writers do not infer ethical skepticism from the variability of moral codes; they draw quite a different conclusion—that a person's ethical values and moral standards are correct when they conform to the values and standards of their social group. According to this view, it was really correct and justified for, say, a Spartan to think that infanticide is morally all right, since infanticide was accepted in Sparta; but it also is correct and justified for a contemporary Englishman to believe that infanticide is wrong, since infanticide is morally repellent to his countrymen. This somewhat strange position may be called "ethical relativism." According to this view, the status of values and moral standards is like that of a person's grammar: there is nothing inherently wrong about the use of "you is," but if educated people generally say "you are," an individual is mistaken if he says "you is." The moral views of an individual are subject to objective testing, but the moral standards of a group are not.

In Reading 12 Ruth Benedict, an anthropologist, provides a good example of the sort of comparative anthropological material from which inferences have been made to both ethical skepticism and ethical relativism. (We will leave it as an exercise for the reader to determine whether Benedict clearly espouses either of these positions.)

Facts about the diversity of moral codes among different peoples, although they have been taken by some to support a sceptical or relativist view about ethical principles, actually do not support such a view except in the context of some meta-ethical theory. If some meta-ethical views are correct, such facts can have no such force. We will see how this is, by looking at some complete meta-ethical theories that comprise both proposals about how ethical words/statements are to be construed and correspondingly how ethical beliefs can be rationally supported (if they can be). Three main types of theories are usually distinguished: Definism, Nonnaturalism or Intuitionism, and the Noncognitive or Emotive theory. These views are all represented among our readings.

Definism

The first theory affirms that there is no special mode of reasoning appropriate to supporting ethical beliefs. The reason is that ethical statements are best construed as synonymous with some type of nonethical statement—ethical words best defined in terms of some less problematic nonethical expressions (hence the term "definism")—so that if we already know how to appraise rationally these nonethical statements, we are in a position to appraise the ethical statements. Consider a simple version. Suppose we believe, with some, that "X is a good thing" just means, "X is conducive to the survival of the species." Then not only must we think that statements about what is good are true or false in the same sense as statements are in science, but also in principle biology can determine which statements are true. If we want to know whether knowledge is a good thing, all we have to do is determine whether knowledge is conducive to the survival of the species. (Presumably it is.) A view often is called "definist" if it asserts only that one (presumably more problematic) ethical statement means the same as another (presumably less problematic) ethical statement: for instance, "X is right" has been said to mean "X will produce at least as much good as any other action open to the agent."

Definists differ widely among themselves as to what ethical statements mean. The above version is accepted by neither of our two representative definists, Henry and Sharp; nor do they agree with each other. Henry thinks that all the important ethical words ("right," "good," "ought") are to be construed as functioning to make some assertion about what is willed or commanded by God; his is a "theological" definism. (Henry's view, incidentally, is not typical of theological writers, or of writers in the Christian tradition. His view has been defended by various, particularly Protestant, writers both contemporary and earlier, and a form of it may be present in some parts of both the Old and New Testament. But it was not held by St. Thomas Aquinas, or by the majority of writers in the religious, or Christian, tradition.) Sharp thinks that "X is right" means "X is an action which I, if I were vividly aware of the total situation and significant consequences; would be willing to have everyone perform under these same circumstances." A definism sometimes is called "naturalism" if it implies that ethical statements can be appraised by the methods of the natural sciences; in contrast, Henry's view would be a "supernaturalist" variety of definism.

There is a subtle complication that we should not overlook. Some definists such as Sharp think that what ordinary people *in fact do mean* by ethical words is the kind of thing the definist says is the meaning of these terms. Sharp would agree that a person on the street might not think of a definist explanation of his meaning if he were asked, but he believes that his view is a reasonable interpretation of what the person on the street means, in view of how he actually uses ethical words. Others, however, are not so concerned to ferret out the ordinary understanding of ethical terms. This may be because they despair of discovering exactly what this ordinary meaning is, or it may be because they consider the ordinary understanding too vague, indeterminate, or otherwise deficient. What they do instead is to maintain that a certain meaning has to be assigned to ethical words, if they are to have a sensible use—if they are to be used to say something that an intelligent and informed person would want to say. Such forms of definism are partially *proposals* about how ethical words may sensibly be used. In so far as they are, some arguments (below) about the meaning of ethical words in ordinary usage are hardly relevant to them.

Nonnaturalism or Intuitionism

The second main meta-ethical theory is represented among our readings by Thomas Reid, and also by some of the essays that are primarily on normative ethics, for instance the one by W. D. Ross (Reading 23). The nonnaturalists agree with the definists on one important point: that the meaning of ethical words is such that ethical statements are either true or false. But they disagree with the definists about the sort of meaning they have; and, as a consequence, they deny that ethical statements can be rationally supported in the ways definists think they can be.

On the question of meaning, the nonnaturalist maintains that the naturalist is mistaken in taking ethical statements to assert some kind of nonethical fact. This view is mistaken, he says, because no ethical word (such as "good" or "right") means the same as *any* word or phrase other than *ethical* words or phrases. (Maybe "ought" can be defined in terms of "wrong," but the latter is an ethical word.) How do nonnaturalists support this general claim, a claim made at least implicitly by Reid in the second page of his essay? In the present century, it has often been asserted that this claim can be made out by appeal to the "open question" argument, which is due originally to Richard Price. This argument runs as follows: Let E be some ethical word, and let P be some word or phrase that stands for a non-ethical property. Now ask yourself: "Is everything that is E also P? And is everything that is P also E? The nonnaturalist says that it will never be self-contradictory to answer these questions in the negative; furthermore, the questions are intelligible ones requiring ethical reflection for an answer. For example, it is an intelligible, "open" question whether everything conducive to the survival of the species is good, and a negative answer would not be self-contradictory. One would not be contradicting himself if he asserted that sterilization of those with under average intelligence would be conducive to the survival of the species, but nevertheless would not be a good thing. But, it is argued, if E just *meant* the same as P, it would be self-contradictory to answer in the negative, and the questions would not be intelligible ones requiring ethical reflection for an answer. In the case of "bachelor" and "unmarried male," which do mean roughly the same thing, it is clearly self-contradictory to say, "Not everything that is a bachelor is an unmarried male," and "Is every bachelor an unmarried male?" is not a genuine question. So the nonnaturalist argument runs.

Nonnaturalists are like definists both in thinking that ethical statements are true or false, and in thinking we can sometimes *know* which an ethical statement is. We may properly ask them, then, *how* we know such things. Usually, their answer is that some general ethical statements are *truths of reason,* although not *analytic* truths. They are cases of a *priori synthetic knowledge.* (For an explanation of these terms, see the Introduction to Part VI.) Sometimes, however, nonnaturalists appear to think that a person can be aware of something as being good, or an action as being right or wrong, not by reason, but by a quasi-observation or "moral sense"—by a kind of direct awareness that is not seeing with the eyes or awareness by any of the five senses. Reid discusses all these points in Reading 16.

Noncognitivism or the Emotive Theory

The third main meta-ethical theory is represented among our readings by Ayer (Reading 17), and also by one of the essays on normative ethics, that by Medlin (Reading 21). The noncognitivist agrees with the nonnaturalist that ethical statements cannot be established as true or false by scientific or theological reasoning. His reason for this is that he disagrees with both the preceding theories in a very fundamental way: he thinks ethical statements are not true or false at all—they do not assert any sort of fact, either empirical or nonempirical. They are, rather, like "Come to the party!" or, "I promise to meet you at eight o'clock," or, "I bet you a dollar," all of which are important items in our speech repertory, but none of which asserts a fact. The first of these utterances issues an invitation; the second makes a promise; and the third offers (or seals) a bet. It would be senseless to say of any such remark, "That's true!" or, "That's false!" The noncognitivist holds that ethical statements are like these utterances in not asserting facts. Only, because of their grammatical form, it is easily supposed that they state facts. (Other statements are like them in this respect: "The faculty will wear academic dress" looks like a fact-stating remark but may be used, not to make a prediction, but to issue an order to the faculty.)

What then, according to writers of this persuasion, is it that ethical statements do? Here, there is a good deal of disagreement. It has been said that ethical statements are disguised *commands*. This view is hardly defended today, but a somewhat similar view is that to make an ethical statement is to issue a prescription for choice or action, with the implication that one would issue the same prescription for all similar cases. (Since these views assert that ethical statements *mean* the same as a command or prescription, why is this view not a form of "definism?" The answer is just that historically "definism" has been used to imply that the theory holds that ethical statements are true or false.) According to another view, ethical convictions are essentially attitudes of favoring or disfavoring, and ethical statements are instruments conventionally used for expressing one's attitudes. Again, it is held that an ethical statement may be an instrument for advice-giving in one context, of exhortation in another, of praise in a third, of condemnation in a fourth, of commendation in a fifth, and so on. In Reading 17, Ayer defends the view that the function of ethical statements is to evince feelings of approval or disapproval, to arouse feeling and to stimulate action. (Ayer at present takes a view somewhat more complex than that espoused in the essay reprinted here.) Obviously a view like Ayer's leads to *skepticism* about ethics, in the sense explained above.

Many philosophers today think, as was suggested at the close of the remarks on Definism, that nothing can turn on what ethical words mean in ordinary usage; what is important, they think, is to know what meaning it would be *useful* to assign to them. One could then argue that the *preferred* meaning for ethical statements is what some definists have thought was their actual meaning (or perhaps something else), or what some non-cognitivists have thought is their actual meaning in ordinary usage. This view is a complex one, and the reasons adduced to support it are difficult. Hence we ignore it here.

NORMATIVE ETHICS

We come now to the question of what ethical principles it is rationally justified to believe. A few years ago, it was widely held that philosophers should stop talking about which ethical principles it is justifiable to accept, until the problems of meta-ethics have been resolved—and some noncognitivists affirmed that the proper business of philosophy stops at meta-ethics, nor-mative ethics being properly left to preachers and to common sense. However, at present almost all philosophers take a lively interest in the questions of normative ethics, which had been debated for centuries (for example, even by the characters in the *Iliad*) before anyone explicitly raised the questions about meaning and rational justification.

Theories about What Is Good in Itself

Philosophers have thought that there are two main normative questions: 1) Which kinds of things are good or desirable in themselves? and 2) Which kinds of action are morally right (or wrong)? We begin with theories about the first. These normative theories are not about the *meaning* of "right" or "good"; they are theories about *what is* right or good.

We must distinguish between being good in itself (intrinsically good) and being good for its consequences (extrinsically good). An operation for appendicitis is a good thing on account of its consequences for relief of pain, and for health; we would not say it is worth choosing just for itself. Driving to the airport is nothing one would choose for itself; one does it only because one wants to take, or meet, a plane. But some things we like, and choose, just for themselves: an evening at the symphony, lolling on the beach, a meal with friends. When contemplating an important decision and listing pros and cons of the alternative actions in terms of the results we think likely, it is frequently useful to list just the outcomes we think worthwhile in themselves.

Philosophers, in thinking about what is worthwhile in itself, have con-sidered such things as enjoyment, fame, prestige, wealth, knowledge, character, love, friendship, and just being alive or conscious. Aristotle and Mill (Readings 18 and 19) represent two main traditions. They agree on one point—that the life that is worthy of choice on its own account is a "happy" life; but they differ as to what kind of life is a "happy" one. Mill holds that only enjoyment (pleasure) of some sort is worthwhile; this view is called "hedonism" after the Greek word for enjoyment. Mill might be called a "monist" about the intrinsically good, since he holds that only one thing has this status. Aristotle, on the other hand, is a "pluralist"; he thinks that different things (contemplation of the truth, moderation in action, and certain features of character) are good in themselves. He does not deny that enjoyment is worthy of desire, but he takes a dim view of a life of sensual enjoyments, and he thinks that the life worthy of choice is primarily a life of reflection on truth, and of moderation and order both in desire and emotion. Pluralists differ among themselves about precisely which things are intrinsically good.

The practical implications of these theories are less divergent than one might suppose. Thus, hedonists generally think that one maximizes one's enjoyments in the long run by acquiring knowledge, by moderation in indulgence of the appetites, and even by suppression of some appetites. The hedonist, Epicurus, regarded a diet of bread, milk, and cheese as being as lavish as a rational man would want, and he thought that fame and power, however enjoyable, are apt in the long run to produce more frustration and sadness than they do joy. So hedonists and pluralists may very well advocate the same kind of life; only, what the pluralist may regard as good in itself, the hedonist may regard as only extrinsically good, in view of the enjoyment it brings.

Theories about the Morally Right or Obligatory

These theories are rather more diverse and complicated. There are two broad types of theory: 1) "consequentialist" (or "teleological") theories, which hold that rightness and wrongness are fixed in some way by the value of the consequences of an action, and 2) "formalist" theories, which deny that the value of consequences is all that needs to be considered in determining what is the right action. It is not profitable to classify formalist theories into types, but it is important to subdivide consequentialist theories as follows: 1A) *egoist* theories (which hold that rightness is determined by the intrinsic worth of consequences for the agent) and 1B) *utilitarian* theories (which hold that rightness is determined by the intrinsic worth of consequences for everyone involved). Unfortunately, we must recognize still further subtypes; in particular, we must divide each of the above into an "act" and a "rule" version, thus ending up with four subtypes: 1AI) *act-egoism,* 1AII) *rule-egoism,* 1BI) *act-utilitarianism,* and 1BII) *rule-utilitarianism.* The *act* theorist thinks that the rightness of an act is determined by the intrinsic value of *its* total consequences, either for the agent in the case of egoism, or for everybody in the case of utilitarianism. The *rule* theorist thinks that the rightness of an act is fixed by whether it would be best to have that kind of act always performed in circumstances like the one in question, or, perhaps better put, whether it would be best to have that kind of act made the rule for action in circumstances like the one in question; the rule-*egoist* will of course say that the question is what policy is best for the agent, whereas the rule-*utilitarian* will be considering which rule of conscience will have best consequences for everyone.

In order to see the difference among the consequentialist theories, consider how they might be used to decide whether our pregnant girl should have an abortion. The act-egoist will ask simply whether her doing so in this case will benefit her more in the long run. The rule-egoist will ask whether a policy of having abortions in such a situation (remember that one's policy is apt to become public knowledge) will or will not benefit her most in the long run. The act-utilitarian will ask whether her having an abortion in this case will maximize the welfare of everybody concerned (herself, boyfriend, family, etc.). The rule-utilitarian will ask whether the most good would be done generally if there were a recognized moral rule permitting women to have abortions in such circumstances.

As we have formulated these consequentialist theories, they are not committed to any particular view about what is intrinsically good, either to hedonism or some type of pluralism. Thus, a person who is convinced by one of them will still have to make up his mind about this latter question in order to decide in a concrete case what it is right to do.

In our readings, a partial act-egoism is represented by Nietzsche (Reading 20: his view is complex and not a pure form of egoism); act-egoism is criticized by Medlin (Reading 21), and the view is defended against his and others' criticisms by Kalin (Reading 22). J. S. Mill (Reading 19) often is regarded as an act-utilitarian, although many think that he should be considered a rule-utilitarian of a sort, and debate what kind of rule-utilitarian he might be.

Formalism is represented by Ross (Reading 23) and Kant (Reading 24). Ross centers his critical fire on act-utilitarianism combined with a pluralistic theory of the intrinsic good, since he regards this as the most plausible of the consequentialist theories. It should be noted, however, that the various forms of consequentialist theory usually were not distinguished when he wrote four decades ago, and consequently he does not discuss rule-utilitarianism. Ross himself is more utilitarian than Kant, in that he agrees that the consequences of an action for good or ill are relevant to its rightness, but he thinks that other features of an act also are relevant: whether the action would be a breach of faith, an expression of ingratitude, or incompatible with justice. All these features of an act tend to make it wrong, and whether a particular action is right or wrong is a matter of how weighty these various features are—rather as the resultant force on a body is the sum of the vectors of the forces operating on it.

Kant's view is further removed from any sort of consequentialism, at least as far as express professions go. Kant says that good or ill consequences are totally irrelevant to whether something is right or wrong. His view about when an action is right is rather similar to the Golden Rule; he says, roughly, that an act is right if and only if its agent is prepared to have that kind of action made universal practice or a "law of nature." Thus, for instance, Kant says it is right for a person to lie if and only if he is prepared to have everyone lie in similar circumstances, including those in which *he* is deceived by the lie. Kant thinks that no one is really prepared to espouse a universal practice of suicide, breach of promise, refusal to develop one's own talents, or ignoring the needs of others, and therefore he concludes that the corresponding actions are wrong. (Kant offers two other formulations of his thesis, one of which is included in our selection. It requires one always to treat humanity as an end in itself, never merely as a means. Kant asserts that this principle is equivalent to the one requiring universalizability, but it is doubtful that he has established this.) Kant's view sharply contrasts with act-utilitarianism, but it is not so different from rule-utilitarianism (which has been much influenced by Kant), since willingness to have some kind of act made a universal practice is not far from thinking that its universal practice will have good consequences.

All of these writers on normative ethics have some view or other on the problems of meta-ethics; the reader may find it interesting to try to identify these views.

Thus far, we have said nothing of Sartre's existentialist ethics (Reading no. 25). Sartre's thinking about ethics has had virtually no influence among philosophers, but his paper is included here because it has been exciting to many writers and to the general public. It is not easy to classify Sartre's view: one can say what he is *not* but not what he *is.* He is clearly not a definist; nor is he a nonnaturalist (he thinks nonnaturalism makes sense only if there is a God, and he is an atheist). He seems rather Kantian when he implies that a person should do something only if he is prepared to have his act taken as an exemplar by all men. (In that sense, a choice is for all people and in a sense "involves" them.) But this restriction is not really a restriction; you are still free what to choose, both for yourself and others. Is there *no* type of reflection, then, that can guide a person to a correct or rational or moral choice? Sartre certainly does not espouse one of the listed normative theories: egoism or utilitarianism or formalism. (He would probably favor formalism just because it is so plural, the opposite of the cut-and-dried.) But on the other hand, he does not say they are all wrong; rather, he says that none of them is sufficiently specific to provide any directive for hard choices, and that any inference you draw from one of them, for a hard choice, is really *your* decision, not an implication of the theory. (This judgment is not quite fair: the theories *do* have implications for many situations, and some of them for *all* situations—such as act-utilitarianism—although the facts required to apply the theory may be hard to come by.) Since we can't, then, find rational guidance for what to do, should we withdraw into our shells and avoid acting, or getting involved? Not at all: Sartre ends with a ringing recommendation to get involved; if you don't get involved, don't *do* anything, your life, and you, are nothing. By now you will see that Sartre's view is puzzling. Since he is a writer, he allows himself overstatements. For instance, when he says there is no such thing as "human nature," he hardly should be taken to mean that the sciences of human physiology and psychology do not have a subject matter, or that laws they come up with are not true for all human beings. Perhaps it is Sartrean in spirit for us to advise each reader to make what he/she can of Sartre's theory, for him/herself!

IS IT ALWAYS RATIONAL TO ACT RIGHTLY?

Many people think that, after we have made up our minds about whether a given line of action is morally right or obligatory, there is a further problem outstanding. This is the question of whether it is reasonable for the agent to perform the right action if doing so conflicts with her own interests, and if so, why. It has been held by intelligent writers, for instance Plato, that a person can never hurt herself by doing what is right or morally obligatory, but this view does seem too optimistic. Unless one is a strict ethical egoist, one will have to recognize situations in which it is one's obligation to sacrifice one's own interests for the overriding needs of others. The most extreme examples of this come when one recognizes an obligation to sacrifice one's life for a cause. The last two readings, by Baier and Frankena (Readings 26 and 27), are attempts to deal with this problem. Obviously a great deal turns on what is meant by acting "reasonably." If to act "reasonably" means to act in a manner calculated to maximize one's own welfare, then it is self-contradictory to say it can be reasonable for a man to do what is morally obligatory when this conflicts with his personal interests. On the other hand, if to act "reasonably" means to act in such a manner as to fulfill one's moral obligations, then it is self-contradictory to say that it could be *un*reasonable for a man to do what is morally obligatory even when this conflicts with his personal welfare. If there is a genuine problem here, there must be some sense of "reasonable" other than the two mentioned above. The reader is invited to consider what Baier and Frankena mean by "reasonable" in their discussions.

12. Ruth Fulton Benedict

Ruth F. Benedict (1887–1948) was Professor of Anthropology at Columbia University.

An Anthropologist's View of Values and Morality

Modern social anthropology has become more and more a study of the varieties and common elements of cultural environment and the consequences of these in human behavior. For such a study of diverse social orders primitive peoples fortunately provide a laboratory not yet entirely vitiated by the spread of a standardized worldwide civilization. Dyaks and Hopis, Fijians and Yakuts are significant for psychological and sociological study because only among these simpler peoples has there been sufficient isolation to give opportunity for the development of localized social forms. In the higher cultures the standardization of custom and belief over a couple of continents has given a false sense of the inevitability of the particular forms that have gained currency, and we need to turn to a wider survey in order to check the conclusions we hastily base upon this near-universality of familiar customs. Most of the simpler cultures did not gain the wide currency of the one which, out of our experience, we identify with human nature, but this was for various historical reasons, and certainly not for any that gives us as its carriers a monopoly of social good or of social sanity. Modern civilization, from

From Ruth Fulton Benedict, "Anthropology and the Abnormal," *Journal of General Psychology*, X (1934), pp. 59–80. Reprinted by permission of The Journal Press, Provincetown, Mass.

this point of view, becomes not a necessary pinnacle of human achieve-ment but one entry in a long series of possible adjustments.

These adjustments, whether they are in mannerisms like the ways of showing anger, or joy, or grief in any society, or in major human drives like those of sex, prove to be far more variable than experience in any one culture would suggest. In certain fields, such as that of religion or of formal marriage arrangements, these wide limits of variability are well known and can be fairly described. In others it is not yet possible to give a generalized account, but that does not absolve us of the task of indicating the significance of the work that has been done and of the problems that have arisen.

One of these problems relates to the customary modern normal-abnormal categories and our conclusions regarding them. In how far are such categories culturally determined, or in how far can we with assur-ance regard them as absolute? In how far can we regard inability to function socially as diagnostic of abnormality, or in how far is it neces-sary to regard this as a function of the culture? . . .

The most spectacular illustrations of the extent to which normality may be culturally defined are those cultures where an abnormality of our culture is the cornerstone of their social structure. It is not possible to do justice to these possibilities in a short discussion. A recent study of an island of northwest Melanesia by Fortune describes a society built upon traits which we regard as beyond the border of paranoia. In this tribe the exogamic groups look upon each other as prime manipulators of black magic, so that one marries always into an enemy group which remains for life one's deadly and unappeasable foes. They look upon a good garden crop as a confession of theft, for everyone is engaged in making magic to induce into his garden the productiveness of his neigh-bor's; therefore no secrecy in the island is so rigidly insisted upon as the secrecy of a man's harvesting of his yams. Their polite phrase at the ac-ceptance of a gift is, "And if you now poison me, how shall I repay you this present?" Their preoccupation with poisoning is constant; no woman ever leaves her cooking pot for a moment unattended. Even the great affinal economic exchanges that are characteristic of this Melanesian culture area are quite altered in Dobu since they are incompatible with this fear and distrust that pervades the culture. . . . They go farther and people the whole world outside their own quarters with such malignant spirits that all-night feasts and ceremonials simply do not occur here. They have even religiously enforced customs that forbid the sharing of seed even in one family group. Anyone else's food is deadly poison to you, so that communality of stores is out of the question. For some months before harvest the whole society is on the verge of starvation, but if one falls to the temptation and eats up one's seed yams, one is an outcast and a beachcomber for life. There is no coming back. It involves, as a matter of course, divorce and the breaking of all social ties.

Now in this society where no one may work with another and no one may share with another, Fortune describes the individual who was re-garded by all his fellows as crazy. He was not one of those who periodi-cally ran amok and, beside himself and frothing at the mouth, fell with a knife upon anyone he could reach. Such behavior they did not regard as putting anyone outside the pale. They did not even put the individuals who were known to be liable to these attacks under any kind of control. They merely fled when they saw the attack coming on and kept out of the way. "He would be all right tomorrow." But there was one man of sunny, kindly disposition who liked work and liked to be helpful. The compulsion was too strong for him to repress it in favor of the opposite tendencies of his culture. Men and women never spoke of him without laughing; he was silly and simple and definitely crazy. Nevertheless, to the ethnologist used to a culture that has, in Christianity, made his type the model of all virtue, he seemed a pleasant fellow.

An even more extreme example, because it is of a culture that has built itself upon a more complex abnormality, is that of the North Pacific Coast of North America. The civilization of the Kwakiutl, at the time when it was first recorded in the last decades of the nineteenth century, was one of the most vigorous in North America. It was built up on an ample economic supply of goods, the fish which furnished their food staple being practically inexhaustible and obtainable with comparatively small labor, and the wood which furnished the material for their houses, their furnishings, and their arts being, with however much labor, always procurable. They lived in coastal villages that compared favorably in size with those of any other American Indians and they kept up constant communication by means of sea-going dug-out canoes.

It was one of the most vigorous and zestful of the aboriginal cultures of North America, with complex crafts and ceremonials, and elaborate and striking arts. It certainly had none of the earmarks of a sick civilization. The tribes of the Northwest Coast had wealth, and exactly in our terms. That is, they had not only a surplus of economic goods, but they made a game of the manipulation of wealth. It was by no means a mere direct transcription of economic needs and the filling of those needs. It involved the idea of capital, of interest, and of conspicuous waste. It was a game with all the binding rules of a game, and a person entered it as a child. His father distributed wealth for him, according to his ability, at a small feast or potlatch, and each gift the receiver was obliged to accept and to return after a short interval with interest that ran to about 100 per cent a year. By the time the child was grown, therefore, he was well launched, a larger potlatch had been given for him on various occasions of exploit or initiation, and he had wealth either out at usury or in his own possession. Nothing in the civilization could be enjoyed without validating it by the distribution of this wealth. Everything that was valued, names and songs as well as material objects were passed down in family lines, but they were always publicly assumed with accompanying sufficient distributions of property. It was the game of validating and exercising all the privileges one could accumulate from one's various forebears, or by gift, or by marriage, that made the chief interest of the culture. Everyone in his degree took part in it, but many, of course, mainly as spectators. In its highest form it was played out between rival chiefs representing not only themselves and their family lines but their communities, and the object of the contest was to glorify oneself and to humiliate one's opponent. On this level of greatness the property involved was no longer represented by blankets, so many thousand of them to a potlatch, but by higher units of value. These higher units were like our bank notes. They were incised copper tablets, each of them named, and having a value that depended upon their illustrious history. This was as high as ten thousand blankets, and to possess one of them, still more to enhance its value at a great potlatch, was one of the greatest glories within the compass of the chiefs of the Northwest Coast. . . .

Every contingency of life was dealt with in . . . two traditional ways. To them the two were equivalent. Whether one fought with weapons or "fought with property," as they say, the same idea was at the bottom of both. In the olden times, they say, they fought with spears, but now they fight with property. One overcomes one's opponents in equivalent fashion in both, matching forces and seeing that one comes out ahead, and one can thumb one's nose at the vanquished rather more satisfactorily at a potlatch than on a battlefield. Every occasion in life was noticed, not in its own terms, as a stage in the sex life of the individual or as a climax of joy or of grief, but as furthering this drama of consolidating one's own prestige and bringing shame to one's guests. Whether it was the occasion of the birth of a child, or a daughter's adolescence, or of the marriage of one's son, they were all equivalent raw material for the culture to use for this one traditionally selected end. They were all to raise one's own personal status and to entrench oneself by the humiliation of one's fellows. A girl's adolescence among the Nootka was an event for which her father gathered property from the time she was first able to run about. When she was adolescent he would demonstrate his greatness by an unheard of distribution of these goods, and put down all his rivals. It was not as a fact of the girl's sex life that it figured in their culture, but as the occasion for a major move in the great game of vindicating one's own greatness and humiliating one's associates.

In their behavior at great bereavements this set of the culture comes out most strongly. Among the Kwakiutl it did not matter whether a relative had died in bed of disease, or by the hand of an enemy; in either case death was an affront to be wiped out by the death of another person. The fact that one had been caused to mourn was proof that one had been put upon. A chief's sister and her daughter had gone up to Victoria, and either because they drank bad whiskey or because their boat capsized they never came back. The chief called together his warriors. "Now I ask you, tribes, who shall wail? Shall I do it or shall another?" The spokesman answered, of course, "Not you, Chief. Let some other of the tribes." Immediately they set up the war pole to announce their intention of wiping out the injury, and gathered a war party. They set out, and found seven men and two children asleep and killed them. "Then they felt good when they arrived at Sebaa in the evening."

The point which is of interest to us is that in our society those who on that occasion would feel good when they arrived at Sebaa that evening would be the definitely abnormal. There would be some, even in our society, but it is not a recognized and approved mood under the circumstances. On the Northwest Coast those are favored and fortunate to whom that mood under those circumstances is congenial, and those to whom it is repugnant are unlucky. This latter minority can register in their own culture only by doing violence to their congenial responses and acquiring others that are difficult for them. The person, for instance, who, like a Plains Indian whose wife has been taken from him, is too proud to fight, can deal with the Northwest Coast civilization only by ignoring its strongest bents. If he cannot achieve it, he is the deviant in that culture, their instance of abnormality.

This head-hunting that takes place on the Northwest Coast after a death is no matter of blood revenge or of organized vengeance. There is no effort to tie up the subsequent killing with any responsibility on the part of the victim for the death of the person who is being mourned. A chief whose son has died goes visiting wherever his fancy dictates, and he says to his host, "My prince has died today, and you go with him." Then he kills him. In this, according to their interpretation, he acts nobly because he has not been downed. He has thrust back in return. The whole procedure is meaningless without the fundamental paranoid reading of bereavement. Death, like all the other untoward accidents of existence, confounds man's pride and can only be handled in the category of insults. . . .

These illustrations, which it has been possible to indicate only in the briefest manner, force upon us the fact that normality is culturally defined. An adult shaped to the drives and standards of either of these cultures, if he were transported into our civilization, would fall into our categories of abnormality. He would be faced with the psychic dilemmas of the socially unavailable. In his own culture, however, he is the pillar of society, the end result of socially inculcated mores, and the problem of personal instability in his case simply does not arise.

No one civilization can possibly utilize in its mores the whole potential range of human behavior. Just as there are great numbers of possible phonetic articulations, and the possibility of language depends on a selection and standardization of a few of these in order that speech communication may be possible at all, so the possibility of organized behavior of every sort, from the fashions of local dress and houses to the dicta of a people's ethics and religion, depends upon a similar selection among the possible behavior traits. In the field of recognized economic obligations or sex tabus this selection is as nonrational and subconscious a process as it is in the field of phonetics. It is a process which goes on in the group for long periods of time and is historically conditioned by innumerable accidents of isolation or of contact of peoples. In any comprehensive study of psychology, the selection that different cultures have made in the course of history within the great circumference of potential behavior is of great significance.

Every society, beginning with some slight inclination in one direction or another, carries its preference farther and farther, integrating itself more and more completely upon its chosen basis, and discarding those types of behavior that are uncongenial. Most of those organizations of personality that seem to us most incontrovertibly abnormal have been used by different civilizations in the very foundations of their institutional

147

life. Conversely the most valued traits of our normal individuals have been looked on in differently organized cultures as aberrant. Normality, in short, within a very wide range, is culturally defined. It is primarily a term for the socially elaborated segment of human behavior in any culture; and abnormality, a term for the segment that that particular civilization does not use. The very eyes with which we see the problem are conditioned by the long traditional habits of our own society.

It is a point that has been made more often in relation to ethics than in relation to psychiatry. We do not any longer make the mistake of deriving the morality of our own locality and decade directly from the inevitable constitution of human nature. We do not elevate it to the dignity of a first principle. We recognize that morality differs in every society, and is a convenient term for socially approved habits. Mankind has always preferred to say, "It is morally good," rather than "It is habitual," and the fact of this preference is matter enough for a critical science of ethics. But historically the two phrases are synonymous.

The concept of the normal is properly a variant of the concept of the good. It is that which society has approved. A normal action is one which falls well within the limits of expected behavior for a particular society. Its variability among different peoples is essentially a function of the variability of the behavior patterns that different societies have created for themselves, and can never be wholly divorced from a consideration of culturally institutionalized types of behavior.

Each culture is a more or less elaborate working-out of the potentialities of the segment it has chosen. In so far as a civilization is well integrated and consistent within itself, it will tend to carry farther and farther, according to its nature, its initial impulse toward a particular type of action, and from the point of view of any other culture those elaborations will include more and more extreme and aberrant traits.

Each of these traits, in proportion as it reinforces the chosen behavior patterns of that culture, is for that culture normal. Those individuals to whom it is congenial either congenitally, or as the result of childhood sets, are accorded prestige in that culture, and are not visited with the social contempt or disapproval which their traits would call down upon them in a society that was differently organized. On the other hand, those individuals whose characteristics are not congenial to the selected type of human behavior in that community are the deviants, no matter how valued their personality traits may be in a contrasted civilization. . . .

The problem of understanding abnormal human behavior in any absolute sense independent of cultural factors is still far in the future. The categories of borderline behavior which we derive from the study of the neuroses and psychoses of our civilization are categories of prevailing local types of instability. They give much information about the stresses and strains of Western civilization, but no final picture of inevitable human behavior. Any conclusions about such behavior must await the collection by trained observers of psychiatric data from other cultures. Since no adequate work of the kind has been done at the present time, it is impossible to say what core of definition of abnormality may be found valid from the comparative material. It is as it is in ethics; all our local conventions of moral behavior and of immoral are without absolute validity, and yet it is quite possible that a modicum of what is considered right and what wrong could be disentangled that is shared by the whole human race. When data are available in psychiatry, this minimum definition of abnormal human tendencies will be probably quite unlike our culturally conditioned, highly elaborated psychoses such as those that are described, for instance, under the terms of schizophrenia and manic-depressive.

13. Carl F. H. Henry

C. F. Henry (b. 1913) has been editor of "Christianity Today."

The Divine Will Theory

The good in Hebrew-Christian theistic ethics is not that which is adapted to human nature, but it is that to which the Creator obliges human nature.

The doctrine that the good is to be identified with the will of God cuts across secular ethics at almost every point. It protests against Utilitarianism, and its validation of the good by an appeal to consequences alone. It indicts Kant's supposition that duty and obligation rest upon a wholly immanental basis. According to Kant, the human will alone imposes man's duties upon him and affirms for him the categorical imperative. This theory of morality mediated to the modern man the artificial hope that the objectivity of the moral order could be maintained by a deliberate *severance* of duty and the good *from* the will of God. The Hebrew-Christian ethical perspective also challenges the many species of humanistic ethics so influential in the Western world today. Biblical ethics discredits an autonomous morality. It gives theonomous ethics its classic form—the identification of the moral law with the Divine will. In Hebrew-Christian revelation, distinctions in ethics reduce to what is good or what is pleasing, and to what is wicked or displeasing to the Creator-God alone. The biblical view maintains always a dynamic statement of values, refusing to sever the elements of morality from the will of God.

That the essence of true morality is to be found primarily in com-

This selection is taken from Carl F. H. Henry, *Christian Personal Ethics*, Wm. B. Eerdmans Publishing Co., Grand Rapids, Mich., 1957. Reprinted by permission of the publisher.

plete obedience to the sovereign Lord provided the climate of thought which Hobbes secularized and perverted in the *Leviathan*. His contemporary, Ralph Cudworth (1617–1688), who wrote *Eternal and Immutable Morality*, sought to place all men, including Hobbes and his sovereign, under an obligation to act for the common good. Cudworth argued that the distinction between right and wrong does not depend upon sovereign will, but on the moral order which confronts the whole of reality. Cudworth did not hesitate to insist that the principles of morality are addressed even to the Divine will and hence are determinative of it. By moralists under Cudworth's influence, man's obligation to obey the injunctions of Scripture was no longer suspended exclusively on the fact that God commands obedience, but correlative reasons for man's conformity were introduced, *e.g.*, that obedience involves the common good. British moralists especially contributed to this Platonic rather than Hebraic orientation of values. The erroneous notion gained ground swiftly that the best device for thwarting political Naturalism, and for protecting the idea of duty from arbitrary perversion, is to assert the independent existence of moral values, rather than to defend the good as the will of God. God is himself thereby assertedly obliged to uphold these values, and hence precluded from acting in an arbitrary way. Hence the detachment of the content of morality from the will of God became the optimistic basis of a reply to political Naturalism and all forms of moral autonomy.

Thereafter, the phrase "I ought" no longer means "the sovereign Lord commands." Rather, it is informed by self-evident truths or by intuitions of the moral order, as by the Cambridge Platonists, and finally it loses its connection with a transcendent moral order no less than with the sovereign Divine will. Thus the Christian West enters into a non-Christian orientation of the account of duty, and the outcome of this transition is that the doctrine of obligation is sketched independently of both the will of God and of theism. At first it was thought that, while separated from the will of God, moral obligations were as secure as mathematical axioms. They were safeguarded by universal and necessary implications of conscience or by some other immanentistic device. In place of the God-spoken moral imperative there arose a categorical imperative. This endured as an effective rallying point for ethical Idealism for less than a century. When the empirical and evolutionary movements in modern thought were felt, the attempt to secure the absolute obligation to perform every duty within an autonomous ethics dissolved, and with it the absoluteness of duty. Instead of exhibiting the inner unity of duty and goodness in their ultimate basis in the will of God, it lost the sanctity of moral obligation.

Yet the failure to identify duty and the good with the will of God is characteristic of idealistic ethics both in ancient and in modern times. Even those moral philosophies that professed hostility to an autonomous ethic and championed the transcendent objectivity of the moral order regarded the good as something given to God. They viewed the good as something to which God was bound rather than as something legislated by him. This prepared the way for an objectionable doctrine of the "good in itself." The good then is superior to God. It is a content which is externally addressed to him as it is to us. This thesis runs through Oriental religion as well as early Western philosophy. It underlies the Zoroastrian notion that Ormazd becomes supreme through his furtherance of the good. This view assumes the existence of an ethical law superior to God himself. It is found also in the Hindu conception of the law of Karma. God is the author of sovereign causality in an impersonal moral universe. Yet not even he can interfere with its autonomous operation now that it is in movement. The same idea becomes influential in Western thought through the moral philosophy of Plato, as expressed in the *Euthyphro.* . . .

This notion of an "intrinsic good" is alien to biblical theology. The God of Hebrew-Christian revelation is the ground of ethics. He is the supreme rule of right. He defines the whole content of morality by his own revealed will. It is not merely because "in God is the perfect realization of the Ideal Righteousness," but because God legislates the nature of the good that biblical ethics is a radical departure from the pagan view of the moral order. . . .

. . . .

The will of God is the source of the ethical law and supplies the content of morality. It alone is intrinsically good. Man's life is not to be oriented to impersonal eternal values, to objective norms, to ethical laws, to principles of conduct, to abiding virtues, viewed abstractly or independently of the Divine will. These place obligation upon men only insofar as they may be traced to the will of God.

. . . .

. . . The good is what God wills, and what he freely wills. The good is what the Creator-Lord does and commands. He is the creator of the moral law, and defines its very nature.

At the same time no suggestion is conveyed that the good is arbitrary or a matter of Divine "caprice." That term frequently suits the propaganda purposes of those who caricature Divine sovereignty. Biblical morality itself has supplied a perspective from which the capriciousness of the polytheistic gods of Greek mythology may be judged. The moral activity of God is a closer definition of his nature. It is the constancy of God's will in its ethical affirmations and claims that supplies the durable basis for moral distinctions. Hovey declares, "The moral law is a free expression of his will to others, and therefore in the fullest and strictest sense it is from him, under him, dependent on him, and immutable only as he is immutable; while the same law comes down upon us from his mind and will, imposing itself on our consciences, and therefore is over us, and independent of us." In stipulating the moral law, the Creator-God lay under no necessity other than to form it according to his own pleasure, and hence in conformity with his real character and purpose. The will of God so reveals his character that the man who conforms to his commandments will exhibit the image of God in his life. The Hebrew-Christian knowledge of God is a knowledge of the Righteous One. The commandments are manifestations of his character, and righteousness is what he prizes as his special glory (Ex. 33:18f., 34:6f.). . . .

The question what makes an act a duty has been answered ambiguously throughout the whole history of ethics. The view that finds in consequences or good results the obligatory basis of our actions, and conceives the ethical act merely as instrumentally good is inadequate. The view that regards an action itself as intrinsically good with total indifference to its consequences, and derives goodness from obligation, is equally inadequate. Both views fail to grasp the fact that obligation and virtue, goodness and happiness, find their common ground in the Divine will. They also fail to recognize that the notions of duty and goodness cannot be analyzed so as to enforce their interlocking nature when this fundamental reference is ignored. Why should man be obliged to do what is regarded as intrinsically good without regard to the consequences? Why is he obliged to do what leads to good consequences if he is in doubt regarding the basic rightness of his action? Speculative ethics furnishes a running commentary on this tension and fails to resolve it. . . .

The appeal to the Divine better explains man's feeling about his moral duties, so that "as soon as we come to regard our duty as a fulfillment of God's will, we begin to see a value in it that was previously hidden, and indeed to understand how it may have a greater value than any alternative act that is possible." Moreover, such a concept formally achieves "a real union of the two fundamental concepts of moral philosophy, duty and value.". . .

[But] the Hebrew-Christian God-concept is not a philosophical device which is used as leverage to extricate philosophical ethics from an insoluble inner difficulty by furnishing a supernatural sanction for a speculative ethics. The reality of the self-revealing God and of the good as the will of God stand or fall together in biblical revelation. God reveals himself in a once-for-all prophetic and apostolic disclosure of his purposes. And he declares a specific moral content which shows his will for man. He summons men to obedience. . . .

Hebrew-Christian ethics centers in the Divine revelation of the statutes, commandments, and precepts of the Living God. Its whole orientation of the moral life may be summarized by what the Holy Lord commands and what he forbids: what accords with his edicts is right, what opposes his holy will is wicked. . . .

The moral law that lays an imperative on the human conscience is nothing more or less than the manifested will of God. For man nothing is good but union with the sovereign holy will of God. Sin therefore must not be defined primarily as social irresponsibility. Rather, it is repudiation of a Divine claim. David's words "against thee only have I sinned" (Psa. 51:4) echo the penitent's confession at its deepest level. Since God fashioned man to bear his moral likeness, nothing other than the fulfillment of this Divine purpose is man's supreme good. This purpose of God is the moral standard by which man throughout all history will be judged. Society in all its breadth and depth is responsible to the will of God. According to Christianity, to be morally good is to obey God's commands. The performance of God's will alone constitutes man's highest good. The rule of life is to "seek first the kingdom of God and his righteousness" (Mt. 6:33).

14. Alfred Cyril Ewing

Alfred Cyril Ewing (1899–1973) was Reader in Philosophy in
Cambridge University, England, and a fellow of Jesus College.

A Reply to the Theological Definition of Moral Concepts

However, before going on to this, I have a word to say about a quite
different way of defining ethical concepts, that is, in terms of metaphysics. A metaphysical definition is a definition by reference to the ultimate
nature of the real as distinguished from the less ultimate aspect in which
reality is conceived as appearing for natural science. Of metaphysical
definitions we need only trouble about one here, which is by far the
clearest and the best known. I refer to the attempt to define ethical concepts in terms of religion by maintaining that to say something is good
or right is to say that it is commanded by God. At first sight it may well
seem that such a theory is refuted at once by the mere fact that agnostics
and atheists can make rational judgements in ethics, but it will be replied that what even the atheist really has in mind when he thinks of
obligation is some confused idea of a command, and that a command implies a commander and a perfect moral law a perfectly good commander
on whose mind the whole moral law depends, so that the atheist is inconsistent in affirming the validity of the moral law and yet denying the
existence of God. It may be doubted whether this argument, if valid,
would make the theological statement an analysis of what the man

This passage is taken from A. C. Ewing, *Ethics*, English Universities Press, Ltd.,
London, 1953. Reprinted by permission of the present publisher, Hodder & Stoughton, Ltd.

meant and not rather of the logical consequences of what he meant, but there are other objections to such a definition.

(a) If "right" and "good" are themselves defined in terms of the commands of God, God cannot command anything because it is right or good, since this would only mean that He commanded it because He commanded it, and therefore there is no reason whatever for His commands, which become purely arbitrary. It would follow that God might just as rationally will that our whole duty should consist in cheating, torturing and killing people to the best of our ability, and that in that case it would be our duty to act in this fashion.

(b) And why are we to obey God's commands? Because we ought to do so? Since "we ought to do A" is held to mean "God commands us to do A," this can only mean that we are commanded by God to obey God's commands, which supplies no further reason. Because we love God? But this involves the assumptions that we ought to obey God if we love Him, and that we ought to love Him. So it again presupposes ethical propositions which cannot without a vicious circle be validated by once more referring to God's commands. Because God is good? This could only mean that God carries out His own commands. Because God will punish us if we do not obey Him? This might be a very good reason from the point of view of self-interest, but self-interest cannot, as we have seen, be an adequate basis for ethics. Without a prior conception of God being good or His commands being right God would have no more claim on our obedience than Hitler except that He would have more power to make things uncomfortable for us if we disobeyed Him than Hitler ever had, and that is not an ethical reason. A moral obligation cannot be created by mere power and threat of punishment. No doubt if we first grant the fundamental concepts of ethics, the existence of God may put us under certain obligations which we otherwise would not have had, e.g. that of thinking of God, as the existence of a man's parents puts him under certain obligations under which he would not stand if they were dead, but we cannot possibly derive all obligations in this fashion from the concept of God. No doubt, if God is perfectly good, we ought to obey His will, but how can we know what His will for us is in a particular case without first knowing what we ought to do?

What I have said of course constitutes no objection to the belief in God or even to the view that we can have a valid argument from ethics to the existence of God, but these views can be held without holding that our ethical terms have to be defined in terms of God. It has been held that the existence of anything implies the existence of God, but it would not therefore be concluded that the meaning of all our words includes a reference to God. Nor is what I have said meant to imply that religion can have no important bearing on ethics, but I think its influence should lie more in helping people to bring themselves to do what would be their duty in any case and in influencing the general spirit in which it is done than in prescribing what our duty is. While it is quite contrary to fact to suggest that an agnostic or atheist cannot be a good man, the influence in the former respects of religious belief, whether true or false, cannot be denied to have been exceedingly strong.

15. Frank Chapman Sharp

F. C. Sharp (1866–1943) was Professor of Philosophy at the
University of Wisconsin.

The Ideal Observer Theory

The moral judgment takes the form: Action S is right—or wrong. It thus
consists in the application of the predicate "right" to conduct. We have
now to inquire into the meaning of this predicate.

The subject matter of our studies is still the man on the street. It is
what *he* means by "right" that interests us. And the difficulty we face is
that he cannot tell us. Ask him to define the term, and he will not even
understand what you are driving at. This difficulty, however, is not one
peculiar to the vocabulary of ethics. John Smith cannot tell you what he
means by "cause," "probable," or "now"; he cannot give a really satisfactory answer to so apparently simple a question as "What is 'money'?"

This difficulty we can meet today as we met it again and again when
we were three years old. We heard the people about us using such terms
as "very" or "if"; and we wanted to know what they meant. Undoubtedly
we were very far from persistent or systematic in our search for enlightenment; indeed, perhaps we did not *search* at all. But, at any rate,
when we had been told that this milk was very hot, this stool very heavy,
this glass very easily broken, and that we had been very naughty, the
meaning of "very" dawned upon our minds, not in the sense that we
could define it but that we could use it intelligently. It is in precisely
this same way that we can discover what the layman means by the fundamental terms in the moral vocabulary. We watch his use of them.

Thereupon, proceeding one step farther than the child, we generalize our observations and in doing so form a definition.

It is indeed a curious fact that men can go through life using words with a fair degree of definiteness and consistency with no formulated definition before the mind. But it is fact, nonetheless. "I cannot define poetry," says A. E. Housman in effect, "but I know it when I see it. In the same way a terrier cannot define rat, but he knows one when he sees it."

If the analysis of this chapter is correct, "right" must be definable in terms of desire, or approbation, that is to say, in terms of "feeling." When John Smith calls an action "right" or "wrong," however, he means something other than that he happens to feel about it in a certain way at that particular moment. This was clearly pointed out by Hume two hundred years ago and should have become commonplace among moralists by this time. A successful swindle may arouse feelings of very different intensity according to who happens to be the victim—myself, my son, my intimate friend, an acquaintance, a stranger, a foreigner, a man who died a hundred years ago. Indeed, in some of the latter cases the feeling component may drop out entirely. Again, an incident I myself have witnessed, such as an act of malicious cruelty or the bullying of the weak by the strong, makes me feel very different from that about which I have only read or heard. And my feelings in the latter case are likely to depend on the vividness and completeness with which the narrator brings the situation home to my imagination. An incident which I can realize because I have been through just such an experience myself appeals to me far otherwise than one which I know only through having viewed it from the outside. The robbery or oppression of those whom I see from day to day or am personally acquainted with arouses in me far more indignation than if they are merely unknown people living for all practical purposes in a world other than my own. With all these variations in my feelings, I recognize upon reflection that what is really right or wrong in the premises remains unchanged. Wrong does not become innocent or right merely because the act took place a hundred years ago instead of this morning, because I did not happen to see it myself, because I myself have never happened to be in that position, or because one of the persons involved happens to be an acquaintance, a member of my family, or myself.

In view of these facts, we must define "right," if we are to use the term in the sense in which the ordinary man uses it, as *that which arouses approbation under certain conditions.* Accordingly the question arises: What are these conditions?

We shall not expect to discover them by asking John Smith to enumerate and describe them. The man in the street does not carry about with him in his mental kit a set of formulas covering these conditions, any more than when he cuts a corner he says to himself, "A straight line is the shortest distance between two points." That the conditions in question represent real forces may be shown empirically by what John Smith does when in doubt or when he changes his mind or when the correctness of his predication is challenged by others.

In the first place, then, John Smith does not apply the predicates right and wrong to conduct unless he supposes himself to be viewing it from an impersonal standpoint. This means that he supposes, negatively, that his attitude is not determined by his egoistic interests or by any purely personal relations to the parties concerned; positively, that the act is one that he would approve of anyone's performing under the same conditions. This attitude is expressed in the familiar maxim: What is right for one is right for everyone else under the same conditions. This maxim is an analytic, not a synthetic, proposition. It is no discovery of moralists, least of all Kant, to whom it is often attributed, for its governing role in the moral world was noted in effect by Cumberland and quite explicitly by Clarke before Kant was born. As a matter of fact, the "discovery" has been made countless millions of times, for it is a dull-witted seven-year-old who does not remind his parents that what they require him to do they are bound to do themselves.

Here, again, enters the all-important distinction between correct and incorrect moral judgments, or, as I should prefer to say, between valid and invalid; for, as we have seen in this chapter, John Smith frequently regards an action as innocent or even obligatory when he profits by it and wrong when he happens to be the sufferer. In calling it "wrong" instead of "harmful," he implies that it is an act which, performed under the conditions, he would condemn in anyone, including himself. His supposition being false, his judgment expresses an opinion which can only be called "incorrect."

As soon as John Smith realizes this lack of impersonality, he recognizes at once the incorrectness of the judgment and therewith the necessity of modifying or abandoning it. In a certain city, the university YMCA, having included a barber shop among the attractions of its new building, engaged as its manager the popular head-barber of the city's leading "tonsorial parlor"; whereupon the proprietor complained loudly of the action of the association in attracting his most valuable employee away from him as being "unfair." When he was reminded that he himself had obtained this same employee in precisely the same way, by attracting him from another shop by a better financial offer, nothing more was heard from him on this subject.

Common sense thus recognizes the existence of such a thing as a mistaken moral judgment. Those moralists who ignore this fact thereby show that their picture of the workings of the moral consciousness is an arbitrary construction, out of touch with the realities of life.

Impersonality, however, is not the only condition which John Smith recognizes the moral judgment must meet if it is to conform to the implications involved in this conception of right. The second condition is a consequence of the essential character of the evaluating judgment as such. When we pass judgment upon anything whatever, whether it be a candidate for public office or Titian's "Assumption of the Virgin," we suppose that we know what it is. Really to know what anything is, is to have an apprehension of its nature, which is at once accurate and complete. In practice, of course, this ideal is ordinarily incapable of attainment. But, in proportion as we approach certainty of conviction, our confidence increases that our view possesses an amount of accuracy and completeness such that any correction of or addition to the data in our possession would make no difference in the conclusion reached. And our task is lightened by growing insight into what kinds of data are relevant and what are not. A datum is relevant when its introduction would tend to make any difference in the resulting judgment.

The application of these observations to the moral judgment is obvious. The subject of the moral judgment is voluntary action. A voluntary act is an attempt to produce certain effects. The moral judgment, accordingly, is supposed, with varying degrees of confidence, by the judger to be based upon an accurate and complete knowledge of these effects or upon as much knowledge as would involve no change of opinion if the rest of the effects were displayed accurately and in order before the mind's eye. If this supposition is true, the judgment is in so far forth correct or valid. On the other hand, if the judgment turns on an incomplete or otherwise inaccurate view of these effects, including, of course, a view of the situation in which they operate, it may properly be termed incorrect or invalid, because it is not what the judger supposes it to be.

Observation verifies this analysis. Our study of the causes that lead to the diversities in moral judgments has shown that a leading cause is difference of opinion as to what the consequences of the act will be. And in the majority of instances when John Smith begins to doubt the correctness of one of his past judgments, it is upon the consequences believed to be involved that his decision turns. Under such and such circumstances is a man justified in lying? in breaking a promise or a contract? in helping himself to someone else's property? in giving a dose of poison to a hopeless invalid? in making a true statement injurious to the reputation of a neighbor? in giving money to a street beggar? Whatever decision is reached turns fundamentally upon what are believed to be the good or evil consequences involved.

If, then, we are to conform to the implications of everyday usage in applying the predicates right and wrong to the effects of volitions, we must know what these effects are. Now, knowledge is of two kinds; or, if you prefer, it has two levels. Using Professor James's terminology, one is acquaintance with; the other, knowledge about. The former is given in immediate experience, whether in the world of sense or in the inner world of pleasure, pain, emotion, or desire. It may be recreated, when past, in those persons who are fortunate enough to possess the capacity for full and vivid imagery. We may call this "realization." The second kind, or level, reveals reality through the instrumentality of concepts. Now, the concept is an abstract idea, such as "length" or "walking" or "very." It represents one or a group of aspects torn from the concrete objects that make up the real world and held before the mind in more or less complete isolation from such objects.

The ability to form and use concepts is the most powerful instrument in the possession of the human mind. Among other things, as a constituent of desire it determines the direction of every voluntary action we perform. But, like everything else in the world, the concept has its limitations. In its very nature as an abstraction, it reveals only a part, usually only a very small part, of the object at which it points. It may report truth but never the whole truth. In this respect it is like a map. Show a map of Switzerland to a person who has never been away from a North Dakota prairie or even seen a picture of a mountain. Compare the knowledge thus gained with that of a Swiss who has spent his vacations for many years exploring his native country. Or, again, let some one who has never come in contact with death and has never had to carry crushing financial burdens read in the newspaper that some stranger, formerly a clerk in a certain grocery store, died yesterday after a painful and lingering illness; he was thirty-five years old; a widow and three children survive him. How small a fraction of the grim realities at which these words hint would enter our consciousness!

Quite apart from poverty of detail, conceptual thought, again like a map, has another limitation. It reveals relations but can never reveal the things related. In other words, thought at its best, conceptual thought, merely performs the functions of a mathematical formula. It is a commonplace that a person born blind may know all the laws of light and yet have no acquaintance with color.

Thus, notwithstanding its marvelous range, conceptual thought is a very inadequate substitute for "acquaintance with" as a revelation of reality. There is only one road to genuine acquaintance with the world outside the consciousness of the moment, and it is through imagery, the power to realize. If, then, a moral judgment is to be valid, it must be either a judgment based upon a complete acquaintance with the whole situation in all its relevant details or, since this is rarely or perhaps never attainable, such a judgment as would result from an acquaintance with the whole situation.

The influence of realization upon the processes of moral judgment exhibits itself frequently in those pseudo-moral judgments in which the predicates right and wrong follow the judger's personal interests, and a vivid sense of his own gain or loss eclipses the vague concept of the loss or gain of the other part. Let the other side of the case come home to him and the victim's plight be fully realized, he "changes his mind," thereby bringing his judgment into conformity with his new insight. This phenomenon has been abundantly illustrated in this chapter.

The definition emerging from the preceding analysis is the following: When John Smith calls an action "right," he means that complete acquaintance with its results would evoke impersonal approval. Exchanging the negative term "impersonal" for a positive one, "right" characterizes the kind of action he would want all human beings to perform under the given conditions if he had a complete acquaintance with all the relevant consequences. The evidence for the correctness of this analysis is that when John Smith discovers that he has failed to meet some one of these conditions, he recognizes that his judgment calls for reconsideration.

Thomas Reid (1710–1796) was first a minister, then taught
philosophy at King's College, Aberdeen, and at the University
of Glasgow.

Nonnaturalism: Intuitive Knowledge of Ethical Facts

Of the Notion of Duty, Rectitude, Moral Obligation

A Being endowed with the animal principles of action only, may be capable of being trained to certain purposes by discipline, as we see many brute-animals are, but would be altogether incapable of being governed by law.

The subject of law must have the conception of a general rule of conduct, which, without some degree of reason, he cannot have. He must likewise have a sufficient inducement to obey the law, even when his strongest animal desires draw him the contrary way.

This inducement may be a sense of interest, or a sense of duty, or both concurring.

These are the only principles I am able to conceive which can reasonably induce a man to regulate all his actions according to a certain general rule, or law. They may therefore be justly called the *rational* principles of action, since they can have no place but in a being endowed with reason, and since it is by them only, that man is capable either of political or of moral government.

From Thomas Reid, *Essays on the Active Powers of Man,* first published 1788. Essay III, Chapters 5 to 7.

Without them, human life would be like a ship at sea without hands, left to be carried by winds and tides as they happen. It belongs to the rational part of our nature to intend a certain port, as the end of the voyage of life; to take the advantage of winds and tides when they are favourable, and to bear up against them when they are unfavourable.

A sense of interest may induce us to do this, when a suitable reward is set before us. But there is a nobler principle in the constitution of man, which, in many cases, gives a clearer and more certain rule of conduct, than a regard merely to interest would give, and a principle, without which man would not be a moral agent.

A man is prudent when he consults his real interest, but he cannot be virtuous, if he has no regard to duty.

I proceed now to consider this regard to duty as a rational principle of action in man, and as that principle alone by which he is capable either of virtue or vice.

I shall first offer some observations with regard to the general notion of duty, and its contrary, or of right and wrong in human conduct; and then consider how we come to judge and determine certain things in human conduct to be right, and others to be wrong.

With regard to the notion or conception of duty, I take it to be too simple to admit of a logical definition.

We can define it only by synonymous words or phrases, or by its properties and necessary concomitants; as when we say that it is what we ought to do, what is fair and honest, what is approvable, what every man professes to be the rule of his conduct, what all men praise, and what is in itself laudable, though no man should praise it.

I observe, in the *next* place, That the notion of duty cannot be resolved into that of interest, or what is most for our happiness.

Every man may be satisfied of this who attends to his own conceptions, and the language of all mankind shews it. When I say this is my interest, I mean one thing; when I say it is my duty, I mean another thing. And though the same course of action, when rightly understood, may be both my duty and my interest, the conceptions are very different. Both are reasonable motives to action, but quite distinct in their nature.

I presume it will be granted, that in every man of real worth, there is a principle of honour, a regard to what is honourable or dishonourable, very distinct from a regard to his interest. It is folly in a man to disregard his interest, but to do what is dishonourable is baseness. The first may move our pity, or, in some cases, our contempt, but the last provokes our indignation.

As these two principles are different in their nature, and not resolvable into one, so the principle of honour is evidently superior in dignity to that of interest.

No man would allow him to be a man of honour, who should plead his interest to justify what he acknowledged to be dishonourable; but to sacrifice interest to honour never costs a blush.

It likewise will be allowed by every man of honour, that this principle is not to be resolved into a regard to our reputation among men, otherwise the man of honour would not deserve to be trusted in the dark. He would have no aversion to lie, or cheat, or play the coward, when he had no dread of being discovered.

I take it for granted, therefore, that every man of real honour feels an abhorrence of certain actions, because they are in themselves base, and feels an obligation to certain other actions, because they are in themselves what honour requires, and this, independently of any consideration of interest or reputation.

This is an immediate moral obligation. This principle ·of honour, which is acknowledged by all men who pretend to character, is only another name for what we call a regard to duty, to rectitude, to propriety of conduct. It is a moral obligation which obliges a man to do certain things because they are right, and not to do other things because they are wrong.

Ask the man of honour, why he thinks himself obliged to pay a debt of honour? The very question shocks him. To suppose that he needs any other inducement to do it but the principle of honour, is to suppose that he has no honour, no worth, and deserves no esteem.

There is therefore a principle in man, which, when he acts according to it, gives him a consciousness of worth, and when he acts contrary to it, a sense of demerit.

From the varieties of education, of fashion, of prejudices, and of habits, men may differ much in opinion with regard to the extent of this principle, and of what it commands and forbids; but the notion of it, as far as it is carried, is the same in all. It is that which gives a man real worth, and is the object of moral approbation.

Men of rank call it *honour*, and too often confine it to certain virtues that are thought most essential to their rank. The vulgar call it *honesty, probity, virtue, conscience*. Philosophers have given it the names of *the moral sense, the moral faculty, rectitude*.

The universality of this principle in men that are grown up to years of understanding and reflection, is evident. The words that express it, the names of the virtues which it commands, and of the vices which it forbids, the *ought* and *ought not* which express its dictates, make an essential part of every language. The natural affections of respect to worthy characters, of resentment of injuries, of gratitude for favours, of indignation against the worthless, are parts of the human constitution which suppose a right and a wrong in conduct. Many transactions that are found necessary in the rudest societies go upon the same supposition. In all testimony, in all promises, and in all contracts, there is necessarily implied a moral obligation on one party, and a trust in the other, grounded upon this obligation.

The variety of opinions among men in points of morality, is not greater, but, as I apprehend, much less than in speculative points; and this variety is as easily accounted for from the common causes of error, in the one case as in the other; so that it is not more evident, that there is a real distinction between true and false, in matters of speculation, than that there is a real distinction between right and wrong in human conduct. . . .

If we examine the abstract notion of duty, or moral obligation, it appears to be neither any real quality of the action, considered by itself, nor of the agent considered without respect to the action, but a certain relation between the one and the other.

When we say a man ought to do such things, the *ought*, which expresses the moral obligation, has a respect, on the one hand, to the person who ought, and, on the other, to the action which he ought to do. Those two correlates are essential to every moral obligation; take away either, and it has no existence. So that, if we seek the place of moral obligation among the categories, it belongs to the category of *relation*.

There are many relations of things, of which we have the most distinct conception, without being able to define them logically. Equality and proportion are relations between quantities, which every man understands, but no man can define.

Moral obligation is a relation of its own kind, which every man understands, but is perhaps too simple to admit of logical definition. Like all other relations, it may be changed or annihilated by a change in any of the two related things, I mean the agent or the action.

Perhaps it may not be improper to point out briefly the circumstances, both in the action and in the agent, which are necessary to constitute moral obligation. The universal agreement of men in these, shews that they have one and the same notion of it.

With regard to the action, it must be a voluntary action . . . of the person obliged, and not of another. There can be no moral obligation upon a man to be six feet high. Nor can I be under a moral obligation that another person should do such a thing. His actions must be imputed to himself, and mine only to me, either for praise or blame.

I need hardly mention, that a person can be under a moral obligation, only to things within the sphere of his natural power.

As to the party obliged, it is evident, there can be no moral obligation upon an inanimate thing. To speak of moral obligation upon a stone or a tree is ridiculous, because it contradicts every man's notion of moral obligation.

The person obliged must have understanding and will, and some degree of active power. He must not only have the natural faculty of understanding, but the means of knowing his obligation. An invincible ignorance of this destroys all moral obligation. . . .

Of the Sense of Duty

We are next to consider, how we learn to judge and determine, that this is right, and that is wrong.

The abstract notion of moral good and ill would be of no use to direct our life, if we had not the power of applying it to particular actions, and determining what is morally good, and what is morally ill.

Some philosophers, with whom I agree, ascribe this to an original power or faculty in man, which they call the *moral sense*, the *moral faculty, conscience*. Others think, that our moral sentiments may be accounted for without supposing any original sense or faculty appropriated to that purpose, and go into very different systems to account for them.

I am not, at present, to take any notice of those systems, because the opinion first mentioned seems to me to be the truth, to wit, That, by an original power of the mind, when we come to years of understanding and reflection, we not only have the notions of right and wrong in conduct, but perceive certain things to be right, and others to be wrong.

The name of the *moral sense*, though more frequently given to conscience since Lord SHAFTSBURY and Dr. HUTCHESON wrote, is not new. The *sensus recti et honesti* is a phrase not unfrequent among the ancients, neither is the *sense of duty* among us.

It has got this name *of sense*, no doubt, from some analogy which it is conceived to bear to the external senses. And if we have just notions of the office of the external senses, the analogy is very evident, and I see no reason to take offence, as some have done, at the name of the *moral sense*. . . .

A man who has totally lost the sense of seeing, may retain very distinct notions of the various colours; but he cannot judge of colours, because he has lost the sense by which alone he could judge. By my eyes I not only have the ideas of a square and a circle, but I perceive this surface to be a square, that to be a circle.

By my ear, I not only have the idea of sounds, loud and soft, acute and grave, but I immediately perceive and judge this sound to be loud, that to be soft, this to be acute, that to be grave. Two or more synchronous sounds I perceive to be concordant, others to be discordant.

These are judgments of the senses. They have always been called and accounted such, by those whose minds are not tinctured by philosophical theories. They are the immediate testimony of nature by our senses; and we are so constituted by nature, that we must receive their testimony, for no other reason but because it is given by our senses.

In vain do Sceptics endeavour to overturn this evidence by metaphysical reasoning. Though we should not be able to answer their arguments, we believe our senses still, and rest our most important concerns upon their testimony.

If this be a just notion of our external senses, as I conceive it is, our moral faculty may, I think, without impropriety, be called the *moral sense*.

In its dignity it is, without doubt, far superior to every other power of the mind; but there is this analogy between it and the external senses, That, as by them we have not only the original conceptions of the various qualities of bodies, but the original judgments that this body has such a quality, that such another; so by our moral faculty, we have both the original conceptions of right and wrong in conduct, of merit and demerit, and the original judgments that this conduct is right, that is wrong; that this character has worth, that, demerit.

The testimony of our moral faculty, like that of the external senses, is the testimony of nature, and we have the same reason to rely upon it.

The truths immediately testified by the external senses are the first principles from which we reason, with regard to the material world, and from which all our knowledge of it is deduced.

The truths immediately testified by our moral faculty, are the first principles of all moral reasoning, from which all our knowledge of our duty must be deduced. . . .

All reasoning must be grounded on first principles. This holds in moral reasoning, as in all other kinds. There must therefore be in morals, as in all other sciences, first or self-evident principles, on which all moral reasoning is grounded, and on which it ultimately rests. From such self-evident principles, conclusions may be drawn synthetically with regard to the moral conduct of life; and particular duties or virtues may be traced back to such principles analytically. But, without such principles, we can no more establish any conclusion in morals, than we can build a castle in the air, without any foundation.

An example or two will serve to illustrate this.

It is a first principle in morals. That we ought not to do to another, what we should think wrong to be done to us in like circumstances. If a man is not capable of perceiving this in his cool moments, when he reflects seriously, he is not a moral agent, nor is he capable of being convinced of it by reasoning.

From what topic can you reason with such a man? You may possibly convince him by reasoning, that it is his interest to observe this rule; but this is not to convince him that it is his duty. To reason about justice with a man who sees nothing to be just or unjust; or about benevolence with a man who sees nothing in benevolence preferable to malice, is like reasoning with a blind man about colour, or with a deaf man about sound.

It is a question in morals that admits of reasoning, Whether, by the law of nature, a man ought to have only one wife?

We reason upon this question, by balancing the advantages and disadvantages to the family, and to society in general, that are naturally consequent both upon monogamy and polygamy. And if it can be shewn that the advantages are greatly upon the side of monogamy, we think the point is determined.

But, if a man does not perceive that he ought to regard the good of society, and the good of his wife and children, the reasoning can have no effect upon him, because he denies the first principles upon which it is grounded.

Suppose again, that we reason for monogamy from the intention of nature, discovered by the proportion of males and of females that are born; a proportion which corresponds perfectly with monogamy but by no means with polygamy. This argument can have no weight with a man who does not perceive that he ought to have a regard to the intention of nature.

Thus we shall find that all moral reasonings rest upon one or more first principles of morals, whose truth is immediately perceived without reasoning, by all men come to years of understanding.

And this indeed is common to every branch of human knowledge that deserves the name of science. There must be first principles proper to that science, by which the whole superstructure is supported.

The first principles of all the sciences, must be the immediate dictates of our natural faculties; nor is it possible that we should have any other evidence of their truth. And in different sciences the faculties which dictate their first principles are very different.

The first principles of morals are the immediate dictates of the moral faculty. They shew us, not what man is, but what we ought to be. Whatever is immediately perceived to be just, honest, and honourable, in human conduct, carries moral obligation along with it, and the contrary carries demerit and blame; and, from those moral obligations that are immediately perceived, all other moral obligations must be deduced by reasoning.

He that will judge of the colour of an object, must consult his eyes, in a good light, when there is no medium or contiguous objects that may give it a false tinge. But in vain will he consult every other faculty in this matter.

In like manner, he that will judge of the first principles of morals, must consult his conscience, or moral faculty, when he is calm and dispassionate, unbiassed by interest, affection, or fashion.

As we rely upon the clear and distinct testimony of our eyes, concerning the colours and figures of the bodies about us, we have the same reason to rely with security upon the clear and unbiassed testimony of our conscience, with regard to what we ought, and ought not to do. In many cases, moral worth and demerit are discerned no less clearly by the last of those natural faculties, than figure and colour by the first.

The faculties which nature hath given us, are the only engines we can use to find out the truth. We cannot indeed prove that those faculties are not fallacious, unless GOD should give us new faculties to sit in judgment upon the old. But we are born under a necessity of trusting them.

Every man in his senses believes his eyes, his ears, and his other senses. He believes his consciousness, with respect to his own thoughts and purposes, his memory, with regard to what is past, his understanding, with regard to abstract relations of things, and his taste, with regard to what is elegant and beautiful. And he has the same reason, and, indeed, is under the same necessity of believing the clear and unbiassed dictates of his conscience, with regard to what is honourable and what is base.

Observations Concerning Conscience

I shall now conclude this Essay with some observations concerning this power of the mind which we call *conscience*, by which its nature may be better understood.

The *first* is, That like all our other powers, it comes to maturity by insensible degrees, and may be much aided in its strength and vigour by proper culture. . . .

The seeds, as it were, of moral discernment are planted in the mind by him that made us. They grow up in their proper season, and are at first tender and delicate, and easily warped. Their progress depends very much upon their being duly cultivated and properly exercised.

It is so with the power of reasoning, which all acknowledge to be one of the most eminent natural faculties of man. It appears not in infancy. It springs up, by insensible degrees, as we grow to maturity. But its strength and vigour depend so much upon its being duly cultivated and exercised, that we see many individuals, nay, many nations, in which it is hardly to be perceived.

Our intellectual discernment is not so strong and vigorous by nature, as to secure us from errors in speculation. On the contrary, we see a great part of mankind, in every age, sunk in gross ignorance of things that are obvious to the more enlightened, and fettered by errors and false notions, which the human understanding, duly improved, easily throws off.

It would be extremely absurd, from the errors and ignorance of mankind, to conclude that there is no such thing as truth; or that man has not a natural faculty of discerning it, and distinguishing it from error.

In like manner, our moral discernment of what we ought, and what we ought not to do, is not so strong and vigorous by nature, as to secure us from very gross mistakes with regard to our duty.

In matters of conduct, as well as in matters of speculation, we are liable to be misled by prejudices of education, or by wrong instruction. But, in matters of conduct, we are also very liable to have our judgment warped by our appetites and passions, by fashion, and by the contagion of evil example.

We must not therefore think, because man has the natural power of discerning what is right, and what is wrong, that he has no need of instruction; that this power has no need of cultivation and improvement; that he may safely rely upon the suggestions of his mind, or upon opinions he has got, he knows not how.

What should we think of a man who because he has by nature the power of moving all his limbs, should therefore conclude that he needs not be taught to dance, or to fence, to ride, or to swim? All these exercises are performed by that power of moving our limbs, which we have by nature; but they will be performed very awkwardly and imperfectly by those who have not been trained to them, and practised in them.

It may be observed, That there are truths, both speculative and moral, which a man left to himself would never discover; yet, when they are fairly laid before him, he owns and adopts them, not barely upon the authority of his teacher, but upon their own intrinsic evidence, and perhaps wonders that he could be so blind as not to see them before.

Like a man whose son has been long abroad, and supposed dead. After many years the son returns, and is not known by his father. He would never find that this is his son. But, when he discovers himself, the father soon finds, by many circumstances, that this is his son who was lost, and can be no other person.

Truth has an affinity with the human understanding, which error hath not. And right principles of conduct have an affinity with a candid mind, which wrong principles have not. When they are set before it in a just light, a well disposed mind recognises this affinity, feels their authority, and perceives them to be genuine. It was this, I apprehend, that led PLATO to conceive that the knowledge we acquire in the present state, is only reminiscence of what, in a former state, we were acquainted with.

A man born and brought up in a savage nation, may be taught to pursue injury with unrelenting malice, to the destruction of his enemy. Perhaps when he does so, his heart does not condemn him.

Yet, if he be fair and candid, and, when the tumult of passion is over, have the virtues of clemency, generosity, and forgiveness, laid before him, as they were taught and exemplified by the divine Author of our religion, he will see, that it is more noble to overcome himself, and subdue a savage passion, than to destroy his enemy. He will see, that to make a friend of an enemy, and to overcome evil with good, is the greatest of all victories, and gives a manly and a rational delight, with which the brutish passion of revenge deserves not to be compared. He will see that hitherto he acted like a man to his friends, but like a brute to his enemies; now he knows how to make his whole character consistent, and one part of it to harmonize with another.

He must indeed be a great stranger to his own heart, and to the state of human nature, who does not see that he has need of all the aid which his situation affords him, in order to know how he ought to act in many cases that occur.

17. Alfred Jules Ayer

**A. J. Ayer was Professor of Philosophy at the University of
London, and since 1946 has been Professor of Philosophy at
Oxford University.**

A Noncognitive Theory

There is still one objection to be met before we can claim to have justified
our view that all synthetic propositions are empirical hypotheses. This
objection is based on the common supposition that our speculative knowledge is of two distinct kinds—that which relates to questions of empirical
fact, and that which relates to questions of value. It will be said that
"statements of value" are genuine synthetic propositions, but that they
cannot with any show of justice be represented as hypotheses, which
are used to predict the course of our sensations; and, accordingly, that
the existence of ethics and aesthetics as branches of speculative knowledge presents an insuperable objection to our radical empiricist thesis.

In face of this objection, it is our business to give an account of
"judgements of value" which is both satisfactory in itself and consistent
with our general empiricist principles. We shall set ourselves to show
that in so far as statements of value are significant, they are ordinary
"scientific" statements; and that in so far as they are not scientific, they
are not in the literal sense significant, but are simply expressions of emotion which can be neither true nor false. In maintaining this view, we
may confine ourselves for the present to the case of ethical statements.
What is said about them will be found to apply, *mutatis mutandis*, to the
case of aesthetic statements also.

From A. J. Ayer, *Language, Truth and Logic*, Chapter 6. Published by Victor Gollancz, Ltd., London, 1936; and by Dover Publications, Inc., New York, 1936. Reprinted
by permission of the publishers.

The ordinary system of ethics, as elaborated in the works of ethical philosophers, is very far from being a homogeneous whole. Not only is it apt to contain pieces of metaphysics, and analyses of non-ethical concepts: its actual ethical contents are themselves of very different kinds. We may divide them, indeed, into four main classes. There are, first of all, propositions which express definitions of ethical terms, or judgements about the legitimacy or possibility of certain definitions. Secondly, there are propositions describing the phenomena of moral experience, and their causes. Thirdly, there are exhortations to moral virtue. And, lastly, there are actual ethical judgements. It is unfortunately the case that the distinction between these four classes, plain as it is, is commonly ignored by ethical philosophers; with the result that it is often very difficult to tell from their works what it is that they are seeking to discover or prove.

In fact, it is easy to see that only the first of our four classes, namely that which comprises the propositions relating to the definitions of ethical terms, can be said to constitute ethical philosophy. The propositions which describe the phenomena of moral experience, and their causes, must be assigned to the science of psychology, or sociology. The exhortations to moral virtue are not propositions at all, but ejaculations or commands which are designed to provoke the reader to action of a certain sort. Accordingly, they do not belong to any branch of philosophy or science. As for the expressions of ethical judgements, we have not yet determined how they should be classified. But inasmuch as they are certainly neither definitions nor comments upon definitions, nor quotations, we may say decisively that they do not belong to ethical philosophy. A strictly philosophical treatise on ethics should therefore make no ethical pronouncements. But it should, by giving an analysis of ethical terms, show what is the category to which all such pronouncements belong. And this is what we are now about to do.

A question which is often discussed by ethical philosophers is whether it is possible to find definitions which would reduce all ethical terms to one or two fundamental terms. But this question, though it undeniably belongs to ethical philosophy, is not relevant to our present enquiry. We are not now concerned to discover which term, within the sphere of ethical terms, is to be taken as fundamental; whether, for example, "good" can be defined in terms of "right" or "right" in terms of "good," or both in terms of "value." What we are interested in is the possibility of reducing the whole sphere of ethical terms to non-ethical terms. We are enquiring whether statements of ethical value can be translated into statements of empirical fact.

That they can be so translated is the contention of those ethical philosophers who are commonly called subjectivists, and of those who are known as utilitarians. For the utilitarian defines the rightness of actions, and the goodness of ends, in terms of the pleasure, or happiness, or satisfaction, to which they give rise; the subjectivist, in terms of the feelings of approval which a certain person, or group of people, has towards them. Each of these types of definition makes moral judgements into a sub-class of psychological or sociological judgements; and for this reason they are very attractive to us. For, if either was correct, it would follow that

171

ethical assertions were not generically different from the factual assertions which are ordinarily contrasted with them; and the account which
we have already given of empirical hypotheses would apply to them also.

Nevertheless we shall not adopt either a subjectivist or a utilitarian
analysis of ethical terms. We reject the subjectivist view that to call an
action right, or a thing good, is to say that it is generally approved of,
because it is not self-contradictory to assert that some actions which
are generally approved of are not right, or that some things which are
generally approved of are not good. And we reject the alternative subjectivist view that a man who asserts that a certain action is right, or
that a certain thing is good, is saying that he himself approves of it, on
the ground that a man who confessed that he sometimes approved of
what was bad or wrong would not be contradicting himself. And a similar
argument is fatal to utilitarianism. We cannot agree that to call an action
right is to say that of all the actions possible in the circumstances it
would cause, or be likely to cause, the greatest happiness, or the greatest
balance of pleasure over pain, or the greatest balance of satisfied over
unsatisfied desire, because we find that it is not self-contradictory to say
that it is sometimes wrong to perform the action which would actually or
probably cause the greatest happiness, or the greatest balance of pleasure
over pain, or of satisfied over unsatisfied desire. And since it is not self-
contradictory to say that some pleasant things are not good, or that some
bad things are desired, it cannot be the case that the sentence "x is good"
is equivalent to "x is pleasant," or "x is desired." And to every other variant of utilitarianism with which I am acquainted the same objection can
be made. And therefore we should, I think, conclude that the validity of
ethical judgements is not determined by the felicific tendencies of actions, any more than by the nature of people's feelings; but that it must
be regarded as "absolute" or "intrinsic," and not empirically calculable.

If we say this, we are not, of course, denying that it is possible to invent a language in which all ethical symbols are definable in non-ethical
terms, or even that it is desirable to invent such a language and adopt
it in place of our own; what we are denying is that the suggested reduction of ethical to non-ethical statements is consistent with the conventions of our actual language. That is, we reject utilitarianism and
subjectivism, not as proposals to replace our existing ethical notions by
new ones, but as analyses of our existing ethical notions. Our contention
is simply that, in our language, sentences which contain normative ethical symbols are not equivalent to sentences which express psychological
propositions, or indeed empirical propositions of any kind.

It is advisable here to make it plain that it is only normative ethical
symbols, and not descriptive ethical symbols, that are held by us to be
indefinable in factual terms. There is a danger of confusing these two
types of symbols, because they are commonly constituted by signs of
the same sensible form. Thus a complex sign of the form "x is wrong"
may constitute a sentence which expresses a moral judgement concerning
a certain type of conduct, or it may constitute a sentence which states
that a certain type of conduct is repugnant to the moral sense of a particular society. In the latter case, the symbol "wrong" is a descriptive

ethical symbol, and the sentence in which it occurs expresses an ordinary sociological proposition; in the former case, the symbol "wrong" is a normative ethical symbol, and the sentence in which it occurs does not, we maintain, express an empirical proposition at all. It is only with normative ethics that we are at present concerned; so that whenever ethical symbols are used in the course of this argument without qualification, they are always to be interpreted as symbols of the normative type.

In admitting that normative ethical concepts are irreducible to empirical concepts, we seem to be leaving the way clear for the "absolutist" view of ethics—that is, the view that statements of value are not controlled by observation, as ordinary empirical propositions are, but only by a mysterious "intellectual intuition." A feature of this theory, which is seldom recognized by its advocates, is that it makes statements of value unverifiable. For it is notorious that what seems intuitively certain to one person may seem doubtful, or even false, to another. So that unless it is possible to provide some criterion by which one may decide between conflicting intuitions, a mere appeal to intuition is worthless as a test of a proposition's validity. But in the case of moral judgements, no such criterion can be given. Some moralists claim to settle the matter by saying that they "know" that their own moral judgements are correct. But such an assertion is of purely psychological interest, and has not the slightest tendency to prove the validity of any moral judgement. For dissentient moralists may equally well "know" that their ethical views are correct. And, as far as subjective certainty goes, there will be nothing to choose between them. When such differences of opinion arise in connection with an ordinary empirical proposition, one may attempt to resolve them by referring to, or actually carrying out, some relevant empirical test. But with regard to ethical statements, there is, on the "absolutist" or "intuitionist" theory, no relevant empirical test. We are therefore justified in saying that on this theory ethical statements are held to be unverifiable. They are, of course, also held to be genuine synthetic propositions.

Considering the use which we have made of the principle that a synthetic proposition is significant only if it is empirically verifiable, it is clear that the acceptance of an "absolutist" theory of ethics would undermine the whole of our main argument. And as we have already rejected the "naturalistic" theories which are commonly supposed to provide the only alternative to "absolutism" in ethics, we seem to have reached a difficult position. We shall meet the difficulty by showing that the correct treatment of ethical statements is afforded by a third theory, which is wholly compatible with our radical empiricism.

We begin by admitting that the fundamental ethical concepts are unanalysable, inasmuch as there is no criterion by which one can test the validity of the judgements in which they occur. So far we are in agreement with the absolutists. But, unlike the absolutists, we are able to give an explanation of this fact about ethical concepts. We say that the reason why they are unanalysable is that they are mere pseudo-concepts. The presence of an ethical symbol in a proposition adds nothing to its factual content. Thus if I say to someone, "You acted wrongly in stealing that money," I am not stating anything more than if I had simply said, "You stole that money." In adding that this action is wrong I am not making any further statement about it. I am simply evincing my moral disapproval of it. It is as if I had said, "You stole that money," in a peculiar tone of horror, or written it with the addition of some special exclamation marks. The tone, or the exclamation marks, adds nothing to the literal meaning of the sentence. It merely serves to show that the expression of it is attended by certain feelings in the speaker.

If now I generalise my previous statement and say, "Stealing money is wrong," I produce a sentence which has no factual meaning—that is, expresses no proposition which can be either true or false. It is as if I had written "Stealing money!!"—where the shape and thickness of the exclamation marks show, by a suitable convention, that a special sort of moral disapproval is the feeling which is being expressed. It is clear that there is nothing said here which can be true or false. Another man may disagree with me about the wrongness of stealing, in the sense that he may not have the same feelings about stealing as I have, and he may quarrel with me on account of my moral sentiments. But he cannot, strictly speaking, contradict me. For in saying that a certain type of action is right or wrong, I am not making any factual statement, not even a statement about my own state of mind. I am merely expressing certain moral sentiments. And the man who is ostensibly contradicting me is merely expressing his moral sentiments. So that there is plainly no sense in asking which of us is in the right. For neither of us is asserting a genuine proposition.

What we have just been saying about the symbol "wrong" applies to all normative ethical symbols. Sometimes they occur in sentences which record ordinary empirical facts besides expressing ethical feeling about those facts: sometimes they occur in sentences which simply express ethical feeling about a certain type of action, or situation, without making any statement of fact. But in every case in which one would commonly be said to be making an ethical judgement, the function of the relevant ethical word is purely "emotive." It is used to express feeling about certain objects, but not to make any assertion about them.

It is worth mentioning that ethical terms do not serve only to express feeling. They are calculated also to arouse feeling, and so to stimulate action. Indeed some of them are used in such a way as to give the sentences in which they occur the effect of commands. Thus the sentence "It is your duty to tell the truth" may be regarded both as the expression of a certain sort of ethical feeling about truthfulness and as the expression of the command "Tell the truth." The sentence "You ought to tell the truth" also involves the command "Tell the truth," but here the tone of the command is less emphatic. In the sentence "It is good to tell the truth" the command has become little more than a suggestion. And thus the "meaning" of the word "good," in its ethical usage, is differentiated from that of the word "duty" or the word "ought." In fact we may define the meaning of the various ethical words in terms both of the different feelings they are ordinarily taken to express, and also the different responses which they are calculated to provoke.

We can now see why it is impossible to find a criterion for determining the validity of ethical judgements. It is not because they have an "absolute" validity which is mysteriously independent of ordinary sense-experience, but because they have no objective validity whatsoever. If a sentence makes no statement at all, there is obviously no sense in asking whether what it says is true or false. And we have seen that sentences which simply express moral judgements do not say anything. They are pure expressions of feelings and as such do not come under the category of truth and falsehood. They are unverifiable for the same reason as a cry of pain or a word of command is unverifiable—because they do not express genuine propositions.

Thus, although our theory of ethics might fairly be said to be radically subjectivist, it differs in a very important respect from the orthodox subjectivist theory. For the orthodox subjectivist does not deny, as we do, that the sentences of a moralizer express genuine propositions. All he denies is that they express propositions of a unique non-empirical character. His own view is that they express propositions about the speaker's feelings. If this were so, ethical judgements clearly would be capable of being true or false. They would be true if the speaker had the relevant feelings and false if he had not. And this is a matter which is, in principle, empirically verifiable. Furthermore they could be significantly contradicted. For if I say, "Tolerance is a virtue," and someone answers, "You don't approve of it," he would, on the ordinary subjectivist theory, be contradicting me. On our theory, he would not be contradicting me, because, in saying that tolerance was a virtue, I should not be making any statement about my own feelings or about anything else. I should simply be evincing my feelings, which is not at all the same thing as saying that I have them.

The distinction between the expression of feeling and the assertion of feeling is complicated by the fact that the assertion that one has a certain feeling often accompanies the expression of that feeling, and is then, indeed, a factor in the expression of that feeling. Thus I may simultaneously express boredom and say that I am bored, and in that case my utterance of the words, "I am bored," is one of the circumstances which make it true to say that I am expressing or evincing boredom. But I can express boredom without actually saying that I am bored. I can express it by my tone and gestures, while making a statement about something wholly unconnected with it, or by an ejaculation, or without uttering any words at all. So that even if the assertion that one has a certain feeling always involves the expression of that feeling, the expression of a feeling assuredly does not always involve the assertion that one has it. And this is the important point to grasp in considering the distinction between our theory and the ordinary subjectivist theory. For whereas the subjectivist holds that ethical statements actually assert the existence of certain feelings, we hold that ethical statements are expressions and excitants of feeling which do not necessarily involve assertions.

We have already remarked that the main objection to the ordinary subjectivist theory is that the validity of ethical judgements is not determined by the nature of their author's feelings. And this is an objection which our theory escapes. For it does not imply that the existence of any feelings is a necessary and sufficient condition of the validity of an ethical judgement. It implies, on the contrary, that ethical judgements have no validity.

There is, however, a celebrated argument against subjectivist theories which our theory does not escape. It has been pointed out by Moore that if ethical statements were simply statements about the speaker's feelings, it would be impossible to argue about questions of value.[1] To take a typical example: if a man said that thrift was a virtue, and another replied that it was a vice, they would not, on this theory, be disputing with one another. One would be saying that he approved of thrift, and the other that *he* didn't; and there is no reason why both these statements should not be true. Now Moore held it to be obvious that we do dispute about questions of value, and accordingly concluded that the particular form of subjectivism which he was discussing was false.

It is plain that the conclusion that it is impossible to dispute about questions of value follows from our theory also. For as we hold that such sentences as "Thrift is a virtue" and "Thrift is a vice" do not express propositions at all, we clearly cannot hold that they express incompatible propositions. We must therefore admit that if Moore's argument really refutes the ordinary subjectivist theory, it also refutes ours. But, in fact, we deny that it does refute even the ordinary subjectivist theory. For we hold that one really never does dispute about questions of value.

This may seem, at first sight, to be a very paradoxical assertion. For we certainly do engage in disputes which are ordinarily regarded as disputes about questions of value. But, in all such cases, we find if we consider the matter closely, that the dispute is not really about a question of value, but about a question of fact. When someone disagrees with us about the moral value of a certain action or type of action, we do admittedly resort to argument in order to win him over to our way of thinking. But we do not attempt to show by our arguments that he has the "wrong" ethical feeling towards a situation whose nature he has correctly apprehended. What we attempt to show is that he is mistaken about the facts of the case. We argue that he has misconceived the agent's motive: or that he has misjudged the effects of the action, or its probable effects in view of the agent's knowledge; or that he has failed to take into account the special circumstances in which the agent was placed. Or else we employ more general arguments about the effects which actions of a certain type tend to produce, or the qualities which are usually manifested in their performance. We do this in the hope that we have only to get our opponent to agree with us about the nature of the empirical facts for him to adopt the same moral attitude towards them as we do. And as the people with whom we argue have generally received the same moral education as ourselves, and live in the same social order, our expectation is usually justified. But if our opponent happens to have undergone a different process of moral "conditioning" from ourselves, so that, even when he acknowledges all the facts, he

1. Cf. *Philosophical Studies*, "The Nature of Moral Philosophy."

still disagrees with us about the moral value of the actions under discussion, then we abandon the attempt to convince him by argument. We say that it is impossible to argue with him because he has a distorted or undeveloped moral sense; which signifies merely that he employs a different set of values from our own. We feel that our own system of values is superior, and therefore speak in such derogatory terms of his. But we cannot bring forward any arguments to show that our system is superior. For our judgement that it is so is itself a judgement of value, and accordingly outside the scope of argument. It is because argument fails us when we come to deal with pure questions of value, as distinct from questions of fact, that we finally resort to mere abuse.

In short, we find that argument is possible on moral questions only if some system of values is presupposed. If our opponent concurs with us in expressing moral disapproval of all actions of a given type *t*, then we may get him to condemn a particular action A, by bringing forward argument to show that A is of type *t*. For the question whether A does or does not belong to that type is a plain question of fact. Given that a man has certain moral principles, we argue that he must, in order to be consistent, react morally to certain things in a certain way. What we do not and cannot argue about is the validity of these moral principles. We merely praise or condemn them in the light of our own feelings.

If anyone doubts the accuracy of this account of moral disputes, let him try to construct even an imaginary argument on a question of value which does not reduce itself to an argument about a question of logic or about an empirical matter of fact. I am confident that he will not succeed in producing a single example. And if that is the case, he must allow that its involving the impossibility of purely ethical arguments is not, as Moore thought, a ground of objection to our theory, but rather a point in favour of it.

Having upheld our theory against the only criticism which appeared to threaten it, we may now use it to define the nature of all ethical enquiries. We find that ethical philosophy consists simply in saying that ethical concepts are pseudo-concepts and therefore unanalysable. The further task of describing the different feelings that the different ethical terms are used to express, and the different reactions that they customarily provoke, is a task for the psychologist. There cannot be such a thing as ethical science, if by ethical science one means the elaboration of a "true" system of morals. For we have seen that, as ethical judgements are mere expressions of feeling, there can be no way of determining the validity of any ethical system, and, indeed, no sense in asking whether any such system is true. All that one may legitimately enquire in this connection is, What are the moral habits of a given person or group of people, and what causes them to have precisely those habits and feelings? And this enquiry falls wholly within the scope of the existing social sciences.

It appears, then, that ethics, as a branch of knowledge, is nothing more than a department of psychology and sociology. And in case anyone thinks that we are overlooking the existence of casuistry, we may remark that casuistry is not a science, but is a purely analytical investigation of the structure of a given moral system. In other words, it is an exercise in formal logic.

When one comes to pursue the psychological enquiries which constitute ethical science, one is immediately enabled to account for the Kantian and hedonistic theories of morals. For one finds that one of the chief causes of moral behavior is fear, both conscious and unconscious, of a god's displeasure, and fear of the enmity of society. And this, indeed, is the reason why moral precepts present themselves to some people as "categorical" commands. And one finds, also, that the moral code of a society is partly determined by the beliefs of that society concerning the conditions of its own happiness—or, in other words, that a society tends to encourage or discourage a given type of conduct by the use of moral sanctions according as it appears to promote or detract from the contentment of the society as a whole. And this is the reason why altruism is recommended in most moral codes and egotism condemned. It is from the observation of this connection between morality and happiness that hedonistic or eudæmonistic theories of morals ultimately spring, just as the moral theory of Kant is based on the fact, previously explained, that moral precepts have for some people the force of inexorable commands. As each of these theories ignores the fact which lies at the root of the other, both may be criticized as being onesided; but this is not the main objection to either of them. Their essential defect is that they treat propositions which refer to the causes and attributes of our ethical feelings as if they were definitions of ethical concepts. And thus they fail to recognize that ethical concepts are pseudo-concepts and consequently indefinable.

As we have already said, our conclusions about the nature of ethics apply to æsthetics also. Aesthetic terms are used in exactly the same way as ethical terms. Such æsthetic words as "beautiful" and "hideous" are employed, as ethical words are employed, not to make statements of fact, but simply to express certain feelings and evoke a certain response. It follows, as in ethics, that there is no sense in attributing objective validity to æsthetic judgements, and no possibility of arguing about questions of value in æsthetics, but only about questions of fact. A scientific treatment of æsthetics would show us what in general were the causes of æsthetic feeling, why various societies produced and admired the works of art they did, why taste varies as it does within a given society, and so forth. And these are ordinary psychological or sociological questions. They have, of course, little or nothing to do with æsthetic criticism as we understand it. But that is because the purpose of æsthetic criticism is not so much to give knowledge as to communicate emotion. The critic, by calling attention to certain features of the work under review, and expressing his own feelings about them, endeavours to make us share his attitude towards the work as a whole. The only relevant propositions that he formulates are propositions describing the nature of the work. And these are plain records of fact. We conclude, therefore, that there is nothing in æsthetics, any more than there is in ethics, to justify the view that it embodies a unique type of knowledge.

18. Aristotle

Aristotle (384–322 B.C.) was a student of Plato, tutor of
Alexander of Macedon, and founder of a school in Athens
known as the Lyceum.

The Good Life Is Rational Activity

1. The Good is What People Desire for Itself.

If, therefore, among the ends at which our conduct aims there is one
which we will for its own sake, whereas we will the other ends only for
the sake of this one, and if we do not choose everything for the sake of
some other thing—that would clearly be an endless process, making all
desire futile and idle—, it is clear that this one ultimate end will be the
good, and the greatest good. Then will not a knowledge of this ultimate
end be of more than theoretic interest? Will it not also have great practical importance for the conduct of life? Shall we not be more likely to
attain our needs if like archers we have a target before us to aim at?
If this be so, an attempt must be made to ascertain at all events in outline what precisely this supreme good is, and under which of the theoretical or practical sciences it falls.

From Aristotle, *Ethics for English Readers*, Books I, II, and X, translated by
H. Rackham, published by Basil Blackwell, Publisher, Oxford, 1952. These paragraphs
have been rearranged in order to present a consecutive discussion. The headings now
used are by the present editors.

2. It is Generally Thought that the Good is Happiness, and We Need Not Deny This; but If We Accept It, It is a Mistake to Identify Happiness with Pleasure, Honor, Wealth, or Having a Fine Character.

To resume: inasmuch as all study and all deliberate action is aimed at some good object, let us state what is the good which is in our view the aim of political science, and what is the highest of the goods obtainable by action.

Now as far as the name goes there is virtual agreement about this among the vast majority of mankind. Both ordinary people and persons of trained mind define the good as happiness. But as to what constitutes happiness opinions differ; the answer given by ordinary people is not the same as the verdict of the philosopher. Ordinary men identify happiness with something obvious and visible, such as pleasure or wealth or hon-our—everybody gives a different definition, and sometimes the same person's own definition alters: when a man has fallen ill he thinks that happiness is health, if he is poor he thinks it is wealth. And when people realise their own ignorance they regard with admiration those who propound some grand theory that is above their heads. The view has been held by some thinkers that besides the many good things alluded to above there also exists something that is good in itself, which is the fundamental cause of the goodness of all the others.

Now to review the whole of these opinions would perhaps be a rather thankless task. It may be enough to examine those that are most widely held, or that appear to have some considerable argument in their favour.

To judge by men's mode of living, the mass of mankind think that good and happiness consist in pleasure, and consequently are content with a life of mere enjoyment. There are in fact three principal modes of life—the one just mentioned, the life of active citizenship and the life of contemplation. The masses, being utterly servile, obviously prefer the life of mere cattle; and indeed they have some reason for this, inasmuch as many men of high station share the tastes of Sardanapalus. The bet-ter people, on the other hand, and men of action, give the highest value to honour, since honour may be said to be the object aimed at in a public career. Nevertheless, it would seem that honour is a more superficial thing than the good which we are in search of, because honour seems to depend more on the people who render it than on the person who re-ceives it, whereas we dimly feel that good must be something inherent in oneself and inalienable. Moreover men's object in pursuing honour ap-pears to be to convince themselves of their own worth; at all events they seek to be honoured by persons of insight and by people who are well acquainted with them, and to be honoured for their merit. It therefore seems that at all events in the opinions of these men goodness is more valuable than honour, and probably one may suppose that it has a better claim than honour to be deemed the end at which the life of politics aims. But even virtue appears to lack completeness as an end, inasmuch as it seems to be possible to possess it while one is asleep or living a life of perpetual inactivity, and moreover one can be virtuous and yet suffer

180

extreme sorrow and misfortune; but nobody except for the sake of maintaining a paradox would call a man happy in those circumstances.

The life of money-making is a cramped way of living, and clearly
wealth is not the good we are in search of, as it is only valuable as a
means to something else. Consequently a stronger case might be made
for the objects previously specified, because they are valued for their own
sake; but even they appear to be inadequate, although a great deal of
discussion has been devoted to them.

3. Happiness Is Desired for Itself, and Never for the Sake of Anything Else; It Is Sufficient in Itself to Make Life Desirable.

Now the objects at which our actions aim are manifestly several, and
some of these objects, for instance money, and instruments in general,
we adopt as means to the attainment of something else. This shows that
not all the objects we pursue are final ends. But the greatest good manifestly is a final end. Consequently if there is only one thing which is final,
that will be the object for which we are now seeking, or if there are
several, it will be that one among them which possesses the most complete finality.

Now a thing that is pursued for its own sake we pronounce to be
more final than one pursued as a means to some other thing, and a thing
that is never desired for the sake of something else we call more final
than those which are desired for the sake of something else as well as
for their own sake. In fact the absolutely final is something that is always
desired on its own account and never as a means for obtaining something
else. Now this description appears to apply in the highest degree to happiness, since we always desire happiness for its own sake and never on
account of something else; whereas honour and pleasure and intelligence
and each of the virtues, though we do indeed desire them on their own
account as well, for we should desire each of them even if it produced no
external result, we also desire for the sake of happiness, because we believe that they will bring it to us, whereas nobody desires happiness for
the sake of those things, nor for anything else but itself.

The same result seems to follow from a consideration of the subject
of self-sufficiency, which is felt to be a necessary attribute of the final
good. The term self-sufficient denotes not merely being sufficient for
oneself alone as if one lived the life of a hermit, but also being sufficient
for the needs of one's parents and children and wife, and one's friends
and fellow-countrymen in general, inasmuch as man is by nature a social
being.

Yet we are bound to assume some limit in these relationships, since
if one extends the connexion to include one's children's children and
friends' friends, it will go on *ad infinitum*. But that is a matter which
must be deferred for later consideration. Let us define self-sufficiency as
the quality which makes life to be desirable and lacking in nothing even
when considered by itself; and this quality we assume to belong to happiness. Moreover when we pronounce happiness to be the most desirable

of all things, we do not mean that it stands as one in a list of good things—were it so it would obviously be more desirable in combination with even the smallest of the other goods, inasmuch as that addition would increase the total of good, and of two good things the larger must always be the more desirable.

Thus it appears that happiness is something final and complete in itself, as being the aim and end of all practical activites whatever.

4. In Order to Acquire a Clearer Concept of Human Happiness, We Do Well to Ask Whether Human Beings Have a Function, As the Eye, or a Carpenter, Has One. What Is Distinctive in Man Is Reason, So His Happiness Must Be the Exercise of Reason in Living.

Possibly, however, the student may feel that the statement that happiness is the greatest good is a mere truism, and he may want a clearer explanation of what the precise nature of happiness is. This may perhaps be achieved by ascertaining what is the proper function of man. In the case of flute-players or sculptors or other artists, and generally of all persons who have a particular work to perform, it is felt that their good and their well-being are found in that work. It may be supposed that this similarly holds good in the case of a human being, if we may assume that there is some work which constitutes the proper function of a human being as such. Can it then be the case that whereas a carpenter and a shoemaker have definite functions or businesses to perform, a man as such has none, and is not designed by nature to perform any function? Should we not rather assume that, just as the eye and hand and foot and every part of the body manifestly have functions assigned to them, so also there is a function that belongs to a man, over and above all the special functions that belong to his members? If so, what precisely will that function be? It is clear that the mere activity of living is shared by man even with the vegetable kingdom, whereas we are looking for some function that belongs specially to man. We must therefore set aside the vital activity of nutrition and growth. Next perhaps comes the life of the senses; but this also is manifestly shared by the horse and the ox and all the animals. There remains therefore what may be designated the practical life of the rational faculty.

But the term "rational" life has two meanings: it denotes both the mere possession of reason, and its active exercise. Let us take it that we here mean the latter, as that appears to be the more proper signification of the term. Granted then that the special function of man is the active exercise of the mind's faculties in accordance with rational principle, or at all events not in detachment from rational principle, and that the function of anything, for example, a harper, is generally the same as the function of a good specimen of that thing, for example a good harper (the specification of the function merely being augmented in the latter case with the statement of excellence—a harper is a man who plays the harp, a good harper one who plays the harp well)—granted, I say, the truth of these assumptions, it follows that the good of man consists in the active exercise of the faculties in conformity with excellence or virtue, or if there are several virtues in conformity with the best and most perfect among them.

Moreover, happiness requires an entire life-time. One swallow does not make a summer, nor does a single fine day; and similarly one day or a brief period of prosperity does not make a man supremely fortunate and happy.

Happiness then we define as the active exercise of the mind in conformity with perfect goodness or virtue.

5. The Rationally Ordered Life Will Necessarily Be Pleasant, but It Must Be Admitted That Happiness Also Requires Some External Goods.

In consequence of this their life has no need of pleasure as an external appendage; it contains pleasures within itself. For in addition to what has been said, if a man does not enjoy performing noble actions he is not a good man at all. Nobody would call a man just who did not enjoy acting justly, nor liberal if he did not enjoy acting liberally, and similarly with the other virtues. But if this is so, actions in conformity with virtue will be intrinsically pleasant. Moreover, they are also good and noble; and good and noble in the highest degree, inasmuch as the virtuous man must be a good judge of these matters, and his judgement is as we have said.

Consequently happiness is at once the best and the noblest and the pleasantest thing there is, and these qualities do not exist in separate compartments, as is implied by the inscription at Delos:

> *The noblest thing is justice, health the best,*
> *But getting your desire the pleasantest.*

For all these qualities are combined in the highest activities, and it is these activities or the best one among them which according to our definition constitutes happiness. All the same it is manifest that happiness requires external goods in addition, since it is impossible, or at all events difficult, to perform noble actions without resources. Many of them require the aid of friends and of wealth and power in the state. Also a lack of such advantages as good birth or a fine family of children or good looks is a blot on a man's supreme felicity. A very ugly man or one of low birth or without children cannot be classed as completely happy; and still less perhaps can a man whose children or friends are utterly base, or though worthy have died. . . .

6. Some Have Thought That Sheer Pleasure, Just As Such, Is the Ultimate Good; But This Is a Mistake.

It was the opinion of Eudoxus, that pleasure is the good. His reason was as follows. Observation showed him that all creatures, rational and irrational alike, desire to obtain pleasure, and he held the view that in every department of life what is desired is good, and what is most desired is the greatest good. Consequently, he argued, the fact that all things "gravitate in the direction of" the same object proves that object to be the greatest good for all, inasmuch as everything finds out its own particular good, just as every creature discovers what food is nourishing for it; but that which is good for all things and which all things try to obtain must be *the* good. This argument won acceptance more because of its author's excellence of character than from its own merits. Eudoxus had the reputation of being an exceptionally temperate man, and so his theory was not supposed to be suggested by love of pleasure but to be a correct statement of the facts.

Eudoxus also held that the truth of this estimate of pleasure is equally attested by considering its opposite. Pain, he argued, was an object of intrinsic aversion to all living things, so that the opposite of pain must be intrinsically desirable. Moreover those things are most desirable which we choose for their own sake and not for the sake of something else, and to this class, he said, pleasure admittedly belongs, because we never ask anybody *why* he wants pleasure: we assume that pleasure is desirable in itself. He also argued that the value of just or temperate conduct is enhanced if we enjoy acting justly or temperately; but a good thing can only be augmented by something else that is good.

But this argument at all events only seems to show that pleasure is *a* good, not that it is a greater good than any other; for every good thing is better and more desirable if some other good thing is added to it than it is by itself. This argument resembles the one used by Plato to prove that the good is not pleasure, since the pleasant life is more desirable if combined with wisdom than it is without it, but if pleasure is improved by combination with something else, pleasure is not the good.

In reply to those who bring forward the degrading pleasures one might say that these are not really pleasant; if they are pleasant to ill-conditioned persons, it must not be thought that they are really pleasant, except to those persons, any more than the things that are wholesome for invalids or that taste sweet or bitter to them, or that look white to people suffering from disease of the eye, are really so. Or one might express the point by saying that, though pleasures are desirable, yet they are not desirable when derived from those sources, just as wealth is desirable, but not if won by treachery, and health, but not at the cost of eating any diet the doctor may prescribe. Or one might say that pleasures differ in kind, those derived from honourable sources not being the same as those from base sources; and that one cannot experience the pleasure of justice without being a just man, nor enjoy music without being a musician, and similarly with the other pleasures.

Moreover the difference that exists between a friend and a flatterer seems to show clearly that pleasure is not a good, or else that there are different kinds of pleasure. A friend is thought to aim at doing good to his associates, but a flatterer at giving them pleasure; to be a flatterer is a reproach, but a friend is praised, because his motives for seeking society are different. Also nobody would like to pass the whole of his life with the intellect of a child, however much pleasure he might get from things that please children, nor to enjoy doing something very disgraceful even though it brought no painful consequences. And there are many things that we should be eager to possess even if they brought us no pleasure, for instance, sight, memory, knowledge, virtue. If these things do as a matter of fact necessarily bring pleasure, that makes no difference; we should prefer to possess them even if we got no pleasure from them.

It seems therefore that pleasure is not the good, and also that not all pleasure is desirable, but that some pleasures of various kinds and derived from various sources are desirable in themselves.

7. The Place of Pleasure in the Good Life Is Indicated By the Fact That Pleasure Occurs When Some Sense or Faculty Is Functioning Well; Pleasure Completes This Activity. Consequently, There Are Different Kinds' of Pleasure.

Each of the senses acts in relation to its object, and acts perfectly when in good condition and when directed to the finest of the objects that come under it—this seems to be the best description of a perfect activity, it being assumed that it makes no difference whether we speak of the sense itself acting or the organ which contains it. Consequently each of the senses acts best when its sense-organ is in its best condition and is directed to the best of its objects. And this activity will be the most complete and the most pleasant. For every sensation is accompanied by pleasure, as also are thought and contemplation, and the pleasantest sensation is the most complete. The most complete sensation is that of the sense-organ when in good condition and directed to its worthiest object; and the activity of sensation is completed by the pleasure, though not in the same way as it is completed by the combination of object and sense, both being in good condition, any more than health is the cause of a man's being healthy in the same sense as the doctor is the cause of it.

(It is clear that each of the senses has a particular pleasure corresponding to it; we speak of pleasant sights and sounds as well as of sweet tastes and scents. And it is also clear that the pleasure is greatest when the sense faculty is in the best condition and is directed to the best object; there will always be pleasure when there is an object to cause it and a subject to feel it, if both the object perceived and the percipient organ are good.)

But the pleasure completes the activity not in the way in which it is completed by a fixed disposition of character already present in the agent, but as a supervening consummation, in the same way as a good complexion gives a finishing touch to the young and healthy. Consequently the activity will be attended by pleasure as long as both the object thought of or perceived and the subject discerning or judging are in a proper condition, inasmuch as in any relationship as long as both the passive and the active parties remain the same and stand in the same position as regards each other, the same result is naturally produced.

How is it then that nobody can go on feeling a pleasure continuously?

Is it that we grow tired? No human activity can continue working without a break, and consequently pleasure also is not continuous, as it accompanies the exercise of a faculty. Also some things give pleasure when they are new but do not give similar pleasure later, for the same reason; at the outset the mind is stimulated and acts vigorously in regard to the object, just as in the case of sight when people fix their gaze on something very intently. Subsequently however the activity is not so vigorous, but relaxes; and this damps down the pleasure which the activity gives.

This moreover is ground for believing that pleasures vary in specific quality. We feel that different kinds of things must have a different sort of perfection; we see this both with natural objects like animals and trees and with the products of art such as a picture or a statue or a building or an implement. Similarly we feel that the thing which perfects one kind of activity must itself be of a different sort from that which perfects another kind. But the activities of the intellect are different in kind from those of the senses, and also differ among themselves. So also therefore do the pleasures that complete them. . . .

8. The Rationally Ordered Activity That Constitutes Happiness Is of Two Kinds: The Practical and the Purely Intellectual or Scientific. Rational Practical Activity Consists in the Choice of the Mean, As Determined By a Man with Practical Wisdom.

In the case of every whole that is divisible into parts, it is possible to take a larger or a smaller share of it, or an equal share; and those amounts may be measured either in relation to the thing itself or in relation to us. I mean that whereas the middle of an object is the point equally distant from each of its extremes, which is one and the same for everybody, the medium quantity in its relation to us is the amount that is not excessive and not deficient, and this is not the same for everybody. For instance, if ten is many and two is few, to take the actual middle amount between them gives six (because 6 is the arithmetic mean between 2 and 10: $6 - 2 = 10 - 6$); but a medium quantity relative to us cannot be arrived at in this same way. For instance, supposing that for an athlete in training ten pounds of food is too large a ration and two pounds too small, the trainer will not necessarily advise six pounds, as possibly that will be too large or too small an allowance for the particular person—a small ration for a Milo but a large one for a novice in athletics; and the same applies to the amount of running or wrestling prescribed in training. This is how every expert avoids excess and deficiency and adopts the middle amount—not the exact half of the object he is dealing with, but a medium quantity in relation to the person concerned.

Such then is the manner in which every kind of skill operates successfully, by looking to the middle point and making its products conform with it. This accounts for the remark commonly made about successful productions, that you cannot take anything away from them or add anything to them. The implication is that excess and deficiency impair excellence, and a middle quantity secures it. If then we are right in saying that good craftsmen when at work keep their eyes fixed on a middle point, and if virtue, no less than nature herself, surpasses all the arts and crafts in accuracy and excellence, it follows that excellence will be the faculty of hitting a middle point. I refer to moral excellence or virtue; and this is concerned with emotions and actions, in which it is possible to have excess, or deficiency, or a medium amount. For instance you can feel either more or less than a moderate amount of fear and boldness, and of desire and anger and pity, and of pleasant or painful emotions generally; and in both cases the feelings will be wrong. But to feel these emotions at the right time and on the right occasion and towards the right people and for the right motives and in the right manner is a middle course, and the best course; and this is the mark of goodness. And similarly there is excess and deficiency or a middle amount in the case of actions. Now it is with emotions and actions that virtue is concerned; excess and deficiency in them are wrong, and a middle amount receives praise and achieves success, both of which are marks of virtue. It follows that virtue is a sort of middle state, in the sense that it aims at the middle.

Moreover, though it is possible to go wrong in many ways (according to the conjecture of the Pythagorean school evil is a property of the infinite and good of the finite), it is only possible to go right in one way:

Goodness is one, but badness manifold.

This is why to go wrong is easy but to go right difficult; it is easy to miss the target but difficult to hit it. Here then is another reason why vice is a matter of excess and deficiency and virtue a middle state.

It follows that virtue is a fixed quality of the will, consisting essentially in a middle state—middle in relation to ourselves, and as determined by principle, by the standard that a man of practical wisdom would apply. And it is a middle state between two vices, one of excess and one of deficiency: and this in view of the fact that vices either exceed or fall short of the right amount in emotions or actions, whereas virtue ascertains the mean and chooses that. Consequently while in its essence and by the principle defining its fundamental nature virtue is a middle state, in point of excellence and rightness it is an extreme.

But not every action or every emotion admits of a middle state: the very names of some of them suggest wickedness—for instance spite, shamelessness, envy, and among actions, adultery, theft, murder; all of these and similar emotions and actions are blamed as being wicked intrinsically and not merely when practised to excess or insufficiently. Consequently it is not possible ever to feel or commit them rightly: they are always wrong, nor are the qualifications "well" or "ill" applicable to them—for instance, you cannot commit adultery with the right woman and at the right time and in the right place: the mere commission of adultery with any woman anywhere at any time is an offence. Similarly, it is equally erroneous to think that there can be a middle amount and an excess and a deficiency of injustice or cowardice or self-indulgence, as that would mean that you can have a medium quantity of excess and deficiency or too much excess or too little deficiency. So just as there is no such thing as an excess or a deficiency of self-control and courage, because in these the middle is in a sense the top point, so there can be no middle amount or excess or deficiency of self-indulgence or cowardice, but actions of that sort however committed are an offence. There is no such thing as a medium amount of excess or deficiency, nor an excessive or insufficient amount of observance of a mean.

It is not enough, however, merely to give a general definition of moral goodness; it is necessary to show how our definition applies to particular virtues. In theories of conduct although general principles have a wider application, particular rules are more accurate, inasmuch as actual conduct deals with particular cases, and theory must be in agreement with these. Let us then take the particular virtues and vices from the diagram.

The middle state as regards fear and boldness is courage. Excessive fearlessness has no name (as is the case with many types of character); excessive boldness is called rashness, and excessive fear and insufficient boldness cowardice.

In regard to pleasure, and.in a less degree to pain, the middle state is self-control, and the excess self-indulgence. Persons deficient in sensibility to pleasure are scarcely to be found, so that this class has no recognized name; they may however be called insensitive.

The middle disposition in respect of giving and getting money is liberality; the excess and the deficiency are extravagance and meanness, both of these vices in opposite ways displaying both excess and deficiency —the extravagant man exceeds in spending money and is deficient in acquiring it, and the mean man exceeds in acquiring money but is deficient in spending it.

There are also other dispositions in regard to money—the middle state called munificence (which is not the same as liberality, as munificence is concerned with large sums of money whereas liberality is displayed in dealing with minor amounts), the excess which is tasteless vulgarity and the deficiency shabbiness in the use of money. . . .

9. The Pleasure of Virtuous Activity Is Better, Indeed in a Sense More Real, Than the Pleasure of Bad Activity.

Activities differ in moral value. Some are to be adopted, others to be avoided, and others are neutral. And the same is the case with the sort of pleasure they afford, as every activity has a special kind of pleasure connected with it. The pleasure of doing a worthy action is morally good and that of doing a base action is morally evil: in fact even to desire what is honourable is praiseworthy and to desire what is disgraceful is reprehensible; but the pleasures contained in our activities are more intimately connected with them than are the desires which prompt them: these are both separate in time and distinct in nature from the activities themselves, whereas the pleasures are closely united with them, and indeed they are so closely linked together as to make it difficult to distinguish the pleasure of doing a thing from the action itself. Nevertheless we must not regard pleasure as actually identical with the sensation or the thought which it accompanies—that would be absurd; although as they occur simultaneously, some people suppose that they are the same thing.

But we hold that in all such matters the thing really is what it appears to be to the good man. And if this rule is sound, as it is generally taken to be, and if the standard of everything is goodness or the good man as such, then the things that appear to him to be pleasures will be real pleasures and the things that he enjoys will be really pleasant. Nor need it surprise us if things which the good man dislikes seem pleasant to some people. Human nature is liable to many corruptions and perversions, and the things referred to are not really pleasant but only pleasant to people who are in a condition to fancy them to be pleasant. It is clear therefore that pleasures which are admittedly disgraceful cannot properly be called pleasant at all, but only pleasant to a corrupt taste.

10. Since the Intellect Is the Highest Part of Human Nature, Contemplation Must Be the Most Perfect Form of Happiness.

But if happiness is activity in conformity with virtue, it is reasonable to suppose that it is in conformity with the highest virtue, which must be the virtue belonging to the highest part of our nature. This is our intellect, or whatever part of us is held to be our natural ruler and guide, and to apprehend things noble and divine, as being itself divine, or nearest to the divine of all the parts of our nature. It will consequently be the activity of this part, in conformity with the virtue that belongs to it, which will constitute perfect happiness; and it has already been stated that this activity is the activity of contemplation.

This view may be accepted as in agreement both with the conclusions reached before and with the truth. Contemplation is the highest form of activity, because the intellect is the highest part of our nature, and the things apprehended by it are the highest objects of knowledge. Also it is the most continuous form of activity; we can go on reflecting more continuously than we can pursue any form of practical activity. Moreover we feel that happiness is bound to contain an element of pleasure; but the activity of philosophic contemplation is admittedly the most pleasurable of all the activities in conformity with virtue. Philosophy is thought to comprise pleasures of marvellous purity and permanence; and it is reasonable to hold that the enjoyment of knowledge already acquired is a more pleasant occupation than research directed to the acquirement of new knowledge. Also the activity of contemplation will be found to possess in the highest degree the quality designated self-sufficiency. It is of course true that the wise man as well as the just man and those possessing all the other virtues requires the necessities of life; but given a sufficient supply of these, whereas the just man needs people towards whom and in partnership with whom he may act justly, and similarly the self-controlled man and the brave man and the others, the wise man can practise contemplation by himself, and the wiser he is the better he can do this. No doubt he can do this better if he has fellow-workers, but nevertheless he is the most self-sufficient of all men.

It would appear that philosophic speculation is the only occupation that is pursued for its own sake. It produces no result beyond the act of contemplation itself, whereas from our practical pursuits we look to gain more or less advantage apart from the activities themselves.

Also happiness is thought to involve leisure. We practice business in order to gain leisure, and we go to war in order to secure peace. Thus the practical virtues are exhibited in the activities of politics or of warfare, and the actions connected with these seem to be essentially unleisurely. Military activities are entirely a business matter: nobody goes to war for choice, just in order to have a war, or takes deliberate steps to cause one. A man would be thought to be an absolutely bloodthirsty person if he made war on a friendly state in order to bring about battles and blood-shed. The life of active citizenship also is devoid of leisure; besides the actual business of politics it aims at winning posts of authority and hon-our, or at all events at securing happiness for oneself and one's friends— objects which are clearly not the same thing as mere political activity in itself. We see therefore that the occupations connected with politics and with war, although standing highest in nobility and importance among activities in conformity with the virtues, are devoid of leisure, and are not adopted for their own sakes but as means to attaining some objects outside themselves. But the exercise of the intellect in contemplation seems to be pre-eminent in point of leisure and to aim at no result exter-nal to itself; the pleasure it contains is inherent, and augments its ac-tivity. Consequently self-sufficiency and leisure, as well as such freedom from fatigue as lies within the capacity of human nature, and all the other advantages that we think of as belonging to complete bliss, appear to be contained in this activity. Therefore the activity of contemplation will be the perfect happiness of man,—provided that it continues through-out a complete lifetime, since in happiness there must be nothing in-complete.

The following consideration will also show that perfect happiness is found in contemplation. The gods as we conceive them are supremely blessed and happy. But what kind of actions must we attribute to them? Just actions? or would it not be absurd to imagine them as making con-tracts and repaying deposits and so on? Then shall we say brave actions —enduring alarms and facing dangers in a noble cause? Or liberal ac-tions? but who will receive their gifts? Moreover it is curious to think of the gods as having money or tokens of value. And what would be the meaning in their case of conduct exhibiting self-control? would it not be a poor compliment to the gods to say that they have no base appetites? If we went through the whole list, all the various forms of virtuous conduct would appear to be too trivial to be worthy of divine beings. Nevertheless everybody conceives of the gods as at all events alive, and therefore active,—they are certainly not imagined as always asleep, like Endymion. But take away action, and particularly productive action, and what remains for a living being except contemplation? It follows that the divine activity, since it is supremely blissful, will be the activity of con-templation. Therefore among human activities the only one most nearly akin to divine contemplation is the activity that contains the largest amount of happiness.

And it appears that one who lives the life of the mind, and cultivates his intellect and keeps that in its best condition, is the man whom the gods love best. It is the common belief that the gods pay heed to the affairs of men. If this is true, it is reasonable to assume that the gods take pleasure in what is best and most akin to themselves, namely man's intellect, and that they requite with benefits those who pay the highest respect to the life of the mind, because these men care for the things that are dear to themselves and these men act rightly and nobly. But manifestly all these attributes belong in the highest degree to the wise man. He therefore is the man dearest to the gods, and consequently it is he who will presumably be supremely happy. This is another indication that the philosopher is the happiest of mankind.

19. John Stuart Mill

John Stuart Mill (1806–1873) was the most important British philosopher of the nineteenth century. He made significant contributions to virtually every branch of philosophy.

A Form of Hedonism and Utilitarianism

Chapter I: General Remarks

There are few circumstances among those which make up the present condition of human knowledge, more unlike what might have been expected, or more significant of the backward state in which speculation on the most important subjects still lingers, than the little progress which has been made in the decision of the controversy respecting the criterion of right and wrong. From the dawn of philosophy, the question concerning the *summum bonum*, or, what is the same thing, concerning the foundation of morality, has been accounted the main problem in speculative thought, has occupied the most gifted intellects, and divided them into sects and schools, carrying on a vigorous warfare against one another. And after more than two thousand years the same discussions continue, philosophers are still ranged under the same contending banners, and neither thinkers nor mankind at large seem nearer to being unanimous on the subject, than when the youth Socrates listened to the old Protagoras, and asserted (if Plato's dialogue be grounded on a real

The following pages are taken from his *Utilitarianism*, first published in 1863.

conversation) the theory of utilitarianism against the popular morality of the so-called sophist.

It is true that similar confusion and uncertainty, and in some cases similar discordance, exist respecting the first principles of all the sciences, not excepting that which is deemed the most certain of them, mathematics; without much impairing, generally indeed without impairing at all, the trustworthiness of the conclusions of those sciences. An apparent anomaly, the explanation of which is, that the detailed doctrines of a science are not usually deduced from, nor depend for their evidence upon, what are called its first principles. Were it not so, there would be no science more precarious, or whose conclusions were more insufficiently made out, than algebra; which derives none of its certainty from what are commonly taught to learners as its elements, since these, as laid down by some of its most eminent teachers, are as full of fictions as English law, and of mysteries as theology. The truths which are ultimately accepted as the first principles of a science, are really the last results of metaphysical analysis, practised on the elementary notions with which the science is conversant; and their relation to the science is not that of foundations to an edifice, but of roots to a tree, which may perform their office equally well though they be never dug down to and exposed to light. But though in science the particular truths precede the general theory, the contrary might be expected to be the case with a practical art, such as morals or legislation. All action is for the sake of some end, the rules of action, it seems natural to suppose, must take their whole character and colour from the end to which they are subservient. When we engage in a pursuit, a clear and precise conception of what we are pursuing would seem to be the first thing we need, instead of the last we are to look forward to. A test of right and wrong must be the means, one would think, of ascertaining what is right or wrong, and not a consequence of having already ascertained it.

The difficulty is not avoided by having recourse to the popular theory of a natural faculty, a sense or instinct, informing us of right and wrong. For—besides that the existence of such a moral instinct is itself one of the matters in dispute—those believers in it who have any pretensions to philosophy, have been obliged to abandon the idea that it discerns what is right or wrong in the particular case in hand, as our other senses discern the sight or sound actually present. Our moral faculty, according to all those of its interpreters who are entitled to the name of thinkers, supplies us only with the general principles of moral judgments; it is a branch of our reason, not of our sensitive faculty; and must be looked to for the abstract doctrines of morality, not for perception of it in the concrete. The intuitive, no less than what may be termed the inductive, school of ethics, insists on the necessity of general laws. They both agree that the morality of an individual action is not a question of direct perception, but of the application of a law to an individual case. They recognise also, to a great extent, the same moral laws; but differ as to their evidence, and the source from which they derive their authority. According to the one opinion, the principles of morals are evident *a priori*, requiring nothing to command assent, except that the meaning of the

193

terms be understood. According to the other doctrine, right and wrong, as well as truth and falsehood, are questions of observation and experience. But both hold equally that morality must be deduced from principles; and the intuitive school affirm as strongly as the inductive, that there is a science of morals. Yet they seldom attempt to make out a list of the *a priori* principles which are to serve as the premises of the science; still more rarely do they make any effort to reduce those various principles to one first principle, or common ground of obligation. They either assume the ordinary precepts of morals as of *a priori* authority, or they lay down as the common groundwork of those maxims, some generality much less obviously authoritative than the maxims themselves, and which has never succeeded in gaining popular acceptance. Yet to support their pretensions there ought either to be some one fundamental principle or law, at the root of all morality, or if there be several, there should be a determinate order of precedence among them; and the one principle, or the rule for deciding between the various principles when they conflict, ought to be self-evident.

To inquire how far the bad effects of this deficiency have been mitigated in practice, or to what extent the moral beliefs of mankind have been vitiated or made uncertain by the absence of any distinct recognition of an ultimate standard, would imply a complete survey and criticism of past and present ethical doctrine. It would, however, be easy to show that whatever steadiness or consistency these moral beliefs have attained, has been mainly due to the tacit influence of a standard not recognised. Although the non-existence of an acknowledged first principle has made ethics not so much a guide as a consecration of men's actual sentiments, still, as men's sentiments, both of favour and of aversion, are greatly influenced by what they suppose to be the effects of things upon their happiness, the principle of utility, or as Bentham latterly called it, the greatest happiness principle, has had a large share in forming the moral doctrines even of those who most scornfully reject its authority. Nor is there any school of thought which refuses to admit that the influence of actions on happiness is a most material and even predominant consideration in many of the details of morals, however unwilling to acknowledge it as the fundamental principle of morality, and the source of moral obligation. I might go much further, and say that to all those *a priori* moralists who deem it necessary to argue at all, utilitarian arguments are indispensable. It is not my present purpose to criticise these thinkers; but I cannot help referring, for illustration, to a systematic treatise by one of the most illustrious of them, the *Metaphysics of Ethics*, by Kant. This remarkable man, whose system of thought will long remain one of the landmarks in the history of philosophical speculation, does, in the treatise in question, lay down a universal first principle as the origin and ground of moral obligation; it is this: "So act, that the rule on which thou actest would admit of being adopted as a law by all rational beings." But when he begins to deduce from this precept any of the actual duties of morality, he fails, almost grotesquely, to show that there would be any contradiction, any logical (not to say physical) impossibility, in the adoption by all rational beings of the most outrageously immoral rules of conduct. All he shows is that the *consequences* of their universal adoption would be such as no one would choose to incur.

On the present occasion, I shall, without further discussion of the other theories, attempt to contribute something towards the understanding and appreciation of the Utilitarian or Happiness theory, and towards such proof as it is susceptible of. It is evident that this cannot be proof in the ordinary and popular meaning of the term. Questions of ultimate ends are not amenable to direct proof. Whatever can be proved to be good, must be so by being shown to be a means to something admitted to be good without proof. The medical art is proved to be good by its conducing to health; but how is it possible to prove that health is good? The art of music is good, for the reason, among others, that it produces pleasure; but what proof is it possible to give that pleasure is good? If, then, it is asserted that there is a comprehensive formula, including all things which are in themselves good, and that whatever else is good, is not so as an end, but as a means, the formula may be accepted or rejected, but is not a subject of what is commonly understood by proof. We are not, however, to infer that its acceptance or rejection must depend on blind impulse, or arbitrary choice. There is a larger meaning of the word proof, in which this question is as amenable to it as any other of the disputed questions of philosophy. The subject is within the cognisance of the rational faculty; and neither does that faculty deal with it solely in the way of intuition. Considerations may be presented capable of determining the intellect either to give or withhold its assent to the doctrine; and this is equivalent to proof. . . .

Chapter II: What Utilitarianism Is

The creed which accepts as the foundation of morals, Utility, or the Greatest Happiness Principle, holds that actions are right in proportion as they tend to promote happiness, wrong as they tend to produce the reverse of happiness. By happiness is intended pleasure, and the absence of pain; by unhappiness, pain, and the privation of pleasure. To give a clear view of the moral standard set up by the theory, much more requires to be said; in particular, what things it includes in the ideas of pain and pleasure; and to what extent this is left an open question. But these supplementary explanations do not affect the theory of life on which this theory of morality is grounded—namely, that pleasure, and freedom from pain, are the only things desirable as ends; and that all desirable things (which are as numerous in the utilitarian as in any other scheme) are desirable either for the pleasure inherent in themselves, or as means to the promotion of pleasure and the prevention of pain.

Now, such a theory of life excites in many minds, and among them in some of the most estimable in feeling and purpose, inveterate dislike. To suppose that life has (as they express it) no higher end than pleasure —no better and nobler object of desire and pursuit—they designate as utterly mean and grovelling; as a doctrine worthy only of swine, to whom the followers of Epicurus were, at a very early period, contemptuously likened; and modern holders of the doctrine are occasionally made the subject of equally polite comparisons by its German, French, and English assailants.

When thus attacked, the Epicureans have always answered, that it is not they, but their accusers, who represent human nature in a degrading light; since the accusation supposes human beings to be capable of no pleasures except those of which swine are capable. If this supposition were true, the charge could not be gainsaid, but would then be no longer an imputation; for if the sources of pleasure were precisely the same to human beings and to swine, the rule of life which is good enough for the one would be good enough for the other. The comparison of the Epicurean life to that of beasts is felt as degrading, precisely because a beast's pleasures do not satisfy a human being's conceptions of happiness. Human beings have faculties more elevated than the animal appetites, and when once made conscious of them, do not regard anything as happiness which does not include their gratification. I do not, indeed, consider the Epicureans to have been by any means faultless in drawing out their scheme of consequences from the utilitarian principle. To do this in any sufficient manner, many Stoic, as well as Christian elements, require to be included. But there is no known Epicurean theory of life which does not assign to the pleasures of the intellect, of the feelings and imagination, and of the moral sentiments, a much higher value as pleasures than to those of mere sensation. It must be admitted, however, that utilitarian writers in general have placed the superiority of mental over bodily pleasures chiefly in the greater permanency, safety, un-costliness, etc., of the former—that is, in their circumstantial advantages rather than in their intrinsic nature. And on all these points utilitarians have fully proved their case; but they might have taken the other, and, as it may be called, higher ground, with entire consistency. It is quite compatible with the principle of utility to recognise the fact, that some *kinds* of pleasure are more desirable and more valuable than others. It would be absurd that while, in estimating all other things, quality is considered as well as quantity, the estimation of pleasures should be supposed to depend on quantity alone.

If I am asked, what I mean by difference of quality in pleasures, or what makes one pleasure more valuable than another, merely as a pleasure, except its being greater in amount, there is but one possible answer. Of two pleasures, if there be one to which all or almost all who have experience of both give a decided preference, irrespective of any feeling of moral obligation to prefer it, that is the more desirable pleasure. If one of the two is, by those who are competently acquainted with both, placed so far above the other that they prefer it, even though knowing it to be attended with a greater amount of discontent, and would not resign it for any quantity of the other pleasure which their nature is capable of, we are justified in ascribing to the preferred enjoyment a superiority in quality, so far outweighing quantity as to render it, in comparison, of small account.

Now it is an unquestionable fact that those who are equally ac-quainted with, and equally capable of appreciating and enjoying, both, do give a most marked preference to the manner of existence which employs their higher faculties. Few human creatures would consent to be changed into any of the lower animals, for a promise of the fullest allowance of a beast's pleasures; no intelligent human being would consent to be a fool, no instructed person would be an ignoramus, no person of feeling and conscience would be selfish and base, even though they should be persuaded that the fool, the dunce, or the rascal is better satisfied with his lot than they are with theirs. They would not resign what they possess more than he for the most complete satisfaction of all the desires which they have in common with him. If they ever fancy they would, it is only in cases of unhappiness so extreme, that to escape from it they would exchange their lot for almost any other, however undesirable in their own eyes. A being of higher faculties requires more to make him happy, is capable probably of more acute suffering, and certainly accessible to it at more points, than one of an inferior type; but in spite of these liabilities, he can never really wish to sink into what he feels to be a lower grade of existence. We may give what ex-planation we please of this unwillingness; we may attribute it to pride, a name which is given indiscriminately to some of the most and to some of the least estimable feelings of which mankind are capable: we may refer it to the love of liberty and personal independence, an appeal to which was with the Stoics one of the most effective means for the inculca-tion of it; to the love of power, or to the love of excitement, both of which do really enter into and contribute to it: but its most appropriate appellation is a sense of dignity, which all human beings possess in one form or other, and in some, though by no means in exact, proportion to their higher faculties, and which is so essential a part of the happiness of those in whom it is strong, that nothing which conflicts with it could be, otherwise than momentarily, an object of desire to them. Whoever supposes that this preference takes place at a sacrifice of happiness— that the superior being, in anything like equal circumstances, is not hap-pier than the inferior—confounds the two very different ideas, of hap-piness, and content. It is indisputable that the being whose capacities of enjoyment are low, has the greatest chance of having them fully satisfied; and a highly endowed being will always feel that any happiness which he can look for, as the world is constituted, is imperfect. But he can learn to bear its imperfections, if they are at all bearable; and they will not make him envy the being who is indeed unconscious of the imperfections, but only because he feels not at all the good which those imperfections qualify. It is better to be a human being dissatisfied than a pig satisfied; better to be Socrates dissatisfied than a fool satisfied. And if the fool, or the pig, are of a different opinion, it is because they only know their own side of the question. The other party to the com-parison knows both sides. . . .

According to the Greatest Happiness Principle, as above explained, the ultimate end, with reference to and for the sake of which all other things are desirable (whether we are considering our own good or that of other people), is an existence exempt as far as possible from pain, and as rich as possible in enjoyments, both in point of quantity and quality; the test of quality, and the rule for measuring it against quantity, being the preference felt by those who in their opportunities of experience, to which must be added their habits of self-consciousness and self-observation, are best furnished with the means of comparison. This, being, according to the utilitarian opinion, the end of human action, is necessarily also the standard of morality; which may accordingly be defined, the rules and precepts for human conduct, by the observance of which an existence such as has been described might be, to the greatest extent possible, secured to all mankind; and not to them only, but, so far as the nature of things admits, to the whole sentient creation.

Against this doctrine, however, arises another class of objectors, who say that happiness, in any form, cannot be the rational purpose of human life and action; because, in the first place, it is unattainable: and they contemptuously ask, what right hast thou to be happy? a question which Mr. Carlyle clenches by the addition, What right, a short time ago, hadst thou even *to be?* Next, they say, that men can do *without* happiness; that all noble human beings have felt this, and could not have become noble but by learning the lesson of Entsagen, or renunciation; which lesson, thoroughly learnt and submitted to, they affirm to be the beginning and necessary condition of all virtue.

The first of these objections would go to the root of the matter were it well founded; for if no happiness is to be had at all by human beings, the attainment of it cannot be the end of morality, or of any rational conduct. Though, even in that case, something might still be said for the utilitarian theory; since utility includes not solely the pursuit of happiness, but the prevention or mitigation of unhappiness; and if the former aim be chimerical, there will be all the greater scope and more imperative need for the latter, so long at least as mankind think fit to live, and do not take refuge in the simultaneous act of suicide recommended under certain conditions by Novalis. When, however, it is thus positively asserted to be impossible that human life should be happy, the assertion, if not something like a verbal quibble, is at least an exaggeration. If by happiness he meant a continuity of highly pleasurable excitement, it is evident enough that this is impossible. A state of exalted pleasure lasts only moments, or in some cases, and with some intermissions, hours or days, and is the occasional brilliant flash of enjoyment, not its permanent and steady flame. Of this the philosophers who have taught that happiness is the end of life were as fully aware as those who taunt them. The happiness which they meant was not a life of rapture; but moments of such, in an existence made up of few and transitory pains, many and various pleasures, with a decided predominance of the active over the passive, and having as the foundation of the whole, not to expect more from life than it is capable of bestowing. A life thus composed, to those who have been fortunate enough to obtain it, has always appeared worthy of the name of happiness. And such an existence is even now the lot of many, during some considerable portion of their lives. The present wretched education, and wretched social arrangements, are the only real hindrance to its being attainable by almost all.

The objectors perhaps may doubt whether human beings, if taught to consider happiness as the end of life, would be satisfied with such a moderate share of it. But great numbers of mankind have been satisfied with much less. The main constituents of a satisfied life appear to be two, either of which by itself is often found sufficient for the purpose: tranquillity, and excitement. With much tranquillity, many find that they can be content with very little pleasure: with much excitement, many can reconcile themselves to a considerable quantity of pain. There is assuredly no inherent impossibility in enabling even the mass of mankind to unite both; since the two are so far from being incompatible that they are in natural alliance, the prolongation of either being a preparation for, and exciting a wish for, the other. It is only those in whom indolence amounts to a vice, that do not desire excitement after an interval of repose: it is only those in whom the need of excitement is a disease, that feel the tranquillity which follows excitement dull and insipid, instead of pleasurable in direct proportion to the excitement which preceded it. When people who are tolerably fortunate in their outward lot do not find in life sufficient enjoyment to make it valuable to them, the cause generally is, caring for nobody but themselves. To those who have neither public nor private affections, the excitements of life are much curtailed, and in any case dwindle in value as the time approaches when all selfish interests must be terminated by death: while those who leave after them objects of personal affection, and especially those who have also cultivated a fellow-feeling with the collective interests of mankind, retain as lively an interest in life on the eve of death as in the vigour of youth and health. Next to selfishness, the principal cause which makes life unsatisfactory is want of mental cultivation. A cultivated mind—I do not mean that of a philosopher, but any mind to which the fountains of knowledge have been opened, and which has been taught, in any tolerable degree, to exercise its faculties—finds sources of inexhaustible interest in all that surrounds it; in the objects of nature, the achievements of art, the imaginations of poetry, the incidents of history, the ways of mankind, past and present, and their prospects in the future. It is possible, indeed, to become indifferent to all this, and that too without having exhausted a thousandth part of it; but only when one has had from the beginning no moral or human interest in these things, and has sought in them only the gratification of curiosity. . . .

And this leads to the true estimation of what is said by the objectors concerning the possibility, and the obligation, of learning to do without happiness. Unquestionably it is possible to do without happiness; it is done involuntarily by nineteen-twentieths of mankind, even in those parts of our present world which are deep in barbarism; and it often has to be done voluntarily by the hero or the martyr, for the sake of something which he prizes more than his individual happiness. But this something, what is it, unless the happiness of others, or some of the requisites of happiness? It is noble to be capable of resigning entirely one's own portion of happiness, or chances of it: but, after all, this self-sacrifice must be for some end; it is not its own end; and if we are told that its end is not happiness, but virtue, which is better than happiness, I ask, would the sacrifice be made if the hero or martyr did not believe that it would earn for others immunity from similar sacrifices? Would it be made if he thought that his renunciation of happiness for himself would produce no fruit for any of his fellow creatures, but to make their lot like his, and place them also in the condition of persons who have renounced happiness? All honour to those who can abnegate for themselves the personal enjoyment of life, when by such renunciation they contribute worthily to increase the amount of happiness in the world; but he who does it, or professes to do it, for any other purpose, is no more deserving of admiration than the ascetic mounted on his pillar. He may be an inspiriting proof of what men *can* do, but assuredly not an example of what they *should*.

Though it is only in a very imperfect state of the world's arrangements that any one can best serve the happiness of others by the absolute sacrifice of his own, yet so long as the world is in that imperfect state, I fully acknowledge that the readiness to make such a sacrifice is the highest virtue which can be found in man. I will add, that in this condition of the world, paradoxical as the assertion may be, the conscious ability to do without happiness gives the best prospect of realising such happiness as is attainable. For nothing except that consciousness can raise a person above the chances of life, by making him feel that, let fate and fortune do their worst, they have not power to subdue him: which, once felt, frees him from excess of anxiety concerning the evils of life, and enables him, like many a Stoic in the worst times of the Roman Empire, to cultivate in tranquillity the sources of satisfaction accessible to him, without concerning himself about the uncertainty of their duration, any more than about their inevitable end.

Meanwhile, let utilitarians never cease to claim the morality of self-devotion as a possession which belongs by as good a right to them, as either to the Stoic or to the Transcendentalist. The utilitarian morality does recognise in human beings the power of sacrificing their own greatest good for the good of others. It only refuses to admit that the sacrifice is itself a good. A sacrifice which does not increase, or tend to increase, the sum total of happiness, it considers as wasted. The only self-renunciation which it applauds, is devotion to the happiness, or to some of the means of happiness, of others; either of mankind collectively, or of individuals within the limits imposed by the collective interests of mankind.

I must again repeat, what the assailants of utilitarianism seldom have the justice to acknowledge, that the happiness which forms the utilitarian standard of what is right in conduct, is not the agent's own happiness, but that of all concerned. As between his own happiness and that of others, utilitarianism requires him to be as strictly impartial as a disinterested and benevolent spectator. In the golden rule of Jesus of Nazareth, we read the complete spirit of the ethics of utility. To do as you would be done by, and to love your neighbour as yourself, constitute the ideal perfection of utilitarian morality. As the means of making the nearest approach to this ideal, utility would enjoin, first, that laws and social arrangements should place the happiness, or (as speaking practically it may be called) the interest, of every individual, as nearly as possible in harmony with the interest of the whole; and secondly, that education and opinion, which have so vast a power over human character, should so use that power as to establish in the mind of every individual an indissoluble association between his own happiness and the good of the whole; especially between his own happiness and the practice of such modes of conduct, negative and positive, as regard for the universal happiness prescribes; so that not only he may be unable to conceive the possibility of happiness to himself, consistently with conduct opposed to the general good, but also that a direct impulse to promote the general good may be in every individual one of the habitual motives of action, and the sentiments connected therewith may fill a large and prominent place in every human being's sentient existence. If the impugners of the utilitarian morality represented it to their own minds in this its true character, I know not what recommendation possessed by any other morality they could possibly affirm to be wanting to it; what more beautiful or more exalted developments of human nature any other ethical system can be supposed to foster, or what springs of action, not accessible to the utilitarian, such systems rely on for giving effect to their mandates.

The objectors to utilitarianism cannot always be charged with representing it in a discreditable light. On the contrary, those among them who entertain anything like a just idea of its disinterested character, sometimes find fault with its standard as being too high for humanity. They say it is exacting too much to require that people shall always act from the inducement of promoting the general interests of society. But this is to mistake the very meaning of a standard of morals, and confound the rule of action with the motive of it. It is the business of ethics to tell us what are our duties, or by what test we may know them; but no system of ethics requires that the sole motive of all we do shall be a feeling of duty; on the contrary, ninety-nine hundredths of all our actions are done from other motives, and rightly so done, if the rule of duty does not condemn them. It is the more unjust to utilitarianism that this particular misapprehension should be made a ground of objection to it, inasmuch as utilitarian moralists have gone beyond almost all others in affirming that the motive has nothing to do with the morality of the action, though much with the worth of the agent. He who saves a fellow creature from drowning does what is morally right, whether his motive be duty, or the hope of being paid for his trouble; he who betrays the friend that trusts him, is guilty of a crime, even if his object be to serve another friend to whom he is under greater obligations. But to speak only of actions done from the motive of duty, and in direct obedience to principle: it is a misapprehension of the utilitarian mode of thought, to conceive it as implying that people should fix their minds upon so wide a generality as the world, or society at large. The great majority of good actions are intended not for the benefit of the world, but for that of individuals, of which the good of the world is made up; and the thoughts of the most virtuous man need not on these occasions travel beyond the particular persons concerned, except so far as is necessary to assure himself that in benefiting them he is not violating the rights, that is, the legitimate and authorised expectations, of any one else. The multiplication of happiness is, according to the utilitarian ethics, the object of virtue: the occasions on which any person (except one in a thousand) has it in his power to do this on an extended scale, in other words to be a public benefactor, are but exceptional; and on these occasions alone is he called on to consider public utility; in every other case, private utility, the interest or happiness of some few persons, is all he has to attend to. Those alone the influence of whose actions extends to society in general, need concern themselves habitually about so large an object. In the case of abstinences indeed—of things which people forbear to do from moral considerations, though the consequences in the particular case might be beneficial—it would be unworthy of an intelligent agent not to be consciously aware that the action is of a class which, if practised generally, would be generally injurious, and that this is the ground of the obligation to abstain from it. The amount of regard for the public interest implied in this recognition, is no greater than is demanded by every system of morals, for they all enjoin to abstain from whatever is manifestly pernicious to society. . . .

Again, Utility is often summarily stigmatised as an immoral doctrine by giving it the name of Expediency, and taking advantage of the popular use of that term to contrast it with Principle. But the Expedient, in the sense in which it is opposed to the Right, generally means that which is expedient for the particular interest of the agent himself; as when a minister sacrifices the interests of his country to keep himself in place. When it means anything better than this, it means that which is expedient for some immediate object, some temporary purpose, but which violates a rule whose observance is expedient in a much higher degree. The Expedient, in this sense, instead of being the same thing with the useful, is a branch of the hurtful. Thus, it would often be expedient, for the purpose of getting over some momentary embarrassment, or attaining some object immediately useful to ourselves or others, to tell a lie. But inasmuch as the cultivation in ourselves of a sensitive feeling on the subject of veracity, is one of the most useful, and the enfeeblement of that feeling one of the most hurtful, things to which our conduct can be instrumental; and inasmuch as any, even unintentional, deviation from truth, does that much towards weakening the trustworthiness of human assertion, which is not only the principal support of all present social well-being, but the insufficiency of which does more than any one thing that can be named to keep back civilisation, virtue, everything on which human happiness on the largest scale depends; we feel that the violation, for a present advantage, of a rule of such transcendant expediency, is not expedient, and that he who, for the sake of a convenience to himself or to some other individual, does what depends on him to deprive mankind of the good, and inflict upon them the evil, involved in the greater or less reliance which they can place in each other's word, acts the part of one of their worst enemies. Yet that even this rule, sacred as it is, admits of possible exceptions, is acknowledged by all moralists; the chief of which is when the withholding of some fact (as of information from a malefactor, or of bad news from a person dangerously ill) would save an individual (especially an individual other than oneself) from great and unmerited evil, and when the withholding can only be effected by denial. But in order that the exception may not extend itself beyond the need, and may have the least possible effect in weakening reliance on veracity, it ought to be recognised, and, if possible, its limits defined; and if the principle of utility is good for anything, it must be good for weighing these conflicting utilities against one another, and marking out the region within which one or the other preponderates.

Again, defenders of utility often find themselves called upon to reply to such objections as this—that there is not time, previous to action, for calculating and weighing the effects of any line of conduct on the general happiness. This is exactly as if any one were to say that it is impossible to guide our conduct by Christianity, because there is not time, on every occasion on which anything has to be done, to read through the Old and New Testaments. The answer to the objection is, that there has been ample time, namely, the whole past duration of the human species. During all that time, mankind have been learning by experience the tendencies of actions; on which experience all the prudence, as well as all the morality of life, are dependent. People talk as if the commencement of this course of experience had hitherto been put off, and as if, at the moment when some man feels tempted to meddle with the property or life of another, he had to begin considering for the first time whether murder and theft are injurious to human happiness. Even then I do not think that he would find the question very puzzling; but, at all events, the matter is now done to his hand. It is truly a whimsical supposition that, if mankind were agreed to considering utility to be the test of morality, they would remain without any agreement as to what *is* useful, and would take no measures for having their notions on the subject taught to the young, and enforced by law and opinion. There is no difficulty in proving any ethical standard whatever to work ill, if we suppose universal idiocy to be conjoined with it; but on any hypothesis short of that, mankind must by this time have acquired positive beliefs as to the effects of some actions on their happiness; and the beliefs which have thus come down are the rules of morality for the multitude, and for the philosopher until he has succeeded in finding better. That philosophers might easily do this, even now, on many subjects; that the received code of ethics is by no means of divine right; and that mankind have still much to learn as to the effects of actions on the general happiness, I admit, or rather, earnestly maintain. The corollaries from the principle of utility, like the precepts of every practical art, admit of indefinite improvement, and, in a progressive state of the human mind, their improvement is perpetually going on. But to consider the rules of morality as improvable, is one thing; to pass over the intermediate generalisations entirely, and endeavour to test each individual action directly by the first principle, is another. It is a strange notion that the acknowledgment of a first principle is inconsistent with the admission of secondary ones. To inform a traveller respecting the place of his ultimate destination, is not to forbid the use of landmarks and direction-posts on the way. The proposition that happiness is the end and aim of morality, does not mean that no road ought to be laid down to that goal, or that persons going thither should not be advised to take one direction rather than another. Men really ought to leave off talking a kind of nonsense on this subject, which they would neither talk nor listen to on other matters of practical concernment. Nobody argues that the art of navigation is not founded on astronomy, because sailors cannot wait to calculate the Nautical Almanack. Being rational creatures, they go to sea with it ready calculated; and all rational creatures go out upon the sea of life with their minds made up on the common questions of right and wrong, as well as on many of the far more difficult questions of wise and foolish. And this, as long as foresight is a human quality, it is to be presumed they will continue to do. Whatever we adopt as the fundamental principle of morality, we require subordinate principles to apply it by; the impossibility of doing without them, being common to all systems, can afford no argument against any one in particular; but gravely to argue as if no such secondary principles could be had, and as if mankind had remained till now, and always must remain, without drawing any general conclusions from the experience of human life, is as high a pitch, I think, as absurdity has ever reached in philosophical controversy.

The remainder of the stock arguments against utilitarianism mostly consist in laying to its charge the common infirmities of human nature, and the general difficulties which embarrass conscientious persons in shaping their course through life. We are told that a utilitarian will be apt to make his own particular case an exception to moral rules, and when under temptation, will see a utility in the breach of a rule, greater than he will see in its observance. But is utility the only creed which is able to furnish us with excuses for evil doing, and means of cheating our own conscience? They are afforded in abundance by all doctrines which recognise as a fact in morals the existence of conflicting considerations; which all doctrines do, that have been believed by sane persons. It is not the fault of any creed, but of the complicated nature of human affairs, that rules of conduct cannot be so framed as to require no exceptions, and that hardly any kind of action can safely be laid down as either always obligatory or always condemnable. There is no ethical creed which does not temper the rigidity of its laws, by giving a certain latitude, under the moral responsibility of the agent, for accommodation to peculiarities of circumstances; and under every creed, at the opening thus made, self-deception and dishonest casuistry get in. There exists no moral system under which there do not arise unequivocal cases of conflicting obligation. These are the real difficulties, the knotty points both in the theory of ethics, and in the conscientious guidance of personal conduct. They are overcome practically, with greater or with less success, according to the intellect and virtue of the individual; but it can hardly be pretended that any one will be the less qualified for dealing with them, from possessing an ultimate standard to which conflicting rights and duties can be referred. If utility is the ultimate source of moral obligations, utility may be invoked to decide between them when their demands are incompatible. Though the application of the standard may be difficult, it is better than none at all: while in other systems, the moral laws all claiming independent authority, there is no common umpire entitled to interfere between them; their claims to precedence one over another rest on little better than sophistry, and unless determined, as they generally are, by the unacknowledged influence of considerations of utility, afford a free scope for the action of personal desires and partialities. We must remember that only in these cases of conflict between secondary principles is it requisite that first principles should be appealed to. There is no case of moral obligation in which some secondary principle is not involved; and if only one, there can seldom be any real doubt which one it is, in the mind of any person by whom the principle itself is recognised.

Chapter IV: Of What Sort of Proof the Principle of Utility Is Susceptible

It has already been remarked, that questions of ultimate ends do not admit of proof, in the ordinary acceptation of the term. To be incapable of proof by reasoning is common to all first principles; to the first premises of our knowledge, as well as to those of our conduct. But the former, being matters of fact, may be the subject of a direct appeal to the faculties which judge of fact—namely, our senses, and our internal consciousness. Can an appeal be made to the same faculties on questions of practical ends? Or by what other faculty is cognisance taken of them?

Questions about ends are, in other words, questions what things are desirable. The utilitarian doctrine is, that happiness is desirable, and the only thing desirable, as an end; all other things being only desirable as means to that end. What ought to be required of this doctrine—what conditions is it requisite that the doctrine should fulfil—to make good its claim to be believed?

The only proof capable of being given that an object is visible, is that people actually see it. The only proof that a sound is audible, is that people hear it: and so of the other sources of our experience. In like manner, I apprehend, the sole evidence it is possible to produce that anything is desirable, is that people do actually desire it. If the end which the utilitarian doctrine proposes to itself were not, in theory and in practice, acknowledged to be an end, nothing could ever convince any person that it was so. No reason can be given why the general happiness is desirable, except that each person, so far as he believes it to be attainable, desires his own happiness. This, however, being a fact, we have not only all the proof which the case admits of, but all which it is possible to require, that happiness is a good: that each person's happiness is a good to that person, and the general happiness, therefore, a good to the aggregate of all persons. Happiness has made out its title as *one* of the ends of conduct, and consequently one of the criteria of morality.

But it has not, by this alone, proved itself to be the sole criterion. To do that, it would seem, by the same rule, necessary to show, not only that people desire happiness, but that they never desire anything else. Now it is palpable that they do desire things which, in common language, are decidedly distinguished from happiness. They desire, for example, virtue, and the absence of vice, no less really than pleasure and the absence of pain. The desire of virtue is not as universal, but it is as authentic a fact, as the desire of happiness. And hence the opponents of the utilitarian standard deem that they have a right to infer that there are other ends of human action besides happiness, and that happiness is not the standard of approbation and disapprobation.

But does the utilitarian doctrine deny that people desire virtue, or maintain that virtue is not a thing to be desired? The very reverse. It maintains not only that virtue is to be desired, but that it is to be desired disinterestedly, for itself. Whatever may be the opinion of utilitarian moralists as to the original conditions by which virtue is made virtue; however they may believe (as they do) that actions and dispositions are only virtuous because they promote another end than virtue; yet this being granted, and it having been decided, from considerations of this description, what *is* virtuous, they not only place virtue at the very head of the things which are good as means to the ultimate end, but they also recognise as a psychological fact the possibility of its being, to the individual, a good in itself, without looking to any end beyond it; and hold, that the mind is not in a right state, not in a state conformable to Utility, not in the state most conducive to the general happiness, unless it does love virtue in this manner—as a thing desirable in itself, even although, in the individual instance, it should not produce those other desirable consequences which it tends to produce, and on account of which it is held to be virtue. This opinion is not, in the smallest degree, a departure from the Happiness principle. The ingredients of happiness are very various, and each of them is desirable in itself, and not merely when considered as swelling an aggregate. The principle of utility does not mean that any given pleasure, as music, for instance, or any given exemption from pain, as for example health, is to be looked upon as means to a collective something termed happiness, and to be desired on that account. They are desired and desirable in and for themselves; besides being means, they are a part of the end. Virtue, according to the utilitarian doctrine, is not naturally and originally part of the end, but it is capable of becoming so; and in those who love it disinterestedly it has become so, and is desired and cherished, not as a means to happiness, but as a part of their happiness.

To illustrate this farther, we may remember that virtue is not the only thing, originally a means, and which if it were not a means to anything else, would be and remain indifferent, but which by association with what it is a means to, comes to be desired for itself, and that too with the utmost intensity. What, for example, shall we say of the love of

206

money? There is nothing originally more desirable about money than about any heap of glittering pebbles. Its worth is solely that of the things which it will buy; the desires for other things than itself, which it is a means of gratifying. Yet the love of money is not only one of the strongest moving forces of human life, but money is, in many cases, desired in and for itself; the desire to possess it is often stronger than the desire to use it, and goes on increasing when all the desires which point to ends beyond it, to be compassed by it, are falling off. It may, then, be said truly, that money is desired not for the sake of an end, but as part of the end. From being a means to happiness, it has come to be itself a principal ingredient of the individual's conception of happiness. The same may be said of the majority of the great objects of human life— power, for example, or fame; except that to each of these there is a certain amount of immediate pleasure annexed, which has at least the semblance of being naturally inherent in them; a thing which cannot be said of money. Still, however, the strongest natural attraction, both of power and of fame, is the immense aid they give to the attainment of our other wishes; and it is the strong association thus generated between them and all our objects of desire, which gives to the direct desire of them the intensity it often assumes, so as in some characters to surpass in strength all other desires. In these cases the means have become a part of the end, and a more important part of it than any of the things which they are means to. What was once desired as an instrument for the attainment of happiness, has come to be desired for its own sake. In being desired for its own sake it is, however, desired as *part* of happiness. The person is made, or thinks he would be made, happy by its mere possession; and is made unhappy by failure to obtain it. The desire of it is not a different thing from the desire of happiness, any more than the love of music, or the desire of health. They are included in happiness. They are some of the elements of which the desire of happiness is made up. Happiness is not an abstract idea, but a concrete whole; and these are some of its parts. And the utilitarian standard sanctions and approves their being so. Life would be a poor thing, very ill provided with sources of happiness, if there were not this provision of nature, by which things originally indifferent, but conducive to, or otherwise associated with, the satisfaction of our primitive desires, become in themselves sources of pleasure more valuable than the primitive pleasures, both in permanency, in the space of human existence that they are capable of covering, and even in intensity.

Virtue, according to the utilitarian conception, is a good of this description. There was no original desire of it, or motive to it, save its conduciveness to pleasure, and especially to protection from pain. But through the association thus formed, it may be felt a good in itself, and desired as such with as great intensity as any other good; and with this difference between it and the love of money, of power, or of fame, that all of these may, and often do, render the individual noxious to the other members of the society to which he belongs whereas there is nothing which makes him so much a blessing to them as the cultivation of the disinterested love of virtue. And consequently, the utilitarian standard, while it tolerates and approves those other acquired desires, up to the point beyond which they would be more injurious to the general happiness than promotive of it, enjoins and requires the cultivation of the love of virtue up to the greatest strength possible, as being above all things important to the general happiness.

It results from the preceding considerations, that there is in reality nothing desired except happiness. Whatever is desired otherwise than as a means to some end beyond itself, and ultimately to happiness, is desired as itself a part of happiness, and is not desired for itself until it has become so. Those who desire virtue for its own sake, desire it either because the consciousness of it is a pleasure, or because the consciousness of being without it is a pain, or for both reasons united; as in truth the pleasure and pain seldom exist separately, but almost always together, the same person feeling pleasure in the degree of virtue attained, and pain in not having attained more. If one of these gave him no pleasure, and the other no pain, he would not love or desire virtue, or would desire it only for the other benefits which it might produce to himself or to persons whom he cared for.

We have now, then, an answer to the question, of what sort of proof the principle of utility is susceptible. If the opinion which I have now stated is psychologically true—if human nature is so constituted as to desire nothing which is not either a part of happiness or a means of happiness, we can have no other proof, and we require no other, that these are the only things desirable. If so, happiness is the sole end of human action, and the promotion of it the test by which to judge of all human conduct; from whence it necessarily follows that it must be the criterion of morality, since a part is included in the whole.

And now to decide whether this is really so; whether mankind do desire nothing for itself but that which is a pleasure to them, or of which the absence is a pain; we have evidently arrived at a question of fact and experience, dependent, like all similar questions, upon evidence. It can only be determined by practised self-consciousness and self-observation, assisted by observation of others. I believe that these sources of evidence, impartially consulted, will declare that desiring a thing and finding it pleasant, aversion to it and thinking of it as painful, are phenomena entirely inseparable, or rather two parts of the same phenomenon; in strictness of language, two different modes of naming the same psychological fact: that to think of an object as desirable (unless for the sake of its consequences), and to think of it as pleasant, are one and the same thing; and that to desire anything, except in proportion as the idea of it is pleasant, is a physical and metaphysical impossibility.

So obvious does this appear to me, that I expect it will hardly be disputed: and the objections made will be, not that desire can possibly be directed to anything ultimately except pleasure and exemption from pain, but that the will is a different thing from desire, that a person of confirmed virtue, or any other person whose purposes are fixed, carries out his purposes without any thought of the pleasure he has in contemplating them, or expects to derive from their fulfilment; and persists in acting on them, even though these pleasures are much diminished, by changes in his character or decay of his passive sensibilities, or are outweighed by the pains which the pursuit of the purposes may bring upon him. All this I fully admit, and have stated it elsewhere, as positively and emphatically as any one. Will, the active phenomenon, is a different thing from desire, the state of passive sensibility, and though originally an offshoot from it, may in time take root and detach itself from the parent stock; so much so, that in the case of an habitual purpose, instead of willing the thing because we desire it, we often desire it only because we will it. This, however, is but an instance of that familiar fact, the power of habit, and is nowise confined to the case of virtuous actions. Many indifferent things, which men originally did from a motive of some sort, they continue to do from habit. Sometimes this is done unconsciously, the consciousness coming only after the action: at other times with conscious volition, but volition which has become habitual, and is put in operation by the force of habit, in opposition perhaps to the deliberate preference, as often happens with those who have contracted habits of vicious or hurtful indulgence. Third and last comes the case in which the habitual act of will in the individual instance is not in contradiction to the general intention prevailing at other times, but in fulfilment of it; as in the case of the person of confirmed virtue, and of all who pursue deliberately and consistently any determinate end. The distinction between will and desire thus understood is an authentic and highly important psychological fact; but the fact consists solely in this—that will, like all other parts of our constitution, is amenable to habit, and that we may will from habit what we no longer desire for itself, or desire only because we will it. It is not the less true that will, in the beginning, is entirely produced by desire; including in that term the repelling influence of pain as well as the attractive one of pleasure. Let us take into consideration, no longer the person who has a confirmed will to do right, but him in whom that virtuous will is still feeble, conquerable by temptation, and not to be fully relied on; by what means can it be strengthened? How can the will to be virtuous, where it does not exist in sufficient force, be implanted or awakened? Only by making the person *desire* virtue—by making him think of it in a pleasurable light, or of its absence in a painful one. It is by associating the doing right with pleasure, or the doing wrong with pain, or by eliciting and impressing and bringing home to the person's experience the pleasure naturally involved in the one or the pain in the other, that it is possible to call forth that will to be virtuous, which, when confirmed, acts without any thought of either pleasure or pain. Will is the child of desire, and passes out of the dominion of its parent only to come under that of habit. That which is the result of habit affords no presumption of being intrinsically good; and there would be no reason for wishing that the purpose of virtue should become independent of pleasure and pain, were it not that the influence of the pleasurable and painful associations which prompt to virtue is not sufficiently to be depended on for unerring constancy of action until it has acquired the support of habit. Both in feeling and in conduct, habit is the only thing which imparts certainty; and it is because of the importance to others of being able to rely absolutely on one's feelings and conduct, and to oneself of being able to rely on one's own, that the will to do right ought to be cultivated into this habitual independence. In other words, this state of the will is a means to good, not intrinsically a good; and does not contradict the doctrine that nothing is good to human beings but in so far as it is either itself pleasurable, or a means of attaining pleasure or averting pain.

But if this doctrine be true, the principle of utility is proved. Whether it is so or not, must now be left to the consideration of the thoughtful reader.

20. Friedrich Nietzsche

Friedrich Nietzsche (1844–1900) taught at the University of Basel. He was obviously something of a rebel against the values of his day.

A Form of Egoism

259

To refrain mutually from injury, from violence, from exploitation, and put one's will on a par with that of others: this may result in a certain rough sense in good conduct among individuals when the necessary conditions are given (namely, the actual similarity of the individuals in amount of force and degree of worth, and their co-relation within one organisation). As soon, however, as one wished to take this principle more generally, and if possible even as *the fundamental principle of society*, it would immediately disclose what it really is—namely, a Will to the *denial* of life, a principle of dissolution and decay. Here one must think profoundly to the very basis and resist all sentimental weakness: life itself is *essentially* appropriation, injury, conquest of the strange and weak, suppression, severity, obtrusion of peculiar forms, incorporation, and at the least, putting it mildest, exploitation;—but why should one forever use precisely these words on which for ages a disparaging purpose has been stamped? Even the organisation within which, as was previously supposed, the individuals treat each other as equal—it takes place in every healthy aristocracy—must itself, if it be a living and not

These excerpts are taken from his *Beyond Good and Evil*, first published in 1887, translated by Helen Zimmern, published by George Allen & Unwin Ltd., London. Reprinted by permission of George Allen & Unwin Ltd.

a dying organisation, do all that towards other bodies, which the individuals within it refrain from doing to each other: it will have to be the incarnated Will to Power, it will endeavour to grow, to gain ground, attract to itself and acquire ascendency—not owing to any morality or immorality, but because it *lives,* and because life *is* precisely Will to Power. On no point, however, is the ordinary consciousness of Europeans more unwilling to be corrected than on this matter; people now rave everywhere, even under the guise of science, about coming conditions of society in which "the exploiting character" is to be absent:—that sounds to my ears as if they promised to invent a mode of life which should refrain from all organic functions. "Exploitation" does not belong to a depraved, or imperfect and primitive society: it belongs to the *nature* of the living being as a primary organic function; it is a consequence of the intrinsic Will to Power, which is precisely the Will to Life.— Granting that as a theory this is a novelty—as a reality it is the *fundamental fact* of all history: let us be so far honest towards ourselves!

260

In a tour through the many finer and coarser moralities which have hitherto prevailed or still prevail on the earth, I found certain traits recurring regularly together, and connected with one another, until finally two primary types revealed themselves to me, and a radical distinction was brought to light. There is *master-morality* and *slave-morality;*—I would at once add, however, that in all higher and mixed civilisations, there are also attempts at the reconciliation of the two moralities; but one finds still oftener the confusion and mutual misunderstanding of them, indeed, sometimes their close juxtaposition— even in the same man, within one soul. The distinctions of moral values have either originated in a ruling caste, pleasantly conscious of being different from the ruled—or among the ruled class, the slaves and dependents of all sorts. In the first case, when it is the rulers who determine the conception "good," it is the exalted, proud disposition which is regarded as the distinguishing feature, and that which determines the order of rank. The noble type of man separates from himself the beings in whom the opposite of this exalted, proud disposition displays itself: he despises them. Let it at once be noted that in this first kind of morality the antithesis "good" and "bad" means practically the same as "noble" and "despicable";—the antithesis "good" and *"evil"* is of a different origin. The cowardly, the timid, the insignificant, and those thinking merely of narrow utility are despised; moreover, also, the distrustful, with their constrained glances, the self-abasing, the dog-like kind of men who let themselves be abused, the mendicant flatterers, and above all the liars:—it is a fundamental belief of all aristocrats that the common people are untruthful. "We truthful ones"—the nobility in ancient Greece called themselves. It is obvious that everywhere the designations of moral value were at first applied to *men,* and were only derivatively and at a later period applied to *actions;* it is a gross mistake, therefore, when historians of morals start questions like, "Why have sympathetic actions been praised?" The noble type of man regards *himself* as a determiner of values; he does not require to be approved of; he passes the judgment: "What is injurious to me is injurious in itself"; he knows that it is he himself only who confers honour on things; he is a *creator of values.* He honours whatever he recognises in himself: such morality is self-glorification. In the foreground there is the feeling of plenitude, of power, which seeks to overflow, the happiness of high tension, the consciousness of a wealth which would fain give and bestow:—the noble man also helps the unfortunate, but not—or scarcely—out of pity, but rather from an impulse generated by the super-abundance of power. The noble man honours in himself the powerful one, him also who has power over himself, who knows how to speak and how to keep silence, who takes pleasure in subjecting himself to severity and hardness, and has reverence for all that is severe and hard. "Wotan placed a hard heart in my breast," says an old Scandinavian Saga: it is thus rightly expressed from the soul of a proud Viking. Such a type of man is even proud of *not* being made for sympathy; the hero of the Saga therefore adds warningly: "He who has not a hard heart when young, will never have one." The noble and brave who think thus are the furthest removed from the morality which sees precisely in sympathy, or in acting for the good of others, or in *désintéressement*, the characteristic of the moral; faith in oneself, pride in oneself, a radical enmity and irony towards "selflessness," belong as definitely to noble morality, as do a careless scorn and precaution in presence of sympathy and the "warm heart."—It is the powerful who *know* how to honour, it is their art, their domain for invention. The profound reverence for age and for tradition—all law rests on this double reverence,—the belief and prejudice in favour of ancestors and unfavourable to newcomers, is typical in the morality of the powerful; and if, reversely, men of "modern ideas" believe almost instinctively in "progress" and the "future," and are more and more lacking in respect for old age, the ignoble origin of these "ideas" has complacently betrayed itself thereby. A morality of the ruling class, however, is more especially foreign and irritating to present-day taste in the sternness of its principle that one has duties only to one's equals; that one may act towards beings of a lower rank, towards all that is foreign, just as seems good to one, or "as the heart desires," and in any case "beyond good and evil": it is here that sympathy and similar sentiments can have a place. The ability and obligation to exercise prolonged gratitude and prolonged revenge—both only within the circle of equals,—artfulness in retaliation, *raffinement* of the idea in friendship, a certain necessity to have enemies (as outlets for the emotions of envy, quarrelsomeness, arrogance—in fact, in order to be a good *friend*): all these are typical characteristics of the noble morality, which, as has been pointed out, is not the morality of "modern ideas," and is therefore at present difficult to realise, and also to unearth and disclose.—It is otherwise with the second type of morality, *slave-morality*. Supposing that the abused, the oppressed, the suffering, the unemancipated, the weary, and those uncertain of themselves, should moralise, what will be the common ele-

213

ment in their moral estimates? Probably a pessimistic suspicion with regard to the entire situation of man will find expression, perhaps a
condemnation of man, together with his situation. The slave has an unfavourable eye for the virtues of the powerful; he has a scepticism and
distrust, a *refinement* of distrust of everything "good" that is there honoured—he would fain persuade himself that the very happiness there is
not genuine. On the other hand, *those* qualities which serve to alleviate
the existence of sufferers are brought into prominence and flooded with
light; it is here that sympathy, the kind, helping hand, the warm heart,
patience, diligence, humility, and friendliness attain to honour; for here
these are the most useful qualities, and almost the only means of supporting the burden of existence. Slave-morality is essentially the morality
of utility. Here is the seat of the origin of the famous antithesis "good"
and "evil":—power and dangerousness are assumed to reside in the evil,
a certain dreadfulness, subtlety, and strength, which do not admit of
being despised. According to slave-morality, therefore, the "evil" man
arouses fear; according to master-morality, it is precisely the "good" man
who arouses fear and seeks to arouse it, while the bad man is regarded
as the despicable being. The contrast attains its maximum when, in accordance with the logical consequences of slave-morality, a shade of de-
preciation—it may be slight and well-intentioned—at last attaches itself
to the "good" man of this morality; because, according to the servile
mode of thought, the good man must in any case be the *safe* man: he is
good-natured, easily deceived, perhaps a little stupid, *un bonhomme.*
Everywhere that slave-morality gains the ascendency, language shows a
tendency to approximate the significations of the words "good" and
"stupid."—A last fundamental difference: the desire for *freedom,* the
instinct for happiness and the refinements of the feeling of liberty belong
as necessarily to slave-morals and morality, as artifice and enthusiasm in
reverence and devotion are the regular symptoms of an aristocratic mode
of thinking and estimating.—Hence we can understand without further
detail why love *as a passion*—it is our European specialty—must absolutely be of noble origin; as is well known, its invention is due to the
Provençal poet-cavaliers, those brilliant, ingenious men of the *"gai saber,"*
to whom Europe owes so much, and almost owes itself.

262

A *species* originates, and a type becomes established and strong in the
long struggle with essentially constant *unfavourable* conditions. On the
other hand, it is known by the experience of breeders that species which
receive superabundant nourishment, and in general a surplus of protection and care, immediately tend in the most marked way to develop
variations, and are fertile in prodigies and monstrosities (also in monstrous vices). Now look at an aristocratic commonwealth, say an ancient
Greek *polis,* or Venice, as a voluntary or involuntary contrivance for the
purpose of *rearing* human beings; there are there men beside one another, thrown upon their own resources, who want to make their species

prevail, chiefly because they *must* prevail, or else run the terrible danger of being exterminated. The favour, the superabundance, the protection are there lacking under which variations are fostered; the species needs itself as species, as something which, precisely by virtue of its hardness, its uniformity, and simplicity of structure, can in general prevail and make itself permanent in constant struggle with its neighbours, or with rebellious or rebellion-threatening vassals. The most varied experience teaches it what are the qualities to which it principally owes the fact that it still exists, in spite of all gods and men, and has hitherto been victorious: these qualities it calls virtues, and these virtues alone it develops to maturity. It does so with severity, indeed it desires severity; every aristocratic morality is intolerant in the education of youth, in the control of women, in the marriage customs, in the relations of old and young, in the penal laws (which have an eye only for the degenerating): it counts intolerance itself among the virtues, under the name of "justice." A type with few, but very marked features, a species of severe, warlike, wisely silent, reserved and reticent men (and as such, with the most delicate sensibility for the charm and *nuances* of society) is thus established, unaffected by the vicissitudes of generations; the constant struggle with uniform *unfavourable* conditions is, as already remarked, the cause of a type becoming stable and hard. Finally, however, a happy state of things results, the enormous tension is relaxed; there are perhaps no more enemies among the neighbouring peoples, and the means of life, even of the enjoyment of life, are present in superabundance. With one stroke the bond and constraint of the old discipline severs: it is no longer regarded as necessary, as a condition of existence—if it would continue, it can only do so as a form of *luxury*, as an archaïsing *taste*. Variations, whether they be deviations (into the higher, finer, and rare), or deteriorations and monstrosities, appear suddenly on the scene in the greatest exuberance and splendour; the individual dares to be individual and detach himself. At this turning-point of history there manifest themselves, side by side, and often mixed and entangled together, a magnificent, manifold, virgin-forest-like up-growth and up-striving, a kind of *tropical tempo* in the rivalry of growth, and an extraordinary decay and self-destruction, owing to the savagely opposing and seemingly exploding egoisms, which strive with one another "for sun and light," and can no longer assign any limit, restraint, or forbearance for themselves by means of the hitherto existing morality. It was this morality itself which piled up the strength so enormously, which bent the bow in so threatening a manner:—it is now "out of date," it is getting "out of date." The dangerous and disquieting point has been reached when the greater, more manifold, more comprehensive life *is lived beyond* the old morality; the "individual" stands out, and is obliged to have recourse to his own law-giving, his own arts and artifices for self-preservation, self-elevation, and self-deliverance. Nothing but new "Whys," nothing but new "Hows," no common formulas any longer, misunderstanding and disregard in league with each other, decay, deterioration, and the loftiest desires frightfully entangled, the genius of the race overflowing from all the cornucopias of good and bad, a portentous simultaneousness of Spring and Autumn, full of new charms and mysteries peculiar to the fresh, still inexhausted, still unwearied corruption. Danger is again present, the mother of morality, great danger; this time shifted into the individual, into the neighbour and friend, into the street, into their own child, into their own heart, into all the most personal and secret recesses of their desires and volitions. What will the moral philosophers who appear at this time have to preach? They discover, these sharp onlookers and loafers, that the end is quickly approaching, that everything around them decays and produces decay, that nothing will endure until the day after tomorrow, except one species of man, the incurably *mediocre*. The mediocre alone have a prospect of continuing and propagating themselves—they will be the men of the future, the sole survivors; "be like them! become mediocre!" is now the only morality which has still a significance, which still obtains a hearing.— But it is difficult to preach this morality of mediocrity! it can never avow what it is and what it desires! it has to talk of moderation and dignity and duty and brotherly love—it will have difficuity *in concealing its irony!*

265

At the risk of displeasing innocent ears, I submit that egoism belongs to the essence of a noble soul, I mean the unalterable belief that to a being such as "we," other beings must naturally be in subjection, and have to sacrifice themselves. The noble soul accepts the fact of his egoism without question, and also without consciousness of harshness, constraint, or arbitrariness therein, but rather as something that may have its basis in the primary law of things:—if he sought a designation for it he would say: "It is justice itself." He acknowledges under certain circumstances, which made him hesitate at first, that there are other equally privileged ones; as soon as he has settled this question of rank, he moves among those equals and equally privileged ones with the same assurance, as regards modesty and delicate respect, which he enjoys in intercourse with himself—in accordance with an innate heavenly mechanism which all the stars understand. It is an *additional* instance of his egoism, this artfulness and self-limitation in intercourse with his equals—every star is a similar egoist; he honours *himself* in them, and in the rights which he concedes to them, he has no doubt that the exchange of honours and rights, as the *essence* of all intercourse, belongs also to the natural condition of things. The noble soul gives as he takes, prompted by the passionate and sensitive instinct of requital, which is at the root of his nature. The notion of "favour" has, *inter pares*, neither significance nor good repute; there may be a sublime way of letting gifts as it were light upon one from above, and of drinking them thirstily like dew-drops; but for those arts and displays the noble soul has no aptitude. His egoism hinders him here: in general, he looks "aloft" unwillingly—he looks either *forward*, horizontally and deliberately, or downwards—*he knows that he is on a height.*

21. Brian Medlin

Brian Medlin was a Fellow in New College, Oxford.

Egoism Claimed Inconsistent

I believe that it is now pretty generally accepted by professional philosophers that ultimate ethical principles must be arbitrary. One cannot derive conclusions about what should be merely from accounts of what is the case; one cannot decide how people ought to behave merely from one's knowledge of how they do behave. To arrive at a conclusion in ethics one must have at least one ethical premiss. This premiss, if it be in turn a conclusion, must be the conclusion of an argument containing at least one ethical premiss. And so we can go back, indefinitely but not for ever. Sooner or later, we must come to at least one ethical premiss which is not deduced but baldly asserted. Here we must be a-rational; neither rational nor irrational, for here there is no room for reason even to go wrong.

But the triumph of Hume in ethics has been a limited one. What appears quite natural to a handful of specialists appears quite monstrous to the majority of decent intelligent men. At any rate, it has been my experience that people who are normally rational resist the above account of the logic of moral language, not by argument—for that can't be done—but by tooth and nail. And they resist from the best motives. They see the philosopher wantonly unravelling the whole fabric of morality. If our ultimate principles are arbitrary, they say, if those principles came out of thin air, then anyone can hold any principle he pleases. Unless

From Brian Medlin, "Ultimate Principles and Ethical Egoism," *Australasian Journal of Philosophy*, 35 (1957), pp. 111–18. Reprinted by kind permission of the author and of the editor of the *Australasian Journal of Philosophy*.

moral assertions are statements of fact about the world and either true or false, we can't claim that any man is wrong, whatever his principles may be, whatever his behaviour. We have to surrender the luxury of calling one another scoundrels. That this anxiety flourishes because its roots are in confusion is evident when we consider that we don't call people scoundrels, anyhow, for being mistaken about their facts. Fools, perhaps, but that's another matter. Nevertheless, it doesn't become us to be high-up. The layman's uneasiness, however irrational it may be, is very natural and he must be reassured.

People cling to objectivist theories of morality from moral motives. It's a very queer thing that by doing so they often thwart their own purposes. There are evil opinions abroad, as anyone who walks abroad knows. The one we meet with most often, whether in pub or parlour, is the doctrine that everyone should look after himself. However refreshing he may find it after the high-minded pomposities of this morning's editorial, the good fellow knows this doctrine is wrong and he wants to knock it down. But while he believes that moral language is used to make statements either true or false, the best he can do is to claim that what the egoist says is false. Unfortunately, the egoist can claim that it's true. And since the supposed fact in question between them is not a publicly ascertainable one, their disagreement can never be resolved. And it is here that even good fellows waver, when they find they have no refutation available. The egoist's word seems as reliable as their own. Some begin half to believe that perhaps it is possible to supply an egoistic basis for conventional morality, some that it may be impossible to supply any other basis. I'm not going to try to prop up our conventional morality, which I fear to be a task beyond my strength, but in what follows I do want to refute the doctrine of ethical egoism. I want to resolve this disagreement by showing that what the egoist says is inconsistent. It is true that there are moral disagreements which can never be resolved, but this isn't one of them. The proper objection to the man who says 'Everyone should look after his own interests regardless of the interest of others' is not that he isn't speaking the truth, but simply that he isn't speaking.

We should first make two distinctions. This done, ethical egoism will lose much of its plausibility.

1. Universal and Individual Egoism

Universal egoism maintains that everyone (including the speaker) ought to look after his own interests and to disregard those of other people except in so far as their interests contribute towards his own.

Individual egoism is the attitude that the egoist is going to look after himself and no one else. The egoist cannot promulgate that he is going to look after himself. He can't even preach that he *should* look after himself and preach this alone. When he tries to convince me that he should look after himself, he is attempting so to dispose me that I shall approve when he drinks my beer and steals Tom's wife. I cannot approve of his looking after himself and himself alone without so far approving of his achieving his happiness, regardless of the happiness of myself and others. So that when he sets out to persuade me that he should look after himself regardless of others, he must also set out to persuade me that I should look after him regardless of myself and others. Very small chance he has! And if the individual egoist cannot promulgate his doctrine without enlarging it, what he has is no doctrine at all.

A person enjoying such an attitude may believe that other people are fools not to look after themselves. Yet he himself would be a fool to tell them so. If he did tell them, though, he wouldn't consider that he was giving them *moral* advice. Persuasion to the effect that one should ignore the claims of morality because morality doesn't pay, to the effect that one has insufficient selfish motive and, therefore, insufficient motive for moral behaviour is not moral persuasion. For this reason I doubt that we should call the individual egoist's attitude an ethical one. And I don't doubt this in the way someone may doubt whether to call the ethical standards of Satan "ethical" standards. A malign morality is none the less a morality for being malign. But the attitude we're considering is one of mere contempt for all moral considerations whatsoever. An indifference to morals may be wicked, but it is not a perverse morality. So far as I am aware, most egoists imagine that they are putting forward a doctrine in ethics, though there may be a few who are prepared to proclaim themselves individual egoists. If the good fellow wants to know how he should justify conventional morality to an individual egoist, the answer is that he shouldn't and can't. Buy your car elsewhere, blackguard him whenever you meet, and let it go at that.

2. Categorical and Hypothetical Egoism

Categorical egoism is the doctrine that we all ought to observe our own interests, *because that is what we ought to do.* For the categorical egoist the egoistic dogma is the ultimate principle in ethics.

The hypothetical egoist, on the other hand, maintains that we all ought to observe our own interest, because. . . . If we want such and such an end, we must do so and so (look after ourselves). The hypothetical egoist is not a real egoist at all. He is very likely an unwitting utilitarian who believes mistakenly that the general happiness will be increased if each man looks wisely to his own. Of course, a man may believe that egoism is enjoined on us by God and he may therefore promulgate the doctrine and observe it in his conduct, not in the hope of achieving thereby a remote end, but simply in order to obey God. But neither is *he* a real egoist. He believes, ultimately, that we should obey God, even should God command us to altruism.

An ethical egoist will have to maintain the doctrine in both its universal and categorical form. Should he retreat to hypothetical egoism he is no longer an egoist. Should he retreat to individual egoism his doctrine, while logically impregnable, is no longer ethical, no longer even a doctrine. He may wish to quarrel with this and if so, I submit peacefully. Let him call himself what he will, it makes no difference. I'm a philosopher, not a ratcatcher, and I don't see it as my job to dig vermin out of such burrows as individual egoism.

Obviously something strange goes on as soon as the ethical egoist tries to promulgate his doctrine. What is he doing when he urges upon his audience that they should each observe his own interests and those interests alone? Is he not acting contrary to the egoistic principle? It cannot be to his advantage to convince them, for seizing always their own advantage they will impair his. Surely if he does believe what he says, he should try to persuade them otherwise. Not perhaps that they should devote themselves to his interests, for they'd hardly swallow that; but that everyone should devote himself to the service of others. But is not to believe that someone should act in a certain way to try to persuade him to do so? Of course, we don't always try to persuade people to act as we think they should act. We may be lazy, for instance. But in so far as we believe that Tom should do so and so, we have a tendency to induce him to do so and so. Does it make sense to say: "Of course you should do this, but for goodness' sake don't?" Only where we mean: "You should do this for certain reasons, but here are even more persuasive reasons for not doing it." If the egoist believes ultimately that others should mind themselves alone, then, he must persuade them accordingly. If he doesn't persuade them, he is no universal egoist. It certainly makes sense to say: "I know very well that Tom should act in such and such a way. But I know also that it's not to my advantage that he should so act. So I'd better dissuade him from it." And this is just what the egoist must say, if he is to consider his own advantage and disregard everyone else's. That is, he must behave as an individual egoist, if he is to be an egoist at all.

He may want to make two kinds of objection here:

1. That it will not be to his disadvantage to promulgate the doctrine, provided that his audience fully understand what is to their ultimate advantage. This objection can be developed in a number of ways, but I think that it will always be possible to push the egoist into either individual or hypothetical egoism.
2. That it is to the egoist's advantage to preach the doctrine if the pleasure he gets out of doing this more than pays for the injuries he must endure at the hands of his converts. It is hard to believe that many people would be satisfied with a doctrine which they could only consistently promulgate in very special circumstances. Besides, this looks suspiciously like individual egoism in disguise.

I shall say no more on these two points because I want to advance a further criticism which seems to me at once fatal and irrefutable.

Now it is time to show the anxious layman that we have means of dealing with ethical egoism which are denied him; and denied him by just that objectivism which he thinks essential to morality. For the very fact that our ultimate principles must be arbitrary means they can't be anything we please. Just because they come out of thin air they can't come out of hot air. Because these principles are not propositions about matters of fact and cannot be deduced from propositions about matters of fact, they must be the fruit of our own attitudes. We assert them largely to modify the attitudes of our fellows but by asserting them we express our own desires and purposes. This means that we cannot use moral language cavalierly. Evidently, we cannot say something like "All human desires and purposes are bad." This would be to express our own desires and purposes, thereby committing a kind of absurdity. Nor, I shall argue, can we say "Everyone should observe his own interests regardless of the interests of others."

Remembering that the principle is meant to be both universal and categorical, let us ask what kind of attitude the egoist is expressing. Wouldn't that attitude be equally well expressed by the conjunction of an infinite number of avowals thus?—

I want myself to come out on top	and	I don't care about Tom, Dick, Harry . . .
and		and
I want Tom to come out on top	and	I don't care about myself, Dick, Harry . . .
and		and
I want Dick to come out on top	and	I don't care about myself, Tom, Harry . . .
and		and
I want Harry to come out on top	and	I don't care about myself, Dick, Tom . . .
etc.		etc.

From this analysis it is obvious that the principle expressing such an attitude must be inconsistent.

But now the egoist may claim that he hasn't been properly understood. When he says "Everyone should look after himself and himself alone," he means "Let each man do what he wants regardless of what anyone else wants." The egoist may claim that what he values is merely that he and Tom and Dick and Harry should each do what he wants and not care about what anyone else may want and that this doesn't involve his principle in any inconsistency. Nor need it. But even if it doesn't, he's no better off. Just what does he value? Is it the well-being of himself, Tom, Dick and Harry or merely their going on in a certain way regardless of whether or not this is going to promote their well-being? When he urges Tom, say, to do what he wants, is he appealing to Tom's self-interest? If so, his attitude can be expressed thus:

I want myself to be happy		I want myself not to care about Tom, Dick, Harry . . .
and	and	
I want Tom to be happy		

We need go no further to see that the principle expressing such an attitude must be inconsistent. I have made this kind of move already. What concerns me now is the alternative position the egoist must take up to be safe from it. If the egoist values merely that people should go on in a certain way, regardless of whether or not this is going to promote their well-being, then he is not appealing to the self-interest of his audience when he urges them to regard their own interests. If Tom has any regard for himself at all, the egoist's blandishments will leave him cold.

Further, the egoist doesn't even have his own interest in mind when he says that, like everyone else, he should look after himself. A funny kind of egoism this turns out to be.

Perhaps now, claiming that he is indeed appealing to the self-interest of his audience, the egoist may attempt to counter the objection of the previous paragraph. He may move into "Let each man do what he wants and let each man disregard what others want when their desires clash with his own. "Now his attitude may be expressed thus:

I want everyone to be happy   I want everyone to dis-
                              and   regard the happiness
                                        of others when their
                                        happiness clashes
                                        with his own.

The egoist may claim justly that a man can have such an attitude and also that in a certain kind of world such a man could get what he wanted. Our objection to the egoist has been that his desires are incompatible. And this is still so. If he and Tom and Dick and Harry did go on as he recommends by saying "Let each man disregard the happiness of others, when their happiness conflicts with his own," then assuredly they'd all be completely miserable. Yet he wants them to be happy. He is attempting to counter this by saying that it is merely a fact about the world that they'd make one another miserable by going on as he recommends. The world could conceivably have been different. For this reason, he says, this principle is not inconsistent. This argument may not seem very compelling, but I advance it on the egoist's behalf because I'm interested in the reply to it. For now we don't even need to tell him that the world isn't in fact like that. (What it's like makes no difference.) Now we can point out to him that he is arguing not as an egoist but as a utilitarian. He has slipped into hypothetical egoism to save his principle from inconsistency. If the world were such that we always made ourselves and others happy by doing one another down, then we could find good utilitarian reasons for urging that we should do one another down.

If, then, he is to save his principle, the egoist must do one of two things. He must give up the claim that he is appealing to the self-interest of his audience, that he has even his own interest in mind. Or he must admit that, in the conjunction above, although "I want everyone to be happy" refers to ends, nevertheless "I want everyone to disregard the happiness of others when their happiness conflicts with his own" can refer only to means. That is, his so-called ultimate principle is really compounded of a principle and a moral rule subordinate to that principle. That is, he is really a utilitarian who is urging everyone to go on in a certain way so that everyone may be happy. A utilitarian, what's more, who is ludicrously mistaken about the nature of the world. Things being as they are, his moral rule is a very bad one. Things being as they are, it can only be deduced from his principle by means of an empirical premiss which is manifestly false. Good fellows don't need to fear him. They may rest easy that the world is and must be on their side and the best thing they can do is be good.

It may be worth pointing out that objections similar to those I have brought against the egoist can be made to the altruist. The man who holds that the principle "Let everyone observe the interests of others" is both universal and categorical can be compelled to choose between two alternatives, equally repugnant. He must give up the claim that he is concerned for the well-being of himself and others. Or he must admit that, though "I want everyone to be happy" refers to ends, nevertheless "I want everyone to disregard his own happiness when it conflicts with the happiness of others" can refer only to means.

I have said from time to time that the egoistic principle is inconsistent. I have not said it is contradictory. This for the reason that we can, without contradiction, express inconsistent desires and purposes. To do so is not to say anything like "Goliath was ten feet tall and not ten feet tall." Don't we all want to eat our cake and have it too? And when we say we do we aren't asserting a contradiction. We are not asserting a contradiction whether we be making an avowal of our attitudes or stating a fact about them. We all have conflicting motives. As a utilitarian exuding benevolence I want the man who mows my landlord's grass to be happy, but as a slug-a-bed I should like to see him scourged. None of this, however, can do the egoist any good. For we assert our ultimate principles not only to express our own attitudes but also to induce similar attitudes in others, to dispose them to conduct themselves as we wish. In so far as their desires conflict, people don't know what to do. And, therefore, no expression of incompatible desires can ever serve for an ultimate principle of human conduct.

22. **Jesse Kalin**

Jesse Kalin is Professor of Philosophy at Vassar College.

A Defense of Egoism

I

Ethical egoism is the view that it is morally right—that is, morally permissible, indeed, morally obligatory—for a person to act in his own self-interest even when his self-interest conflicts or is irreconcilable with the self-interest of another. The point people normally have in mind in accepting and advocating this ethical principle is that of justifying or excusing their own self-interested actions by giving them a moral sanction.

This position is sometimes construed as saying that selfishness is moral, but such an interpretation is not quite correct. "Self-interest" is a general term usually used as a synonym for "personal happiness" and "personal welfare," and what would pass as selfish behavior frequently would not pass as self-interested behavior in this sense. Indeed, we have the suspicion that selfish people are characteristically, if not always, unhappy. Thus, in cases where selfishness tends to a person's unhappiness it is not in his self-interest, and as an egoist he ought not to be selfish. As a consequence, ethical egoism does not preclude other-interested, nonselfish, or altruistic behavior, as long as such behavior also leads to the individual's own welfare.

That the egoist may reasonably find himself taking an interest in others and promoting their welfare perhaps sounds nonegoistic, but it is

This selection is taken from his "In Defense of Egoism," an essay in David P. Gauthier (editor), *Morality and Rational Self-Interest*, Englewood Cliffs, N.J., 1970, Prentice-Hall, Inc. Reprinted by permission of the author.

not. Ethical egoism's justification of such behavior differs from other accounts in the following way: The ethical egoist acknowledges no general obligation to help people in need. Benevolence is never justified unconditionally or "categorically." The egoist has an obligation to promote the welfare only of those whom he likes, loves, needs, or can use. The source of this obligation is his interest in them. No interest, no obligation. And when his interest conflicts or is irreconcilable with theirs, he will reasonably pursue his own well-being at their expense, even when this other person is his wife, child, mother, or friend, as well as when it is a stranger or enemy.

Such a pursuit of one's own self-interest is considered *enlightened*. The name Butler provides for ethical egoism so interpreted is "cool self-love."[1] On this view, a person is to harmonize his natural interests, perhaps cultivate some new interests, and optimize their satisfaction. Usually among these interests will be such things as friendships and families (or perhaps one gets his greatest kicks from working for UNICEF). And, of course, it is a part of such enlightenment to consider the "long run" rather than just the present and immediate future.

Given this account of ethical egoism plus the proper circumstances, a person could be morally justified in cheating on tests, padding expense accounts, swindling a business partner, being a slum landlord, draft-dodging, lying, and breaking promises, as well as in contributing to charity, helping friends, being generous or civic minded, and even undergoing hardship to put his children through college. Judged from inside "standard morality," the first actions would clearly be immoral, while the preceding paragraphs suggest the latter actions would be immoral as well, being done from a vicious or improper motive.

With this informal account as background, I shall now introduce a formal definition of ethical egoism, whose coherence will be the topic of the subsequent discussion:

(i) (x) (y) (x ought to do y if and only if y is in x's overall self-interest)

In this formalization, "x" ranges over persons and "y" over particular actions, or kinds of action; "ought" has the sense "ought, all things considered." (i) may be translated as: "A person ought to do a specific action, all things considered, if and only if that action is in that person's overall (enlightened) self-interest."

(i) represents what Medlin calls "universal egoism."[2] The majority

---

1. Butler, Joseph, *Fifteen Sermons Preached at the Rolls Chapel*, 1726. Standard anthologies of moral philosophy include the most important of these sermons; or see the Library of Liberal Arts Selection, *Five Sermons* (New York: The Bobbs-Merrill Company, Inc., 1950). See particularly Sermons I and XI. In XI, Butler says of rational self-love that "the object the former pursues is something internal—our own happiness, enjoyment, satisfaction . . . The principle we call "self-love" never seeks anything external for the sake of the thing, but only as a means of happiness or good." Butler is not, however, an egoist for there is also in man conscience and "a natural principle of benevolence" (see Sermon I).

2. Medlin, Brian, "Ultimate Principles and Ethical Egoism," *Australasian Journal of Philosophy*, XXXV (1957), 111–18; reprinted in this volume, pp. 217–23.

of philosophers have considered universalization to be necessary for a sound moral theory, though few have considered it sufficient. This requirement may be expressed as follows: If it is reasonable for A to do s in C, it is also reasonable for any similar person to do similar things in similar circumstances. Since everyone has a self-interest and since the egoist is arguing that his actions are right simply because they are self-interested, it is intuitively plausible to hold that he is committed to regarding everyone as morally similar and as morally entitled (or even morally obligated) to be egoists. His claim that his own self-interested actions are right thus entails the claim that all self-interested actions are right. If the egoist is to reject this universalization, he must show that there are considerations in addition to self-interest justifying his action, considerations making him relevantly different from all others such that his self-interested behavior is justified while theirs is not. I can't imagine what such considerations would be. In any case, egoism has usually been advanced and defended in its universalized form, and it is in this form that it will most repay careful examination. Thus, for the purposes of this paper, I shall assume without further defense the correctness of the universalization requirement.

It has also been the case that the major objections to ethical egoism have been derived from this requirement. Opponents have argued that once egoism is universalized, it can readily be seen to be incoherent. Frankena[3] and Medlin each advance an argument of this sort. In discussing their positions, I shall argue that the universalization of egoism given by (i) is coherent. . . . The result will be that egoism can with some plausibility be defended as an ultimate practical principle. At the least, if egoism is incorrect, this is not due to any incoherence arising from the universalization requirement.

II

One purpose of a moral theory is to provide criteria for first person moral judgments (such as "I ought to do s in C"); another purpose is to provide criteria for second and third person moral judgments (such as "Jones ought to do s in C"). Any theory which cannot coherently provide such criteria must be rejected as a moral theory. Can ethical egoism do this? Frankena argues that it cannot.

Frankena formulates egoism as consisting of two principles:

a) If A is judging about himself, then A is to use this criterion: A ought to do y if and only if y is in A's overall self-interest.
b) If A is a spectator judging about anyone else, B, then A is to use this criterion: B ought to do y if and only if y is in A's overall self-interest.

Frankena thinks that [(a) & (b)] is the only interpretation of (i) "consistent with the spirit of ethical egoism."

3. Frankena, William, *Ethics* (Englewood Cliffs, New Jersey: Prentice-Hall, Inc., 1963), pp. 16–18. References to Frankena in section II are to this book.

But isn't it the case that (a) and (b) taken together produce contradictory moral judgments about an important subset of cases, namely, those where people's self-interests conflict or are irreconcilable? If this is so, egoism as formulated by Frankena is incoherent and must be rejected.

To illustrate, let us suppose that B does *s*, and that *s* is in B's overall self-interest, but not in A's. Is *s* right or wrong? Ought, or ought not B do *s*? The answer depends on who is making the judgment. If A is making the judgment, then "B ought not to do *s*" is correct. If B is making the judgment, then "B ought to do *s*" is correct. And, of course, when both make judgments, both "B ought to do *s*" and "B ought not to do *s*" are correct. Surely any principle which has this result as a possibility is incoherent.

This objection may be put another way. The ethical egoist claims that there is one ultimate moral principle applicable to everyone. This is to claim that (i) is adequate for all moral issues, and that all applications of it can fit into a logically coherent system. Given the above illustration, "B ought to do *s*" does follow from (a), and "B ought not to do *s*" does follow from (b), but the fact that they cannot coherently be included in a set of judgements shows that (a) and (b) are not parts of the same ultimate moral principle. Indeed, these respective judgments can be said to follow from a moral principle at all only if they follow from *different* moral principles. Apparently, the ethical egoist must choose between (i)'s parts if he is to have a coherent ethical system, but he can make no satisfactory choice. If (a) is chosen, second and third person judgments become impossible. His moral theory, however, must provide for both kinds of judgment. Ethical egoism needs what it logically cannot have. Therefore, it can only be rejected.

The incompatibility between (a) and (b) and the consequent incoherence of (i) manifests itself in still a third way. Interpreted as a system of judgments, [(a) & (b)] is equivalent to: Everyone ought to pursue A's self-interest, and everyone ought to pursue B's self-interest, and everyone ought to pursue C's self-interest, and. . . .[4] When the inter-

---

4. This can be shown as follows:
   i. Suppose A is the evaluator, then
      What ought A to do? A ought to do what's in A's interest. (by (a))
      What ought B to do? B ought to do what's in A's interest. (by (b))
      What ought C to do? C ought to do what's in A's interest. (by (b))
      etc.
      Therefore, everyone ought to do what's in A's interest. (by (a) & (b))
   ii. Suppose B is the evaluator, then
      What ought A to do? A ought to do what's in B's interest. (by (b))
      What ought B to do? B ought to do what's in B's interest. (by (a))
      What ought C to do? C ought to do what's in B's interest. (by (b))
      etc.
      Therefore, everyone ought to do what's in B's interest. (by (a) & (b))
   iii. Suppose C is the evaluator, then
      .
      .
      .
      etc.
   Conclusion: Everyone ought to do what's in A's interest, and everyone ought to do what's in B's interest, and . . . *etc.*

ests of A and B are incompatible, one must pursue both of these incompatible goals, which, of course, is impossible. On this interpretation, ethical egoism must fail in its function of guiding conduct (one of the most important uses of moral judgments). In particular, it must fail with respect to just those cases for which the guidance is most wanted—conflicts of interests. In such situations, the theory implies that one must both do and not do a certain thing. Therefore, since ethical egoism cannot guide conduct in these crucial cases, it is inadequate as a moral theory and must be rejected.

Ethical egoism suffers from three serious defects if it is interpreted as [(a) & (b)]. These defects are closely related. The first is that the theory implies a contradiction, namely, that some actions are both right *and* wrong. The second defect is that the theory, if altered and made coherent by rejecting one of its parts, cannot fulfill one of its essential tasks: Altered, it can provide for first person moral judgments *or* for second and third person moral judgments, but not for both. The third defect is that the theory cannot guide conduct and must fail in its advice-giving function because it advises (remember: advises, all things considered) a person to do what it advises him not to do.

Any one of these defects would be sufficient to refute the theory, and indeed they do refute ethical egoism when it is defined as [(a) & (b)]. The only plausible way to escape these arguments is to abandon Frankena's definition and reformulate egoism so that they are no longer applicable. Clearly, (a) must remain, for it seems central to any egoistic position. However, we can replace (b) with the following:

c) If A is a spectator judging about anyone else, then A is to use this criterion: B ought to do *y* if and only if *y* is in B's overall self-interest.

The objections to [(a) & (b)] given above do not apply to [(a) & (c)]. [(a) & (c)] yields no contradictions, even in cases where self-interests conflict or are irreconcilable. When we suppose that B is the agent, that *s* is in B's overall self-interest, and that *s* is against A's overall self-interest, both B and A will agree in their moral judgments about this case, that is, both will agree that B ought to do *s*. And, of course, the theory provides for all moral judgments, whether first, second, or third person; since it yields no contradictions, there is no need to make it coherent by choosing between its parts and thereby making it inadequate.

Finally, this interpretation avoids the charge that ethical egoism cannot adequately fulfill its conduct guiding function. Given [(a) & (c)], it will never truly be the case that an agent ought to pursue anyone's self-interest except his own. Any judgment of the form "A ought to pursue B's self-interest" will be false, unless it is understood to mean that pursuit of B's self-interest is a part of the pursuit of A's self-interest (and this, of course, would not contribute to any incoherence in the theory). Thus, the theory will have no difficulty in being an effective practical theory; it will not give contradictory advice, even in situations where interests conflict. True, it will not remove such conflicts—indeed, in practice it might well encourage them; but a conflict is not a contradiction.

The theory tells A to pursue a certain goal, and it tells B to pursue another goal, and does this unequivocally. That both cannot succeed in their pursuits is irrelevant to the coherence of the theory and its capacity to guide conduct, since both *can* do what they are advised to do, all things considered—pursue their own self-interests. . . .

There remains the question whether [(a) & (c)] is a plausible interpretation of (i), that is, whether it is "consistent with the spirit of ethical egoism." It is certainly consistent with the "spirit" behind the "ethical" part of egoism in its willingness to universalize the doctrine. It is also consistent with the "egoistic" part of the theory in that if a person does faithfully follow (a) he will behave as an egoist. Adding the fact that [(a) & (c)] is a coherent theory adequate to the special ethical chores so far discussed, do we have any reason for rejecting it as an interpretation of (i) and ethical egoism? So far, I think not. Therefore, I conclude that Frankena has failed to refute egoism. It has thus far survived the test of universalization and still remains as a candidate for "the one true moral theory."

III

In his article, "Ultimate Principles and Ethical Egoism," Brian Medlin maintains that ethical egoism cannot be an ultimate moral principle because it fails to guide our actions, tell us what to do, or determine our choice between alternatives.[5] He bases this charge on his view that because ethical egoism is the expression of inconsistent desires, it will always tell people to do incompatible things. Thus:

> I have said from time to time that the egoistic principle is inconsistent. I have not said it is contradictory. This for the reason that we can, without contradiction, express inconsistent desires and purposes. To do so is not to say anything like "Goliath was ten feet tall and not ten feet tall." Don't we all want to have our cake and eat it too? And when we say we do we aren't asserting a contradiction whether we be making an avowal of our attitudes or stating a fact about them. We all have conflicting motives. None of this, however, can do the egoist any good. For we assert our ultimate principles not only to express our own attitudes but also to induce similar attitudes in others, to dispose them to conduct themselves as we wish. In so far as their desires conflict, people don't know what to do. And, therefore, no expression of incompatible desires can ever serve for an ultimate principle of human conduct.

That egoism could not successfully guide one's conduct was a criticism discussed and rebutted in section II. There, it rested upon Frankena's formulation of egoism as equal to [(a) & (b)] and was easily circumvented by replacing principle (b) with principle (c). Medlin's charge is significant, however, because it appears to be applicable to

5. All references to Medlin are to the reprint in this volume, pp. 217–23.

[(a) & (c)] as well[6] and therefore must be directly refuted if egoism is to be maintained.

The heart of Medlin's argument is his position that to affirm a moral principle is to express approval of any and all actions following from that principle. This means for Medlin not only that the egoist is committed to approving all egoistic actions but also that such approval will involve wanting those actions to occur and trying to bring them about, even when they would be to one's own detriment.

> But is not to believe that someone should act in a certain way to try to persuade him to do so? Of course, we don't always try to persuade people to act as we think they should act. We may be lazy, for instance. But insofar as we believe that Tom should do so and so, we have a tendency to induce him to do so and so. Does it make sense to say: "Of course you should do this, but for goodness' sake don't"? Only where we mean: "You should do this for certain reasons, but here are even more persuasive reasons for not doing it." If the egoist believes ultimately that others should mind themselves alone, then, he must persuade them accordingly. If he doesn't persuade them, he is no universal egoist.

According to Medlin, if I adopt ethical egoism and am thereby led to approve of A's egoistic actions (as would follow from (c)), I must also *want* A to behave in that way and must want him to be happy, to come out on top, and so forth where wanting is interpreted as setting an end for my own actions and where it tends (according to the intensity of the want, presumably) to issue in my "looking after him."

Of course, I will also approve of my pursuing my own welfare (as would follow from (a)) and will want myself to be happy, to come out on top, and so forth. Since I want my own success, I will want A's noninterference. Indeed, what I will want A to do, and will therefore approve of A's doing, is to pursue my welfare, rather than his own.

It is thus the case that whenever my interest conflicts with A's interest, I will approve of inconsistent ends and will want incompatible things ("I want myself to come out on top and I want Tom to come

---

6. Medlin himself does nct distinguish between (b) and (c). Some of his remarks suggest (c). Thus, at one point he says:

> When he [the egoist] tries to convince me that he should look after himself, he is attempting so to dispose me that I shall approve when he drinks my beer and steals Tom's wife. I cannot approve of his looking after himself and himself alone without so far approving of his achieving his happiness, regardless of the happiness of myself and others.

This passage implies that as a spectator assessing another's conduct, I should employ principle (c) and approve of A's doing y whenever y promotes A's interest, even if this is at the expense of my welfare.

But other of his remarks suggest (b). Thus, the above passage continues:

> So that when he sets out to persuade me that he should look after himself regardless of others, he must also set out to persuade me that I should look after him regardless of myself and others. Very small chance he has!

Here, the implication is that the egoist as spectator and judge of another should assess the other's behavior according to his own interests, not the other's, which would be in accordance with (b).

Perhaps Medlin is arguing that the egoist is committed to accepting both (b) and (c), as well as (a). This interpretation is consistent with his analysis of "approval."

out on top"). Since I approve of incompatible ends, I will be motivated in contrary directions—both away from and toward my own welfare, for instance. However, this incompatibility of desires is not sufficient to produce inaction and does not itself prove Medlin's point, for one desire may be stronger than the other. If the egoist's approval of his own well-being were always greater than his approval of anyone else's well-being, the inconsistent desires constituting egoism would not prevent (i) from decisively guiding conduct. Unfortunately for the egoist, his principle will in fact lead him to inaction, for in being universal (i) expresses equal approval of each person's pursuing his own self-interest, and therefore, insofar as his desires follow from this principle, none will be stronger than another.

We can now explain Medlin's conclusion that "the proper objection to the man who says 'Everyone should look after his own interests regardless of the interests of others' is not that he isn't speaking the truth, but simply that he isn't speaking." Upon analysis, it is clear that the egoist is "saying" that others should act so that he himself comes out on top and should not care about Tom, Dick, *et al.*, but they should also act so that Tom comes out on top and should not care about himself, Dick, the others, and so forth. This person *appears* to be saying how people should act, and that they should act in a definite way. But his "directions" can guide no one. They give one nothing to do. Therefore, such a man has in fact said nothing.

I think Medlin's argument can be shown to be unsuccessful without a discussion of the emotivism in which it is framed. The egoist can grant that there is a correct sense in which affirmation of a moral principle is the expression of approval. The crux of the issue is Medlin's particular analysis of approbation, and this can be shown to be incorrect.

We may grant that the egoist is committed to approving of anyone's egoistic behavior at least to the extent of believing that the person ought so to behave. Such approval will hold of all egoistic actions, even those that endanger his own welfare. But does believing that A ought to do y commit one to wanting A to do y? Surely not. This is made clear by the analogy with competitive games. Team A has no difficulty in believing that team B ought to make or try to make a field goal while not wanting team B to succeed, while hoping that team B fails, and, indeed, while trying to prevent team B's success. Or consider this example: I may see how my chess opponent can put my king in check. That is how he ought to move. But believing that he ought to move his bishop and check my king does not commit me to wanting him to do that, nor to persuading him to do so. What *I* ought to do is sit there quietly, hoping he does not move as he ought.

Medlin's mistake is to think that believing that A ought to do y commits one to *wanting* A to do y and hence to encouraging or otherwise helping A to do y. The examples from competitive games show that this needn't be so. The egoist's reply to Medlin is that just as team A's belief that team B ought to do so and so is compatible with their not wanting team B to do so and so, so the egoist's belief that A ought to do y is compatible with the egoist's not wanting A to do y. Once this is understood, egoism has no difficulty in decisively guiding conduct, for insofar as (i) commits the egoist to wanting anything, it only commits him to wanting his own welfare. Since he does not want incompatible goals, he has no trouble in deciding what to do according to (a) and in judging what others ought to do according to (c).

IV

There is in Medlin's paper confusion concerning what the egoist wants or values and why he believes in ethical egoism. The egoist does not believe that everyone ought to pursue their own self-interest merely because *he* wants to get *his* goodies out of life. If this were all there were to his position, the egoist would not bother with (i) or with moral concepts at all. He would simply go about doing what he wants. What reason, then, does he have to go beyond wanting his own welfare to ethical egoism? On Medlin's emotivist account, his reason must be that he also wants B to have B's goodies, and wants D to have his, and so forth, even when it is impossible that everybody be satisfied. But I argued in the preceding section that the egoist is not committed to wanting such states, and that it is not nonsense for him to affirm (i) and desire his own welfare yet not desire the welfare of others. Therefore, the question remains —why affirm egoism at all?

The egoist's affirmation of (i) rests upon both teleological and deontological elements. What *he* finds to be of ultimate value is his own welfare. He needn't be selfish or egocentric in the ordinary sense (as Medlin sometimes suggests by such paraphrases as "Let each man do what he wants regardless of what anyone else wants"), but he will value his own interest above that of others. Such an egoist would share Sidgwick's view that when "the painful necessity comes for another man to choose between his own happiness and the general happiness, he must as a reasonable being prefer his own."[7] When this occasion does arise, the egoist will want the other's welfare less than he wants his own, and this will have the practical effect of not wanting the other's welfare at all. It is in terms of this personal value that he guides his actions, judging that he ought to do y if and only if y is in his overall self-interest. This is the teleological element in his position.

However, there is no reason that others should find his well-being to be of value to them, less more to be of ultimate value; and it is much more likely that each will find his own welfare to be his own ultimate value. But if it is reasonable for the egoist to justify his behavior in terms of what he finds to be of ultimate value, then it is also reasonable for others to justify their behavior in terms of what they find to be of ultimate value. This follows from the requirement of universalization and provides the deontological element. Interpreted as "Similar things are right for similar people in similar circumstances," the universalization

7. Henry Sidgwick, *The Methods of Ethics*, 7th ed. (London: Macmillan and Co., 1907), preface to the 6th edition, p. xvii.

principle seems undeniable. Failing to find any relevant difference between himself and others, the egoist must admit that it can be morally permissible for him to pursue his self-interest only if it is morally permissible for each person to pursue his self-interest. He therefore finds himself committed to (i), even though he does not *want* others to compete with him for life's goods.

23. William David Ross

Sir William David Ross was, until his retirement, Provost of Oriel College, Oxford.

Many Self-Evident Obligations

The real point at issue between hedonism and utilitarianism on the one hand and their opponents on the other is not whether 'right' means 'productive of so and so'; for it cannot with any plausibility be maintained that it does. The point at issue is that to which we now pass, viz. whether there is any general character which makes right acts right, and if so, what it is. Among the main historical attempts to state a single characteristic of all right actions which is the foundation of their rightness are those made by egoism and utilitarianism. But I do not propose to discuss these, not because the subject is unimportant, but because it has been dealt with so often and so well already, and because there has come to be so much agreement among moral philosophers that neither of these theories is satisfactory. A much more attractive theory has been put forward by Professor Moore: that what makes actions right is that they are productive of more *good* than could have been produced by any other action open to the agent.

This theory is in fact the culmination of all the attempts to base rightness on productivity of some sort of result. The first form this attempt takes is the attempt to base rightness on conduciveness to the advantage or pleasure of the agent. This theory comes to grief over the fact, which stares us in the face, that a great part of duty consists in an

From W. D. Ross, *The Right and the Good*, published by The Clarendon Press, Oxford, 1930. From Chapter 2. Reprinted by permission of Oxford University Press.

observance of the rights and a furtherance of the interests of others, whatever the cost to ourselves may be. Plato and others may be right in holding that a regard for the rights of others never in the long run involves a loss of happiness for the agent, that 'the just life profits a man.' But this, even if true, is irrelevant to the rightness of the act. As soon as a man does an action *because* he thinks he will promote his own interests thereby, he is acting not from a sense of its rightness but from self-interest.

To the egoistic theory hedonistic utilitarianism supplies a much-needed amendment. It points out correctly that the fact that a certain pleasure will be enjoyed by the agent is no reason why he *ought* to bring it into being rather than an equal or greater pleasure to be enjoyed by another, though, human nature being what it is, it makes it not unlikely that he *will* try to bring it into being. But hedonistic utilitarianism in its turn needs a correction. On reflection it seems clear that pleasure is not the only thing in life that we think good in itself, that for instance we think the possession of a good character, or an intelligent understanding of the world, as good or better. A great advance is made by the substitution of 'productive of the greatest good' for 'productive of the greatest pleasure.'

Not only is this theory more attractive than hedonistic utilitarianism, but its logical relation to that theory is such that the latter could not be true unless *it* were true, while it might be true though hedonistic utilitarianism were not. It is in fact one of the logical bases of hedonistic utilitarianism. For the view that what produces the maximum pleasure is right has for its bases the views 1) that what produces the maximum good is right, and 2) that pleasure is the only thing good in itself. . . . If, therefore, it can be shown that productivity of the maximum good is not what makes all right actions right, we shall *a fortiori* have refuted hedonistic utilitarianism.

When a plain man fulfils a promise because he thinks he ought to do so, it seems clear that he does so with no thought of its total consequences, still less with any opinion that these are likely to be the best possible. He thinks in fact much more of the past than of the future. What makes him think it right to act in a certain way is the fact that he has promised to do so—that and, usually, nothing more. That his act will produce the best possible consequences is not his reason for calling it right. What lends colour to the theory we are examining, then, is not the actions (which form probably a great majority of our actions) in which some such reflection as 'I have promised' is the only reason we give ourselves for thinking a certain action right, but the exceptional cases in which the consequences of fulfilling a promise (for instance) would be so disastrous to others that we judge it right not to do so. It must of course be admitted that such cases exist. If I have promised to meet a friend at a particular time for some trivial purpose, I should certainly think myself justified in breaking my engagement if by doing so I could prevent a serious accident or bring relief to the victims of one. And the supporters of the view we are examining hold that my thinking so is due to my thinking that I shall bring more good into existence by the one action than by the other. A different account may, however, be given of the matter, an account which will, I believe, show itself to be the true one. It may be said that besides the duty of fulfilling promises I have and recognize a duty of relieving distress, and that when I think it right to do the latter at the cost of not doing the former, it is not because I think I shall produce more good thereby but because I think it the duty which is in the circumstances more of a duty. This account surely corresponds much more closely with what we really think in such a situation. If, so far as I can see, I could bring equal amounts of good into being by fulfilling my promise and by helping some one to whom I had made no promise, I should not hesitate to regard the former as my duty. Yet on the view that what is right is right because it is productive of the most good I should not so regard it.

There are two theories, each in its way simple, that offer a solution of such cases of conscience. One is the view of Kant, that there are certain duties of perfect obligation, such as those of fulfilling promises, of paying debts, of telling the truth, which admit of no exception whatever in favour of duties of imperfect obligation, such as that of relieving distress. The other is the view of, for instance, Professor Moore and Dr. Rashdall, that there is only the duty of producing good, and that all 'conflicts of duties' should be resolved by asking 'by which action will most good be produced?' But it is more important that our theory fit the facts than that it be simple, and the account we have given above corresponds (it seems to me) better than either of the simpler theories with what we really think, viz. that normally promise-keeping, for example, should come before benevolence, but that when and only when the good to be produced by the benevolent act is very great and the promise comparatively trivial, the act of benevolence becomes our duty.

In fact the theory of 'ideal utilitarianism,' if I may for brevity refer so to the theory of Professor Moore, seems to simplify unduly our relations to our fellows. It says, in effect, that the only morally significant relation in which my neighbours stand to me is that of being possible beneficiaries by my action.[1] They do stand in this relation to me, and this relation is morally significant. But they may also stand to me in the relation of promisee to promiser, of creditor to debtor, of wife to husband, of child to parent, of friend to friend, of fellow countryman to fellow countryman, and the like; and each of these relations is the foundation of a *prima facie* duty, which is more or less incumbent on me according to the circumstances of the case. When I am in a situation, as perhaps I always am, in which more than one of these *prima facie* duties is incumbent on me, what I have to do is to study the situation as fully as I can until I form the considered opinion (it is never more) that in the circumstances one of them is more incumbent than any other; then I am bound to think that to do this *prima facie* duty is my duty *sans phrase* in the situation.

I suggest '*prima facie* duty' or 'conditional duty' as a brief way of referring to the characteristic (quite distinct from that of being a duty

1. Some will think it, apart from other considerations, a sufficient refutation of this view to point out that I also stand in that relation to myself, so that for this view the distinction of oneself from others is morally insignificant.

proper) which an act has, in virtue of being of a certain kind (e.g. the keeping of a promise), of being an act which would be a duty proper if it were not at the same time of another kind which is morally significant. Whether an act is a duty proper or actual duty depends on *all* the morally significant kinds it is an instance of. . . .

There is nothing arbitrary about these *prima facie* duties. Each rests on a definite circumstance which cannot seriously be held to be without moral significance. Of *prima facie* duties I suggest, without claiming completeness or finality for it, the following division.[2]

1) Some duties rest on previous acts of my own. These duties seem to include two kinds, *a*) those resting on a promise or what may fairly be called an implicit promise, such as the implicit undertaking not to tell lies which seems to be implied in the act of entering into conversation (at any rate by civilized men), or of writing books that purport to be history and not fiction. These may be called the duties of fidelity. *b*) Those resting on a previous wrongful act. These may be called the duties of reparation. 2) Some rest on previous acts of other men, i.e. services done by them to me. These may be loosely described as the duties of gratitude. 3) Some rest on the fact or possibility of a distribution of pleasure or happiness (or of the means thereto) which is not in accordance with the merit of the persons concerned; in such cases there arises a duty to upset or prevent such a distribution. These are the duties of justice. 4) Some rest on the mere fact that there are other beings in the world whose condition we can make better in respect of virtue, or of intelligence, or of pleasure. These are the duties of beneficence. 5) Some rest on the fact that we can improve our own condition in respect of virtue or of intelligence. These are the duties of self-improvement. 6) I think that we should distinguish from 4) the duties that may be summed up under the title of 'not injuring others.' No doubt to injure others is incidentally to fail to do them good; but it seems to me clear that nonmaleficence is apprehended as a duty distinct from that of beneficence, and as a duty of a more stringent character. It will be noticed that this alone among the types of duty has been stated in a negative way. An attempt might no doubt be made to state this duty, like the others, in a positive way. It might be said that it is really the duty to prevent ourselves from acting either from an inclination to harm others or from an inclination to seek our own pleasure, in doing which we should incidentally harm them. But on reflection it seems clear that the primary duty here is the duty not to harm others, this being a duty whether or

2. I should make it plain at this stage that I am *assuming* the correctness of some of our main convictions as to *prima facie* duties, or, more strictly, am claiming that we *know* them to be true. To me it seems as self-evident as anything could be, that to make a promise, for instance, is to create a moral claim on us in someone else. Many readers will perhaps say that they do *not* know this to be true. If so, I certainly cannot prove it to them; I can only ask them to reflect again, in the hope that they will ultimately agree that they also know it to be true. The main moral convictions of the plain man seem to me to be, not opinions which it is for philosophy to prove or disprove, but knowledge from the start; and in my own case I seem to find little difficulty in distinguishing these essential convictions from other moral convictions which I also have, which are merely fallible opinions based on an imperfect study of the working for good or evil of certain institutions or types of action.

not we have an inclination that if followed would lead to our harming them; and that when we have such an inclination the primary duty not to harm others gives rise to a consequential duty to resist the inclination. The recognition of this duty of nonmaleficence is the first step on the way to the recognition of the duty of beneficence; and that accounts for the prominence of the commands 'thou shalt not kill,' 'thou shalt not commit adultery,' 'thou shalt not steal,' 'thou shalt not bear false witness,' in so early a code as the Decalogue. But even when we have come to recognize the duty of beneficence, it appears to me that the duty of nonmaleficence is recognized as a distinct one, and as *prima facie* more binding. We should not in general consider it justifiable to kill one person in order to keep another alive, or to steal from one in order to give alms to another.

The essential defect of the 'ideal utilitarian' theory is that it ignores, or at least does not do full justice to, the highly personal character of duty. If the only duty is to produce the maximum of good, the question who is to have the good—whether it is myself, or my benefactor, or a person to whom I have made a promise to confer that good on him, or a mere fellow man to whom I stand in no such special relation—should make no difference to my having a duty to produce that good. But we are all in fact sure that it makes a vast difference. . . .

If the objection be made, that this catalogue of the main types of duty is an unsystematic one resting on no logical principle, it may be replied, first, that it makes no claim to being ultimate. It is a *prima facie* classification of the duties which reflection on our moral convictions seems actually to reveal. And if these convictions are, as I would claim that they are, of the nature of knowledge, and if I have not misstated them, the list will be a list of authentic conditional duties, correct as far as it goes though not necessarily complete. The list of *goods* put forward by the rival theory is reached by exactly the same method—the only sound one in the circumstances—viz. that of direct reflection on what we really think. Loyalty to the facts is worth more than a symmetrical architectonic or a hastily reached simplicity. If further reflection discovers a perfect logical basis for this or for a better classification, so much the better.

It may, again, be objected that our theory that there are these various and often conflicting types of *prima facie* duty leaves us with no principle upon which to discern what is our actual duty in particular circumstances. But this objection is not one which the rival theory is in a position to bring forward. For when we have to choose between the production of two heterogeneous goods, say knowledge and pleasure, the 'ideal utilitarian' theory can only fall back on an opinion, for which no logical basis can be offered, that one of the goods is the greater; and this is no better than a similar opinion that one of two duties is the more urgent. And again, when we consider the infinite variety of the effects of our actions in the way of pleasure, it must surely be admitted that the claim which *hedonism* sometimes makes, that it offers a readily applicable criterion of right conduct, is quite illusory.

I am unwilling, however, to content myself with an *argumentum ad hominem*, and I would contend that in principle there is no reason to anticipate that every act that is our duty is so for one and the same reason. Why should two sets of circumstances, or one set of circumstances, *not* possess different characteristics, any one of which makes a certain act our *prima facie* duty? When I ask what it is that makes me in certain cases sure that I have a *prima facie* duty to do so and so, I find that it lies in the fact that I have made a promise; when I ask the same question in another case, I find the answer lies in the fact that I have done a wrong. And if on reflection I find (as I think I do) that neither of these reasons is reducible to the other, I must not on any *a priori* ground assume that such a reduction is possible. . . .

It is necessary to say something by way of clearing up the relation between *prima facie* duties and the actual or absolute duty to do one particular act in particular circumstances. If, as almost all moralists except Kant are agreed, and as most plain men think, it is sometimes right to tell a lie or to break a promise, it must be maintained that there is a difference between *prima facie* duty and actual or absolute duty. When we think ourselves justified in breaking, and indeed morally obliged to break, a promise in order to relieve some one's distress, we do not for a moment cease to recognize a *prima facie* duty to keep our promise, and this leads us to feel, not indeed shame or repentance, but certainly compunction, for behaving as we do; we recognize further, that it is our duty to make up somehow to the promisee for the breaking of the promise. We have to distinguish from the characteristic of being our duty that of tending to be our duty. Any act that we do contains various elements in virtue of which it falls under various categories. In virtue of being the breaking of a promise, for instance, it tends to be wrong; in virtue of being an instance of relieving distress it tends to be right. Tendency to be one's duty may be called a parti-resultant attribute, i.e. one which belongs to an act in virtue of some one component in its nature. *Being* one's duty is a toti-resultant attribute, one which belongs to an act in virtue of its whole nature and of nothing less than this. . . .

Another instance of the same distinction may be found in the operation of natural laws. *Qua* subject to the force of gravitation towards some other body, each body tends to move in a particular direction with a particular velocity; but its actual movement depends on *all* the forces to which it is subject. It is only by recognizing this distinction that we can preserve the absoluteness of laws of nature, and only by recognizing a corresponding distinction that we can preserve the absoluteness of the general principles of morality. But an important difference between the two cases must be pointed out. When we say that in virtue of gravitation a body tends to move in a certain way, we are referring to a causal influence actually exercised on it by another body or other bodies. When we say that in virtue of being deliberately untrue a certain remark tends to be wrong, we are referring to no causal relation, to no relation that involves succession in time, but to such a relation as connects the various attributes of a mathematical figure. And if the word 'tendency' is thought to suggest too much a causal relation, it is better to talk of certain types of act as being *prima facie* right or wrong (or of different persons as having different and possibly conflicting claims upon us), than of their tending to be right or wrong.

Something should be said of the relation between our apprehension of the *prima facie* rightness of certain types of act and our mental attitude towards particular acts. It is proper to use the word 'apprehension' in the former case and not in the latter. That an act, *qua* fulfilling a promise, or *qua* effecting a just distribution of goods, or *qua* returning services rendered, or *qua* promoting the good of others, or *qua* promoting the virtue or insight of the agent, is *prima facie* right, is self-evident; not in the sense that it is evident from the beginning of our lives, or as soon as we attend to the proposition for the first time, but in the sense that when we have reached sufficient mental maturity and have given sufficient attention to the proposition it is evident without any need of proof, or of evidence beyond itself. It is self-evident just as a mathematical axiom, or the validity of a form of inference, is evident. The moral order expressed in these propositions is just as much part of the fundamental nature of the universe (and, we may add, of any possible universe in which there were moral agents at all) as is the spatial or numerical structure expressed in the axioms of geometry or arithmetic. In our confidence that these propositions are true there is involved the same trust in our reason that is involved in our confidence in mathematics; and we should have no justification for trusting it in the latter sphere and distrusting it in the former. In both cases we are dealing with propositions that cannot be proved, but that just as certainly need no proof. . . .

Our judgements about our actual duty in concrete situations have none of the certainty that attaches to our recognition of the general principles of duty. A statement is certain, i.e. is an expression of knowledge, only in one or other of two cases: when it is either self-evident, or a valid conclusion from self-evident premises. And our judgements about our particular duties have neither of these characters. 1) They are not self-evident. Where a possible act is seen to have two characteristics, in virtue of one of which it is *prima facie* right, and in virtue of the other *prima facie* wrong, we are (I think) well aware that we are not certain whether we ought or ought not to do it; that whether we do it or not, we are taking a moral risk. We come in the long run, after consideration, to think one duty more pressing than the other, but we do not feel certain that it is so. And though we do not always recognize that a possible act has two such characteristics, and though there *may* be cases in which it has not, we are never certain that any particular possible act has not, and therefore never certain that it is right, nor certain that it is wrong. For, to go no further in the analysis, it is enough to point out that any particular act will in all probability in the course of time contribute to the bringing about of good or of evil for many human beings and thus have a *prima facie* rightness or wrongness of which we know nothing. 2) Again, our judgements about our particular duties are not logical conclusions from self-evident premises. The only possible premises would be the general principles stating their *prima facie* rightness or wrongness *qua* having the different characteristics they do have; and even if we could (as we cannot) apprehend the extent to which an act will tend on the one hand, for example, to bring about advantages for our benefactors, and on the other hand to bring about disadvantages for fellow men who are not our benefactors, there is no principle by which we can draw the conclusion that it is on the whole right or on the whole wrong. In this respect the judgement as to the rightness of a particular act is just like the judgement as to the beauty of a particular natural object or work of art. A poem is, for instance, in respect of certain qualities beautiful and in respect of certain others not beautiful; and our judgement as to the degree of beauty it possesses on the whole is never reached by logical reasoning from the apprehension of its particular beauties or particular defects. Both in this and in the moral case we have more or less probable opinions which are not logically justified conclusions from the general principles that are recognized as self-evident.

There is therefore much truth in the description of the right act as a fortunate act. If we cannot be certain that it is right, it is our good fortune if the act we do is the right act. This consideration does not, however, make the doing of our duty a mere matter of chance. There is a parallel here between the doing of duty and the doing of what will be to our personal advantage. We never *know* what act will in the long run be to our advantage. Yet it is certain that we are more likely in general to secure our advantage if we estimate to the best of our ability the probable tendencies of our actions in this respect, than if we act on caprice. And similarly we are more likely to do our duty if we reflect to the best of our ability on the *prima facie* rightness or wrongness of various possible acts in virtue of the characteristics we perceive them to have, than if we act without reflection. With this greater likelihood we must be content.

Many people would be inclined to say that the right act for me is not that whose general nature I have been describing, viz. that which if I were omniscient I should see to be my duty, but that which on all the evidence available to me I should think to be my duty. But suppose that from the state of partial knowledge in which I think act A to be my duty, I could pass to a state of perfect knowledge in which I saw act B to be my duty, should I not say 'act B was the right act for me to do'? I should no doubt add 'though I am not to be blamed for doing act A.' But in adding this, am I not passing from the question 'what is right' to the question 'what is morally good'? At the same time I am not making the *full* passage from the one notion to the other; for in order that the act should be morally good, or an act I am not to be blamed for doing, it must not merely be the act which it is reasonable for me to think my duty; it must also be done for that reason, or from some other morally good motive. Thus the conception of the right act as the act which it is reasonable for me to think my duty is an unsatisfactory compromise between the true notion and the right act and the notion of the morally good action.

The general principles of duty are obviously not self-evident from the beginning of our lives. How do they come to be so? The answer is, that they come to be self-evident to us just as mathematical axioms do. We find by experience that this couple of matches and that couple make four matches, that this couple of balls on a wire and that couple make four balls; and by reflection on these and similar discoveries we come to see that it is of the nature of two and two to make four. In a precisely similar way, we see the *prima facie* rightness of an act which would be the fulfilment of a particular promise, and of another which would be the fulfilment of another promise, and when we have reached sufficient maturity to think in general terms, we apprehend *prima facie* rightness to belong to the nature of any fulfilment of promise. What comes first in time is the apprehension of the self-evident *prima facie* rightness of an individual act of a particular type. From this we come by reflection to apprehend the self-evident general principle of *prima facie* duty. From this, too, perhaps along with the apprehension of the self-evident *prima facie* rightness of the same act in virtue of its having another characteristic as well, and perhaps in spite of the apprehension of its *prima facie* wrongness in virtue of its having some third characteristic, we come to believe something not self-evident at all, but an object of probable opinion, viz. that this particular act is (not *prima facie* but) actually right. . . .

Supposing it to be agreed, as I think on reflection it must, that no one *means* by 'right' just 'productive of the best possible consequences,' or 'optimific,' the attributes 'right' and 'optimific' might stand in either of two kinds of relation to each other. 1) They might be so related that we could apprehend *a priori*, either immediately or deductively, that any act that is optimific is right and any act that is right is optimific, as we can apprehend that any triangle that is equilateral is equiangular and *vice versa*. Professor Moore's view is, I think, that the coextensiveness of 'right' and 'optimific' is apprehended immediately. He rejects the possibility of any proof of it. Or 2) the two attributes might be such that the question whether they are invariably connected had to be answered by means of an inductive inquiry. Now at first sight it might seem as if the constant connexion of the two attributes could be immediately apprehended. It might seem absurd to suggest that it could be right for any one to do an act which would produce consequences less good than those which would be produced by some other act in his power. Yet a little thought will convince us that this is not absurd. The type of case in which it is easiest to see that this is so is, perhaps, that in which one has made a promise. In such a case we all think that *prima facie* it is our duty to fulfill the promise irrespective of the precise goodness of the total consequences. And though we do not think it is necessarily our actual or absolute duty to do so, we are far from thinking that any, even the slightest, gain in the value of the total consequences will necessarily justify us in doing something else instead. Suppose, to simplify the case by abstraction, that the fulfilment of a promise to *A* would produce 1,000 units of good[3] for him, but that by doing some other act I could produce 1,001 units of good for *B*, to whom I have made no promise, the other consequences of the two acts being of equal value; should we really think it self-evident that it was our duty to do the second act and not the first?

---

3. I am assuming that good is objectively quantitative, but not that we can accurately assign an exact quantitative measure to it. Since it is of a definite amount, we can make the *supposition* that its amount is so-and-so, though we cannot with any confidence *assert* that it is.

I think not. We should, I fancy, hold that only a much greater disparity of value between the total consequences would justify us in failing to discharge our *prima facie* duty to A. After all, a promise is a promise, and is not to be treated so lightly as the theory we are examining would imply. What, exactly, a promise is, is not so easy to determine, but we are surely agreed that it constitutes a serious moral limitation to our freedom of action. To produce the 1,001 units of good for B rather than fulfill our promise to A would be to take, not perhaps our duty as philanthropists too seriously, but certainly our duty as makers of promises too lightly. . . .

Such instances—and they might easily be added to—make it clear that there is no self-evident connexion between the attributes 'right' and 'optimific.' The theory we are examining has a certain attractiveness when applied to our decision that a particular act is our duty (though I have tried to show that it does not agree with our actual moral judgements even here). But it is not even plausible when applied to our recognition of *prima facie* duty. For if it were self-evident that the right coincides with the optimific, it should be self-evident that what is *prima facie* right is *prima facie* optimific. But whereas we are certain that keeping a promise is *prima facie* right, we are not certain that it is *prima facie* optimific (though we are perhaps certain that it is *prima facie* bonific). Our certainty that it is *prima facie* right depends not on its consequences but on its being the fulfilment of a promise. The theory we are examining involves too much difference between the evident ground of our conviction about *prima facie* duty and alleged ground of our conviction about actual duty. . . .

I conclude that the attributes 'right' and 'optimific' are not identical, and that we do not know either by intuition, by deduction, or by induction that they coincide in their application, still less that the latter is the foundation of the former. It must be added, however, that if we are ever under no special obligation such as that of fidelity to a promisee or of gratitude to a benefactor, we ought to do what will produce most good; and that even when we are under a special obligation the tendency of acts to promote general good is one of the main factors in determining whether they are right.

In what has preceded, a good deal of use has been made of 'what we really think' about moral questions; a certain theory has been rejected because it does not agree with what we really think. It might be said that this is in principle wrong; that we should not be content to expound what our present moral consciousness tells us but should aim at a criticism of our existing moral consciousness in the light of theory. Now I do not doubt that the moral consciousness of men has in detail undergone a good deal of modification as regards the things we think right, at the hands of moral theory. But if we are told, for instance, that we should give up our view that there is a special obligatoriness attaching to the keeping of promises because it is self-evident that the only duty is to produce as much good as possible, we have to ask ourselves whether we really, when we reflect, *are* convinced that this is self-evident, and whether we really *can* get rid of our view that promise-keeping has a bindingness independent of productiveness of maximum good. In my own experience I find that I cannot, in spite of a very genuine attempt to do so; and I venture to think that most people will find the same, and that just because they cannot lose the sense of special obligation, they cannot accept as self-evident, or even as true, the theory which would require them to do so. In fact it seems, on reflection, self-evident that a promise, simply as such, is something that *prima facie* ought to be kept, and it does *not*, on reflection, seem self-evident that production of maximum good is the only thing that makes an act obligatory. And to ask us to give up at the bidding of a theory our actual apprehension of what is right and what is wrong seems like asking people to repudiate their actual experience of beauty, at the bidding of a theory which says 'only that which satisfies such and such conditions can be beautiful.' If what I have called our actual apprehension is (as I would maintain that it is) truly an apprehension, i.e. an instance of knowledge, the request is nothing less than absurd.

I would maintain, in fact, that what we are apt to describe as 'what we think' about moral questions contains a considerable amount that we do not think but know, and that this forms the standard by reference to which the truth of any moral theory has to be tested, instead of having itself to be tested by reference to any theory. I hope that I have in what precedes indicated what in my view these elements of knowledge are that are involved in our ordinary moral consciousness.

It would be a mistake to found a natural science on 'what we really think,' i.e. on what reasonably thoughtful and well-educated people think about the subjects of the science before they have studied them scientifically. For such opinions are interpretations, and often misinterpretations, of sense-experience; and the man of science must appeal from these to sense-experience itself, which furnishes his real data. In ethics no such appeal is possible. We have no more direct way of access to the facts about rightness and goodness and about what things are right or good, than by thinking about them; the moral convictions of thoughtful and well-educated people are the data of ethics just as sense-perceptions are the data of a natural science. Just as some of the latter have to be rejected as illusory, so have some of the former; but as the latter are rejected only when they are in conflict with other more accurate sense-perceptions, the former are rejected only when they are in conflict with other convictions which stand better the test of reflection. The existing body of moral convictions of the best people is the cumulative product of the moral reflection of many generations, which has developed an extremely delicate power of appreciation of moral distinctions; and this the theorist cannot afford to treat with anything other than the greatest respect. The verdicts of the moral consciousness of the best people are the foundation on which he must build; though he must first compare them with one another and eliminate any contradictions they may contain.

24. Immanuel Kant

Immanuel Kant (1724–1804), the most influential philosopher
of the modern period, was a professor at the University
of Königsberg.

Right Acts Must Be Universalizable

. . . Unless we wish to deny to the concept of morality all truth and all
relation to a possible object, we cannot dispute that its law is of such
widespread significance as to hold, not merely for men, but for all *rational beings as such*—not merely subject to contingent conditions and
exceptions, but *with absolute necessity*. It is therefore clear that no experience can give us occasion to infer even the possibility of such
apodeictic laws. For by what right can we make what is perhaps valid
only under the contingent conditions of humanity into an object of unlimited reverence as a universal precept for every rational nature? And
how could laws for determining *our* will be taken as laws for determining the will of a rational being as such—and only because of this for
determining ours—if these laws were merely empirical and did not have
their source completely *a priori* in pure, but practical, reason?

What is more, we cannot do morality a worse service than by seeking
to derive it from examples. Every example of it presented to me must

From Immanuel Kant, *The Fundamental Principles of the Metaphysic of Morals*,
translated by H. J. Paton, 1948. Published by the Hutchinson Publishing Group Ltd.,
London, and by Harper Torchbooks, New York. Reprinted by permission of the
Hutchinson Publishing Group Ltd. The foregoing volume is a translation of Immanuel Kant, *Grundlegung zur Metaphysik der Sitten*, first published in 1785.

first itself be judged by moral principles in order to decide if it is fit to serve as an original example—that is, as a model: it can in no way supply the prime source for the concept of morality. Even the Holy One of the gospel must first be compared with our ideal of moral perfection before we can recognize him to be such. He also says of himself: 'Why callest thou me (whom thou seest) good? There is none good (the archetype of the good) but one, that is, God (whom thou seest not).' But where do we get the concept of God as the highest good? Solely from the *Idea* of moral perfection, which reason traces *a priori* and conjoins inseparably with the concept of a free will. Imitation has no place in morality, and examples serve us only for encouragement. . . .

From these considerations the following conclusions emerge. All moral concepts have their seat and origin in reason completely *a priori*, and indeed in the most ordinary human reason just as much as in the most highly speculative: they cannot be abstracted from any empirical, and therefore merely contingent, knowledge. In this purity of their origin is to be found their very worthiness to serve as supreme practical principles, and everything empirical added to them is just so much taken away from their genuine influence and from the absolute value of the corresponding actions. It is not only a requirement of the utmost necessity in respect of theory, where our concern is solely with speculation, but is also of the utmost practical importance, to draw these concepts and laws from pure reason, to set them forth pure and unmixed, and indeed to determine the extent of this whole practical, but pure, rational knowledge—that is, to determine the whole power of pure practical reason. We ought never—as speculative philosophy does allow and even at times finds necessary—to make principles depend on the special nature of human reason. Since moral laws have to hold for every rational being as such, we ought rather to derive our principles from the general concept of a rational being as such, and on this basis to expound the whole of ethics—which requires anthropology for its *application* to man—at first independently as pure philosophy, that is, entirely as metaphysics (which we can very well do in this wholly abstract kind of knowledge). We know well that without possessing such a metaphysics it is a futile endeavor, I will not say to determine accurately for speculative judgement the moral element of duty in all that accords with duty—but that it is impossible, even in ordinary and practical usage, particularly in that of moral instruction, to base morals on their genuine principles and so to bring about pure moral dispositions and engraft them on men's minds for the highest good of the world.

In this task of ours we have to progress by natural stages, not merely from ordinary moral judgement (which is here worthy of great respect) to philosophical judgement, . . . but from popular philosophy, which goes no further than it can get by fumbling about with the aid of examples, to metaphysics. (This no longer lets itself be held back by anything empirical, and indeed—since it must survey the complete totality of this kind of knowledge—goes right to Ideas, where examples themselves fail.) For this purpose we must follow—and must portray in detail—the power of practical reason from the general rules determining it right up to the point where there springs from it the concept of duty.

[Imperatives in General]

Everything in nature works in accordance with laws. Only a rational being has the power to act *in accordance with his idea* of laws—that is, in accordance with principles—and only so has he a *will*. Since *reason* is required in order to derive actions from laws, the will is nothing but practical reason. If reason infallibly determines the will, then in a being of this kind the actions which are recognized to be objectively necessary are also subjectively necessary—that is to say, the will is then a power to choose *only that* which reason independently of inclination recognizes to be practically necessary, that is, to be good. But if reason solely by itself is not sufficient to determine the will; if the will is exposed also to subjective conditions (certain impulsions) which do not always harmonize with the objective ones; if, in a word, the will is not *in itself* completely in accord with reason (as actually happens in the case of men); then actions which are recognized to be objectively necessary are subjectively contingent, and the determining of such a will in accordance with objective laws is *necessitation*. That is to say, the relation of objective laws to a will not good through and through is conceived as one in which the will of a rational being, although it is determined by principles of reason, does not necessarily follow these principles in virtue of its own nature.

The conception of an objective principle so far as this principle is necessitating for a will is called a command (of reason), and the formula of this command is called an *Imperative*.

All imperatives are expressed by an *'ought'* (*Sollen*). By this they mark the relation of an objective law of reason to a will which is not necessarily determined by this law in virtue of its subjective constitution (the relation of necessitation). They say that something would be good to do or to leave undone; only they say it to a will which does not always do a thing because it has been informed that this is a good thing to do. . . .

A perfectly good will would thus stand quite as much under objective laws (laws of the good), but it could not on this account be conceived as *necessitated* to act in conformity with law, since of itself, in accordance with its subjective constitution, it can be determined only by the concept of the good. Hence for the *divine* will, and in general for a *holy* will, there are no imperatives: *'I ought'* is here out of place, because *'I will'* is already of itself necessarily in harmony with the law. Imperatives are in consequence only formulae for expressing the relation of objective laws of willing to the subjective imperfection of the will of this or that rational being—for example, of the human will.

[Classification of Imperatives]

All *imperatives* command either *hypothetically* or *categorically*. Hypothetical imperatives declare a possible action to be practically necessary as a means to the attainment of something else that one wills (or that one may will). A categorical imperative would be one which represented an action as objectively necessary in itself apart from its relation to a further end. . . . [Hence] if the action would be good solely as a means to *something else*, the imperative is *hypothetical*; if the action is represented as good *in itself* and therefore as necessary, in virtue of its principle, for a will which of itself accords with reason, then the imperative is *categorical*.

An imperative therefore tells me which of my possible actions would be good; and it formulates a practical rule for a will that does not perform an action straight away because the action is good—whether because the subject does not always know that it is good or because, even if he did know this, he might still act on maxims contrary to the objective principles of practical reason.

A hypothetical imperative thus says only that an action is good for some purpose or other, either *possible* or *actual*. In the first case it is a *problematic* practical principle; in the second case an *assertoric* practical principle. A categorical imperative, which declares an action to be objectively necessary in itself without reference to some purpose—that is, even without any further end—ranks as an *apodeictic* practical principle. . . .

All sciences have a practical part consisting of problems which suppose that some end is possible for us and of imperatives which tell us how it is to be attained. Hence the latter can in general be called imperatives of *skill*. Here there is absolutely no question about the rationality or goodness of the end, but only about what must be done to attain it. A prescription required by a doctor in order to cure his man completely and one required by a poisoner in order to make sure of killing him are of equal value so far as each serves to effect its purpose perfectly. Since in early youth we do not know what ends may present themselves to us in the course of life, parents seek above all to make their children learn things *of many kinds;* they provide carefully for *skill* in the use of means to all sorts of *arbitrary* ends, of none of which can they be certain that it could not in the future become an actual purpose of their ward, while it is always *possible* that he might adopt it. Their care in this matter is so great that they commonly neglect on this account to form and correct the judgement of their children about the worth of the things which they might possibly adopt as ends.

There is, however, *one* end that can be presupposed as actual in all rational beings (so far they are dependent beings to whom imperatives apply); and thus there is one purpose which they not only *can* have, but which we can assume with certainty that they all *do* have by a natural necessity—the purpose, namely, of *happiness*. A hypothetical imperative which affirms the practical necessity of an action as a means to the furtherance of happiness is *assertoric*. We may represent it, not simply as necessary to an uncertain, merely possible purpose, but as necessary to a purpose which we can presuppose *a priori* and with certainty to be present in every man because it belongs to his very being. Now skill in the choice of means to one's own greatest well-being can be called *prudence* in the narrowest sense. Thus an imperative concerned with the choice of means to one's own happiness—that is, a precept of prudence —still remains *hypothetical:* an action is commanded, not absolutely, but only as a means to a further purpose.

Finally, there is an imperative which, without being based on, and conditioned by, any further purpose to be attained by a certain line of conduct, enjoins this conduct immediately. This imperative is *categorical.* It is concerned, not with the matter of the action and its presumed results, but with its form and with the principle from which it follows; and what is essentially good in the action consists in the mental disposition, let the consequences be what they may. This imperative may be called the imperative of *morality.* . . .

[How Are Imperatives Possible?]

The question now arises 'How are all these imperatives possible?' This question does not ask how we can conceive the execution of an action commanded by the imperative, but merely how we can conceive the necessitation of the will expressed by the imperative in setting us a task. How an imperative of skill is possible requires no special discussion. Who wills the end, wills (so far as reason has decisive influence on his actions) also the means which are indispensably necessary and in his power. So far as willing is concerned, this proposition is analytic: for in my willing of an object as an effect there is already conceived the causality of myself as an acting cause—that is, the use of means; and from the concept of willing an end the imperative merely extracts the concept of actions necessary to this end. (Synthetic propositions are required in order to determine the means to a proposed end, but these are concerned, not with the reason for performing the act of will, but with the cause which produces the object.) That in order to divide a line into two equal parts on a sure principle I must from its ends describe two intersecting arcs —this is admittedly taught by mathematics only in synthetic propositions; but when I know that the aforesaid effect can be produced only by such an action, the proposition 'If I fully will the effect, I also will the action required for it' is analytic; for it is one and the same thing to conceive something as an effect possible in a certain way through me and to conceive myself as acting in the same way with respect to it. . . .

[With the] categorical imperative or law of morality the reason for our difficulty (in comprehending its possibility) is a very serious one. We have here a synthetic *a priori practical* proposition,[1] and since in theoretical knowledge there is so much difficulty in comprehending the possi-

---

1. Without presupposing a condition taken from some inclination I connect an action with the will *a priori* and therefore necessarily (although only objectively so— that is, only subject to the Idea of a reason having full power over all subjective impulses to action). Here we have a practical proposition in which the willing of an action is not derived analytically from some other willing already presupposed (for we do not possess any such perfect will), but is on the contrary connected immediately with the concept of the will of a rational being as something which is not contained in this concept.

bility of propositions of this kind, it may readily be gathered that in practical knowledge the difficulty will be no less.

[The Formula of Universal Law]

In this task we wish first to enquire whether perhaps the mere concept of a categorical imperative may not also provide us with the formula containing the only proposition that can be a categorical imperative; for even when we know the purport of such an absolute command, the question of its possibility will still require a special and troublesome effort, which we postpone to the final chapter.

When I conceive a *hypothetical* imperative in general, I do not know beforehand what it will contain—until its condition is given. But if I conceive a *categorical* imperative, I know at once what it contains. For since besides the law this imperative contains only the necessity that our maxim[2] should conform to this law, while the law, as we have seen, contains no condition to limit it, there remains nothing over to which the maxim has to conform except the universality of a law as such; and it is this conformity alone that the imperative properly asserts to be necessary.

There is therefore only a single categorical imperative and it is this: *'Act only on that maxim through which you can at the same time will that it should become a universal law.'*

Now if all imperatives of duty can be derived from this one imperative as their principle, then even although we leave it unsettled whether what we call duty may not be an empty concept, we shall still be able to show at least what we understand by it and what the concept means.

[The Formula of the Law of Nature]

Since the universality of the law governing the production of effects constitutes what is properly called *nature* in its most general sense (nature as regards its form)—that is, the existence of things so far as determined by universal laws—the universal imperative of duty may also run as follows: *'Act as if the maxim of your action were to become through your will a universal law of nature.'*

[*Illustrations*]

We will now enumerate a few duties, following their customary division into duties towards self and duties towards others and into perfect and imperfect duties.

---

2. A *maxim* is a subjective principle of action and must be distinguished from an *objective principle*—namely, a practical law. The former contains a practical rule determined by reason in accordance with the conditions of the subject (often his ignorance or again his inclinations): it is thus a principle on which the subject *acts*. A law, on the other hand, is an objective principle valid for every rational being; and it is a principle on which he *ought to act*—that is, an imperative.

1. A man feels sick of life as the result of a series of misfortunes that has mounted to the point of despair, but he is still so far in possession of his reason as to ask himself whether taking his own life may not be contrary to his duty to himself. He now applies the test 'Can the maxim of my action really become a universal law of nature?' His maxim is 'From self-love I make it my principle to shorten my life if its continuance threatens more evil than it promises pleasure.' The only further question to ask is whether this principle of self-love can become a universal law of nature. It is then seen at once that a system of nature by whose law the very same feeling whose function (*Bestimmung*) is to stimulate the furtherance of life should actually destroy life would contradict itself and consequently could not subsist as a system of nature. Hence this maxim cannot possibly hold as a universal law of nature and is therefore entirely opposed to the supreme principle of all duty.

2. Another finds himself driven to borrowing money because of need. He well knows that he will not be able to pay it back; but he sees too that he will get no loans unless he gives a firm promise to pay it back within a fixed time. He is inclined to make such a promise; but he has still enough conscience to ask 'Is it not unlawful and contrary to duty to get out of difficulties in this way?' Supposing, however, he did resolve to do so, the maxim of his action would run thus: 'Whenever I believe myself short of money, I will borrow money and promise to pay it back, though I know that this will never be done.' Now this principle of self-love or personal advantage is perhaps quite compatible with my own entire future welfare; only there remains the question 'Is it right?' I therefore transform the demand of self-love into a universal law and frame my question thus: 'How would things stand if my maxim became a universal law?' I then see straight away that this maxim can never rank as a universal law of nature and be self-consistent, but must necessarily contradict itself. For the universality of a law that every one believing himself to be in need can make any promise he pleases with the intention not to keep it would make promising, and the very purpose of promising, itself impossible, since no one would believe he was being promised anything, but would laugh at utterances of this kind as empty shams.

3. A third finds in himself a talent whose cultivation would make him a useful man for all sorts of purposes. But he sees himself in comfortable circumstances, and he prefers to give himself up to pleasure rather than to bother about increasing and improving his fortunate natural aptitudes. Yet he asks himself further 'Does my maxim of neglecting my natural gifts, besides agreeing in itself with my tendency to indulgence, agree also with what is called duty?' He then sees that a system of nature coud indeed aways subsist under such a universal law, although (like the South Sea Islanders) every man should let his talents rust and should be bent on devoting his life solely to idleness, indulgence, procreation, and, in a word, to enjoyment. Only he cannot possibly *will* that this should become a universal law of nature or should be implanted in us as such a law by a natural instinct. For as a rational being he necessarily wills that all his powers should be developed, since they serve him, and are given him, for all sorts of possible ends.

4. Yet a *fourth* is himself flourishing, but he sees others who have to struggle with great hardships (and whom he could easily help); and he thinks 'What does it matter to me? Let every one be as happy as Heaven wills or as he can make himself; I won't deprive him of anything; I won't even envy him; only I have no wish to contribute anything to his well-being or to his support in distress!' Now admittedly if such an attitude were a universal law of nature, mankind could get on perfectly well —better no doubt than if everybody prates about sympathy and goodwill, and even takes pains, on occasion, to practise them, but on the other hand cheats where he can, traffics in human rights, or violates them in other ways. But although it is possible that a universal law of nature could subsist in harmony with this maxim, yet it is impossible to *will* that such a principle should hold everywhere as a law of nature. For a will which decides in this way would be in conflict with itself, since many a situation might arise in which the man needed love and sympathy from others, and in which, by such a law of nature sprung from his own will, he would rob himself of all hope of the help he wants for himself.

[The Canon of Moral Judgement]

These are some of the many actual duties—or at least of what we take to be such—whose derivation from the single principle cited above leaps to the eye. We must *be able to will* that a maxim of our action should become a universal law—this is the general canon for all moral judgement of action. Some actions are so constituted that their maxim cannot even be *conceived* as a universal law of nature without contradiction, let alone be *willed* as what *ought* to become one. In the case of others we do not find this inner impossibility, but it is still impossible to *will* that their maxim should be raised to the universality of a law of nature, because such a will would contradict itself. It is easily seen that the first kind of action is opposed to strict or narrow (rigorous) duty, the second only to wider (meritorious) duty; and thus that by these examples all duties—so far as the type of obligation is concerned (not the object of dutiful action)—are fully set out in their dependence on our single principle.

If we now attend to ourselves whenever we transgress a duty, we find that we in fact do not will that our maxim should become a universal law—since this is impossible for us—but rather that its opposite should remain a law universally: we only take the liberty of making an *exception* to it for ourselves (or even just for this once) to the advantage of our inclination. . . .

We have thus at least shown this much—that if duty is a concept which is to have meaning and real legislative authority for our actions, this can be expressed only in categorical imperatives and by no means in hypothetical ones. At the same time—and this is already a great deal— we have set forth distinctly, and determinately for every type of application, the content of the categorical imperative, which must contain the principle of all duty (if there is to be such a thing at all). But we are still not so far advanced as to prove *a priori* that there actually is an imperative of this kind—that there is a practical law which by itself commands absolutely and without any further motives, and that the following of this law is duty. . . .

Our question therefore is this: 'Is it a necessary law *for all rational beings* always to judge their actions by reference to those maxims of which they can themselves will that they should serve as universal laws?' If there is such a law, it must already be connected (entirely *a priori*) with the concept of the will of a rational being as such. But in order to discover this connexion we must, however much we may bristle, take a step beyond it—that is, into metaphysics, although into a region of it different from that of speculative philosophy, namely, the metaphysic of morals. . . . Here . . . we are discussing objective practical laws, and consequently the relation of a will to itself as determined solely by reason. Everything related to the empirical then falls away of itself; for if *reason entirely by itself* determines conduct (and it is the possibility of this which we now wish to investigate), it must necessarily do so *a priori*.

[The Formula of the End in Itself]

The will is conceived as a power of determining oneself to action in *accordance with the idea of certain laws*. And such a power can be found only in rational beings. Now what serves the will as a subjective ground of its self-determination is an *end;* and this, if it is given by reason alone, must be equally valid for all rational beings. What, on the other hand, contains merely the ground of the possibility of an action whose effect is an end is called a *means*. The subjective ground of a desire is an *impulsion (Triebfeder)*; the objective ground of a volition is a *motive (Bewegungsgrund)*. Hence the difference between subjective ends, which are based on impulsions, and objective ends, which depend on motives valid for every rational being. Practical principles are *formal* if they abstract from all subjective ends; they are *material*, on the other hand, if they are based on such ends and consequently on certain impulsions. Ends that a rational being adopts arbitrarily as *effects* of his action (material ends) are in every case only relative; for it is solely their relation to special characteristics in the subject's power of appetition which gives them their value. Hence this value can provide no universal principles, no principles valid and necessary for all rational beings and also for every volition—that is, no practical laws. Consequently all these relative ends can be the ground only of hypothetical imperatives.

Suppose, however, there were something *whose existence* has *in itself* an absolute value, something which as *an end in itself* could be a ground of determinate laws; then in it, and in it alone, would there be the ground of a possible categorical imperative—that is, of a practical law.

Now I say that man, and in general every rational being, *exists* as an end in himself, *not merely as a means* for arbitrary use by this or that will: he must in all his actions, whether they are directed to himself or to other rational beings, always be viewed *at the same time as an end*.

All the objects of inclination have only a conditioned value; for if there were not these inclinations and the needs grounded on them, their object would be valueless. Inclinations themselves, as sources of needs, are so far from having an absolute value to make them desirable for their own sake that it must rather be the universal wish of every rational being to be wholly free from them. Thus the value of all objects that can *be produced* by our action is always conditioned. Beings whose existence depends, not on our will, but on nature, have none the less, if they are non-rational beings, only a relative value as means and are consequently called *things*. Rational beings, on the other hand, are called *persons* because their nature already marks them out as ends in themselves—that is, as something which ought not to be used merely as a means—and consequently imposes to that extent a limit on all arbitrary treatment of them (and is an object of reverence). Persons therefore, are not merely subjective ends whose existence as an object of our actions has a value *for us:* they are *objective ends*—that is, things whose existence is in itself an end, and indeed an end such that in its place we can put no other end to which they should serve *simply* as means; for unless this is so, nothing at all of *absolute* value would be found anywhere. But if all value were conditioned—that is, contingent—then no supreme principle could be found for reason at all.

If then there is to be a supreme practical principle and—so far as the human will is concerned—a categorical imperative, it must be such that from the idea of something which is necessarily an end for every one because it is an *end in itself* it forms an *objective* principle of the will and consequently can serve as a practical law. The ground of this principle is: *Rational nature exists as an end in itself*. This is the way in which a man necessarily conceives his own existence: it is therefore so far a *subjective* principle of human actions. But it is also the way in which every other rational being conceives his existence on the same rational ground which is valid also for me; hence it is at the same time an *objective* principle, from which, as a supreme practical ground, it must be possible to derive all laws for the will. The practical imperative will therefore be as follows: *Act in such a way that you always treat humanity, whether in your own person or in the person of any other, never simply as a means, but always at the same time as an end.* We will now consider whether this can be carried out in practice.

[*Illustrations*]

Let us keep to our previous examples.

First, as regards the concept of necessary duty to oneself, the man who contemplates suicide will ask 'Can my action be compatible with the Idea of humanity *as an end in itself?*' If he does away with himself in order to escape from a painful situation, he is making use of a person merely as *a means* to maintain a tolerable state of affairs till the end of his life. But man is not a thing—not something to be used *merely* as a means: he must always in all his actions be regarded as an end in himself. Hence I cannot dispose of man in my person by maiming, spoiling, or killing. (A more precise determination of this principle in order to avoid all misunderstanding—for example, about having limbs amputated to save myself or about exposing my life to danger in order to preserve it, and so on—I must here forego: this question belongs to morals proper.)

Secondly, so far as necessary or strict duty to others is concerned, the man who has a mind to make a false promise to others will see at once that he is intending to make use of another man *merely as a means* to an end he does not share. For the man whom I seek to use for my own purposes by such a promise cannot possibly agree with my way of behaving to him, and so cannot himself share the end of the action. This incompatibility with the principle of duty to others leaps to the eye more obviously when we bring in examples of attempts on the freedom and property of others. For then it is manifest that a violator of the rights of man intends to use the person of others merely as a means without taking into consideration that, as rational beings, they ought always at the same time to be rated as ends—that is, only as beings who must themselves be able to share in the end of the very same action.

Thirdly, in regard to contingent (meritorious) duty to oneself, it is not enough that an action should refrain from conflicting with humanity in our own person as an end in itself: it must also *harmonize with this end*. Now there are in humanity capacities for greater perfection which form part of nature's purpose for humanity in our person. To neglect these can admittedly be compatible with the *maintenance* of humanity as an end in itself, but not with the *promotion* of this end.

Fourthly, as regards meritorious duties to others, the natural end which all men seek is their own happiness. Now humanity could no doubt subsist if everybody contributed nothing to the happiness of others but at the same time refrained from deliberately impairing their happiness. This is, however, merely to agree negatively and not positively with *humanity as an end in itself* unless every one endeavours also, so far as in him lies, to further the ends of others. For the ends of a subject who is an end in himself must, if this conception is to have its *full* effect in me, be also, as far as possible, *my* ends.

25. Jean-Paul Sartre

Jean-Paul Sartre (b. 1905) is an influential French
philosopher, novelist, and political activist. He
declined the Nobel Prize for Literature in 1964.

The Ethics of Existentialism

What is meant by the term *existentialism?*

Most people who use the word would be rather embarrassed if they
had to explain it, since, now that the word is all the rage, even the work
of a musician or painter is being called existentialist. A gossip columnist
in *Clartés* signs himself *The Existentialist*, so that by this time the word
has been so stretched and has taken on so broad a meaning, that it no
longer means anything at all. It seems that for want of an advance-guard
doctrine analogous to surrealism, the kind of people who are eager for
scandal and flurry turn to this philosophy which in other respects does
not at all serve their purposes in this sphere.

Actually, it is the least scandalous, the most austere of doctrines. It
is intended strictly for specialists and philosophers. Yet it can be defined
easily. What complicates matters is that there are two kinds of existentialist; first, those who are Christian, among whom I would include Jas-
pers and Gabriel Marcel, both Catholic; and on the other hand the
atheistic existentialists, among whom I class Heidegger, and then the
French existentialists and myself. What they have in common is that they
think that existence precedes essence, or, if you prefer, that subjectivity
must be the starting point.

Just what does that mean? Let us consider some object that is manu-

Reprinted from Jean-Paul Sartre, *The Philosophy of Existentialism*, Philosophical
Library, New York, 1965, pp. 33–49. Reprinted by permission of the publisher.

factured, for example, a book or a paper-cutter: here is an object which has been made by an artisan whose inspiration came from a concept. He referred to the concept of what a paper-cutter is and likewise to a known method of production, which is part of the concept, something which is, by and large, a routine. Thus, the paper-cutter is at once an object produced in a certain way and, on the other hand, one having a specific use; and one can not postulate a man who produces a paper-cutter but does not know what it is used for. Therefore, let us say that, for the paper-cutter, essence—that is, the ensemble of both the production routines and the properties which enable it to be both produced and defined—precedes existence. Thus, the presence of the paper-cutter or book in front of me is determined. Therefore, we have here a technical view of the world whereby it can be said that production precedes existence.

When we conceive God as the Creator, He is generally thought of as a superior sort of artisan. Whatever doctrine we may be considering, whether one like that of Descartes or that of Leibnitz, we always grant that will more or less follows understanding or, at the very least, accompanies it, and that when God creates He knows exactly what He is creating. Thus, the concept of man in the mind of God is comparable to the concept of paper-cutter in the mind of the manufacturer, and, following certain techniques and a conception, God produces man, just as the artisan, following a definition and a technique, makes a paper-cutter. Thus, the individual man is the realization of a certain concept in the divine intelligence.

In the eighteenth century, the atheism of the *philosophes* discarded the idea of God, but not so much for the notion that essence precedes existence. To a certain extent, this idea is found everywhere; we find it in Diderot, in Voltaire, and even in Kant. Man has a human nature; this human nature, which is the concept of the human, is found in all men, which means that each man is a particular example of a universal concept, man. In Kant, the result of this universality is that the wild-man, the natural man, as well as the bourgeois, are circumscribed by the same definition and have the same basic qualities. Thus, here too the essence of man precedes the historical existence that we find in nature.

Atheistic existentialism, which I represent, is more coherent. It states that if God does not exist, there is at least one being in whom existence precedes essence, a being who exists before he can be defined by any concept, and that this being is man, or, as Heidegger says, human reality. What is meant here by saying that existence precedes essence? It means that, first of all, man exists, turns up, appears on the scene, and, only afterwards, defines himself. If man, as the existentialist conceives him, is indefinable, it is because at first he is nothing. Only afterward will he be something, and he himself will have made what he will be. Thus, there is no human nature, since there is no God to conceive it. Not only is man what he conceives himself to be, but he is also only what he wills himself to be after this thrust toward existence.

Man is nothing else but what he makes of himself. Such is the first principle of existentialism. It is also what is called subjectivity, the name we are labeled with when charges are brought against us. But what do we mean by this, if not that man has a greater dignity than a stone or table? For we mean that man first exists, that is, that man first of all is the being who hurls himself toward a future and who is conscious of imagining himself as being in the future. Man is at the start a plan which is aware of itself, rather than a patch of moss, a piece of garbage, or a cauliflower; nothing exists prior to this plan; there is nothing in heaven; man will be what he will have planned to be. Not what he will want to be. Because by the word "will" we generally mean a conscious decision, which is subsequent to what we have already made of ourselves. I may want to belong to a political party, write a book, get married; but all that is only a manifestation of an earlier, more spontaneous choice that is called "will." But if existence really does precede essence, man is responsible for what he is. Thus, existentialism's first move is to make every man aware of what he is and to make the full responsibility of his existence rest on him. And when we say that a man is responsible for himself, we do not only mean that he is responsible for his own individuality, but that he is responsible for all men.

The word subjectivism has two meanings, and our opponents play on the two. Subjectivism means, on the one hand, that an individual chooses and makes himself; and, on the other, that it is impossible for man to transcend human subjectivity. The second of these is the essential meaning of existentialism. When we say that man chooses his own self, we mean that every one of us does likewise; but we also mean by that that in making this choice he also chooses all men. In fact, in creating the man that we want to be, there is not a single one of our acts which does not at the same time create an image of man as we think he ought to be. To choose to be this or that is to affirm at the same time the value of what we choose, because we can never choose evil. We always choose the good, and nothing can be good for us without being good for all.

If, on the other hand, existence precedes essence, and if we grant that we exist and fashion our image at one and the same time, the image is valid for everybody and for our whole age. Thus, our responsibility is much greater than we might have supposed, because it involves all mankind. If I am a workingman and choose to join a Christian trade-union rather than be a communist, and if by being a member I want to show that the best thing for man is resignation, that the kingdom of man is not of this world, I am not only involving my own case—I want to be resigned for everyone. As a result, my action has involved all humanity. To take a more individual matter, if I want to marry, to have children; even if this marriage depends solely on my own circumstances or passion or wish, I am involving all humanity in monogamy and not merely myself. Therefore, I am responsible for myself and for everyone else. I am creating a certain image of man of my own choosing. In choosing myself, I choose man.

This helps us understand what the actual content is of such rather grandiloquent words as anguish, forlornness, despair. As you will see, it's all quite simple.

First, what is meant by anguish? The existentialists say at once that man is anguish. What that means is this: the man who involves himself and who realizes that he is not only the person he chooses to be, but also a lawmaker who is, at the same time, choosing all mankind as well as himself, can not help escape the feeling of his total and deep responsibility. Of course, there are many people who are not anxious; but we claim that they are hiding their anxiety, that they are fleeing from it. Certainly, many people believe that when they do something, they themselves are the only ones involved, and when someone says to them, "What if everyone acted that way?" they shrug their shoulders and answer, "Everyone doesn't act that way." But really, one should always ask himself, "What would happen if everybody looked at things that way?" There is no escaping this disturbing thought except by a kind of double-dealing. A man who lies and makes excuses for himself by saying "not everybody does that," is someone with an uneasy conscience, because the act of lying implies that a universal value is conferred upon the lie.

Anguish is evident even when it conceals itself. This is the anguish that Kierkegaard called the anguish of Abraham. You know the story: an angel has ordered Abraham to sacrifice his son; if it really were an angel who has come and said, "You are Abraham, you shall sacrifice your son," everything would be all right. But everyone might first wonder, "Is it really an angel, and am I really Abraham? What proof do I have?"

There was a madwoman who had hallucinations; someone used to speak to her on the telephone and give her orders. Her doctor asked her, "Who is it who talks to you?" She answered, "He says it's God." What proof did she really have that it was God? If an angel comes to me, what proof is there that it's an angel? And if I hear voices, what proof is there that they come from heaven and not from hell, or from the subconscious, or a pathological condition? What proves that they are addressed to me? What proof is there that I have been appointed to impose my choice and my conception of man on humanity? I'll never find any proof or sign to convince me of that. If a voice addresses me, it is always for me to decide that this is the angel's voice; if I consider that such an act is a good one, it is I who will choose to say that it is good rather than bad.

Now, I'm not being singled out as an Abraham, and yet at every moment I'm obliged to perform exemplary acts. For every man, everything happens as if all mankind had its eyes fixed on him and were guiding itself by what he does. And every man ought to say to himself, "Am I really the kind of man who has the right to act in such a way that humanity might guide itself by my actions?" And if he does not say that to himself, he is masking his anguish.

There is no question here of the kind of anguish which would lead to quietism, to inaction. It is a matter of a simple sort of anguish that anybody who has had responsibilities is familiar with. For example, when a military officer takes the responsibility for an attack and sends a certain number of men to death, he chooses to do so, and in the main he alone makes the choice. Doubtless, orders come from above, but they are too broad; he interprets them, and on this interpretation depend the lives of ten or fourteen or twenty men. In making a decision he can not help having a certain anguish. All leaders know this anguish. That doesn't keep them from acting; on the contrary, it is the very condition of their action. For it implies that they envisage a number of possibilities, and when they choose one, they realize that it has value only because it is chosen. We shall see that this kind of anguish, which is the kind that existentialism describes, is explained, in addition, by a direct responsibility to the other men whom it involves. It is not a curtain separating us from action, but is part of action itself.

When we speak of forlornness, a term Heidegger was fond of, we mean only that God does not exist and that we have to face all the consequences of this. The existentialist is strongly opposed to a certain kind of secular ethics which would like to abolish God with the least possible expense. About 1880, some French teachers tried to set up a secular ethics which went something like this: God is a useless and costly hypothesis; we are discarding it; but, meanwhile, in order for there to be an ethics, a society, a civilization, it is essential that certain values be taken seriously and that they be considered as having an *a priori* existence. It must be obligatory, *a priori*, to be honest, not to lie, not to beat your wife, to have children, etc., etc. So we're going to try a little device which will make it possible to show that values exist all the same, inscribed in a heaven of ideas, though otherwise God does not exist. In other words—and this, I believe, is the tendency of everything called reformism in France—nothing will be changed if God does not exist. We shall find ourselves with the same norms of honesty, progress, and humanism, and we shall have made of God an outdated hypothesis which will peacefully die off by itself.

The existentialist, on the contrary, thinks it very distressing that God does not exist, because all possibility of finding values in a heaven of ideas disappears along with Him; there can no longer be an *a priori* Good, since there is no infinite and perfect consciousness to think it. Nowhere is it written that the Good exists, that we must be honest, that we must not lie; because the fact is we are on a plane where there are only men. Dostoevsky said, "If God didn't exist, everything would be possible." That is the very starting point of existentialism. Indeed, everything is permissible if God does not exist, and as a result man is forlorn, because neither within him nor without does he find anything to cling to. He can't start making excuses for himself.

If existence really does precede essence, there is no explaining things away by reference to a fixed and given human nature. In other words, there is no determinism, man is free, man is freedom. On the other hand, if God does not exist, we find no values or commands to turn to which legitimize our conduct. So, in the bright realm of values, we have no excuse behind us, nor justification before us. We are alone, with no excuses.

That is the idea I shall try to convey when I say that man is condemned to be free. Condemned, because he did not create himself, yet, in other respects is free; because, once thrown into the world, he is responsible for everything he does. The existentialist does not believe in the power of passion. He will never agree that a sweeping passion is a ravaging torrent which fatally leads a man to certain acts and is therefore an excuse. He thinks that man is responsible for his passion.

The existentialist does not think that man is going to help himself by finding in the world some omen by which to orient himself. Because he thinks that man will interpret the omen to suit himself. Therefore, he thinks that man, with no support and no aid, is condemned every moment to invent man. Ponge, in a very fine article, has said, "Man is the future of man." That's exactly it. But if it is taken to mean that this future is recorded in heaven, that God sees it, then it is false, because it would really no longer be a future. If it is taken to mean that, whatever a man may be, there is a future to be forged, a virgin future before him, then this remark is sound. But then we are forlorn.

To give you an example which will enable you to understand forlornness better, I shall cite the case of one of my students who came to see me under the following circumstances: his father was on bad terms with his mother, and, moreover, was inclined to be a collaborationist; his older brother had been killed in the German offensive of 1940, and the young man, with somewhat immature but generous feelings, wanted to avenge him. His mother lived alone with him, very much upset by the half-treason of her husband and the death of her older son; the boy was her only consolation.

The boy was faced with the choice of leaving for England and joining the Free French Forces—that is, leaving his mother behind—or remaining with his mother and helping her to carry on. He was fully aware that the woman lived only for him and that his going-off—and perhaps his death—would plunge her into despair. He was also aware that every act that he did for his mother's sake was a sure thing, in the sense that it was helping her to carry on, whereas every effort he made toward going off and fighting was an uncertain move which might run aground and prove completely useless; for example, on his way to England he might, while passing through Spain, be detained indefinitely in a Spanish camp; he might reach England or Algiers and be stuck in an office at a desk job. As a result, he was faced with two very different kinds of action: one, concrete, immediate, but concerning only one individual; the other concerned an incomparably vaster group, a national collectivity, but for that very reason was dubious, and might be interrupted en route. And, at the same time, he was wavering between two kinds of ethics. On the one hand, an ethics of sympathy, of personal devotion; on the other, a broader ethics, but one whose efficacy was more dubious. He had to choose between the two.

Who could help him choose? Christian doctrine? No. Christian doctrine says, "Be charitable, love your neighbor, take the more rugged path, etc., etc." But which is the more rugged path? Whom should he love as a brother? The fighting man or his mother? Which does the greater good, the vague act of fighting in a group, or the concrete one of helping a particular human being to go on living? Who can decide a priori? Nobody. No book of ethics can tell him. The Kantian ethics says, "Never treat any person as a means, but as an end." Very well, if I stay with my mother, I'll treat her as an end and not as a means; but by virtue of this very fact, I'm running the risk of treating the people around me who are fighting, as means; and, conversely, if I go to join those who are fighting,

I'll be treating them as an end, and, by doing that, I run the risk of treating my mother as a means.

If values are vague, and if they are always too broad for the concrete and specific case that we are considering, the only thing left for us is to trust our instincts. That's what this young man tried to do; and when I saw him, "In the end, feeling is what counts. I ought to choose whichever pushes me in one direction. If I feel that I love my mother enough to sacrifice everything else for her—my desire for vengeance, for action, for adventure—then I'll stay with her. If, on the contrary, I feel that my love for my mother isn't enough, I'll leave."

But how is the value of a feeling determined? What gives his feeling for his mother value? Precisely the fact that he remained with her. I may say that I like so-and-so well enough to sacrifice a certain amount of money for him, but I may say so only if I've done it. I may say "I love my mother well enough to remain with her" if I have remained with her. The only way to determine the value of this affection is, precisely, to perform an act which confirms and defines it. But, since I require this affection to justify my act, I find myself caught in a vicious circle.

On the other hand, Gide has well said that a mock feeling and a true feeling are almost indistinguishable; to decide that I love my mother and will remain with her, or to remain with her by putting on an act, amount somewhat to the same thing. In other words, the feeling is formed by the acts one performs; so, I can not refer to it in order to act upon it. Which means that I can neither seek within myself the true condition which will impel me to act, nor apply to a system of ethics for concepts which will permit me to act. You will say, "At least, he did go to a teacher for advice." But if you seek advice from a priest, for example, you have chosen this priest; you already knew, more or less, just about what advice he was going to give you. In other words, choosing your adviser is involving yourself. The proof of this is that if you are a Christian, you will say, "Consult a priest." But some priests are collaborating, some are just marking time, some are resisting. Which to choose? If the young man chooses a priest who is resisting or collaborating, he has already decided on the kind of advice he's going to get. Therefore, in coming to see me he knew the answer I was going to give him, and I had only one answer to give: "You're free, choose, that is, invent." No general ethics can show you what is to be done; there are no omens in the world. The Catholics will reply, "But there are." Granted—but, in any case, I myself choose the meaning they have.

When I was a prisoner, I knew a rather remarkable young man who was a Jesuit. He had entered the Jesuit order in the following way: he had had a number of very bad breaks; in childhood, his father died, leaving him in poverty, and he was a scholarship student at a religious institution where he was constantly made to feel that he was being kept out of charity; then, he failed to get any of the honors and distinctions that children like; later on, at about eighteen, he bungled a love affair; finally at twenty-two, he failed in military training, a childish enough matter, but it was the last straw.

This young fellow might well have felt that he had botched everything. It was a sign of something, but of what? He might have taken refuge in bitterness or despair. But he very wisely looked upon all this as a sign that he was not made for secular triumphs, and that only the triumphs of religion, holiness, and faith were open to him. He saw the hand of God in all this, and so he entered the order. Who can help seeing that he alone decided what the sign meant?

Some other interpretation might have been drawn from this series of setbacks; for example, that he might have done better to turn carpenter or revolutionist. Therefore, he is fully responsible for the interpretation. Forlornness implies that we ourselves choose our being. Forlornness and anguish go together.

As for despair, the term has a very simple meaning. It means that we shall confine ourselves to reckoning only with what depends upon our will, or on the ensemble of probabilities which make our action possible. When we want something, we always have to reckon with probabilities. I may be counting on the arrival of a friend. The friend is coming by rail or street-car; this supposes that the train will arrive on schedule, or that the street-car will not jump the track. I am left in the realm of possibility; but possibilities are to be reckoned with only to the point where my action comports with the ensemble of these possibilities, and no further. The moment the possibilities I am considering are not rigorously involved by my action, I ought to disengage myself from them, because no God, no scheme, can adapt the world and its possibilities to my will. When Descartes said, "Conquer yourself rather than the world," he meant essentially the same thing.

The Marxists to whom I have spoken reply, "You can rely on the support of others in your action, which obviously has certain limits because you're not going to live forever. That means: rely on both what others are doing elsewhere to help you, in China, in Russia, and what they will do later on, after your death, to carry on the action and lead it to its fulfillment, which will be the revolution. You even *have* to rely upon that, otherwise you're immoral." I reply at once that I will always rely on fellow-fighters insofar as these comrades are involved with me in a common struggle, in the unity of a party or a group in which I can more or less make my weight felt; that is, one whose ranks I am in as a fighter and whose movements I am aware of at every moment. In such a situation, relying on the unity and will of the party is exactly like counting on the fact that the train will arrive on time or that the car won't jump the track. But, given that man is free and that there is no human nature for me to depend on, I can not count on men whom I do not know by relying on human goodness or man's concern for the good of society. I don't know what will become of the Russian revolution; I may make an example of it to the extent that at the present time it is apparent that the proletariat plays a part in Russia that it plays in no other nation. But I can't swear that this will inevitably lead to a triumph of the proletariat. I've got to limit myself to what I see.

Given that men are free and that tomorrow they will freely decide what man will be, I can not be sure that, after my death, fellow-fighters will carry on my work to bring it to its maximum perfection. Tomorrow, after my death, some men may decide to set up Fascism, and the others may be cowardly and muddled enough to let them do it. Fascism will then be the human reality, so much the worse for us.

Actually, things will be as man will have decided they are to be. Does that mean that I should abandon myself to quietism? No. First, I should involve myself; then, act on the old saw, "Nothing ventured, nothing gained." Nor does it mean that I shouldn't belong to a party, but rather that I shall have no illusions and shall do what I can. For example, suppose I ask myself, "Will socialization, as such, ever come about?" I know nothing about it. All I know is that I'm going to do everything in my power to bring it about. Beyond that, I can't count on anything. Quietism is the attitude of people who say, "Let others do what I can't do." The doctrine I am presenting is the very opposite of quietism, since it declares, "There is no reality except in action." Moreover, it goes further, since it adds, "Man is nothing else than his plan; he exists only to the extent that he fulfills himself; he is therefore nothing else than the ensemble of his acts, nothing else than his life."

According to this, we can understand why our doctrine horrifies certain people. Because often the only way they can bear their wretchedness is to think, "Circumstances have been against me. What I've been and done doesn't show my true worth. To be sure, I've had no great love, no great friendship, but that's because I haven't met a man or woman who was worthy. The books I've written haven't been very good because I haven't had the proper leisure. I haven't had children to devote myself to because I didn't find a man with whom I could have spent my life. So there remains within me, unused and quite viable, a host of propensities, inclinations, possibilities, that one wouldn't guess from the mere series of things I've done."

Now, for the existentialist there is really no love other than one which manifests itself in a person's being in love. There is no genius other than one which is expressed in works of art; the genius of Proust is the sum of Proust's works; the genius of Racine is his series of tragedies. Outside of that, there is nothing. Why say that Racine could have written another tragedy, when he didn't write it? A man is involved in life, leaves his impress on it, and outside of that there is nothing. To be sure, this may seem a harsh thought to someone whose life hasn't been a success. But, on the other hand, it prompts people to understand that reality alone is what counts, that dreams, expectations, and hopes warrant no more than to define a man as a disappointed dream, as miscarried hopes, as vain expectations. In other words, to define him negatively and not positively. However, when we say, "You are nothing else than your life," that does not imply that the artist will be judged solely on the basis of his works of art; a thousand other things will contribute toward summing him up. What we mean is that a man is nothing else than a series of undertakings, that he is the sum, the organization, the ensemble of the relationships which make up these undertakings. . . .

26. Kurt Baier

**Kurt Baier is Professor of Philosophy at the University
of Pittsburgh.**

It Is Rational to Act Morally

The Supremacy of Moral Reasons

Are moral reasons really superior to reasons of self-interest as we all believe? Do we really have reason on our side when we follow moral reasons
against self-interest? What reasons could there be for being moral? Can
we really give an answer to "Why should we be moral?" It is obvious that
all these questions come to the same thing. When we ask, "Should we be
moral?" or "Why should we be moral?" or "Are moral reasons superior to
all others?" we ask to be shown the reason for being moral. What is this
reason?

Let us begin with a state of affairs in which reasons of self-interest are
supreme. In such a state everyone keeps his impulses and inclinations in
check when and only when they would lead him into behavior detrimental
to his own interest. Everyone who follows reason will discipline himself
to rise early, to do his exercises, to refrain from excessive drinking and
smoking, to keep good company, to marry the right sort of girl, to work
and study hard in order to get on, and so on. However, it will often happen that people's interests conflict. In such a case, they will have to resort
to ruses or force to get their own way. As this becomes known, men will
become suspicious, for they will regard one another as scheming com-

petitors for the good things in life. The universal supremacy of the rules of self-interest must lead to what Hobbes called the state of nature. At the same time, it will be clear to everyone that universal obedience to certain rules overriding self-interest would produce a state of affairs which serves everyone's interest much better than his unaided pursuit of it in a state where everyone does the same. Moral rules are universal rules designed to override those of self-interest when following the latter is harmful to others. "Thou shalt not kill," "Thou shalt not lie," "Thou shalt not steal" are rules which forbid the inflicting of harm on someone else even when this might be in one's interest.

The very *raison d'être* of a morality is to yield reasons which overrule the reasons of self-interest in those cases when everyone's following self-interest would be harmful to everyone. Hence moral reasons are superior to all others.

"But what does this mean?" it might be objected. "If it merely means that we do so regard them, then you are of course right, but your contention is useless, a mere point of usage. And how could it mean any more? If it means that we not only do so regard them, but *ought* so to regard them, then there must be *reasons* for saying this. But there could not be any reasons for it. If you offer reasons of self-interest you are arguing in a circle. Moreover, it cannot be true that it is always in my interest to treat moral reasons as superior to reasons of self-interest. If it were, self-interest and morality could never conflict, but they notoriously do. It is equally circular to argue that there are moral reasons for saying that one ought to treat moral reasons as superior to reasons of self-interest. And what other reasons are there?"

The answer is that we are now looking at the world from the point of view of *anyone*. We are not examining particular alternative courses of action before this or that person; we are examining two alternative worlds, one in which moral reasons are always treated by everyone as superior to reasons of self-interest and one in which the reverse is the practice. And we can see that the first world is the better world, because we can see that the second world would be the sort which Hobbes describes as the state of nature.

This shows that I ought to be moral, for when I ask the question "What ought I to do?" I am asking, "Which is the course of action supported by the best reasons?" But since it has just been shown that moral reasons are superior to reasons of self-interest, I have been given a reason for being moral, for following moral reasons rather than any other, namely, they are better reasons than any other.

But is this always so? Do we have a reason for being moral whatever the conditions we find ourselves in? Could there not be situations in which it is not true that we have reasons for being moral, that, on the contrary, we have reasons for ignoring the demands of morality? Is not Hobbes right in saying that in a state of nature the laws of nature, that is, the rules of morality, bind only *in foro interno*?

Hobbes argues as follows.

i) To live in a state of nature is to live outside society. It is to live in conditions in which there are no common ways of life and, therefore, no reliable expectations about other people's behavior other than that they will follow their inclination or their interest.

ii) In such a state reason will be the enemy of co-operation and mutual trust. For it is too risky to hope that other people will refrain from protecting their own interests by the preventive elimination of probable or even possible dangers to them. Hence reason will counsel everyone to avoid these risks by preventive action. But this leads to war.

iii) It is obvious that everyone's following self-interest leads to a state of affairs which is desirable from no one's point of view. It is, on the contrary, desirable that everybody should follow rules overriding self-interest whenever that is to the detriment of others. In other words, it is desirable to bring about a state of affairs in which all obey the rules of morality.

iv) However, Hobbes claims that in the state of nature it helps nobody if a single person or a small group of persons begins to follow the rules of morality, for this could only lead to the extinction of such individuals or groups. In such a state, it is therefore contrary to reason to be moral.

v) The situation can change, reason can support morality, only when the presumption about other people's behavior is reversed. Hobbes thought that this could be achieved only by the creation of an absolute ruler with absolute power to enforce his laws. We have already seen that this is not true and that it is quite different if people live in a society, that is, if they have common ways of life, which are taught to all members and somehow enforced by the group. Its members have reason to expect their fellows generally to obey its rules, that is, its religion, morality, customs, and law, even when doing so is not, on certain occasions, in their interest. Hence they too have reason to follow these rules.

Is this argument sound? One might, of course, object to step i) on the grounds that this is an empirical proposition for which there is little or no evidence. For how can we know whether it is true that people in a state of nature would follow only their inclinations or, at best, reasons of self-interest, when nobody now lives in that state or has ever lived in it?

However, there is some empirical evidence to support this claim. For in the family of nations, individual states are placed very much like individual persons in a state of nature. The doctrine of the sovereignty of nations and the absence of an effective international law and police force are a guarantee that nations live in a state of nature, without commonly accepted rules that are somehow enforced. Hence it must be granted that living in a state of nature leads to living in a state in which individuals act either on impulse or as they think their interest dictates. For states pay only lip service to morality. They attack their hated neighbors when the opportunity arises. They start preventive wars in order to destroy the enemy before he can deliver his knockout blow. Where interests conflict, the stronger party usually has his way, whether his claims are justified or not. And where the relative strength of the parties is not obvious, they usually resort to arms in order to determine "whose side God is on." Treaties are frequently concluded but, morally speaking, they are not worth the paper they are written on. Nor do the partners regard them as contracts binding in the ordinary way, but rather as public expressions of the belief of the governments concerned that for the time being their alliance is in the interest of the allies. It is well understood that such treaties may be canceled before they reach their predetermined end or simply broken when it suits one partner. In international affairs, there are very few examples of *Nibelungentreue*, although statesmen whose countries have profited from keeping their treaties usually make such high moral claims.

It is, moreover, difficult to justify morality in international affairs. For suppose a highly moral statesman were to demand that his country adhere to a treaty obligation even though this meant its ruin or possibly its extinction. Suppose he were to say that treaty obligations are sacred and must be kept whatever the consequences. How could he defend such a policy? Perhaps one might argue that someone has to make a start in order to create mutual confidence in international affairs. Or one might say that setting a good example is the best way of inducing others to follow suit. But such a defense would hardly be sound. The less skeptical one is about the genuineness of the cases in which nations have adhered to their treaties from a sense of moral obligation, the more skeptical one must be about the effectiveness of such examples of virtue in effecting a change of international practice. Power politics still govern in international affairs.

We must, therefore, grant Hobbes the first step in his argument and admit that in a state of nature people, as a matter of psychological fact, would not follow the dictates of morality. But we might object to the next step that knowing this psychological fact about other people's behavior constitutes a reason for behaving in the same way. Would it not still be immoral for anyone to ignore the demands of morality even though he knows that others are likely or certain to do so, too? Can we offer as a justification for morality the fact that no one is entitled to do wrong just because someone else is doing wrong? This argument begs the question whether it *is* wrong for anyone in this state to disregard the demands of morality. It cannot be wrong to break a treaty or make preventive war if we have no reason to obey the moral rules. For to say that it is wrong to do so is to say that we ought not to do so. But if we have no reason for obeying the moral rule, then we have no reason overruling self-interest, hence no reason for keeping the treaty when keeping it is not in our interest, hence it is not true that we ought to keep it, hence not true that it is wrong not to keep it.

I conclude that Hobbes's argument is sound. Moralities are systems of principles whose acceptance by everyone as overruling the dictates of self-interest is in the interest of everyone alike, though following the rules of a morality is not of course identical with following self-interest. If it were, there could be no conflict between a morality and self-interest and no point in having moral rules overriding self-interest. Hobbes is also right in saying that the application of this system of rules is in accordance with reason only in social conditions, that is, when they are well-established ways of behavior.

The answer to our question "Why should we be moral?" is therefore as follows. We should be moral because being moral is following rules designed to overrule self-interest whenever it is in the interest of every-one alike that everyone should set aside his interest. It is not self-contradictory to say this, because it may be in one's interest *not* to follow one's interest at times. We have already seen that enlightened self-interest acknowledges this point. But while enlightened self-interest does not require any genuine sacrifice from anyone, morality does. In the interest of the possibility of the good life for everyone, voluntary sacri-fices are sometimes required from everybody. Thus, a person might do better for himself by following enlightened self-interest rather than morality. The best possible life *for everyone* is possible only by every-one's following the rules of morality, that is, rules which quite frequently may require individuals to make genuine sacrifices.

It must be added to this, however, that such a system of rules has the support of reason only where people live in societies, that is, in conditions in which there are established common ways of behavior. Outside society, people have no reason for following such rules, that is, for being moral. In other words, outside society, the very distinction between right and wrong vanishes.

27. William K. Frankena

W. K. Frankena is Professor of Philosophy at the University of Michigan.

Reasons for Acting Morally

Why Be Moral?

Another problem that remains has been mentioned before. Why should we be moral? Why should we take part in the moral institution of life? Why should we adopt the moral point of view? We have already seen that the question, "Why should . . . ?" is ambiguous, and may be a request either for motivation or for justification. Here, then, one may be asking for (1) the motives for doing what is morally right, (2) a justification for doing what is morally right, (3) motivation for adopting the moral point of view and otherwise subscribing to the moral institution of life, or (4) a justification of morality and the moral point of view. It is easy to see the form an answer to a request for (1) and (3) must take; it will consist in pointing out the various prudential and nonprudential motives for doing what is right or for participating in the moral institution of life. Most of these are familiar or readily thought of and need not be detailed here. A request for (2) might be taken as a request for a *moral* justification for doing what is right. Then, the answer is that doing what is morally right does not need a justification, since the justification has already been given in showing that it is right. On this interpretation, a request for (2) is like asking, "Why morally ought I to do what is morally right?" A request for (2) may also, however, be meant as a demand for a nonmoral justification

From William K. Frankena, ETHICS, 2nd edition. © 1973, pp. 114–117. Reprinted by permission of Prentice-Hall, Inc., Englewood Cliffs, New Jersey.

of doing what is morally right; then, the answer to it will be like the answer to a request for (4). For a request for (4), being a request for reasons for subscribing to the moral way of thinking, judging, and living, must be a request for a nonmoral justification of morality. What will this be like?

There seem to be two questions here. First, why should *society* adopt such an institution as morality? Why should it foster such a system for the guidance of conduct in addition to convention, law, and prudence? To this the answer seems clear. The conditions of a satisfactory human life for people living in groups could hardly obtain otherwise. The alternatives would seem to be either a state of nature in which all or most of us would be worse off than we are, even if Hobbes is wrong in thinking that life in such a state would be "solitary, poor, nasty, brutish, and short"; or a leviathan civil state more totalitarian than any yet dreamed of, one in which the laws would cover all aspects of life and every possible deviation by the individual would be closed off by an effective threat of force.

The other question has to do with the nonmoral reasons (not just motives) there are for an *individual's* adopting the moral way of thinking and living. To some extent, the answer has just been given, but only to some extent. For on reading the last paragraph an individual might say, "Yes. This shows that society requires morality and even that it is to my advantage to have others adopt the moral way of life. But it does not show that I should adopt it and certainly not that I should *always* act according to it. And it is no use arguing on moral grounds that I should. I want a nonmoral justification for thinking I should." Now, if this means that he wants to be shown that it is always to his advantage—that is, that his life will invariably be better or, at least, not worse in the prudential sense of better and worse—if he thoroughly adopts the moral way of life, then I doubt that his demand can always be met. Through the use of various familiar arguments, one can show that the moral way of life is likely to be to his advantage, but it must be admitted in all honesty that one who takes the moral road may be called upon to make a sacrifice and, hence, may not have as good a life in the nonmoral sense as he would otherwise have had.

The point made at the end of Chapter 5 must be recalled here, namely, that morally good or right action is one kind of excellent activity and hence is a prime candidate for election as part of any good life, especially since it is a kind of excellent activity of which all normal people are capable. It does seem to me that this is an important consideration in the answer to our present question. Even if we add it to the usual arguments, however, we still do not have a conclusive proof that every individual should in the nonmoral sense under discussion, always do the morally excellent thing. For, as far as I can see, from a prudential point of view, some individuals might have nonmorally better lives if they sometimes did what is not morally excellent, for example in cases in which a considerable self-sacrifice is morally required. A TV speaker once said of his subject, "He was too good for his good," and it seems to me that this may sometimes be true.

It does not follow that one cannot justify the ways of morality to an individual, although it may follow that one cannot justify morality to some individuals. For nonmoral justification is not necessarily egoistic or prudential. If A asks B why he, A, should be moral, B may reply by asking A to try to decide in a rational way what kind of life he wishes to live or what kind of a person he wishes to be. That is, B may ask A what way of life A would choose if he were to choose rationally, or in other words, freely, impartially, and in full knowledge of what it is like to live the various alternative ways of life, including the moral one. B may then be able to convince A, when he is calm and cool in this way, that the way of life he prefers, all things considered, includes the moral way of life. If so, then he has justified the moral way of life to A. A may even, when he considers matters in such a way, prefer a life that includes self-sacrifice on his part.

Of course, A may refuse to be rational, calm, and cool. He may retort, "But why should I be rational?" However, if this was his posture in originally asking for justification, he had no business asking for it. For one can only ask for justification if one is willing to be rational. One cannot consistently ask for reasons unless one is ready to accept reasons of some sort. Even in asking, "Why should I be rational?" one is implicitly committing oneself to rationality, for such a commitment is part of the connotation of the word "should."

What kind of a life A would choose if he were fully rational and knew all about himself and the world will, of course, depend on what sort of a person he is (and people are different), but if psychological egoism is not true of any of us, it may always be that A would then choose a way of life that would be moral. As Bertrand Russell once wrote:

> We have wishes which are not purely personal . . . The sort of life that most of us admire is one which is guided by large, impersonal desires . . . Our desires are, in fact, more general and less purely selfish than many moralists imagine. . . .[1]

Perhaps A has yet one more question: Is society justified in demanding that I adopt the moral way of life, and in blaming and censuring me if I do not?" But this is a moral question; and A can hardly expect it to be allowed that society is justified in doing this to A only if it can show that doing so is to A's advantage. However, if A is asking whether society is morally justified in requiring of him at least a certain minimal subscription to the moral institution of life, then the answer surely is that society sometimes is justified in this, as Socrates argued in the *Crito*. But society must be careful here. For it is itself morally required to respect the individual's autonomy and liberty, and in general to treat him justly; and it must remember that morality is made to minister to the good lives of individuals and not to interfere with them any more than is necessary. Morality is made for man, not man for morality.

1. *Religion and Science* (New York: Henry Holt and Co., 1935), pp. 252–54.

SUGGESTED READINGS

Value and Obligation

General Books on Ethics

Brandt, R. B. *Ethical Theory*. Englewood Cliffs, N.J.: Prentice-Hall, Inc., 1959.
Dewey, John. *Theory of the Moral Life*. New York: Holt, Rinehart and Winston, Inc., 1960.
Ewing, A. C. *Ethics*. New York: The Macmillan Company, 1953. (elementary)
Frankena, W. K. *Ethics*. Englewood Cliffs, N.J.: Prentice-Hall, Inc., 1973. (beginning)
Garner, R. T., and Rosen, B. *Moral Philosophy*. The Macmillan Company, New York, 1967. (introductory)
Grice, G. R. *The Grounds of Moral Judgment*. Cambridge: Cambridge University Press, 1967. (advanced)
Hare, R. M. *Freedom and Reason*. Oxford University Press, 1963.
Harrison, Jonathan. *Our Knowledge of Right and Wrong*. London: George Allen and Unwin, Ltd., 1971.
Hospers, John. *Human Conduct*. New York: Harcourt, Brace & World, Inc., 1972.
Nowell-Smith, P. H. *Ethics*. Baltimore: Penguin Books, 1954.
Rawls, John. *A Theory of Justice*. Cambridge, Mass.: Harvard University Press, 1971. (advanced)
Sartorius, R. *Individual Conduct and Social Norms.*
Sidgwick, Henry. *The Methods of Ethics*. London: Macmillan and Co., Ltd., 1922. (advanced)
Stace, W. T. *The Concept of Morals*. New York: The Macmillan Company, 1937.
Taylor, P. W. *Principles of Ethics*. Encino, Calif.: Dickenson Pub. Co., 1975. (introductory)
Taylor, Richard. *Good and Evil*. New York: The Macmillan Company, 1970.
Zink, S. *The Concepts of Ethics.* New York: St. Martin's Press, 1962. (advanced)

Anthologies in Ethics

Abelson, R., and Friquegnon, M. L. *Ethics for Modern Life*. New York: St. Martin's Press, 1975.
Bayles, Michael D. *Contemporary Utilitarianism*. New York: Doubleday and Company, Inc., 1968.
Brandt, R. B. *Value and Obligation*. New York: Harcourt, Brace, and World, 1961.
Brody, B. A. *Moral Rules and Particular Circumstances*. Englewood Cliffs., N.J., Prentice-Hall, Inc., 1970.
Dewey, R. E., Gramlich, F. W., and Loftsgordon, D. *Problems of Ethics*. New York: The Macmillan Company, 1961.
Exman, Rosalind. *Readings in the Problems of Ethics*. New York: Charles Scribner's Sons, 1965.

Feinberg, J., and West, H. *Moral Philosophy.* Encino, Calif.: Dickenson Publishing Co., Inc., 1977.

Frankena, W. K., and Granrose, J. T. *Introductory Readings in Ethics.* Englewood Cliffs, N.J.: Prentice-Hall, Inc., 1974.

Gauthier, David P. *Morality and Rational Self-Interest.* Englewood Cliffs, N.J.: Prentice-Hall, Inc., 1970.

Gorovitz, Samuel. *Utilitarianism: John Stuart Mill.* Indianapolis, Ind.: The Bobbs-Merrill Company, Inc., 1971.

Hearn, T. K. *Studies in Utilitarianism.* New York: Appleton-Century-Crofts, 1971.

Johnson, Oliver. *Ethics: Selections from Classical and Contemporary Writers.* New York: Holt, Rinehart and Winston, 1965.

Jones, W. T., Sontag, F., and Beckner, Morton O. *Approaches to Ethics.* New York: McGraw-Hill Book Company, 1969.

Melden, A. I. *Ethical Theories.* Englewood Cliffs, N.J.: Prentice-Hall, Inc., 1955.

Pahel, Kenneth, and Schiller, Marvin. *Readings in Contemporary Ethical Theory.* Englewood Cliffs, N.J.: Prentice-Hall, Inc., 1970.

Rachels, J. *Moral Problems.* New York: Harper & Row, Publishers, 1975.

Sellars, W., and Hospers, J. *Readings in Ethical Theory.* New York: Appleton-Century-Crofts, 1971.

Smith, J. M., and Sosa, Ernest. *Mill's Utilitarianism.* Belmont, Calif.: Wadsworth Publishing Company, Inc., 1969.

Taylor, Paul W. *Problems of Moral Philosophy.* Encino, Calif.: Dickenson Publishing Company, Inc., 1972.

Wasserstrom, Richard. *Today's Moral Problems.* New York: The Macmillan Company, 1975.

Ethical Relativism

Benedict, Ruth. *Patterns of Culture.* New York: Pelican Books, 1946.

Brandt, R. B. *Ethical Theory.* Englewood Cliffs, N.J.: Prentice-Hall, Inc., 1959.

——————————. *Hopi Ethics: A Theoretical Analysis.* Chicago: The University of Chicago Press, 1954.

Herskovits, M. J. *Cultural Anthropology.* New York: Knopf, 1955.

Ladd, John (ed.), *Ethical Relativism.* Belmont, Calif.: Wadsworth Publishing Company, 1973.

Linton, Ralph. "The Problem of Universal Values," in R. F. Spencer (ed.), *Method and Perspective in Anthropology.* Minneapolis: University of Minnesota Press, 1954. [Reprinted in Brandt, *Value and Obligation.*]

Stace, W. T. *The Concept of Morals.* Chaps. 1 and 2. [Reprinted in Tillman, Berofsky, and O'Connor.]

Sumner, W. G. *Folkways.* Boston: Ginn & Co., 1934. [Excerpted in Brandt and Johnson.]

Taylor, P. "Four Types of Ethical Relativism," *Philosophical Review,* 63 (1954), 500–16.

——————————. "Social Science and Ethical Relativism," *Journal of Philosophy,* 55 (1958), 32–43. [Reprinted in Taylor.]

Wellman, Carl. "The Ethical Implications of Cultural Relativity," *Journal of Philosophy,* 60 (1963), 169–84.

Westermarck, E. *The Origin and Development of the Moral Ideas.* Vol. I. New York: The Macmillan Company, 1906. Chaps. 1 to 5.

Theology and Ethics

Augustine, St. "The Morals of the Catholic Church." In *Basic Writings of Saint Augustine,* ed. Whitney J. Oates. New York: Random House, 1948. [Excerpted in Brandt, and Johnson, *Ethics.*]

Brandt, R. B. *Ethical Theory.* Englewood Cliffs, N.J.: Prentice-Hall, Inc., 1959. Chap. 4.

Brunner, Emil. *The Divine Imperative.* Philadelphia: Westminster Press, 1947. [Excerpted in Johnson, *Ethics,* and Dewey-Gramlich-Loftsgordon.]

Ewing, A. C. "Ethics and Belief in God," *The Hibbert Journal,* 39 (1941), 375–88.

Hospers, John. *Human Conduct.* New York: Harcourt, Brace & World, Inc., 1972.

Mortimer, R. C. *Christian Ethics.* London: Hutchinson's University Library, 1950.

Paley, William. *The Principles of Moral and Political Philosophy.* 1785. Many editions.

Plato. *Euthyphro,* in *Plato on the Trial and Death of Socrates,* trans. by Lane Cooper. Ithaca, N.Y.: Cornell University Press, 1941. [Reprinted in Brandt.]

Ramsey, I. T., ed. *Christian Ethics and Contemporary Philosophy.* London: SCM Press, 1966.

Rashdall, H. *Conscience and Christ.* London: Gerald Duckworth & Co., Ltd., 1933.

Thomas, George W. *Christian Ethics and Moral Philosophy.* New York: Charles Scribner's Sons, 1955. [Excerpted in Brandt.]

Intuitionist or Rationalist Views

Broad, C. D. *Five Types of Ethical Theory.* New York: Humanities Press, Inc., 1956, 266–73.

Ewing, A. C. *Ethics.* New York: The Macmillan Company, 1947. Chaps. 6 and 7. [Excerpted in Ekman.]

——————————. *The Definition of Good.* New York: The Macmillan Company, 1947.

Hudson, W. D. *Ethical Intuitionism.* New York: St. Martin's Press, 1967.

Moore, G. E. *Principia Ethica.* Cambridge: Cambridge University Press, 1929. [Excerpted in Dewey-Gramlich-Loftsgordon; Melden.]

Price, Richard. *A Review of the Principal Questions in Morals.* Oxford: The Clarendon Press, 1948. [Excerpted in Brandt.]

Critics:

Brandt, R. B. *Ethical Theory.* Englewood Cliffs, N.J.: Prentice-Hall, Inc., 1959. Chap. 8.

Frankena, W. K. *Ethics.* Englewood Cliffs, N.J.: Prentice-Hall, Inc., 1963, 85–88.

Nowell-Smith, P. H *Ethics*. Baltimore: Penguin Books, 1954. Chaps. 2–4.
Strawson, P. F. "Ethical Intuitionism," *Philosophy*, 24 (1949), 23–33.
  [Excerpted in Brandt; Sellars and Hospers.]

Naturalism

Blanshard, Brand. *Reason and Goodness*. New York: The Macmillan
  Company, 1947.
Firth, R. "Ethical Absolutism and the Ideal Observer," *Philosophy and
  Phenomenological Research*, 12 (1952), 317–45.
Hume, David. *Enquiry Concerning the Principles of Morals*. Many editions.
  [Excerpted in Melden; Brandt; Johnson; Ekman; Dewey-Gramlich-
  Anderson.] [May be classified as a noncognitive theory.]
James, William. "The Moral Philosophers and the Moral Life" (first published
  1891), in *Essays in Pragmatism*. New York: Hafner, 1948.
Lewis, C. I. *Analysis of Knowledge and Valuation*. La Salle, Ill.: Open Court
  Publishing Company, 1946. Chaps. 12, 13, 16, 17.
Perry, R. B. *Realms of Value: A Critique of Human Civilization*. Cambridge,
  Mass.: Harvard University Press, 1954. [Excerpted in Brandt; Johnson;
  Dewey-Gramlich-Loftsgordon.]
Sparshott, F. E. *An Inquiry into Goodness*. Chicago: University of Chicago
  Press, 1958.
von Wright, G. H. *The Varieties of Goodness*. London: Routledge & Kegan
  Paul, 1963.

Critics:

Brandt, R. B. *Ethical Theory*. Englewood Cliffs, N.J.: Prentice-Hall, Inc., 1959.
  Chap. 7.
Edwards, Paul. *The Logic of Moral Discourse.* Glencoe, Ill.: The Free Press,
  1955. Chap. 2.
Ewing, A. C. *Ethics*. New York: The Macmillan Company, 1953. Chap. 6.
——————————. *The Definition of Good*. New York: The Macmillan Company,
  1947. Chaps. 1 and 2.
Hare, R. M. *The Language of Morals*. Oxford: The Clarendon Press, 1952.
  Chap. 5.
Russell, Bertrand. "The Elements of Ethics," originally in *Philosophical
  Essays*. London, George Allen & Unwin, Ltd., 1910. [Reprinted in Sellars
  and Hospers.]

Noncognitive Theories

Hare, R. M. *Freedom and Reason*. Oxford: The Clarendon Press, 1963.
  Chap. 6.
Nowell-Smith, P. H. *Ethics*. Baltimore: Penguin Books, 1954. [Excerpted in
  Brandt; Johnson, *Selections*.]
Russell, B. *Religion and Science*. New York: Henry Holt & Company, Inc.,
  1935. Chap. 9. [Reprinted in Brandt.]
Stevenson, C. L. "The Emotive Meaning of Ethical Terms," *Mind*, 46 (1937),
  14–31. [Reprinted in Ekman; Johnson, *Selections;* Dewey-Gramlich-
  Loftsgordon.]

——————————. "The Nature of Ethical Disagreement," *Sigma,* 1–2n, nos. 8–9, 1947–48. [Reprinted in Sellars and Hospers; Brandt.]

——————————. "The Emotive Conception of Ethics and Its Cognitive Implications," *Philosophical Review,* 59 (1950), 291–304.

——————————. *Ethics and Language.* New Haven: Yale University Press, 1944. Chaps. 1, 2, 4–7, 9. [Excerpted in Ekman.]

——————————. *Facts and Values.* New Haven: Yale University Press, 1963.

Urmson, J. O. *The Emotive Theory of Ethics.* London: Hutchinson's University Library, 1968.

Critics

Aiken, Henry. "Emotive 'Meanings' and Ethical Terms," *Journal of Philosophy,* 41 (1944), 456–70.

Brandt, R. B. *Ethical Theory.* Englewood Cliffs, N.J.: Prentice-Hall, Inc., 1959. Chap. 9.

Falk, W. D. "Goading and Guiding," *Mind,* 62 (1953), 145–69. [Reprinted in Ekman.]

Ladd, John. "Value Judgments, Emotive Meaning and Attitudes," *Journal of Philosophy,* XLVI (1949), 119–29.

Kerner, George. *The Revolution in Ethical Theory.* New York: Oxford University Press, 1966.

Hedonism and Pluralism

Hedonists:

Bentham, Jeremy. *Principles of Morals and Legislation.* Many editions. [Excerpted in Melden; Brandt; Dewey-Gramlich-Loftsgordon.]

Blake, R. "Why Not Hedonism?" *Ethics,* 37 (1926), 1–18.

Epicurus. From Diogenes Laertius, *Lives of Eminent Philosophers,* trans. by R. D. Hicks. Cambridge, Mass.: Harvard University Press, 1925. [Excerpted in Brandt; Johnson; Melden.]

Sharp, F. C. *Ethics.* New York: Appleton-Century Company, 1928. Chap. 19.

Sidgwick, Henry. *Methods of Ethics.* London: Macmillan & Co., Ltd., 1922. Bk. III, Chap. 14. [Excerpted in Melden.]

Critics and Pluralists:

Brandt, R. B. *Ethical Theory.* Englewood Cliffs, N.J.: Prentice-Hall, Inc., 1959. Chaps. 12 and 13.

Broad, C. D. *Five Types of Ethical Theory.* New York: Harcourt, Brace & World, Inc., 1934, 180–91. [Reprinted in Brandt.]

Carritt, E. F. *Ethical and Political Thinking.* Oxford: Clarendon Press, 1947. Chap. 8.

Ewing, A. C. *Ethics.* New York: The Macmillan Company, 1953. Chap. 3.

Hospers, John. *Human Conduct.* New York: Harcourt, Brace & World, Inc., 1961. Chap. 3.

Moore, G. E. *Principia Ethica.* Cambridge: Cambridge University Press, 1929. Sections 36–57. [Excerpted in Johnson, *Ethics.*]

——————————. *Ethics.* Oxford: Oxford University Press, 1949. Chaps. 1 and 2.

Nietzsche, F. *Beyond Good and Evil,* trans. Helen Zimmern. London: George Allen & Unwin, Ltd., 1924. [Excerpted in Brandt; Dewey-Gramlich-Loftsgordon; Johnson.]

Ross, W. D. *The Right and the Good.* Oxford: The Clarendon Press, 1930. Chap. 5. [Reprinted in Brandt.]

Egoism

Hobbes, Thomas. *Leviathan.* First published 1651; many editions. [Excerpted in Johnson, *Selections.*]

——————————. *Philosophical Rudiments Concerning Government and Society.* Reprinted in Sir William Molesworth, ed., *The English Works of Thomas Hobbes.* London: Bohn, 1841. [Excerpted in Brandt.]

Hospers, J. "Baier and Medlin on Ethical Egoism," *Philosophical Studies,* 12: 10–16. [Reprinted in Taylor.]

Olson, R. G. *The Morality of Self-Interest.* New York: Harcourt, Brace & World, Inc., 1965.

Williams, Gardner. "Individual, Social, and Universal Ethics," *The Journal of Philosophy,* XLV (1948), pp. 645–55.

Critics:

Brandt, R. B. *Ethical Theory.* Englewood Cliffs, N.J.: Prentice-Hall, Inc., 1959. Chap. 14.

Broad, C. D. *Five Types of Ethical Theory.* New York: Humanities Press, Inc., 1956, 161–77.

Butler, Joseph. *Fifteen Sermons upon Human Nature.* First published 1726. Many editions. [Excerpted in Brandt; Johnson; Melden.]

Ewing, A. C. *Ethics.* New York: The Macmillan Company, 1953. Chap. 2.

Frankena, W. K. *Ethics.* Englewood Cliffs, N.J.: Prentice-Hall, Inc., 1963. Chap. 2.

Hospers, John. *Human Conduct.* New York: Harcourt, Brace & World, Inc., 1961. Chap. 4.

Kading, D., and Kramer, M. "Mr. Hospers' Defense of Impersonal Egoism," *Philosophical Studies,* 15 (1964), 44–46.

Sharp, F. C. *Ethics.* New York: D. Appleton-Century Company, 1928. Chaps. 22 and 23.

Utilitarianism

General:

Quinton, A. M. *Utilitarian Ethics.* Macmillan, London, 1973. (introductory)

Classical Utilitarianism:

Bentham, Jeremy. *Principles of Morals and Legislation.* Many editions. [Excerpted in Melden; Brandt; Dewey-Gramlich-Loftsgordon.]

Mill, J. S. *Utilitarianism.* Many editions. [Excerpted in Brandt; Melden; Johnson.]

Sidgwick, Henry. *Methods of Ethics.* London: Macmillan & Co., Ltd., 1922. Bk. I, Chap. 9; Bk. II, Chap. 1; Bk. III, Chaps. 11, 13; Bk. IV, Chaps. 2–5.

Analyzed in C. D. Broad, *Five Types of Ethical Theory.* New York: Harcourt, Brace & World, Inc., 1934. Chap. 6.

Smart, J. J. C. *An Outline of a System of Utilitarian Ethics.* Melbourne: Melbourne University Press, 1961.

———————. "Extreme and Restricted Utilitarianism," *Philosophical Quarterly,* 6 (1956). [Reprinted in Bayles.]

——————— and Williams, B. *Utilitarianism: For and Against.* Cambridge: Cambridge University Press 1973.

Rule-Utilitarianism:

Baier, Kurt. *The Moral Point of View.* Ithaca: Cornell University Press, 1958. Chap. 8.

Brandt, R. B. "Some Merits of One Form of Rule-Utilitarianism," *University of Colorado Series in Philosophy,* No. 3 (1967), pp. 39–65. [Reprinted in Bobbs-Merrill Reprint Series; Hearn; Pahel and Schiller.]

Donagan, Alan. "Is There a Credible Form of Utilitarianism?" in Bayles. [Reprinted in Tillman, Berofsky, and O'Connor.]

Harrison, J. "Utilitarianism, Universalization, and Our Duty to Be Just," *Proceedings,* The Aristotelian Society, 1952–53. [Reprinted in Bayles.]

Mabbott, J. D. "Moral Rules," *Proceedings of the British Academy,* 39 (1953), 97–117. [Reprinted in Hearn, Pahel and Schiller.]

Rawls, John. "Two Concepts of Rules," *Philosophical Review,* 64 (1955), 3–32. [Excerpted in Brandt; Taylor; reprinted in Hearn; Pahel and Schiller, and Bayles.]

Discussions and Critics:

Brandt, R. B. *Ethical Theory.* Englewood Cliffs, N.J.: Prentice-Hall, Inc., 1959. Chap. 15.

Ewing, A. C. *Ethics.* New York: The Macmillan Company, 1947. Chap. 5.

Frankena, W. K. *Ethics.* Englewood Cliffs, N.J.: Prentice-Hall, Inc., 1963. Chap. 3.

Hodgson, D. H. *Consequences of Utilitarianism.* Oxford: The Clarendon Press, 1967.

Hospers, John. *Human Conduct.* New York: Harcourt, Brace & World, Inc., 1961. Chaps. 12–17.

Lyons, David. *Forms and Limits of Utilitarianism.* Oxford: The Clarendon Press, 1965.

Singer, M. G. *Generalization in Ethics.* New York: Alfred A. Knopf, 1961.

Why Be Moral?

Brandt, R. B. *Ethical Theory.* Englewood Cliffs, N.J.: Prentice-Hall, Inc., 1959, 375–78.

Gauthier, D. P. "Morality and Advantage," *Philosophical Review,* 76 (1967), 460–75. [Reprinted in Gauthier, Taylor.]

Hospers, John. *Human Conduct.* New York: Harcourt, Brace & World, Inc., 1961, 174–98.

Melden, A. I. "Why Be Moral?" *Journal of Philosophy,* 45 (1948), 449–56.

Pahel, K., and Schiller, M. (eds.), *Readings on Contemporary Ethical Theory.* Englewood Cliffs, N.J.: Prentice-Hall, Inc., 1970. Part IV, especially papers by Thornton and Nielsen.

Scriven, Michael. *Primary Philosophy.* New York: McGraw-Hill Book Company, 1966, 238–59.

Singer, M. G. *Generalization in Ethics.* New York: Alfred A. Knopf, 1961, 319–27.

Stace, W. T. *The Concept of Morals.* New York: The Macmillan Company, 1937. Chaps. 11 and 12.

Taylor, Paul. *Normative Discourse.* Englewood Cliffs, N.J.: Prentice-Hall, Inc., 1961, 164–88.

PART III

Some Personal Actions and Political Structures: An Ethical Appraisal

Introduction

The normative theories defended in the preceding Part may seem abstract and general, and the reader may well wonder how they could ever be used as guides to a serious moral appraisal of either personal behavior or public policy. In this Part, we shall see how. The authors of the readings in this section do not, however, espouse the same general normative principles: there are utilitarians, at least one egoist, defenders of appeal to a plurality of "intuitions," and in some cases, argument based on assumptions about God's will for people. Thus, the various arguments are to be read with caution; the reader may wish to set some aside as relying on a general normative principle that he has already decided must be abandoned. It may be, however, that the reader will feel happier (or unhappier) about his tentative decisions about general principles when he sees what they imply for the analysis of complex personal or social problems.

The appraisal of a personal moral action or a social policy will normally call for a good deal of purely factual information as well as general moral principles. If you have tentatively espoused act-utilitarianism, for example, you will need to know, in order to decide what it is morally right to do in a particular case, how many persons are apt to be injured, or benefited, by a given action, and how much. Only then can one know whether on balance a proposed action is harmful or beneficial, and be able to infer whether the principle of act-utilitarianism would recommend or prohibit it. In some cases, especially when the issue is a proposed social policy, such relevant information may be complex and hard to get.

One benefit of the Watergate affair is that many persons are now convinced, as formerly many were not convinced, that social and political problems are *moral* problems and need assessment from a moral point of view. But even now it is not clear that this fact is as obvious to everyone as it ought to be. The authors have seen only one philosopher interviewed on the *Today* show (that one on the moral treatment of animals); and even though government regularly calls for advice from economists, anthropologists, sociologists, criminologists, and legal experts, no philosopher is an adviser in the White House or occupies a position in the Cabinet or a seat in the Senate. It may be that this fact simply reflects the belief in high quarters that the relevant moral principles are well known and that what is needed from experts is information about complex facts needed to apply the principles. (If such a belief is widespread it is unfortunately not quite accurate, since government officials sometimes issue pronouncements on moral issues that are not ideally sophisticated!) However, it is obvious that many or most political decisions do raise moral questions, and that these moral questions can be answered only on the basis of both knowledge of the relevant moral principles and knowledge of the relevant facts. Which sorts of questions? Whether income taxes should be more or less steeply progressive and what should be allowable deductions. Whether available school funds should be diverted from athletics into expanded programs of music and drama. Whether the United States has a moral obligation to put more money into aid for underdeveloped nations, at least approximating Sweden's policy of contributing 1% of the gross national product. Whether automobile manufacturers should be permitted to encourage irrational values in consumers by the advertising used to promote the sale of luxury models. Whether there should be general price and wage controls, or whether inflation should be accepted as the price of full employment. Whether capital punishment should be continued, and more generally whether the whole system of criminal justice should not be radically revised.

The readings in this Part fall into two groups. First are four readings about personal behavior: suicide and abortion. The remaining five readings are about larger social issues, primarily about the moral justification of some structures of government. Four of these latter readings are not about specific acts or policies; the last one is. It concerns the moral permissibility of governments' legally requiring conformity to the moral code of the society, specifically whether it is permissible to make homosexual behavior illegal just because it is widely thought to be immoral. Most of the readings deal with questions about the proper structure, function, and authority of governments. Is the government ever justified morally in coercing the behavior of individuals through the military, police, and system of criminal justice? If so, under what circumstances (e.g., when the government has the consent of the governed)? Ought individuals to submit to this coercion—or, in other words, do citizens have a moral obligation to obey the law? Are there restrictions on the legitimate activities of government? For instance, is it right for governments to censor the newspapers, deprive citizens of freedom or property without "due process," or infringe on the "privacy" of individuals? What control, if any, should the citizens of a country have over their government? Should there be some form of political democracy, which at least provides adults a periodic opportunity to replace a government, so that the decisions of a party in power can be influenced by the threat of dismissal? These questions are not as much in the headlines today as some listed above, but they are more fundamental, being about the proper functions of the most important social institution—the government.

The first reading, by St. Thomas Aquinas, is an argument that suicide is immoral. This argument has been very influential on the teaching of the Catholic Church. It should be noticed that St. Thomas does not adopt a divine-command theory of the meaning of ethical statements; nor does he regard the issue as settled by appeal to the divine will as revealed in the Ten Commandments. Reading the text shows that St. Thomas employed a good many ethical principles as the basis for his condemnation: that one should not do what is "unnatural," that one should not do what injures the community, that life is God's gift and hence it is His decision when it is to end; that a man is bound not to embrace a lesser good for himself in place of a greater one; that evil may not be done for the sake of good. The plurality of these principles reminds one of W. D. Ross. Which principles are convincing? If suicide really does harm the community, then perhaps it is wrong. But the others?

Hume's essay is aimed to defend suicide against some of these charges. Most of the article is devoted to arguing that there is no special duty to God to refrain from taking one's own life when there are good reasons for doing so. But Hume also argues that one does not injure society by taking leave of this life, when the individual has the reasons, of ill health, for example, that normally prompt suicide; he does not, however, argue that there are *no* cases in which one would be wronging others in taking such a step. Finally, he thinks that suicide is not normally contrary to the individual's own interests; he says that people do not throw away life when it is "worth keeping." Here one may question Hume's psychology and his knowledge of the motivation of suicides; for it appears that many persons commit suicide in moods of depression when they have the possibility of a very good life ahead but do not appreciate the fact because of their temporary despair. The reader may wish to consult a contemporary volume on the motivations of suicide.

The first of the two papers on abortion, by Judith Thomson, begins by making a concession for the sake of the argument: that the fetus is a person with a right to life from the moment of conception. But Thomson argues that this fact proves nothing about abortion until we have examined the rights the woman may have. Thomson argues that it is evident (like W. D. Ross?) that she has a right to defend herself if the fetus threatens her life; she has further rights deriving from the fact that it is her body the fetus is inhabiting. Further, she argues that the "right to life" can hardly reach so far as to include a right to *anything* necessary to sustain life, when the means necessary to sustain life affect seriously the lives of others, especially when it requires the use of another's body. There is no *injustice* in restricting the right to life in this way, on behalf of the decisions of the mother, especially if pregnancy occurred contrary to her will or by accident. She argues, however, that some late abortions, for trivial reasons, would be indecent and wrong. What are her basic moral principles?

Warren, in the second reading on abortion, is unconvinced by Thomson's argument. She thinks Thomson overlooks the fact that a woman has special responsibility for the fetus she has conceived, except, say, in case of rape. She wants to argue for a stronger thesis: that abortion is a morally neutral act such as cutting one's hair, not an act that can be justified only by balancing rights of the mother against the right to life of a fetus. She argues that a fetus has no "full-fledged right to life" at all. Why not? She thinks arguments to show that a fetus is *human* are not to the point, that it must be shown that a fetus is a *person,* in order to show that it is a subject of moral rights. Her "intuition" is that nothing has moral rights unless it has a capacity to feel pain, a developed capacity to reason, and self-motivated activity. (She *may* be claiming that this is an *analytic* truth: that it is analytic that only persons have moral rights, and also that a person must have these listed properties.) A fetus is not a person; hence, it has no moral rights at all, and specifically no right to life. It is true that a fetus is *potentially* a person, but this fact has little moral force.

The reader might well ask what an egoist would say about such matters. Or would J. S. Mill concede that the welfare of society is best preserved by a morality that permits, or one that prohibits, abortion? Would one of the *"prima facie* duties" that Ross lists cover this problem, or is there another duty that he should list but does not, which is equally self-evident and relevant? Given what Kant says about suicide, one can speculate with some reason what he would say about abortion; but can he show that a rational person would not want abortion permitted, as a universal rule? And what might Sartre be for? These same questions, of course, may be raised for the case of suicide.

We turn now to the readings on the moral justification of the authority of governments and of its limitations. Of these five readings, the first four have historically been influential and are among the classical documents of Western political philosophy, although they do not advocate the same things.

The first reading, by Thomas Hobbes, is a defense of virtually un- limited powers of government (even power to prescribe what may be printed or said) on the ground that such a government is the only serious alternative to a situation of chaotic competition and violence among individuals. Hobbes is the classic "law and order" philosopher. He thinks that the moral authority of government rests in the fact that a rational and selfish person would prefer dictatorial government with such powers to the chaos of a "state of nature." The second reading, by John Locke, contrasts sharply with this, not only in its conclusion, to the effect that governments are severely restricted in their rightful powers over the citizens, but also in the premises from which he starts. Locke begins with the basic principle that one person is not morally free to harm another in respect of his life, liberty, health, or possessions, except to punish someone who himself has violated the welfare or property of others. But it would be chaotic for each person to be both judge and executioner with respect to anyone's violations of these rights of others; hence, men have compacted together to hand over the right to punish to a supreme authority, and this act of consent or contract is the source of the authority of government. Men do not, however, transfer to government their other basic rights, to be left alone in respect of life, liberty, health, and property; and this fact sets a restriction on what governments are morally justified in doing. Locke allows, however, that even these rights are, by rational consent, transferred to the society or government to some extent, that is, where the good, prosperity, and safety of society demand it; Locke tries to fix, as carefully as possible, just how far the power of govern- ment, e.g., to tax property, may go.

The third and fourth readings, by J. S. Mill, are similar to Locke in their conclusions; but Mill is a utilitarian and bases these conclusions on consider- ations of general utility, not on supposed basic fundamental rights of in- dividuals, or on the consent of individuals to a transfer of some of their rights to the government. The first of Mill's readings defends a democratic representative form of government, not on the ground that only such a government could have authority, in view of the basic rights of individuals, but on the ground of its many advantages. The second excerpt from Mill is a defense of freedom of speech and of the press, and in general of freedom of action insofar as it is not harmful to other persons. Again, he appeals not to any supposed basic right, but to the great benefits that flow from people being secured in these freedoms.

The final reading, by Lord Patrick Devlin, a justice on the British bench, is a direct criticism of Mill's theory of the right to freedom of action as going much too far; in particular, he attacks Mill's thesis that society rightfully can restrict a person's freedom of action only for the purpose of preventing harm to others, except to exact a person's just contribution to the common defense and other proper services of the state. Devlin thinks traditional Anglo-American practice does not, and should not, go so far. He takes as his example homosexual behavior between consenting adults, which admittedly is not injurious to other specific persons. Can this be a proper matter for legal regulation? Devlin thinks it is. For one thing, he thinks that indulgence in "private vice" may weaken the self-discipline of a community; a nation of debauchees, he thinks, would not have won the Second World War. Moreover, he says "some shared morality" is an essential element in a healthy society. Since the destruction of any part tends to weaken the whole, it is proper for the law to support any part of morality. This is not to say that the law is to aim to "freeze into immobility" the morality of a particular time; the law must give ground when conscientious people demand a change. So in principle it is not improper, not necessarily outside the scope of the law, for homosexual behavior to be prohibited by law, although such a prohibition might reasonably be attacked on the pragmatic ground that such a prohibition, in the particular circumstances, would do more harm than good. The proper decision, in all such cases, should be made by balancing the merits of the individual situations. But there is no general blanket limitation on the extent to which society may invade the privacy of the individual.

28. St. Thomas Aquinas

St. Thomas Aquinas (1225–1274) was a philosopher and theologian who was much influenced by Aristotle. Aquinas' teaching is uniquely revered within the Catholic Church, his doctrines having been recommended by encyclicals by Leo XIII (Aeterni patris, 1879) and Pius XI (Studiorem ducem, 1923). He wrote prodigiously on almost all philosophical topics.

The Immorality of Suicide

We proceed thus to the Fifth Article:

Objection 1. It would seem lawful for a man to kill himself. For murder is a sin in so far as it is contrary to justice. But no man can do an injustice to himself, as is proved in *Ethic.*v.11.[1] Therefore no man sins by killing himself.

Obj. 2. Further, It is lawful, for one who exercises public authority, to kill evildoers. Now he who exercises public authority is sometimes an evildoer. Therefore he may lawfully kill himself.

Obj. 3. Further, It is lawful for a man to suffer spontaneously a lesser danger that he may avoid a greater. Thus it is lawful for a man to cut off a decayed limb even from himself, that he may save his whole body. Now sometimes a man, by killing himself, avoids a greater evil, for example an unhappy life, or the shame of sin. Therefore a man may kill himself.

Obj. 4. Further, Samson killed himself, as related in Judges xvi, and yet he is numbered among the saints (Heb.xi). Therefore it is lawful for a man to kill himself.

This article is taken from the *Summa Theologica*, Second Part of the Second Part, Question 64, Article 5. Published by Benziger Brothers, New York, 1925, and reprinted by their permission.

1. The reference is to Aristotle.

Obj. 5. Further, It is related (2 Mach.xiv.42) that a certain Razias killed himself, *choosing to die nobly rather than to fall into the hands of the wicked, and to suffer abuses unbecoming his noble birth.* Now nothing that is done nobly and bravely is unlawful. Therefore suicide is not unlawful.

On the contrary, Augustine says (*De Civ. Dei* i.20): *Hence it follows that the words "Thou shalt not kill" refer to the killing of a man; not another man; therefore, not even thyself. For he who kills himself, kills nothing else than a man.*

I answer that, It is altogether unlawful to kill oneself, for three reasons. First, because everything naturally loves itself, the result being that everything naturally keeps itself in being, and resists corruption so far as it can. Wherefore suicide is contrary to the inclination of nature and to charity, whereby every man should love himself. Hence suicide is always a mortal sin, as being contrary to the natural law and to charity.

Secondly, because every part, as such, belongs to the whole. Now every man is part of the community, and so, as such, he belongs to the community. Hence by killing himself he injures the community as the Philosopher declares (*Ethic.*v.ii).

Thirdly, because life is God's gift to man, and is subject to His power, Who kills and makes to live. Hence whoever takes his own life sins against God, even as he who kills another's slave sins against that slave's master, and as he who usurps himself judgment of a matter not entrusted to him. For it belongs to God alone to pronounce sentence of death and life, according to Deut.xxxii.39, *I will kill and I will make to live.*

Reply Obj. 1. Murder is a sin, not only because it is contrary to justice, but also because it is opposed to charity, which a man should have towards himself; in this respect suicide is a sin in relation to oneself. In relation to the community and to God, it is sinful, by reason also of its opposition to justice.

Reply Obj. 2. One who exercises public authority may lawfully put to death an evildoer, since he can pass judgment on him. But no man is judge of himself. Wherefore it is not lawful for one who exercises public authority to put himself to death for any sin whatever, although he may lawfully commit himself to the judgment of others.

Reply Obj. 3. Man is made master of himself through his free will: wherefore he can lawfully dispose of himself as to those matters which pertain to this life, which is ruled by man's free will. But the passage from this life to another and happier one is subject not to man's free will but to the power of God. Hence it is not lawful for man to take his own life that he may pass to a happier life, nor that he may escape any unhappiness whatsoever of the present life, because the ultimate and most fearsome evil of this life is death, as the Philosopher states (*Ethic.*iii. 6). Therefore to bring death upon oneself in order to escape the other afflictions of this life is to adopt a greater evil in order to avoid a lesser. In like manner it is unlawful to take one's own life on account of one's having committed a sin, both because by so doing one does oneself a very great injury, by depriving oneself of the time needful for repentance, and because it is not lawful to slay an evildoer except by the sentence of the public authority. Again it is unlawful for woman to kill herself lest she be violated, because she ought not to commit on herself the very great sin of suicide to avoid the lesser sin of another. For she commits no sin in being violated by force, provided she does not consent, since *without consent of the mind there is no stain on the body,* as the Blessed Lucy declared. Now it is evident that fornication and adultery are less grievous sins than taking a man's, especially one's own, life, since the latter is most grievous, because one injures oneself, to whom one owes the greatest love. Moreover it is most dangerous since no time is left wherein to expiate it by repentance. Again it is not lawful for anyone to take his own life for fear he should consent to sin, because *evil must not be done that good may come* (Rom.iii.8) or that evil may be avoided, especially if the evil be of small account and an uncertain event, for it is uncertain whether one will at some future time consent to a sin, since God is able to deliver man from sin under any temptation whatever.

Reply Obj. 4. As Augustine says (*De Civ. Dei* i.21), *not even Samson is to be excused that he crushed himself together with his enemies under the ruins of the house, except the Holy Ghost, Who had wrought many wonders through him, had secretly commanded him to do this.* He assigns the same reason in the case of certain holy women who at the time of persecution took their own lives and who are commemorated by the Church.

Reply Obj. 5. It belongs to fortitude that a man does not shrink from being slain by another, for the sake of the good of virtue and that he may avoid sin. But that a man take his own life in order to avoid penal evils has indeed an appearance of fortitude (for which reason some . . . have killed themselves, thinking to act from fortitude), yet it is not true fortitude, but rather a weakness of soul unable to bear penal evils, as the Philosopher (*Ethic.*iii.7) and Augustine (*De Civ. Dei* i.22,23) declare.

29. David Hume

David Hume (1711–1776) was perhaps the greatest of the British empiricist philosophers of the seventeenth and eighteenth centuries.

The Justifiability of Suicide

If Suicide be criminal, it must be a transgression of our duty either to God, our neighbour, or ourselves.—To prove that suicide is no transgression of our duty to God, the following considerations may perhaps suffice. In order to govern the material world, the almighty Creator has established general and immutable laws by which all bodies, from the greatest planet to the smallest particle of matter, are maintained in their proper sphere and function. To govern the animal world, he has endowed all living creatures with bodily and mental powers; with senses, passions, appetites, memory and judgment, by which they are impelled or regulated in that course of life to which they are destined. These two distinct principles of the material and animal world, continually encroach upon each other, and mutually retard or forward each others operations. The powers of men and of all other animals are restrained and directed by the nature and qualities of the surrounding bodies; and the modifications and actions of these bodies are incessantly altered by the operation of all animals. Man is stopt by rivers in his passage over the surface of the earth; and rivers, when properly directed, lend their force to the motion of machines, which serve to the use of man. But tho' the provinces of the material and animal powers are not kept entirely separate, there results from thence no discord or disorder in the creation; on the contrary, from the mixture, union and contrast of all the various powers

The following is taken from David Hume's essay, *On Suicide* (1777).

of inanimate bodies and living creatures, arises that surprizing harmony and proportion which affords the surest argument of supreme wisdom. The providence of the Deity appears not immediately in any operation, but governs everything by those general and immutable laws, which have been established from the beginning of time. All events, in one sense, may be pronounced the action of the Almighty; they all proceed from those powers with which he has endowed his creatures. A house which falls by its own weight is not brought to ruin by his providence more than one destroyed by the hands of men; nor are the human faculties less his workmanship, than the laws of motion and gravitation. When the passions play, when the judgment dictates, when the limbs obey; this is all the operation of God, and upon these animate principles, as well as upon the inanimate, has he established the government of the universe. Every event is alike important in the eyes of that infinite being, who takes in at one glance the most distant regions of space and remotest periods of time. There is no event, however important to us, which he has exempted from the general laws that govern the universe, or which he has peculiarly reserved for his own immediate action and operation. The revolution of states and empires depends upon the smallest caprice or passion of single men; and the lives of men are shortened or extended by the smallest accident of air or diet, sunshine or tempest. Nature still continues her progress and operation; and if general laws be ever broke by particular volitions of the Deity, 'tis after a manner which entirely escapes human observation. As, on the one hand, the elements and other inanimate parts of the creation carry on their action without regard to the particular interest and situation of men; so men are entrusted to their own judgment and discretion, in the various shocks of matter, and may employ every faculty with which they are endowed, in order to provide for their ease, happiness, or preservation. What is the meaning then of that principle, that a man who, tired of life, and hunted by pain and misery, bravely overcomes all the natural terrors of death and makes his escape from this cruel scene; that such a man, I say, has incurred the indignation of his Creator by encroaching on the office of divine providence, and disturbing the order of the universe? Shall we assert that the Almighty has reserved to himself in any peculiar manner the disposal of the lives of men, and has not submitted that event, in common with others, to the general laws by which the universe is governed? This is plainly false; the lives of men depend upon the same laws as the lives of all other animals; and these are subjected to the general laws of matter and motion. The fall of a tower, or the infusion of a poison will destroy a man equally with the meanest creature; an inundation sweeps away every thing without distinction that comes within the reach of its fury. Since therefore the lives of men are for ever dependant on the general laws of matter and motion, is a man's disposing of his life criminal, because in every case it is criminal to encroach upon these laws, or disturb their operation? But this seems absurd; all animals are entrusted to their own prudence and skill for their conduct in the world, and have full authority, as far as their power extends, to alter all the operations of nature. Without the exercise of this authority they could not subsist a moment; every action, every motion of a man, innovates on the order of some parts of matter, and diverts from their ordinary course the general laws of motion. Putting together, therefore, these conclusions, we find that human life depends upon the general laws of matter and motion, and that it is no encroachment on the office of providence to disturb or alter these general laws: Has not every one, of consequence, the free disposal of his own life? And may he not lawfully employ that power with which nature has endowed him? In order to destroy the evidence of this conclusion, we must shew a reason, why this particular case is excepted: is it because human life is of so great importance, that 'tis a presumption for human prudence to dispose of it? But the life of a man is of no greater importance to the universe than that of an oyster. And were it of ever so great importance, the order of nature has actually submitted it to human prudence, and reduced us to a necessity in every incident of determining concerning it. Were the disposal of human life so much reserved as the peculiar province of the Almighty that it were an encroachment on his right, for men to dispose of their own lives; it would be equally criminal to act for the preservation of life as for its destruction. If I turn aside a stone which is falling upon my head, I disturb the course of nature, and I invade the peculiar province of the Almighty by lengthening out my life beyond the period which by the general laws of matter and motion he had assigned it.

A hair, a fly, an insect is able to destroy this mighty being whose life is of such importance. Is it an absurdity to suppose that human prudence may lawfully dispose of what depends on such insignificant causes? It would be no crime in me to divert the *Nile* or *Danube* from its course, were I able to effect such purposes. Where then is the crime of turning a few ounces of blood from their natural channel?—Do you imagine that I repine at providence or curse my creation, because I go out of life, and put a period to a being, which, were it to continue, would render me miserable? Far be such sentiments from me; I am only convinced of a matter of fact which you yourself acknowledge possible, that human life may be unhappy, and that my existence, if further prolonged, would become ineligible: but I thank providence, both for the good which I have already enjoyed, and for the power with which I am endowed of escaping the ill that threatens me. To you it belongs to repine at providence, who foolishly imagine that you have no such power, and who must still prolong a hated life, tho' loaded with pain and sickness, with shame and poverty.—Do you not teach, that when any ill befalls me, tho' by the malice of my enemies, I ought to be resigned to providence, and that the actions of men are the operations of the Almighty as much as the actions of inanimate beings? When I fall upon my own sword, therefore, I receive my death equally from the hands of the Deity as if it had proceeded from a lion, a precipice, or a fever. The submission which you require to providence, in every calamity that befalls me, excludes not human skill and industry, if possibly by their means I can avoid or escape the calamity: And why may I not employ one remedy as well as another?—If my life be not my own, it were criminal for me to put it in danger, as well as to dispose of it; nor could one man deserve the appellation of *hero* whom glory or friendship transports into the greatest dangers, and another merit the reproach of *wretch* or *miscreant* who puts a period to his life from the same or like motives.—There is no being, which possesses any power or faculty, that it receives not from its Creator, nor is there any one, which by ever so irregular an action can encroach upon the plan of his providence, or disorder the universe. Its operations are his works equally with that chain of events, which it invades, and which ever principle prevails, we may for that very reason conclude it to be most favoured by him. Be it animate, or inanimate, rational, or irrational; 'tis all a case: Its power is still derived from the supreme creator, and is alike comprehended in the order of his providence. When the horror of pain prevails over the love of life; when a voluntary action anticipates the effects of blind causes; 'tis only in consequence of those powers and principles, which he has implanted in his creatures. Divine providence is still inviolate and placed far beyond the reach of human injuries. 'Tis impious, says the old Roman superstition, to divert rivers from their course, or invade the prerogatives of nature. 'Tis impious, says the French superstition, to inoculate for the small-pox, or usurp the business of providence, by voluntarily producing distempers and maladies. 'Tis impious, says the modern *European* superstition, to put a period to our own life, and thereby rebel against our creator; and why not impious, say I, to build houses, cultivate the ground, or sail upon the ocean? In all these actions we employ our powers of mind and body, to produce some innovation in the course of nature; and in none of them do we any more. They are all of them therefore equally innocent, or equally criminal.—*But you are placed by providence, like a sentinel in a particular station, and when you desert it without being recalled, you are equally guilty of rebellion against your almighty sovereign, and have incurred his displeasure.*—I ask, why do you conclude that providence has placed me in this station? For my part I find that I owe my birth to a long chain of causes, of which many depended upon voluntary actions of men. *But Providence guided all these Causes, and nothing happens in the universe without its consent and Co-operation.* If so, then neither does my death, however voluntary, happen without its consent; and whenever pain or sorrow so far overcome my patience, as to make me tired of life, I may conclude that I am recalled from my station in the clearest and most express terms. 'Tis Providence surely that has placed me at this present moment in this chamber: But may I not leave it when I think proper, without being liable to the imputation of having deserted my post or station? When I shall be dead, the principles of which I am composed will still perform their part in the universe, and will be equally useful in the grand fabric, as when they composed this individual creature. The difference to the whole will be no greater than betwixt my being in a chamber and in the open air. The one change is of more importance to me than the other; but not more so to the universe.

'Tis a kind of blasphemy to imagine that any created being can disturb the order of the world or invade the business of providence! It supposes, that that Being possesses powers and faculties, which it received not from its creator, and which are not subordinate to his government and authority. A man may disturb society no doubt, and thereby incur the displeasure of the Almighty: But the government of the world is placed far beyond his reach and violence. And how does it appear that the Almighty is displeased with those actions that disturb society? By the principles which he has implanted in human nature, and which inspire us with a sentiment of remorse if we ourselves have been guilty of such actions, and with that of blame and disapprobation, if we ever observe them in others.—Let us now examine, according to the method proposed, whether Suicide be of this kind of actions, and be a breach of our duty to our *neighbour* and to *society*.

A man, who retires from life, does no harm to society: He only ceases to do good; which, if it is an injury, is of the lowest kind.—All our obligations to do good to society seem to imply something reciprocal. I receive the benefits of society and therefore ought to promote its interests, but when I withdraw myself altogether from society, can I be bound any longer? But, allowing that our obligations to do good were perpetual, they have certainly some bounds; I am not obliged to do a small good to society at the expense of a great harm to myself; why then should I prolong a miserable existence, because of some frivolous advantage which the public may perhaps receive from me? If upon account of age and infirmities I may lawfully resign any office, and employ my time altogether in fencing against these calamities, and alleviating as much as possible the miseries of my future life: Why may I not cut short these miseries at once by an action which is no more prejudicial to society?—But suppose that it is no longer in my power to promote the interest of society; suppose that I am a burthen to it; suppose that my life hinders some person from being much more useful to society. In such cases my resignation of life must not only be innocent but laudable. And most people who lie under any temptation to abandon existence, are in some such situation; those, who have health, or power, or authority, have commonly better reason to be in humour with the world.

A man is engaged in a conspiracy for the public interest is seized upon suspicion, is threatened with the rack; and knows from his own weakness that the secret will be extorted from him: Could such a one consult the public interest better than by putting a quick period to a miserable life? This was the case of the famous and brave *Strozi of Florence.*—Again, suppose a malefactor is justly condemned to a shameful death; can any reason be imagined, why he may not anticipate his punishment, and save himself all the anguish of thinking on its dreadful approaches? He invades the business of providence no more than the magistrate did, who ordered his execution; and his voluntary death is equally advantageous to society by ridding it of a pernicious member. That suicide may often be consistent with interest and with our duty to ourselves, no one can question, who allows that age, sickness, or misfortune may render life a burthen, and make it worse even than annihilation. I believe that no man ever threw away life, while it was worth keeping. For such is our natural horror of death, that small motives will never be able to reconcile us to it; and though perhaps the situation of a man's health or fortune did not seem to require this remedy, we may at least be assured, that any one who, without apparent reason, has had recourse to it, was curst with such an incurable depravity or gloominess of temper as must poison all enjoyment, and render him equally miserable as if he had been loaded with the most grievous misfortunes.—If suicide be supposed a crime, 'tis only cowardice can impel us to it. If it be no crime, both prudence and courage should engage us to rid ourselves at once of existence, when it becomes a burthen. 'Tis the only way that we can then be useful to society, by setting an example, which, if imitated, would preserve to every one his chance for happiness in life and would effectually free him from all danger or misery.

30. Judith Jarvis Thomson

Judith Jarvis Thomson is professor of philosophy at the
Massachusetts Institute of Technology.

A Woman's Right to Abortion

Most opposition to abortion relies on the premise that the fetus is a
human being, a person, from the moment of conception.[1] The premise
is argued for, but, as I think, not well. Take, for example, the most common argument. We are asked to notice that the development of a human
being from conception through birth into childhood is continuous; then
it is said that to draw a line, to choose a point in this development and
say "before this point the thing is not a person, after this point it is a
person" is to make an arbitrary choice, a choice for which in the nature
of things no good reason can be given. It is concluded that the fetus is,
or anyway that we had better say it is, a person from the moment of
conception. But this conclusion does not follow. Similar things might be
said about the development of an acorn into an oak tree, and it does not
follow that acorns are oak trees, or that we had better say they are.
Arguments of this form are sometimes called "slippery slope arguments"
—the phrase is perhaps self-explanatory—and it is dismaying that opponents of abortion rely on them so heavily and uncritically.

I am inclined to agree, however, that the prospects for "drawing a
line" in the development of the fetus look dim. I am inclined to think
also that we shall probably have to agree that the fetus has already be-

From Judith Jarvis Thomson, "A Defense of Abortion," *Philosophy and Public
Affairs*, Vol. 1, No. 1 (1971), 47–66. Copyright © 1971 by Princeton University Press.
Reprinted by permission of Princeton University Press.
    1. I am very much indebted to James Thomson for discussion, criticism, and
many helpful suggestions.

come a human person well before birth. Indeed, it comes as a surprise when one first learns how early in its life it begins to acquire human characteristics. By the tenth week, for example, it already has a face, arms and legs, fingers and toes; it has internal organs, and brain activity is detectable.[2] On the other hand, I think that the premise is false, that the fetus is not a person from the moment of conception. A newly fertilized ovum, a newly implanted clump of cells, is no more a person than an acorn is an oak tree. But I shall not discuss any of this. For it seems to me to be of great interest to ask what happens if, for the sake of argument, we allow the premise. How, precisely, are we supposed to get from there to the conclusion that abortion is morally impermissible? Opponents of abortion commonly spend most of their time establishing that the fetus is a person, and hardly any time explaining the step from there to the impermissibility of abortion. Perhaps they think the step too simple and obvious to require much comment. Or perhaps instead they are simply being economical in argument. Many of those who defend abortion rely on the premise that the fetus is not a person, but only a bit of tissue that will become a person at birth; and why pay out more arguments than you have to? Whatever the explanation, I suggest that the step they take is neither easy nor obvious, that it calls for closer examination than it is commonly given, and that when we do give it this closer examination we shall feel inclined to reject it.

I propose, then, that we grant that the fetus is a person from the moment of conception. How does the argument go from here? Something like this, I take it. Every person has a right to life. So the fetus has a right to life. No doubt the mother has a right to decide what shall happen in and to her body; everyone would grant that. But surely a person's right to life is stronger and more stringent than the mother's right to decide what happens in and to her body, and so outweighs it. So the fetus may not be killed; an abortion may not be performed.

It sounds plausible. But now let me ask you to imagine this. You wake up in the morning and find yourself back to back in bed with an unconscious violinist. A famous unconscious violinist. He has been found to have a fatal kidney ailment, and the Society of Music Lovers has canvassed all the available medical records and found that you alone have the right blood type to help. They have therefore kidnapped you, and last night the violinist's circulatory system was plugged into yours, so that your kidneys can be used to extract poisons from his blood as well as your own. The director of the hospital now tells you, "Look, we're sorry the Society of Music Lovers did this to you—we would never have permitted it if we had known. But still, they did it, and the violinist now is plugged into you. To unplug you would be to kill him. But never mind, it's only for nine months. By then he will have recovered from his ail-

2. Daniel Callahan, *Abortion: Law, Choice and Morality* (New York, 1970), p. 373. This book gives a fascinating survey of the available information on abortion. The Jewish tradition is surveyed in David M. Feldman, *Birth Control in Jewish Law* (New York, 1968), Part 5, the Catholic tradition in John T. Noonan, Jr., "An Almost Absolute Value in History," in *The Morality of Abortion*, ed. John T. Noonan, Jr. (Cambridge, Mass., 1970).

ment, and can safely be unplugged from you." Is it morally incumbent on you to accede to this situation? No doubt it would be very nice of you if you did, a great kindness. But do you *have* to accede to it? What if it were not nine months, but nine years? Or longer still? What if the director of the hospital says, "Tough luck, I agree, but you've now got to stay in bed, with the violinist plugged into you, for the rest of your life. Because remember this. All persons have a right to life, and violinists are persons. Granted you have a right to decide what happens in and to your body, but a person's right to life outweighs your right to decide what happens in and to your body. So you cannot ever be unplugged from him." I imagine you would regard this as outrageous, which suggests that something really is wrong with that plausible-sounding argument I mentioned a moment ago.

In this case, of course, you were kidnapped; you didn't volunteer for the operation that plugged the violinist into your kidneys. Can those who oppose abortion on the ground I mentioned make an exception for a pregnancy due to rape? Certainly. They can say that persons have a right to life only if they didn't come into existence because of rape; or they can say that all persons have a right to life, but that some have less of a right to life than others, in particular, that those who came into existence because of rape have less. But these statements have a rather unpleasant sound. Surely the question of whether you have a right to life at all, or how much of it you have, shouldn't turn on the question of whether or not you are the product of a rape. And in fact the people who oppose abortion on the ground I mentioned do not make this distinction, and hence do not make an exception in case of rape.

Nor do they make an exception for a case in which the mother has to spend the nine months of her pregnancy in bed. They would agree that would be a great pity, and hard on the mother; but all the same, all persons have a right to life, the fetus is a person, and so on. I suspect, in fact, that they would not make an exception for a case in which, miraculously enough, the pregnancy went on for nine years, or even the rest of the mother's life.

Some won't even make an exception for a case in which continuation of the pregnancy is likely to shorten the mother's life; they regard abortion as impermissible even to save the mother's life. Such cases are nowadays very rare, and many opponents of abortion do not accept this extreme view. All the same, it is a good place to begin: a number of points of interest come out in respect to it.

1. Let us call the view that abortion is impermissible even to save the mother's life "the extreme view." I want to suggest first that it does not issue from the argument I mentioned earlier without the addition of some fairly powerful premises. Suppose a woman has become pregnant, and now learns that she has a cardiac condition such that she will die if she carries the baby to term. What may be done for her? The fetus, being a person, has a right to life, but as the mother is a person too, so has she a right to life. Presumably they have an equal right to life. How is it supposed to come out that an abortion may not be performed? If mother and child have an equal right to life, shouldn't we perhaps flip

a coin? Or should we add to the mother's right to life her right to decide what happens in and to her body, which everybody seems to be ready to grant—the sum of her rights now outweighing the fetus' right to life?

The most familiar argument here is the following. We are told that performing the abortion would be directly killing[3] the child, whereas doing nothing would not be killing the mother, but only letting her die. Moreover, in killing the child, one would be killing an innocent person, for the child has committed no crime, and is not aiming at his mother's death. And then there are a variety of ways in which this might be continued. (1) But as directly killing an innocent person is always and absolutely impermissible, an abortion may not be performed. Or, (2) as directly killing an innocent person is murder, and murder is always and absolutely impermissible, an abortion may not be performed.[4] Or, (3) as one's duty to refrain from directly killing an innocent person is more stringent than one's duty to keep a person from dying, an abortion may not be performed. Or, (4) if one's only options are directly killing an innocent person or letting a person die, one must prefer letting the person die, and thus an abortion may not be performed.[5]

Some people seem to have thought that these are not further premises which must be added if the conclusion is to be reached, but that they follow from the very fact that an innocent person has a right to life.[6] But this seems to me to be a mistake, and perhaps the simplest way to show this is to bring out that while we must certainly grant that innocent persons have a right to life, the theses in (1) through (4) are all false. Take (2), for example. If directly killing an innocent person is murder, and thus is impermissible, then the mother's directly killing the innocent person inside her is murder, and thus is impermissible. But it cannot seriously be thought to be murder if the mother performs an abortion on herself to save her life. It cannot seriously be said that

3. The term "direct" in the arguments I refer to is a technical one. Roughly, what is meant by "direct killing" is either killing as an end in itself, or killing as a means to some end, for example, the end of saving someone else's life. See note 6, below, for an example of its use.

4. Cf. *Encyclical Letter of Pope Pius XI on Christian Marriage*, St. Paul Editions (Boston, n.d.), p. 32: "however much we may pity the mother whose health and even life is gravely imperiled in the performance of the duty allotted to her by nature, nevertheless what could ever be a sufficient reason for excusing in any way the direct murder of the innocent? This is precisely what we are dealing with here." Noonan (*The Morality of Abortion*, p. 43) reads this as follows: "What cause can ever avail to excuse in any way the direct killing of the innocent? For it is a question of that."

5. The thesis in (4) is in an interesting way weaker than those in (1), (2), and (3): they rule out abortion even in cases in which both mother *and* child will die if the abortion is not performed. By contrast, one who held the view expressed in (4) could consistently say that one needn't prefer letting two persons die to killing one.

6. Cf. the following passage from Pius XII, *Address to the Italian Catholic Society of Midwives:* "The baby in the maternal breast has the right to life immediately from God.—Hence there is no man, no human authority, no science, no medical, eugenic, social, economic or moral 'indication' which can establish or grant a valid juridical ground for a direct deliberate disposition of an innocent human life, that is a disposition which looks to its destruction either as an end or as a means to another end perhaps in itself not illicit.—The baby, still not born, is a man in the same degree and for the same reason as the mother" (quoted in Noonan, *The Morality of Abortion*, p. 45).

she *must* refrain, that she *must* sit passively by and wait for her death. Let us look again at the case of you and the violinist. There you are, in bed with the violinist, and the director of the hospital says to you, "It's all most distressing, and I deeply sympathize, but you see this is putting an additional strain on your kidneys, and you'll be dead within the month. But you *have* to stay where you are all the same. Because unplugging you would be directly killing an innocent violinist, and that's murder, and that's impermissible." If anything in the world is true, it is that you do not commit murder, you do not do what is impermissible, if you reach around to your back and unplug yourself from that violinist to save your life.

The main focus of attention in writings on abortion has been on what a third party may or may not do in answer to a request from a woman for an abortion. This is in a way understandable. Things being as they are, there isn't much a woman can safely do to abort herself. So the question asked is what a third party may do, and what the mother may do, if it is mentioned at all, is deduced, almost as an afterthought, from what it is concluded that third parties may do. But it seems to me that to treat the matter in this way is to refuse to grant to the mother that very status of person which is so firmly insisted on for the fetus. For we cannot simply read off what a person may do from what a third party may do. Suppose you find yourself trapped in a tiny house with a growing child. I mean a very tiny house, and a rapidly growing child—you are already up against the wall of the house and in a few minutes you'll be crushed to death. The child on the other hand won't be crushed to death; if nothing is done to stop him from growing he'll be hurt, but in the end he'll simply burst open the house and walk out a free man. Now I could well understand it if a bystander were to say, "There's nothing we can do for you. We cannot choose between your life and his, we cannot be the ones to decide who is to live, we cannot intervene." But it cannot be concluded that you too can do nothing, that you cannot attack it to save your life. However innocent the child may be, you do not have to wait passively while it crushes you to death. Perhaps a pregnant woman is vaguely felt to have the status of house, to which we don't allow the right of self-defense. But if the woman houses the child, it should be remembered that she is a person who houses it.

I should perhaps stop to say explicitly that I am not claiming that people have a right to do anything whatever to save their lives. I think, rather, that there are drastic limits to the right of self-defense. If someone threatens you with death unless you torture someone else to death, I think you have not the right, even to save your life, to do so. But the case under consideration here is very different. In our case there are only two people involved, one whose life is threatened, and one who threatens it. Both are innocent: the one who is threatened is not threatened because of any fault, the one who threatens does not threaten because of any fault. For this reason we may feel that we bystanders cannot intervene. But the person threatened can.

In sum, a woman surely can defend her life against the threat to it posed by the unborn child, even if doing so involves its death. And this shows not merely that the theses in (1) through (4) are false; it shows also that the extreme view of abortion is false, and so we need not canvass any other possible ways of arriving at it from the argument I mentioned at the outset.

2. The extreme view could of course be weakened to say that while abortion is permissible to save the mother's life, it may not be performed by a third party, but only by the mother herself. But this cannot be right either. For what we have to keep in mind is that the mother and the unborn child are not like two tenants in a small house which has, by an unfortunate mistake, been rented to both: the mother *owns* the house. The fact that she does adds to the offensiveness of deducing that the mother can do nothing from the supposition that third parties can do nothing. But it does more than this: it casts a bright light on the supposition that third parties can do nothing. Certainly it lets us see that a third party who says "I cannot choose between you" is fooling himself if he thinks this is impartiality. If Jones has found and fastened on a certain coat, which he needs to keep him from freezing, but which Smith also needs to keep him from freezing, then it is not impartiality that says "I cannot choose between you" when Smith owns the coat. Women have said again and again "This body is *my* body!" and they have reason to feel angry, reason to feel that it has been like shouting into the wind. Smith, after all, is hardly likely to bless us if we say to him, "Of course it's your coat, anybody would grant that it is. But no one may choose between you and Jones who is to have it."

We should really ask what it is that says "no one may choose" in the face of the fact that the body that houses the child is the mother's body. It may be simply a failure to appreciate this fact. But it may be something more interesting, namely the sense that one has a right to refuse to lay hands on people, even where it would be just and fair to do so, even where justice seems to require that somebody do so. Thus justice might call for somebody to get Smith's coat back from Jones, and yet you have a right to refuse to be the one to lay hands on Jones, a right to refuse to do physical violence to him. This, I think, must be granted. But then what should be said is not "no one may choose," but only "*I* cannot choose," and indeed not even this, but "*I* will not *act*," leaving it open that somebody else can or should, and in particular that anyone in a position of authority, with the job of securing people's rights, both can and should. So this is no difficulty. I have not been arguing that any given third party must accede to the mother's request that he perform an abortion to save her life, but only that he may.

I suppose that in some views of human life the mother's body is only on loan to her, the loan not being one which gives her any prior claim to it. One who held this view might well think it impartiality to say "I cannot choose." But I shall simply ignore this possibility. My own view is that if a human being has any just, prior claim to anything at all, he has a just, prior claim to his own body. And perhaps this needn't be argued for here anyway, since, as I mentioned, the arguments against abortion we are looking at do grant that the woman has a right to decide what happens in and to her body.

But although they do grant it, I have tried to show that they do not take seriously what is done in granting it. I suggest the same thing will reappear even more clearly when we turn away from cases in which the mother's life is at stake, and attend, as I propose we now do, to the vastly more common cases in which a woman wants an abortion for some less weighty reason than preserving her own life.

3. Where the mother's life is not at stake, the argument I mentioned at the outset seems to have a much stronger pull. "Everyone has a right to life, so the unborn person has a right to life." And isn't the child's right to life weightier than anything other than the mother's own right to life, which she might put forward as ground for an abortion?

This argument treats the right to life as if it were unproblematic. It is not, and this seems to me to be precisely the source of the mistake.

For we should now, at long last, ask what it comes to, to have a right to life. In some views having a right to life includes having a right to be given at least the bare minimum one needs for continued life. But suppose that what in fact *is* the bare minimum a man needs for continued life is something he has no right at all to be given? If I am sick unto death, and the only thing that will save my life is the touch of Henry Fonda's cool hand on my fevered brow, then all the same, I have no right to be given the touch of Henry Fonda's cool hand on my fevered brow. It would be frightfully nice of him to fly in from the West Coast to provide it. It would be less nice, though no doubt well meant, if my friends flew out to the West Coast and carried Henry Fonda back with them. But I have no right at all against anybody that he should do this for me. Or again, to return to the story I told earlier, the fact that for continued life that violinist needs the continued use of your kidneys does not establish that he has a right to be given the continued use of your kidneys. He certainly has no right against you that *you* should give him continued use of your kidneys. For nobody has any right to use your kidneys unless you give him such a right; and nobody has the right against you that you shall give him this right—if you do allow him to go on using your kidneys, this is a kindness on your part, and not something he can claim from you as his due. Nor has he any right against anybody else that *they* should give him continued use of your kidneys. Certainly he had no right against the Society of Music Lovers that they should plug him into you in the first place. And if you now start to unplug yourself, having learned that you will otherwise have to spend nine years in bed with him, there is nobody in the world who must try to prevent you, in order to see to it that he is given something he has a right to be given.

Some people are rather stricter about the right to life. In their view, it does not include the right to be given anything, but amounts to, and only to, the right not to be killed by anybody. But here a related difficulty arises. If everybody is to refrain from killing that violinist, then everybody must refrain from doing a great many different sorts of things. Everybody must refrain from slitting his throat, everybody must refrain from shooting him—and everybody must refrain from unplugging you from him. But does he have a right against everybody that they shall refrain from unplugging you from him? To refrain from doing this is to allow him to continue to use your kidneys. It could be argued that he has a right against us that *we* should allow him to continue to use your kidneys. That is, while he had no right against us that we should give him the use of your kidneys, it might be argued that he anyway has a right against us that we shall not now intervene and deprive him of the use of your kidneys. I shall come back to third-party interventions later. But certainly the violinist has no right against you that *you* shall allow him to continue to use your kidneys. As I said, if you do allow him to use them, it is a kindness on your part, and not something you owe him.

The difficulty I point to here is not peculiar to the right to life. It reappears in connection with all the other natural rights; and it is something which an adequate account of rights must deal with. For present purposes it is enough just to draw attention to it. But I would stress that I am not arguing that people do not have a right to life—quite to the contrary, it seems to me that the primary control we must place on the acceptability of an account of rights is that it should turn out in that account to be a truth that all persons have a right to life. I am arguing only that having a right to life does not guarantee having either a right to be given the use of or a right to be allowed continued use of another person's body—even if one needs it for life itself. So the right to life will not serve the opponents of abortion in the very simple and clear way in which they seem to have thought it would.

4. There is another way to bring out the difficulty. In the most ordinary sort of case, to deprive someone of what he has a right to is to treat him unjustly. Suppose a boy and his small brother are jointly given a box of chocolates for Christmas. If the older boy takes the box and refuses to give his brother any of the chocolates, he is unjust to him, for the brother has been given a right to half of them. But suppose that, having learned that otherwise it means nine years in bed with that violinist, you unplug yourself from him. You surely are not being unjust to him, for you gave him no right to use your kidneys, and no one else can have given him any such right. But we have to notice that in unplugging yourself, you are killing him; and violinists, like everybody else, have a right to life, and thus in the view we were considering just now, the right not to be killed. So here you do what he supposedly has a right you shall not do, but you do not act unjustly to him in doing it.

The emendation which may be made at this point is this: the right to life consists not in the right not to be killed, but rather in the right not to be killed unjustly. This runs a risk of circularity, but never mind: it would enable us to square the fact that the violinist has a right to life with the fact that you do not act unjustly toward him in unplugging yourself, thereby killing him. For if you do not kill him unjustly, you do not violate his right to life, and so it is no wonder you do him no injustice.

But if this emendation is accepted, the gap in the argument against abortion stares us plainly in the face: it is by no means enough to show that the fetus is a person, and to remind us that all persons have a right to life—we need to be shown also that killing the fetus violates its right to life, i.e., that abortion is unjust killing. And is it?

I suppose we may take it as a datum that in a case of pregnancy due

305

to rape the mother has not given the unborn person a right to the use of her body for food and shelter. Indeed, in what pregnancy could it be supposed that the mother has given the unborn person such a right? It is not as if there were unborn persons drifting about the world, to whom a woman who wants a child says "I invite you in."

But it might be argued that there are other ways one can have acquired a right to the use of another person's body than by having been invited to use it by that person. Suppose a woman voluntarily indulges in intercourse, knowing of the chance it will issue in pregnancy, and then she does become pregnant; is she not in part responsible for the presence, in fact the very existence, of the unborn person inside her? No doubt she did not invite it in. But doesn't her partial responsibility for its being there itself give it a right to the use of her body?[7] If so, then her aborting it would be more like the boy's taking away the chocolates, and less like your unplugging yourself from the violinist—doing so would be depriving it of what it does have a right to, and thus would be doing it an injustice.

And then, too, it might be asked whether or not she can kill it even to save her own life: If she voluntarily called it into existence, how can she now kill it, even in self-defense?

The first thing to be said about this is that it is something new. Opponents of abortion have been so concerned to make out the independence of the fetus, in order to establish that it has a right to life, just as its mother does, that they have tended to overlook the possible support they might gain from making out that the fetus is *dependent* on the mother, in order to establish that she has a special kind of responsibility for it, a responsibility that gives it rights against her which are not possessed by any independent person—such as an ailing violinist who is a stranger to her.

On the other hand, this argument would give the unborn person a right to its mother's body only if her pregnancy resulted from a voluntary act, undertaken in full knowledge of the chance a pregnancy might result from it. It would leave out entirely the unborn person whose existence is due to rape. Pending the availability of some further argument, then, we would be left with the conclusion that unborn persons whose existence is due to rape have no right to the use of their mothers' bodies, and thus that aborting them is not depriving them of anything they have a right to and hence is not unjust killing.

And we should also notice that it is not at all plain that this argument really does go even as far as it purports to. For there are cases and cases, and the details make a difference. If the room is stuffy, and I therefore open a window to air it, and a burglar climbs in, it would be absurd to say, "Ah, now he can stay, she's given him a right to the use of her house —for she is partially responsible for his presence there, having voluntarily done what enabled him to get in, in full knowledge that there are such things as burglars, and that burglars burgle." It would be still more absurd to say this if I had had bars installed outside my windows, pre-

---

7. The need for a discussion of this argument was brought home to me by members of the Society for Ethical and Legal Philosophy, to whom this paper was originally presented.

cisely to prevent burglars from getting in, and a burglar got in only because of a defect in the bars. It remains equally absurd if we imagine it is
not a burglar who climbs in, but an innocent person who blunders or
falls in. Again, suppose it were like this: people-seeds drift about in the
air like pollen, and if you open your windows, one may drift in and take
root in your carpets or upholstery. You don't want children, so you fix up
your windows with fine mesh screens, the very best you can buy. As can
happen, however, and on very, very rare occasions does happen, one of
the screens is defective; and a seed drifts in and takes root. Does the
person-plant who now develops have a right to the use of your house?
Surely not—despite the fact that you voluntarily opened your windows,
you knowingly kept carpets and upholstered furniture, and you knew
that screens were sometimes defective. Someone may argue that you are
responsible for its rooting, that it does have a right to your house, because after all you *could* have lived out your life with bare floors and
furniture, or with sealed windows and doors. But this won't do—for by
the same token anyone can avoid a pregnancy due to rape by having a
hysterectomy, or anyway by never leaving home without a (reliable!)
army.

It seems to me that the argument we are looking at can establish at
most that there are *some* cases in which the unborn person has a right to
the use of its mother's body, and therefore *some* cases in which abortion
is unjust killing. There is room for much discussion and argument as to
precisely which, if any. But I think we should sidestep this issue and
leave it open, for at any rate the argument certainly does not establish
that all abortion is unjust killing.

5. There is room for yet another argument here, however. We surely
must all grant that there may be cases in which it would be morally indecent to detach a person from your body at the cost of his life. Suppose
you learn that what the violinist needs is not nine years of your life, but
only one hour: all you need do to save his life is to spend one hour in
bed with him. Suppose also that letting him use your kidneys for that
one hour would not affect your health in the slightest. Admittedly you
were kidnapped. Admittedly you did not give anyone permission to plug
him into you. Nevertheless it seems to me plain you *ought* to allow him
to use your kidneys for that hour—it would be indecent to refuse.

Again, suppose pregnancy lasted only an hour, and constituted no
threat to life or health. And suppose that a woman becomes pregnant as
a result of rape. Admittedly she did not voluntarily do anything to bring
about the existence of a child. Admittedly she did nothing at all which
would give the unborn person a right to the use of her body. All the same
it might well be said, as in the newly emended violinist story, that she
ought to allow it to remain for that hour—that it would be indecent in
her to refuse.

Now some people are inclined to use the term "right" in such a way
that it follows from the fact that you ought to allow a person to use your
body for the hour he needs, that he has a right to use your body for the
hour he needs, even though he has not been given that right by any
person or act. They may say that it follows also that if you refuse, you act

unjustly toward him. This use of the term is perhaps so common that it cannot be called wrong; nevertheless it seems to me to be an unfortunate loosening of what we would do better to keep a tight rein on. Suppose that box of chocolates I mentioned earlier had not been given to both boys jointly, but was given only to the older boy. There he sits, stolidly eating his way through the box, his small brother watching enviously. Here we are likely to say "You ought not to be so mean. You ought to give your brother some of those chocolates." My own view is that it just does not follow from the truth of this that the brother has any right to any of the chocolates. If the boy refuses to give his brother any, he is greedy, stingy, callous—but not unjust. I suppose that the people I have in mind will say it does follow that the brother has a right to some of the chocolates, and thus that the boy does act unjustly if he refuses to give his brother any. But the effect of saying this is to obscure what we should keep distinct, namely the difference between the boy's refusal in this case and the boy's refusal in the earlier case, in which the box was given to both boys jointly, and in which the small brother thus had what was from any point of view clear title to half.

A further objection to so using the term "right" that from the fact that A ought to do a thing for B, it follows that B has a right against A that A do it for him, is that it is going to make the question of whether or not a man has a right to a thing turn on how easy it is to provide him with it; and this seems not merely unfortunate, but morally unacceptable. Take the case of Henry Fonda again. I said earlier that I had no right to the touch of his cool hand on my fevered brow, even though I needed it to save my life. I said it would be frightfully nice of him to fly in from the West Coast to provide me with it, but that I had no right against him that he should do so. But suppose he isn't on the West Coast. Suppose he has only to walk across the room, place a hand briefly on my brow—and lo, my life is saved. Then surely he ought to do it, it would be indecent to refuse. Is it to be said "Ah, well, it follows that in this case she has a right to the touch of his hand on her brow, and so it would be an injustice in him to refuse"? So that I have a right to it when it is easy for him to provide it, though no right when it's hard? It's rather a shocking idea that anyone's rights should fade away and disappear as it gets harder and harder to accord them to him.

So my own view is that even though you ought to let the violinist use your kidneys for the one hour he needs, we should not conclude that he has a right to do so—we would say that if you refuse, you are, like the boy who owns all the chocolates and will give none away, self-centered and callous, indecent in fact, but not unjust. And similarly, that even supposing a case in which a woman pregnant due to rape ought to allow the unborn person to use her body for the hour he needs, we should not conclude that he has a right to do so; we should conclude that she is self-centered, callous, indecent, but not unjust, if she refuses. The complaints are no less grave; they are just different. However, there is no need to insist on this point. If anyone does wish to deduce "he has a right" from "you ought," then all the same he must surely grant that there are cases in which it is not morally required of you that you allow that violinist to use your kidneys, and in which he does not have a right to use them, and in which you do not do him an injustice if you refuse. And so also for mother and unborn child. Except in such cases as the unborn person has a right to demand it—and we were leaving open the possibility that there may be such cases—nobody is morally *required* to make large sacrifices, of health, of all other interests and concerns, of all other duties and commitments, for nine years, or even for nine months, in order to keep another person alive.

6. We have in fact to distinguish between two kinds of Samaritan: the Good Samaritan and what we might call the Minimally Decent Samaritan. The story of the Good Samaritan, you will remember, goes like this:

> A certain man went down from Jerusalem to Jericho, and fell among thieves, which stripped him of his raiment, and wounded him, and departed, leaving him half dead.
>
> And by chance there came down a certain priest that way; and when he saw him, he passed by on the other side.
>
> And likewise a Levite, when he was at the place, came and looked on him, and passed by on the other side.
>
> But a certain Samaritan, as he journeyed, came where he was; and when he saw him he had compassion on him.
>
> And went to him, and bound up his wounds, pouring in oil and wine, and set him on his own beast, and brought him to an inn, and took care of him.
>
> And on the morrow, when he departed, he took out two pence, and gave them to the host, and said unto him, "Take care of him; and whatsoever thou spendest more, when I come again, I will repay thee."
>
> (Luke 10:30–35)

The Good Samaritan went out of his way, at some cost to himself, to help one in need of it. We are not told what the options were, that is, whether or not the priest and the Levite could have helped by doing less than the Good Samaritan did, but assuming they could have, then the fact they did nothing at all shows they were not even Minimally Decent Samaritans, not because they were not Samaritans, but because they were not even minimally decent.

These things are a matter of degree, of course, but there is a difference, and it comes out perhaps most clearly in the story of Kitty Genovese, who, as you will remember, was murdered while thirty-eight people watched or listened, and did nothing at all to help her. A Good Samaritan would have rushed out to give direct assistance against the murderer. Or perhaps we had better allow that it would have been a Splendid Samaritan who did this, on the ground that it would have involved a risk of death for himself. But the thirty-eight not only did not do this, they did not even trouble to pick up a phone to call the police. Minimally Decent Samaritanism would call for doing at least that, and their not having done it was monstrous.

After telling the story of the Good Samaritan, Jesus said "Go, and do thou likewise." Perhaps he meant that we are morally required to act as the Good Samaritan did. Perhaps he was urging people to do more than is morally required of them. At all events it seems plain that it was not morally required of any of the thirty-eight that he rush out to give direct assistance at the risk of his own life, and that it is not morally required of anyone that he give long stretches of his life—nine years or nine months—to sustaining the life of a person who has no special right (we were leaving open the possibility of this) to demand it.

Indeed, with one rather striking class of exceptions, no one in any country in the world is *legally* required to do anywhere near as much as this for anyone else. The class of exceptions is obvious. My main concern here is not the state of the law in respect to abortion, but it is worth drawing attention to the fact that in no state in this country is any man compelled by law to be even a Minimally Decent Samaritan to any person; there is no law under which charges could be brought against the thirty-eight who stood by while Kitty Genovese died. By contrast, in most states in this country women are compelled by law to be not merely Minimally Decent Samaritans, but Good Samaritans to unborn persons inside them. This doesn't by itself settle anything one way or the other, because it may well be argued that there should be laws in this country —as there are in many European countries—compelling at least Minimally Decent Samaritanism.[8] But it does show that there is a gross injustice in the existing state of the law. And it shows also that the groups currently working against liberalization of abortion laws, in fact working toward having it declared unconstitutional for a state to permit abortion, had better start working for the adoption of Good Samaritan laws generally, or earn the charge that they are acting in bad faith.

I should think, myself, that Minimally Decent Samaritan laws would be one thing, Good Samaritan laws quite another, and in fact highly improper. But we are not here concerned with the law. What we should ask is not whether anybody should be compelled by law to be a Good Samaritan, but whether we must accede to a situation in which somebody is being compelled—by nature, perhaps—to be a Good Samaritan. We have, in other words, to look now at third-party interventions. I have been arguing that no person is morally required to make large sacrifices to sustain the life of another who has no right to demand them, and this even where the sacrifices do not include life itself; we are not morally required to be Good Samaritans or anyway Very Good Samaritans to one another. But what if a man cannot extricate himself from such a situation? What if he appeals to us to extricate him? It seems to me plain that there are cases in which we can, cases in which a Good Samaritan would extricate him. There you are, you were kidnapped, and nine years in bed with that violinist lie ahead of you. You have your own life to lead. You are sorry, but you simply cannot see giving up so much of your life to the sustaining of his. You cannot extricate yourself, and ask us to do so. I should have thought that—in light of his having no right to the use of your body—it was obvious that we do not have to accede to your

8. For a discussion of the difficulties involved, and a survey of the European experience with such laws, see *The Good Samaritan and the Law*, ed. James M. Ratcliffe (New York, 1966).

being forced to give up so much. We can do what you ask. There is no injustice to the violinist in our doing so.

7. Following the lead of the opponents of abortion, I have throughout been speaking of the fetus merely as a person, and what I have been asking is whether or not the argument we began with, which proceeds only from the fetus' being a person, really does establish its conclusion. I have argued that it does not.

But of course there are arguments and arguments, and it may be said that I have simply fastened on the wrong one. It may be said that what is important is not merely the fact that the fetus is a person, but that it is a person for whom the woman has a special kind of responsibility issuing from the fact that she is its mother. And it might be argued that all my analogies are therefore irrelevant—for you do not have that special kind of responsibility for that violinist, Henry Fonda does not have that special kind of responsibility for me. And our attention might be drawn to the fact that men and women both *are* compelled by law to provide support for their children.

I have in effect dealt (briefly) with this argument in section 4 above; but a (still briefer) recapitulation now may be in order. Surely we do not have any such "special responsibility" for a person unless we have assumed it, explicitly or implicitly. If a set of parents do not try to prevent pregnancy, do not obtain an abortion, and then at the time of birth of the child do not put it out for adoption, but rather take it home with them, then they have assumed responsibility for it, they have given it rights, and they cannot *now* withdraw support from it at the cost of its life because they now find it difficult to go on providing for it. But if they have taken all reasonable precautions against having a child, they do not simply by virtue of their biological relationship to the child who comes into existence have a special responsibility for it. They may wish to assume responsibility for it, or they may not wish to. And I am suggesting that if assuming responsibility for it would require large sacrifices, then they may refuse. A Good Samaritan would not refuse—or anyway, a Splendid Samaritan, if the sacrifices that had to be made were enormous. But then so would a Good Samaritan assume responsibility for that violinist; so would Henry Fonda, if he is a Good Samaritan, fly in from the West Coast and assume responsibility for me.

8. My argument will be found unsatisfactory on two counts by many of those who want to regard abortion as morally permissible. First, while I do argue that abortion is not impermissible, I do not argue that it is always permissible. There may well be cases in which carrying the child to term requires only Minimally Decent Samaritanism of the mother, and this is a standard we must not fall below. I am inclined to think it a merit of my account precisely that it does *not* give a general yes or a general no. It allows for and supports our sense that, for example, a sick and desperately frightened fourteen-year-old schoolgirl, pregnant due to rape, may *of course* choose abortion, and that any law which rules this out is an insane law. And it also allows for and supports our sense that in other cases resort to abortion is even positively indecent. It would be indecent in the woman to request an abortion, and indecent in a doctor

to perform it, if she is in her seventh month, and wants the abortion just to avoid the nuisance of postponing a trip abroad. The very fact that the arguments I have been drawing attention to treat all cases of abortion, or even all cases of abortion in which the mother's life is not at stake, as morally on a par ought to have made them suspect at the outset.

Secondly, while I am arguing for the permissibility of abortion in some cases, I am not arguing for the right to secure the death of the unborn child. It is easy to confuse these two things in that up to a certain point in the life of the fetus it is not able to survive outside the mother's body; hence removing it from her body guarantees its death. But they are importantly different. I have argued that you are not morally required to spend nine months in bed, sustaining the life of that violinist; but to say this is by no means to say that if, when you unplug yourself, there is a miracle and he survives, you then have a right to turn round and slit his throat. You may detach yourself even if this costs him his life; you have no right to be guaranteed his death, by some other means, if unplugging yourself does not kill him. There are some people who will feel dissatis-fied by this feature of my argument. A woman may be utterly devastated by the thought of a child, a bit of herself, put out for adoption and never seen or heard of again. She may therefore want not merely that the child be detached from her, but more, that it die. Some opponents of abortion are inclined to regard this as beneath contempt—thereby showing in-sensitivity to what is surely a powerful source of despair. All the same, I agree that the desire for the child's death is not one which anybody may gratify, should it turn out to be possible to detach the child alive.

At this place, however, it should be remembered that we have only been pretending throughout that the fetus is a human being from the moment of conception. A very early abortion is surely not the killing of a person, and so is not dealt with by anything I have said here.

31. Mary Anne Warren

Mary Anne Warren is professor of philosophy at Sonoma
State College, California.

Abortion and the Scope of the Right to Life

. . . Judith Thomson . . . has argued that, even if we grant the antiabortionist his claim that a fetus is a human being, with the same right
to life as any other human being, we can still demonstrate that, in at least
some and perhaps most cases, a woman is under no moral obligation to
complete an unwanted pregnancy.[1] Her argument is worth examining,
since if it holds up it may enable us to establish the moral permissibility
of abortion without becoming involved in problems about what entitles
an entity to be considered human, and accorded full moral rights. To be
able to do this would be a great gain in the power and simplicity of the
proabortion position, since, although I will argue that these problems
can be solved at least as decisively as can any other moral problem, we
should certainly be pleased to be able to avoid having to solve them as
part of the justification of abortion.

On the other hand, even if Thomson's argument does not hold up,
her insight, i.e., that it requires *argument* to show that if fetuses are

From Mary Anne Warren, "On the Moral and Legal Status of Abortion." Reprinted
from THE MONIST, Vol 57 No. 1, with the permission of the author and the publisher. The "Postscript on Infanticide" first appeared in Richard Wasserstrom (ed.),
Today's Moral Problems, published by Macmillan Publishing Co., Inc., New York, and
Collier Macmillan Publishers, London. Reprinted by permission of the author and
the publishers.

1. "A Defense of Abortion."

human then abortion is properly classified as murder, is an extremely valuable one. The assumption she attacks is particularly invidious, for it amounts to the decision that it is appropriate, in deciding the moral status of abortion, to leave the rights of the pregnant woman out of consideration entirely, except possibly when her life is threatened. Obviously, this will not do; determining what moral rights, if any, a fetus possesses is only the first step in determining the moral status of abortion. Step two, which is at least equally essential, is finding a just solution to the conflict between whatever rights the fetus may have, and the rights of the woman who is unwillingly pregnant. While the historical error has been to pay far too little attention to the second step, Ms. Thomson's suggestion is that if we look at the second step first we may find that a woman has a right to obtain an abortion *regardless* of what rights the fetus has.

Our own inquiry will also have two stages. In Section I, we will consider whether or not it is possible to establish that abortion is morally permissible even on the assumption that a fetus is an entity with a full-fledged right to life. I will argue that in fact this cannot be established, at least not with the conclusiveness which is essential to our hopes of convincing those who are skeptical about the morality of abortion, and that we therefore cannot avoid dealing with the question of whether or not a fetus really does have the same right to life as a (more fully developed) human being.

In Section II, I will propose an answer to this question, namely, that a fetus cannot be considered a member of the moral community, the set of beings with full and equal moral rights, for the simple reason that it is not a person, and that it is personhood, and not genetic humanity, i.e., humanity as defined by Noonan, which is the basis for membership in this community. I will argue that a fetus, whatever its stage of development, satisfies none of the basic criteria of personhood, and is not even enough *like* a person to be accorded even some of the same rights on the basis of this resemblance. Nor, as we will see, is a fetus's *potential* personhood a threat to the morality of abortion, since, whatever the rights of potential people may be, they are invariably overriden in any conflict with the moral rights of actual people.

I

We turn now to Professor Thomson's case for the claim that even if a fetus has full moral rights, abortion is still morally permissible, at least sometimes, and for some reasons other than to save the woman's life. Her argument is based upon a clever, but I think faulty, analogy. She asks us to picture ourselves waking up one day, in bed with a famous violinist. Imagine that you have been kidnapped, and your bloodstream hooked up to that of the violinist, who happens to have an ailment which will certainly kill him unless he is permitted to share your kidneys for a period of nine months. No one else can save him, since you alone have the right type of blood. He will be unconscious all that time, and you will have to stay in bed with him, but after the nine months are over he may be unplugged, completely cured, that is provided that you have cooperated.

Now then, she continues, what are your obligations in this situation? The antiabortionist, if he is consistent, will have to say that you are obligated to stay in bed with the violinist: for all people have a right to life, and violinists are people, and therefore it would be murder for you to disconnect yourself from him and let him die (pp. 299–300). But this is outrageous, and so there must be something wrong with the same argument when it is applied to abortion. It would certainly be commendable of you to agree to save the violinist, but it is absurd to suggest that your refusal to do so would be murder. His right to life does not obligate you to do whatever is required to keep him alive; nor does it justify anyone else in forcing you to do so. A law which required you to stay in bed with the violinist would clearly be an unjust law, since it is no proper function of the law to force unwilling people to make huge sacrifices for the sake of other people toward whom they have no such prior obligation.

Thomson concludes that, if this analogy is an apt one, then we can grant the antiabortionist his claim that a fetus is a human being, and still hold that it is at least sometimes the case that a pregnant woman has the right to refuse to be a Good Samaritan towards the fetus, i.e., to obtain an abortion. For there is a great gap between the claim that x has a right to life, and the claim that y is obligated to do whatever is necessary to keep x alive, let alone that he ought to be forced to do so. It is y's duty to keep x alive only if he has somehow contracted a *special* obligation to do so; and a woman who is unwillingly pregnant, e.g., who was raped, has done nothing which obligates her to make the enormous sacrifice which is necessary to preserve the conceptus.

This argument is initially quite plausible, and in the extreme case of pregnancy due to rape it is probably conclusive. Difficulties arise, however, when we try to specify more exactly the range of cases in which abortion is clearly justifiable even on the assumption that the fetus is human. Professor Thomson considers it a virtue of her argument that it does not enable us to conclude that abortion is *always* permissible. It would, she says, be "indecent" for a woman in her seventh month to obtain an abortion just to avoid having to postpone a trip to Europe. On the other hand, her argument enables us to see that "a sick and desperately frightened schoolgirl pregnant due to rape may *of course* choose abortion, and that any law which rules this out is an insane law" (p. 311–12). So far, so good; but what are we to say about the woman who becomes pregnant not through rape but as a result of her own carelessness, or because of contraceptive failure, or who gets pregnant intentionally and then changes her mind about wanting a child? With respect to such cases, the violinist analogy is of much less use to the defender of the woman's right to obtain an abortion.

Indeed, the choice of a pregnancy due to rape, as an example of a case in which abortion is permissible even if a fetus is considered a human being, is extremely significant; for it is only in the case of pregnancy due to rape that the woman's situation is adequately analogous to the violinist case for our intuitions about the latter to transfer convincingly. The crucial difference beween a pregnancy due to rape and the *normal* case of an unwanted pregnancy is that in the normal case we cannot claim that the woman is in no way responsible for her predicament; she could have remained chaste, or taken her pills more faithfully, or abstained on dangerous days, and so on. If, on the other hand, you are kidnapped by strangers, and hooked up to a strange violinist, then you are free of any shred of responsibility for the situation, on the basis of which it could be argued that you are obligated to keep the violinist alive. Only when her pregnancy is due to rape is a woman clearly just as nonresponsible.[2]

Consequently, there is room for the antiabortionist to argue that in the normal case of unwanted pregnancy a woman has, by her own actions, assumed responsibility for the fetus. For if x behaves in a way which he could have avoided, and which he knows involves, let us say, a one percent chance of bringing into existence a human being, with a right to life, and does so knowing that if this should happen then that human being will perish unless x does certain things to keep him alive, then it is by no means clear that when it does happen x is free of any obligation to what he knew in advance would be required to keep that human being alive.

The plausibility of such an argument is enough to show that the Thomson analogy can provide a clear and persuasive defense of a woman's right to obtain an abortion only with respect to those cases in which the woman is in no way responsible for her pregnancy, e.g., where it is due to rape. In all other cases, we would almost certainly conclude that it was necessary to look carefully at the particular circumstances in order to determine the extent of the woman's responsibility, and hence the extent of her obligation. This is an extremely unsatisfactory outcome, from the viewpoint of the opponents of restrictive abortion laws, most of whom are convinced that a woman has a right to obtain an abortion regardless of how and why she got pregnant.

Of course a supporter of the violinist analogy might point out that it is absurd to suggest that forgetting her pill one day might be sufficient to obligate a woman to complete an unwanted pregnancy. And indeed it *is* absurd to suggest this. As we will see, the moral right to obtain an abortion is not in the least dependent upon the extent to which the woman is responsible for her pregnancy. But unfortunately, once we alllow the assumption that a fetus has full moral rights, we cannot avoid taking this absurd suggestion seriously. Perhaps we can make this point more clear by altering the violinist story just enough to make it more analogous to a normal unwanted pregnancy and less to a pregnancy due to rape, and then seeing whether it is still obvious that you are not obligated to stay in bed with the fellow.

Suppose, then, that violinists are peculiarly prone to the sort of ill-

2. We may safely ignore the fact that she might have avoided getting raped, e.g., by carrying a gun, since by similar means you might likewise have avoided getting kidnapped, and in neither case does the victim's failure to take all possible precautions against a highly unlikely event (as opposed to reasonable precautions against a rather likely event) mean that he is morally responsible for what happens.

ness the only cure for which is the use of someone else's bloodstream for nine months, and that because of this there has been formed a society of music lovers who agree that whenever a violinist is stricken they will draw lots and the loser will, by some means, be made the one and only person capable of saving him. Now then, would you be obligated to cooperate in curing the violinist if you had voluntarily joined this society, knowing the possible consequences, and then your name had been drawn and you had been kidnapped? Admittedly, you did not promise ahead of time that you would, but you did deliberately place yourself in a position in which it might happen that a human life would be lost if you did not. Surely this is at least a prima facie reason for supposing that you have an obligation to stay in bed with the violinist. Suppose that you had gotten your name drawn deliberately; surely *that* would be quite a strong reason for thinking that you had such an obligation.

It might be suggested that there is one important disanalogy between the modified violinist case and the case of an unwanted pregnancy, which makes the woman's responsibility significantly less, namely, the fact that the fetus *comes into existence* as the result of the result of the woman's actions. This fact might give her a right to refuse to keep it alive, whereas she would not have had this right had it existed previously, independently, and then as a result of her actions become dependent upon her for its survival.

My own intuition, however, is that x has no more right to bring into existence, either deliberately or as a foreseeable result of actions he could have avoided, a being with full moral rights (y), and then refuse to do what he knew beforehand would be required to keep that being alive, than he has to enter into an agreement with an existing person, whereby he may be called upon to save that person's life, and then refuse to do so when so called upon. Thus, x's responsibility for y's existence does not seem to lessen his obligation to keep y alive, if he is also responsible for y's being in a situation in which only he can save him.

Whether or not this intuition is entirely correct, it brings us back once again to the conclusion that once we allow the assumption that a fetus has full moral rights it becomes an extremely complex and difficult question whether and when abortion is justifiable. Thus the Thomson analogy cannot help us produce a clear and persuasive proof of the moral permissibility of abortion. Nor will the opponents of the restrictive laws thank us for anything less; for their conviction (for the most part) is that abortion is obviously *not* a morally serious and extremely unfortunate, even though sometimes justified act, comparable to killing in self-defense or to letting the violinist die, but rather is closer to being a morally neutral act, like cutting one's hair.

The basis of this conviction, I believe, is the realization that a fetus is not a person, and thus does not have a full-fledged right to life. Perhaps the reason why this claim has been so inadequately defended is that it seems self-evident to those who accept it. And so it is, insofar as it follows from what I take to be perfectly obvious claims about the nature of personhood, and about the proper grounds for ascribing moral rights, claims which ought, indeed, to be obvious to both the friends and foes of abortion. Nevertheless, it is worth examining these claims, and showing how they demonstrate the moral innocuousness of abortion, since this apparently has not been adequately done before.

II

The question which we must answer in order to produce a satisfactory solution to the problem of the moral status of abortion is this: How are we to define the moral community, the set of beings with full and equal moral rights, such that we can decide whether a human fetus is a member of this community or not? What sort of entity, exactly, has the inalienable rights to life, liberty, and the pursuit of happiness? Jefferson attributed these rights to all *men*, and it may or may not be fair to suggest that he intended to attribute them *only* to men. Perhaps he ought to have attributed them to all human beings. If so, then we arrive, first, at Noonan's problem of defining what makes a being human, and, second, at the equally vital question which Noonan does not consider, namely, What reason is there for identifying the moral community with the set of all human beings, in whatever way we have chosen to define that term?

1. *On the Definition of 'Human'*

One reason why this vital second question is so frequently overlooked in the debate over the moral status of abortion is that the term 'human' has two distinct, but not often distinguished, senses. This fact results in a slide of meaning, which serves to conceal the fallaciousness of the traditional argument that since (1) it is wrong to kill innocent human beings, and (2) fetuses are innocent human beings, then (3) it is wrong to kill fetuses. For if 'human' is used in the same sense in both (1) and (2) then, whichever of the two senses is meant, one of these premises is question-begging. And if it is used in two different senses then of course the conclusion doesn't follow.

Thus, (1) is a self-evident moral truth,[3] and avoids begging the question about abortion, only if 'human being' is used to mean something like 'a full-fledged member of the moral community.' (It may or may not also be meant to refer exclusively to members of the species *Homo sapiens*.) We may call this the *moral* sense of 'human.' It is not to be confused with what we will call the *genetic* sense, i.e., the sense in which *any* member of the species is a human being, and no member of any other species could be. If (1) is acceptable only if the moral sense is intended, (2) is non-question-begging only if what is intended is the genetic sense.

In "Deciding Who is Human," Noonan argues for the classification of fetuses with human beings by pointing to the presence of the full genetic

3. Of course, the principle that it is (always) wrong to kill innocent human beings is in need of many other modifications, e.g., that it may be permissible to do so to save a greater number of other innocent human beings, but we may safely ignore these complications here.

code, and the potential capacity for rational thought (p. 135). It is clear that what he needs to show, for his version of the traditional argument to be valid, is that fetuses are human in the moral sense, the sense in which it is analytically true that all human beings have full moral rights. But, in the absence of any argument showing that whatever is genetically human is also morally human, and he gives none, nothing more than genetic humanity can be demonstrated by the presence of the human genetic code. And, as we will see, the *potential* capacity for rational thought can at most show that an entity has the potential for *becoming* human in the moral sense.

2. *Defining the Moral Community*

Can it be established that genetic humanity is sufficient for moral humanity? I think that there are very good reasons for not defining the moral community in this way. I would like to suggest an alternative way of defining the moral community, which I will argue for only to the extent of explaining why it is, or should be, self-evident. The suggestion is simply that the moral community consists of all and only *people*, rather than all and only human beings;[4] and probably the best way of demonstrating its self-evidence is by considering the concept of personhood, to see what sorts of entity are and are not persons, and what the decision that a being is or is not a person implies about its moral rights.

What characteristics entitle an entity to be considered a person? This is obviously not the place to attempt a complete analysis of the concept of personhood, but we do not need such a fully adequate analysis just to determine whether and why a fetus is or isn't a person. All we need is a rough and approximate list of the most basic criteria of personhood, and some idea of which, or how many, of these an entity must satisfy in order to properly be considered a person.

In searching for such criteria, it is useful to look beyond the set of people with whom we are acquainted, and ask how we would decide whether a totally alien being was a person or not. (For we have no right to assume that genetic humanity is necessary for personhood.) Imagine a space traveler who lands on an unknown planet and encounters a race of beings utterly unlike any he has ever seen or heard of. If he wants to be sure of behaving morally toward these beings, he has to somehow decide whether they are people, and hence have full moral rights, or whether they are the sort of thing which he need not feel guilty about treating as, for example, a source of food.

How should he go about making this decision? If he has some anthropological background, he might look for such things as religion, art, and the manufacturing of tools, weapons, or shelters, since these factors have been used to distinguish our human from our prehuman ancestors, in what seems to be closer to the moral than the genetic sense of 'human.' And no doubt he would be right to consider the presence of such factors

4. From here on, we will use 'human' to mean genetically human, since the moral sense seems closely connected to, and perhaps derived from, the assumption that genetic humanity is sufficient for membership in the moral community.

as good evidence that the alien beings were people, and morally human. It would, however, be overly anthropocentric of him to take the absence of these things as adequate evidence that they were not, since we can imagine people who have progressed beyond, or evolved without ever developing, these cultural characteristics.

I suggest that the traits which are most central to the concept of personhood, or humanity in the moral sense, are, very roughly, the following:

1. consciousness (of objects and events external and/or internal to the being), and in particular the capacity to feel pain;
2. reasoning (the *developed* capacity to solve new and relatively complex problems);
3. self-motivated activity (activity which is relatively independent of either genetic or direct external control);
4. the capacity to communicate, by whatever means, messages of an indefinite variety of types, that is, not just with an indefinite number of possible contents, but on indefinitely many possible topics;
5. the presence of self-concepts, and self-awareness, either individual or racial, or both.

Admittedly, there are apt to be a great many problems involved in formulating precise definitions of these criteria, let alone in developing universally valid behavioral criteria for deciding when they apply. But I will assume that both we and our explorer know approximately what (1)–(5) mean, and that he is also able to determine whether or not they apply. How, then, should he use his findings to decide whether or not the alien beings are people? We needn't suppose that an entity must have *all* of these attributes to be properly considered a person; (1) and (2) alone may well be sufficient for personhood, and quite probably (1)–(3) are sufficient. Neither do we need to insist that any one of these criteria is *necessary* for personhood, although once again (1) and (2) look like fairly good candidates for necessary conditions, as does (3), if 'activity' is construed so as to include the activity of reasoning.

All we need to claim, to demonstrate that a fetus is not a person, is that any being which satisfies *none* of (1)–(5) is certainly not a person. I consider this claim to be so obvious that I think anyone who denied it, and claimed that a being which satisfied one of (1)–(5) was a person all the same, would thereby demonstrate that he had no notion at all of what a person is—perhaps because he had confused the concept of a person with that of genetic humanity. If the opponents of abortion were to deny the appropriateness of these five criteria, I do not know what further arguments would convince them. We would probably have to admit that our conceptual schemes were indeed irreconcilably different, and that our dispute could not be settled objectively.

I do not expect this to happen, however, since I think that the concept of a person is one which is very nearly universal (to people), and that it is common to both proabortionists and antiabortionists, even though neither group has fully realized the relevance of this concept to the resolution of their dispute. Furthermore, I think that on reflection even the antiabortionists ought to agree not only that (1)–(5) are central to the concept of personhood, but also that it is a part of this concept that all and only people have full moral rights. The concept of a person is in part a moral concept; once we have admitted that *x* is a person we have recognized, even if we have not agreed to respect, *x*'s right to be treated as a member of the moral community. It is true that the claim that *x* is a *human being* is more commonly voiced as part of an appeal to treat *x* decently than is the claim that *x* is a person, but this is either because 'human being' is here used in the sense which implies personhood, or because the genetic and moral senses of 'human' have been confused.

Now if (1)–(5) are indeed the primary criteria of personhood, then it is clear that genetic humanity is neither necessary nor sufficient for establishing that an entity is a person. Some human beings are not people, and there may well be people who are not human beings. A man or woman whose consciousness has been permanently obliterated but who remains alive is a human being which is no longer a person; defective human beings, with no appreciable mental capacity, are not and presumably never will be people; and a fetus is a human being which is not yet a person, and which therefore cannot coherently be said to have full moral rights. Citizens of the next century should be prepared to recognize highly advanced, self-aware robots or computers, should such be developed, and intelligent inhabitants of other worlds, should such be found, as people in the fullest sense, and to respect their moral rights. But to ascribe full moral rights to an entity which is not a person is as absurd as to ascribe moral obligations and responsibilities to such an entity.

3. *Fetal Development and the Right to Life*

Two problems arise in the application of these suggestions for the definition of the moral community to the determination of the precise moral status of a human fetus. Given that the paradigm example of a person is a normal adult human being, then (1) How like this paradigm, in particular how far advanced since conception, does a human being need to be before it begins to have a right to life by virtue, not of being fully a person as of yet, but of being *like* a person? and (2) To what extent, if any, does the fact that a fetus has the *potential* for becoming a person endow it with some of the same rights? Each of these questions requires some comment.

In answering the first question, we need not attempt a detailed consideration of the moral rights of organisms which are not developed enough, aware enough, intelligent enough, etc., to be considered people, but which resemble people in some respects. It does seem reasonable to suggest that the more like a person, in the relevant respects, a being is, the stronger is the case for regarding it as having a right to life, and indeed the stronger its right to life is. Thus we ought to take seriously the suggestion that, insofar as "the human individual develops biologically in a continuous fashion . . . the rights of a human person might

321

develop in the same way."[5] But we must keep in mind that the attributes which are relevant in determining whether or not an entity is enough like a person to be regarded as having some of the same moral rights are no different from those which are relevant to determining whether or not it is fully a person—i.e., are no different from (1)–(5)—and that being genetically human, or having recognizably human facial and other physical features, or detectable brain activity, or the capacity to survive outside the uterus, are simply not among these relevant attributes.

Thus it is clear that even though a seven- or eight-month fetus has features which make it apt to arouse in us almost the same powerful protective instinct as is commonly aroused by a small infant, nevertheless it is not significantly more personlike than is a very small embryo. It is *somewhat* more personlike; it can apparently feel and respond to pain, and it may even have a rudimentary form of consciousness, insofar as its brain is quite active. Nevertheless, it seems safe to say that it is not fully conscious, in the way that an infant of a few months is, and that it cannot reason, or communicate messages of indefinitely many sorts, does not engage in self-motivated activity, and has no self-awareness. Thus, in the *relevant* respects, a fetus, even a fully developed one, is considerably less personlike than is the average mature mammal, indeed the average fish. And I think that a rational person must conclude that if the right to life of a fetus is to be based upon its resemblance to a person, then it cannot be said to have any more right to life than, let us say, a newborn guppy (which also seems to be capable of feeling pain), and that a right of that magnitude could never override a woman's right to obtain an abortion, at any stage of her pregnancy.

There may, of course, be other arguments in favor of placing legal limits upon the stage of pregnancy in which an abortion may be performed. Given the relative safety of the new techniques of artificially inducing labor during the third trimester, the danger to the woman's life or health is no longer such an argument. Neither is the fact that people tend to respond to the thought of abortion in the later stages of pregnancy with emotional repulsion, since mere emotional responses cannot take the place of moral reasoning in determining what ought to be permitted. Nor, finally, is the frequently heard argument that legalizing abortion, especially late in the pregnancy, may erode the level of respect for human life, leading, perhaps, to an increase in unjustified euthanasia and other crimes. For this threat, if it is a threat, can be better met by educating people to the kinds of moral distinctions which we are making here than by limiting access to abortion (which limitation may, in its disregard for the rights of women, be just as damaging to the level of respect for human rights).

Thus, since the fact that even a fully developed fetus is not personlike enough to have any significant right to life on the basis of its personlikeness shows that no legal restrictions upon the stage of pregnancy in which an abortion may be performed can be justified on the grounds

5. Thomas L. Hayes, "A Biological View," *Commonweal*, 85 (March 17, 1967), 677–78; quoted by Daniel Callahan, in *Abortion, Law, Choice, and Morality* (London: Macmillan & Co., 1970).

that we should protect the rights of the older fetus; and since there is no other apparent justification for such restrictions, we may conclude that they are entirely unjustified. Whether or not it would be *indecent* (whatever that means) for a woman in her seventh month to obtain an abortion just to avoid having to postpone a trip to Europe, it would not, in itself, be *immoral*, and therefore it ought to be permitted.

4. *Potential Personhood and the Right to Life*

We have seen that a fetus does not resemble a person in any way which can support the claim that it has even some of the same rights. But what about its *potential*, the fact that if nurtured and allowed to develop naturally it will very probably become a person? Doesn't that alone give it at least some right to life? It is hard to deny that the fact that an entity is a potential person is a strong prima facie reason for not destroying it; but we need not conclude from this that a potential person has a right to life, by virtue of that potential. It may be that our feeling that it is better, other things being equal, not to destroy a potential person is better explained by the fact that potential people are still (felt to be) an invaluable resource, not to be lightly squandered. Surely, if every speck of dust were a potential person, we would be much less apt to conclude that every potential person has a right to become actual.

Still, we do not need to insist that a potential person has no right to life whatever. There may well be something immoral, and not just imprudent, about wantonly destroying potential people, when doing so isn't necessary to protect anyone's rights. But even if a potential person does have some prima facie right to life, such a right could not possibly outweigh the right of a woman to obtain an abortion, since the rights of any actual person invariably outweigh those of any potential person, whenever the two conflict. Since this may not be immediately obvious in the case of a human fetus, let us look at another case.

Suppose that our space explorer falls into the hands of an alien culture, whose scientists decide to create a few hundred thousand or more human beings, by breaking his body into its component cells, and using these to create fully developed human beings, with, of course, his genetic code. We may imagine that each of these newly created men will have all of the original man's abilities, skills, knowledge, and so on, and also have an individual self-concept, in short that each of them will be a bona fide (though hardly unique) person. Imagine that the whole project will take only seconds, and that its chances of success are extremely high, and that our explorer knows all of this, and also knows that these people will be treated fairly. I maintain that in such a situation he would have every right to escape if he could, and thus to deprive all of these potential people of their potential lives; for his right to life outweighs all of theirs together, in spite of the fact that they are all genetically human, all innocent, and all have a very high probability of becoming people very soon, if only he refrains from acting.

Indeed, I think he would have a right to escape even if it were not his life which the alien scientists planned to take, but only a year of his freedom, or, indeed, only a day. Nor would he be obligated to stay if he had gotten captured (thus bringing all these people-potentials into existence) because of his own carelessness, or even if he had done so deliberately, knowing the consequences. Regardless of how he got captured, he is not morally obligated to remain in captivity for *any* period of time for the sake of permitting any number of potential people to come into actuality, so great is the margin by which one actual person's right to liberty outweighs whatever right to life even a hundred thousand potential people have. And it seems reasonable to conclude that the rights of a woman will outweigh by a similar margin whatever right to life a fetus may have by virtue of its potential personhood.

Thus, neither a fetus's resemblance to a person, nor its potential for becoming a person provides any basis whatever for the claim that it has any significant right to life. Consequently, a woman's right to protect her health, happiness, freedom, and even her life,[6] by terminating an unwanted pregnancy, will always override whatever right to life it may be appropriate to ascribe to a fetus, even a fully developed one. And thus, in the absence of any overwhelming social need for every possible child, the laws which restrict the right to obtain an abortion, or limit the period of pregnancy during which an abortion may be performed, are a wholly unjustified violation of a woman's most basic moral and constitutional rights.[7]

POSTSCRIPT ON INFANTICIDE. Since the publication of this article, many people have written to point out that my argument appears to justify not only abortion, but infanticide as well. For a new-born infant is not significantly more person-like than an advanced fetus, and consequently it would seem that if the destruction of the latter is permissible so too must be that of the former. Inasmuch as most people, regardless of how they feel about the morality of abortion, consider infanticide a form of murder, this might appear to represent a serious flaw in my argument.

Now, if I am right in holding that it is only people who have a full-fledged right to life, and who can be murdered, and if the criteria of personhood are as I have described them, then it obviously follows that killing a new-born infant isn't murder. It does *not* follow, however, that infanticide is permissible, for two reasons. In the first place, it would be wrong, at least in this country and in this period of history, and other things being equal, to kill a new-born infant, because even if its parents do not want it and would not suffer from its destruction, there are other people who would like to have it, and would, in all probability, be deprived of a great deal of pleasure by its destruction. Thus, infanticide is wrong for reasons analogous to those which make it wrong to wantonly destroy natural resources, or great works of art.

Secondly, most people, at least in this country, value infants and

6. That is, insofar as the death rate, for the woman, is higher for childbirth than for early abortion.

7. My thanks to the following people, who were kind enough to read and criticize an earlier version of this paper: Herbert Gold, Gene Glass, Anne Lauterbach, Judith Thomson, Mary Mothersill, and Timothy Binkley.

would much prefer that they be preserved, even if foster parents are not immediately available. Most of us would rather be taxed to support orphanages than allow unwanted infants to be destroyed. So long as there are people who want an infant preserved, and who are willing and able to provide the means of caring for it, under reasonably humane conditions, it is, *ceteris paribis*, wrong to destroy it.

But, it might be replied, if this argument shows that infanticide is wrong, at least at this time and in this country, doesn't it also show that abortion is wrong? After all, many people value fetuses, are disturbed by their destruction, and would much prefer that they be preserved, even at some cost to themselves. Furthermore, as a potential source of pleasure to some foster family, a fetus is just as valuable as an infant. There is, however, a crucial difference between the two cases: so long as the fetus is unborn, its preservation, contrary to the wishes of the pregnant woman, violates her rights to freedom, happiness, and self-determination. Her rights override the rights of those who would like the fetus preserved, just as if someone's life or limb is threatened by a wild animal, his right to protect himself by destroying the animal overrides the rights of those who would prefer that the animal not be harmed.

The minute the infant is born, however, its preservation no longer violates any of its mother's rights, even if she wants it destroyed, because she is free to put it up for adoption. Consequently, while the moment of birth does not mark any sharp discontinuity in the degree to which an infant possesses the right to life, it does mark the end of its mother's right to determine its fate. Indeed, if abortion could be performed without killing the fetus, she would never possess the right to have the fetus destroyed, for the same reasons that she has no right to have an infant destroyed.

On the other hand, it follows from my argument that when an unwanted or defective infant is born into a society which cannot afford and/or is not willing to care for it, then its destruction is permissible. This conclusion will, no doubt, strike many people as heartless and immoral, but remember that the very existence of people who feel this way, and who are willing and able to provide care for unwanted infants, is reason enough to conclude that they should be preserved.

32. Thomas Hobbes

Thomas Hobbes (1588–1679) wrote on various philosophical topics. His theory of government has been highly influential, and, in one interpretation, is thought by some contemporary philosophers to be correct in its main outline.

An Egoist's Justification of Unlimited Monarchy

Chapter XIII: Of the Natural Condition of Mankind as Concerning Their Felicity, and Misery

Nature hath made men so equal, in the faculties of the body, and mind; as that though there be found one man sometimes manifestly stronger in body, or of quicker mind than another; yet when all is reckoned together, the difference between man, and man, is not so considerable, as that one man can thereupon claim to himself any benefit, to which another may not pretend, as well as he. For as to the strength of body, the weakest has strength enough to kill the strongest, either by secret machination, or by confederacy with others, that are in the same danger with himself.

And as to the faculties of the mind, setting aside the arts grounded upon words, and especially that skill of proceeding upon general, and infallible rules, called science; which very few have, and but in few things; as being not a native faculty, born with us; nor attained, as

From *Leviathan*, first published 1651; printed here as edited by Michael Oakeshott, Basil Blackwell, Oxford, no date.

prudence, while we look after somewhat else, I find yet a greater equality amongst men, than that of strength. For prudence, is but experience; which equal time, equally bestows on all men, in those things they equally apply themselves unto. That which may perhaps make such equality incredible, is but a vain conceit of one's own wisdom, which almost all men think they have in a greater degree, than the vulgar; that is, than all men but themselves, and a few others, whom by fame, or for concurring with themselves, they approve. For such is the nature of men, that howsoever they may acknowledge many others to be more witty, or more eloquent, or more learned; yet they will hardly believe there be many so wise as themselves, for they see their own wit at hand, and other men's at a distance. But this proveth rather that men are in that point equal, than unequal. For there is not ordinarily a greater sign of the equal distribution of any thing, than that every man is contented with his share.

From this equality of ability, ariseth equality of hope in the attaining of our ends. And therefore if any two men desire the same thing, which nevertheless they cannot both enjoy, they become enemies; and in the way to their end, which is principally their own conservation, and sometimes their delectation only, endeavour to destroy, or subdue one another. And from hence it comes to pass, that where an invader hath no more to fear, than another man's single power; if one plant, sow, build, or possess a convenient seat, others may probably be expected to come prepared with forces united, to dispossess, and deprive him, not only of the fruit of his labour, but also of his life, or liberty. And the invader again is in the like danger of another.

And from this diffidence of one another, there is no way for any man to secure himself, so reasonable, as anticipation; that is, by force, or wiles, to master the persons of all men he can, so long, till he see no other power great enough to endanger him: and this is no more than his own conservation requireth, and is generally allowed. Also because there be some, that taking pleasure in contemplating their own power in the acts of conquest, which they pursue farther than their security requires; if others, that otherwise would be glad to be at ease within modest bounds, should not by invasion increase their power, they would not be able, long time, by standing only on their defence, to subsist. And by consequence, such augmentation of dominion over men being necessary to a man's conservation, it ought to be allowed him.

Again, men have no pleasure, but on the contrary a great deal of grief, in keeping company, where there is no power able to over-awe them all. For every man looketh that his companion should value him at the same rate he sets upon himself: and upon all signs of contempt, or undervaluing, naturally endeavours, as far as he dares, (which amongst them that have no common power to keep them in quiet, is far enough to make them destroy each other), to extort a greater value from his contemners, by damage; and from others, by the example.

So that in the nature of man, we find three principal causes of quarrel. First, competition; secondly, diffidence; thirdly, glory.

The first, maketh men invade for gain, the second, for safety, and the third, for reputation. The first use violence, to make themselves masters of other men's persons, wives, children, and cattle; the second, to defend them; the third, for trifles, as a word, a smile, a different opinion, and any other sign of undervalue, either direct in their persons, or by reflection in their kindred, their friends, their nation, their profession, or their name.

Hereby it is manifest, that during the time men live without a common power to keep them all in awe, they are in that condition which is called war; and such a war, as is of every man, against every man. For WAR, consisteth not in battle only, or the act of fighting; but in a tract of time, wherein the will to contend by battle is sufficiently known: and therefore the notion of *time*, is to be considered in the nature of war; as it is in the nature of weather. For as the nature of foul weather, lieth not in a shower or two of rain; but in an inclination thereto of many days together: so the nature of war, consisteth not in actual fighting; but in the known disposition thereto, during all the time there is no assurance to the contrary. All other time is PEACE.

Whatsoever therefore is consequent to a time of war, where every man is enemy to every man; the same is consequent to the time, wherein men live without other security, than what their own strength, and their own invention shall furnish them withal. In such condition, there is no place for industry; because the fruit thereof is uncertain: and consequently no culture of the earth; no navigation, nor use of the commodities that may be imported by sea; no commodious building; no instruments of moving, and removing, such things as require much force; no knowledge of the face of the earth; no account of time; no arts; no letters; no society; and which is worst of all, continual fear, and danger of violent death; and the life of man, solitary, poor, nasty, brutish, and short.

It may seem strange to some man, that has not well weighed these things; that nature should thus dissociate, and render men apt to invade, and destroy one another: and he may therefore, not trusting to this inference, made from the passions, desire perhaps to have the same confirmed by experience. Let him therefore consider with himself, when taking a journey, he arms himself, and seeks to go well accompanied; when going to sleep, he locks his doors; when even in his house he locks his chests; and this when he knows there be laws, and public officers, armed, to revenge all injuries shall be done him; what opinion he has of his fellow-subjects, when he rides armed; of his fellow citizens, when he locks his doors; and of his children, and servants, when he locks his chests. Does he not there as much accuse mankind by his actions, as I do by my words? But neither of us accuse man's nature in it. The desires, and other passions of man, are in themselves no sin. No more are the actions, that proceed from those passions, till they know a law that forbids them: which till laws be made they cannot know: nor can any law be made, till they have agreed upon the person that shall make it.

It may peradventure be thought, there was never such a time, nor condition of war as this; and I believe it was never generally so, over all the world: but there are many places, where they live so now. For the savage people in many places of America, except the government of small families, the concord whereof dependeth on natural lust, have no government at all; and live at this day in that brutish manner, as I said before. Howsoever, it may be perceived what manner of life there would be, where there were no common power to fear, by the manner of life, which men that have formerly lived under a peaceful government, use to degenerate into, in a civil war.

But though there had never been any time, wherein particular men were in a condition of war one against another; yet in all times, kings, and persons of sovereign authority, because of their independency, are in continual jealousies, and in the state and posture of gladiators; having their weapons pointing, and their eyes fixed on one another; that is, their forts, garrisons, and guns upon the frontiers of their kingdoms; and continual spies upon their neighbours; which is a posture of war. But because they uphold thereby, the industry of their subjects; there does not follow from it, that misery, which accompanies the liberty of particular men.

To this war of every man, against every man, this also is consequent; that nothing can be unjust. The notions of right and wrong, justice and injustice have there no place. Where there is no common power, there is no law: where no law, no injustice. Force, and fraud, are in war the two cardinal virtues. Justice, and injustice are none of the faculties neither of the body, nor mind. If they were, they might be in a man that were alone in the world, as well as his senses, and passions. They are qualities, that relate to men in society, not in solitude. It is consequent also to the same condition, that there be no propriety, no dominion, no *mine* and *thine* distinct; but only that to be every man's, that he can get: and for so long, as he can keep it. And thus much for the ill condition, which man by mere nature is actually placed in; though with a possibility to come out of it, consisting partly in the passions, partly in his reason.

The passions that incline men to peace, are fear of death; desire of such things as are necessary to commodious living; and a hope by their industry to obtain them. And reason suggesteth convenient articles of peace, upon which men may be drawn to agreement. These articles, are they, which otherwise are called the Laws of Nature: whereof I shall speak more particularly, in the two following chapters.

Chapter XIV: Of the First and Second Natural Laws, and of Contracts

The RIGHT OF NATURE, which writers commonly call *jus naturale*, is the liberty each man hath, to use his own power, as he will himself, for the preservation of his own nature; that is to say, of his own life; and consequently, of doing any thing, which in his own judgment, and reason, he shall conceive to be the aptest means thereunto.

By LIBERTY, is understood, according to the proper signification of the word, the absence of external impediments: which impediments, may oft take away part of a man's power to do what he would; but cannot hinder him from using the power left him, according as his judgment, and reason shall dictate to him.

329

A LAW OF NATURE, *lex naturalis,* is a precept or general rule, found out by reason, by which a man is forbidden to do that, which is destructive of his life, or taketh away the means of preserving the same; and to omit that, by which he thinketh it may be best preserved. For though they that speak of this subject, use to confound *jus,* and *lex, right* and *law:* yet they ought to be distinguished; because RIGHT, consisteth in liberty to do, or to forbear: whereas LAW, determineth, and bindeth to one of them: so that law, and right, differ as much, as obligation, and liberty; which in one and the same matter are inconsistent.

And because the condition of man, as hath been declared in the precedent chapter, is a condition of war of every one against every one; in which case every one is governed by his own reason; and there is nothing he can make use of, that may not be a help unto him, in preserving his life against his enemies; it followeth, that in such a condition, every man has a right to every thing; even to one another's body. And therefore, as long as this natural right of every man to every thing endureth, there can be no security to any man, how strong or wise soever he be, of living out the time, which nature ordinarily alloweth men to live. And consequently it is a precept, or general rule of reason, *that every man, ought to endeavor peace, as far as he has hope of obtaining it; and when he cannot obtain it, that he may seek, and use, all helps, and advantages of war.* The first branch of which rule, containeth the first, and fundamental law of nature; which is, *to seek peace, and follow it.* The second, the sum of the right of nature; which is, *by all means we can, to defend ourselves.*

From this fundamental law of nature, by which men are commanded to endeavour peace, is derived this second law; *that a man be willing, when others are so too, as far-forth, as for peace, and defence of himself he shall think it necessary, to lay down this right to all things; and be contented with so much liberty against other men, as he would allow other men against himself.* For as long as every man holdeth this right, of doing any thing he liketh; so long are all men in the condition of war. But if other men will not lay down their right, as well as he; then there is no reason for any one, to divest himself of his: for that were to expose himself to prey, which no man is bound to, rather than to dispose himself to peace. This is that law of the Gospel; *whatsoever you require that others should do to you, that do ye to them.* And that law of all men, *quod tibi fieri non vis, alteri ne feceris.*

To *lay down* a man's *right* to any thing, is to *divest* himself of the *liberty,* of hindering another of the benefit of his own right to the same. For he that renounceth, or passeth away his right, giveth not to any other man a right which he had not before; because there is nothing to which every man had not right by nature: but only standeth out of his way, that he may enjoy his own original right, without hindrance from him; not without hindrance from another. So that the effect which redoundeth to one man, by another man's defect of right, is but so much diminution of impediments to the use of his own right original. Right is laid aside, either by simply renouncing it; or by transferring it to another. By *simply* RENOUNCING; when he cares not to whom the benefit thereof redoundeth. By TRANSFERRING; when he intendeth the benefit thereof to some certain person, or persons. And when a man hath in either manner abandoned, or granted away his right; then he is said to be OBLIGED, or BOUND, not to hinder those, to whom such right is granted, or abandoned, from the benefit of it: and that he *ought*, and it is his DUTY, not to make void that voluntary act of his own: and that such hindrance is INJUSTICE, and INJURY, as being *sine jure*; the right being before renounced, or transferred. So that *injury*, or *injustice*, in the controversies of the world, is somewhat like to that, which in the disputations of scholars is called *absurdity*. For as it is there called an absurdity, to contradict what one maintained in the beginning: so in the world, it is called injustice, and injury, voluntarily to undo that, which from the beginning he had voluntarily done. The way by which a man either simply renounceth, or transferreth his right, is a declaration, or signification, by some voluntary and sufficient sign, or signs, that he doth so renounce, or transfer; or hath so renounced, or transferred the same, to him that accepteth it. And these signs are either words only, or actions only; or, as it happeneth most often, both words, and actions. And the same are the BONDS, by which men are bound, and obliged: bonds, that have their strength, not from their own nature, for nothing is more easily broken than a man's word, but from fear of some evil consequence upon the rupture.

Whensoever a man transferreth his right, or renounceth it; it is either in consideration of some right reciprocally transferred to himself; or for some other good he hopeth for thereby. For it is a voluntary act: and of the voluntary acts of every man, the object is some *good to himself*. And therefore there be some rights, which no man can be understood by any words, or other signs, to have abandoned, or transferred. As first a man cannot lay down the right of resisting them, that assault him by force, to take away his life; because he cannot be understood to aim thereby, at any good to himself. The same may be said of wounds, and chains, and imprisonment; both because there is no benefit consequent to such patience; as there is to the patience of suffering another to be wounded, or imprisoned: as also because a man cannot tell, when he seeth men proceed against him by violence, whether they intend his death or not. And lastly the motive, and end for which this renouncing, and transferring of right is introduced, is nothing else but the security of a man's person, in his life, and in the means of so preserving life, as not to be weary of it. And therefore if a man by words, or other signs, seem to despoil himself of the end, for which those signs were intended; he is not to be understood as if he meant it, or that it was his will; but that he was ignorant of how such words and actions were to be interpreted. . . .

If a covenant be made, wherein neither of the parties perform presently, but trust one another; in the condition of mere nature, which is a condition of war of every man against every man, upon any reasonable suspicion, it is void: but if there be a common power set over them both, with right and force sufficient to compel performance, it is not void. For he that performeth first, has not assurance the other will perform after; because the bonds of words are too weak to bridle men's ambition, avarice, anger, and other passions, without the fear of some coercive power; which in the condition of mere nature, where all men are equal, and judges of the justness of their own fears, cannot possibly be supposed. And therefore he which performeth first, does but betray himself to his enemy; contrary to the right, he can never abandon, of defending his life, and means of living.

But in a civil estate, where there is a power set up to constrain those that would otherwise violate their faith, that fear is no more reasonable; and for that cause, he which by the covenant is to perform first, is obliged so to do. . . .

Chapter XV: Of Other Laws of Nature

From that law of nature, by which we are obliged to transfer to another, such rights as being retained, hinder the peace of mankind, there followeth a third; which is this, *that men perform their covenants made:* without which, covenants are in vain, and but empty words; and the right of all men to all things remaining, we are still in the condition of war.

And in this law of nature, consisteth the fountain and original of JUSTICE. For where no covenant hath preceded, there hath no right been transferred, and every man has right to every thing; and consequently, no action can be unjust. But when a covenant is made, then to break it is *unjust:* and the definition of INJUSTICE, is no other than *the not performance of covenant.* And whatsoever is not unjust, is *just.*

But because covenants of mutual trust, where there is a fear of not performance on either part, as hath been said in the former chapter, are invalid; though the original of justice be the making of covenants; yet injustice actually there can be none, till the cause of such fear be taken away; which while men are in the natural condition of war, cannot be done. Therefore before the names of just, and unjust can have place, there must be some coercive power, to compel men equally to the performance of their covenants, by the terror of some punishment, greater than the benefit they expect by the breach of their covenant; and to make good that propriety, which by mutual contract men acquire, in recompense of the universal right they abandon: and such power there is none before the erection of a commonwealth. And this is also to be gathered out of the ordinary definition of justice in the Schools: for they say, that *justice is the constant will of giving to every man his own.* And therefore where there is no *own,* that is no propriety, there is no injustice; and where there is no coercive power erected, that is, where there is no commonwealth, there is no propriety; all men having right to all things: therefore where there is no commonwealth, there nothing is unjust. So that the nature of justice, consisteth in keeping of valid covenants: but the validity of covenants begins not with the constitution of a civil power, sufficient to compel men to keep them: and then it is also that propriety begins. . . .

These are the laws of nature, dictating peace, for a means of the conservation of men in multitudes; and which only concern the doctrine of civil society. There be other things tending to the destruction of particular men; as drunkenness, and all other parts of intemperance; which may therefore also be reckoned amongst those things which the law of nature hath forbidden; but are not necessary to be mentioned, nor are pertinent enough to this place.

And though this may seem too subtle a deduction of the laws of nature, to be taken notice of by all men; whereof the most part are too busy in getting food, and the rest too negligent to understand; yet to leave all men inexcusable, they have been contracted into one easy sum, intelligible even to the meanest capacity; and that is, *Do not that to another, which thou wouldest not have done to thyself;* which sheweth him, that he has no more to do in learning the laws of nature, but, when weighing the actions of other men with his own, they seem too heavy, to put them into the other part of the balance, and his own into their place, that his own passions, and self-love, may add nothing to the weight; and then there is none of these laws of nature that will not appear unto him very reasonable.

The laws of nature oblige *in foro interno;* that is to say, they bind to a desire they should take place: but *in foro externo;* that is, to the putting them in act, not always. For he that should be modest, and tractable, and perform all he promises, in such time, and place, where no man else should do so, should but make himself a prey to others, and procure his own certain ruin, contrary to the ground of all laws of nature, which tend to nature's preservation. And again, he that having sufficient security, that others shall observe the same laws towards him, observes them not himself, seeketh not peace, but war; and consequently the destruction of his nature by violence.

And whatsoever laws bind *in foro interno*, may be broken, not only by a fact contrary to the law, but also by a fact according to it, in case a man think it contrary. For though his action in this case, be according to the law; yet his purpose was against the law; which, where the obligation is *in foro interno*, is a breach.

The laws of nature are immutable and eternal; for injustice, ingratitude, arrogance, pride, iniquity, acception of persons, and the rest, can never be made lawful. For it can never be that war shall preserve life, and peace destroy it.

The same laws, because they oblige only to a desire, and endeavour, I mean an unfeigned and constant endeavour, are easy to be observed. For in that they require nothing but endeavour, he that endeavoureth their performance, fulfilleth them; and he that fulfilleth the law, is just.

And the science of them is the true and only moral philosophy. For moral philosophy is nothing else but the science of what is *good*, and *evil*, in the conversation, and society of mankind. *Good*, and *evil*, are names that signify our appetites, and aversions; which in different tempers, customs, and doctrines of men, are different: and divers men, differ not only in their judgment, on the senses of what is pleasant, and unpleasant to the taste, smell, hearing, touch, and sight; but also of what is conformable, or disagreeable to reason, in the actions of common life. Nay, the same man, in divers times, differs from himself; and one time praiseth, that is, calleth good, what another time he dispraiseth, and calleth evil: from whence arise disputes, controversies, and at last war. And therefore so long as a man is in the condition of mere nature, which is a condition of war, as private appetite is the measure of good, and evil: and consequently all men agree on this, that peace is good, and therefore also the way, or means of peace, which, as I have shewed before, are *justice, gratitude, modesty, equity, mercy*, and the rest of the laws of nature, are good; that is to say; *moral virtues;* and their contrary *vices,* evil. Now the science of virtue and vice, is moral philosophy; and therefore the true doctrine of the laws of nature, is the true moral philosophy. But the writers of moral philosophy, though they acknowledge the same virtues and vices; yet not seeing wherein consisted their goodness; nor that they come to be praised, as the means of peaceable, sociable, and comfortable living, place them in a mediocrity of passions: as if not the cause, but the degree of daring, made fortitude; or not the cause, but the quantity of a gift, made liberality. . . .

Chapter XVII: Of the Causes, Generation, and Definition of a Commonwealth

The final cause, end, or design of men, who naturally love liberty, and dominion over others, in the introduction of that restraint upon themselves, in which we see them live in commonwealths, is the foresight of their own preservation, and of a more contented life thereby; that is to say, of getting themselves out from that miserable condition of war, which is necessarily consequent, as hath been shown (chapter XIII), to the natural passions of men, when there is no visible power to keep them in awe, and tie them by fear of punishment to the performance of their covenants, and observation of those laws of nature set down in the fourteenth and fifteenth chapters.

For the laws of nature, as *justice, equity, modesty, mercy*, and, in sum, *doing to others, as we would be done to*, of themselves, without the terror of some power, to cause them to be observed, are contrary to our natural passions, that carry us to partiality, pride, revenge, and the like. And covenants, without the sword, are but words, and of no strength to secure a man at all. Therefore notwithstanding the laws of nature (which every one hath then kept, when he has the will to keep them, when he can do it safely) if there be no power erected, or not great enough for our security; every man will, and may lawfully rely on his own strength and art, for caution against all other men. . . . there be somewhat else required, besides covenant, to make their agreement constant and lasting; which is a common power, to keep them in awe, and to direct their actions to the common benefit.

The only way to erect such a common power, as may be able to defend them from the invasion of foreigners, and the injuries of one another, and thereby to secure them in such sort, as that by their own industry, and by the fruits of the earth, they may nourish themselves and live contentedly; is, to confer all their power and strength upon one man, or upon one assembly of men, that may reduce all their wills, by plurality of voices, unto one will: which is as much as to say, to appoint one man, or assembly of men, to bear their person; and every one to own, and acknowledge himself to be author of whatsoever he that so beareth their person, shall act, or cause to be acted, in those things which concern the common peace and safety; and therein to submit their wills, every one to his will, and their judgments, to his judgment. This is more than consent, or concord; it is a real unity of them all, in one and the same person, made by covenant of every man with every man, in such manner, as if every man should say to every man, *I authorize and give up my right of governing myself, to this man, or to this assembly of men, on this condition, that thou give up thy right to him, and authorize all his actions in like manner.* This done, the multitude so united in one person, is called a COMMONWEALTH, in Latin CIVITAS. This is the generation of that great LEVIATHAN, or rather, to speak more reverently, of that *mortal god,* to which we owe under the *immortal God,* our peace and defence. For by this authority, given him by every particular man in the commonwealth, he hath the use of so much power and strength conferred on him, that by terror thereof, he is enabled to form the wills of them all, to peace at home, and mutual aid against their enemies abroad. And in him consisteth the essence of the commonwealth; which, to define it, is *one person, of whose acts a great multitude, by mutual covenants one with another, have made themselves every one the author, to the end he may use the strength and means of them all, as he shall think expedient, for their peace and common defence.*

And he that carrieth this person, is called SOVEREIGN, and said to have *sovereign power;* and every one besides, his SUBJECT.

The attaining to this sovereign power, is by two ways. One, by natural force; as when a man maketh his children, to submit themselves, and their children to his government, as being able to destroy them if they refuse; or by war subdueth his enemies to his will, giving them their lives on that condition. The other, is when men agree amongst themselves, to submit to some man, or assembly of men, voluntarily, on confidence to be protected by him against all others. This latter, may be called a political commonwealth, or commonwealth by *institution;* and the former, a commonwealth by *acquisition.* And first, I shall speak of a commonwealth by institution.

Chapter XVIII: Of the Rights of Sovereigns by Institution

A *commonwealth* is said to be *instituted,* when a *multitude* of men do agree, and *covenant, every one, with every one,* that to whatsoever *man,* or *assembly of men,* shall be given by the major part, the *right to present* the person of them all, that is to say, to be their *representative;* every one, as well he that *voted for it,* as he that *voted against it,* shall *authorize* all the actions and judgments, of that man, or assembly of men, in the same manner, as if they were his own, to the end, to live peaceably amongst themselves, and be protected against other men.

From this institution of a commonwealth are derived all the *rights*, and *faculties* of him, or them, on whom the sovereign power is conferred by the consent of the people assembled.

First, because they covenant, it is to be understood, they are not obliged by former covenant to any thing repugnant hereunto. And consequently they that have already instituted a commonwealth, being thereby bound by covenant, to own the actions, and judgments of one, cannot lawfully make a new covenant, amongst themselves, to be obedient to any other, in any thing whatsoever, without his permission. And therefore, they that are subjects to a monarch, cannot without his leave cast off monarchy, and return to the confusion of a disunited multitude; nor transfer their person from him that beareth it, to another man, or other assembly of men: for they are bound every man to every man, to own, and be reputed author of all, that he that already is their sovereign, shall do, and judge fit to be done: so that any one man dissenting, all the rest should break their covenant made to that man, which is injustice: and they have also every man given the sovereignty to him that beareth their person; and therefore if they depose him, they take from him that which is his own, and so again it is injustice. Besides, if he that attempteth to depose his sovereign, be killed, or punished by him for such attempt, he is author of his own punishment, as being by the institution, author of all his sovereign shall do: and because it is injustice for a man to do any thing, for which he may be punished by his own authority, he is also upon that title, unjust. And whereas some men have pretended for their disobedience to their sovereign, a new covenant, made, not with men, but with God; this also is unjust: for there is no covenant with God, but by mediation of somebody that representeth God's person; which none doth but God's lieutenant, who hath the sovereignty under God. But this pretence of covenant with God, is so evident a lie, even in the pretenders' own consciences, that it is not only an act of an unjust, but also of a vile, and unmanly disposition. . . .

Fourthly, because every subject is by this institution author of all the actions, and judgments of the sovereign instituted; it follows, that whatsoever he doth, it can be no injury to any of his subjects; nor ought he to be by any of them accused of injustice. For he that doth anything by authority from another, doth therein no injury to him by whose authority he acteth: but by this institution of a commonwealth, every particular man is author of all the sovereign doth: and consequently he that complaineth of injury from his sovereign, complaineth of that whereof he himself is author; and therefore ought not to accuse any man but himself; no nor himself of injury; because to do injury to one's self, is impossible. It is true that they that have sovereign power may commit iniquity; but not injustice, or injury in the proper signification.

Fifthly, and consequently to that which was said last, no man that hath sovereign power can justly be put to death, or otherwise in any manner by his subjects punished. For seeing every subject is author of the actions of his sovereign; he punisheth another for the actions committed by himself.

And because the end of this institution, is the peace and defence of them all; and whosoever has right to the end, has right to the means; it belongeth of right, to whatsoever man, or assembly that hath the sovereignty, to be judge both of the means of peace and defence, and also of the hindrances, and disturbances of the same; and to do whatsoever he shall think necessary to be done, both beforehand, for the preserving of peace and security, by prevention of discord at home, and hostility from abroad; and, when peace and security are lost, for the recovery of the same. And therefore,

Sixthly, it is annexed to the sovereignty, to be judge of what opinions and doctrines are averse, and what conducing to peace; and consequently, on what occasions, how far, and what men are to be trusted withal, in speaking to multitudes of people; and who shall examine the doctrines of all books before they be published. For the actions of men proceed from their opinions; and in the well-governing of opinions, consisteth the well-governing of men's actions, in order to their peace, and concord. And though in matter of doctrine, nothing ought to be regarded but the truth; yet this is not repugnant to regulating the same by peace. For doctrine repugnant to peace, can no more be true, than peace and concord can be against the law of nature. It is true, that in a commonwealth, where by the negligence, or unskilfulness of governors, and teachers, false doctrines are by time generally received; the contrary truths may be generally offensive. Yet the most sudden, and rough busling in of a new truth, that can be, does never break the peace, but only sometimes awake the war. For those men that are so remissly governed, that they dare take up arms to defend, or introduce an opinion, are still in war; and their condition not peace, but only a cessation of arms for fear of one another; and they live, as it were, in the precincts of battle continually. It belongeth therefore to him that hath the sovereign power, to be judge, or constitute all judges of opinions and doctrines, as a thing necessary to peace; thereby to prevent discord and civil war.

33. John Locke

John Locke (1632–1704) has influenced philosophy most in
the areas of epistemology and the philosophy of language
through his Essay Concerning Human Understanding (1690).
His Two Treatises of Government (also 1690) is one of the
great defenses of the thesis that government derives its
authority from a transfer or delegation of rights by
members of the community, and that this authority reaches
only as far as the purposes for which the transfer
was made.

Consent and Natural Law the Sources of Limited Powers of Governments

Two Treatises of Government

Chapter 2: Of the State of Nature

4. To understand political power aright, and derive it from its original,
we must consider what estate all men are naturally in, and that is, a state
of perfect freedom to order their actions, and dispose of their possessions
and persons as they think fit, within the bounds of the law of Nature,
without asking leave or depending upon the will of any other man.

A state also of equality, wherein all the power and jurisdiction is
reciprocal, no one having more than another, there being nothing more
evident than that creatures of the same species and rank, promiscuously

born to all the same advantages of Nature, and the use of the same faculties, should also be equal one amongst another, without subordination or subjection, unless the lord and master of them all should, by any manifest declaration of his will, set one above another, and confer on him, by an evident and clear appointment, an undoubted right to dominion and sovereignty. . . .

6. But though this be a state of liberty, yet it is not a state of licence; though man in that state have an uncontrollable liberty to dispose of his person or possessions, yet he has not liberty to destroy himself, or so much as any creature in his possession, but where some nobler use than its bare preservation calls for it. The state of Nature has a law of Nature to govern it, which obliges every one, and reason, which is that law, teaches all mankind who will but consult it, that being all equal and independent, no one ought to harm another in his life, health, liberty or possessions; for men being all the workmanship of one omnipotent and infinitely wise Maker; all the servants of one sovereign Master, sent into the world by His order and about His business; they are His property, whose workmanship they are made to last during His, not one another's pleasure. And, being furnished with like faculties, sharing all in one community of Nature, there cannot be supposed any such subordination among us that may authorise us to destroy one another, as if we were made for one another's uses, as the inferior ranks of creatures are for ours. Every one as he is bound to preserve himself, and not to quit his station wilfully, so by the like reason, when his own preservation comes not in competition, ought he as much as he can to preserve the rest of mankind, and not unless it be to do justice on an offender, take away or impair the life, or what tends to the preservation of the life, the liberty, health, limb, or goods of another.

7. And that all men may be restrained from invading others' rights, and from doing hurt to one another, and the law of Nature be observed, which willeth the peace and preservation of all mankind, the execution of the law of Nature is in that state put into every man's hands, whereby every one has a right to punish the transgressors of that law to such a degree as may hinder its violation. For the law of Nature would, as all other laws that concern men in this world, be in vain if there were nobody that in the state of Nature had a power to execute that law, and thereby preserve the innocent and restrain offenders; and if any one in the state of Nature may punish another for any evil he has done, every one may do so. For in that state of perfect equality, where naturally there is no superiority or jurisdiction of one over another, what any may do in prosecution of that law, every one must needs have a right to do.

8. And thus, in the state of Nature, one man comes by a power over another, but yet no absolute or arbitrary power to use a criminal, when he has got him in his hands, according to the passionate heats or boundless extravagancy of his own will, but only to retribute to him so far as calm reason and conscience dictate, what is proportionate to his transgression, which is so much as may serve for reparation and restraint. For these two are the only reasons why one man may lawfully do harm to another, which is that we call punishment. In transgressing the law of

Nature, the offender declares himself to live by another rule than that of reason and common equity, which is that measure God has set to the actions of men for their mutual security, and so he becomes dangerous to mankind; the tie which is to secure them from injury and violence being slighted and broken by him, which being a trespass against the whole species, and the peace and safety of it, provided for by the law of Nature, every man upon this score, by the right he hath to preserve mankind in general, may restrain, or where it is necessary, destroy things noxious to them, and so may bring such evil on any one who hath transgressed that law, as may make him repent the doing of it, and thereby deter him, and, by his example, others from doing the like mischief. And in this case, and upon this ground, every man hath a right to punish the offender, and be executioner of the law of Nature.

9. I doubt not but this will seem a very strange doctrine to some men; but before they condemn it, I desire them to resolve me by what right any prince or state can put to death or punish an alien for any crime he commits in their country? It is certain their laws, by virtue of any sanction they receive from the promulgated will of the legislature, reach not a stranger. They speak not to him, nor, if they did, is he bound to hearken to them. The legislative authority by which they are in force over the subjects of that commonwealth hath no power over him. Those who have the supreme power of making laws in England, France, or Holland are, to an Indian, but like the rest of the world—men without authority. And therefore, if by the law of Nature every man hath not a power to punish offences against it, as he soberly judges the case to require, I see not how the magistrates of any community can punish an alien of another country, since, in reference to him, they can have no more power than what every man naturally may have over another.

10. Besides the crime which consists in violating the laws, and varying from the right rule of reason, whereby a man so far becomes degenerate, and declares himself to quit the principles of human nature and to be a noxious creature, there is commonly injury done, and some person or other, some other man, receives damage by his transgression; in which case, he who hath received any damage has (besides the right of punishment common to him, with other men) a particular right to seek reparation from him that hath done it. And any other person who finds it just may also join with him that is injured, and assist him in recovering from the offender so much as may make satisfaction for the harm he hath suffered.

11. From these two distinct rights (the one of punishing the crime, for restraint and preventing the like offence, which right of punishing is in everybody, the other of taking reparation, which belongs only to the injured party) comes it to pass that the magistrate, who by being magistrate hath the common right of punishing put into his hands, can often, where the public good demands not the execution of the law, remit the punishment of criminal offences by his own authority, but yet cannot remit the satisfaction due to any private man for the damage he has received. That he who hath suffered the damage has a right to demand in his own name, and he alone can remit. The damnified person has this

power of appropriating to himself the goods or service of the offender by right of self-preservation, as every man has a power to punish the crime to prevent its being committed again, by the right he has of preserving all mankind, and doing all reasonable things he can in order to that end. And thus it is that every man in the state of Nature has a power to kill a murderer, both to deter others from doing the like injury (which no reparation can compensate) by the example of the punishment that attends it from everybody, and also to secure men from the attempts of a criminal who, having renounced reason, the common rule and measure God hath given to mankind, hath, by the unjust violence and slaughter he hath committed upon one, declared war against all mankind, and therefore may be destroyed as a lion or a tiger, one of those wild savage beasts with whom men can have no society nor security. And upon this is grounded that great law of Nature, "Whoso sheddeth man's blood, by man shall his blood be shed." And Cain was so fully convinced that every one had a right to destroy such a criminal, that, after the murder of his brother, he cries out, "Every one that findeth me shall slay me," so plain was it writ in the hearts of all mankind.

12. By the same reason may a man in the state of Nature punish the lesser breaches of that law, it will, perhaps, be demanded, with death? I answer: Each transgression may be punished to that degree, and with so much severity, as will suffice to make it an ill bargain to the offender, give him cause to repent, and terrify others from doing the like. Every offence that can be committed in the state of Nature may, in the state of Nature, be also punished equally, and as far forth, as it may, in a commonwealth. For though it would be beside my present purpose to enter here into the particulars of the law of Nature, or its measures of punishment, yet it is certain there is such a law, and that too as intelligible and plain to a rational creature and a studier of that law as the positive laws of commonwealths, nay, possibly plainer; as much as reason is easier to be understood than the fancies and intricate contrivances of men, following contrary and hidden interests put into words; for truly so are a great part of the municipal laws of countries, which are only so far right as they are founded on the law of Nature, by which they are to be regulated and interpreted.

13. To this strange doctrine—viz., That in the state of Nature every one has the executive power of the law of Nature—I doubt not but it will be objected that it is unreasonable for men to be judges in their own cases, that self-love will make men partial to themselves and their friends; and, on the other side, ill-nature, passion, and revenge will carry them too far in punishing others, and hence nothing but confusion and disorder will follow, and that therefore God hath certainly appointed government to restrain the partiality and violence of men. I easily grant that civil government is the proper remedy for the inconveniences of the state of Nature, which must certainly be great where men may be judges in their own case, since it is easy to be imagined that he who was so unjust as to do his brother an injury will scarce be so just as to condemn himself for it. But I shall desire those who make this objection to remember that absolute monarchs are but men; and if government is to be

the remedy of those evils which necessarily follow from men being judges in their own cases, and the state of Nature is therefore not to be endured, I desire to know what kind of government that is, and how much better it is than the state of Nature, where one man commanding a multitude has the liberty to be judge in his own case, and may do to all his subjects whatever he pleases without the least question or control of those who execute his pleasure? and in whatsoever he doth, whether led by reason, mistake, or passion, must be submitted to? which men in the state of Nature are not bound to do one to another. And if he that judges, judges amiss in his own or any other case, he is answerable for it to the rest of mankind.

14. It is often asked as a mighty objection, where are, or ever were, there any men in such a state of Nature? To which it may suffice as an answer at present, that since all princes and rulers of "independent" governments all through the world are in a state of Nature, it is plain the world never was, nor never will be, without numbers of men in that state. I have named all governors of "independent" communities, whether they are, or are not, in league with others, for it is not every compact that puts an end to the state of Nature between men, but only this one of agreeing together mutually to enter into one community, and make one body politic; other promises and compacts men may make one with another, and yet still be in the state of Nature. The promises and bargains for truck, etc., between the two men in Soldania, or between a Swiss and an Indian, in the woods of America, are binding to them, though they are perfectly in a state of Nature in reference to one another for truth, and keeping of faith belongs to men as men, and not as members of society. . . .

Chapter 7: Of Political or Civil Society

. . . 87. Man being born, as has been proved, with a title to perfect freedom and an uncontrolled enjoyment of all the rights and privileges of the law of Nature, equally with any other man, or number of men in the world, hath by nature a power not only to preserve his property—that is, his life, liberty, and estate, against the injuries and attempts of other men, but to judge of and punish the breaches of that law in others, as he is persuaded the offence deserves, even with death itself, in crimes where the heinousness of the fact, in his opinion, requires it. But because no political society can be, nor subsist, without having in itself the power to preserve the property, and in order thereunto punish the offences of all those of that society, there, and there only, is political society where every one of the members hath quitted this natural power, resigned it up into the hands of the community in all cases that exclude him not from appealing for protection to the law established by it. And thus all private judgment of every particular member being excluded, the community comes to be umpire, and by understanding indifferent rules and men authorised by the community for their execution, decides all the differences that may happen between any members of that society concerning any matter of right, and punishes those offences which any member hath committed against the society with such penalties as the law has established; whereby it is easy to discern who are, and are not, in political society together. Those who are united into one body, and have a common established law and judicature to appeal to, with authority to decide controversies between them and punish offenders, are in civil society one with another; but those who have no such common appeal, I mean on earth, are still in the state of Nature, each being where there is no other, judge for himself and executioner; which is, as I have before showed it, the perfect state of Nature.

88. And thus the commonwealth comes by a power to set down what punishment shall belong to the several transgressions they think worthy of it, committed amongst the members of that society (which is the power of making laws), as well as it has the power to punish any injury done unto any of its members by any one that is not of it (which is the power of war and peace); and all this for the preservation of the property of all the members of that society, as far as is possible. But though every man entered into society has quitted his power to punish offences against the law of Nature in prosecution of his own private judgment, yet with the judgment of offences which he has given up to the legislative, in all cases where he can appeal to the magistrate, he has given up a right to the commonwealth to employ his force for the execution of the judgments of the commonwealth whenever he shall be called to it, which, indeed, are his own judgments, they being made by himself or his representative. And herein we have the original of the legislative and executive power of civil society, which is to judge by standing laws how far offences are to be punished when committed within the commonwealth; and also by occasional judgments founded on the present circumstances of the fact, how far injuries from without are to be vindicated, and in both these to employ all the force of all the members when there shall be need.

89. Wherever, therefore, any number of men so unite into one society as to quit every one his executive power of the law of Nature, and to resign it to the public, there and there only is a political or civil society. And this is done wherever any number of men, in the state of Nature, enter into society to make one people one body politic under one supreme government: or else when any one joins himself to, and incorporates with any government already made. For hereby he authorises the society, or which is all one, the legislative thereof, to make laws for him as the public good of the society shall require, to the execution whereof his own assistance (as to his own decrees) is due. And this puts men out of a state of Nature into that of a commonwealth, by setting up a judge on earth with authority to determine all the controversies and redress the injuries that may happen to any member of the commonwealth, which judge is the legislative or magistrates appointed by it. And wherever there are any number of men, however associated, that have no such decisive power to appeal to, there they are still in the state of Nature.

90. And hence it is evident that absolute monarchy, which by some men is counted for the only government in the world, is indeed inconsistent with civil society, and so can be no form of civil government at

all. For the end of civil society being to avoid and remedy those inconveniences of the state of Nature which necessarily follow from every man's being judge in his own case, by setting up a known authority to which every one of that society may appeal upon any injury received, or controversy that may arise, and which every one of the society ought to obey. Wherever any persons are who have not such an authority to appeal to, and decide any difference between them there, those persons are still in the state of Nature. And so is every absolute prince in respect of those who are under his dominion.

Chapter 8: Of the Beginning of Political Societies

95. Men being, as has been said, by nature all free, equal, and independent, no one can be put out of this estate and subjected to the political power of another without his own consent, which is done by agreeing with other men, to join and unite into a community for their comfortable, safe, and peaceable living, one amongst another, in a secure enjoyment of their properties, and a greater security against any that are not of it. This any number of men may do, because it injures not the freedom of the rest; they are left, as they were, in the liberty of the state of Nature. When any number of men have so consented to make one community or government, they are thereby presently incorporated, and make one body politic, wherein the majority have a right to act and conclude the rest.

96. For, when any number of men have, by the consent of every individual, made a community, they have thereby made that community one body, with a power to act as one body, which is only by the will and determination of the majority. For that which acts any community, being only the consent of the individuals of it, and it being one body, must move one way, it is necessary the body should move that way whither the greater force carries it, which is the consent of the majority, or else it is impossible it should act or continue one body, one community, which the consent of every individual that united into it agreed that it should; and so every one is bound by that consent to be concluded by the majority. And therefore we see that in assemblies empowered to act by positive laws where no number is set by that positive law which empowers them, the act of the majority passes for the act of the whole, and of course determines as having, by the law of Nature and reason, the power of the whole.

97. And thus every man, by consenting with others to make one body politic under one government, puts himself under an obligation to every one of that society to submit to the determination of the majority, and to be concluded by it; or else this original compact, whereby he with others incorporates into one society, would signify nothing, and be no compact if he be left free and under no other ties than he was in before in the state of Nature. For what appearance would there be of any compact? What new engagement if he were no farther tied by any decrees of the society than he himself thought fit and did actually consent to? This would be still as great a liberty as he himself had before his compact, or

any one else in the state of Nature, who may submit himself and consent to any acts of it if he thinks fit.

98. For if the consent of the majority shall not in reason be received as the act of the whole, and conclude every individual, nothing but the consent of every individual can make anything to be the act of the whole, which, considering the infirmities of health and avocations of business, which in a number though much less than that of a commonwealth, will necessarily keep many away from the public assembly; and the variety of opinions and contrariety of interests which unavoidably happen in all collections of men, it is next to impossible ever to be had. And, therefore, if coming into society be upon such terms, it will be only like Cato's coming into the theatre, *tantum ut exiret*. Such a constitution as this would make the mighty leviathan of a shorter duration than the feeblest creatures, and not let it outlast the day it was born in, which cannot be supposed till we can think that rational creatures should desire and constitute societies only to be dissolved. For where the majority cannot conclude the rest, there they cannot act as one body, and consequently will be immediately dissolved again.

99. Whosoever, therefore, out of a state of Nature unite into a community, must be understood to give up all the power necessary to the ends for which they unite into society to the majority of the community, unless they expressly agreed in any number greater than the majority. And this is done by barely agreeing to unite into one political society, which is all the compact that is, or needs be, between the individuals that enter into or make up a commonwealth. And thus, that which begins and actually constitutes any political society is nothing but the consent of any number of freemen capable of majority, to unite and incorporate into such a society. And this is that, and that only, which did or could give beginning to any lawful government in the world. . . .

Chapter 9: Of the Ends of Political Society and Government

123. If man in the state of Nature be so free as has been said, if he be absolute lord of his own person and possessions, equal to the greatest and subject to nobody, why will he part with his freedom, this empire, and subject himself to the dominion and control of any other power? To which it is obvious to answer, that though in the state of Nature he hath such a right, yet the enjoyment of it is very uncertain and constantly exposed to the invasion of others; for all being kings as much as he, every man his equal, and the greater part no strict observers of equity and justice, the enjoyment of the property he has in this state is very unsafe, very insecure. This makes him willing to quit this condition which, however free, is full of fears and continual dangers; and it is not without reason that he seeks out and is willing to join in society with others who are already united, or have a mind to unite for the mutual preservation of their lives, liberties and estates, which I call by the general name—property.

124. The great and chief end, therefore, of men uniting into com-

monwealths, and putting themselves under government, is the preservation of their property; to which in the state of Nature there are many
things wanting.

Firstly, there wants an established, settled, known law, received and
allowed by common consent to be the standard of right and wrong, and
the common measure to decide all controversies between them. For
though the law of Nature be plain and intelligible to all rational creatures,
yet men, being biased by their interest, as well as ignorant for want of
study of it, are not apt to allow of it as a law binding to them in the application of it to their particular cases.

125. Secondly, in the state of Nature there wants a known and indifferent judge, with authority to determine all differences according to
the established law. For every one in that state being both judge and
executioner of the law of Nature, men being partial to themselves, passion and revenge is very apt to carry them too far, and with too much
heat in their own cases, as well as negligence and unconcernedness, make
them too remiss in other men's.

126. Thirdly, in the state of Nature there often wants power to back
and support the sentence when right, and to give it due execution. They
who by any injustice offended will seldom fail where they are able by
force to make good their injustice. Such resistance many times makes
the punishment dangerous, and frequently destructive to those who attempt it.

127. Thus mankind, notwithstanding all the privileges of the state of
Nature, being but in an ill condition while they remain in it are quickly
driven into society. Hence it comes to pass, that we seldom find any
number of men live any time together in this state. The inconveniencies
that they are therein exposed to by the irregular and uncertain exercise
of the power every man has of punishing the transgressions of others,
make them take sanctuary under the established laws of government,
and therein seek the preservation of their property. It is this makes them
so willingly give up every one his single power of punishing to be exercised by such alone as shall be appointed to it amongst them, and by
such rules as the community, or those authorised by them to that purpose, shall agree on. And in this we have the original right and rise of
both the legislative and executive power as well as of the governments
and societies themselves.

128. For in the state of Nature to omit the liberty he has of innocent
delights, a man has two powers. The first is to do whatsoever he thinks
fit for the preservation of himself and others within the permission of the
law of Nature; by which law, common to them all, he and all the rest of
mankind are one community, make up one society distinct from all other
creatures, and were it not for the corruption and viciousness of degenerate men, there would be no need of any other, no necessity that men
should separate from this great and natural community, and associate
into lesser combinations. The other power a man has in the state of
Nature is the power to punish the crimes committed against that law.
Both these he gives up when he joins in a private, if I may so call it, or

particular political society, and incorporates into any commonwealth separate from the rest of mankind.

129. The first power—viz., of doing whatsoever he thought fit for the preservation of himself and the rest of mankind, he gives up to be regulated by laws made by the society, so far forth as the preservation of himself and the rest of that society shall require; which laws of the society in many things confine the liberty he had by the law of Nature.

130. Secondly, the power of punishing he wholly gives up, and engages his natural force, which he might before employ in the execution of the law of Nature, by his own single authority, as he thought fit, to assist the executive power of the society as the law thereof shall require. For being now in a new state, wherein he is to enjoy many conveniencies from the labour, assistance, and society of others in the same community, as well as protection from its whole strength, he is to part also with as much of his natural liberty, in providing for himself, as the good, prosperity, and safety of the society shall require, which is not only necessary but just, since the other members of the society do the like.

131. But though men when they enter into society give up the equality, liberty, and executive power they had in the state of Nature into the hands of the society, to be so far disposed of by the legislative as the good of the society shall require, yet it being only with an intention in every one the better to preserve himself, his liberty and property (for no rational creature can be supposed to change his condition with an intention to be worse), the power of the society or legislative constituted by them can never be supposed to extend farther than the common good, but is obliged to secure every one's property by providing against those three defects above mentioned that made the state of Nature so unsafe and uneasy. And so, whoever has the legislative or supreme power of any commonwealth, is bound to govern by established standing laws, promulgated and known to the people, and not by extemporary decrees, by indifferent and upright judges, who are to decide controversies by those laws; and to employ the force of the community at home only in the execution of such laws, or abroad to prevent or redress foreign injuries and secure the community from inroads and invasion. And all this to be directed to no other end but the peace, safety, and public good of the people.

Chapter II: Of the Extent of the Legislative Power

134. The great end of men's entering into society being the enjoyment of their properties in peace and safety, and the great instrument and means of that being the laws established in that society, the first and fundamental positive law of all commonwealths is the establishing of the legislative power, as the first and fundamental natural law which is to govern even the legislative. . . . This legislative is not only the supreme power of the commonwealth, but sacred and unalterable in the hands where the community have once placed it. Nor can any edict of anybody

else, in what form soever conceived, or by what power soever backed, have the force and obligation of a law which has not its sanction from that legislative which the public has chosen and appointed; for without this the law could not have that which is absolutely necessary to its being a law, the consent of the society, over whom nobody can have a power to make laws but by their own consent and by authority received from them; and therefore all the obedience, which by the most solemn ties any one can be obliged to pay, ultimately terminates in this supreme power, and is directed by those laws which it enacts. . . .

135. Though the legislative, whether placed in one or more, whether it be always in being or only by intervals, though it be the supreme power in every commonwealth, yet, first, it is not, nor can possibly be, absolutely arbitrary over the lives and fortunes of the people. For it being but the joint power of every member of the society given up to that person or assembly which is legislator, it can be no more than those persons had in a state of Nature before they entered into society, and gave it up to the community. For nobody can transfer to another more power than he has in himself, and nobody has an absolute arbitrary power over himself, or over any other, to destroy his own life, or take away the life or property of another. A man, as has been proved, cannot subject himself to the arbitrary power of another; and having, in the state of Nature, no arbitrary power over the life, liberty, or possession of another, but only so much as the law of Nature gave him for the preservation of himself and the rest of mankind, this is all he doth, or can give up to the commonwealth, and by it to the legislative power, so that the legislative can have no more than this. Their power in the utmost bounds of it is limited to the public good of the society. It is a power that hath no other end but preservation, and therefore can never have a right to destroy, enslave, or designedly to impoverish the subjects; the obligations of the law of Nature cease not in society, but only in many cases are drawn closer, and have, by human laws, known penalties annexed to them to enforce their observation. Thus the law of Nature stands as an eternal rule to all men, legislators as well as others. The rules that they make for other men's actions must, as well as their own and other men's actions, be conformable to the law of Nature—*i.e.*, to the will of God, of which that is a declaration, and the fundamental law of Nature being the preservation of mankind, no human sanction can be good or valid against it.

136. Secondly, the legislative or supreme authority cannot assume to itself a power to rule by extemporary arbitrary decrees, but is bound to dispense justice and decide the rights of the subject by promulgated standing laws, and known authorised judges. For the law of Nature being unwritten, and so nowhere to be found but in the minds of men, they who, through passion or interest, shall miscite or misapply it, cannot so easily be convinced of their mistake where there is no established judge; and so it serves not as it aught, to determine the rights and fence the properties of those that live under it, especially where every one is judge, interpreter, and executioner of it too, and that in his own case; and he that has right on his side, having ordinarily but his own single strength,

hath not force enough to defend himself from injuries or punish delinquents. To avoid these inconveniencies which disorder men's properties in the state of Nature, men unite into societies that they may have the united strength of the whole society to secure and defend their properties, and may have standing rules to bound it by which every one may know what is his. To this end it is that men give up all their natural power to the society they enter into, and the community put the legislative power into such hands as they think fit, with this trust, that they shall be governed by declared laws, or else their peace, quiet, and property will still be at the same uncertainty as it was in the state of Nature.

137. Absolute arbitrary power, or governing without settled standing laws, can neither of them consist with the ends of society and government, which men would not quit the freedom of the state of Nature for, and tie themselves up under, were it not to preserve their lives, liberties, and fortunes, and by stated rules of right and property to secure their peace and quiet. It cannot be supposed that they should intend, had they a power so to do, to give any one or more an absolute arbitrary power over their persons and estates, and put a force into the magistrate's hand to execute his unlimited will arbitrarily upon them; this were to put themselves into a worse condition than the state of Nature, wherein they had a liberty to defend their right against the injuries of others, and were upon equal terms of force to maintain it, whether invaded by a single man or many in combination. Whereas by supposing they have given up themselves to the absolute arbitrary power and will of a legislator, they have disarmed themselves, and armed him to make a prey of them when he pleases; he being in a much worse condition that is exposed to the arbitrary power of one man who has the command of a hundred thousand than he that is exposed to the arbitrary power of a hundred thousand single men, nobody being secure, that his will who has such a command is better than that of other men, though his force be a hundred thousand times stronger. And, therefore, whatever form the commonwealth is under, the ruling power ought to govern by declared and received laws, and not by extemporary dictates and undetermined resolutions, for then mankind will be in a far worse condition than in the state of Nature if they shall have armed one or a few men with the joint power of a multitude, to force them to obey at pleasure the exorbitant and unlimited decrees of their sudden thoughts, or unrestrained, and till that moment, unknown wills, without having any measures set down which may guide and justify their actions. For all the power the government has, being only for the good of the society, as it ought not to be arbitrary and at pleasure, so it ought to be exercised by established and promulgated laws, that both the people may know their duty, and be safe and secure within the limits of the law, and the rulers, too, kept within their due bounds, and not be tempted by the power they have in their hands to employ it to purposes, and by such measures as they would not have known, and own not willingly.

138. Thirdly, the supreme power cannot take from any man any part of his property without his own consent. For the preservation of property being the end of government, and that for which men enter into society,

it necessarily supposes and requires that the people should have property, without which they must be supposed to lose that by entering into society which was the end for which they entered into it; too gross an absurdity for any man to own. Men, therefore, in society having property, they have such a right to the goods, which by the law of the community are theirs, that nobody hath a right to take them, or any part of them, from them without their own consent; without this they have no property at all. For I have truly no property in that which another can by right take from me when he pleases against my consent. Hence it is a mistake to think that the supreme or legislative power of any commonwealth can do what it will, and dispose of the estates of the subject arbitrarily, or take any part of them at pleasure. This is not much to be feared in governments where the legislative consists wholly or in part in assemblies which are variable, whose members upon the dissolution of the assembly are subjects under the common laws of their country, equally with the rest. But in governments where the legislative is in one lasting assembly, always in being, or in one man as in absolute monarchies, there is danger still, that they will think themselves to have a distinct interest from the rest of the community, and so will be apt to increase their own riches and power by taking what they think fit from the people. For a man's property is not at all secure, though there be good and equitable laws to set the bounds of it between him and his fellow-subjects, if he who commands those subjects have power to take from any private man what part he pleases of his property, and use and dispose of it as he thinks good. . . .

140. It is true governments cannot be supported without great charge, and it is fit every one who enjoys his share of the protection should pay out of his estate his proportion for the maintenance of it. But still it must be with his own consent—*i.e.*, the consent of the majority, giving it either by themselves or their representatives chosen by them; for if any one shall claim a power to lay and levy taxes on the people by his own authority, and without such consent of the people, he thereby invades the fundamental law of property, and subverts the end of government. For what property have I in that which another may by right take when he pleases to himself?

141. Fourthly. The legislative cannot transfer the power of making laws to any other hands, for it being but a delegated power from the people, they who have it cannot pass it over to others. The people alone can appoint the form of the commonwealth, which is by constituting the legislative, and appointing in whose hands that shall be. And when the people have said, "We will submit, and be governed by laws made by such men, and in such forms," nobody else can say other men shall make laws for them; nor can they be bound by any laws but such as are enacted by those whom they have chosen and authorised to make laws for them.

142. These are the bounds which the trust that is put in them by the society and the law of God and Nature have set to the legislative power of every commonwealth, in all forms of government. First: They are to govern by promulgated established laws, not to be varied in particular

cases, but to have one rule for rich and poor, for the favourite at Court, and the countryman at plough. Secondly: These laws also ought to be designed for no other end ultimately but the good of the people. Thirdly: They must not raise taxes on the property of the people without the consent of the people given by themselves or their deputies. And this properly concerns only such governments where the legislative is always in being, or at least where the people have not reserved any part of the legislative to deputies, to be from time to time chosen by themselves. Fourthly: Legislative neither must nor can transfer the power of making laws to anybody else, or place it anywhere but where the people have.

34. John Stuart Mill

John Stuart Mill (1806–1873) contributed to almost every
branch of philosophy, and was the most influential British
philosopher of the last century. He was politically active
and served in Parliament.

The Justification of Political Democracy

Chapter 3: That the Ideally Best Form of Government Is Representative Government

... There is no difficulty in showing that the ideally best form of government is that in which the sovereignty, or supreme controlling power in the last resort, is vested in the entire aggregate of the community; every citizen not only having a voice in the exercise of that ultimate sovereignty, but being, at least occasionally, called on to take an actual part in the government, by the personal discharge of some public function, local or general.

To test this proposition, it has to be examined in reference to the two branches into which, as pointed out in the last chapter, the inquiry into the goodness of a government conveniently divides itself, namely, how far it promotes the good management of the affairs of society by means of the existing faculties, moral, intellectual, and active, of its various members, and what is its effect in improving or deteriorating those faculties.

This excerpt is taken from *Considerations on Representative Government*. First published 1861. Many editions.

The ideally best form of government, it is scarcely necessary to say, does not mean one which is practicable or eligible in all states of civilisation, but the one which, in the circumstances in which it is practicable and eligible, is attended with the greatest amount of beneficial consequences, immediate and prospective. A completely popular government is the only polity which can make out any claim to this character. It is pre-eminent in both the departments between which the excellence of a political constitution is divided. It is both more favourable to present good government, and promotes a better and higher form of national character, than any other polity whatsoever.

Its superiority in reference to present well-being rests upon two principles, of as universal truth and applicability as any general propositions which can be laid down respecting human affairs. The first is, that the rights and interests of every or any person are only secure from being disregarded when the person interested is himself able, and habitually disposed, to stand up for them. The second is, that the general prosperity attains a greater height, and is more widely diffused, in proportion to the amount and variety of the personal energies enlisted in promoting it.

Putting these two propositions into a shape more special to their present application; human beings are only secure from evil at the hands of others in proportion as they have the power of being, and are, *self-protecting;* and they only achieve a high degree of success in their struggle with Nature in proportion as they are *self-dependent*, relying on what they themselves can do, either separately or in concert, rather than on what others do for them.

The former proposition—that each is the only safe guardian of his own rights and interests—is one of those elementary maxims of prudence, which every person, capable of conducting his own affairs, implicitly acts upon, wherever he himself is interested. Many, indeed, have a great dislike to it as a political doctrine, and are fond of holding it up to obloquy, as a doctrine of universal selfishness. To which we may answer, that whenever it ceases to be true that mankind, as a rule, prefer themselves to others, and those nearest to them to those more remote, from that moment Communism is not only practicable, but the only defensible form of society; and will, when that time arrives, be assuredly carried into effect. For my own part, not believing in universal selfishness, I have no difficulty in admitting that Communism would even now be practicable among the *élite* of mankind, and may become so among the rest. But as this opinion is anything but popular with those defenders of existing institutions who find fault with the doctrine of the general predominance of self-interest, I am inclined to think they do in reality believe that most men consider themselves before other people. It is not, however, necessary to affirm even thus much in order to support the claim of all to participate in the sovereign power. We need not suppose that when power resides in an exclusive class, that class will knowingly and deliberately sacrifice the other classes to themselves: it suffices that, in the absence of its natural defenders, the interest of the excluded is always in danger of being overlooked; and, when looked at, is seen with very different eyes from those of the persons whom it directly concerns.

In this country, for example, what are called the working classes may be considered as excluded from all direct participation in the government. I do not believe that the classes who do participate in it have in general any intention of sacrificing the working classes to themselves. They once had that intention; witness the persevering attempts so long made to keep down wages by law. But in the present day their ordinary disposition is the very opposite: they willingly make considerable sacrifices, especially of their pecuniary interest, for the benefit of the working classes, and err rather by too lavish and indiscriminating beneficence; nor do I believe that any rulers in history have been actuated by a more sincere desire to do their duty towards the poorer portion of their countrymen. Yet does Parliament, or almost any of the members composing it, ever for an instant look at any question with the eyes of a working man? When a subject arises in which the labourers as such have an interest, is it regarded from any point of view but that of the employers of labour? I do not say that the working men's view of these questions is in general nearer to the truth than the other: but it is sometimes quite as near; and in any case it ought to be respectfully listened to, instead of being, as it is, not merely turned away from, but ignored. On the question of strikes, for instance, it is doubtful if there is so much as one among the leading members of either House who is not firmly convinced that the reason of the matter is unqualifiedly on the side of the masters, and that the men's view of it is simply absurd. Those who have studied the question know well how far this is from being the case; and in how different, and how infinitely less superficial a manner the point would have to be argued, if the classes who strike were able to make themselves heard in Parliament.

It is an adherent condition of human affairs that no intention, however sincere, of protecting the interests of others can make it safe or salutary to tie up their own hands. Still more obviously true is it, that by their own hands only can any positive and durable improvement of their circumstances in life be worked out. Through the joint influence of these two principles, all free communities have both been more exempt from social injustice and crime, and have attained more brilliant prosperity, than any others, or than they themselves after they lost their freedom. Contrast the free states of the world, while their freedom lasted, with the contemporary subjects of monarchical or oligarchical despotism: the Greek cities with the Persian satrapies; the Italian republics and the free towns of Flanders and Germany, with the feudal monarchies of Europe; Switzerland, Holland, and England, with Austria or anterevolutionary France. Their superior prosperity was too obvious ever to have been gainsaid: while their superiority in good government and social relations is proved by the prosperity, and is manifest besides in every page of history. If we compare, not one age with another, but the different governments which co-existed in the same age, no amount of disorder which exaggeration itself can pretend to have existed amidst the publicity of the free states can be compared for a moment with the contemptuous trampling upon the mass of the people which pervaded the whole life of the monarchical countries, or the disgusting individual tyranny which was of more than daily occurrence under the systems of plunder which they called fiscal arrangements, and in the secrecy of their frightful courts of justice.

It must be acknowledged that the benefits of freedom, so far as they have hitherto been enjoyed, were obtained by the extension of its privileges to a part only of the community; and that a government in which they are extended impartially to all is a desideratum still unrealised. But though every approach to this has an independent value, and in many cases more than an approach could not, in the existing state of general improvement, be made, the participation of all in these benefits is the ideally perfect conception of free government. In proportion as any, no matter who, are excluded from it, the interests of the excluded are left without the guarantee accorded to the rest, and they themselves have less scope and encouragement than they might otherwise have to that exertion of their energies for the good of themselves and of the community, to which the general prosperity is always proportioned.

Thus stands the case as regards present well-being; the good management of the affairs of the existing generation. If we now pass to the influence of the form of government upon character, we shall find the superiority of popular government over every other to be, if possible, still more decided and indisputable.

This question really depends upon a still more fundamental one, viz., which of two common types of character, for the general good of humanity, it is most desirable should predominate—the active, or the passive type; that which struggles against evils, or that which endures them; that which bends to circumstances, or that which endeavours to make circumstances bend to itself.

The commonplaces of moralists, and the general sympathies of mankind, are in favour of the passive type. Energetic characters may be admired, but the acquiescent and submissive are those which most men personally prefer. The passiveness of our neighbours increases our sense of security, and plays into the hands of our wilfulness. Passive characters, if we do not happen to need their activity, seem an obstruction the less in our own path. A contented character is not a dangerous rival. Yet nothing is more certain than that improvement in human affairs is wholly the work of the uncontented characters; and, moreover, that it is much easier for an active mind to acquire the virtues of patience than for a passive one to assume those of energy.

Of the three varieties of mental excellence, intellectual, practical, and moral, there never could be any doubt in regard to the first two which side had the advantage. All intellectual superiority is the fruit of active effort. Enterprise, the desire to keep moving, to be trying and accomplishing new things for our own benefit or that of others, is the parent even of speculative, and much more of practical, talent. The intellectual culture compatible with the other type is of that feeble and vague description which belongs to a mind that stops at amusement, or at simple contemplation. The test of real and vigorous thinking, the thinking which ascertains truths instead of dreaming dreams, is successful application to practice. Where that purpose does not exist, to give definiteness, precision, and an intelligible meaning to thought, it generates nothing better than the mystical metaphysics of the Pythagoreans or the Vedas. With respect to practical improvement, the case is still more evident. The character which improves human life is that which struggles with natural powers and tendencies, not that which gives way to them. The self-benefiting qualities are all on the side of the active and energetic character: and the habits and conduct which promote the advantage of each individual member of the community must be at least a part of those which conduce most in the end to the advancement of the community as a whole.

The striving, go-ahead character of England and the United States is only a fit subject of disapproving criticism on account of the very secondary objects on which it commonly expends its strength. In itself it is the foundation of the best hopes for the general improvement of mankind. It has been acutely remarked that whenever anything goes amiss the habitual impulse of French people is to say, "Il faut de la patience"; and of English people, "What a shame." The people who think it a shame when anything goes wrong—who rush to the conclusion that the evil could and ought to have been prevented, are those who, in the long run, do most to make the world better. If the desires are low placed, if they extend to little beyond physical comfort, and the show of riches, the immediate results of the energy will not be much more than the continual extension of man's power over material objects; but even this makes room, and prepares the mechanical appliances, for the greatest intellectual and social achievements; and while the energy is there, some persons will apply it, and it will be applied more and more, to the perfecting not of outward circumstances alone, but of man's inward nature. Inactivity, unaspiringness, absence of desire, are a more fatal hindrance to improvement than any misdirection of energy; and are that through which alone, when existing in the mass, any very formidable misdirection by an energetic few becomes possible. It is this, mainly, which retains in a savage or semi-savage state the great majority of the human race.

Now there can be no kind of doubt that the passive type of character is favoured by the government of one or a few, and the active self-helping type by that of the Many. Irresponsible rulers need the quiescence of the ruled more than they need any activity but that which they can compel. Submissiveness to the prescriptions of men as necessities of nature is the lesson inculcated by all governments upon those who are wholly without participation in them. The will of superiors, and the law as the will of superiors, must be passively yielded to. But no men are mere instruments or materials in the hands of their rulers who have will or spirit or a spring of internal activity in the rest of their proceedings: and any manifestation of these qualities, instead of receiving encouragement from despots, has to get itself forgiven by them. Even when irresponsible rulers are not sufficiently conscious of danger from the mental activity of their subjects to be desirous of repressing it, the position itself is a repression. Endeavour is even more effectually restrained by the certainty of its impotence than by any positive discouragement. Between subjection to the will of others, and the virtues of self-help and self-government, there is a natural incompatibility. This is more or less complete, according as the bondage is strained or relaxed. Rulers differ very much in the length to which they carry the control of the free agency of their subjects, or the supersession of it by managing their business for them. But the difference is in degree, not in principle; and the best despots often go the greatest lengths in chaining up the free agency of their subjects. A bad despot, when his own personal indulgences have been provided for, may sometimes be willing to let the people alone; but a good despot insists on doing them good, by making them do their own business in a better way than they themselves know of. The regulations which restricted to fixed processes all the leading branches of French manufactures were the work of the great Colbert.

Very different is the state of the human faculties where a human being feels himself under no other external restraint than the necessities of nature, or mandates of society which he has his share in imposing, and which it is open to him, if he thinks them wrong, publicly to dissent from, and exert himself actively to get altered. No doubt, under a government partially popular, this freedom may be exercised even by those who are not partakers in the full privileges of citizenship. But it is a great additional stimulus to any one's self-help and self-reliance when he starts from even ground, and has not to feel that his success depends on the impression he can make upon the sentiments and dispositions of a body of whom he is not one. It is a great discouragement to an individual, and a still greater one to a class, to be left out of the constitution; to be reduced to plead from outside the door to the arbiters of their destiny, not taken into consultation within. The maximum of the invigorating effect of freedom upon the character is only obtained when the person acted on either is, or is looking forward to becoming, a citizen as fully privileged as any other. What is still more important than even this matter of feeling is the practical discipline which the character obtains from the occasional demand made upon the citizens to exercise, for a time and in their turn, some social function. It is not sufficiently considered how little there is in most men's ordinary life to give any largeness either to their conceptions or to their sentiments. Their work is a routine; not a labour of love, but of self-interest in the most elementary form, the satisfaction of daily wants; neither the thing done, nor the process of doing it, introduces the mind to thoughts or feelings extending beyond individuals; if instructive books are within their reach, there is no stimulus to read them; and in most cases the individual has no access to any person of cultivation much superior to his own. Giving him something to do for the public, supplies, in a measure, all these deficiencies. If circumstances allow the amount of public duty assigned him to be considerable, it makes him an educated man. Notwithstanding the defects of the social system and moral ideas of antiquity, the practice of the dicastery and the ecclesia raised the intellectual standard of an average Athenian citizen far beyond anything of which there is yet an example in any other mass of men, ancient or modern. The proofs of this are apparent in every page of our great historian of Greece; but we need scarcely look further than to the high quality of the addresses which their great orators deemed best calculated to act with effect on their understanding and will. A benefit of the same kind, though far less in degree, is produced on Englishmen of the lower middle class by their liability to be placed on juries and to serve parish offices; which, though it does not occur to so many, nor is so continuous, nor introduces them to so great a variety of elevated considerations, as to admit of comparison with the public education which every citizen of Athens obtained from her democratic institutions, must make them nevertheless very different beings, in range of ideas and development of faculties, from those who have done nothing in their lives but drive a quill, or sell goods over a counter. Still more salutary is the moral part of the instruction afforded by the participation of the private citizen, if even rarely, in public functions. He is called upon, while so engaged, to weigh interests not his own; to be guided, in case of conflicting claims, by another rule than his private partialities; to apply, at every turn, principles and maxims which have for their reason of existence the common good: and he usually finds associated with him in the same work minds more familiarised than his own with these ideas and operations, whose study it will be to supply reasons to his understanding, and stimulation to his feeling for the general interest. He is made to feel himself one of the public, and whatever is for their benefit to be for his benefit. Where this school of public spirit does not exist, scarcely any sense is entertained that private persons, in no eminent social situation, owe any duties to society, except to obey the laws and submit to the government. There is no unselfish sentiment of identification with the public. Every thought or feeling, either of interest or of duty, is absorbed in the individual and in the family. The man never thinks of any collective interest, of any objects to be pursued jointly with others, but only in competition with them, and in some measure at their expense. A neighbour, not being an ally or an associate, since he is never engaged in any common undertaking for joint benefit, is therefore only a rival. Thus even private morality suffers, while public is actually extinct. Were this the universal and only possible state of things, the utmost aspirations of the lawgiver or the moralist could only stretch to make the bulk of the community a flock of sheep innocently nibbling the grass side by side.

From these accumulated considerations it is evident that the only government which can fully satisfy all the exigencies of the social state is one in which the whole people participate; that any participation, even in the smallest public function, is useful; that the participation should everywhere be as great as the general degree of improvement of the community will allow; and that nothing less can be ultimately desirable than the admission of all to a share in the sovereign power of the state. But since all cannot, in a community exceeding a single small town, participate personally in any but some very minor portions of the public business, it follows that the ideal type of a perfect government must be representative.

35. **John Stuart Mill**

The Scope of the Right to Freedom

The subject of this Essay is not the so-called Liberty of the Will, so unfortunately opposed to the misnamed doctrine of Philosophical Necessity; but Civil, or Social Liberty: the nature and limits of the power which can be legitimately exercised by society over the individual. A question seldom stated, and hardly ever discussed, in general terms, but which profoundly influences the practical controversies of the age by its latent presence, and is likely soon to make itself recognised as the vital question of the future. It is so far from being new, that, in a certain sense, it has divided mankind, almost from the remotest ages; but in the stage of progress into which the more civilised portions of the species have now entered, it presents itself under new conditions, and requires a different and more fundamental treatment.

The struggle between Liberty and Authority is the most conspicuous feature in the portions of history with which we are earliest familiar, particularly in that of Greece, Rome, and England. But in old times this contest was between subjects, or some classes of subjects, and the Government. By liberty, was meant protection against the tyranny of the political rulers. The rulers were conceived (except in some of the popular governments of Greece) as in a necessarily antagonistic position to the people whom they ruled. They consisted of a governing One, or a governing tribe or caste, who derived their authority from inheritance or conquest, who, at all events, did not hold it at the pleasure of the governed, and whose supremacy men did not venture, perhaps did not desire, to

From John Stuart Mill, *On Liberty*. London: Parker, 1859. Many editions.

contest, whatever precautions might be taken against its oppressive exercise. Their power was regarded as necessary, but also as highly dangerous; as a weapon which they would attempt to use against their subjects, no less than against external enemies. To prevent the weaker members of the community from being preyed upon by innumerable vultures, it was needful that there should be an animal of prey stronger than the rest, commissioned to keep them down. But as the king of the vultures would be no less bent upon preying on the flock than any of the minor harpies, it was indispensable to be in a perpetual attitude of defence against his beak and claws. The aim, therefore, of patriots was to set limits to the power which the ruler should be suffered to exercise over the community; and this limitation was what they meant by liberty. It was attempted in two ways. First, by obtaining a recognition of certain immunities, called political liberties or rights, which it was to be regarded as a breach of duty in the ruler to infringe, and which if he did infringe, specific resistance, or general rebellion, was held to be justifiable. A second, and generally a later expedient, was the establishment of constitutional checks, by which the consent of the community, or of a body of some sort, supposed to represent its interests, was made a necessary condition to some of the more important acts of the governing power. To the first of these modes of limitation, the ruling power, in most European countries, was compelled, more or less, to submit. It was not so with the second; and, to attain this, or when already in some degree possessed, to attain it more completely, became everywhere the principal object of the lovers of liberty. And so long as mankind were content to combat one enemy by another, and to be ruled by a master, on condition of being guaranteed more or less efficaciously against his tyranny, they did not carry their aspirations beyond this point.

A time, however, came, in the progress of human affairs, when men ceased to think it a necessity of nature that their governors should be an independent power, opposed in interest to themselves. It appeared to them much better that the various magistrates of the State should be their tenants or delegates, revocable at their pleasure. In that way alone, it seemed, could they have complete security that the powers of government would never be abused to their disadvantage. By degrees this new demand for elective and temporary rulers became the prominent object of the exertions of the popular party, wherever any such party existed; and superseded, to a considerable extent, the previous efforts to limit the power of rulers. As the struggle proceeded for making the ruling power emanate from the periodical choice of the ruled, some persons began to think that too much importance had been attached to the limitation of the power itself. *That* (it might seem) was a resource against rulers whose interests were habitually opposed to those of the people. What was now wanted was, that the rulers should be identified with the people; that their interest and will should be the interest and will of the nation. The nation did not need to be protected against its own will. There was no fear of its tyrannising over itself. Let the rulers be effectually responsible to it, promptly removable by it, and it could afford to trust them with power of which it could itself dictate the use to be made. Their power was but the nation's own power, concentrated, and in a form convenient for exercise. This mode of thought, or rather perhaps of feeling, was common among the last generation of European liberalism, in the Continental section of which it still apparently predominates. Those who admit any limit to what a government may do, except in the case of such governments as they think ought not to exist, stand out as brilliant exceptions among the political thinkers of the Continent. A similar tone of sentiment might by this time have been prevalent in our own country, if the circumstances which for a time encouraged it, had continued unaltered.

But, in political and philosophical theories, as well as in persons, success discloses faults and infirmities which failure might have concealed from observation. The notion, that the people have no need to limit their power over themselves, might seem axiomatic, when popular government was a thing only dreamed about, or read of as having existed at some distant period of the past. Neither was that notion necessarily disturbed by such temporary aberrations as those of the French Revolution, the worst of which were the work of a usurping few, and which, in any case, belonged, not to the permanent working of popular institutions, but to a sudden and convulsive outbreak against monarchical and aristocratic despotism. In time, however, a democratic republic came to occupy a large portion of the earth's surface, and made itself felt as one of the most powerful members of the community of nations; and elective and responsible government became subject to the observations and criticisms which wait upon a great existing fact. It was now perceived that such phrases as "self-government," and "the power of the people over themselves," do not express the true state of the case. The "people" who exercise the power are not always the same people with those over whom it is exercised; and the "self-government" spoken of is not the government of each by himself, but of each by all the rest. The will of the people, moreover, practically means the will of the most numerous or the most active *part* of the people; the majority, or those who succeed in making themselves accepted as the majority; the people, consequently *may* desire to oppress a part of their number; and precautions are as much needed against this as against any other abuse of power. The limitation, therefore, of the power of government over individuals loses none of its importance when the holders of power are regularly accountable to the community, that is, to the strongest party therein. This view of things, recommending itself equally to the intelligence of thinkers and to the inclination of those important classes in European society to whose real or supposed interests democracy is adverse, has had no difficulty in establishing itself; and in political speculations "the tyranny of the majority" is now generally included among the evils against which society requires to be on its guard.

Like other tyrannies, the tyranny of the majority was at first, and is still vulgarly, held in dread, chiefly as operating through the acts of the public authorities. But reflecting persons perceived that when society is itself the tyrant—society collectively over the separate individuals who compose it—its means of tyrannising are not restricted to the acts which it may do by the hands of its political functionaries. Society can and does execute its own mandates: and if it issues wrong mandates instead of right, or any mandates at all in things with which it ought not to meddle, it practises a social tyranny more formidable than many kinds of political oppression, since, though not usually upheld by such extreme penalties, it leaves fewer means of escape, penetrating much more deeply into the details of life, and enslaving the soul itself. Protection, therefore, against the tyranny of the magistrate is not enough: there needs protection also against the tyranny of the prevailing opinion and feeling; against the tendency of society to impose, by other means than civil penalties, its own ideas and practices as rules of conduct on those who dissent from them; to fetter the development, and, if possible, prevent the formation, of any individuality not in harmony with its ways, and compels all characters to fashion themselves upon the model of its own. There is a limit to the legitimate interference of collective opinion with individual independence: and to find that limit, and maintain it against encroachment, is as indispensable to a good condition of human affairs, as protection against political despotism.

But though this proposition is not likely to be contested in general terms, the practical question, where to place the limit—how to make the fitting adjustment between individual independence and social control—is a subject on which nearly everything remains to be done. All that makes existence valuable to any one, depends on the enforcement of restraints upon the actions of other people. Some rules of conduct, therefore, must be imposed, by law in the first place, and by opinion on many things which are not fit subjects for the operation of law. What these rules should be is the principal question in human affairs. . . .

. . . There is, in fact, no recognized principle by which the propriety or impropriety of government interference is customarily tested. People decide according to their personal preferences. Some, whenever they see any good to be done, or evil to be remedied, would willingly instigate the government to undertake the business; while others prefer to bear almost any amount of social evil, rather than add one to the departments of human interests amenable to governmental control. And men range themselves on one or the other side in any particular case, according to this general direction of their sentiments; or according to the degree of interest which they feel in the particular thing which it is proposed that the government should do, or according to the belief they entertain that the government would, or would not, do it in the manner they prefer; but very rarely on account of any opinion to which they consistently adhere, as to what things are fit to be done by a government. And it seems to me that in consequence of this absence of rule or principle, one side is at present as often wrong as the other; the interference of government is, with about equal frequency, improperly invoked and improperly condemned.

The object of this Essay is to assert one very simple principle, as entitled to govern absolutely the dealings of society with the individual in the way of compulsion and control, whether the means used be physical force in the form of legal penalties, or the moral coercion of public opinion. That principle is, that the sole end for which mankind are warranted, individually or collectively, in interfering with the liberty of action of any of their number, is self-protection. That the only purpose for which power can be rightfully exercised over any member of a civilised community, against his will, is to prevent harm to others. His own good, either physical or moral, is not a sufficient warrant. He cannot rightfully be compelled to do or forebear because it will be better for him to do so, because it will make him happier, because, in the opinions of others, to do so would be wise, or even right. These are good reasons for remonstrating with him, or reasoning with him, or persuading him, or entreating him, but not for compelling him, or visiting him with any evil in case he do otherwise. To justify that, the conduct from which it is desired to deter him must be calculated to produce evil to some one else. The only part of the conduct of any one, for which he is amenable to society, is that which concerns others. In the part which merely concerns himself, his independence is, of right, absolute. Over himself, over his own body and mind, the individual is sovereign.

It is, perhaps, hardly necessary to say that this doctrine is meant to apply only to human beings in the maturity of their faculties. We are not speaking of children, or of young persons below the age which the law may fix as that of manhood or womanhood. Those who are still in a state to require being taken care of by others, must be protected against their own actions as well as against external injury. For the same reason, we may leave out of consideration those backward states of society in which the race itself may be considered as in its nonage. The early difficulties in the way of spontaneous progress are so great, that there is seldom any choice of means for overcoming them; and a rule full of the spirit of improvement is warranted in the use of any expedients that will attain an end, perhaps otherwise unattainable. Despotism is a legitimate mode of government in dealing with barbarians, provided the end be their improvement, and the means justified by actually effecting that end. Liberty, as a principle, has no application to any state of things anterior to the time when mankind have become capable of being improved by free and equal discussion. Until then, there is nothing for them but implicit obedience to an Akbar or a Charlemagne, if they are so fortunate as to find one. But as soon as mankind have attained the capacity of being guided to their own improvement by convictions or persuasion (a period long since reached in all nations with whom we need here concern ourselves), compulsion, either in the direct form or in that of pains and penalties for non-compliance, is no longer admissible as a means to their own good, and justifiable only for the security of others.

It is proper to state that I forego any advantage which could be derived to my argument from the idea of abstract right, as a thing independent of utility. I regard utility as the ultimate appeal on all ethical questions; but it must be utility in the largest sense, grounded on the permanent interests of a man as a progressive being. Those interests, I contend, authorise the subjection of individual spontaneity to external control, only in respect to those actions of each, which concern the interest of other people. If any one does an act hurtful to others, there is a *prima facie* case for punishing him, by law, or, where legal penalties are not safely applicable, by general disapprobation. There are also many positive acts for the benefit of others, which he may rightfully be compelled to perform; such as to give evidence in a court of justice; to bear his fair share in the common defence, or in any other joint work necessary to the interest of the society of which he enjoys the protection; and to perform certain acts of individual beneficence, such as saving a fellow-creature's life, or interposing to protect the defenceless against ill-usage, things which whenever it is obviously a man's duty to do, he may rightfully be made responsible to society for not doing. A person may cause evil to others not only by his actions but by his inaction, and in either case he is justly accountable to them for the injury. The latter case, it is true, requires a much more cautious exercise of compulsion than the former. To make any one answerable for doing evil to others is the rule; to make him answerable for not preventing evil is, comparatively speaking, the exception. Yet there are many cases clear enough and grave enough to justify that exception. In all things which regard the external relations of the individual, he is *de jure* amenable to those whose interests are concerned, and, if need be, to society as their protector. There are often good reasons for not holding him to the responsibility; but these reasons must arise from the special expediencies of the case: either because it is a kind of case in which he is on the whole likely to act better, when left to his own discretion, than when controlled in any way in which society have it in their power to control him; or because the attempt to exercise control would produce other evils, greater than those which it would prevent. When such reasons as these preclude the enforcement of responsibility, the conscience of the agent himself should step into the vacant judgment seat, and protect those interests of others which have no external protection; judging himself all the more rigidly, because the case does not admit of his being made accountable to the judgment of his fellow-creatures.

But there is a sphere of action in which society, as distinguished from the individual, has, if any, only an indirect interest; comprehending all that portion of a person's life and conduct which affects only himself, or if it also affects others, only with their free, voluntary, and undeceived consent and participation. When I say only himself, I mean directly, and in the first instance; for whatever affects himself, may affect others through himself; and the objection which may be grounded on this contingency, will receive consideration in the sequel. This, then, is the appropriate region of human liberty. It comprises, first, the inward domain of consciousness; demanding liberty of conscience in the most comprehensive sense; liberty of thought and feeling; absolute freedom of opinion and sentiment on all subjects, practical or speculative, scientific, moral, or theological. The liberty of expressing and publishing opinions may seem to fall under a different principle, since it belongs to that part of the conduct of an individual which concerns other people; but, being almost of as much importance as the liberty of thought itself, and resting in great part on the same reasons, is practically inseparable from it. Secondly, the principle requires liberty of tastes and pursuits; of framing the plan of our life to suit our own character; of doing as we like, subject to such consequences as may follow: without impediment from our fellow-creatures, so long as what we do does not harm them, even though they should think our conduct foolish, perverse, or wrong. Thirdly, from this liberty of each individual, follows the liberty, within the same limits, of combination among individuals; freedom to unite, for any purpose not involving harm to others: the persons combining being supposed to be of full age, and not forced or deceived.

No society in which these liberties are not, on the whole, respected, is free, whatever may be its form of government; and none is completely free in which they do not exist absolute and unqualified. The only freedom which deserves the name, is that of pursuing our own good in our own way, so long as we do not attempt to deprive others of theirs, or impede their efforts to obtain it. Each is the proper guardian of his own health, whether bodily, *or* mental and spiritual. Mankind are greater gainers by suffering each other to live as seems good to themselves, than by compelling each to live as seems good to the rest.

Of the Liberty of Thought and Discussion

The time, it is to be hoped, is gone by, when any defence would be necessary of the "liberty of the press" as one of the securities against corrupt or tyrannical government. No argument, we may suppose, can now be needed, against permitting a legislature or an executive, not identified in interest with the people, to prescribe opinions to them, and determine what doctrines or what arguments they shall be allowed to hear. This aspect of the question, besides, has been so often and so triumphantly enforced by preceding writers, that it needs not be specially insisted on in this place. Though the law of England, on the subject of the press, is as servile to this day as it was in the time of the Tudors, there is little danger of its being actually put in force against political discussion, except during some temporary panic, when fear of insurrection drives ministers and judges from their propriety; and, speaking generally, it is not, in constitutional countries, to be apprehended, that the government, whether completely responsible to the people or not, will often attempt to control the expression of opinion, except when in doing so it makes itself the organ of the general intolerance of the public. Let us suppose, therefore, that the government is entirely at one with the people, and never thinks of exerting any power of coercion unless in agreement with what it conceives to be their voice. But I deny the right of the people to exercise such coercion, either by themselves or by their government. The power itself is illegitimate. The best government has no more title to it than the worst. It is as noxious, or more noxious, when exerted in accordance with public opinion, than when in opposition to it. If all mankind minus one were of one opinion, and only one person were of the contrary opinion, mankind would be no more justified in silencing that one person, than he, if he had the power, would be justified in silencing mankind. Were an opinion a personal possession of no value except to the owner; if to be obstructed in the enjoyment of it were simply a private injury, it would make some difference whether the injury was inflicted only on a few persons or on many. But the peculiar evil of silencing the expression of an opinion is, that it is robbing the human race; posterity as well as the existing generation; those who dissent from the opinion, still more than those who hold it. If the opinion is right, they are deprived of the opportunity of exchanging error for truth: if wrong, they lose, what is almost as great a benefit, the clearer perception and livelier impression of truth, produced by its collision with error.

It is necessary to consider separately these two hypotheses, each of which has a distinct branch of the argument corresponding to it. We can never be sure that the opinion we are endeavouring to stifle is a false opinion; and if we were sure, stifling it would be an evil still.

First: the opinion which it is attempted to suppress by authority may possibly be true. Those who desire to suppress it, of course deny its truth; but they are not infallible. They have no authority to decide the question for all mankind, and exclude every other person from the means of judging. To refuse a hearing to an opinion, because they are sure that it is false, is to assume that *their* certainty is the same thing as *absolute* certainty. All silencing of discussion is an assumption of infallibility. Its condemnation may be allowed to rest on this common argument, not the worse for being common.

Unfortunately for the good sense of mankind, the fact of their fallibility is far from carrying the weight in their practical judgment which is always allowed to it in theory; for while every one well knows himself to be fallible, few think it necessary to take any precautions against their own fallibility, or admit the supposition that any opinion, of which they feel very certain, may be one of the examples of the error to which they acknowledge themselves to be liable. Absolute princes, or others who are accustomed to unlimited deference, usually feel this complete confidence in their own opinions on nearly all subjects. People more happily situated, who sometimes hear their opinions disputed, and are not wholly unused to be set right when they are wrong, place the same unbounded reliance only on such of their opinions as are shared by all who surround them, or to whom they habitually defer; for in proportion to a man's want of confidence in his own solitary judgment, does he usually repose, with implicit trust, on the infallibility of "the world" in general. And the world, to each individual, means the part of it with which he comes in contact; his party, his sect, his church, his class of society; the man may be called, by comparison, almost liberal and large-minded to whom it means anything so comprehensive as his own country or his own age. Nor is his faith in this collective authority at all shaken by his being aware that other ages, countries, sects, churches, classes, and parties have thought, and even now think, the exact reverse. He devolves upon his own world the responsibility of being in the right against the dissentient worlds of other people; and it never troubles him that mere accident has decided which of these numerous worlds is the object of his reliance, and that the same causes which make him a Churchman in London, would have made him a Buddhist or a Confucian in Peking. Yet it is as evident in itself, as any amount of argument can make it, that

366

ages are no more infallible than individuals; every age having held many opinions which subsequent ages have deemed not only false but absurd; and it is as certain that many opinions now general will be rejected by future ages, as it is that many, once general, are rejected by the present.

The objection likely to be made to this argument would probably take some such form as the following. There is no greater assumption of infallibility in forbidding the propagation of error, than in any other thing which is done by public authority on its own judgment and responsibility. Judgment is given to men that they may use it. Because it may be used erroneously, are men to be told that they ought not to use it at all? To prohibit what they think pernicious, is not claiming exemption from error, but fulfilling the duty incumbent on them, although fallible, of acting on their conscientious conviction. If we were never to act on our opinions, because those opinions may be wrong, we should leave all our interests uncared for, and all our duties unperformed. An objection which applies to all conduct can be no valid objection to any conduct in particular. It is the duty of governments, and of individuals, to form the truest opinions they can; to form them carefully, and never impose them upon others unless they are quite sure of being right. But when they are sure (such reasoners may say), it is not conscientiousness but cowardice to shrink from acting on their opinions, and allow doctrines which they honestly think dangerous to the welfare of mankind, either in this life or in another, to be scattered abroad without restraint, because other people, in less enlightened times, have persecuted opinions now believed to be true. Let us take care, it may be said, not to make the same mistake: but governments and nations have made mistakes in other things, which are not denied to be fit subjects for the exercise of authority: they have laid on bad taxes, made unjust wars. Ought we therefore to lay on no taxes, and, under whatever provocation, make no wars? Men, and governments, must act to the best of their ability. There is no such thing as absolute certainty, but there is assurance sufficient for the purposes of human life. We may, and must, assume our opinion to be true for the guidance of our own conduct: and it is assuming no more when we forbid bad men to pervert society by the propagation of opinions which we regard as false and pernicious.

I answer, that it is assuming very much more. There is the greatest difference between presuming an opinion to be true, because, with every opportunity for contesting it, it has not been refuted, and assuming its truth for the purpose of not permitting its refutation. Complete liberty of contradicting and disproving our opinion is the very condition which justifies us in assuming its truth for purposes of action; and on no other terms can a being with human faculties have any rational assurance of being right.

When we consider either the history of opinion, or the ordinary conduct of human life, to what is it to be ascribed that the one and the other are no worse than they are? Not certainly to the inherent force of the human understanding; for, on any matter not self-evident, there are ninety-nine persons totally incapable of judging of it for one who is capable; and the capacity of the hundredth person is only comparative; for the majority of the eminent men of every past generation held many opinions now known to be erroneous, and did or approved numerous things which no one will now justify. Why is it, then, that there is on the whole a preponderance among mankind of rational opinions and rational conduct? If there really is this preponderance—which there must be unless human affairs are, and have always been, in an almost desperate state—it is owing to a quality of the human mind, the source of everything respectable in man either as an intellectual or as a moral being, namely, that his errors are corrigible. He is capable of rectifying his mistakes, by discussion and experience. Not by experience alone. There must be discussion, to show how experience is to be interpreted. Wrong opinions and practices gradually yield to fact and argument; but facts and arguments, to produce any effect on the mind, must be brought before it. Very few facts are able to tell their own story, without comments to bring out their meaning. The whole strength and value, then, of human judgment, depending on the one property, that it can be set right when it is wrong, reliance can be placed on it only when the means of setting it right are kept constantly at hand. In the case of any person whose judgment is really deserving of confidence, how has it become so? Because he has kept his mind open to criticism of his opinions and conduct. Because it has been his practice to listen to all that could be said against him; to profit by as much of it as was just, and expound to himself, and upon occasion to others, the fallacy of what was fallacious. Because he has felt, that the only way in which a human being can make some approach to knowing the whole of a subject, is by hearing what can be said about it by persons of every variety of opinion, and studying all modes in which it can be looked at by every character of mind. No wise man ever acquired his wisdom in any mode but this. . . .

In order more fully to illustrate the mischief of denying a hearing to opinions because we, in our own judgment, have condemned them, it will be desirable to fix down the discussion to a concrete case; and I choose, by preference, the cases which are least favourable to me—in which the argument against freedom of opinion, both on the score of truth and on that of utility, is considered the strongest. Let the opinions impugned be the belief in a God and in a future state, or any of the commonly received doctrines of morality. To fight the battle on such ground gives a great advantage to an unfair antagonist; since he will be sure to say (and many who have no desire to be unfair will say it internally), Are these the doctrines which you do not deem sufficiently certain to be taken under the protection of law? Is the belief in a God one of the opinions to feel sure of which you hold to be assuming infallibility? But I must be permitted to observe, that it is not the feeling sure of a doctrine (be it what it may) which I call an assumption of infallibility. It is the undertaking to decide that question *for others*, without allowing them to hear what can be said on the contrary side. And I denounce and reprobate this pretension not the less, if put forth on the side of my most solemn convictions. However positive any one's persuasion may be, not only of the falsity but of the pernicious consequences—not only of the pernicious consequences, but (to adopt expressions which I altogether condemn) the immorality and impiety of an opinion; yet if, in pursuance of that private judgment, though backed by the public judgment of his country or his contemporaries, he prevents the opinion from being heard in its defence, he assumes infallibility. And so far from the assumption being less objectionable or less dangerous because the opinion is called immoral or impious, this is the case of all others in which it is most fatal. These are exactly the occasions on which the men of one generation commit those dreadful mistakes which excite the astonishment and horror of posterity. It is among such that we find the instances memorable in history, when the arm of the law has been employed to root out the best men and the noblest doctrines; with deplorable success as to the men, though some of the doctrines have survived to be (as if in mockery) invoked in defence of similar conduct towards those who dissent from *them*, or from their received interpretation.

Mankind can hardly be too often reminded, that there was once a man named Socrates, between whom and the legal authorities and public opinion of his time there took place a memorable collision. Born in an age and country abounding in individual greatness, this man has been handed down to us by those who best knew both him and the age, as the most virtuous man in it; while *we* know him as the head and prototype of all subsequent teachers of virtue, the source equally of the lofty inspiration of Plato and the judicious utilitarianism of Aristotle, "*i maëstri di color che sanno,*" the two headsprings of ethical as of all other philosophy. This acknowledged master of all the eminent thinkers who have since lived—whose fame, still growing after more than two thousand years, all but outweighs the whole remainder of the names which make his native city illustrious—was put to death by his countrymen, after a judicial conviction, for impiety and immorality. Impiety, in denying the gods recognised by the State; indeed his accuser asserted (see the "Apologia") that he believed in no gods at all. Immorality, in being, by his doctrines and instructions, a "corruptor of youth." Of these charges the tribunal, there is every ground for believing, honestly found him guilty, and condemned the man who probably of all then born had deserved best of mankind to be put to death as a criminal. . . .

Let us now pass to the second division of the argument, and dismissing the supposition that any of the received opinions may be false, let us assume them to be true, and examine into the worth of the manner in which they are likely to be held, when their truth is not freely and openly canvassed. However unwillingly a person who has a strong opinion may admit the possibility that his opinion may be false, he ought to be moved by the consideration that, however true it may be, if it is not fully, frequently, and fearlessly discussed, it will be held as a dead dogma, not a living truth.

There is a class of persons (happily not quite so numerous as formerly) who think it enough if a person assents undoubtingly to what they think true, though he has no knowledge whatever on the grounds of the opinion, and could not make a tenable defence of it against the most superficial objections. Such persons, if they can once get their creed taught from authority, naturally think that no good, and some harm, comes of its being allowed to be questioned. Where their influence prevails, they make it nearly impossible for the received opinion to be rejected wisely and considerately, though it may still be rejected rashly and ignorantly; for to shut out discussion entirely is seldom possible, and when it once gets in, beliefs not grounded on conviction are apt to give way before the slightest semblance of an argument. Waiving, however, this possibility—assuming that the true opinion abides in the mind, but abides as a prejudice, a belief independent of, and proof against, argument—this is not the way in which truth ought to be held by a rational being. This is not knowing the truth. Truth, thus held, is but one superstition the more, accidentally clinging to the words which enunciate a truth. . . .

He who knows only his own side of the case, knows little of that. His reasons may be good, and no one may have been able to refute them. But if he is equally unable to refute the reasons on the opposite side; if he does not so much as know what they are, he has no ground for preferring either opinion. The rational position for him would be suspension of judgment, and unless he contents himself with that, he is either led by authority, or adopts, like the generality of the world, the side to which he feels most inclination. Nor is it enough that he should hear the arguments of adversaries from his own teachers, presented as they state them, and accompanied by what they offer as refutations. That is not the way to do justice to the arguments, or bring them into real contact with his own mind. He must be able to hear them from persons who actually believe them; who defend them in earnest, and do their very utmost for them. He must know them in their most plausible and persuasive form; he must feel the whole force of the difficulty which the true view of the subject has to encounter and dispose of; else he will never really possess himself of the portion of truth which meets and removes that difficulty. Ninety-nine in a hundred of what are called educated men are in this condition; even of those who can argue fluently for their opinions. Their conclusion may be true, but it might be false for anything they know: they have never thrown themselves into the mental position of those who think differently from them, and considered what such persons may have to say; and consequently they do not, in any proper sense of the word, know the doctrine which they themselves profess. . . .

But what! (it may be asked) Is the absence of unanimity an indispensable condition of true knowledge? Is it necessary that some part of mankind should persist in error to enable any to realise the truth? Does a belief cease to be real and vital as soon as it is generally received—and is a proposition never thoroughly understood and felt unless some doubt of it remains? As soon as mankind have unanimously accepted a truth, does the truth perish within them? The highest aim and best result of improved intelligence, it has hitherto been thought, is to unite mankind more and more in the acknowledgment of all important truths; and does the intelligence only last as long as it has not achieved its object? Do the fruits of conquest perish by the very completeness of the victory?

I affirm no such thing. As mankind improve, the number of doctrines which are no longer disputed or doubted will be constantly on the increase: and the well-being of mankind may almost be measured by the number and gravity of the truths which have reached the point of being uncontested. The cessation, on one question after another, of serious controversy, is one of the necessary incidents of the consolidation of opinion; a consolidation as salutary in the case of true opinions, as it is dangerous and noxious when the opinions are erroneous. But though this gradual narrowing of the bounds of diversity of opinion is necessary in both senses of the term, being at once inevitable and indispensable, we are not therefore obliged to conclude that all its consequences must be beneficial. The loss of so important an aid to the intelligent and living apprehension of a truth, as is afforded by the necessity of explaining it to, or defending it against, opponents, though not sufficient to outweigh, is no trifling drawback from, the benefit of its universal recognition. Where this advantage can no longer be had, I confess I should like to see the teachers of mankind endeavouring to provide a substitute for it; some contrivance for making the difficulties of the question as present to the learner's consciousness, as if they were pressed upon him by a dissentient champion, eager for his conversion.

But instead of seeking contrivances for this purpose, they have lost those they formerly had. The Socratic dialectics, so magnificently exemplified in the dialogues of Plato, were a contrivance of this description. They were essentially a negative discussion of the great question of philosophy and life, directed with consummate skill to the purpose of convincing any one who had merely adopted the commonplaces of received opinion that he did not understand the subject—that he as yet attached no definite meaning to the doctrines he professed; in order that, becoming aware of his ignorance, he might be put in the way to obtain a stable belief, resting on a clear apprehension both of the meaning of doctrines and of their evidence. The school disputations of the Middle Ages had a somewhat similar object. They were intended to make sure that the pupil understood his own opinion, and (by necessary correlation) the opinion opposed to it, and could enforce the grounds of the one and confute those of the other. These last-mentioned contests had indeed the incurable defect, that the premises appealed to were taken from authority, not from reason; and, as a discipline to the mind, they were in every respect inferior to the powerful dialectics which formed the intellects of the "Socratici viri"; but the modern mind owes far more to both than it is generally willing to admit, and the present modes of education contain nothing which in the smallest degree supplies the place either of the one or of the other. A person who derives all his instruction from teachers or books, even if he escapes the besetting temptation of contenting himself with cram, is under no compulsion to hear both sides; accordingly it is far from a frequent accomplishment, even among thinkers, to know both sides; and the weakest part of what everybody says in defence of his opinion is what he intends as a reply to antagonists. It is the fashion of the present time to disparage negative logic—that which points out weaknesses in theory or errors in practice, without establishing positive truths. Such negative criticism would indeed be poor enough as an ultimate result; but as a means to attaining any positive knowledge or conviction worthy the name, it cannot be valued too highly; and until people are again systematically trained to it, there will be few great thinkers, and a low general average of intellect, in any but the mathematical and physical departments of speculation. On any other subject no one's opinions deserve the name of knowledge, except so far as he has either had forced upon him by others, or gone through of himself, the same mental process which would have been required of him in carrying on an active controversy with opponents. That, therefore, which when absent, it is so indispensable, but so difficult, to create, how worse than absurd it is to forego, when spontaneously offering itself! If there are any persons who contest a received opinion, or who will do so if law or opinion will let them, let us thank them for it, open our minds to listen to them, and rejoice that there is some one to do for us what we otherwise ought, if we have any regard for either the certainty or the vitality of our convictions, to do with much greater labour for ourselves. . . .

We have now recognised the necessity to the mental well-being of mankind (on which all their other well-being depends) of freedom of opinion, and freedom of the expression of opinion, on four distinct grounds; which we will now briefly recapitulate.

First, if any opinion is compelled to silence, that opinion may, for aught we can certainly know, be true. To deny this is to assume our own infallibility.

Secondly, though the silenced opinion be an error, it may, and very commonly does, contain a portion of truth; and since the general or prevailing opinion on any subject is rarely or never the whole truth, it is only by the collision of adverse opinions that the remainder of the truth has any chance of being supplied.

Thirdly, even if the received opinion be not only true, but the whole truth; unless it is suffered to be, and actually is, vigorously and earnestly contested, it will, by most of those who receive it, be held in the manner of a prejudice, with little comprehension or feeling of its rational grounds. And not only this, but, fourthly, the meaning of the doctrine itself will be in danger of being lost, or enfeebled, and deprived of its vital effect on the character and conduct: the dogma becoming a mere formal profession, inefficacious for good, but cumbering the ground, and preventing the growth of any real and heartfelt conviction, from reason or personal experience.

Of Individuality, As One of the Elements of Well-Being

Such being the reasons which make it imperative that human beings should be free to form opinions, and to express their opinions without reserve; and such the baneful consequences to the intellectual, and through that to the moral nature of man, unless this liberty is either conceded, or asserted in spite of prohibition; let us next examine whether the same reasons do not require that men should be free to act upon their opinions—to carry these out in their lives, without hindrance, either physical or moral, from their fellow-men, so long as it is at their own risk and peril. This last proviso is of course indispensable. No one pretends that actions should be as free as opinions. On the contrary, even opinions lose their immunity when the circumstances in which they are expressed are such as to constitute their expression a positive instigation to some mischievous act. An opinion that corn-dealers are starvers of the poor, or that private property is robbery, ought to be unmolested when simply circulated through the press, but may justly incur punishment when delivered orally to an excited mob assembled before the house of a corn-dealer, or when handed about among the same mob in the form of a placard. Acts, of whatever kind, which, without justifiable cause, do harm to others, may be, and in the more important cases absolutely require to be, controlled by the unfavourable sentiments, and, when needful, by the active interference of mankind. The liberty of the individual must be thus far limited; he must not make himself a nuisance to other people. But if he refrains from molesting others in what concerns them, and merely acts according to his own inclination and judgment in things which concern himself, the same reasons which show that opinion should be free, prove also that he should be allowed, without molestation, to carry his opinions into practice at his own cost. That mankind are not infallible; that their truths, for the most part, are only half-truths; that unity of opinion, unless resulting from the fullest and freest comparison of opposite opinions, is not desirable, and diversity not an evil, but a good, until mankind are much more capable than at present of recognising all sides of the truth, are principles applicable to men's modes of action, not less than to their opinions. As it is useful that while mankind are imperfect there should be different opinions, so it is that there should be different experiments of living; that free scope should be given to varieties of character, short of injury to others; and that the worth of different modes of life should be proved practically, when any one thinks fit to try them. It is desirable, in short, that in things which do not primarily concern others, individuality should assert itself. Where, not the person's own character, but the traditions or customs of other people are the rule of conduct, there is wanting one of the principal ingredients of human happiness, and quite the chief ingredient of individual and social progress.

In maintaining this principle, the greatest difficulty to be encountered does not lie in the appreciation of means towards an acknowledged end, but in the indifference of persons in general to the end itself. If it were felt that the free development of individuality is one of the leading essentials of well-being; that it is not only a co-ordinate element with all that is designated by the terms civilisation, instruction, education, culture, but is itself a necessary part and condition of all those things; there would be no danger that liberty should be undervalued, and the adjustment of the boundaries between it and social control would present no extraordinary difficulty. But the evil is, the individual spontaneity is hardly recognised by the common modes of thinking as having any intrinsic worth, or deserving any regard on its own account. . . .

It is not by wearing down into uniformity all that is individual in themselves, but by cultivating it, and calling it forth, within the limits imposed by the rights and interests of others, that human beings become a noble and beautiful object of contemplation; and as the works partake the character of those who do them, by the same process human life also becomes rich, diversified, and animating, furnishing more abundant aliment to high thoughts and elevating feelings, and strengthening the tie which binds every individual to the race, by making the race infinitely better worth belonging to. In proportion to the development of his individuality, each person becomes more valuable to himself, and is therefore capable of being more valuable to others. There is a greater fulness of life about his own existence, and when there is more life in the units there is more in the mass which is composed of them. As much compression as is necessary to prevent the stronger specimens of human nature from encroaching on the rights of others cannot be dispensed with; but for this there is ample compensation even in the point of view of human development. The means of development which the individual loses by being prevented from gratifying his inclinations to the injury of others, are chiefly obtained at the expense of the development of other people. And even to himself there is a full equivalent in the better development of the social part of his nature, rendered possible by the restraint put upon the selfish part. To be held to rigid rules of justice for the sake of others, develops the feelings and capacities which have the good of others for their object. But to be restrained in things not affecting their good, by their mere displeasure, develops nothing valuable, except such force of character as may unfold itself in resisting the restraint. If acquiesced in, it dulls and blunts the whole nature. To give any fair play to the nature of each, it is essential that different persons should be allowed to lead different lives. In proportion as this latitude has been exercised in any age, has that age been noteworthy to posterity. Even despotism does not produce its worst effects, so long as individuality exists under it; and whatever crushes individuality is despotism, by whatever name it may be called, and whether it professes to be enforcing the will of God or the injunctions of men. . . .

36. Lord Patrick Devlin

Patrick Devlin (born, 1905) was educated at Christ's College, Cambridge. He has served as Justice of the High Court, 1948–1960; Lord Justice of Appeal, 1960–61; and Lord of Appeal in Ordinary, 1961–63. He is the author of five books on various topics pertaining to the law.

Society's Right to Enforce Morality

John Stuart Mill thought to resolve the struggle between liberty and authority that is inherent in every society. We who belong to the societies of the United States or of the British Commonwealth or of other like-minded peoples say that we belong to a free society. By this I think we mean no more than that we strike a balance in favour of individual freedom. The law is the boundary that marks the limit of authority and it is not drawn in a straight line. As it traverses the field of human activities it inclines from side to side, in some allowing much more freedom than in others. At each point we try to strike the right balance. What I mean by striking it in favour of freedom is that the question to be asked in each case is: 'How much authority is necessary?' and not: 'How much liberty is to be conceded?' That the question should be put in that form, that authority should be a grant and liberty not a privilege, is, I think, the true mark of a free society.

Taken from Patrick Devlin, "Mill on Liberty in Morals," published in the University of Chicago *Law Review* 32, no. 2; and in *The Enforcement of Morals*, Oxford University Press, London, 1965. Copyright by the Oxford University Press. Reprinted by permission of the Oxford University Press.

Is it possible to drive a straight line across the field running from one end to the other, marking out for all time the private domain on one side and the public on the other? If it is, the value to the individual in the minority would be immense. As things are, in the constant struggle between liberty and authority the individual is at a disadvantage. Each time the Government, backed by the power of the majority, brings forward some new piece of legislation designed to benefit the majority and involving some further invasions of the private domain, the minority can only appeal to an undefined concept of liberty. Lack of definition suits the stronger party. What is wanted, if it can be got, is a comprehensive principle, clear and precise, by which any proposed law can be tested. . . .

Mill . . . set out to define once and for all 'the nature and limits of the power which can be legitimately exercised by society over the individual.' He did this by asserting 'one very simple principle, as entitled to cover absolutely the dealings of society with the individual in the way of compulsion and control. . . . That principle is, that the sole end for which mankind are warranted, individually or collectively, in interfering with the liberty of action of any of their number, is self-protection. That the only purpose for which power can be rightfully exercised over any member of a civilised community, against his will, is to prevent harm to others. His own good, either physical or moral, is not a sufficient warrant. He cannot rightfully be compelled to do or forbear because it will be better for him to do so, because it will make him happier, because, in the opinion of others, to do so would be wise, or even right.'

The core of this principle is that a man must be allowed to pursue his own good in his own way. Its opposite has come to be identified as paternalism. But an identifying mark is not a line. To secure the citadel of freedom Mill flung a line beyond which the law must not trespass. The law was not to interfere with a man unless what he did caused harm to others. What Mill included in 'harm to others' was chiefly physical harm to other individuals.

Now if a man lives in society it is not simply his own concern whether or not he keeps himself physically, mentally, and morally fit. He owes in these respects a duty to others as well as to himself. Mill accepted the duty as owing to 'assignable individuals,' such as a man's family or his creditors. He did not see it as a debt due to society at large. The only right he allowed to society as a collective entity, i.e., to the State, and which it might enforce by law, was the right to exact contributions to common defence and protection. 'But with regard to the merely contingent, or, as it may be called, constructive injury which a person causes to society, by conduct which neither violates any specific duty to the public, nor occasions perceptible hurt to any assignable individual except himself, the inconvenience is one which society can afford to bear, for the sake of the greater good of human freedom.' . . .

As Mill noted, this conception of liberty was not accepted in his own time which we now look back upon as an age of individualism triumphant. In the hundred years that have passed since then it has over and over again been decisively rejected in economic matters. Its weakness in practice is that it enables one man in a hundred to hold up indefinitely projects which would benefit the other ninety-nine. So we have laws that allow the compulsory acquisition of property. We have also social schemes that an individual is not allowed to contract out of because he cannot be excluded from the benefits of the scheme without wrecking it. Contracting out may be an expression of in-dividuality and proceed from the pure desire for liberty, but we have come to think that it proceeds from selfishness or laziness, indifference to the common good, or a desire to get something for nothing. So we have health laws, thinking it wrong that a man should receive the benefit of modern sanitation in the town in which he lives and keep his own home as a pigsty. . . .

This does not mean that necessarily we have witnessed the triumph of paternalism. We would still, I think, most of us deeply resent a law that was passed avowedly for our own good and treated us as if we were in need of care and protection. What it means is that the citadel has not been secured from attack in the way in which Mill proposed. His outer line enclosed territory which has had to be yielded, and authority has not decisively, as he hoped, been kept at bay.

The incident in England which has recently revived interest in Mill's doctrine is the publication of the Wolfenden Report in 1957. The Report based its proposals for the reform of criminal law on homosexuality upon the principle of the realm of private morality which is not the law's business. This use of the principle is, as Professor Hart observed, 'strikingly similar' to Mill's doctrine. Professor Hart immediately con-ferred upon it his full approval with all the authority which that carries and in 1963 devoted a series of comprehensive and penetrating lectures to expounding it. The idea that in a free society a man's morals should be his own affair is superficially at least an attractive one. We have built a society in which a man's religion is his own affair: can we not go a step further and build one in which his morals are his own affair too? The law knows nothing of any religion. Is there any need for it to know anything of morals?

Let me for a moment stop talking about society as an abstract conception and talk instead about a hundred men and women. Ninety are virtuous and ten are vicious. Are the virtuous to be compelled to associate with the vicious? The natural answer is—certainly not. For even granted that the vicious do no physical harm to others against their will, association with them may cause the vice to be spread. Moreover, the object of the association being to share the burdens and benefits of life among the community as a whole, it is likely that the vicious will be more benefited than burdened; men who are constantly drunk, drugged or debauched are not likely to be useful members of the community.

What then are the ninety to do about it? If all that was involved was the membership of a social club, the situation would be simple. The vicious ten would be expelled and no one would think the expulsion harsh. But a society in which a man has his whole social life is something more than a club. Men can no longer be driven into the desert; outlawry and banishment are things of the past. Even when in use they were as punishments so severe that mercy enjoined, at least at first, a lesser penalty. Is it therefore permissible for the ninety to deprive the ten of their liberty for the purpose at best of reformation and at worst of restraint? Or must they in the name of freedom leave the ten at large, relying on the strength of their own virtue to resist contamination and in time to convert the vicious?

I do not suppose that any secular society has ever existed which sought to control vice simply by passive resistance and good works. But this is what Mill's conception of a free society demands. Mill's opinion of what was virtuous did not substantially differ from that of his contemporaries. But no one, he felt, could be sure. In a free society full scope must be given to individuality as one of the elements of well-being and the individual must be free to question, challenge and experiment. 'The liberty of the individual must be thus far limited; he must not make himself a nuisance to other people. But if he refrains from molesting others in what concerns them, and merely acts according to his own inclination and judgement in things which concern himself, the same reasons which show that opinion should be free, prove also that he should be allowed, without molestation, to carry his opinions into practice at his own cost. That mankind are not infallible; that their truths, for the most part, are only half-truths; that unity of opinion, unless resulting from the fullest and freest comparison of opposite opinions, is not desirable, and diversity not an evil, but a good, until mankind are much more capable than at present of recognising all sides of the truth, are principles applicable to men's modes of action, not less than to their opinions. As it is useful that while mankind are imperfect there should be different opinions, so it is that there should be different experiments of living; that free scope should be given to varieties of character, short of injury to others; and that the worth of different modes of life should be proved practically, when anyone thinks fit to try them.'

It is with freedom of opinion and discussion that Mill is primarily concerned. Freedom of action follows naturally on that; men must be allowed to do what they are allowed to talk about doing. Evidently what Mill visualizes is a number of people doing things he himself would disapprove of, but doing them earnestly and openly and after thought and discussion in an endeavour to find the way of life best suited to them as individuals. This seems to me on the whole an idealistic picture. It has happened to some extent in the growth of free love. Although for many it is just the indulgence of the flesh, for some it is a serious decision to break the constraint of chastity outside marriage. In the area of morals touched by the law I find it difficult to think of any other example of high-mindedness. A man does not as a rule commit bigamy because he wants to experiment with two wives instead of one. He does not as a rule lie with his daughter or sister because he thinks that an incestuous relationship can be a good one but because he finds in it a way of satisfying his lust in the home. He does not keep a brothel so as to prove the value of promiscuity but so as to make money. There must be some homosexuals who believe theirs to be a good way of life but many more who would like to get free of it if only they could. Certainly no one in his senses can think that habitual drunkenness or drugging leads to any good at all.

Such are the vices that the law seeks to control. If the ninety men, who sincerely believe all this to be depravity, are to be convinced that they must put up with it in their society because after all they are not infallible, their truths may be only half-truths, and that it is only by diversity of precept and practice that the whole truth can be found, surely they must be persuaded that there is at least one man among the ten seeking after the truth and proclaiming that what is commonly received as a vice is in truth a virtue. Freedom is not a good in itself. We believe it to be good because out of freedom there comes more good than bad. If a free society is better than a disciplined one, it is because—and this certainly was Mill's view—it is better for a man himself that he should be free to seek his own good in his own way and better too for the society to which he belongs, since thereby a way may be found to a greater good for all. But no good can come from a man doing what he acknowledges to be evil. The freedom that is worth having is freedom to do what you think to be good notwithstanding that others think it to be bad. Freedom to do what you know to be bad is worthless.

Mill believed that diversity in morals and the removal of restraint on what was traditionally held to be immorality would liberate men to prove what they thought to be good. He would have been the last man to have advocated the removal of restraint so as to permit self-indulgence. He conceived of an old morality being replaced by a new and perhaps better morality; he would not have approved of those who did not care whether there was any morality at all. But he did not really grapple with the fact that along the paths that depart from traditional morals, pimps leading the weak astray far outnumber spiritual explorers at the head of the strong. It is significant that when Mill touched on this problem—the commercialization of vice—his teaching wavered.

Should a person, he asked, be free to be a pimp or to keep a gambling-house? Against the affirmative answer which flows logically from his doctrine, Mill put the following argument. If society believes conduct to be bad, it must be at least a disputable question whether it is good or bad: that being so, society is entitled to exclude the influence of solicitations which are not disinterested. There was, he thought, considerable force in this argument and he would not venture to decide the point.

But there are other reasons than a desire to make money which may make a person indulge in vice and solicit others to join with him. Disinterestedness is not proved because money is not demanded. Mill's doctrine caters bountifully for good men who are unorthodox. The only bad men he sees at his table are those who are trading in vice and then he does not quite know what to do with them. I think that the true distinction does not lie between those who trade in vice and those who do not, but between those who practise what they know to be vice and those who practise what they believe to be virtue. Only the latter are truly disinterested.

Let us suppose that in the mass of the iniquitous there are some righteous and disinterested men. If then the law is used to suppress immorality, it may suppress also new morality which its advocates sincerely claim to be better than the old. The suppression of any new beliefs sincerely held and purposefully translated into action is injurious to a free society. On this two questions arise. First, can the wheat be separated from the chaff, the chaff burnt, and the wheat made into bread? If not, how is the injury done to society by the suppression of a new morality to be balanced against the injury done by the toleration of acknowledged vice?

I shall begin with the second question because Mill's disciples think that they have an easy answer to it which will make it unnecessary to trouble about the first. Their answer is that the toleration of acknowledged vice, provided that it is confined to private immorality, does not injure society at all; or that if it does, the law is useless as an instrument for suppression. So there is no need for separation and nothing to balance. It may be disagreeable for the ninety virtuous men to have to associate with the vicious ones, or at least to have to extend the benefit and protection of their society to those who are undeserving of it; but that, as Mill says in the passage I have quoted, is an inconvenience which society can afford to bear for the sake of the greater good of human freedom.

The twin arguments that the law is useless against private immorality and that the damage done by private immorality to society is insignificant, have much in common. One thing that they have in common is that their supporters tend, consciously or unconsciously, to apply them in particular to one sort of private immorality which is now much in the public notice, namely, homosexuality between consenting adults. It is argued that the enforcement of the laws against homosexuals causes great misery to men who are morally incapable of changing their way of life. The argument has in this instance an appeal which it altogether lacks when applied to pimps and brothel-keepers. Their supporters tend also, consciously or unconsciously, to forget that what is in dispute is not whether a particular law should be on the statute book but whether it is a condition of a free society that private immorality should altogether and always be immune from interference by the law. No one suggests that all private immorality should be punished by the law as a matter of course. You can grant that private immorality is within the competence of the legislature in a free society and still advance many powerful arguments why the law should not try to punish particular vices in particular circumstances. . . .

Granted then that the law can play some part in the war against vice, ought it to be excluded for the reason that private vice cannot do any harm to society? I think that it is capable of doing both physical harm and spiritual harm. Tangible and intangible may be better words; body and soul a better simile.

Let me consider first the tangible harm. It is obvious that an individual may by unrestricted indulgence in vice so weaken himself that he ceases to be a useful member of society. It is obvious also that if a sufficient number of individuals so weaken themselves, society will thereby be weakened. That is what I mean by tangible harm to society. If the proportion grows sufficiently large, society will succumb either to its own disease or to external pressure. A nation of debauchees would not in 1940 have responded satisfactorily to Winston Churchill's call to blood and toil and sweat and tears. I doubt if any of this would be denied. The answer that is made to it is that the danger, if private immorality were tolerated, of vice spreading to such an extent as to affect society as a whole is negligible and in a free society ought to be ignored.

There is here a distinction to be made. As I have said, the question is not whether at any given time the spread of a particular vice has reached such proportions as to constitute a danger, but whether all vice that can be committed in private is of its nature harmless to society. It is therefore proper to distinguish between natural and unnatural vice; and it is usually an example, such as homosexuality, selected from unnatural vice that is taken to illustrate the absurdity of supposing that private immorality could ever develop into a menace to society. Of course, looking at the thing in the crudest way, a completely homosexual society would, unless continuously reinforced from outside, soon cease to exist because it would not breed. But, as has been pointed out, the same might be said of a completely celibate society, yet no one regards celibacy as injurious to society. The natural demand for heterosexual intercourse, it is argued, will always be strong enough to ensure that homosexuality is kept to a harmless minority.

This is, within limits, a formidable argument and I shall return to consider the curious results which flow from it. It does not however apply to natural vice where the pressure is the other way. There may be those who argue that men and women are inherently virtuous so that the vicious few, even if allowed free rein, will always be in a harmless and unattractive minority. This seems to me like arguing that the vast majority of men and women in society are inherently loyal so that it would be quite safe to ignore the treacherous few. No doubt traitors, as also vice-mongers, are often in it only for money and no one would applaud that. But there are noble as well as ignoble traitors; and—it might well be argued on the lines of Mill—it is worth putting up with the almost negligible harm that is caused by treachery as it is ordinarily practised so as to make sure that we do not stifle some new political conception, which although now regarded with abhorrence by all right-minded people, may in the end, because we are all fallible, turn out to be a great improvement. The danger that some traitors or spies may deliver up to the enemy some vital secrets is, it can be urged, an imaginary one existing only in story books. In real life the damage they do, at any rate in peacetime, is hardly likely to do more than dent the structure of a strong society.

But this is not the way in which treachery is considered. We do not estimate the achievements of treason over the last century and ask what they have amounted to. So with incitement to mutiny; we do not ask how much can safely be permitted without seriously endangering the discipline of the armed forces. So with sedition; we do not argue that the loyalty of the robust majority and its belief in the merits of our polity is all that is necessary for the safety of the realm. When we are constitution-making—whether what is being formulated is a clause in writing or a principle supported by tacit consent—it is the nature of the subject-matter that is the determinant. Whether society should have the power to restrain any activity depends on the nature of the activity. Whether it should exercise the power at any given time in its history depends on the situation at that time and requires a balance to be struck between the foreseeable danger to society and the foreseeable damage to the freedom and happiness of the individual. . . .

I move now to the consideration of intangible harm to society and begin by noting a significant distinction. When considering tangible damage to society we are concerned chiefly with immoral activity. Moral belief is relevant only in so far as the lack of it contributes to immoral activity. A vicious minority dimishes the physical strength of society even if all its members believe themselves to be sinning. But if they all believed that, they would not diminish the common belief in right and wrong which is the intangible property of society. When considering intangible injury to society it is moral belief that matters; immoral activity is relevant only in so far as it promotes disbelief.

It is generally accepted that some shared morality, that is, some common agreement about what is right and what is wrong, is an essential element in the constitution of any society. Without it there would be no cohesion. But polygamy can be as cohesive as monogamy and I am prepared to believe that a society based on free love and a community of children could be just as strong (though according to our ideas it could not be as good) as one based on the family. What is important is not the quality of the creed but the strength of the belief in it. The enemy of society is not error but indifference.

But no one, it will be said, wants to subvert a whole morality. All that is sought is freedom to make peripheral changes or, if not quite peripheral, changes that will leave the bulk of morality intact; nothing will be done that will seriously diminish the cohesive force of a common morality. That brings us back to the old difficulty: how much can be allowed and how can it be measured? If it is proper and indeed necessary for the law to guard some part of public morality, how shall we determine what part to leave unguarded? There is in this respect a special difficulty due to the nature of moral belief. It is not for most men based on a number of separate rational judgements arrived at after weighing the arguments for and against chastity, for and against honesty, for and against homosexuality, and so on. Most men take their morality as a whole and in fact derive it, though this is irrelevant, from some religious doctrine. To destroy the belief in one part of it will probably result in weakening the belief in the whole. . . .

But then if the law is required to guard the whole of public morality, is that not, as Professor Hart puts it graphically, using 'legal punishment to freeze into immobility the morality dominant at a particular time in a society's existence'? I do not see why it should have that effect. At the worst it leaves morality as mobile as the law; and though it may not be easy to change the law, it is far easier than to change a moral belief of a community. In fact, for practical reasons the law never attempts to cover the whole of public morality and the area left uncovered is naturally that which is most susceptible to change. But assume that it did cover the whole of public morality, its effect would be not to freeze but to regulate the process of liquefaction and to help distinguish the changes which are motivated by a genuine search after moral improvement from those which are relaxation into vice. It is in this way that the law acts as a winnower, if I may return to the metaphor of the wheat and the chaff. Admittedly it is an unscientific way. There is no phased programme, no planners to say that if free love is let in in the 60's, the homosexualist must wait until the 70's. But relaxation, if it seems to be going too far, sets off a movement for tightening up what is left. The law is brought in to do the tightening as well as to hold off the evil-doers who flourish whenever moral principle is uncertain. A detached observer, who favoured neither the old nor the new morality, would see this as a natural, albeit a rough and ready, method of regulation.

In any society in which the members have a deeply-rooted desire for individual freedom—and where there is not that desire, it is useless to devise methods for securing it—there is also a natural respect for opinions that are sincerely held. When such opinions accumulate enough weight, the law must either yield or it is broken. In a democratic society, especially one like ours in which laymen play a conspicuous part in the enforcement of the law, there will be a strong tendency for it to yield—not to abandon all defences so as to let in the horde, but to give ground to those who are prepared to fight for something that they prize. To fight may be to suffer. A willingness to suffer is the most convincing proof of sincerity. Without the law there would be no proof. The law is the anvil on which the hammer strikes.

Much of what I have just said is more appropriate to a society in which freedom is still young than to ours. In England today there is no question of the law being used to suppress any activity which is not generally thought to be immoral. The climate of a free society is naturally clement to individuality of any sort and uncongenial to compulsion, so that the criminal law will withdraw its support, if it has ever given it, from a moral belief which is seriously challenged.

It may be that in the case of homosexuality this is too sweeping a statement. I do not think that there is anyone who asserts vocally that homosexuality is a good way of life but there may be those who believe it to be so. This brings me back to the point where I left that subject when distinguishing between natural and unnatural vice. That distinction does not affect the intangible harm that immorality does to society but it is relevant, I suggested, to assessing the likelihood of tangible injury. If the intangible harm is ignored, there is a strong case for arguing that homosexuality between adults should be excluded altogether from the ambit of the law on the ground that as a practice it is incapable of causing appreciable injury to society. I cannot say more than that there is a strong case, for many would argue that homosexuality if tolerated would spread to significant proportions. If one ignores that argument as well, the result would be that the charter of freedom should not encompass the whole of morality but only so much of it as is concerned with un-natural vice—freedom of morality in matters unnatural.

Is this the sort of result that is really worth striving for on a high theoretical plane? Any law reformer who raises this sort of issue must be the sort of man who likes to bang his head against a brick wall in the hope that he will be able to get through on his own terms and so avoid a little argument at the gate. It will not improve his chances of getting through the gate if he tells the janitor that there ought not to be a wall there at all. So it is much easier to obtain the repeal of a law by persuad-ing the law-maker that on balance it is doing more harm than good than by denouncing him as a meddler who ought to be minding his own business.

Whether or not I am right in thinking that this is the only way in which the case for reform can be put, it is certainly the most attractive way. It is put thus cogently by Professor Hart in the preface to his book where, after mentioning proposals for the reform of the law on abortion, homosexuality, and euthanasia, he refers to them as cases where 'the misery caused directly and indirectly by legal punishment outweighs any conceivable harm these practices may do.' This is the balancing process. There are other factors besides human misery (which inevitably accom-panies any serious punishment for any breach of the law) to be taken into account; and in my first lecture I enumerated some which it seemed to me the law-maker, whether it be a parliamentary majority or a mon-arch, ought to weigh before it uses its powers. This applies to every exercise of the criminal law. If the law on abortion causes unnecessary misery, let it be amended, not abolished on the ground that abortion is not the law's business. So with obscenity. It is one thing to amend the law, if we can, so that it will distinguish more effectively between art and obscenity, and another thing to remove altogether the restraint of the law, admitting a flood of pornography, so as to make quite sure that no creative work is left outside. In all these cases the appointed law-makers of society have the duty to balance conflicting values—the value of diver-sity against the value of conformity—and to form a judgement according to the merits of each case. They cannot be constrained by rule. They cannot suffer a definite limitation on their powers. They cannot be denied entry into some private realm.

It can be said in general terms, and often is, that law-makers are bound to legislate for the common good. The common good is perhaps a useful and compendious, if vague, description of all the things law-makers should have in mind when they legislate. But it does not constitute a clear limitation on the right to legislate. There may be a difference of opinion about what is for the common good which can be solved only by a judgement upon the conflicting values. Society alone can make that judgement and if it makes it honestly, it is a judgement that cannot be impugned.

Can then the judgement of society sanction every invasion of a man's privacy, however extreme? Theoretically that must be so; there is no theoretical limitation. Society must be the judge of what is necessary to its own integrity if only because there is no other tribunal to which the question can be submitted. In a free society the understanding that men have with each other is that each shall retain for himself the greatest measure of personal freedom that is compatible with the integrity and good government of his society. In a free society men must trust each other and each man must put his trust in his fellows that they will not interfere with him unless in their honest judgement it is necessary to do so. Furthermore, in a free society checks are usually put upon the government, both the executive and the legislature, so that it is difficult for them to enact and enforce a law that takes away another's freedom unless in the honest judgement of society it is necessary to do so. One sort of check consists in the safeguarding of certain specific freedoms by the articles of a constitution; another consists in trial by jury. But the only certain security is the understanding in the heart of every man that he must not condemn what another does unless he honestly considers that it is a threat to the integrity or good government of their society.

If one man practises what he calls virtue and the others call vice and if he fails to convince the others that they are wrong, he has the right to make a further appeal. He has, in a free society, a right to claim that however much the others dislike and deplore what he does, they should allow him to do it unless they are genuinely convinced that it threatens the integrity of society. If the others reject that appeal, constitutionally that is the end. He must either submit or reject society.

SUGGESTED READINGS

Personal Actions and Political Structures: An Ethical Appraisal

The Morality of Suicide

Brandt, R. B. "The Morality and Rationality of Suicide" in E. S. Shneidman (ed.), *Suicidology: Contemporary Developments.* New York: Grune & Stratton, 1976. [Reprinted in James Rachels (ed.), *Moral Problems.* New York: Harper & Row, 1975.]

Douglas, J. D. *Social Meanings of Suicide.* Princeton, N.J.: Princeton University Press, 1967.

Durkheim, E. *Suicide.* New York: Free Press, 1960.

Gibbs, J. P. (ed.) *Suicide.* New York: Harper & Row, 1968.

Hillman, J. *Suicide and the Soul.* New York: Harper & Row, 1973.

Holland, R. F. "Suicide," in J. Rachels (ed.), *Moral Problems.* New York: Harper & Row, 1975.

Kant, I. "Suicide," in *Lectures on Ethics.* New York: Harper & Row, 1963.

Nagel, Thomas. "Death," in J. Rachels (ed.), *Moral Problems.* New York: Harper & Row, 1975.

Perlin, S. (ed.) *A Handbook for the Study of Suicide.* New York: Oxford University Press, 1975.

St. John-Stevas, N., *Life, Death, and the Law.* Bloomington, Ind.: Indiana University Press, 1961.

Shneidman, E. S. (ed.) *On the Nature of Suicide.* San Francisco: Jossey Bass, 1969.

——————. *Suicidology: Contemporary Developments.* New York: Grune & Stratton, 1976.

Sprott, S. E. *Suicide.* Chicago: Open Court, 1973.

Szasz, T. "The Ethics of Suicide," *Antioch Review* 31 (1971).

Westermarck, E. *The Origin and Development of the Moral Ideas.* London: Macmillan, 1926.

Williams, B. "The Makropulos Case: Reflections on the Tedium of Immortality," in James Rachels, (ed.), *Moral Problems.* New York: Harper & Row, 1975.

Williams, Glanville. *The Sanctity of Life and the Criminal Law.* New York: Knopf, 1968.

The Morality of Abortion

Bennett, John C., and others, *Christianity and Crisis* 32 (1973), 287–98.

Bok, Sissela, "Who shall Count as a Human Being?" in R. L. Perkins (ed.), *Abortion: Pro and Con.* Cambridge, Mass.: Schenkman Publishing Co., 1974.

Brandt, R. B. "The Morality of Abortion," *Monist* 56 (1972), 504–26 [Reprinted in R. L. Perkins, *op.cit.*]

Brody, B. A. "Abortion and the Sanctity of Human Life," *American Philosophical Quarterly* 10 (1973), 133–40.

Callahan, Daniel, *Abortion: Law, Choice, and Morality.* New York: Macmillan and Company, 1970.

Curran, C. E., "Abortion: Law and Morality in Recent Roman Catholic Thought," *The Jurist* 33 (1973).

Cutler, Donald R. (ed.), *Updating Life and Death: Essays in Ethics and Medicine.* Boston: Beacon Press, 1969.

Feinberg, Joel (ed.), *The Problem of Abortion.* Belmont, Calif.: Wadsworth Publishing Co., 1973.

Grisez, G. G. "Toward a Consistent Natural Law Ethics of Killing," *American Journal of Jurisprudence* 15 (1970), 64–96.

Kohl, Marvin, *The Morality of Killing.* New York: Humanities Press, 1974.

Noonan, John T. (ed.), *The Morality of Abortion; Legal and Historical Perspectives.* Cambridge: Harvard University Press, 1970.

Purdy, L., and Tooley, M. "Is Abortion Murder?" in R. L. Perkins, *op.cit.*

Rachels, James (ed.), *Moral Problems.* New York: Harper & Row, 1975.

Ramsey, Paul, "The Morality of Abortion," in D. H. Labby (ed.), *Life or Death: Ethics and Options.* Seattle: University of Washington Press, 1968. [Reprinted in James Rachels (ed.), *Moral Problems,* Harper & Row, New York, 1975.]

St. John-Stevas, N. *The Right to Life.* London: Hodder and Stoughton, 1963.

Tooley, Michael. "Abortion and Infanticide," *Philosophy and Public Affairs,* 2 (1972), 37–65.

Wertheimer, Roger, "Understanding the Abortion Argument," *Philosophy and Public Affairs* 1 (1971), 67–95. [Reprinted in James Rachels, *op.cit.*]

Williams, Glanville, *The Sanctity of Life and Criminal Law.* New York: Knopf, 1968.

General Books on Political Philosophy

Benn, S. I., and Peters, R. S. *Social Principles and the Democratic State.* London: George Allen and Unwin, Ltd., 1959.

Mabbott, J. D. *The State and the Citizen.* London: Hutchinson's University Library, 1948.

Raphael, D. D. *Problems of Political Philosophy.* London: Pall Mall Press, 1970.

The foregoing are relatively elementary, and clearly written.

Barker, Ernest. *Principles of Social and Political Theory.* Oxford: Clarendon Press, 1951.

Barry, Brian. *Political Argument.* New York: Humanities Press, 1965.

Brecht, Arnold. *Political Theory: The Foundation of Twentieth Century Political Thought.* Princeton: Princeton University Press, 1959.

Carritt, E. F. *Morals and Politics.* Oxford: Clarendon Press, 1935.

——————. *Ethical and Political Thinking. Oxford:* Clarendon Press, 1947.

Ewing, A. C. *The Individual, the State, and World Government.* London: The Macmillan Company, 1947.

Laslett, P. (ed.) *Philosophy, Politics, and Society,* first series. Oxford: Blackwell, 1956.

Laslett, P., and Runciman, W. G. (eds.) *Philosophy, Politics, and Society,* second series. Oxford: Blackwell, 1964.

——————————. *Philosophy, Politics, and Society,* third series. Oxford: Blackwell, 1967.

Lucas, J. R. *The Principles of Politics.* Oxford: Clarendon Press, 1966.

Olafson, F. (ed.) *Society, Law, and Morality.* Englewood Cliffs, N.J.: Prentice-Hall, Inc., 1961.

Plamenatz, J. P. *Man and Society.* London: Longman's, 1963.

Popper, K. R. *The Open Society and Its Enemies.* Princeton: Princeton University Press, 1950.

Quinton, A. M. (ed.) *Political Philosophy.* London: Oxford University Press, 1967.

Russell, Bertrand. *Human Society in Ethics and Politics.* London: George Allen & Unwin, Ltd., 1962.

Sabine, G. H. *History of Political Theory.* New York: Holt, 1950.

Strauss, Leo. *What Is Political Theory?* Glencoe, Ill.: Free Press, 1959.

The Authority of the State and the Obligation to Obey the Law

Blanshard, Brand. *Reason and Goodness.* London: George Allen & Unwin, Ltd., 1961, pp. 375–408.

Carnes, J. R. "Why should I obey the law?" *Ethics,* 1960.

Gough, J. W. *The Social Contract.* Oxford: The Clarendon Press, 1936. Chap. 15.

Green, T. H. *Lectures on the Principles of Political Obligation.* London: Longman's Green and Co., 1950.

Lewis, H. D. "Is there a social contract?" *Philosophy,* 1940.

MacPherson, Thomas. *Political Obligation.* London: Routledge and Kegan Paul, 1968.

Pennock, J. R., and Chapman, J. (eds.) *Political and Legal Obligation. Nomos,* Vol. XII. New York: Atherton Press, 1970.

Pitkin, Hanna. "Obligation and consent," *American Political Science Review,* 1966.

Plamenatz, John. *Consent, Freedom, and Political Obligation.* London: Oxford University Press, 1938.

Raphael, D. D. *Problems of Political Philosophy.* London: Pall Mall Press, 1970. Chaps. 3 and 4.

Rawls, John. "Legal obligation and the duty of fair play," in Sidney Hook (ed.), *Law and Philosophy.* New York: New York University Press, 1964.

Rousseau, J. J. *The Social Contract.* Many editions.

Tussman, Joseph. *Obligation and the Body Politic.* New York: Oxford University Press, 1960.

Wasserstrom, R. A. "The obligation to obey the law," *U.C.L.A. Law Review,* 1963, reprinted in Summers, R. S., *Essays in Legal Philosophy.* Oxford: Blackwell, 1968.

——————————. "Disobeying the law," *Journal of Philosophy,* 1961, 641–53.

Democracy

Cohen, Carl. (ed.) *Communism, Fascism, and Democracy.* New York: Random House, 1966.
——————. *Democracy.* Athens, Ga.: University of Georgia Press, 1971.
Dahl, R. A. *Preface to Democratic Theory.* Chicago: University of Chicago Press, 1961.
Hospers, John. *Human Conduct.* New York: Harcourt, Brace and World, Inc., 1961. Chap. 18.
MacPherson, C. B. *The Real World of Democracy.* Oxford: Clarendon Press, 1966.
Mayo, H. B. *An Introduction to Democratic Theory.* New York: Oxford University Press, 1960.
Pennock, J. R. *Liberal Democracy.* New York: Rinehart, 1950.
——————. "Responsiveness, responsibility, and majority rule," *American Political Science Review,* 1952.
Raphael, D. D. *Problems of Political Philosophy.* London: Pall Mall Press, 1970. Chap. 6.
Schumpeter, Joseph. "Two concepts of democracy," in A. M. Quinton (ed.), *Political Philosophy.* London: Oxford University Press, 1967.
Wollheim, R. "A paradox in the theory of democracy," in P. Laslett and W. G. Runciman (eds.), *Philosophy, Politics, and Society,* second series. Oxford: Blackwell, 1962.

Liberty and the Enforcement of Morality

Beauchamp, T. L. (ed.) *Ethics and Public Policy.* Englewood Cliffs, N.J.: Prentice-Hall, Inc., 1975.
Berlin, Isaiah. "Two Concepts of Liberty" in A. M. Quinton (ed.), *Political Philosophy.* Oxford: Blackwell, 1967.
Care, N. S., and Trelogan, T. K. (eds.) *Issues in Law and Morality.* Cleveland: Case-Western Reserve Press, 1973.
Carritt, E. F. "Liberty and Equality" in A. M. Quinton, *op.cit.*
Devlin, Patrick, *The Enforcement of Morals.* Oxford: Oxford University Press, 1964.
——————. "Law, Democracy, and Morality," *University of Pennsylvania Law Review,* 110 (1962).
Dworkin, Ronald, "Lord Devlin and the Enforcement of Morals," *Yale Law Journal* 75 (1966).
Feinberg, Joel, "Moral Enforcement and the Harm Principle," in T. L. Beauchamp, *op.cit.*
Friedrich, C. J. (ed.) *Liberty. Nomos* IV. New York: Atherton Press, 1962.
Hart, H. L. A. *Law, Liberty and Morality.* Stanford: Stanford University Press, 1963.
——————. "Social Solidarity and the Enforcement of Morality," in T. L. Beauchamp, *op.cit.*
Hughes, G. "Morals and the Criminal Law," *Yale Law Journal* 71 (1962).
Lewis, C. I. "The Meaning of Liberty," *Revue Internationale de Philosophie,* 1948.

Mitchell, B. *Law, Morality and Religion in a Secular Society.* London: Oxford University Press, 1967.

Nagel, Ernest. "The Enforcement of Morals" in T. L. Beauchamp, *op.cit.*

Plamenatz, John. *Consent, Freedom, and Political Obligation.* London: Oxford University Press, 1938.

Raphael, D. D. *Problems of Political Philosophy.* London: Pall Mall Press, 1970.

Rostow, E. *The Sovereign Prerogative: The Supreme Court and the Quest for Law.* New Haven: Yale University Press, 1962.

Schur, E. M. *Crimes Without Victims.* Englewood Cliffs, N.J.: Prentice-Hall, Inc., 1965.

Wasserstrom, Richard (ed.). *Morality and the Law.* Belmont, Calif.: Wadsworth Publishing Company Inc., 1971.

Wollheim, R. "Crime, Sin, and Mr. Justice Devlin," *Encounter,* Nov. 1959.

PART IV

Free Will and Determinism

Introduction

DETERMINISM

If I place an ice tray filled with water in the freezer, where the temperature is below 32 degrees Fahrenheit, the water will, of course, freeze. And it is not just that it does in fact become solid. It *must* freeze; no other outcome is possible. The drop in temperature uniquely determines (causes) a transition to the solid state.

This example is a particular application of the thesis of determinism, which may be stated generally as follows:

I. *Every event is causally determined, by preceding events and circumstances, to happen just as it does happen.*

Another way of expressing the same idea is in terms of lawfulness or uniformity. To say that the drop in temperature caused the water to freeze is to say that there is a general law to the effect that *whenever* the temperature of water is reduced to below 32°F (and conditions are normal in relevant respects) the water will freeze. The notion of a uniform sequence in events, the notion that the same causes will always be followed by the same effects, is an essential part of the modern scientific concept of causation. Thus, a deterministic universe has a definite kind of *intelligibility;* we can understand why things happen as they do, in the sense that we can see their occurrence (the way they issue from what precedes them) as examples of general regularities. Determinism also guarantees *predictability* in principle. If we know the laws governing a system (such as the solar system), and know enough about the present state of the system (such as the position of each planet), we can predict any future state of the system. We will be able to determine what next state will follow from any given state.

REASONS FOR DETERMINISM

Why should we believe that every event is causally determined? Our main reason comes from the success of science in establishing many causal laws.

In the past few centuries, science has made dramatic advances in increasing our knowledge of what causes what. For example, think of the increased knowledge of the causes of contagious diseases and of genetic defects, a matter in which we were in almost complete ignorance as recently as one hundred and fifty years ago.

To be sure, science provides *direct* evidence for the reign of causal law only in areas in which it can exhibit a clear record of success; human behavior, the topic under consideration in this part of the book, is not one of those. Psychology and allied disciplines have not been notably successful up to now in discovering rigid deterministic laws that specify conditions from which behavior of a certain sort *invariably* follows. We do not know any general laws of the form: *"Whenever* a man _____, he will leave his wife." It is not even clear what *sorts* of causal factors determine human behavior. Some theorists favor a rather traditional scheme (exemplified in our readings by Holbach, Reading 37), in which choice is determined by such things as desires, aversions, fears, and scruples; others advocate a physiological scheme, in which the determinants are such things as patterns of neural excitation in the brain. Nevertheless, it is not unreasonable to extrapolate from the areas in which science already has been successful to relatively undeveloped areas such as psychology. That is, it is not unreasonable to suppose that our relative ignorance of causal laws governing human behavior is due to the complexity of the causal network (or to the fact that we have not yet happened onto the right conceptual scheme), rather than to any lack of causal determination in the subject matter itself. If we only knew enough, we would see that my decision to ask Sally's hand in marriage is as uniquely determined by causal factors as the downward motion of a ball I release is uniquely determined by gravitational forces.

Determinism is not entirely a creation of modern science. Holbach presents arguments for the causal determination of human behavior that are not based on scientific results. Holbach's argument is based on his position that "man is a being purely physical." (See Readings 44 and 45 for discussions of a materialist view of human nature.) Since the will is a modification of the brain, its operations are physically determined. A more general support for determinism in the area of human behavior is provided by the fact that men's actions usually conform to simple regularities. Most people with jobs show up for work most working days. Even Campbell, who rejects determinism, argues in Section 9 of Reading 38 that his position allows for a great deal of uniformity and predictability in human conduct.

FREE WILL

However plausible it may be otherwise, the deterministic picture of man runs head-on into the notion that men have "free will," that is, that in many situations they have a free choice between two or more alternative lines of action.[1] It does *seem* perfectly obvious that in many situations *there is more than one thing I can choose, that each of these alternatives is a real pos-*

1. Two terminological notes. The term "will" is now more or less archaic. Although we will continue to use the traditional term "free will" as a label for the conviction just

sibility for me. Consider the case of Sue, who is trying to decide whether to have an abortion. In a typical situation of that sort, we would all assume, including Sue, that *she can choose either to have the abortion or not; that both choices are within her power;* that *she has a "free choice" between them; that whichever one she does choose, it will remain true that she could have chosen otherwise.* Indeed, if she were not convinced that both alternatives were real possibilities, then she would not be engaged in trying to make up her mind *which one* to choose; where there is only one possibility, there is nothing to deliberate about. The conviction that one is often in such a position, we may term the *Free Will Thesis,* and formulate as follows:

II. *There are situations in which there is more than one action a person can choose (in which he has a free choice between alternative actions)*[2]

There are both "psychological" and "moral" reasons for believing in free will. We have already indicated the psychological reasons—the well-nigh irresistible sense we have in situations of choice that more than one alternative is open, plus the fact that this is a necessary presupposition of deliberation. This "sense of freedom" is especially stressed by Campbell (Reading 38), and it is also recognized by Hobart (Reading 39). Note that Campbell restricts his discussion to a very special sort of case—a person struggling with moral temptation; only in cases of this sort does he insist on the existence of alternative possibilities.

The moral argument is that free will is a necessary presupposition of moral responsibility. The notion of moral responsibility is a complex one, and perhaps not completely clear-cut, but at least it involves the notion of susceptibility to praise and blame, reward and punishment. When I hold a person morally responsible for something he did, such as joining a demonstration, I thereby take him to be subject to moral approval or disapproval, moral praise or blame for doing what he did. That is, to hold someone morally responsible for an action is to suppose that moral praise and blame would be *appropriate* in this case. But how can I be justified in holding someone morally responsible for something he did unless he freely chose to do it, unless he *could have done otherwise?* This is perhaps most obvious in the case of blame. In blaming a person for having lied, I imply that he *ought not to have lied.* But if the person could not refrain from lying, how could it have been his obligation not to have lied? One is not obliged to do something he cannot do, or to refrain from something he cannot refrain from. If I supposed that he had no choice but to lie, I should no more blame him for it than I would blame him for other things he cannot help, such as being pushed against me in a crowd.

---

expressed, the discussions will be carried on in terms of "choice" or "decision," rather than "will."

To say I have a *free choice* between going and staying away may mean that I am able to actually *do* both (actually carry out either choice), or it may only mean that I am able to perform either inner mental act of choice. In this discussion, we will employ the former, more inclusive sense, since it is the whole package—a choice issuing in the act chosen—in which we are interested. Note that Hobart, in the section of Reading 39 headed *"Can,"* distinguishes the inner "act of will" from the outer behavior, and discusses freedom with respect to each of these.

2. The various italicized phrases in the above paragraph can be regarded as formulations of the same idea.

CONFLICT OF DETERMINISM AND FREE WILL

It *seems* clear that the Free Will Thesis flatly contradicts determinism. The former asserts, while the latter denies, that there are situations in which more than one action is a real possibility for an agent. According to determinism, in every situation only one outcome is possible; the causal factors at work uniquely determine a particular result. If, for example, Todd is trying to decide whether to drop out of college, the determinist maintains that, given all his desires, fears, beliefs, moral convictions, and whatever other causal factors are relevant, one decision is uniquely determined by those causes; no other decision is possible, whatever Todd himself may suppose. According to the Free Will Thesis, before the moment of choice, either alternative is a possibility. Thus, we seem to be confronted with an irreconcilable opposition between two fundamental convictions, each of which is deeply rooted in human thought and experience. The "free will problem" is the problem of what to do about this opposition.

NECESSITARIANISM

The simplest reaction to the conflict is to choose up sides. That is, one may either accept determinism and reject free will (Necessitarianism) or accept free will and reject determinism, at least with respect to human choice (Libertarianism).

Holbach (Reading 37) is our Necessitarian. In addition to arguing that a person's motives necessitate his actions, Holbach tries to dismiss our sense of freedom as an illusion generated by our ignorance of the complex network of causal factors. When confronted with a job offer I believe that I can either accept it or reject it; but that is only because I am unable to trace the complex interplay of desires, fears, and so forth that determine my choice. Holbach does not really discuss the moral argument for free will; the usual Necessitarian line is to dismiss the traditional concept of moral responsibility as so much prescientific superstition. The Necessitarian agrees with his opponent that free will is a necessary presupposition of moral responsibility and draws the conclusion that we are never justified in holding anyone responsible. The Necessitarian can still admit that praise and blame, reward and punishment may be justified in terms of socially beneficial effects, but denies that they can be justified on the grounds that the agent acted freely and therefore *deserves* approval or disapproval. Hospers (Reading 40) approximates to this position, with qualifications to be noted later.

LIBERTARIANISM

Our main representative of Libertarianism, C. A. Campbell (Reading 38), is not wholly typical of the position; he supposes determinism to fail only in a very limited range of cases—viz., situations of moral temptation, in which

396

a person is more or less strongly inclined to do something other than what she realizes her duty to be. If no conflict between duty and inclination is involved, Campbell concedes that human choices are causally determined by the agent's "character." However, within this special range, he uses both the main arguments for free will. He maintains that in a moral struggle, the agent is conscious that she has the power either to put forth or to withhold the amount of "moral effort" required to resist temptation. And he maintains that we hold persons morally responsible only to the extent that we believe they have these options open to them.

Some Libertarians mount a counterattack against determinism by arguing that human volition and/or conduct is unpredictable in principle. In Reading 41, Alvin Goldman considers a number of such arguments. He contends that causal determinism does not require predictability by anyone under any and all circumstances, and he also maintains that human actions are not unpredictable in any way in which physical events are predictable.

It also has been maintained by many recent philosophers that reflection on the concept of action (and the other concepts involved) will reveal conceptual confusions in the supposition that actions are causally determined. For example, it is argued that if my behavior is determined by causes, then *I* had nothing to do with it; I am a passive spectator of the operation of the causes involved. In that case, the behavior would not count as *my action.* (For a presentation of some of these arguments and responses to them, see the bibliography at the end of this part.)

THE RECONCILIST TWIST

So far, we, along with Holbach and Campbell, have been proceeding on the assumption that determinism and free will are mutually contradictory and hence that we must choose between them. However, a long line of philosophers, including Hume, Locke, and Mill, have challenged this assumption; they have maintained that, contrary to first appearances, the two theses are quite compatible and hence there is no need to choose; we can have both. We may term this position *Reconcilism.* It is represented here by Hobart (Reading 39). But how can the two positions be compatible when one asserts, while the other denies, a plurality of possibilities in a situation of choice?

Whether they are incompatible depends, of course, on how they are interpreted, and more specifically (since the import of determinism is not at issue at this point), on how free will is interpreted. Up to this point, we have supposed that "possibility" in the Free Will Thesis is to be understood as "causal possibility"; on that interpretation, to say that a person *can* make any one of several choices (any one of these choices is a *possibility*) is to say that the causes operative in the situation leave all these possibilities open; they do not uniquely determine one and rule out the others. So understood, the Free Will Thesis does indeed flatly contradict determinism. Let's spell out this interpretation.

IIA. Free Will Thesis: "Categorical" or "Contra-Causal" Interpretation. In some situations, a person *can* choose more than one action *in the sense*

*that the causes operative in the situation do not uniquely determine
one and only one choice.*

We may use the term "freedom from determinism" for the kind of freedom
defined by this formulation.

According to the Reconcilist, this is the wrong way to construe free will.
The alternative is clearly set out by Hobart in the section of Reading 39
headed *"Can."* There, he maintains that to say that a person has a certain
power is simply to say that if he wants to do something, then, in the absence
of interferences, it will forthwith be done. And to say that one is *free* in
exercising a power is to deny that there are any obstacles sufficient to prevent that power from being exercised. Thus, to say that one is free to choose
any one of several alternatives is simply to say that one has the power to
make such choices and that nothing is preventing one from exercising that
power. In other words, the person is so situated that whichever of these
choices he prefers (most wants) to make, that choice will in fact be made.
In making this assertion, we are saying something hypothetical about the
person; we are saying, with respect to each of the choices in question, that
if he prefers (most wants) to make that choice, he will in fact do so; nothing
is preventing his carrying out his preference. We may embody this idea in a
second interpretation of the Free Will Thesis.

IIB. Free Will Thesis: "Hypothetical" Interpretation. In some situations, a
person can choose more than one action *in the sense that for each of
these actions it is true that if the person prefers to choose that action,
he will do so.*

This interpretation is called the "hypothetical interpretation" for obvious
reasons; we have followed Campbell's terminology in calling IIA, by contrast,
the "categorical interpretation."

Clearly, free will in the hypothetical sense is compatible with determinism. To say of each of several alternative actions, that *if* I prefer that
action then I will choose it, implies nothing as to whether my preferences,
choices, actions, or anything else are causally determined. It is simply to say
something about the *consequences* that one or another preference will have.
This is quite compatible with that preference, and the resulting decision and action, being causally determined by desires, motives, brain
processes, or whatever. What freedom in this sense does rule out is *constraint,* something that would prevent me from carrying out a given choice.
Thus, we may term this kind of freedom, "freedom from constraint," in contrast to "freedom from determinism."

ARGUMENTS FOR RECONCILISM

Of course, the Reconcilist is not concerned just to point out that the Free
Will Thesis *might* be given the hypothetical interpretation. The Reconcilist
wants to show that it is in his sense, and not in the categorical sense, that
human beings do have free will. How does he seek to do this?

Hobart frequently insists that the whole issue (of the compatibility or incompatibility of determinism and free will) hangs on the "meanings of

words." He thinks that by examining words such as "can" and "free" he can establish that when we affirm our ability to make any one of several choices, we mean this in the hypothetical sense. Other reconcilists argue that when, in ordinary life, we *distinguish* between cases in which we have and cases in which we do not have a free choice, we do so on the basis of the hypothetical interpretation. Consider a student, Anna, who is trying to decide whether to go to class or go to a movie, in contrast with another student, Beth, who also is supposed to be in class soon but has been bound, hand and foot, by burglars. Clearly, Anna feels that she has a real choice[3] as to whether to attend class, whereas Beth does not. We would all agree that, in some sense, both going to the movie and attending class are real possibilities for Anna, whereas, in that same sense, staying where she is and going to class are not both real possibilities for Beth. Furthermore, whichever choice Anna makes, it will remain true that she "could have done otherwise," whereas this is not true of Beth. Now, when we make these contrasts, are we employing the crucial terms in the categorical or the hypothetical sense? If the former, then we would be saying that the causes acting on Beth determine one unique response, whereas this is not true of Anna. But it seems that *this* is not the basis of the contrast. We do not have to go into the causal question at all in order to make this distinction. In order to assure ourselves that Anna had a free choice, whereas Beth did not, we do not have to determine whether Anna's desires, fears, and scruples causally determined her to make the choice she made. All we have to ascertain is that Anna *was in a position to carry out whichever line of action she preferred,* whereas Beth was not. That is, the crucial difference lies in whether or not there were forces strong enough to prevent the person from carrying out a preference. We are contrasting Anna and Beth in terms of *freedom from constraint,* not in terms of *freedom from determinism.*

So far, the Reconcilist is merely arguing that we ordinarily employ the hypothetical sense in our everyday talk about human conduct. If he could establish this, it would be quite significant, for it would dispose of the assumption, made by both Necessitarians and Libertarians, that we ordinarily ascribe free will to ourselves in the categorical sense. Nevertheless, it would not definitively settle the matter. For the question would still remain as to whether there are sufficient reasons for supposing that human beings also have a free choice in the categorical sense. This issue is explicitly raised by Campbell in section 2 of Reading 38. Out of the various ways of expressing the Free Will Thesis we distinguished on p. 395, Campbell focuses on "Whichever he chooses, he could have chosen otherwise" (except that Campbell says, "could have *acted* otherwise"). Campbell recognizes both interpretations of "could have acted otherwise," but he argues that what moral responsibility requires, and what we are aware of in situations of moral choice, is that one *could have acted otherwise* in the categorical sense. Thus, in order to fully make out a case, the Reconcilist must go on to show that the psychological and moral arguments support free will in the hypothetical sense.

3. In the strong sense of "choice" in which it includes overt behavior. *Both* students can make either "choice" in the sense of inner mental acts of decision.

A considerable part of Hobart's essay is devoted to doing just that. His discussion of the "sense of freedom" (in the section headed *"Can"*) is rather brief, but he gives a full-dress treatment of the moral argument. He takes each idea associated with moral responsibility—responsibility, praise and blame, moral indignation, "desert" (i.e., the deserving of reward or punishment)— and tries to show for each that free will in the hypothetical sense provides an adequate foundation. With respect to praise and blame, for instance, he maintains that moral blame is directed to the person's character from which we take the choice in question to have sprung. When I reproach myself for having gratuitously wounded someone else's feelings, I am disapproving of myself (my character) for being of the sort to produce such an action. So far from requiring indeterminism, such a reproach presupposes that my action was determined by my character at the time; otherwise, I could not take the act as an indication of the nature of that self.

With respect to reward and punishment, Hobart takes a Utilitarian position. (See Reading 19 for a presentation of Utilitarianism.) The question of whether a person *deserves* reward or punishment is the question of whether he *should be* rewarded or punished, and that question is to be answered (this is where Utilitarianism comes in) on the basis of the social consequences of the reward or punishment. If, for example, punishing a person for selling heroin will make it less likely that he, and others, will sell heroin in the future, and this benefit is not outweighed by unfortunate results of the punishment, then we are justified in punishing him. Clearly, this kind of justification does not require the assumption of free will in the categorical sense of freedom from determinism. If the person's act of selling heroin is causally determined, the punishment could still make it less likely that he will do it again.

Let's go back to our two students. It would be silly to penalize Beth for missing class, but not silly to penalize Anna; this is just because Anna, but not Beth, enjoyed freedom from constraint. Anna was in a situation in which the relative strengths of various motives determined the overall preference, which she was able to carry out in choice and action. Hence, if the penalty has the desired effect of strengthening her fear of penalties for missing class, this means that her overall preference is less likely to be for missing class the next time she is in a similar situation, and hence that she is less likely to miss class next time. With Beth, on the other hand, her motives and preferences had no influence on her behavior; so that even if her fear of penalties for missing class is strengthened, that will have no tendency to make her less likely to miss class the next time she is bound hand and foot. Thus, the appropriateness of punishment (on Utilitarian grounds) seems to be strictly a function of whether the wrongdoer enjoyed freedom from constraint.

Hobart's position is more extreme than that of many Reconcilists. Not content with maintaining that free will is *compatible* with determinism, he argues that free will *requires* determinism (that it is incompatible with *indeterminism*). His main argument for this is that an action that is not causally determined by the character of the agent (together with the situation in which he is acting) cannot be said to have stemmed from *him,* from the particular person that he is, and hence is not anything for which *he* can be held responsible. If it is causally determined by something independent of the person's character, it is not *his* act; if it is not causally determined

400

at all, it is a chance happening, and again, something for which the person cannot be held responsible. The reader is invited to scrutinize Campbell's rejoinder in section 10 of Reading 38.

BEYOND RESPONSIBILITY

Hosper's essay (Reading 40), in which the topic of responsibility is the center of attention, occupies a sort of middle position between Reconcilism and Necessitarianism. In the first section, he considers a number of criteria of responsibility (all of which are compatible with determinism, although Hospers does not stress this point), including freedom from constraint (Hospers speaks of "compulsion" rather than "constraint"). He opts for a criterion in terms of one's behavior being influenceable by reasons. So far, he is proceeding in the spirit of Reconcilism. But in his second section he suggests that determinism implies that in a "deeper sense" we are never responsible for our actions. Here, Hospers brings out the point that moral blame involves an element of "moral superiority" and "righteous indignation." When we morally blame someone, we seem to imply that he is some sort of monster who deliberately and willfully chose to be a person of bad character. But according to determinism, there is an unbroken causal chain stretching from conditions that existed before our birth (such as our parents, their genes, and their personalities, the circumstances into which we were born) to our present characters. This means that our characters are causally determined by conditions that antedated our birth, conditions over which we obviously had no sort of control. This being the case, it ill behooves the "good" to look down on the "evil," when both simply are acting out the characters that necessarily result from conditions beyond their control. A thoughtful person, Hospers suggests, will have inescapably ambivalent attitudes toward wrongdoers. On the one hand, he feels indignant, feels inclined to snarl and criticize; and he feels justified in this, as Hobart says, because the wrongdoer *does* have a defective character and because these reactions do, to some extent, serve to decrease wrongdoing. On the other hand, when he gets fully and vividly in mind the causal processes that have produced this socially undesirable character, he finds himself inclined to feel sorry for him, and to feel that he himself is fortunate in having more fortunate causal influences in *his* background. "There, but for the grace of my causal antecedents, go I." Thus, in this part of his essay, Hospers is agreeing with Holbach (and Campbell) that moral responsibility, as usually conceived, is incompatible with determinism.

401

37. Baron d'Holbach

Baron P. H. D. d'Holbach (1725–1789) was a leading figure in the French enlightenment.

Determinism Rules Out Free Will

Those who have pretended that the *soul* is distinguished from the body, is immaterial, draws its ideas from its own peculiar source, acts by its own energies, without the aid of any exterior object, have, by a consequence of their own system, enfranchised it from those physical laws according to which all beings of which we have a knowledge are obliged to act. They have believed that the soul is mistress of its own conduct, is able to regulate its own peculiar operations, has the faculty to determine its will by its own natural energy; in a word, they have pretended that man is a *free agent*.

It has been already sufficiently proved that the soul is nothing more than the body considered relatively to some of its functions more concealed than others: it has been shown that this soul, even when it shall be supposed immaterial, is continually modified conjointly with the body, is submitted to all its motion, and that without this it would remain inert and dead: that, consequently, it is subjected to the influence of those material and physical causes which give impulse to the body; of which the mode of existence, whether habitual or transitory, depends upon the material elements by which it is surrounded, that form its texture, con-

From Chapter XI, "Of the System of Man's Free Agency," of *The System of Nature* (1770). The translation is by H. D. Robinson.

stitute its temperament, enter into it by means of the aliments, and penetrate it by their subtility. The faculties which are called *intellectual*, and those qualities which are styled *moral*, have been explained in a manner purely physical and natural. In the last place it has been demonstrated that all the ideas, all the systems, all the affections, all the opinions, whether true or false, which man forms to himself, are to be attributed to his physical and material senses. Thus man is a being purely physical; in whatever manner he is considered, he is connected to universal nature, and submitted to the necessary and immutable laws that she imposes on all the beings she contains, according to their peculiar essences or to the respective properties with which, without consulting them, she endows each particular species. Man's life is a line that nature commands him to describe upon the surface of the earth, without his ever being able to swerve from it, even for an instant. He is born without his own consent; his organization does in nowise depend upon himself; his ideas come to him involuntarily; his habits are in the power of those who cause him to contract them; he is unceasingly modified by causes, whether visible or concealed, over which he has no control, which necessarily regulate his mode of existence, give the hue to his way of thinking, and determine his manner of acting. He is good or bad, happy or miserable, wise or foolish, reasonable or irrational, without his will being for any thing in these various states. Nevertheless, in despite of the shackles by which he is bound, it is pretended he is a free agent, or that independent of the causes by which he is moved, he determines his own will, and regulates his own condition.

However slender the foundation of this opinion, of which every thing ought to point out to him the errour, it is current at this day and passes for an incontestable truth with a great number of people, otherwise extremely enlightened; it is the basis of religion, which, supposing relations between man and the unknown being she has placed above nature, has been incapable of imagining how man could either merit reward or deserve punishment from this being, if he was not a free agent. Society has been believed interested in this system; because an idea has gone abroad, that if all the actions of man were to be contemplated as necessary, the right of punishing those who injure their associates would no longer exist. At length human vanity accommodated itself to a hypothesis which, unquestionably, appears to distinguish man from all other physical beings, by assigning to him the special privilege of a total independence of all other causes, but of which a very little reflection would have shown him the impossibility.

. . . .

The will, as we have elsewhere said, is a modification of the brain, by which it is disposed to action, or prepared to give play to the organs. This will is necessarily determined by the qualities, good or bad, agreeable or painful, of the object or the motive that acts upon his senses, or of which the idea remains with him, and is resuscitated by his memory. In consequence, he acts necessarily, his action is the result of the impulse he receives either from the motive, from the object, or from the idea which has modified his brain, or disposed his will. When he does not act according to this impulse, it is because there comes some new cause, some new motive, some new idea, which modifies his brain in a different manner, gives him a new impulse, determines his will in another way, by which the action of the former impulse is suspended: thus, the sight of an agreeable object, or its idea, determines his will to set him in action to procure it; but if a new object or a new idea more powerfully attracts him, it gives a new direction to his will, annihilates the effect of the former, and prevents the action by which it was to be procured. This is the mode in which reflection, experience, reason, necessarily arrests or suspends the action of man's will: without this he would of necessity have followed the anterior impulse which carried him towards a then desirable object. In all this he always acts according to necessary laws, from which he has no means of emancipating himself.

If when tormented with violent thirst, he figures to himself in idea, or really perceives a fountain, whose limpid streams might cool his feverish want, is he sufficient master of himself to desire or not to desire the object competent to satisfy so lively a want? It will no doubt be conceded, that it is impossible he should not be desirous to satisfy it; but it will be said—if at this moment it is announced to him that the water he so ardently desires is poisoned, he will, notwithstanding his vehement thirst, abstain from drinking it: and it has, therefore, been falsely concluded that he is a free agent. The fact, however, is, that the motive in either case is exactly the same: his own conservation. The same necessity that determined him to drink before he knew the water was deleterious, upon this new discovery equally determines him not to drink; the desire of conserving himself either annihilates or suspends the former impulse; the second motive becomes stronger than the preceding, that is, the fear of death, or the desire of preserving himself, necessarily prevails over the painful sensation caused by his eagerness to drink: but, it will be said, if the thirst is very parching, an inconsiderate man without regarding the danger will risk swallowing the water. Nothing is gained by this remark: in this case the anterior impulse only regains the ascendency; he is persuaded that life may possibly be longer preserved, or that he shall derive a greater good by drinking the poisoned water than by enduring the torment, which, to his mind, threatens instant dissolution: thus the first becomes the strongest and necessarily urges him on to action. Nevertheless, in either case, whether he partakes of the water, or whether he does not, the two actions will be equally necessary; they will be the effect of that motive which finds itself most puissant; which consequently acts in the most coercive manner upon his will.

This example will serve to explain the whole phenomena of the human will. This will, or rather the brain, finds itself in the same situation as a bowl, which, although it has received an impulse that drives it forward in a straight line, is deranged in its course whenever a force superior to the first obliges it to change its direction. The man who drinks the poisoned water appears a madman; but the actions of fools are as necessary as those of the most prudent individuals. The motives that determine the voluptuary and the debauchee to risk their health, are as powerful, and their actions are as necessary, as those which decide the wise man to manage his. But, it will be insisted, the debauchee may be prevailed on to change his conduct: this does not imply that he is a free agent; but that motives may be found sufficiently powerful to annihilate the effect of those that previously acted upon him; then these new motives determine his will to the new mode of conduct he may adopt as necessarily as the former did to the old mode.

Man is said to *deliberate*, when the action of the will is suspended; this happens when two opposite motives act alternately upon him. To *deliberate*, is to hate and to love in succession; it is to be alternately attracted and repelled; it is to be moved, sometimes by one motive, sometimes by another. Man only deliberates when he does not distinctly understand the quality of the objects from which he receives impulse, or when experience has not sufficiently apprised him of the effects, more or less remote, which his actions will produce. He would take the air, but the weather is uncertain; he deliberates in consequence; he weighs the various motives that urge his will to go out or to stay at home; he is at length determined by that motive which is most probable; this removes his indecision, which necessarily settles his will, either to remain within or to go abroad: his motive is always either the immediate or ultimate advantage he finds, or thinks he finds, in the action to which he is persuaded.

Man's will frequently fluctuates between two objects, of which either the presence or the ideas move him alternately: he waits until he has contemplated the objects, or the ideas they have left in his brain which solicit him to different actions; he then compares these objects or ideas; but even in the time of deliberation, during the comparison, pending these alternatives of love and hatred which succeed each other, sometimes with the utmost rapidity, he is not a free agent for a single instant; the good or the evil which he believes he finds successively in the objects, are the necessary motives of these momentary wills; of the rapid motion of desire or fear, that he experiences as long as his uncertainty continues. From this it will be obvious that deliberation is necessary; that uncertainty is necessary; that whatever part he takes, in consequence of this deliberation, it will always necessarily be that which he has judged, whether well or ill, is most probable to turn to his advantage.

When the soul is assailed by two motives that act alternately upon it, or modify it successively, it deliberates; the brain is in a sort of equilibrium, accompanied with perpetual oscillations, sometimes towards one object, sometimes towards the other, until the most forcible carries the point, and thereby extricates it from this state of suspense, in which consists the indecision of his will. But when the brain is simultaneously assailed by causes equally strong that move it in opposite directions, agreeable to the general law of all bodies when they are struck equally by contrary powers, it stops, it is in *nisu*; it is neither capable to will nor to act; it waits until one of the two causes has obtained sufficient force to overpower the other; to determine its will; to attract it in such a manner that it may prevail over the efforts of the other cause.

This mechanism, so simple, so natural, suffices to demonstrate why uncertainty is painful, and why suspense is always a violent state for man. The brain, an organ so delicate and so mobile, experiences such rapid modifications that it is fatigued; or when it is urged in contrary directions, by causes equally powerful, it suffers a kind of compression, that prevents the activity which is suitable to the preservation of the whole, and which is necessary to procure what is advantageous to its existence. This mechanism will also explain the irregularity, the indecision, the inconstancy of man, and account for that conduct which frequently appears an inexplicable mystery, and which is, indeed, the effect of the received systems. In consulting experience, it will be found that the soul is submitted to precisely the same physical laws as the material body. If the will of each individual, during a given time, was only moved by a single cause or passion, nothing would be more easy than to foresee his actions; but his heart is frequently assailed by contrary powers, by adverse motives, which either act on him simultaneously or in succession; then his brain, attracted in opposite directions, is either fatigued, or else tormented by a state of compression, which deprives it of activity. Sometimes it is in a state of incommodious inaction; sometimes it is the sport of the alternate shocks it undergoes. Such, no doubt, is the state in which man finds himself when a lively passion solicits him to the commission of crime, whilst fear points out to him the danger by which it is attended: such, also, is the condition of him whom remorse, by the continued labour of his distracted soul, prevents from enjoying the objects he has criminally obtained.

. . . .

Choice by no means proves the free agency of man: he only deliberates when he does not yet know which to choose of the many objects that move him, he is then in an embarrassment, which does not terminate until his will is decided by the greater advantage he believes he shall find in the object he chooses, or the action he undertakes. From whence it may be seen, that choice is necessary, because he would not determine for an object, or for an action, if he did not believe that he should find in it some direct advantage. That man should have free agency it were needful that he should be able to will or choose without motive, or that he could prevent motives coercing his will. Action always being the effect of his will once determined, and as his will cannot be determined but by a motive which is not in his own power, it follows that he is never the master of the determination of his own peculiar will; that consequently he never acts as a free agent. It has been believed that man was a free agent because he had a will with the power of choosing; but attention has not been paid to the fact that even his will is moved by causes independent of himself; is owing to that which is inherent in his own organization, or which belongs to the nature of the beings acting on him.†
Is he the master of willing not to withdraw his hand from the fire when

---

† Man passes a great portion of his life without even willing. His will depends on the motive by which he is determined. If he were to render an exact account of every thing he does in the course of each day—from rising in the morning to lying down at night—he would find that not one of his actions have been in the least voluntary; that they have been mechanical, habitual, determined by causes he was not able to foresee; to which he was either obliged to yield, or with which he was allured to acquiesce: he would discover, that all the motives of his labours, of his amusements, of his discourses, of his thoughts, have been necessary; that they have evidently either seduced him or drawn him along.

407

he fears it will be burnt? Or has he the power to take away from fire the property which makes him fear it? Is he the master of not choosing a dish of meat, which he knows to be agreeable or analogous to his palate; of not preferring it to that which he knows to be disagreeable or dangerous? It is always according to his sensations, to his own peculiar experience, or to his suppositions, that he judges of things, either well or ill; but whatever may be his judgment, it depends necessarily on his mode of feeling, whether habitual or accidental, and the qualities he finds in the causes that move him, which exist in despite of himself.

· ·

It has been believed that man was a free agent, because it has been imagined that his soul could at will recall ideas which sometimes suffice to check his most unruly desires. Thus, the idea of a remote evil, frequently prevents him from enjoying a present and actual good: thus remembrance, which is an almost insensible or slight modification of his brain, annihilates, at each instant, the real objects that act upon his will. But he is not master of recalling to himself his ideas at pleasure; their association is independent of him; they are arranged in his brain in despite of him and without his own knowledge, where they have made an impression more or less profound; his memory itself depends upon his organization; its fidelity depends upon the habitual or momentary state in which he finds himself; when his will is vigorously determined to some object or idea that excites a very lively passion in him, those objects or ideas that would be able to arrest his action, no longer present themselves to his mind; in those moments his eyes are shut to the dangers that menace him; of which the idea ought to make him forbear; he marches forwards headlong towards the object by whose image he is hurried on; reflection cannot operate upon him in any way; he sees nothing but the object of his desires; the salutary ideas which might be able to arrest his progress disappear, or else display themselves either too faintly or too late to prevent his acting. Such is the case with all those who, blinded by some strong passion, are not in a condition to recall to themselves those motives, of which the idea alone, in cooler moments, would be sufficient to deter them from proceeding; the disorder in which they are, prevents their judging soundly; renders them incapable of foreseeing the consequences of their actions; precludes them from applying to their experience; from making use of their reason; natural operations which suppose a justness in the manner of associating their ideas, but to which their brain is then not more competent, in consequence of the momentary delirium it suffers, than their hand is to write whilst they are taking violent exercise.

Man's mode of thinking is necessarily determined by his manner of being; it must therefore depend on his natural organization, and the modification his system receives independently of his will. From this, we are obliged to conclude, that his thoughts, his reflections, his manner of viewing things, of feeling, of judging, of combining ideas, is neither voluntary nor free. In a word, that his soul is neither mistress of the motion excited in it, nor of representing to itself, when wanted, those images or ideas that are capable of counterbalancing the impulse it receives. This is the reason, why man, when in a passion, ceases to reason; at that moment reason is as impossible to be heard, as it is during an ecstacy, or in a fit of drunkenness. The wicked are never more than men who are either drunk or mad; if they reason, it is not until tranquillity is re-established in their machine; then, and not till then, the tardy ideas that present themselves to their mind enable them to see the consequence of their actions, and give birth to ideas that bring on them that trouble, which is designated *shame, regret, remorse.*

The errours of philosophers on the free agency of man, have arisen from their regarding his will as the *primum mobile,* the original motive of his actions; for want of recurring back, they have not perceived the multiplied, the complicated causes which, independently of him, give motion to the will itself; or which dispose and modify his brain, whilst he himself is purely passive in the motion he receives. Is he the master of desiring or not desiring an object that appears desirable to him? Without doubt it will be answered, no: but he is the master of resisting his desire, if he reflects on the consequences. But, I ask, is he capable of reflecting on these consequences, when his soul is hurried along by a very lively passion, which entirely depends upon his natural organization, and the causes by which he is modified? Is it in his power to add to these consequences all the weight necessary to counterbalance his desire? Is he the master of preventing the qualities which render an object desirable from residing in it? I shall be told: he ought to have learned to resist his passions; to contract a habit of putting a curb on his desires. I agree to it without any difficulty. But in reply, I again ask, is his nature susceptible of this modification? Does his boiling blood, his unruly imagination, the igneous fluid that circulates in his veins permit him to make, enable him to apply true experience in the moment when it is wanted? And even when his temperament has capacitated him, has his education, the examples set before him, the ideas with which he has been inspired in early life, been suitable to make him contract this habit of repressing his desires? Have not all these things rather contributed to induce him to seek with avidity, to make him actually desire those objects which you say he ought to resist.

. . . .

In despite of these proofs of the want of free agency in man, so clear to unprejudiced minds, it will, perhaps, be insisted upon with no small feeling of triumph, that if it be proposed to any one, to move or not to move his hand, an action in the number of those called *indifferent,* he evidently appears to be the master of choosing; from which it is concluded that evidence has been offered of his free agency. The reply is, this example is perfectly simple; man in performing some action which he is resolved on doing, does not by any means prove his free agency: the very desire of displaying this quality, excited by the dispute, becomes a necessary motive, which decides his will either for the one or the other of these actions: what deludes him in this instance, or that which persuades him he is a free agent at this moment, is, that he does not discern the true motive which sets him in action, namely, the desire of convincing his opponent: if in the heat of the dispute he insists and asks,

"Am I not the master of throwing myself out of the window?" I shall answer him, no; that whilst he preserves his reason there is no probability that the desire of proving his free agency, will become a motive sufficiently powerful to make him sacrifice his life to the attempt: if, notwithstanding this, to prove he is a free agent, he should actually precipitate himself from the window, it would not be a sufficient warranty to conclude he acted freely, but rather that it was the violence of his temperament which spurred him on to this folly. Madness is a state, that depends upon the heat of the blood, not upon the will. A fanatic or a hero, braves death as necessarily as a more phlegmatic man or a coward flies from it.*

It is said that free agency is the absence of those obstacles competent to oppose themselves to the actions of man, or to the exercise of his faculties: it is pretended that he is a free agent whenever, making use of these faculties, he produces the effect he has proposed to himself. In reply to this reasoning, it is sufficient to consider that it in nowise depends upon himself to place or remove the obstacles that either determine or resist him; the motive that causes his action is no more in his own power than the obstacle that impedes him, whether this obstacle or motive be within his own machine or exterior of his person: he is not master of the thought presented to his mind, which determines his will; this thought is excited by some cause independent of himself.

To be undeceived on the system of his free agency, man has simply to recur to the motive by which his will is determined; he will always find this motive is out of his own control. It is said: that in consequence of an idea to which the mind gives birth, man acts freely if he encounters no obstacle. But the question is, what gives birth to this idea in his brain? was he the master either to prevent it from presenting itself, or from renewing itself in his brain? Does not this idea depend either upon objects that strike him exteriorly and in despite of himself, or upon causes, that without his knowledge, act within himself and modify his brain? Can he prevent his eyes, cast without design upon any object whatever, from giving him an idea of this object, and from moving his brain? He is not more master of the obstacles; they are the necessary effects of either interior or exterior causes, which always act according to their given properties. A man insults a coward, this necessarily irritates him against his insulter, but his will cannot vanquish the obstacle that cowardice places to the object of his desire, because his natural conformation,

---

* There is, in point of fact, no difference between the man that is cast out of the window by another, and the man who throws himself out of it, except that the impulse in the first instance comes immediately from without, whilst that which determines the fall in the second case, springs from within his own peculiar machine, having its more remote cause also exterior. When Mutius Scaevola held his hand in the fire, he was as much acting under the influence of necessity (caused by interior motives) that urged him to this strange action, as if his arm had been held by strong men: pride, despair, the desire of braving his enemy, a wish to astonish him, an anxiety to intimidate him, &c., were the invisible chains that held his hand bound to the fire. The love of glory, enthusiasm for their country, in like manner caused Codrus and Decius to devote themselves for their fellow-citizens. The Indian Colanus and the philosopher Peregrinus were equally obliged to burn themselves, by desire of exciting the astonishment of the Grecian assembly.

which does not depend upon himself, prevents his having courage. In this case, the coward is insulted in despite of himself; and against his will is obliged patiently to brook the insult he has received.

The partisans of the system of free agency appear ever to have confounded constraint with necessity. Man believes he acts as a free agent, every time he does not see any thing that places obstacles to his actions; he does not perceive that the motive which causes him to will, is always necessary and independent of himself. A prisoner loaded with chains is compelled to remain in prison; but he is not a free agent in the desire to emancipate himself; his chains prevent him from acting, but they do not prevent him from willing; he would save himself if they would loose his fetters; but he would not save himself as a free agent; fear or the idea of punishment would be sufficient motives for his action.

Man may, therefore, cease to be restrained, without, for that reason, becoming a free agent: in whatever manner he acts, he will act necessarily, according to motives by which he shall be determined. He may be compared to a heavy body that finds itself arrested in its descent by any obstacle whatever: take away this obstacle, it will gravitate or continue to fall; but who shall say this dense body is free to fall or not? Is not its descent the necessary effect of its own specific gravity? The virtuous Socrates submitted to the laws of his country, although they were unjust; and though the doors of his jail were left open to him, he would not save himself; but in this he did not act as a free agent: the invisible chains of opinion, the secret love of decorum, the inward respect for the laws, even when they are iniquitous, the fear of tarnishing his glory, kept him in his prison; they were motives sufficiently powerful with this enthusiast for virtue, to induce him to wait death with tranquillity; it was not in his power to save himself, because he could find no potential motive to bring him to depart, even for an instant, from those principles to which his mind was accustomed.

Man, it is said, frequently acts against his inclination, from whence it is falsely concluded he is a free agent; but when he appears to act contrary to his inclination, he is always determined to it by some motive sufficiently efficacious to vanquish this inclination. A sick man, with a view to his cure, arrives at conquering his repugnance to the most disgusting remedies: the fear of pain, or the dread of death, then become necessary motives; consequently this sick man cannot be said to act freely.

When it is said, that man is not a free agent, it is not pretended to compare him to a body moved by a simple impulsive cause: he contains within himself causes inherent to his existence; he is moved by an interior organ, which has its own peculiar laws, and is itself necessarily determined in consequence of ideas formed from perceptions resulting from sensations which it receives from exterior objects. As the mechanism of these sensations, of these perceptions, and the manner they engrave ideas on the brain of man, are not known to him; because he is unable to unravel all these motions; because he cannot perceive the chain of operations in his soul, or the motive principle that acts within him, he supposes himself a free agent; which, literally translated, signifies, that he moves himself by himself; that he determines himself without cause: when he rather ought to say, that he is ignorant how or for why he acts in the manner he does. It is true the soul enjoys an activity peculiar to itself; but it is equally certain that this activity would never be displayed, if some motive or some cause did not put it in a condition to exercise itself: at least it will not be pretended that the soul is able either to love or to hate without being moved, without knowing the objects, without having some idea of their qualities. Gunpowder has unquestionably a particular activity, but this activity will never display itself, unless fire be applied to it; this, however, immediately sets it in motion.

It is the great complication of motion in man, it is the variety of his action, it is the multiplicity of causes that move him, whether simultaneously or in continual succession, that persuades him he is a free agent: if all his motions were simple, if the causes that move him did not confound themselves with each other, if they were distinct, if his machine were less complicated, he would perceive that all his actions were necessary, because he would be enabled to recur instantly to the cause that made him act. A man who should be always obliged to go towards the west, would always go on that side; but he would feel that, in so going, he was not a free agent: if he had another sense, as his actions or his motion, augmented by a sixth, would be still more varied and much more complicated, he would believe himself still more a free agent than he does with his five senses.

It is, then, for want of recurring to the causes that move him; for want of being able to analyze, from not being competent to decompose the complicated motion of his machine, that man believes himself a free agent; it is only upon his own ignorance that he founds the profound yet deceitful notion he has of his free agency; that he builds those opinions which he brings forward as a striking proof of his pretended freedom of action. If, for a short time, each man was willing to examine his own peculiar actions, search out their true motives to discover their concatenation, he would remain convinced that the sentiment he has of his natural free agency, is a chimera that must speedily be destroyed by experience.

Nevertheless it must be acknowledged that the multiplicity and diversity of the causes which continually act upon man, frequently without even his knowledge, render it impossible, or at least extremely difficult for him to recur to the true principles of his own peculiar actions, much less the actions of others: they frequently depend upon causes so fugitive, so remote from their effects, and which, superficially examined, appear to have so little analogy, so slender a relation with them, that it requires singular sagacity to bring them into light. This is what renders the study of the moral man a task of such difficulty; this is the reason why his heart is an abyss, of which it is frequently impossible for him to fathom the depth. He is then obliged to content himself with a knowledge of the general and necessary laws by which the human heart is regulated: for the individuals of his own species these laws are pretty nearly the same; they vary only in consequence of the organization that is peculiar to each, and of the modification it undergoes: this, however, cannot be rigorously the same in any two. It suffices to know, that by his essence, man tends to conserve himself, and to render his existence happy: this granted, whatever may be his actions, if he recur back to this first principle, to this general, this necessary tendency of his will, he never can be deceived with regard to his motives.

38. **C. A. Campbell**

C. A. Campbell is Professor Emeritus at the University of Glasgow.

Free Will Rules Out Determinism

1. During the greater part of the last lecture, which was concerned with the defence of the notion of self-activity and with the classification of its main species, we were operating on the very threshold of the problem of Free Will; and in its later stages, particularly in connection with the analysis of moral-decision activity, we may perhaps be judged to have passed beyond the threshold. The present lecture, in which we address ourselves formally to the Free Will problem, is in fact so closely continuous with its predecessor that I should wish the two lectures to be regarded as constituting, in a real sense, a single unit.

In the later, more constructive part of my programme today this intimate dependence upon what has gone before will become very apparent. My initial task, however, must be one of elucidation and definition. The general question I have to try to answer, a question which is very far indeed from admitting of a ready answer is, What precisely *is* the Free Will problem?

It is something of a truism that in philosophic enquiry the exact formulation of a problem often takes one a long way on the road to its

From Lecture IX, "Has the Self 'Free Will'?" of *On Selfhood and Godhood* (1957). Reprinted by permission of the publisher, George Allen & Unwin, Ltd., and Humanities Press, Inc.

solution. In the case of the Free Will problem I think there is a rather special need of careful formulation. For there are many sorts of human freedom; and it can easily happen that one wastes a great deal of labour in proving or disproving a freedom which has almost nothing to do with the freedom which is at issue in the traditional problem of Free Will. The abortiveness of so much of the argument for and against Free Will in contemporary philosophical literature seems to me due in the main to insufficient pains being taken over the preliminary definition of the problem. There is, indeed, one outstanding exception, Professor Broad's brilliant inaugural lecture entitled, 'Determinism, Indeterminism, and Libertarianism,'[1] in which forty-three pages are devoted to setting out the problem, as against seven of its solution! I confess that the solution does not seem to myself to follow upon the formulation quite as easily as all that:[2] but Professor Broad's eminent example fortifies me in my decision to give here what may seem at first sight a disproportionate amount of time to the business of determining the essential characteristics of the kind of freedom with which the traditional problem is concerned.

Fortunately we can at least make a beginning with a certain amount of confidence. It is not seriously disputable that the kind of freedom in question is the freedom which is commonly recognised to be in some sense a precondition of moral responsibility. Clearly, it is on account of this integral connection with moral responsibility that such exceptional importance has always been felt to attach to the Free Will problem. But in what precise sense is free will a precondition of moral responsibility, and thus a postulate of the moral life in general? This is an exceedingly troublesome question; but until we have satisfied ourselves about the answer to it, we are not in a position to state, let alone decide, the question whether 'Free Will' in its traditional, ethical, significance is a reality.

Our first business, then, is to ask, exactly what kind of freedom is it which is required for moral responsibility? And as to method of procedure in this inquiry, there seems to me to be no real choice. I know of only one method that carries with it any hope of success; viz. the critical comparison of those acts for which, on due reflection, we deem it proper to attribute moral praise or blame to the agents, with those acts for which, on due reflection, we deem such judgments to be improper. The ultimate touchstone, as I see it, can only be our moral consciousness as it manifests itself in our more critical and considered moral judgments. The 'linguistic' approach by way of the analysis of moral *sentences* seems to me, despite its present popularity, to be an almost infallible method for reaching wrong results in the moral field; but I must reserve what I have to say about this for the next lecture.

2.   The first point to note is that the freedom at issue (as indeed the very name 'Free *Will* Problem' indicates) pertains primarily not to overt acts but to inner acts. The nature of things has decreed that, save in the case

1. Reprinted in *Ethics and the History of Philosophy, Selected Essays.*
2. I have explained the grounds for my dissent from Broad's final conclusions on pp. 27 ff. of *In Defence of Free Will* (Jackson Son & Co., 1938).

of one's self, it is only overt acts which one can directly observe. But a very little reflection serves to show that in our moral judgments upon others their overt acts are regarded as significant only in so far as they are the expression of inner acts. We do not consider the acts of a robot to be morally responsible acts; nor do we consider the acts of a man to be so save in so far as they are distinguishable from those of a robot by reflecting an inner life of choice. Similarly, from the other side, if we are satisfied (as we may on occasion be, at least in the case of ourselves) that a person has definitely elected to follow a course which he believes to be wrong, but has been prevented by external circumstances from translating his inner choice into an overt act, we still regard him as morally blameworthy. Moral freedom, then, pertains to *inner* acts.

The next point seems at first sight equally obvious and uncontroversial; but, as we shall see, it has awkward implications if we are in real earnest with it (as almost nobody is). It is the simple point that the act must be one of which the person judged can be regarded as the *sole* author. It seems plain enough that if there are any *other* determinants of the act, external to the self, to that extent the act is not an act which the *self* determines, and to that extent not an act for which the self can be held morally responsible. The self is only part-author of the act, and his moral responsibility can logically extend only to those elements within the act (assuming for the moment that these can be isolated) of which he is the *sole* author.

The awkward implications of this apparent truism will be readily appreciated. For, if we are mindful of the influences exerted by heredity and environment, we may well feel some doubt whether there is any act of will at all of which one can truly say that the self is sole author, sole determinant. No man has a voice in determining the raw material of impulses and capacities that constitute his hereditary endowment, and no man has more than a very partial control of the material and social environment in which he is destined to live his life. Yet it would be manifestly absurd to deny that these two factors do constantly and profoundly affect the nature of a man's choices. That this is so we all of us recognise in our moral judgments when we 'make allowances,' as we say, for a bad heredity or a vicious environment, and acknowledge in the victim of them a diminished moral responsibility for evil courses. Evidently we do *try*, in our moral judgments, however crudely, to praise or blame a man only in respect of that of which we can regard him as *wholly* the author. And evidently we do recognise that, for a man to be the author of an act in the full sense required for moral responsibility, it is not enough merely that he 'wills' or 'chooses' the act: since even the most unfortunate victim of heredity or environment does, as a rule, 'will' what he does. It is significant, however, that the ordinary man, though well enough aware of the influence upon choices of heredity and environment, does not feel obliged thereby to give up his assumption that moral predicates *are* somehow applicable. Plainly he still believes that there is *something* for which a man is morally responsible, something of which we can fairly say that he is the sole author. *What is this something?* To that question common-sense is not ready with an explicit answer—

though an answer is, I think, implicit in the line which its moral judgments take. I shall do what I can to give an explicit answer later in this lecture. Meantime it must suffice to observe that, if we are to be true to the deliverances of our moral consciousness, it is very difficult to deny that *sole* authorship is a necessary condition of the morally responsible act.

Thirdly we come to a point over which much recent controversy has raged. We may approach it by raising the following question. Granted an act of which the agent is sole author, does this 'sole authorship' suffice to make the act a morally free act? We may be inclined to think that it does, until we contemplate the possibility that an act of which the agent is sole author might conceivably occur as a necessary expression of the agent's nature; the way in which, e.g. some philosophers have supposed the Divine act of creation to occur. This consideration excites a legitimate doubt; for it is far from easy to see how a person can be regarded as a proper subject for moral praise or blame in respect of an act which he *cannot help* performing—even if it be his own 'nature' which necessitates it. Must we not recognise it as a condition of the morally free act that the agent 'could have acted otherwise' than he in fact did? It is true, indeed, that we sometimes praise or blame a man for an act about which we are prepared to say, in the light of our knowledge of his established character, that he 'could no other.' But I think that a little reflection shows that in such cases we are not praising or blaming the man strictly for what he does *now* (or at any rate we ought not to be), but rather for those past acts of his which have generated the firm habit of mind from which his *present* act follows 'necessarily.' In other words, our praise and blame, so far as justified, are really retrospective, being directed not to the agent *qua* performing *this* act, but to the agent *qua* performing those past acts which have built up his present character, and in respect to which we presume that he *could* have acted otherwise, that there really *were* open possibilities before him. These cases, therefore, seem to me to constitute no valid exception to what I must take to be the rule, viz. that a man can be morally praised or blamed for an act only if he could have acted otherwise.

Now philosophers today are fairly well agreed that it is a postulate of the morally responsible act that the agent 'could have acted otherwise' in *some* sense of that phrase. But sharp differences of opinion have arisen over the way in which the phrase ought to be interpreted. There is a strong disposition to water down its apparent meaning by insisting that it is not (as a postulate of moral responsibility) to be understood as a straightforward categorical proposition, but rather as a disguised hypothetical proposition. All that we really require to be assured of, in order to justify our holding X morally responsible for an act, is, we are told, that X could have acted otherwise *if* he had *chosen* otherwise (Moore, Stevenson); or perhaps that X could have acted otherwise *if* he had had a different character, or *if* he had been placed in different circumstances.

I think it is easy to understand, and even, in a measure, to sympathise with, the motives which induce philosophers to offer these counter-interpretations. It is not just the fact that 'X could have acted otherwise,' as a bald categorical statement, is incompatible with the universal sway of causal law—though this is, to some philosophers, a serious stone of stumbling. The more widespread objection is that it at least looks as though it were incompatible with that causal continuity of an agent's character with his conduct which is implied when we believe (surely with justice) that we can often tell the sort of thing a man will do from our knowledge of the sort of man he is.

We shall have to make our accounts with that particular difficulty later. At this stage I wish merely to show that neither of the hypothetical propositions suggested—and I think the same could be shown for *any* hypothetical alternative—is an acceptable substitute for the categorical proposition 'X could have acted otherwise' as the presupposition of moral responsibility.

Let us look first at the earlier suggestion—'X could have acted otherwise *if* he had chosen otherwise.' Now clearly there are a great many acts with regard to which we are entirely satisfied that the agent is thus situated. We are often perfectly sure that—for this is all it amounts to— if X had chosen otherwise, the circumstances presented no external obstacle to the translation of that choice into action. For example, we often have no doubt at all that X, who in point of fact told a lie, could have told the truth *if* he had so chosen. But does our confidence on this score allay all legitimate doubts about whether X is really blameworthy? Does it entail that X is free in the sense required for moral responsibility? Surely not. The obvious question immediately arises: 'But *could* X have *chosen* otherwise than he did?' It is doubt about the true answer to *that* question which leads most people to doubt the reality of moral responsibility. Yet on this crucial question the hypothetical proposition which is offered as a sufficient statement of the condition justifying the ascription of moral responsibility gives us no information whatsoever.

Indeed this hypothetical substitute for the categorical 'X could have acted otherwise' seems to me to lack all plausibility unless one contrives to forget why it is, after all, that we ever come to feel fundamental doubts about man's moral responsibility. Such doubts are born, surely, when one becomes aware of certain reputable world-views in religion or philosophy, or of certain reputable scientific beliefs, which in their several ways imply that man's actions are necessitated, and thus could not be otherwise than they in fact are. But clearly a doubt so based is not even touched by the recognition that a man could very often act otherwise *if* he so chose. That proposition is entirely compatible with the necessitarian theories which generate our doubt: indeed it is this very compatibility that has recommended it to some philosophers, who are reluctant to give up either moral responsibility or Determinism. The proposition which we *must* be able to affirm if moral praise or blame of X is to be justified is the categorical proposition that X could have acted otherwise because—not if—he could have chosen otherwise; or, since it is essentially the inner side of the act that matters, the proposition simply that X could have chosen otherwise.

For the second of the alternative formulae suggested we cannot spare more than a few moments. But its inability to meet the demands it is required to meet is almost transparent. 'X could have acted otherwise,' as a statement of a precondition of X's moral responsibility, really means (we are told) 'X could have acted otherwise *if* he were differently constituted, or *if* he had been placed in different circumstances.' It seems a sufficient reply to this to point out that the person whose moral responsibility is at issue is X; a specific individual, in a specific set of circumstances. It is totally irrelevant to X's moral responsibility that we should be able to say that some person differently constituted from X, or X in a different set of circumstances, could have done something different from what X did.

3. Let me, then, briefly sum up the answer at which we have arrived to our question about the kind of freedom required to justify moral responsibility. It is that a man can be said to exercise free will in a morally significant sense only in so far as his chosen act is one of which he is the sole cause or author, and only if—in the straightforward, categorical sense of the phrase—he 'could have chosen otherwise.'

I confess that this answer is in some ways a disconcerting one, disconcerting, because most of us, however objective we are in the actual conduct of our thinking, would *like* to be able to believe that moral responsibility is real: whereas the freedom required for moral responsibility, on the analysis we have given, is certainly far more difficult to establish than the freedom required on the analyses we found ourselves obliged to reject. If, e.g., moral freedom entails only that I could have acted otherwise *if* I had chosen otherwise, there is no real 'problem' about it at all. I am 'free' in the normal case where there is no external obstacle to prevent my translating the alternative choice into action, and not free in other cases. Still less is there a problem if all that moral freedom entails is that I could have acted otherwise *if* I had been a differently constituted person, or been in different circumstances. Clearly I am *always* free in *this* sense of freedom. But, as I have argued, these so-called 'freedoms' fail to give us the pre-conditions of moral responsibility, and hence leave the freedom of the traditional free-will problem, the freedom that people are really concerned about, precisely where it was.

5. That brings me to the second, and more constructive, part of this lecture. From now on I shall be considering whether it is reasonable to believe that man does in fact possess a free will of the kind specified in the first part of the lecture. If so, just how and where within the complex fabric of the volitional life are we to locate it?—for although free will must presumably belong (if anywhere) to the volitional side of human experience, it is pretty clear from the way in which we have been forced to define it that it does not pertain simply to volition as such; not even to all volitions that are commonly dignified with the name of 'choices.' It has been, I think, one of the more serious impediments to profitable discussion of the Free Will problem that Libertarians and Determinists alike have so often failed to appreciate the comparatively narrow area within which the free will that is necessary to 'save' morality is required

to operate. It goes without saying that this failure has been gravely prejudicial to the case for Libertarianism. I attach a good deal of importance, therefore, to the problem of locating free will correctly within the volitional orbit. Its solution forestalls and annuls, I believe, some of the more tiresome clichés of Determinist criticism.

We saw earlier that Common Sense's practice of 'making allowances' in its moral judgments for the influence of heredity and environment indicates Common Sense's conviction, both that a just moral judgment must discount determinants of choice over which the agent has no control, and also (since it still accepts moral judgments as legitimate) that *something* of moral relevance survives which can be regarded as genuinely self-originated. We are now to try to discover what this 'something' is. And I think we may still usefully take Common Sense as our guide. Suppose one asks the ordinary intelligent citizen *why* he deems it proper to make allowances for X, whose heredity and/or environment are unfortunate. He will tend to reply, I think, in some such terms as these: that X has more and stronger temptations to deviate from what is right than Y or Z, who are normally circumstanced, so that he must put forth *a stronger moral effort* if he is to achieve the same level of external conduct. The intended implication seems to be that X is just as morally praiseworthy as Y or Z *if* he exerts an equivalent moral effort, even though he may not thereby achieve an equal success in conforming his will to the 'concrete' demands of duty. And this implies, again, Common Sense's belief that *in moral effort* we have something for which a man is responsible *without qualification*, something that is *not* affected by heredity and environment but depends *solely* upon the self itself.

Now in my opinion Common Sense has here, in principle, hit upon the one and only defensible answer. Here, and here alone, so far as I can see, in the act of deciding whether to put forth or withhold the moral effort required to resist temptation and rise to duty, is to be found an act which is free in the sense required for moral responsibility; an act of which the self is sole author, and of which it is true to say that 'it could be' (or, after the event, 'could have been') 'otherwise.' Such is the thesis which we shall now try to establish.

6. The species of argument appropriate to the establishment of a thesis of this sort should fall, I think, into two phases. First, there should be a consideration of the evidence of the moral agent's own inner experience. What *is* the act of moral decision, and what does it imply, from the standpoint of the actual participant? Since there is no way of knowing the act of moral decision—or for that matter any other form of activity —except by actual participation in it, the evidence of the subject, or agent, is on an issue of this kind of primary importance. It can hardly, however, be taken as in itself conclusive. For even if that evidence should be overwhelmingly to the effect that moral decision does have the characteristics required by moral freedom, the question is bound to be raised —and in view of considerations from other quarters pointing in a contrary direction is *rightly* raised—Can we *trust* the evidence of inner experience? That brings us to what will be the second phase of the argu-

ment. We shall have to go on to show, if we are to make good our case, that the extraneous considerations so often supposed to be fatal to the belief in moral freedom are in fact innocuous to it.

In the light of what was said in the last lecture about the self's experience of moral decision as a *creative* activity, we may perhaps be absolved from developing the first phase of the argument at any great length. The appeal is throughout to one's own experience in the actual taking of the moral decision in the situation of moral temptation. 'Is it possible,' we must ask, 'for anyone so circumstanced to *dis*believe that we could be deciding otherwise?' The answer is surely not in doubt. When we decide to exert moral effort to resist a temptation, we feel quite certain that we *could* withhold the effort; just as, if we decide to withhold the effort and yield to our desires, we feel quite certain that we *could* exert it—otherwise we should not blame ourselves afterwards for having succumbed. It may be, indeed, that this conviction is mere self-delusion. But that is not at the moment our concern. It is enough at present to establish that the act of deciding to exert or to withhold moral effort, as we know it from the inside in actual moral living, belongs to the category of acts which 'could have been otherwise.'

Mutatis mutandis, the same reply is forthcoming if we ask, 'Is it possible for the moral agent in the taking of his decision to *dis*believe that he is the *sole* author of that decision?' Clearly he cannot disbelieve that it is *he* who takes the decision. That, however, is not in itself sufficient to enable him, on reflection, to regard himself as *solely* responsible for the act. For his 'character' as so far formed might conceivably be a factor in determining it, and no one can suppose that the constitution of his 'character' is uninfluenced by circumstances of heredity and environment with which *he* has nothing to do. But as we pointed out in the last lecture, the very essence of the moral decision as it is experienced is that it is a decision whether or not to *combat* our strongest desire, and our strongest desire *is* the expression in the situation of our character as so far formed. Now clearly our character cannot be a factor in determining the decision whether or not to *oppose* our character. I think we are entitled to say, therefore, that the act of moral decision is one in which the self is for itself not merely 'author' but 'sole author.'

7. We may pass on, then, to the second phase of our constructive argument; and this will demand more elaborate treatment. Even if a moral agent *qua* making a moral decision in the situation of 'temptation' cannot help believing that he has free will in the sense at issue—a moral freedom between real alternatives, between genuinely open possibilities—are there, nevertheless, objections to a freedom of this kind so cogent that we are bound to distrust the evidence of 'inner experience?'

I begin by drawing attention to a simple point whose significance tends, I think, to be under-estimated. If the phenomenological analysis we have offered is substantially correct, no one while functioning as a moral agent can help believing that he enjoys free will. Theoretically he may be completely convinced by Determinist arguments, but when actually confronted with a personal situation of conflict between duty and desire he is quite certain that it lies with him here and now whether or not he will rise to duty. It follows that if Determinists could produce convincing theoretical arguments against a free will of this kind, the awkward predicament would ensue that man has to deny as a theoretical being what he has to assert as a practical being. Now I think the Determinist ought to be a good deal more worried about this than he usually is. He seems to imagine that a strong case on general theoretical grounds is enough to prove that the 'practical' belief in free will, even if inescapable for us as practical beings, is mere illusion. But in fact it proves nothing of the sort. There is no reason whatever why a belief that we find ourselves obliged to hold *qua* practical beings should be required to give way before a belief which we find ourselves obliged to hold *qua* theoretical beings; or, for that matter, *vice versa*. All that the theoretical arguments of Determinism can prove, unless they are reinforced by a refutation of the phenomenological analysis that supports Libertarianism, is that there is a radical conflict between the theoretical and the practical sides of man's nature, an antimony at the very heart of the self. And this is a state of affairs with which no one can easily rest satisfied. I think therefore that the Determinist ought to concern himself a great deal more than he does with phenomenological analysis, in order to show, if he can, that the assurance of free will is not really an inexpugnable element in man's practical consciousness. There is just as much obligation upon him, convinced though he may be of the soundness of his theoretical arguments, to expose the errors of the Libertarian's phenomenological analysis, as there is upon us, convinced though we may be of the soundness of the Libertarian's phenomenological analysis, to expose the errors of the Determinist's theoretical arguments.

8. However, we must at once begin the discharge of our own obligation. The rest of this lecture will be devoted to trying to show that the arguments which seem to carry most weight with Determinists are, to say the least of it, very far from compulsive.

Fortunately a good many of the arguments which at an earlier time in the history of philosophy would have been strongly urged against us make almost no appeal to the bulk of philosophers today, and we may here pass them by. That applies to any criticism of 'open possibilities' based on a metaphysical theory about the nature of the universe as a whole. Nobody today *has* a metaphysical theory about the nature of the universe as a whole! It applies also, with almost equal force, to criticisms based upon the universality of causal law as a supposed postulate of science. There have always been, in my opinion, sound philosophic reasons for doubting the validity, as distinct from the convenience, of the causal postulate in its universal form, but at the present time, when scientists themselves are deeply divided about the need for postulating causality even within their own special field, we shall do better to concentrate our attention upon criticisms which are more confidently advanced. I propose to ignore also, on different grounds, the type of criticism of free will that is sometimes advanced from the side of religion, based upon religious postulates of Divine Omnipotence and Omniscience. So far as I can see, a postulate of human freedom is every bit as necessary to meet certain religious demands (e.g. to make sense of the 'conviction of sin'), as postulates of Divine Omniscience and Omnipotence are to meet certain other religious demands. If so, then it can hardly be argued that religious experience as such tells more strongly against than for the position we are defending; and we may be satisfied, in the present context, to leave the matter there. It will be more profitable to discuss certain arguments which contemporary philosophers do think important, and which recur with a somewhat monotonous regularity in the literature of anti-Libertarianism.

These arguments can, I think, be reduced in principle to no more than two: first, the argument from 'predictability'; second, the argument from the alleged meaninglessness of an act supposed to be the self's act and yet not an expression of the self's character. Contemporary criticism of free will seems to me to consist almost exclusively of variations of these two themes. I shall deal with each in turn.

9. On the first we touched in passing at an earlier stage. Surely it is beyond question (the critic urges) that when we know a person intimately we can foretell with a high degree of accuracy how he will respond to at least a large number of practical situations. One feels safe in predicting that one's dog-loving friend will not use his boot to repel the little mongrel that comes yapping at his heels; or again that one's wife will not pass with incurious eyes (or indeed pass at all) the new hat-shop in the city. So to behave would not be (as we say) 'in character.' But, so the criticism runs, you with your doctrine of 'genuinely open possibilities,' of a free will by which the self can diverge from its own character, remove all rational basis from such prediction. You require us to make the absurd supposition that the success of countless predictions of the sort in the past has been mere matter of chance. If you *really* believed in your theory, you would not be surprised if tomorrow your friend with the notorious horror of strong drink should suddenly exhibit a passion for whisky and soda, or if your friend whose taste for reading has hitherto been satisfied with the sporting columns of the newspapers should be discovered on a fine Saturday afternoon poring over the works of Hegel. But of course you *would* be surprised. Social life would be sheer chaos if there were not well-grounded social expectations; and social life is not sheer chaos. Your theory is hopelessly wrecked upon obvious facts.

Now whether or not this criticism holds good against some versions of Libertarian theory I need not here discuss. It is sufficient if I can make it clear that against the version advanced in this lecture, according to which free will is localised in a relatively narrow field of operation, the criticism has no relevance whatsoever.

Let us remind ourselves briefly of the setting within which, on our view, free will functions. There is X, the course which we believe we ought to follow, and Y, the course towards which we feel our desire is strongest. The freedom which we ascribe to the agent is the freedom to put forth or refrain from putting forth the moral effort required to resist the pressure of desire and do what he thinks he ought to do.

But then there is surely an immense range of practical situations—covering by far the greater part of life—in which there is no question of a conflict within the self between what he most desires to do and what he thinks he ought to do? Indeed such conflict is a comparatively rare phenomenon for the majority of men. Yet over that whole vast range there is nothing whatever in our version of Libertarianism to prevent our agreeing that character determines conduct. In the absence, real or supposed, of any 'moral' issue, what a man chooses will be simply that course which, after such reflection as seems called for, he deems most likely to bring him what he most strongly desires; and that is the same as to say the course to which his present character inclines him.

Over by far the greater area of human choices, then, our theory offers no more barrier to successful prediction on the basis of character than any other theory. For where there is no clash of strongest desire with duty, the free will we are defending has no business. There is just nothing for it to do.

But what about the situations—rare enough though they may be—in which there *is* this clash and in which free will does therefore operate? Does our theory entail that there at any rate, as the critic seems to suppose, 'anything may happen'?

Not by any manner of means. In the first place, and by the very nature of the case, the range of the agent's possible choices is bounded by what he thinks he ought to do on the one hand, and what he most strongly desires on the other. The freedom claimed for him is a freedom of decision to make or withhold the effort required to do what he thinks he ought to do. There is no question of a freedom to act in some 'wild' fashion, out of all relation to his characteristic beliefs and desires. This so-called 'freedom of caprice,' so often charged against the Libertarian, is, to put it bluntly, a sheer figment of the critic's imagination, with no *habitat* in serious Libertarian theory. Even in situations where free will does come into play it is perfectly possible, on a view like ours, given the appropriate knowledge of a man's character, to predict within certain limits how he will respond.

But 'probable' prediction in such situations can, I think, go further than this. It is obvious that where desire and duty are at odds, the felt 'gap' (as it were) between the two may vary enormously in breadth in different cases. The moderate drinker and the chronic tippler may each want another glass, and each deems it his duty to abstain, but the felt gap between desire and duty in the case of the former is trivial beside the great gulf which is felt to separate them in the case of the latter. Hence it will take a far harder moral effort for the tippler than for the moderate drinker to achieve the same external result of abstention. So much is matter of common agreement. And we are entitled, I think, to take it into account in prediction, on the simple principle that the harder the moral effort required to resist desire the less likely it is to occur. Thus in the example taken, most people would predict that the tippler will very probably succumb to his desires, whereas there is a reasonable likelihood that the moderate drinker will make the comparatively slight effort needed to resist them. So long as the prediction does not pretend to more than a measure of probability, there is nothing in our theory which would disallow it.

I claim, therefore, that the view of free will I have been putting forward is consistent with predictability of conduct on the basis of character over a very wide field indeed. And I make the further claim that that field will cover all the situations in life concerning which there is any empirical evidence that successful prediction is possible.

10. Let us pass on to consider the second main line of criticism. This is, I think, much the more illuminating of the two, if only because it compels the Libertarian to make explicit certain concepts which are indispensable to him, but which, being desperately hard to state clearly, are apt not to be stated at all. The critic's fundamental point might be stated somewhat as follows:

'Free will as you describe it is completely unintelligible. On your own showing no *reason* can be given, because there just *is* no reason, why a man decides to exert rather than to withhold moral effort, or *vice versa*. But such an act—or more properly, such an "occurrence"—it is nonsense to speak of as an act of a *self*. If there is nothing in the self's character to which it is, even in principle, in any way traceable, the self has nothing to do with it. Your so-called "freedom," therefore, so far from supporting the self's moral responsibility, destroys it as surely as the crudest Determinism could do.'

If we are to discuss this criticism usefully, it is important, I think, to begin by getting clear about two different senses of the word 'intelligible.'

If, in the first place, we mean by an 'intelligible' act one whose occurrence is in principle capable of being inferred, since it follows necessarily from something (though we may not know in fact from what), then it is certainly true that the Libertarian's free will is unintelligible. But that is only saying, is it not, that the Libertarian's 'free' act is not an act which follows necessarily from something! This can hardly rank as a *criticism* of Libertarianism. It is just a description of it. That there can be nothing unintelligible in *this* sense is precisely what the Determinist has got to *prove*.

Yet it is surprising how often the critic of Libertarianism involves himself in this circular mode of argument. Repeatedly it is urged against the Libertarian, with a great air of triumph, that on his view he can't say *why* I now decide to rise to duty, or now decide to follow my strongest desire in defiance of duty. Of course he can't. If he could he wouldn't *be* a Libertarian. To 'account for' a 'free' act is a contradiction in terms. A free will is *ex hypothesi* the sort of thing of which the request for an *explanation* is absurd. The assumption that an explanation must be in principle possible for the act of moral decision deserves to rank as a classic example of the ancient fallacy of 'begging the question.'

But the critic usually has in mind another sense of the word 'unintelligible.' He is apt to take it for granted that an act which is unintelligible in the *above* sense (as the morally free act of the Libertarian undoubtedly is) is unintelligible in the *further* sense that we can attach no meaning to it. And this is an altogether more serious matter. If it could really be shown that the Libertarian's 'free will' were unintelligible in this sense of being meaningless, that, for myself at any rate, would be the end of the affair. Libertarianism would have been conclusively refuted.

But it seems to me manifest that this can *not* be shown. The critic has allowed himself, I submit, to become the victim of a widely accepted but fundamentally vicious assumption. He has assumed that whatever is meaningful must exhibit its meaningfulness to those who view it from the standpoint of external observation. Now if one chooses thus to limit one's self to the rôle of external observer, it is, I think, perfectly true that one can attach no meaning to an act which is the act of something we call a 'self' and yet follows from nothing in that self's character. But then *why should we* so limit ourselves, when what is under consideration is a subjective activity? For the apprehension of subjective acts there is *another* standpoint available, that of *inner experience*, of the practical consciousness in its actual functioning. If our free will should turn out to be something to which we can attach a meaning from *this* standpoint, no more is required. And no more ought to be expected. For I must repeat that only from the inner standpoint of living experience *could* anything of the nature of 'activity' be directly grasped. Observation from without is in the nature of the case impotent to apprehend the active *qua* active. We can from without observe sequences of states. If into these we read activity (as we sometimes do), this can only be on the basis of what we discern in ourselves from the inner standpoint. It follows that if anyone insists upon taking his criterion of the meaningful simply from the standpoint of external observation, he is really deciding in advance of the evidence that the notion of activity, and *a fortiori* the notion of a free will, is 'meaningless.' He looks for the free act through a medium which is in the nature of the case incapable of revealing it, and then, because inevitably he doesn't find it, he declares that it doesn't exist!

But if, as we surely ought in this context, we adopt the inner standpoint, then (I am suggesting) things appear in a totally different light. From the inner standpoint, it seems to me plain, there is no difficulty whatever in attaching meaning to an act which is the self's act and which nevertheless does not follow from the self's character. So much I claim has been established by the phenomenological analysis, in this and the previous lecture, of the act of moral decision in face of moral temptation. It is thrown into particularly clear relief where the moral decision is to make the moral effort required to rise to duty. For the very function of moral effort, as it appears to the agent engaged in the act, is to enable the self to act against the line of least resistance, against the line to which his character as so far formed most strongly inclines him. But if the self is thus conscious here of *combating* his formed character, he surely cannot possibly suppose that the act, although his own act, *issues from* his formed character? I submit, therefore, that the self knows very well indeed—from the inner standpoint—what is meant by an act which is the *self's* act and which nevertheless does not follow from the self's *character*.

What this implies—and it seems to me to be an implication of cardinal importance for any theory of the self that aims at being more than superficial—is that the nature of the self is for itself something more than just its character as so far formed. The 'nature' of the self and what we commonly call the 'character' of the self are by no means the same thing, and it is utterly vital that they should not be confused. The 'nature' of the self comprehends, but is not without remainder reducible to, its 'character'; it must, if we are to be true to the testimony of our experience of it, be taken as including *also* the authentic creative power of fashioning and re-fashioning 'character.'

The misguided, and as a rule quite uncritical, belittlement, of the evidence offered by inner experience has, I am convinced, been responsible for more bad argument by the opponents of Free Will than has any other single factor. How often, for example, do we find the Determinist critic saying, in effect, '*Either* the act follows necessarily upon precedent states, *or* it is a mere matter of chance and accordingly of no moral significance.' The disjunction is invalid, for it does not exhaust the possible alternatives. It seems to the critic to do so only because he *will* limit himself to the standpoint which is proper, and indeed alone possible, in dealing with the physical world, the standpoint of the external observer. If only he would allow himself to assume the standpoint which is not merely proper for, but necessary to, the apprehension of subjective activity, the inner standpoint of the practical consciousness in its actual functioning, he would find himself obliged to recognise the falsity of his disjunction. Reflection upon the act of moral decision as apprehended from the inner standpoint would force him to recognise a *third* possibility, as remote from chance as from necessity, that, namely, of *creative activity*, in which (as I have ventured to express it) nothing determines the act save the agent's doing of it.

11. There we must leave the matter. But as this lecture has been, I know, somewhat densely packed, it may be helpful if I conclude by reminding you, in bald summary, of the main things I have been trying to say. Let me set them out in so many successive theses.

1. The freedom which is at issue in the traditional Free Will problem is the freedom which is presupposed in moral responsibility.
2. Critical reflection upon carefully considered attributions of moral responsibility reveals that the only freedom that will do is a freedom which pertains to inner acts of choice, and that these acts must be acts (*a*) of which the self is *sole* author, and (*b*) which the self could have performed otherwise.
3. From phenomenological analysis of the situation of moral temptation we find that the self as engaged in this situation is inescapably convinced that it possesses a freedom of precisely the specified kind, located in the decision to exert or withhold the moral effort needed to rise to duty where the pressure of its desiring nature is felt to urge it in a contrary direction.
   Passing to the question of the *reality* of this moral freedom which the moral agent believes himself to possess, we argued:
4. Of the two types of Determinist criticism which seem to have most influence today, that based on the predictability of much human be-

haviour fails to touch a Libertarianism which confines the area of free will as above indicated. Libertarianism so understood is compatible with all the predictability that the empirical facts warrant. And:

5. The second main type of criticism, which alleges the 'meaninglessness' of an act which is the self's act and which is yet not determined by the self's character, is based on a failure to appreciate that the standpoint of inner experience is not only legitimate but indispensable where what is at issue is the reality and nature of a subjective activity. The creative act of moral decision is inevitably meaningless to the mere external observer; but from the inner standpoint it is as real, and as significant, as anything in human experience.

39. R. E. Hobart

"R. E. Hobart" was a pseudonym used by Dickinson Miller
(1868–1963), an American philosopher and close friend
of William James.

The Harmony of Free Will and Determinism

The thesis of this article is that there has never been any ground for the controversy between the doctrine of free will and determinism, that it is based upon a misapprehension, that the two assertions are entirely consistent, that one of them strictly implies the other, that they have been opposed only because of our natural want of the analytical imagination. In so saying I do not tamper with the meaning of either phrase. That would be unpardonable. I mean free will in the natural and usual sense, in the fullest, the most absolute sense in which for the purposes of the personal and moral life the term is ever employed. I mean it as implying responsibility, merit and demerit, guilt and desert. I mean it as implying, after an act has been performed, that one "could have done otherwise" than one did. I mean it as conveying these things also, not in any subtly modified sense but in exactly the sense in which we conceive them in life and in law and in ethics. These two doctrines have been opposed because we have not realised that free will can be analysed without being destroyed, and that determinism is merely a feature of the analysis of it.

From "Free Will as Involving Determination and Inconceivable Without It," first published in *Mind*, Vol. XLIII, No. 169, January, 1934. Pp. 1-27, *passim*. Reprinted by permission of the editor of *Mind*.

And if we are tempted to take refuge in the thought of an "ultimate," an "innermost" liberty that eludes the analysis, then we have implied a deterministic basis and constitution for this liberty as well. For such a basis and constitution lie in the idea of liberty.

. . . .

I am not maintaining that determinism is true; only that it is true in so far as we have free will. That we are free in willing is, broadly speaking, a fact of experience. That broad fact is more assured than any philosophical analysis. It is therefore surer than the deterministic analysis of it, entirely adequate as that in the end appears to be. But it is not here affirmed that there are no small exceptions, no slight undetermined swervings, no ingredient of absolute chance. All that is here said is that such absence of determination, if and so far as it exists, is no gain to freedom, but sheer loss of it; no advantage to the moral life, but blank subtraction from it.—When I speak below of "the indeterminist" I mean the libertarian indeterminist, that is, him who believes in free will and holds that it involves indetermination.

By the analytical imagination is meant, of course, the power we have, not by nature but by training, of realising that the component parts of a thing or process, taken together, each in its place, with their relations, are identical with the thing or process itself. If it is "more than its parts," then this "more" will appear in the analysis. It is not true, of course, that all facts are susceptible of analysis, but so far as they are, there is occasion for the analytical imagination. We have been accustomed to think of a thing or a person as a whole, not as a combination of parts. We have been accustomed to think of its activities as the way in which, as a whole, it naturally and obviously behaves. It is a new, an unfamiliar and an awkward act on the mind's part to consider it, not as one thing acting in its natural manner, but as a system of parts that work together in a complicated process. Analysis often seems at first to have taken away the individuality of the thing, its unity, the impression of the familiar identity. For a simple mind this is strikingly true of the analysis of a complicated machine. The reader may recall Paulsen's ever significant story about the introduction of the railway into Germany. When it reached the village of a certain enlightened pastor, he took his people to where a locomotive engine was standing, and in the clearest words explained of what parts it consisted and how it worked. He was much pleased by their eager nods of intelligence as he proceeded. But on his finishing they said: "Yes, yes, Herr Pastor, but there's a horse inside, isn't there?" They could not *realise* the analysis. They were wanting in the analytical imagination. Why not? They had never been trained to it. It is in the first instance a great effort to think of all the parts working together to produce the simple result that the engine glides down the track. It is easy to think of a horse inside doing all the work. A horse is a familiar totality that does familiar things. They could no better have grasped the physiological analysis of a horse's movements had it been set forth to them.

Now the position of the indeterminist is that a free act of will is the act of the self. The self becomes through it the author of the physical act that ensues. This volition of the self causes the physical act but it is not in its turn caused, it is "spontaneous." To regard it as caused would be determinism. The causing self to which the indeterminist here refers is to be conceived as distinct from character; distinct from temperament, wishes, habits, impulses. He emphasises two things equally: the physical act springs from the self through its volition, and it does not spring merely from character, it is not simply the result of character and circumstances. If we ask, "Was there anything that induced the self thus to act?" we are answered in effect, "Not definitively. The self feels motives but its act is not determined by them. It can choose between them."

The next thing to notice is that this position of the indeterminist is taken in defence of moral conceptions. There would be no fitness, he says, in our reproaching ourselves, in our feeling remorse, in our holding ourselves or anyone guilty, if the act in question were not the act of the self instead of a product of the machinery of motives.

We have here one of the most remarkable and instructive examples of something in which the history of philosophy abounds—of a persistent, an age-long deadlock due solely to the indisposition of the human mind to look closely into the meaning of its terms.

How do we reproach ourselves? We say to ourselves, "How negligent of me!" "How thoughtless!" "How selfish!" "How hasty and unrestrained!" "That I should have been capable even for a moment of taking such a petty, irritated view!" etc. In other words, we are attributing to ourselves at the time of the act, in some respect and measure, a bad character, and regretting it. And that is the entire point of our self-reproach. We are turning upon ourselves with disapproval and it may be with disgust; we wish we could undo what we did in the past, and, helpless to do that, feel a peculiar thwarted poignant anger and shame at ourselves that we *had it in us* to perpetrate the thing we now condemn. It is self we are reproaching, *i.e.*, self that we are viewing as bad in that it produced bad actions. Except in so far as what-it-is produced these bad actions, there is no ground for reproaching it (calling it bad) and no meaning in doing so. All self-reproach is self-judging, and all judging is imputing a character. We are blaming ourselves. If spoken, what we are thinking would be dispraise. And what are praise and dispraise? Always, everywhere, they are *descriptions* of a person (more or less explicit) with favourable or unfavourable feeling of what is described,— descriptions in terms of value comporting fact, or of fact comporting value, or of both fact and value. In moral instances they are descriptions of his character. We are morally characterising him in our minds (as above) with appropriate feelings. We are attributing to him the character that we approve and like and wish to see more of, or the contrary. All the most intimate terms of the moral life imply that the act has proceeded from *me*, the distinctive me, from the manner of man I am or was. And this is the very thing on which the libertarian lays stress. What the indeterminist prizes with all his heart, what he stoutly affirms and insists upon, is precisely what he denies, namely, that I, the concrete and specific moral being, am the author, the source of my acts. For, of course, that is determinism. To say that they come from the self is to say that they are determined by the self—the moral self, the self with a moral

quality. He gives our preferrings the bad name of the machinery of motives, but they are just what we feel in ourselves when we decide. When
he maintains that the self at the moment of decision may act to some
extent independently of motives, *and is good or bad according as it acts
in this direction or that*, he is simply setting up one character within
another, he is separating the self from what he understands by the person's character as at first mentioned, only thereupon to attribute to it a
character of its own, *in that he judges it good or bad*.

The whole controversy is maintained by the indeterminist in order
to defend the validity of the terms in which we morally judge,—for example, ourselves. But the very essence of all judgment, just so far as it
extends, asserts determination.

If in conceiving the self you detach it from all motives or tendencies,
what you have is not a morally admirable or condemnable, not a morally
characterisable self at all. Hence it is not subject to reproach. You cannot
call a self good because of its courageous free action, and then deny that
its action was determined by its character. In calling it good because
of that action you have implied that the action came from its goodness
(which means its good character) and was a sign thereof. By their fruits
ye shall know them. The indeterminist appears to imagine that he can
distinguish the moral "I" from all its propensities, regard its act as arising in the moment undetermined by them, and yet can then (for the
first time, in his opinion, with propriety!) ascribe to this "I" an admirable
quality. At the very root of his doctrine he contradicts himself. How odd
that he never catches sight of that contradiction! He fights for his doctrine in order that he may call a man morally good, on account of his acts,
with some real meaning; and his doctrine is that a man's acts (precisely
so far as "free" or undetermined) do not come from his goodness. So
they do not entitle us to call him good. He has taken his position in defence of moral conceptions, and it is fatal to all moral conceptions.

We are told, however, that it is under determinism that we should
have no right any more to praise or to blame. At least we could not do
so in the old sense of the terms. We might throw words of praise to a
man, or throw words of blame at him, because we know from observation
that they will affect his action; but the old light of meaning in the terms
has gone out. Well, all we have to do is to keep asking what this old
meaning was. We praise a man by saying that he is a good friend, or a
hard worker, or a competent man of business, or a trusty assistant, or a
judicious minister, or a gifted poet, or one of the noblest of men—one
of the noblest of characters! In other words, he is a being with such and
such qualities. If it is moral praise, he is a being with such and such
tendencies to bring forth good acts. If we describe a single act, saying,
for instance: "Well done!" we mean to praise the person for the act as
being the author of it. It is he who has done well and proved himself
capable of doing so. If the happy act is accidental we say that no praise
is deserved for it. If a person is gratified by praise it is because of the
estimate of him, in some respect or in general, that is conveyed. Praise
(once again) means description, with expressed or implied admiration.
If any instance of it can be found which does not consist in these ele-

ments our analysis fails. "Praise the Lord, O my soul, *and forget not all His benefits*,"—and the Psalm goes on to tell His loving and guarding acts toward humankind. To praise the Lord is to tell His perfections, especially the perfections of His character. This is the old light that has always been in words of praise and there appears no reason for its going out.

Indeterminism maintains that we need not be impelled to action by our wishes, that our active will need not be determined by them. Motives "incline without necessitating." We choose amongst the ideas of action before us, but need not choose solely according to the attraction of desire, in however wide a sense that word is used. Our inmost self may rise up in its autonomy and moral dignity, independently of motives, and register its sovereign decree.

Now, *in so far* as this "interposition of the self" is undetermined, the act is not *its* act, it does not issue from any concrete continuing self; it is born at the moment, of nothing, hence it expresses no quality; it bursts into being from no source. The self does not register *its* decree, for the decree is not the product of just that "*it*." The self does not rise up in *its* moral dignity, for dignity is the quality of an enduring being, influencing its actions, and therefore expressed by them, and that would be determination. *In proportion* as an act of volition starts of itself without cause it is exactly, so far as the freedom of the individual is concerned, as if it had been thrown into his mind from without—"suggested" to him —by a freakish demon. It is exactly like it in this respect, that in neither case does the volition arise from what the man is, cares for or feels allegiance to; it does not come out of him. *In proportion* as it is undetermined, it is just as if his legs should suddenly spring up and carry him off where he did not prefer to go. Far from constituting freedom, that would mean, in the exact measure in which it took place, the loss of freedom. It would be an interference, and an utterly uncontrollable interference, with his power of acting as he prefers. In fine, then, *just so far* as the volition is undetermined, the self can neither be praised nor blamed for it, since it is not the act of the self.

The principle of free will says: "*I* produce my volitions." Determinism says: "My volitions are produced by *me*." Determinism is free will expressed in the passive voice.

After all, it is plain what the indeterminists have done. It has not occurred to them that our free will may be resolved into its component elements. (Thus far a portion only of this resolution has been considered.) When it is thus resolved they do not recognize it. The analytical imagination is considerably taxed to perceive the identity of the free power that we feel with the component parts that analysis shows us. We are gratified by their nods of intelligence and their bright, eager faces as the analysis proceeds, but at the close are a little disheartened to find them falling back on the innocent supposition of a horse inside that does all the essential work. They forget that they may be called upon to analyse the horse. They solve the problem by forgetting analysis. The solution they offer is merely: "There is a self inside which does the deciding." Or, let us say, it is as if the *Pfarrer* were explaining the physiology of a horse's motion. They take the whole thing to be analysed, imagine a duplicate of it reduced in size, so to speak, and place this duplicate-self inside as an explanation—making it the elusive source of the "free decisions." They do not see that they are merely pushing the question a little further back, since the process of deciding, with its constituent factors, must have taken place within that inner self. Either it decided in a particular way because, on the whole, it preferred to decide in that way, or the decision was an underived event, a rootless and sourceless event. It is the same story over again. In neither case is there any gain in imagining a second self inside, however wonderful and elusive. Of course, it is the first alternative that the indeterminist is really imagining. If you tacitly and obscurely conceive the self as deciding *its own way*, *i.e.*, according to its preference, but never admit or recognise this, then you can happily remain a libertarian indeterminist; but upon no other terms. In your theory there is a heart of darkness.

Freedom.   In accordance with the genius of language, free will means freedom of persons in willing, just as "free trade" means freedom of persons (in a certain respect) in trading. The freedom of anyone surely always implies his possession of a power, and means the absence of any interference (whether taking the form of restraint or constraint) with his exercise of that power. Let us consider this in relation to freedom in willing.

"Can."   We say, "I can will this or I can will that, whichever I choose." Two courses of action present themselves to my mind. I think of their consequences, I look on this picture and on that, one of them commends itself more than the other, and I will an act that brings it about. I knew that I could choose either. That means that I had the power to choose either.

What is the meaning of "power"? A person has a power if it is a fact that when he sets himself in the appropriate manner to produce a certain event that event will actually follow. I have the power to lift the lamp; that is, if I grasp it and exert an upward pressure with my arm, *it will rise.* I have the power to will so and so; that is, if I want, that act of will will take place. That and none other is the meaning of power, is it not? A man's being in the proper active posture of body or of mind is the cause, and the sequel in question will be the effect. (Of course, it may be held that the sequel not only does but must follow, in a sense opposed to Hume's doctrine of cause. Very well; the question does not here concern us.)

Thus power depends upon, or rather consists in, a law. The law in question takes the familiar form that if something happens a certain something else will ensue. If A happens then B will happen. The law in this case is that if the man definitively so desires then volition will come to pass. There is a series, wish—will—act. The act follows according to the will (that is a law,—I do not mean an underived law) and the will follows according to the wish (that is another law). A man has the power (sometimes) to act as he wishes. He has the power (whenever he is not physically bound or held) to act as he wills. He has the power always (except in certain morbid states) to will as he wishes. All this depends upon the laws of his being. Wherever there is a power there is a law. In it the power wholly consists. A man's power to will as he wishes is simply the law that his will follows his wish.

What, again, does freedom mean? It means the absence of any interference with all this. Nothing steps in to prevent my exercising my power.[1]

All turns on the meaning of "can." "I can will either this or that" means, I am so constituted that if I definitely incline to this, the appropriate act of will will take place, and if I definitely incline to that, the appropriate act of will will take place. The law connecting preference and will exists, and there is nothing to interfere with it. My free power, then, is not an exemption from law but in its inmost essence an embodiment of law.

Thus it is true, after the act of will, that I could have willed otherwise. It is most natural to add, "if I had wanted to"; but the addition is not required. The point is the meaning of "could." I could have willed whichever way I pleased. I had the power to will otherwise, there was nothing to prevent my doing so, and I should have done so if I had wanted. If someone says that the wish I actually had prevented my willing otherwise, so that I could not have done it, he is merely making a slip in the use of the word "could." He means, that wish could not have produced anything but this volition. But "could" is asserted not of the wish (a transient fact to which power in this sense is not and should not be ascribed) but of the person. And the person *could* have produced something else than that volition. He could have produced any volition he wanted; he had the power to do so.

But the objector will say, "This person as he was at the moment—the person as animated by that wish—could not have produced any other volition." Oh, yes, he could. "Could" has meaning not as applied to a momentary actual phase of a person's life, but to the person himself of whose life that is but a phase; and it means that (even at that moment) he had the power to will just as he preferred. *The idea of power, because it is the idea of a law, is hypothetical, carries in itself hypothesis as part of its very intent and meaning—"if he should prefer this, if he should prefer that,"—and therefore can be truly applied to a person irrespective of what at the moment he does prefer. It remains hypothetical even when*

---

1. A word as to the relation of power and freedom. Strictly power cannot exist without freedom, since the result does not follow without it. Freedom on the other hand is a negative term, meaning the absence of something, and implies a power only because that whose absence it signifies is interference, which implies something to be interfered with. Apart from this peculiarity of the term itself, there might be freedom without any power. Absence of interference (of what would be interference if there were a power) might exist in the absence of a power; a man might be free to do something because there was nothing to interfere with his doing it, but might have no power to do it. Similarly and conveniently we may speak of a power as existing though interfered with; that is, the law may exist that would constitute a power if the interference were away.

applied.[2] This very peculiarity of its meaning is the whole point of the idea of power. It is just because determinism is true, because a law obtains, that one "could have done otherwise."

Sidgwick set over against "the formidable array of cumulative evidence" offered for determinism the "affirmation of consciousness" "that I can now choose to do" what is right and reasonable, "however strong may be my inclination to act unreasonably."[3] But it is not against determinism. It is a true affirmation (surely not of immediate consciousness but of experience), the affirmation of my power to will what I deem right, however intense and insistent my desire for the wrong. I can will anything, and can will effectively anything that my body will enact. I can will it despite an inclination to the contrary of any strength you please —strength as felt by me before decision. We all know cases where we have resisted impulses of great strength in this sense and we can imagine them still stronger. I have the power to do it, and shall do it, shall exercise that power, if I prefer. Obviously in that case (be it psychologically remarked) my solicitude to do what is right will have proved itself even stronger (as measured by ultimate tendency to prevail, though not of necessity by sensible vividness or intensity) than the inclination to the contrary, for that is what is meant by my preferring to do it. I am conscious that the field for willing is open; I can will anything that I elect to will. Sidgwick did not analyse the meaning of "can," that is all. He did not precisely catch the outlook of consciousness when it says, "I can." He did not distinguish the function of the word, which is to express the availability of the alternatives I see when, before I have willed, and perhaps before my preference is decided, I look out on the field of conceivable volition. He did not recognize that I must have a word to express my power to will as I please, quite irrespective of what I shall please, and that "can" is that word. It is no proof that I cannot do something to point out that I shall not do it if I do not prefer. A man, let us say, can turn on the electric light; but he will not turn it on if he walks away from it; though it is still true that he can turn it on. When we attribute power to a man we do not mean that something will accomplish itself without his wanting it to. That would never suggest the idea of power. We mean that if he makes the requisite move the thing will be accomplished. It is part of the idea that the initiative shall rest with him. The initiative for an act of will is a precedent phase of consciousness that we call the definitive inclination, or, in case of conflict, the definitive preference for it. If someone in the throes of struggle with temptation says to himself, "I can put this behind me," he is saying truth and precisely the pertinent truth. He is bringing before his mind the act of will, unprevented, quite open to him, that would deliver him from what he deems noxious. It may still happen that the noxiousness of the temptation does not affect him so powerfully as its allurement, and that he succumbs. It is no whit less true, according to determinism, that he could have willed

2. I am encouraged by finding in effect the same remark in Prof. G. E. Moore's *Ethics*, ch. vi., at least as regards what he terms one sense of the word "could." I should hazard saying, the only sense in this context.

3. *Methods of Ethics*, 7th ed., 65.

otherwise. To analyse the fact expressed by "could" is not to destroy it.

But it may be asked, "Can I will in opposition to my strongest desire at the moment when it is strongest?" If the words "at the moment when it is strongest" qualify "can," the answer has already been given. If they qualify "will," the suggestion is a contradiction in terms. Can I turn-on-the-electric-light-at-a-moment-when-I-am-not-trying-to-do-so? This means, if I try to turn on the light at a moment when I am not trying to, will it be turned on? A possible willing as I do not prefer to will is not a power on my part, hence not to be expressed by "I can."

Everybody knows that we often will what we do not want to will, what we do not prefer. But when we say this we are using words in another sense than that in which I have just used them. In *one* sense of the words, whenever we act we are doing what we prefer, on the whole, in view of all the circumstances. We are acting for the greatest good or the least evil or a mixture of these. In the *other* and more usual sense of the words, we are very often doing what we do not wish to do, *i.e.*, doing some particular thing we do not wish because we are afraid of the consequences or disapprove of the moral complexion of the particular thing we do wish. We do the thing that we do not like because the other thing has aspects that we dislike yet more. We are still doing what we like best on the whole. It is again a question of the meaning of words.

COMPULSION. The indeterminist conceives that according to determinism the self is carried along by wishes to acts which it is thus necessitated to perform. This mode of speaking distinguishes the self from the wishes and represents it as under their dominion. This is the initial error. This is what leads the indeterminist wrong on all the topics of his problem. And the error persists in the most recent writings. In fact, the moral self is the wishing self. The wishes are its own. It cannot be described as under their dominion, for it has no separate predilections to be overborne by them; they themselves are its predilections. To fancy that because the person acts according to them he is compelled, a slave, the victim of a power from whose clutches he cannot extricate himself, is a confusion of ideas, a mere slip of the mind. The answer that has ordinarily been given is surely correct; all compulsion is causation, but not all causation is compulsion. Seize a man and violently force him to do something, and he is compelled—also caused—to do it. But induce him to do it by giving him reasons and his doing it is caused but not compelled.

PASSIVITY. We have to be on our guard even against conceiving the inducement as a cause acting like the impact of a billiard ball, by which the self is precipitated into action like a second billiard ball, as an effect. The case is not so simple. Your reasons have shown him that his own preferences require the action. He does it of his own choice; he acts from his own motives in the light of your reasons. The sequence of cause and effect goes on within the self, with contributory information from without.

It is not clarifying to ask, "Is a volition free or determined?" It is the person who is free, and his particular volition that is determined.

Freedom is something that we can attribute only to a continuing being, and he can have it only so far as the particular transient volitions within him are determined. (According to the strict proprieties of language, it is surely events that are caused, not things or persons; a person or thing can be caused or determined only in the sense that its beginning to be, or changes in it, are caused or determined.)

It is fancied that, owing to the "necessity" with which an effect follows upon its cause, if my acts of will are caused I am not free in thus acting. Consider an analogous matter. When I move I use ligaments. "Ligament" means that which binds, and a ligament does bind bones together. But *I* am not bound. *I* (so far as my organism is concerned) am rendered possible by the fact that my bones are bound one to another; that is part of the secret of my being able to act, to move about and work my will. If my bones ceased to be bound one to another I should be undone indeed. The human organism is detached, but it is distinctly important that its component parts shall not be detached. Just so my free power of willing is built up of tight cause-and-effect connections. The point is that when I employ the power thus constituted nothing determines the particular employment of it but *me*. Each particular act of mine is determined from outside itself, *i.e.*, by a cause, a prior event. But not from outside me. I, the possessor of the power, am not in my acts passively played upon by causes outside me, but am enacting my own wishes in virtue of a chain of causation within me. What is needed is to distinguish broadly between a particular effect, on the one hand, and, on the other, the detached, continuous life of a mental individual and his organism; a life reactive, but reacting according to its own nature.

What makes the other party uncontrollably reject all this—let us never forget—is the words. They smell of sordid detail, of unwinsome psychological machinery. They are not bathed in moral value, not elevated and glowing. In this the opponents' instinct is wholly right; only when they look for the value they fail to focus their eyes aright. It is in the whole act and the whole trait and the whole being that excellence and preciousness inhere; analysis must needs show us elements which, taken severally, are without moral expressiveness; as would be even the celestial anatomy of an angel appearing on earth. The analytic imagination, however, enables us to see the identity of the living fact in its composition with the living fact in its unity and integrity. Hence we can resume the thought of it as a unit and the appropriate feelings without fancying that analysis threatens them or is at enmity with them.

. . . .

PREDICTION. If we knew a man's character thoroughly and the circumstances that he would encounter, determinism (which we are not here completely asserting) says that we could foretell his conduct. This is a thought that repels many libertarians. Yet to predict a person's conduct need not be repellent. If you are to be alone in a room with $1000 belonging to another on the table and can pocket it without anyone knowing the fact, and if I predict that you will surely *not* pocket it, that is not an insult. I say, I know you, I know your character; you will not do it. But if I say that you are "a free being" and that I really do not know whether you will pocket it or not, that is rather an insult. On the other hand, there are cases where prediction is really disparaging. If I say when you make a remark, "I knew you were going to say that," the impression is not agreeable. My exclamation seems to say that your mind is so small and simple that one can predict its ideas. That is the real reason why people resent in such cases our predicting their conduct; that if present human knowledge, which is known to be so limited, can foresee their conduct, it must be more naive and stereotyped than they like to think it. It is no reflection upon the human mind or its freedom to say that one who knew it through and through (a human impossibility) could foreknow its preferences and its spontaneous choice. It is of the very best of men that even we human beings say, "I am sure of him." It has perhaps in this controversy hardly been observed how much at this point is involved, how far the question of prediction reaches. The word "reliable" or "trustworthy" is a prediction of behaviour. Indeed, all judgment of persons whatever, in the measure of its definitude, is such a prediction.

MATERIAL FATE.   The philosopher in the old story, gazing at the stars, falls into a pit. We have to notice the pitfall in our subject to which, similarly occupied, Prof. Eddington has succumbed.

"What significance is there in my mental struggle to-night whether I shall or shall not give up smoking, if the laws which govern the matter of the physical universe already pre-ordain for the morrow a configuration of matter consisting of pipe, tobacco, and smoke connected with my lips?"[4]

No laws, according to determinism, pre-ordain such a configuration, unless I give up the struggle. Let us put the matter aside for the moment, to return to it. Fatalism says that my morrow is determined no matter how I struggle. This is of course a superstition. Determinism says that my morrow is determined through my struggle. There is this significance in my mental effort, that it is deciding the event. The stream of causation runs through my deliberations and decision, and, if it did not run as it does run, the event would be different. The past cannot determine the event except through the present. And no past moment determined it any more truly than does the present moment. In other words, each of the links in the causal chain must be in its place. Determinism (which, the reader will remember, we have not here taken for necessarily true in all detail) says that the coming result is "pre-ordained" (literally, caused) at each stage, and therefore the whole following series for to-morrow may be described as already determined; so that did we know all about the struggler, how strong of purpose he was and how he was influenced (which is humanly impossible) we could tell what he would do. But for the struggler this fact (supposing it to be such) is not pertinent. If, believing it, he ceases to struggle, he is merely revealing that the forces within him have brought about that cessation. If on the other hand he struggles manfully he will reveal the fact that they have

4. *Philosophy*, Jan., 1933, p. 41.

brought about his success. Since the causation of the outcome works through his struggle in either case equally, it cannot become for him a moving consideration in the struggle. In it the question is, "Shall I do this or that?" It must be answered in the light of what there is to recommend to me this or that. To this question the scientific truth (according to determinism) that the deliberation itself is a play of causation is completely irrelevant; it merely draws the mind delusively away from the only considerations that concern it.

. . . .

SELF AS PRODUCT AND PRODUCER.   We can at this stage clearly see the position when a certain very familiar objection is raised. "How can any one be praised or blamed if he was framed by nature as he is, if heredity and circumstance have given him his qualities? A man can surely be blamed only for what he does himself, and he did not make his original character; he simply found it on his hands." A man is to be blamed only for what he does himself, for that alone tells what he is. He did not make his character; no, but he made his acts. Nobody blames him for making such a character, but only for making such acts. And to blame him for that is simply to say that he is a bad act-maker. If he thinks the blame misapplied he has to prove that he is not that sort of an act-maker. Are we to be told that we may not recognise what he is, with appropriate feelings of its quality, because he did not create himself—a mere contortion and intussusception of ideas? The moral self cannot be *causa sui*. To cause his original self a man must have existed before his original self. Is there something humiliating to him in the fact that he is not a contradiction in terms? If there were a being who made his "original character," and made a fine one, and we proceeded to praise him for it, our language would turn out to be a warm ascription to him of a still earlier character, so that the other would not have been original at all. To be praised or blamed you have to be; and be a particular person; and the praise or blame is telling what kind of a person you are. There is no other meaning to be extracted from it. Of course, a man does exist before his later self, and in that other sense he can be a moral *causa sui*. If by unflagging moral effort he achieves for himself better subsequent qualities, what can merit praise but the ingredient in him of aspiration and resolution that was behind the effort? If he should even remake almost his whole character, still there would be a valiant remnant that had done it. These are commonplaces, precisely of the moral outlook upon life. When we come to the moral fountainhead we come to what the man is, at a particular time, as measured by what he does or is disposed to do with his power of volition.

. . . .

The indeterminist, we noticed, requires a man to be "an absolute moral source" if we are to commend him. Well, if he were so, what could we say about him but what kind of a source he was? And he is so in fact. Suppose now that this source has in turn a source—or that it has not! Does that (either way) change what it is?

"But moral severity! How can we justly be severe toward a mere fact in nature—inhuman nature?" Because it is evil; because it must be checked. If somebody takes pleasure in torturing an innocent person, we spring to stop the act; to hold back the perpetrator, if need be with violence; to deter him from doing it again, if need be with violence; to warn any other possible perpetrators: "This shall not be done; we are the enemies of this conduct; this is evil conduct." At what could we be indignant but at a fact in somebody's human nature? Our severity and enmity are an active enmity to the evil; they are all part of that first spring to stop the act. "Society is opposed in every possible manner to such cruelty. You shall be made to feel that society is so, supposing that you cannot be made to feel yourself the vileness of the act." It does not remove our sense of its vileness to reflect that he was acting according to his nature. That is very precisely why we are indignant at him. We intend to make him feel that his nature is in that respect evil and its expression insufferable. We intend to interfere with the expression of his nature. That what he did proceeded from it is not a disturbing and pause-giving consideration in the midst of our conduct, but the entire basis of it. The very epithet "vile" assumes that his behaviour arose from an intention and a moral quality in the man. How can we justly be severe? Because he *ought* to be checked and deterred, made to feel the moral estimate of what he has been doing. This we consider more fully under the topic of Desert.

Compare a case where the wrongdoing, whatever it be, is one's own. Catch a man in a moment of fierce self-reproach, and bring the objection above before him. Would it relieve him of his feeling? It would be an irrelevant frivolity to him. He is shocked at a wrong that was done and at himself for doing it; he repents of the acts of will that brought it about; he would gladly so change himself as never to do the like again; he is ready to "beat himself with rods." With all that the metaphysical entanglement has simply nothing to do.

. . . .

"Still, does not determinism force us to face a fact in some sort new to us, that the offending person came to act so from natural causes; and does not that of necessity alter somewhat our attitude or state of mind about moral judgment?" Why, the fact is not new at all. In daily life we are all determinists, just as we are all libertarians. We are constantly attributing behaviour to the character, the temperament, the peculiarities of the person and expecting him to behave in certain fashions. The very words of our daily converse, as we have so amply observed, are full of determinism. And we see nothing inconsistent in being aware at the same time that he is free in choosing his course, as we know ourselves to be. We merely form expectations as to what he *will* freely choose. Nor do we see anything inconsistent in blaming him. At the very moment when we do so we often shake our heads over the environment or mode of life or ill-omened pursuits that have brought him to such ways and to being a blameworthy person.

. . . .

To be sure, determinism as a philosophic doctrine, determinism so named, may come as a new and repellent idea to us. We have been thinking in the right terms of thought all the while, but we did not identify them with terms of causation; when the philosophical names are put upon them we recoil, not because we have a false conception of the facts, but a false conception of the import of the philosophical terms. When we feel that somebody could have done otherwise but chose to do a wrong act knowingly, then we one and all feel that he is culpable and a proper object of disapproval, as we ought to feel. We merely have not been schooled enough in the application of general terms to call the course of mental events within him causation. So again, goodness consists in qualities, but the qualities express themselves in choosing, which is unfettered and so often trembles in the balance; when we are suddenly confronted with the abstract question, "Can we be blamed for a quality we did not choose?" the colours run and the outlines swim a little; some disentanglement of abstract propositions is required, though we think aright in practice on the concrete cases. So all that philosophic determinism "forces us to face" is the meaning of our terms.

No, it is the opposite doctrine that must revolutionise our attitude toward moral judgments. If it is true, we must come to see that no moral severity towards the helpless subject of an act of will that he suddenly finds discharging itself within him, though not emanating from what he is or prefers, can be deserved or relevant. To comprehend all is to pardon all—so far as it is undetermined. Or, rather, not to pardon but to acquit of all.

However, in face of the actual facts, there is something that does bring us to a larger than the usual frame of mind about indignation and punishment and the mood of severity. And that is thought, sympathetic thought, any thought that enters with humane interest into the inner lives of others and pursues in imagination the course of them. In an outbreak of moral indignation we are prone to take little cognizance of that inner life. We are simply outraged by a noxious act and a noxious trait (conceived rather objectively and as it concerns the persons affected) and feel that such act should not be and that such a trait should be put down. The supervening of a sympathetic mental insight upon moral indignation is not a displacement, but the turning of attention upon facts that call out other feelings too. To comprehend all is neither to pardon all nor to acquit of all; overlooking the disvalue of acts and intentions would not be comprehension; but it is to appreciate the human plight; the capacity for suffering, the poor contracted outlook, the plausibilities that entice the will. This elicits a sympathy or concern co-existing with disapproval. That which is moral in moral indignation and behind it, if we faithfully turn to it and listen, will not let us entirely wash our hands even of the torturer, his feelings and his fate; certainly will not permit us to take satisfaction in seeing him in turn tortured, merely for the torture's sake. His act was execrable because of its effect on sentient beings, but he also is a sentient being. The humanity that made us reprobate his crime has not ceased to have jurisdiction. The morality that hates the sin has in that very fact the secret of its undiscourageable interest in the sinner. We come, not to discredit indignation and penalty, nor to tamper with their meaning, but to see their office and place in life and the implications wrapped up in their very fitness. Of this more presently.

. . . .

RESPONSIBILITY. Again, it is said that determinism takes from man all responsibility. As regards the origin of the term, a man is responsible when he is the person to respond to the question why the act was performed, how it is to be explained or justified. That is what he must answer; he is answerable for the act. The act proceeded from him. He is to say whether it proceeded consciously. He is to give evidence that he did or did not know the moral nature of the act and that he did or did not intend the result. He is to say how he justifies it or if he can justify it. If the act proceeded from him by pure accident, if he can show that he did the damage (if damage it was) by brushing against something by inadvertence, for example, then he has not to respond to the question what he did it for—he is not consciously responsible—nor how it is justified— he is not morally responsible, though of course he may have been responsible in these respects for a habit of carelessness.

But why does the peculiar moral stain of guilt or ennoblement of merit belong to responsibility? If an act proceeds from a man and not merely from his accidental motion but from his mind and moral nature, we judge at once that like acts may be expected from him in the future. The colour of the act for good or bad is reflected on the man. We see him now as a living source of possible acts of the same kind. If we must be on our guard against such acts we must be on our guard against such men. If we must take steps to defend ourselves against such acts we must take steps to defend ourselves against such men. If we detest such acts, we must detest that tendency in such men which produced them. He is guilty in that he knowingly did evil, in that the intentional authorship of evil is in him. Because the act proceeded in every sense from him, for that reason he is (so far) to be accounted bad or good according as the act is bad or good, and he is the one to be punished if punishment is required. And that is moral responsibility.

But how, it is asked, can I be responsible for what I will if a long train of past causes has made me will it—the old query asked anew in relation to another category, responsibility, which must be considered separately. Is it not these causes that are "responsible" for my act—to use the word in the only sense, says the objector, that seems to remain for it?

The parent past produced the man, none the less the man is responsible for his acts. We can truly say that the earth bears apples, but quite as truly that trees bear apples. The earth bears the apples by bearing trees. It does not resent the claim of the trees to bear the apples, or try to take the business out of the trees' hands. Nor need the trees feel their claim nullified by the earth's part in the matter. There is no rivalry between them. A man is a being with free will and responsibility; where this being came from, I repeat, is another story. The past finished its functions in the business when it generated him as he is. So far from interfering with him and coercing him the past does not even exist. If

443

we could imagine it as lingering on into the present, standing over against him and stretching out a ghostly hand to stay his arm, then indeed the past would be interfering with his liberty and responsibility. But so long as it and he are never on the scene together they cannot wrestle; the past cannot overpower him. The whole alarm is an evil dream, a nightmare due to the indigestion of words. The past has created, and left extant, a free-willed being.

DESERT.   But we have not come to any final clearness until we see how a man can be said to *deserve* anything when his acts flow from his wishes, and his wishes flow from other facts further up the stream of his life. There is a peculiar element in the idea of deserving. This is the element of "ought." A man deserves punishment or reward if society ought to give it to him; he deserves the punishment or reward that he ought to receive. We cannot say universally that he deserves what he ought to receive, but only when it is a question of reward or punishment.

What treatment a man should receive from society as a result of wrongdoing is a question of ethics. It is widely held that an evildoer deserves punishment, not only for the defence of society but because there is an ultimate fitness in inflicting natural evil for moral evil. This, as we know, has been maintained by determinists. Since the idea of desert collapses altogether on the indeterminist's conception of conduct, this theory of the ground of desert cannot be said to be logically bound up with indeterminism. For my own part, however, owing to reasons for which I have no space here, I cannot hold the theory. I believe that the ideal ends of the administration of justice are 1) to see that all possible restitution is made, 2) to see as far as possible that the malefactor does not repeat the act, and 3) so far as possible to render the act less likely on the part of others. And these ends should be sought by means that will accomplish them. Morality is humane. It is animated by good-will toward humanity. Our instinctive impulse to retaliation must be interpreted with a view to its function in society, and so employed and regulated to the best purpose. Being a part of the defensive and fighting instinct, its functional aim is evidently to destroy or check the threatening source of evil—to destroy the culprit or change his temper. Our common and natural notion of desert is in harmony with either of these views; only on the second it receives a supplement, a purposive interpretation.

We discover punishment not only in combat but in nature at large. If a child puts its hand into flames it is burnt. After that it puts its hand into flames no more. Nature teaches us to respect her by punishments that deter. Society, to preserve itself, must find deterrents to administer to men. It must say, "I'll teach you not to do that." Already nature has taught it such deterrents. Society must shape men's actions or at least rough-hew them, to the extent of striking off certain jagged and dangerous edges, and the most obvious way to do so is by penalties. A secondary way is by rewards, and these nature has taught also.

When a man needlessly injures others, society by punishment injures him. It administers to him a specimen of what he has given to others.

444

"This," it says, "is the nature of your act; to give men suffering like this. They rebel at it as you rebel at this. You have to be made more acutely conscious of the other side; the side of the feelings and the forces that you have outraged. You have to be made to feel them recoil upon you, that you may know that they are there. You have to be made to respect them in advance. And others like-minded to respect them in some degree better by seeing how they recoil upon you."

But this is only a method of working upon him and them; it is justified by effectiveness alone. It supposes two things; that society has been just in the first instance to these men themselves, that is, that they were not drawn by unjust conditions of life into the acts for which they are made to suffer; and that the suffering will in fact improve their conduct or that of others. The truth is that society often punishes when it is itself the greater malefactor, and that the penalty, instead of reforming, often confirms the criminality. It is due to nothing but the crude state of civilisation that we have added so little of a more sagacious and effectual mode of influencing criminals and preventing crime than the original and natural method of hitting back.

Out of this situation arises a subsidiary sense of deserving. A man may be said to deserve a punishment in the sense that, in view of the offence, it is not too severe to give him if it would work as above conceived; though if we believe it will not so work it ought not to be given him.

· ·

If the general view here taken, which seems forced upon us in the prosaic process of examining words, is correct, then as we look back over the long course of this controversy and the false antithesis that has kept it alive, how can we help exclaiming, "What waste!" Waste is surely the tragic fact above all in life; we contrast it with the narrow areas where reason and its economy of means to ends in some measure reign. But here is huge waste in the region of reasoning itself, the enemy in the citadel. What ingenuity, what resource in fresh shifts of defence, what unshaken loyalty to inward repugnances, what devotion to ideal values, have here been expended in blind opposition instead of analysis. The cause of determinism, seeming to deny freedom, has appeared as the cause of reason, of intelligence itself, and the cause of free will, seeming to exclude determination, has appeared that of morals. The worst waste is the clash of best things. In our subject it is time this waste should end. Just as we find that morality requires intelligence to give effect and remains rudimentary and largely abortive till it places the conscience of the mind in the foreground, so we find that determinism and the faith in freedom meet and are united in the facts, and that the long enmity has been a bad dream.

40. John Hospers

John Hospers is Professor of Philosophy at the University
of Southern California.

Psychoanalysis and Moral Responsibility

. . . As a preparation for developing my own views on the subject, I want
to mention a factor that I think is of enormous importance and relevance: namely, unconscious motivation. There are many actions—not
those of an insane person (however the term "insane" be defined), nor
of a person ignorant of the effects of his action, nor ignorant of some
relevant fact about the situation, nor in any obvious way mentally deranged—for which human beings in general and the courts in particular
are inclined to hold the doer responsible, and for which, I would say,
he should not be held responsible. The deed may be planned, it may be
carried out in cold calculation, it may spring from the agent's character
and be continuous with the rest of his behavior, and it may be perfectly
true that he could have done differently *if* he had wanted to; nonetheless
his behavior was brought about by unconscious conflicts developed in
infancy, over which he had no control and of which (without training
in psychiatry) he does not even have knowledge. He may even *think* he
knows why he acted as he did, he may *think* he has conscious control over
his actions, he may even *think* he is fully responsible for them; but he is

From "What Means This Freedom?" first published in *Determinism and Freedom
in the Age of Modern Science*, ed. Sidney Hook. Reprinted by permission of the
author and the publisher, New York University Press. Copyright © 1958 by New York
University.

not. Psychiatric casebooks provide hundreds of examples. The law and common sense, though puzzled sometimes by such cases, are gradually becoming aware that they exist; but at this early stage countless tragic blunders still occur because neither the law nor the public in general is aware of the genesis of criminal actions. The mother blames her daughter for choosing the wrong men as candidates for husbands; but though the daughter thinks she is choosing freely and spends a considerable amount of time "deciding" among them, the identification with her sick father, resulting from Oedipal fantasies in early childhood, prevents her from caring for any but sick men, twenty or thirty years older than herself. Blaming her is beside the point; she cannot help it, and she cannot change it. Countless criminal acts are thought out in great detail; yet the participants are (without their own knowledge) acting out fantasies, fears, and defenses from early childhood, over whose coming and going they have no conscious control.

Now, I am not saying that none of these persons should be in jails or asylums. Often society must be protected against them. Nor am I saying that people should cease the practices of blaming and praising, punishing and rewarding; in general these devices are justified by the results—although very often they have practically no effect; the deeds are done from inner compulsion, which is not lessened when the threat of punishment is great. I am only saying that frequently persons we think responsible are not properly to be called so; we mistakenly think them responsible because we assume they are like those in whom no unconscious drive (toward this type of behavior) is present, and that their behavior can be changed by reasoning, exhorting, or threatening.

I

I have said that these persons are not responsible. But what is the criterion for responsibility? Under precisely what conditions is a person to be held morally responsible for an action? Disregarding here those conditions that have to do with a person's *ignorance* of the situation or the effects of his action, let us concentrate on those having to do with his "inner state." There are several criteria that might be suggested:

1. The first idea that comes to mind is that responsibility is determined by the presence or absence of *premeditation*—the opposite of "premeditated" being, presumably, "unthinking" or "impulsive." But this will not do—both because some acts are not premeditated but responsible, and because some are premeditated and not responsible.

Many acts we call responsible can be as unthinking or impulsive as you please. If you rush across the street to help the victim of an automobile collision, you are (at least so we would ordinarily say) acting responsibly, but you did not do so out of premeditation; you saw the accident, you didn't think, you rushed to the scene without hesitation. It was like a reflex action. But you acted responsibly: unlike the knee jerk, the act was the result of past training and past thought about situations of this kind; that is why you ran to help instead of ignoring the incident or running away. When something done originally from conviction or training becomes habitual, it becomes *like* a reflex action. As Aristotle said, virtue should become second nature through habit: a virtuous act should be performed *as if* by instinct; this, far from detracting from its moral worth, testifies to one's mastery of the desired type of behavior; one does not have to make a moral effort each time it is repeated.

There are also premeditated acts for which, I would say, the person is not responsible. Premeditation, especially when it is so exaggerated as to issue in no action at all, can be the result of neurotic disturbance or what we sometimes call an emotional "block," which the person inherits from long-past situations. In Hamlet's revenge on his uncle (I use this example because it is familiar to all of us), there was no lack, but rather a surfeit, of premeditation; his actions were so exquisitely premeditated as to make Freud and Dr. Ernest Jones look more closely to find out what lay behind them. The very premeditation camouflaged unconscious motives of which Hamlet himself was not aware. I think this is an important point, since it seems that the courts often assume that premeditation is a criterion of responsibility. If failure to kill his uncle had been considered a crime, every court in the land would have convicted Hamlet. Again: a woman's decision to stay with her husband in spite of endless "mental cruelty" is, if she is the victim of an unconscious masochistic "will to punishment," one for which she is not responsible; she is the victim and not the agent, no matter how profound her conviction that she is the agent; she is caught in a masochistic web (of complicated genesis) dating back to babyhood, perhaps a repetition of a comparable situation involving her own parents, a repetition-compulsion that, as Freud said, goes "beyond the pleasure principle." Again: a criminal whose crime was carefully planned step by step is usually considered responsible, but as we shall see in later examples, the overwhelming impulse toward it, stemming from an unusually humiliating ego defeat in early childhood, was as compulsive as any can be.

2. Shall we say, then, that a person is not responsible for his act unless he can *defend it with reasons*? I am afraid that this criterion is no better than the previous one. First, intellectuals are usually better at giving reasons than nonintellectuals, and according to this criterion would be more responsible than persons acting from moral conviction not implemented by reasoning; yet it is very doubtful whether we should want to say that the latter are the more responsible. Second, the giving of reasons itself may be suspect. The reasons may be rationalizations camouflaging unconscious motives of which the agent knows nothing. Hamlet gave many reasons for not doing what he felt it was his duty to do: the time was not right, his uncle's soul might go to heaven, etc. His various "reasons" contradicted one another, and if an overpowering compulsion had not been present, the highly intellectual Hamlet would not have been taken in for a moment by these rationalizations. The real reason, the Oedipal conflict that made his uncle's crime the accomplishment of his own deepest desire, binding their fates into one and paralyzing him into inaction was unconscious and of course unknown to him. One's intelligence and reasoning power do not enable one to escape from uncon-

sciously motivated behavior; it only gives one greater facility in rationalizing that behavior; one's intelligence is simply used in the interests of the neurosis—it is pressed into service to justify with reasons what one does quite independently of the reasons.

If these two criteria are inadequate, let us seek others.

3. Shall we say that a person is responsible for his action unless it is the *result of unconscious forces* of which he knows nothing? Many psychoanalysts would probably accept this criterion. If it is not largely reflected in the language of responsibility as ordinarily used, this may be due to ignorance of fact: most people do not know that there are such things as unconscious motives and unconscious conflicts causing human beings to act. But it may be that if they did, perhaps they would refrain from holding persons responsible for certain actions.

I do not wish here to quarrel with this criterion of responsibility. I only want to point out the fact that if this criterion is employed a far greater number of actions will be excluded from the domain of responsibility than we might at first suppose. Whether we are neat or untidy, whether we are selfish or unselfish, whether we provoke scenes or avoid them, even whether we can exert our powers of will to change our behavior—all these may, and often do, have their source in our unconscious life.

4. Shall we say that a person is responsible for his act unless it is *compelled?* Here we are reminded of Aristotle's assertion (*Nicomachean Ethics*, Book III) that a person is responsible for his act except for reasons of either ignorance or compulsion. Ignorance is not part of our problem here (unless it is unconsciously induced ignorance of facts previously remembered and selectively forgotten—in which case the forgetting is again compulsive), but compulsion is. How will compulsion do as a criterion? The difficulty is to state just what it means. When we say an act is compelled in a psychological sense, our language is metaphorical —which is not to say that there is no point in it or that, properly interpreted, it is not true. Our actions are compelled in a literal sense if someone has us in chains or is controlling our bodily movements. When we say that the storm compelled us to jettison the cargo of the ship (Aristotle's example), we have a less literal sense of compulsion, for at least it is open to us to go down with the ship. When psychoanalysts say that a man was compelled by unconscious conflicts to wash his hands constantly, this is also not a literal use of "compel"; for nobody forces his hands under the tap. Still, it is a typical example of what psychologists call *compulsive* behavior: it has unconscious causes inaccessible to introspection, and moreover nothing can change it—it is as inevitable for him to do it as it would be if someone were forcing his hands under the tap. In this it is exactly like the action of a powerful external force; it is just as little within one's conscious control.

In its area of application this interpretation of responsibility comes to much the same as the previous one. And this area is very great indeed. For if we cannot be held responsible for the infantile situations (in which we were after all passive victims), then neither, it would seem, can we be held responsible for compulsive actions occurring in adulthood that are inevitable consequences of those infantile situations. And, psychiatrists and psychoanalysts tell us, actions fulfilling this description are characteristic of all people some of the time and some people most of the time. Their occurrence, once the infantile events have taken place, is inevitable, just as the explosion is inevitable once the fuse has been lighted; there is simply more "delayed action" in the psychological explosions than there is in the physical ones.

(I have not used the word "inevitable" here to mean "causally determined," for according to such a definition every event would be inevitable if one accepted the causal principle in some form or other; and probably nobody except certain philosophers uses "inevitable" in this sense. Rather, I use "inevitable" in its ordinary sense of "cannot be avoided." To the extent, therefore, that adult neurotic manifestations *can* be avoided, once the infantile patterns have become set, the assertion that they are inevitable is not true.)

5. There is still another criterion, which I prefer to the previous ones, by which a man's responsibility for an act can be measured: the degree to which that act can (or could have been) *changed by the use of reasons.* Suppose that the man who washes his hands constantly does so, he says, for hygienic reasons, believing that if he doesn't do so he will be poisoned by germs. We now convince him, on the best medical authority, that his belief is groundless. Now, the test of his responsibility is whether the changed belief will result in changed behavior. If it does not, as with the compulsive hand washer, he is not acting responsibly, but if it does, he is. It is not the *use* of reasons, but their *efficacy in changing behavior,* that is being made the criterion of responsibility. And clearly in neurotic cases no such change occurs; in fact, this is often made the defining characteristic of neurotic behavior: it is unchangeable by any rational considerations.

II

I have suggested these criteria to distinguish actions for which we can call the agent responsible from those for which we cannot. Even persons with extensive knowledge of psychiatry do not, I think, use any one of these criteria to the exclusion of the others; a conjunction of two or more may be used at once. But however they may be combined or selected in actual application, I believe we can make the distinction along some such lines as we have suggested.

But is there not still another possible meaning of "responsibility" that we have not yet mentioned? Even after we have made all of the above distinctions, there remains a question in our minds whether we are, in the final analysis, *responsible for any of our actions at all.* The issue may be put this way: How can anyone be responsible for his actions, since they grow out of his character, which is shaped and molded and made what it is by influences—some hereditary, but most of them stemming from early parental environment—that were not of his own making or choosing? This question, I believe, still troubles many people who would agree to all the distinctions we have just made but still have the feeling that "this isn't all." They have the uneasy suspicion that there is a more ultimate sense, a "deeper" sense, in which we are *not* responsible for our actions, since we are not responsible for the character out of which those actions spring. This, of course, is the sense Professor Edwards was describing.

Let us take as an example a criminal who, let us say, strangled several persons and is himself now condemned to die in the electric chair. Jury and public alike hold him fully responsible (at least they utter the words "he is responsible"), for the murders were planned down to the minutest detail, and the defendant tells the jury exactly how he planned them. But now we find out how it all came about; we learn of parents who rejected him from babyhood, of the childhood spent in one foster home after another, where it was always plain to him that he was not wanted; of the constantly frustrated early desire for affection, the hard shell of nonchalance and bitterness that he assumed to cover the painful and humiliating fact of being unwanted, and his subsequent attempts to heal these wounds to his shattered ego through defensive aggression.

> The criminal is the most passive person in this world, helpless as a baby in his motorically inexpressible fury. Not only does he try to wreak revenge on the mother of the earliest period of his babyhood; his criminality is based on the inner feeling of being incapable of making the mother even feel that the child seeks revenge on her. The situation is that of a dwarf trying to annoy a giant who superciliously refuses to see these attempts. . . . Because of his inner feeling of being a dwarf, the criminotic uses, so to speak, dynamite. Of that the giant must take cognizance. True, the "revenge" harms the avenger. He may be legally executed. However, the primary inner aim of forcing the giant to acknowledge the dwarf's fury is fulfilled.[1]

The poor victim is not conscious of the inner forces that exact from him this ghastly toll; he battles, he schemes, he revels in pseudo-aggression, he is miserable, but he does not know what works within him to produce these catastrophic acts of crime. His aggressive actions are the wriggling of a worm on a fisherman's hook. And if this is so, it seems difficult to say any longer, "He is responsible." Rather, we shall put him behind bars for the protection of society, but we shall no longer flatter our feeling of moral superiority by calling him personally responsible for what he did.

Let us suppose it were established that a man commits murder only if, sometime during the previous week, he has eaten a certain combination of foods—say, tuna fish salad at a meal also including peas, mushroom soup, and blueberry pie. What if we were to track down the factors common to all murders committed in this country during the last twenty years and found this factor present in all of them, and only in them? The example is of course empirically absurd; but may it not be that there is *some* combination of factors that regularly leads to homicide, factors

1. Edmund Bergler, *The Basic Neurosis* (New York: Grune and Stratton, 1949), p. 305.

such as are described in general terms in the above quotation? (Indeed the situation in the quotation is less fortunate than in our hypothetical example, for it is easy to avoid certain foods once we have been warned about them, but the situation of the infant is thrust on him; something has already happened to him once and for all, before he knows it has happened.) When such specific factors are discovered, won't they make it clear that it is foolish and pointless, as well as immoral, to hold human beings responsible for crimes? Or, if one prefers biological to psychological factors, suppose a neurologist is called in to testify at a murder trial and produces X-ray pictures of the brain of the criminal; anyone can see, he argues, that the *cella turcica* was already calcified at the age of nineteen; it should be a flexible bone, growing, enabling the gland to grow.[2] All the defendant's disorders might have resulted from this early calcification. Now, this particular explanation may be empirically false; but who can say that no such factors, far more complex, to be sure, exist?

When we know such things as these, we no longer feel so much tempted to say that the criminal is responsible for his crime; and we tend also (do we not?) to excuse him—not legally (we still confine him to prison) but morally; we no longer call him a monster or hold him personally responsible for what he did. Moreover, we do this in general, not merely in the case of crime: "You must excuse Grandmother for being irritable; she's really quite ill and is suffering some pain all the time." Or: "The dog always bites children after she's had a litter of pups; you can't blame her for it: she's not feeling well, and besides she naturally wants to defend them." Or: "She's nervous and jumpy, but do excuse her: she has a severe glandular disturbance."

Let us note that the more *thoroughly* and *in detail* we know the causal factors leading a person to behave as he does, the more we tend to exempt him from responsibility. When we know nothing of the man except what we see him do, we say he is an ungrateful cad who expects much of other people and does nothing in return, and we are usually indignant. When we learn that his parents were the same way and, having no guilt feelings about this mode of behavior themselves, brought him up to be greedy and avaricious, we see that we could hardly expect him to have developed moral feelings in this direction. When we learn, in addition, that he is not aware of being ungrateful or selfish, but unconsciously represses the memory of events unfavorable to himself, we feel that the situation is unfortunate but "not really his fault." When we know that this behavior of his, which makes others angry, occurs more constantly when he feels tense or insecure, and that he now feels tense and insecure, and that relief from pressure will diminish it, then we tend to "feel sorry for the poor guy" and say he's more to be pitied than censured. We no longer want to say that he is personally responsible; we might rather blame nature or his parents for having given him an unfortunate constitution or temperament.

In recent years a new form of punishment has been imposed on middle-aged and elderly parents. Their children, now in their twenties, thirties

2. Meyer Levin, *Compulsion* (New York: Simon and Schuster, 1956), p. 403.

or even forties, present them with a modern grievance: "My analysis proves that *you* are responsible for my neurosis." Overawed by these authoritative statements, the poor tired parents fall easy victims to the newest variations on the scapegoat theory.

In my opinion, this senseless cruelty—which disinters educational sins which had been buried for decades, and uses them as the basis for accusations which the victims cannot answer—is unjustified. Yes "the truth loves to be centrally located" (Melville), and few parents—since they are human—have been perfect. But granting their mistakes, they acted as *their* neurotic difficulties forced them to act. To turn the tables and declare the children not guilty because of the *impersonal* nature of their own neuroses, while at the same time the parents are *personally* blamed, is worse than illogical; it is profoundly unjust.[3]

And so, it would now appear, neither of the parties is responsible: "they acted as their neurotic difficulties forced them to act." The patients are not responsible for their neurotic manifestations, but then neither are the parents responsible for theirs; and so, of course, for their parents in turn, and theirs before them. It is the twentieth-century version of the family curse, the curse on the House of Atreus.

"But," a critic complains, "it's immoral to exonerate people indiscriminately in this way. I might have thought it fit to excuse somebody because he was born on the other side of the tracks, if I didn't know so many bank presidents who were also born on the other side of the tracks." Now, I submit that the most immoral thing in this situation is the critic's caricature of the conditions of the excuse. Nobody is excused merely because he was born on the other side of the tracks. But if he was born on the other side of the tracks *and* was a highly narcissistic infant to begin with *and* was repudiated or neglected by his parents *and* . . . (here we list a finite number of conditions), and if this complex of factors is *regularly* followed by certain behavior traits in adulthood, and moreover *unavoidably* so—that is, they occur no matter what he or anyone else tries to do—then we excuse him morally and say he is not responsible for his deed. If he is not responsible for *A*, a series of events occurring in his babyhood, then neither is he responsible for *B*, a series of things he does in adulthood, provided that *B* inevitably—that is, unavoidably—follows upon the occurrence of *A*. And according to psychiatrists and psychoanalysts, this often happens.

But one may still object that so far we have talked only about neurotic behavior. Isn't nonneurotic or normal or not unconsciously motivated (or whatever you want to call it) behavior still within the area of responsibility? There are reasons for answering "No" even here, for the normal person no more than the neurotic one has caused his own character, which makes him what he is. Granted that neurotics are not responsible for their behavior (that part of it which we call neurotic) because it stems from undigested infantile conflicts that they had no part in bringing about, and that are external to them just as surely as if their behavior had been forced on them by a malevolent deity (which is indeed

3. Edmund Bergler, *The Superego* (New York: Grune and Stratton, 1952), p. 320.

one theory on the subject); but the so-called normal person is equally the product of causes in which his volition took no part. And if, unlike the neurotic's, his behavior is changeable by rational considerations, and if he has the will power to overcome the effects of an unfortunate early environment, this again is no credit to him; he is just lucky. If energy is available to him in a form in which it can be mobilized for constructive purposes, this is no credit to him, for this too is part of his psychic legacy. Those of us who can discipline ourselves and develop habits of concentration of purpose tend to blame those who cannot, and call them lazy and weak-willed; but what we fail to see is that they literally *cannot* do what we expect; if their psyches were structured like ours, they could, but as they are burdened with a tyrannical superego (to use psychoanalytic jargon for the moment), and a weak defenseless ego whose energies are constantly consumed in fighting endless charges of the superego, they simply cannot do it, and it is irrational to expect it of them. We cannot with justification blame them for their inability, any more than we can congratulate ourselves for our ability. This lesson is hard to learn, for we constantly and naively assume that other people are constructed as we ourselves are.

For example: A child raised under slum conditions, whose parents are socially ambitious and envy families with money, but who nevertheless squander the little they have on drink, may simply be unable in later life to mobilize a drive sufficient to overcome these early conditions. Common sense would expect that he would develop the virtue of thrift; he would make quite sure that he would never again endure the grinding poverty he had experienced as a child. But in fact it is not so: the exact conditions are too complex to be specified in detail here, but when certain conditions are fulfilled (concerning the subject's early life), he will always thereafter be a spendthrift, and no rational considerations will be able to change this. He will listen to the rational considerations and see the force of these, but they will not be able to change him, even if he tries; he cannot change his wasteful habits any more than he can lift the Empire State Building with his bare hands. We moralize and plead with him to be thrifty, but we do not see how strong, how utterly overpowering, and how constantly with him, is the opposite drive, which is so easily manageable with us. But he is possessed by the all-consuming, all-encompassing urge to make the world see that he belongs, that he has arrived, that he is just as well off as anyone else, that the awful humiliations were not real, that they never actually occurred, for isn't he now able to spend and spend? The humiliation must be blotted out; and conspicuous, flashy, expensive, and wasteful buying will do this; it shows the world what the world must know! True, it is only for the moment; true, it is in the end self-defeating, for wasteful consumption is the best way to bring poverty back again; but the person with an overpowering drive to mend a lesion to his narcissism cannot resist the avalanche of that drive with his puny rational consideration. A man with his back against the wall and a gun at his throat doesn't think of what may happen ten years hence. (Consciously, of course, he knows nothing of this drive; all that appears to consciousness is its shattering effects; he knows only that he must keep on spending—not why—and that he is unable to resist.) He hasn't in him the psychic capacity, the energy to stem the tide of a drive that at that moment is all-powerful. We, seated comfortably away from this flood, sit in judgment on him and blame him and exhort him and criticize him; but he, carried along by the flood, cannot do otherwise than he does. He may fight with all the strength of which he is capable, but it is not enough. And we, who are rational enough at least to exonerate a man in a situation of "overpowering impulse" when we recognize it to be one, do not even recognize this as an example of it; and so, in addition to being swept away in the flood that childhood conditions rendered inevitable, he must also endure our lectures, our criticisms, and our moral excoriation.

But, one will say, he could have overcome his spendthrift tendencies; some people do. Quite true: some people do. They are lucky. They have it in them to overcome early deficiencies by exerting great effort, and they are capable of exerting the effort. Some of us, luckier still, can overcome them with but little effort; and a few, the luckiest, haven't the deficiencies to overcome. It's all a matter of luck. The least lucky are those who can't overcome them, even with great effort, and those who haven't the ability to exert the effort.

But, one persists, it isn't a matter simply of luck; it *is* a matter of effort. Very well then, it's a matter of effort; without exerting the effort you may not overcome the deficiency. But whether or not you are the kind of person who has it in him to exert the effort is a matter of luck.

All this is well known to psychoanalysts. They can predict, from minimal cues that most of us don't notice, whether a person is going to turn out to be lucky or not. "The analyst," they say, "must be able to use the residue of the patient's unconscious guilt so as to remove the symptom or character trait that creates the guilt. The guilt must not be present, but *available* for use, *mobilizable*. If it is used up (absorbed) in criminal activity, or in an excessive amount of self-damaging tendencies, then it cannot be used for therapeutic purposes, and the prognosis is negative." Not all philosophers will relish the analyst's way of putting the matter, but at least as a physician he can soon detect whether the patient is lucky or unlucky—and he knows that whichever it is, it *isn't the patient's fault*. The patient's conscious volition cannot remedy the deficiency. Even whether he will co-operate with the analyst is really out of the patient's hands: if he continually projects the denying-mother fantasy on the analyst and unconsciously identifies him always with the cruel, harsh forbidder of the nursery, thus frustrating any attempt at impersonal observation, the sessions are useless; yet if it happens that way, he can't help that either. That fatal projection is not under his control; whether it occurs or not depends on how his unconscious identifications have developed since his infancy. He can try, yes—but the ability to try enough for the therapy to have effect is also beyond his control; the capacity to try more than just so much is either there or it isn't—and either way "it's in the lap of the gods."

The position, then, is this: if we *can* overcome the effects of early environment, the ability to do so is itself a product of the early environment. We did not give ourselves this ability; and if we lack it we cannot be blamed for not having it. Sometimes, to be sure, moral exhortation brings out an ability that is there but not being used, and in this lies its *occasional utility;* but very often its use is pointless, because the ability is not there. The only thing that can overcome a desire, as Spinoza said, is a stronger contrary desire; and many times there simply is no where-withal for producing a stronger contrary desire. Those of us who do have the wherewithal are lucky.

There is one possible practical advantage in remembering this. It may prevent us (unless we are compulsive blamers) from indulging in right-eous indignation and committing the sin of spiritual pride, thanking God that we are not as this publican here. And it will protect from our useless moralizings those who are least equipped by nature for enduring them. As with responsibility, so with deserts. Someone commits a crime and is punished by the state; "he deserved it," we say self-righteously—as if we were moral and he immoral, when in fact we are lucky and he is unlucky —forgetting that there, but for the grace of God and a fortunate early environment, go we. Or, as Clarence Darrow said in his speech for the defense in the Loeb-Leopold case:

> I do not believe that people are in jail because they deserve to be. . . . I know what causes the emotional life. . . . I know it is practically left out of some. Without it they cannot act with the rest. They cannot feel the moral shocks which safeguard others. Is [this man] to blame that his machine is imperfect? Who is to blame? I do not know. I have never in my life been interested so much in fixing blame as I have in relieving people from blame. I am not wise enough to fix it.[4]

4. Levin, *op. cit.*, pp. 439–40, 469.

41. Alvin I. Goldman

Alvin I. Goldman is Professor of Philosophy at the
University of Michigan.

Predictability and Determinism

Are actions determined? Since it is difficult to tell "directly" whether or not actions are governed by universal laws, some philosophers resort to the following "indirect" argument:

- If actions are determined, then it is possible in principle to predict them (with certainty).
- It is not possible in principle for actions to be predicted (with certainty).
- Therefore, actions are not determined.

A defender of this argument I shall call an "anti-predictionist"; his position will be called "anti-predictionism." In this paper I shall try to rebut anti-predictionism.

Both premisses of the anti-predictionist argument will come under attack here. The first premiss, affirming that determinism entails predictability, is often accepted without adequate scrutiny. Some writers not only assume that determinism entails predictability but even *define* determinism as the thesis that every event is predictable in principle.[1]

From Alvin I. Goldman, "Actions, Predictions, and Books of Life," *American Philosophical Quarterly*, Vol. 5 (1968), pp. 135–151. Reprinted by kind permission of the author and editor of *American Philosophical Quarterly*.

1. Karl Popper, for example, defines "determined" as "predictable in accordance with the methods of science," in "Indeterminism in Quantum Mechanics and in Classical Physics," *The British Journal for the Philosophy of Science*, Vol. I (1950–51), see p. 120.

I believe, however, that it is essential to distinguish between determinism and predictability. We must first notice that there are various kinds or senses of "possibility" which may be involved in the "possibility of prediction." Moreover, it can be shown that in many of these senses, determinism does *not* entail the possibility of prediction. Many anti-predictionists have failed to notice this, however. Therefore, upon discovering some unpredictability in the arena of human action, they have wrongly concluded that actions must be undetermined. This error will be avoided only if we carefully distinguish between determinism and predictability. Hence, an important aim of this paper will be to differentiate various senses of "possibility of prediction" and to ascertain how they are related to determinism.

Let us assume now that we can find some suitable sense of "possibility of prediction" which is closely related to, if not entailed by, determinism. The second premise of the anti-predictionist argument asserts that, in such a sense, it is impossible for actions to be predicted. Various arguments have been offered in support of this premise. One that I shall consider concerns the possibility of writing a complete description of an agent's life—including his voluntary actions—even before he is born. According to anti-predictionism, if actions were determined, it would be possible to write such books. Indeed, it would be possible for such a "book of life" to be written even if the agent were to read its prediction of a given action before he is to perform that action. It seems clear to the anti-predictionist, however, that such books of life are impossible. Predictions of my actions cannot be made with certainty; for when I read these predictions, I can easily choose to falsify them. So argues the anti-predictionist. But it is far from clear that he is right. I think, on the contrary, that it may well be possible (in a suitable sense) for books of life to be written. And thus it seems to me that the anti-predictionist is unable to establish the truth of his second premise.

In general, anti-predictionists support their second premise by contrasting the predictability of human behavior with that of physical events. It is alleged that special difficulties of a purely conceptual sort arise for the prediction of action and that these difficulties are unparalleled in the realm of merely physical phenomena. I shall claim, however, that there are no essential differences between actions and physical events with respect to the problem of prediction. More precisely, I shall claim that *conceptual* reflection on the nature of human behavior (as opposed to investigation by the special sciences) does not reveal any peculiar immunity to prediction.

It must be emphasized that I offer no proof of the thesis that actions *are* determined; I merely wish to show that the anti-predictionists's arguments fail to prove that they are *not* determined. It is conceivable, of course, that actions are not determined. And if actions are not determined, then I would admit that they are not perfectly predictable (in any sense at all). What I contend, however, is that the arguments of philosophers, based on familiar, common-sense features of human action and human choice, do not prove that actions are undetermined or unpredictable. The basic features of human action are quite compatible with the contention that actions are determined and susceptible of prediction. In other words, my aim here is not to establish the *truth,* but merely the *tenability,* of the thesis that actions are determined.

II

Let us begin with some definitions. I shall define determinism as the view that every event and state of affairs is determined in every detail. An event is determined (in a given detail) if and only if it is deducible from some set of antecedent conditions and laws of nature. A law of nature is, roughly, any true non-analytic universal statement of unlimited scope which supports counterfactual conditionals.[2] Both "low-level" empirical conditions, like all metals expand when heated, and "theoretical" conditions, like F = ma, are included. Antecedent conditions can be either events, like moving at 10 m.p.h., or states of affairs, like having a specific gravity of 1.7. (Throughout I shall be concerned both with events and with states of affairs, but for brevity I shall often omit reference to states of affairs.) Negations of events, like a ball's *not* moving at 10 m.p.h., are also included. Antecedent conditions may be directly observable phenomena, but they need not be. Theoretical, hypothetical, and dispositional states—like being brittle or being intelligent—can serve as antecedent conditions.

Notice that my definition of determinism is in terms of a formal relationship, i.e., the relationship of deducibility holding between events and sets of laws and antecedent conditions. In particular, this definition makes no explicit reference to the ability of anyone to predict these events, and thereby leaves open the question of the connection between determinism and predictability.

If determinism is true, human actions are determined. But determinism alone does not tell us what laws or kinds of laws take human actions as their dependent variables. I shall assume, however, that these laws would include ones with psychological states like desires, beliefs, intentions, etc., as their independent variables. This presupposes—correctly, I think—that statements connecting actions with, for example, wants and beliefs, are not purely analytic.[3] Rather, their logical status would correspond to quasi-analytic, quasi-empirical generalizations like many theoretical statements of science. If determinism is true, wants, beliefs, intentions, etc., are themselves determined by prior events of various sorts. The determinants of these mental states are quite diverse, however, so I shall make no attempt to delineate them.

In ordinary language, not all determining factors of an event are called its "causes." A body's having a certain mass may be a determining

2. There are, of course, numerous problems associated with the concept of a law of nature. But a detailed discussion of these problems would go beyond the scope of this paper.

3. For a defense of this view, see William P. Alston, "Wants, Actions, and Causal Explanations" in H. N. Castañeda, (ed), *Minds, Intentionality, and Perception* (Detroit, 1967) and R. Brandt and J. Kim, "Wants as Explanations of Actions," *The Journal of Philosophy*, Vol. 60 (1963), pp. 425–435.

antecedent condition of that body's moving at a certain velocity after being struck by another object, but its having that mass would not be called a "cause" of its velocity. Similarly, although a person's having a certain intention or desire would not ordinarily be termed a "cause" of his action, it may be an antecedent condition of the relevant sort. Since determinism is often connected with what philosophers call "causal necessity," I shall use the technical term *"causally necessitate"* to apply to antecedent conditions which, together with laws of nature, determine a given event. Thus, I shall say that desires and beliefs (together with other conditions) "causally necessitate" a given action, even though ordinary language would not condone such an expression.

In our discussion of predictability we need a sense of "prediction" distinct from mere lucky guesses or pre-cognition. We must be concerned with predictions made on the basis of laws and antecedent conditions. I shall call a prediction a *"scientific prediction"* if and only if it is made by deducing the predicted event from laws and antecedent conditions. A scientific predictor may learn of the laws and antecedent conditions in any number of ways. (On my definition, most predictions made by actual scientists are not "scientific" predictions, for real scientists seldom, if ever, *deduce* what will occur from laws and prior conditions. Nevertheless, scientific prediction as defined here may be regarded as an ideal of prediction to which scientists can aspire.)

As indicated above, it is important to identify different senses of the phrase "possibility of prediction." I shall now distinguish four relevant species of possibility, though further distinctions will be made later within some of these categories. The four species are: (1) *logical possibility*, (2) *logical compossibility*, (3) *physical possibility*, and (4) *causal compossibility*.

An event is *logically possible* if and only if it is not self-contradictory, and logically impossible if and only if it is self-contradictory. Drawing a square circle is a logically impossible event, while jumping 90 feet is a logically possible event. *Logical compossibility* is defined for two or more events. A set of two or more events is logically compossible if and only if the conjunction of the members of the set is logically consistent. A set is logically incompossible (i.e., not logically compossible) if and only if each of the events is logically possible but their conjunction is logically inconsistent. Thus, the two events, (a) *x*'s being a pumpkin from 11 o'clock to 12 o'clock, and (b) *x*'s turning into a pumpkin at 12 o'clock, are logically incompossible.

An event is *physically possible* if and only if it is not inconsistent with any law or laws of nature; an event is physically impossible if and only if there are laws of nature with which it is inconsistent. Traveling faster than the speed of light, for example, is physically impossible. I shall speak not only of events being physically impossible *in general*, but also as being physically impossible *for* certain kinds of entities. Thus, the act of lifting a ten-ton weight is not, in general, physically impossible; but it is physically impossible for (normal) human beings to lift ten-ton weights. Given the physical constitution of human beings, laws of nature make it impossible for them to lift such weights.

Causal compossibility differs from physical possibility in attending to groups of events rather than events taken singly. Roughly, a set of events is causally compossible just in case laws of nature allow each of them to occur singly and allow them to occur as a group.

III

The most interesting questions concerning the prediction of action are best handled in terms of the notion of causal compossibility. The reflexivity of predictions—the fact that a prediction often has an effect which bears on its own truth—can be understood properly with the use of this notion. But the question of the causal compossibility of predictions of action cannot arise unless the other three species of possibility are satisfied. Our definition of causal compossibility makes a set causally compossible only if its members are logically possible, physically possible, and (jointly) logically compossible. For example, if it is physically impossible to make scientific predictions of actions, the question of causal compossibility does not even arise. Therefore, before turning to the questions of reflexivity, including the question of whether "books of life" can be written, we must focus on certain problems connected with the logical compossibility and the physical possibility of predicting actions.

The logical possibility and compossibility of predictions can be discussed together, since the distinction between them is somewhat blurred. This is because a correct prediction is not really a single event, but a pair of events—a prediction and an event predicted. Two different examples of logical incompossibility have been uncovered in connection with the prediction of behavior. I shall discuss these examples briefly and argue that, contrary to what their authors suppose, they do not prove that actions are undetermined and they do not prove that actions have a peculiar immunity to prediction unparalleled by physical phenomena.

The first logical incompossibility, as discussed by Maurice Cranston,[4] can be summarized as follows. Suppose that Sam invents the corkscrew at time *t*. In the intended sense of "invent," this means (a) that Sam thinks of the corkscrew at *t*, and (b) that no one ever thought of the corkscrew before *t*. Cranston argues that no one could have predicted Sam's inventing the corkscrew. In order for him to make this prediction, he would himself have to think of the corkscrew. And had he thought of the corkscrew, it would be false to say that Sam "invented" the corkscrew. Yet, *ex-hypothesi*, Sam *did* invent the corkscrew. Using the terminology of "logical incompossibility," we can formulate Cranston's problem by saying that the three events, (a) Sam thinks of the corkscrew at *t*, (b) no one ever thought of the corkscrew before *t*, and (c) someone predicted Sam's inventing the corkscrew, are logically incompossible.

The second example poses a problem for predicting not actions, but decisions. However, since the concept of a voluntary action is so closely tied to that of a decision, an unpredictability connected with decisions is

4. *Freedom: A New Analysis* (London, 1954), p. 169.

very important for us to discuss. Carl Ginet claims that it is impossible ("conceptually" impossible) for anyone to predict his own decisions.[5] The argument begins by defining "deciding to do A" as *passing into* a state of knowledge (of a certain kind) that one will do A, or try to do A.[6] Suppose now that Sam, at t, decides to do A. Had Sam predicted that he would make this decision—and had this prediction involved *knowledge*— he could not have decided later to do A. For if, before t, he had known that he would decide to do A, he would have known then that he would do A, or try to do A. But if, before t, he had known that he would do A (or try to do A), then he could not, at t, have *passed into* a state of knowing that he would do A. Thus, according to Ginet, Sam could not have predicted that he would make this decision.

Of course, Sam might make his prediction and then forget it. If so, he can still decide, at t, to do A. However, if Sam not only knows, before t, that he will decide to do A, but also *continues* to know this up until t, then Sam cannot, at t, decide to do A. In other words, the following three events are logically incompossible: (a') Sam decides, at t, to do A, (b') Sam predicts (i.e., knows) that he will decide to do A, and (c') Sam continues to know this until t.

What do these two logical incompossibilities prove? Do they prove that decisions and inventions are undetermined? Do they prove that voluntary actions, including the decisions which lead to them, have a special immunity to prediction? The answer is "No," I believe, to both questions.

Our examples of logical incompossibilities do not establish any special status for human behavior, for precisely analogous incompossibilities can be produced for physical phenomena. Let the expression "a tornado strikes *x by surprise*" mean: (1) a tornado strikes x at a certain time, and (2) before that time nobody ever thought of a tornado striking x. Now suppose that, as a matter of fact, a tornado strikes Peking by surprise. Then it is logically incompossible for this event to have been predicted. That is, the set consisting in the tornado striking Peking by surprise and a prediction of the tornado striking Peking by surprise is a logically incompossible set. In general it is logically incompossible for tornadoes striking places by surprise to be predicted. For if anyone were to predict these events, they could no longer be described as "tornadoes striking places *by surprise*." Nevertheless, there certainly are (or could be) events correctly describable as " a tornado striking x by surprise."

I wish next to argue that the invention and decision incompossibilities do not show that these human phenomena are undetermined. Notice

---

5. "Can the Will Be Caused?," *The Philosophical Review*, Vol. 71 (1962), pp. 49–55.
6. One might challenge Ginet's argument by criticizing this definition of "deciding." This criticism has implicitly been made, along with other criticisms of Ginet's position by various writers. For example, see John Canfield, "Knowing about Future Decisions," *Analysis*, Vol. 22 (1962), and J. W. Roxbee Cox, "Can I Know Beforehand What I Am Going to Decide?," *The Philosophical Review*, Vol. 72 (1963). Here I shall waive these criticisms, however, and accept Ginet's claim that it is impossible to predict one's own decisions. I shall then ask whether this proves that decisions are undetermined and whether they are intrinsically different from physical phenomena.

first that the tornado case, though it has the same logical structure, does not bear on the question of determinism. Although it is logically incompossible for anyone to predict the tornado striking Peking by surprise, I am in no way inclined to suppose that this event is not determined. Similarly, our logical incompossibilities fail to show that inventions and decisions are undetermined. How could such logical incompossibilities demonstrate that these events are not governed by laws of nature? The notion of a law is in no way involved in the concept of logical incompossibility. And hence the presence of logical incompossibilities sheds no light on the question of whether there are laws and antecedent conditions which entail inventions or decisions.

The critical error here is the assumption that if an event is determined (under a given description), it must be possible to predict it (under that description).[7] The falsity of this proposition should be adequately clear from the invention case. Suppose that Sam's thinking of the corkscrew at *t* is deducible from laws and antecedent conditions. And suppose that the fact that no one ever thinks of the corkscrew before *t* is also deducible from laws and antecedent conditions. Then, the event consisting in Sam's *inventing* the corkscrew at *t* would be determined; but it still would be logically incompossible for it to have been predicted under that description. The lesson to be learned here is not that inventions are undetermined actions, but that the alleged entailment between determinism and predictability is not an entailment at all. At any rate, the fact that an event is determined under a given description does not entail that it is *logically compossible* for it to be predicted under that description.[8]

The case of decisions can be handled similarly. It seems to me quite possible that a person's passing into a state of knowing, or intending, to do *A* be deducible from laws and antecedent conditions. But although this event would be determined (under the given description) it would not be logically compossible for Sam to have predicted it (under that description) and continued to know it until *t*.

V

Perhaps the anti-predictionist would think it obvious that it is causally incompossible to predict actions scientifically. He might argue as fol-

7. That this is an error has also been claimed by Arnold S. Kaufman, in "Practical Decision," *Mind*, Vol. 75 (1966), see p. 29.
8. It is also an error—committed at least as frequently—to think that determinism entails the possibility of retrodicting or explaining every event under any description. Suppose that Sam thinks of the corkscrew at *t* and that no one ever thinks of the corkscrew after *t*. Suppose, moreover, that both of these events are deducible from laws and antecedent conditions. Now let us introduce the expression "postventing *x*" to mean "thinking of *x* for the last time" (just as "inventing *x*" means "thinking of *x* for the *first* time"). Clearly, we may say of Sam that he "postvented" the corkscrew and that this action of his is determined. However, it is logically incompossible for anyone to *retrodict* Sam's postventing the corkscrew. To do so, the retrodicter would himself have to think of the corkscrew, and, *ex hypothesi*, Sam thought of the corkscrew for the *last* time at *t*.

lows: "Let us grant, as is likely, that there have never been any genuine scientific predictions of voluntary human actions. If, as my opponent claims, determinism is true, then it is causally incompossible for any predictions to have been made of these actions. For every actual action A, there is an actual event $\bar{P}_A$, the *absence* of a prediction of A. Since each of these events $\bar{P}_A$ is actual, and since determinism is true, each of these events $\bar{P}_A$ must be causally necessitated by some set of actual events prior to it. But if each of these events $\bar{P}_A$ is causally necessitated by actual prior events, then each event $\bar{P}_A$—the prediction of A—is causally incompossible relative to some actual events. In other words, for each actual action A, it is causally incompossible for A to have been predicted."

This argument, like a previous one, proves too much. The anti-predictionist is right in saying that non-actual predictions of actions are causally incompossible with the actual prior events in the world. But this is true simply because, assuming determinism, every non-actual event whatever is causally incompossible with some set of actual prior events. Thus, using the notion of causal-compossibility-relative-to-all-actual-events, we can establish the impossibility of predicting physical phenomena as well as human behavior. We can point to an action that was never predicted and say that, in this sense, it "could not" have been predicted, since its non-prediction was causally necessitated by other actual events. But by the same token, we can point to a physical event which was never predicted and say that it "could not" have been predicted, since its non-prediction was also causally necessitated by other actual events. Using this notion of "possibility of prediction," the anti-predictionist again fails to establish any special immunity of action to prediction.

Apart from this point, however, the notion of "causal-compossibility-relative-to-all-actual-events" does not seem to be a pertinent kind of possibility for our discussion. We have seen that determinism does not entail the possibility of predicting actions in *every* sense of "possible." And here, I believe, we have still another sense of "possible" in which determinism does not entail that it is possible for every action to be predicted. Determinism does not say that, relative to all actual prior events, it is causally compossible for a prediction of an action to be made *even if* those actual prior events causally necessitate that no prediction occur. Thus, the fact that it is impossible, in this sense, for actions to be predicted does not conflict with the thesis that actions are determined. Nor is it surprising that the sense of "possible" here under discussion is not important. Using the notion of "causally-compossible-relative-to-all-actual-prior-events" it turns out, assuming determinism, that only actual events are possible. But it is a strange and unduly restrictive notion of "possible" according to which only actual events are possible!

We need, then, a broader notion of possibility, one which allows for nonactual possibles while also taking into account the notion of causal necessity. We can discover a more relevant notion by examining what is often meant in ordinary contexts when we say, counterfactually, "e could have occurred." Suppose we say, counterfactually, "The picnic could have been a success." This sort of statement would normally be made with a suppressed "if"-clause. We might mean, for example, "The picnic could have been a success if it had not rained." Now if the only thing which prevented the picnic from being a success was the rain, we are also likely to say, "The picnic *would* have been a success if it had not rained." In the first case we mean that the substitution of non-rain for rain in the course of events would have *allowed* the picnic to be a success; in the second case we mean that this substitution would have *ensured* the success of the picnic. In both cases we are saying that a certain event could have or would have occurred *if* the prior course of the world had differed from its actual course in specified ways.

Although in ordinary contexts we might not pursue the matter further, in order to be systematic we must inquire further: "*Could* it *not* have rained?" "Could non-rain have occurred instead of rain?" The actual rain was causally necessitated by actual events prior to the rain. If we are to suppose that it did not rain, we must also make changes (in our imagination) of still earlier events. Carrying this argument to its logical conclusion, it is obvious that whenever a determinist says that a non-actual event *e* "could have" occurred, he must imagine *an entirely new world*. For the picnic to have been a success, it is required that it not have rained. For it not to have rained, the cloud formation would have had to be different. For the cloud formation to have been different, it is required that the wind velocity (or some other factor) have been different. Etc.

Not only must we change conditions prior to *e*, if we are to suppose *e* occurs, but we probably[9] must change events after *e* as well. Had it not rained, a certain other picnic group near us would not have ended their picnic just then. And had they not ended their picnic just then, they would not have left for home just then. And had they not left for home just then, they would not have had an automobile accident when they did.[10] Etc.

The determinist who says, counterfactually, "*e* could have occurred," must construct a whole world to justify his claim. Nevertheless, this gives him a sense of "possible" that allows non-actual possibles. For a determinist, "*e* could have occurred" may be translated as "a causally compossible world can be imagined in which *e* occurs." Normally the determinist will be able to construct worlds resembling the real one to a large extent. But these worlds will never be exactly like our world except for one event only. Any such imagined world will differ from the real world by at least one event for every moment of time. This will be true, at any rate, if the laws governing these imagined worlds are identical with those of the real world. And I shall assume throughout that these laws (whatever they are, exactly) are held constant.

---

9. I say "probably" because the definition of determinism does not entail that every event is a determinant of some subsequent event. Thus, if not-*e* actually occurred but had no effect on any subsequent event, then we might substitute *e* for not-*e* without changing any subsequent events. However, though determinism does not require it, it is reasonable to assume that every event will have some differential effect on *some* later event or events.

10. This is all plausible, at any rate, if we deny fatalism. Fatalism, which is by no means implied by determinism, is the view that certain events will happen at certain times *no matter what* antecedent conditions obtain.

VI

We can now give what I regard as a reasonable formulation of the question: "Is it possible, in principle, to make scientific predictions of voluntary actions?" The formulation is: "Can one construct casually compossible worlds in which scientific predictions are made of voluntary actions?" In saying that this is a "reasonable" formulation of the question, I do not mean that a negative answer to this question would entail that voluntary actions are not determined, but it would suggest a disparity between actions and physical phenomena. For, assuming that scientific predictions are physically possible, it does seem that there are causally compossible worlds in which scientific predictions are made of physical events.

Similar comments are in order on the question, "Can one construct causally compossible worlds in which scientific predictions are made of voluntary actions and in which the agent learns beforehand of the prediction?" Determinism does not entail that there must be such causally compossible worlds. But if no such worlds are constructible—worlds in which "books of life" are found, or things comparable to books of life—one might well claim a disparity between voluntary actions and physical phenomena.

Fortunately, I believe that there *are* causally compossible worlds in which scientific predictions are made of voluntary actions and in which, moreover, the agent learns of (some of these) predictions before he performs the predicted actions. I believe that there are causally compossible worlds in which books of life are written before a man's birth. Inscribed in these books are predictions of the agent's actions, predictions based on laws and antecedent conditions. These predictions are correct even though the agent sometimes reads them before he performs the predicted actions. I shall support my claim that there are such causally compossible worlds by giving a sketch of such a world. Before giving my sketch, however, I wish to examine the structure of prediction-making where the prediction itself has a causal effect on the predicted event. This will be essential in understanding how a "book of life" could be written, even though the writer knows that the agent will read it.

Consider the problem of an election predictor. He may know what the precise results of the upcoming election are going to be, if he makes no public prediction of the election. If he publishes a prediction, however, some of the voters, having found out what the results will be, may change their votes and thereby falsify his prediction. How, then, can a pollster make a genuinely scientific and accurate prediction of an election? Can he take into account the effect of the prediction itself? Herbert Simon has shown that, under specifiable conditions, a predictor can do this.[11] Essentially, what the predictor must know is the propensity of the

---

11. "Bandwagon and Underdog Effects of Election Predictions," reprinted in *Models of Man* (New York, 1957). The requisite condition is that the function relating the actual outcome of the voting to the predicted outcome, given the electorate's original voting intention, be *continuous*.

voters in the community to *change* their voting intention in accordance with their expectations of the outcome. If persons are more likely to vote for a candidate when they expect him to win than when they expect him to lose, we have a "bandwagon" effect; if the opposite holds, we have an "underdog" effect.

Let us suppose that a given pollster has ascertained that, two days before the election, 60 percent of the electorate plans to vote for candidate *A* and 40 percent for *B*. He also knows that, unless he publishes a prediction, the percentages will be the same on election day. Further suppose he knows that there is a certain "bandwagon" effect obtaining in the voting community.[12] When the original intention of the electorate is to vote 60 percent for *A*, this bandwagon effect can be expressed by the equation, $V = 60 + .2(P - 50)$, where P is the percentage vote for *A* publicly predicted by a pollster, and V is the actual resultant vote for *A*. Clearly, if the pollster publicly predicts that *A* will receive 60 percent of the vote, his prediction will be falsified. Putting $P = 60$, the equation tells us that $V = 62$. In other words, the effect of the prediction, combined with the original voting intention of the electorate, would result in a 62 percent vote for *A*. However, the pollster can easily calculate a value for P which will make $P = V$. He need only solve the two equations, $P = V$ and $V = 60 + .2(P - 50)$. Such a solution yields $P = 62.5$. Thus, the pollster can publish a prediction saying that 62.5 percent of the electorate will vote for *A*, knowing that his own prediction will bring an additional 2.5 percent of the electorate into the *A* column, and thereby make his prediction come true.

Notice that all the antecedent conditions relevant to the outcome cannot be known until it is known what prediction (if any) the pollster will make. His prediction (or lack of prediction) is itself an important antecedent condition. However, one of the crucial determinants of the outcome—viz., the original voting intention of the electorate—is given independently of the pollster's prediction. Thus, while holding that factor constant, the pollster calculates what the outcome of the election *would* be, *if* he were to make certain predictions. By solving the equations given above, he discovers a prediction and proceeds to fulfill that intention. Until he forms this intention, he does not know what prediction he will make, and therefore does not know all the requisite antecedent conditions from which to deduce the election outcome. But at the same time he makes the prediction (and perhaps even earlier), he does know all the relevant antecedent conditions and has deduced from these conditions what the results will be. Thus, his prediction of the outcome is a truly scientific prediction.

If someone wishes to predict a single person's behavior and yet let him learn of the prediction, the predictor must employ the same sort of strategy as the pollster. He must take into account what the agent's reaction will be to the prediction. There are several kinds of circumstances in which, having made the appropriate calculations, he will be able to

12. That this bandwagon effect holds in the community could be discovered either by studying previous elections or by deducing it from "higher-level" generalizations found to be true of the community.

make a correct prediction. (A) The agent learns of the prediction but does not want to falsify it. (B) Upon hearing the prediction, the agent decides to falsify it. But later, when the time of the action approaches, he acquires preponderant reasons for doing what was predicted after all. (C) Having decided to refute the prediction, the agent performs the action conforming with it because he doesn't realize that he is conforming with it. (D) At the time of the action the agent lacks either the ability or the opportunity to do anything but conform with the prediction, though he may have believed that he would be able to falsify it. In any of these four kinds of cases, a predictor would be able to calculate that his prediction, together with numerous other antecedent conditions, would casually necessitate that the agent perform the predicted action. In a case of kind (B), for example, the predictor may be able to foresee that the agent will first read his prediction and decide to falsify it. But other factors will crop up—ones which the agent did not originally count on—which will make him change his mind and perform the predicted action after all. And the predictor also foresees this.

In the first three kinds of cases, (A), (B), and (C), the agent performs the predicted action *voluntarily* (though in (C) he does not realize that what he is doing falls under the description "what was predicted"). In other words, in each of these three kinds of cases, the agent *could have* acted otherwise, in at least one sense of "could have" which some philosophers think is relevant to free will. Thus, the possibility of a scientific prediction does not require that the agent be *unable* to act in any way different from the prediction. All that is required is that the agent will not *in fact* act in any way different from the prediction. A predictor might know that an agent will in fact act in a certain way, not because he knows the agent will be incapable of doing otherwise, but because he knows that the agent will *choose* or *decide* to act as predicted. This point will be clarified at the end of the paper in a brief discussion of the indicated sense of "could have."

I shall now give a sketch of a causally compossible world in which a large number of correct predictions are made of an agent's behavior. Since I imagine this world to be governed by the same laws as those of the real world, and since I do not know all the laws of the real world, I cannot *prove* that my imagined world really is causally compossible. But as far as I can tell from common-sense knowledge of psychological and physical regularities, it certainly seems to be causally compossible. In this world, predictions of a man's life are made in great detail and inscribed in a "book of life," (parts of) which the agent subsequently reads. Obviously, I cannot describe the whole of this world, but I shall describe some of its most important and problematic features, namely the interaction between the agent and the book. Unfortunately, I shall have to omit a description of another important part of the world, the part in which the predictor (or predictors) gathers his data and makes his calculations. I am unable to describe this part of the world, first, because I do not know all the laws which the predictor would have at his disposal, and secondly, because I am not able to say just what the structure of this being would be. However, the main features of his *modus operandi* should be clear from our discussion of the pollster, whose technique is at the heart of such predicting.

VII

And now to the description of the world.

While browsing around the library one day, I notice an old dusty tome, quite large, entitled "Alvin I. Goldman." I take it from the shelf and start reading. In great detail, it describes my life as a little boy. It always gibes with my memory and sometimes even revives my memory of forgotten events. I realize that this purports to be a book of my life and I resolve to test it. Turning to the section with today's date on it, I find the following entry for 2:36 P.M. "He discovers me on the shelf. He takes me down and starts reading me. . . ." I look at the clock and see that it is 3:03. It is quite plausible, I say to myself, that I found the book about half an hour ago. I turn now to the entry for 3:03. It reads: "He is reading me. He is reading me. He is reading me." I continue looking at the book in this place, meanwhile thinking how remarkable the book is. The entry reads: "He continues to look at me, meanwhile thinking how remarkable I am."

I decide to defeat the book by looking at a future entry. I turn to an entry 18 minutes hence. It says: "He is reading this sentence." Aha, I say to myself, all I need do is refrain from reading that sentence 18 minutes from now. I check the clock. To ensure that I won't read that sentence, I close the book. My mind wanders; the book has revived a buried memory and I reminisce about it. I decide to reread the book there and relive the experience. That's safe, I tell myself, because it is an earlier part of the book. I read that passage and become lost in reverie and rekindled emotion. Time passes. Suddenly I start. Oh yes, I intended to refute the book. But what was the time of the listed action?, I ask myself. It was 3:19, wasn't it? But it's 3:21 now, which means I have already refuted the book. Let me check and make sure. I inspect the book at the entry for 3:17. Hmm, that seems to be the wrong place for there it says I'm in a reverie. I skip a couple of pages and suddenly my eyes alight on the sentence: "He is reading this sentence." But it's an entry for 3:21, I notice! So I made a mistake. The action I had intended to refute was to occur at 3:21, not 3:19. I look at the clock, and it is still 3:21. I have not refuted the book after all.

I now turn to the entry for 3:28. It reads, "He is leaving the library, on his way to the President's office." Good heavens, I say to myself, I had completely forgotten about my appointment with the President of the University at 3:30. I suppose I could falsify the book by not going, but it is much more important for me not to be late for that appointment. I'll refute the book some other time! Since I do have a few minutes, however, I turn back to the entry for 3:22. Sure enough, it says that my reading the 3:28 entry has reminded me about the appointment. Before putting the book back on the shelf, and leaving, I turn to an entry for tomorrow at 3:30 P.M. "He's still riding the bus bound for Chicago," it reads. Well, I say to myself, *that* prediction will be easy to refute. I have absolutely no intention of going to Chicago tomorrow.

Despite my decision to refute the book, events later induce me to change my mind and to conform to it. For although I want to refute the book on this matter, stronger reasons arise for not refuting it. When I get home that evening I find a note from my wife saying that her father (in Chicago) is ill and that she had to take the car and drive to Chicago. I call her there and she explains what has happened. I tell her about the book. Next morning she calls again with news that her father's condition is deteriorating and that I must come to Chicago immediately. As I hang up I realize that the book may turn out right after all, but the situation nevertheless demands that I go to Chicago. I might still refute it by going by plane or train. However, I call the airlines and am told that the fog is delaying all flights. The railroad says that there are no trains for Chicago till later in the day. So, acquiescing, I take a bus to Chicago, and find myself on it at 3:30.

VIII

Let me interrupt my narrative here. I have given several cases in which the book is not refuted, and the reader should be convinced that I could easily continue this way. But it is important now to reply to several objections which the anti-predictionist is anxious to make against my procedure.

(1) *"Your story clearly presupposes determinism. But whether or not determinism is true is the central matter of dispute. Hence, you are begging the question."* Admittedly, my story does presuppose determinism. Unless determinism were true, the imagined predictor could not have figured out what actions the agent would perform and then written them in the book. However, I do not think that this begs the question. For I am not here trying to prove that determinism *is* true. I am merely trying to show that the thesis of determinism is quite compatible with the world as we know it and with human nature as we know it. The world depicted in my story seems to be very much like the real world except that it contains different antecedent conditions. The fact that this imagined world is determined and contains predictions of actions, and yet it resembles the real world very closely, suggests to me that the real world may also be determined. At any rate, this supposition seems quite tenable, and its tenability is what I seek to establish in this paper.

(2) *"The story you told was fixed. Events might have been different from the way you described them. For example, the fog might not have curtailed all air traffic."* No, events could not be different *in the world I am imagining.* That is, in my world all the events I described were causally necessitated by prior antecedent conditions. I did not describe all the antecedent conditions, so perhaps the reader cannot see that each event I did describe was causally necessitated by them. But, since it is a

deterministic world, that is so. No one can imagine *my* world and also substitute the negation of one of the events I described. I'm not "fixing" the story by saying that the fog curtailed air traffic; that just is the way my imagined world goes.

(3) *"But I can imagine a world in which some putative predictions of actions are refuted."* I have no doubt that you can; that is very easy. You could even imagine a world *somewhat* like the one I have just described, but in which putative predictions are falsified. But this proves nothing at all. I would never deny that one can construct some causally compossible worlds in which putative scientific predictions of actions are not successful. I have only claimed that one can (also) construct *some* causally compossible worlds in which genuine scientific predictions of actions are made (and are successful). The situation with predictions of action is no different from the one with predictions of physical events. We can construct causally compossible worlds in which predictions of physical phenomena are correct. But we can also construct worlds in which putative scientific predictions of physical phenomena are incorrect. If our ability to construct worlds in which predictions are unsuccessful proves the inherent unpredictableness of the kind of phenomena unsuccessfully predicted, then we can prove the unpredictableness of physical phenomena as easily as the unpredictableness of human action.

(4) *"The world you have described, though possible, is a highly improbable world. Worlds in which putative predictions of actions are falsified are much more probable."* The notion of one possible world being "more probable" than another seems to me unintelligible. Surely the statistical sense of probability cannot be intended. There is no way of "sampling" from possible worlds to discover what features most of them have. Perhaps the anti-predictionist means that we can *imagine* more worlds in which putative predictions of actions are falsified. But this too is questionable. I can imagine indefinitely many worlds in which successful predictions of actions are made.

Perhaps the anti-predictionist means that it is improbable that any such sequence of events as I described would occur in the *real* world. He may well be right on this point. However, to talk about what is probable (in the evidential sense) in the real world is just to talk about what has happened, is happening, and will happen *as a matter of fact*. But the dispute between predictionists and anti-predictionists is, presumably, not about what *will* happen, but about what *could* happen *in principle*. This "in principle" goes beyond the particular facts of the actual world.

(5) *"The difference between physical phenomena and action is that predictions of actions can defeat themselves; but predictions of physical events cannot."* This is not so. One can construct worlds in which the causal effect of a putative prediction of a physical event falsifies that prediction. Jones calculates the position of a speck of dust three inches from his nose and the direction and velocity of wind currents in the room. He then announces his prediction that five seconds thence the speck will be in a certain position. He had neglected to account for the wind expelled from his mouth when he made the prediction, however, and this factor changes the expected position of the speck of dust.

Perhaps one can imagine a wider variety of cases in which predictions affect human action more than physical phenomena. But this is only a difference of *degree*, not of kind.

(6) *"Predictions of physical events can refute themselves because the predictor may fail to account for the effect of his own prediction. But were he to take this effect into account, he would make a correct prediction. On the other hand, there are conditions connected with the prediction of action in which, no matter what prediction the predictor makes, his prediction will be falsified. Here there is no question of inaccurate calculation or insufficient information. Whatever he predicts will be incorrect. Yet this situation arises only in connection with human action, not physical events."*

This is an important objection and warrants detailed discussion.

IX

Suppose that I wish to predict what action you will perform 30 seconds from now, but that I shall not try to change or affect your behavior except by making my prediction. (Thus, I shall not, for example, predict that you will perform no action at all and then make that prediction come true by killing you.) Further suppose that the following conditions obtain. At this moment you want to falsify any prediction that I shall make of your action. Moreover, you will still have this desire 30 seconds from now, and it will be stronger than any conflicting desire you will have at that time. Right now you intend to do action A, but you are prepared to perform $\bar{A}$ (not-A) if I predict that you will perform A. Thirty seconds hence you will have the ability and opportunity to do A and the ability and opportunity to do $\bar{A}$. Finally, conditions are such that, if I make a prediction in English in your presence, you will understand it, will remember it for 30 seconds, and will be able to tell whether any of your actions will conform to it or not. Given all these conditions, whatever I predict —at least, if I make the prediction by saying it aloud, in your presence, in English, etc.—will be falsified. If I predict you will do A, then you will do $\bar{A}$, while if I predict that you will do $\bar{A}$, you will proceed to do A. In other words, in these conditions no prediction of mine is causally compossible with the occurrence of the event I predict. Let $C_1, \ldots, C_n$ be the (actual) conditions just delineated, let P_A be my predicting you will do A (announced in the indicated way), and let $P_{\bar{A}}$ be my predicting you will do $\bar{A}$ (announced in the same way). Then *both* sets ($C_1, \ldots, C_n, P_A, A$) and ($C_1, \ldots, C_n, P_{\bar{A}}, \bar{A}$) are causally *in*compossible sets of events.

Notice that this example does not prove that it is causally incompossible "simpliciter" for me to make a scientific prediction of your action. All that it proves is that I cannot make such a prediction *in a certain manner*, viz., by announcing it to you in English. The events P_A and $P_{\bar{A}}$ include this particular manner, and that they do so is important. If I predict your action in some other manner, by thinking it to myself or by saying it aloud in Hindustani, for example, the effect on your action would not be the same as if I say it aloud in English. Assume that, if you do not hear me make any prediction or if you hear me say something you fail to understand, you will proceed to perform action A. Then it is causally composible for me to predict your action correctly by announcing the prediction in Hindustani. In other words, letting P_A' be my predicting that you will do A by announcing this in Hindustani, then the set of events $(C_1, \ldots, C_n, P_A' A)$ is a casually composible set.

In determining whether or not a certain set of events, including (1) a prediction, (2) the event predicted, and (3) certain other assumed conditions, is a causally composible set, it is essential to specify the manner of the prediction. This is true *in general*, not just in the case of predictions of action. A prediction which is "embodied" or expressed in one way will not have the same causal effects as the same prediction expressed in another way. We can see this in the case of the speck of dust. Jones predicted the position of the dust by announcing it orally, and this resulted in the falsification of the prediction. But had he made the same prediction in another fashion—say, by moving his toes in a certain conventional pattern—his prediction would not have been falsified, for the position of the dust would not have been affected.

What is the significance of the fact that it is causally incomposible, in some circumstances, for a (correct) prediction of an action to be made in a specified manner? First, this unpredictability does not prove that these actions are undetermined. Indeed, the very construction of the case in which no prediction is possible *presupposed* the existence of laws of nature which, together with a given prediction, would result in a certain action. In short, the case under discussion should, if anything, support rather than defeat the thesis that actions are determined. The only reason one might have for thinking the contrary is the assumption—which should by now appear very dubious—that determinism entails predictability. What our present case shows, I think, is that under some circumstances, even a determined event may not be susceptible of being correctly predicted in a specified manner. This fact can be further supported by adducing a similar case connected with purely physical events. And this brings me to my second point: the case produced above does not reflect a peculiarity of human action, since parallel examples can be found among physical phenomena.

Imagine a certain physical apparatus placed in front of a piano keyboard. A bar extends from the apparatus and is positioned above a certain key. (Only white keys will be considered.) If the apparatus is not disturbed, the bar will strike that key at a certain time. Now let us suppose that the apparatus is sensitive to sound, and, in particular, can discriminate between sounds of varying pitches. If the apparatus picks up a certain sound, the position of the bar will move to the right and proceed to strike the key immediately to the right of the original one (if there is one). Specifically, if the sound has the same pitch as that of the key over which the bar is poised, the bar will move. If the monitored sound has any other pitch, the bar will remain in its position and proceed to strike that key.

Now suppose that someone (or something) wishes to make predictions of the behavior of the apparatus. He wishes to predict what key the bar will strike. But the following restriction is made on the *manner* in which the prediction is to be made. The prediction must be expressed according to a specific set of conventions or symbols. To predict that the bar will strike middle *C*, for example, the predictor must emit a sound with the pitch of middle *C*. To predict that the bar will strike *D*, he must emit a sound with the pitch of that key, etc. All sound emissions are to be made in the neighborhood of the apparatus. Given this restriction on the manner of prediction, it will be causally incompossible for the predictor to make a correct prediction. For suppose that the bar is poised above middle *C*. If he predicts that it will strike middle *C*—that is, if he emits a sound of that pitch—the bar will move and proceed to strike *D*. But if he predicts any other behavior of the bar, for example, that it will strike *D*, the bar will remain in its original position and strike middle *C*.

Admittedly, the manner of prediction I have allowed to the predictor of this physical phenomenon is much more narrowly restricted than the manner of prediction allowed to the predictor of human action. But we could imagine physical apparatuses with a greater degree of complexity, able to "refute" predictions made in any of a wider variety of manners. In any case, the principle of the situation is the same for both physical phenomena and human actions, though the manners of prediction which affect one phenomenon may be different from the manners of prediction which affect the other. The latter difference simply reflects that fact that physical objects and human beings do not respond in precisely the same ways to the same causes. But this is equally true of different kinds of physical objects and of different pairs of human beings.

The reader should not suppose that the present discussion in any way vitiates my description of the book of life in Sect. VII. Our present discussion shows that under *some* conditions it is *not* causally compossible to predict a man's action in a way which allows him to learn of the prediction. But there are *other* conditions, such as the ones described in Sect. VII, in which such predictions *are* causally compossible. The existence of the latter conditions suffices to establish the possibility (in principle) of scientific predictions of voluntary actions which the agent hears or reads. Admittedly, it is not always possible to make predictions in this manner. But even when it is impossible to let one's prediction become known to the agent, it does not follow that it is impossible to make the prediction "privately." Thus, suppose you are trying to write a book of my life before I am born. Your calculations might show that if you inscribe certain predictions in the book they will be confirmed. For these calculations might reveal that I shall not read the book, or that I shall perform the actions despite the fact that I shall read the book. If so, you may proceed to write the book, having (scientific) knowledge that it will be correct. On the other hand, your calculations might reveal that, no matter what prediction you inscribe in the book, I shall refute it. In this case, you will be unable to write a book of my life. But you may nevertheless have scientific knowledge of what I shall do! Your calculations may reveal that I shall do a certain sequence of actions, as long as I do not come across any (putative) book of my life. If you decide not to write such a book yourself, and if you know that no one else will, you may conclude (deductively) that I shall perform the indicated sequence of acts.

I have shown that there are causally compossible worlds in which voluntary actions are scientifically predicted. Let us now see whether there are causally compossible worlds in which a person scientifically predicts one of his *own* actions. I think that there are such worlds and I shall illustrate by continuing the description of the world I was sketching earlier.

Having tested my book of life on a very large number of occasions during many months and failed to refute it, I become convinced that whatever it says is true. I have about as good inductive evidence for this proposition as I do for many another proposition I could be said to know. Finally, I get up enough courage to look at the very end of the book and, as expected, it tells when and how I shall die. Dated five years hence, it describes my committing suicide by jumping off the 86th floor observation deck of the Empire State Building. From a description of the thoughts which will flash through my mind before jumping, it is clear that the intervening five years will have been terrible. As a result of those experiences, I shall have emotions and desires (and beliefs) which will induce me to jump. Since I trust the book completely, I now conclude that I *shall* commit suicide five years hence. Moreover, I can be said to *know* that I shall commit suicide.

As described so far, we cannot consider my prediction of my suicide a "scientific" prediction. To be a scientific prediction the predicted event must be *deduced* from laws and antecedent conditions, while, as I have described the case, no deduction was involved. However, we might supplement the situation so as to include a deduction. The book may be imagined to list the relevant physical and psychological laws (in a footnote, say) and the relevant conditions which determine my committing suicide (my intention to commit suicide, my proximity to the fence surrounding the observation deck, the absence of guards or other interfering factors, etc.). From these laws and conditions I actually deduce my future action.[13]

This example shows, contrary to the view of some authors, that we can have inductive knowledge of our own future actions, knowledge which is not based on having already made a decision or formed an intention to perform the future action. Stuart Hampshire, for example, has recently written, ". . . I cannot intelligibly justify a claim to certain knowledge of what I shall voluntarily do on a specific occasion by an

---

13. That these conditions will actually obtain is, of course, open to doubt. Moreover, I have not learned of *them* by scientific prediction. I have simply "taken the book's word" that these conditions will obtain; I have not deduced them from other, still earlier, conditions. However, there are no restrictions on the manner in which a predictor comes to know antecedent conditions. One way predictors might learn about antecedent conditions is by using various measuring devices and instruments, the reliability of which is supported by inductive evidence. My book of life may be regarded as such a device, and my inductive evidence supporting its reliability may be as strong as that supporting the reliability of various other devices which scientists commonly use for obtaining knowledge of antecedent conditions.

inductive argument; if I do really know what I shall do, voluntarily, and entirely of my own free will, on a specific occasion, I must know this in virtue of a firm intention to act in a certain way."[14] The case outlined, I believe, shows that Hampshire is mistaken. In that case, there is a time at which I do have certain knowledge of what I shall do (at any rate, about as "certain" as one can be with inductive evidence) and yet I have formed no intention nor made any decision to perform that action. At the time I read the book's prediction, I do not intend to commit suicide. But although I do not intend to commit suicide, I fully believe and know that, five years later, I shall intend to commit suicide. I firmly believe that, at that later time, I shall feel certain emotions and have certain desires which will induce me to jump off the Empire State Building. At the time of my reading the book I do not feel those things, but I commiserate with my future self, much as I commiserate with and understand another person's desires, beliefs, feelings, intentions, etc. Still, my understanding of these states of mind and of the action in which they will issue is the understanding of a spectator; my knowledge of these states and of my future action is purely inductive. Moreover, this knowledge is of a particular *voluntary* act to be performed at a specified time. Though the suicide will be a "desperate" action, it will in no sense be "coerced" or done unknowingly; it will flow from a firm intention, an intention formed very deliberately. But that intention will not be formed until after I have had certain experiences, experiences which, at the time I am reading the book, I have not yet had.

We can imagine two alternative series of events to occur between my reading the book and my suicide. First, I might *forget* what I have learned from the book, and later decide to commit suicide. Secondly, while never forgetting the prediction, the knowledge of my future suicide may gradually change from more inductive knowledge to knowledge based on intention. In this second alternative, there is never any "moment" of decision. I never pass from a state of complete doubt about committing suicide into a sudden intention of committing suicide. Rather, there is a gradual change, over the five-year period, from mere inductive knowledge that I shall commit suicide to an intention to commit suicide. When I first read the book I am fully prepared to assent to the proposition that I shall commit suicide. But I am saddened by the thought; my heart isn't in it. Later, as a result of various tragic experiences, my *will* acquiesces in the idea. I begin to welcome the thought of suicide, to entertain the thought of committing suicide with pleasure and relief. By the time the appointed time comes around, I am *bent* on suicide. This gradual change in attitude constitutes the difference between the kind of knowledge of my future suicide, the difference between mere inductive knowledge and knowledge based on intention. Hampshire claims that the first kind of knowledge of one's own action is impossible. The present case, I believe, shows this claim to be mistaken.

Many philosophers seem to be very uncomfortable with the idea of a book of life. They believe that the existence of such books—or of fore-

---

14. *Freedom of the Individual* (London, 1965), see p. 54.

knowledge of actions in any form—would deprive us of all the essential characteristics of voluntary behavior: choice, decision, deliberation, etc.[15] I do not think this fear is warranted, however. I have just shown that even if a person reads what a book of life predicts, and believes this prediction, he can still perform the indicated action voluntarily. Moreover, the existence of predictions which the agent does *not* read leaves ample opportunity for deliberation and decision. An agent may know that a book of his life exists and yet proceed to make decisions and to deliberate as all of us do now. The agent's belief that there is such a book, and his belief that the book's existence implies that his actions are causally necessitated, is compatible with his deliberating whether to do one action or another. Although his future action is causally necessitated, one of the antecedent conditions which necessitate it is his deliberation. Indeed, the prediction in the book of life was made precisely because its writer knew that the agent would deliberate and then decide to do the predicted action. Thus, the book of life can hardly be said to preclude deliberation. Nor does the book of life imply that the agent's deliberation is "for naught," or "irrelevant." On the contrary, his deliberation is a crucial antecedent condition: were he not to deliberate, he probably would not perform the action he eventually does perform. Deliberation and decision are perfectly compatible with the existence of books of life; and they are perfectly compatible with the thesis that they, and the actions in which they issue, are determined.

15. One such philosopher is Richard Taylor. See his "Deliberation and Foreknowledge," *American Philosophical Quaterly*, Vol. 1 (1964), pp. 73–80. Many others could also be named.

SUGGESTED READINGS

Free Will and Determinism

Collections of Writings on the Free Will Problem

Berofsky, Bernard (ed.). *Free Will and Determinism.* New York: Harper & Row, 1966.

Honderick, Ted (ed.). *Essays on Freedom of Action.* London: Routledge & Kegan Paul, 1973.

Hook, Sidney (ed.). *Determinism and Freedom.* New York: New York University Press, 1961.

Lehrer, Keith (ed.). *Freedom and Determinism.* New York: Random House, 1966.

Morgenbesser, Sidney, and Walsh, James (eds.). *Free Will.* Englewood Cliffs, N.J.: Prentice-Hall, Inc., 1962.

Pears, David F. (ed.). *Freedom and the Will.* New York: St. Martin's Press, 1963.

Libertarianism

Campbell, C. A. *In Defense of Free Will.* Glasgow: Glasgow University Press, 1934 [partly in Bierman-Gould, Brandt, Singer-Ammerman, Tillman-Berofsky-O'Connor].

———————. "Is Free Will a Pseudo-Problem?" *Mind,* Vol. 60 (1951) [partly in Berofsky, Edwards-Pap, Feinberg, Margolis].

Chisholm, Roderick M. "Human Freedom and the Self." University of Kansas, 1964 [in Feinberg].

Foot, Philippa. "Free Will as Involving Determinism," *Philosophical Review,* Vol. 66 (1957) [in Berofsky, Morgenbesser-Walsh, Wolff].

Hartmann, Nicolai, *Ethics.* London: Allen & Unwin, 1932. Vol. III.

James, William. "The Dilemma of Determinism," in *The Will to Believe and Other Essays.* London: Longmans, Green, 1931 [partly in Edwards-Pap, Mandelbaum-Gramlich-Anderson, Bronstein-Krikorian-Wiener].

Lewis, H. D. *Morals and Revelation.* London: Allen & Unwin, 1951.

Sartre, J. P. *Being and Nothingness,* tr. H. E. Barnes. New York: Philosophical Library, 1956. Part 4, Chap. 1 [partly in Berofsky, Morgenbesser-Walsh].

Reconcilism

Brandt, R. B. *Ethical Theory.* Englewood Cliffs, N.J.: Prentice-Hall, Inc., 1959, Chap. 20.

Hobbes, Thomas. "Of Liberty and Necessity."

Hume, David. *An Enquiry Concerning Human Understanding,* Section VIII, "Of Liberty and Necessity."

Locke, John. *Essay Concerning Human Understanding,* Bk. II, Chap. 21.

Mill, J. S. *A System of Logic,* Bk VI, Chap. 2 [in Edwards-Pap, Margolis, Randall-Buchler, Shirk, Singer-Ammerman].

———————. *An Examination of Sir William Hamilton's Philosophy.* Chap. 26 [in Berofsky, Morgenbesser-Walsh, Tillman-Berofsky-O'Connor].

Moore, G. E. *Ethics.* London: Oxford Univ. Press, 1912, Chap. 6.

Nowell-Smith, P. H. *Ethics.* London: Penguin Books, 1954. Chaps. 19, 20 [partly in Berofsky].

Ross, W. D. *Foundations of Ethics.* Oxford: Clarendon Press, 1931. Chap. 10.

Schlick, Moritz. *Problems of Ethics,* tr. David Rynin, Englewood Cliffs, N.J.: Prentice-Hall, Inc., 1939. Chap. 7 [in Berofsky, Edwards-Pap].

Stevenson, C. L. *Ethics and Language.* New Haven, Conn.: Yale University Press, 1944. Chap. 14.

Determinism, Pro and Con

Bergson, Henry. *Time and Free Will.* New York: Macmillan,;1921.

Broad, C. D. *Determinism, Indeterminism, and Libertarianism.* New York: Macmillan, 1934 [in Morgenbesser and Walsh, Berofsky].

Nagel, Ernest. *The Structure of Science.* New York: Harcourt, 1961. Chap. 10.

Pap, Arthur. *An Introduction to the Philosophy of Science.* New York: Free Press, 1962. Chap. 17.

Peirce, C. S. "The Doctrine of Necessity Examined," in M. R. Cohen, ed., *Chance, Love, and Logic.* New York: Harcourt, 1923.

Russell, Bertrand. "On the Notion of Cause," in *Mysticism and Logic.* London: Longmans, Green, 1918. Chap. 9.

——————. *Our Knowledge of the External World.* New York: Norton, 1929. Chap. 8.

Indeterminism in Recent Physics

Eddington, Sir Arthur. *The Nature of the Physical World.* New York: Macmillan, 1928. Chap. 14.

Planck, Max. *Where Is Science Going?* tr. James Murphy. New York: Norton, 1932. Chaps. 4, 5 [in Sprague-Taylor].

Russell, Bertrand. *Religion and Science.* London: Oxford Univ. Press, 1935. Chap. 6.

Stebbing, Susan L. *Philosophy ˋnd the Physicists.* London: Methuen, 1937. Part III.

Determinism and the Concept of Action

Alston, W. P. "Wants, Actions, and Causal Explanations," in H. N. Castañeda, ed., *Intentionality, Minds, and Perception.* Detroit: Wayne State University Press, 1966.

Brandt, R. B., and Kim, J. "Wants as Explanations of Actions," *Journal of Philosophy,* Vol. 60 (1963).

Davidson, Donald. "Actions, Reasons, and Causes," *Journal of Philosophy,* Vol. 60 (1963) [in Berofsky, Margolis].

Goldman, A. I. *A Theory of Human Action.* Englewood Cliffs, N.J.: Prentice-Hall, Inc., 1970. Chap. 3.

Macintyre, A. C. "Determinism," *Mind,* Vol. 66 (1957) [in Berofsky].

Melden, A. I. *Free Action.* London: Routledge & Kegan Paul, 1961.

479

Taylor, R. *Action and Purpose.* Englewood Cliffs, N.J.: Prentice-Hall, Inc., 1966. Pt. II.

Responsibility

Feinberg, Joel. "Problematic Responsibility in Law and Morals," *Philosophical Review,* Vol. 71 (1962).

Hart, H. L. A. "The Ascription of Responsibility and Rights," in Anthony Flew, ed., *Essays in Logic and Language,* First Series. Oxford: Basil Blackwell, 1951.

Mandelbaum, Maurice. "Determinism and Moral Responsibility," *Ethics,* Vol. 71 (1960).

Morris, Herbert (ed.). *Freedom and Responsibility: Readings in Philosophy and Law.* Stanford, Calif.: Stanford University Press, 1961.

Nowell-Smith, P. H. "Free Will and Moral Responsibility," *Mind,* Vol. 57 (1944) [partly in Brandt, Sprague-Taylor].

PART V

Mind and Body

Introduction

People have always been fascinated by questions about their own nature, and philosophers have grappled with a number of problems in this area. The problems represented in this volume include: 1) the nature of the mind, or consciousness, and its relation to the body (the "mind-body problem"); 2) what makes a human being remain the same person through time (criteria of personal identity); 3) whether a person survives bodily death; 4) whether a person ever has a free choice between alternative actions. Part IV was devoted to question 4, and this part is made up of discussions of the first three questions.

THE MIND-BODY PROBLEM

There would be no philosophical problem about the relation of mind and body were it not for a peculiar fact about human beings, and presumably the higher animals as well; that different aspects or features of human beings are known in altogether different ways. Some of them are known "immediately" by the person himself but not by anyone else ("immediate knowledge" is knowledge that is not based on inference). Among the items known in this way are thoughts, daydreams, feelings, longings, pain, and sensory experiences. Other people can tell what I am thinking or feeling only through something else (mediately), only by asking me or by inferring it from my situation and behavior. But I do not have to find out through something else. I do not have to ask myself what I am feeling or observe my behavior. I *just know* what I am thinking or feeling, merely because I am thinking or feeling it. The facts about a person to which he has "privileged access" in this way, we may call "mental" facts. This leaves open the possibility that some individual instances of a type of fact, such as thoughts, may be "unconscious," and so not known immediately by their possessor. Thoughts can still be called "mental" since they are *generally* known immediately by their possessor.

There are other facts about a person to which he and other persons have equal access. These include being six-feet tall, having well-developed muscles, and secreting gastric juices. I do not have any specially privileged access to such facts as these. If I am to find out how tall I am, I will have to juxtapose my body to some standard measuring instrument; and it is clear that anyone else could determine my height in exactly the same way. These are "nonmental" facts.

You should note that, as we have defined these terms, for something to be "mental" is simply for it to be *knowable* in a certain way, and that alone. In calling thoughts "mental" we are not implying anything about their intrinsic nature. In particular, we are not implying anything as to whether they are physical in character. That question is left open.

The mental and nonmental aspects of people are intimately related. For one thing, they are aspects of one and the same being. At least, our way of talking about people is based on the assumption that this is so. It is one and the same person, John Jones, who is both six-feet tall and mentally depressed, who is both digesting his food and thinking about the history assignment. Moreover, it is not just that these aspects happen to exist side by side in the same substance; they influence each other in a variety of ways. One's conscious perceptions depend on physical processes in the sense organs and the brain. One's emotional feelings and states of mind are affected by glandular secretions. On the other side, anxieties and anger can affect the operations of the circulatory and digestive systems, even to the extent of giving rise to psychosomatic disease. And a conscious decision to go to the grocery store gives rise to a complicated series of bodily movements.

The "mind-body problem" is the problem of working out an adequate conception of the nature of a human being, a conception that takes account of the differences between mental and nonmental facts and also takes account of their intimate connection.

Classification of Theories

The sharpest opposition on the mind-body problem is over whether the mental and nonmental are fundamentally different in nature. For the *dualist,* the distinction between mental and nonmental indicates a basic metaphysical distinction between two types of reality. The dualist takes the nonmental side of people to be physical (material) in character and the mental side to be nonphysical, where "being physical in character" means "describable in terms of the concepts of physical science, such as spatial position, velocity, mass, electric charge, chemical composition, and so on." The dualist is flanked by opposing monisms, each of which tries to show that one side of the physical-mental contrast is really a special case of the other. On the one side, the *materialist (physicalist)* maintains that a human being is a purely physical substance, completely describable in physical terms. On this view, mental states are physical states of the brain, as physical in character as digestion or muscular contraction, although undoubtedly more complicated. On the other side, the *idealist* takes the position that matter is not ultimately real; that what we call "matter" or "physical substance" is only an aspect of mind, or somehow derivative from mind. There are many forms of idealism; the version advanced by Berkeley in Part VII (Reading 63) maintains that physical objects (including human bodies as well as tables and chairs) are really nothing more than collections of what would ordinarily be thought of as sensory experiences "of them." Idealism, as a position on the mind-body problem, is not a live option in the present climate of philosophical thought. In this part of the book, we shall restrict our attention to various forms of dualism and materialism.

Types of Dualism. The most extreme form of dualism is *Two-Substance Dualism,* which not only takes mental states to be nonphysical in *character,* but also considers them to be states of a nonphysical *substance,* a substance that is not located in space and has no size, shape, mass, or any other physical characteristics. (The general notion of "substance" being employed here is simply the notion of that which has properties and undergoes changes but is not itself a property or a change, and which remains the same thing through change.) According to this view, a person really is a combination of two "things": a physical thing, the body, and a nonphysical thing, the "mind" or "soul." Mental states are assigned to the latter, nonmental states to the former. It is an immaterial substance that does the thinking and feeling, whereas it is a material substance that does the walking and the digesting. The two-substance dualist generally holds that each of these components is inherently capable of existing on its own, although under the conditions of our earthly life they operate in close dependence on each other. This view of human nature flourished in the "mystery religions" of the ancient Near East, where it was believed that a man is essentially a spiritual substance, which is temporarily imprisoned in the body. When released from its confinement, it will be able to realize its true nature and destiny, provided it can avoid reincarnation in another body.[1] These views were given powerful philosophical expression by Plato, and the Platonic influence has kept this way of thinking alive in the philosophical tradition. Two-substance dualism is represented here by its most influential modern exponent, Descartes (Reading 42). The position is often referred to as "Cartesian dualism," and much philosophizing since Descartes' day has been taken up with extending and modifying his position, or with reacting against it in a variety of ways.

One can deny that mental states are physical in nature without ascribing them to an immaterial *substance* distinct from the body. There are two possibilities here. *One-substance dualism* holds that it is one and the same thing that has both mental and nonmental states, that is both seated on a chair and is feeling resentful. The second possibility is to deny that mental states and processes belong to any substance at all. In this view, a momentary thought or feeling simply *happens;* it is, so to speak, floating in the void, all by itself. There is no continuing thing that is *doing* the thinking and feeling. In this view, the most famous proponent of which was David Hume (1711–1776), what we call a mind is nothing but an aggregate or "bundle" of momentary conscious events. Hence, this position may be termed *"bundle dualism."* Huxley (Reading 43) represents a form of dualism that does not posit an immaterial substance; but his presentation does not

1. The notion of an immaterial soul also has been one strand in the Christian tradition (see Part I).

make clear whether he should be classed as a one-substance dualist or a bundle dualist.

General Reasons for Dualism.   Most philosophers have been dualists of one or another stripe. The popularity of the position has largely stemmed from the fact that conscious states *seem* so different from anything having physical characteristics. Thoughts and feelings do not seem to have exact spatial location, size, or shape. It sounds nonsensical to ask just exactly where my current thoughts about tax reform are located, how large they are, whether they are conical or cylindrical in shape, and how much they weigh. Furthermore, it seems that no matter how much I observed the physical processes going on in someone else's brain, I would fall short of observing his thoughts and feelings themselves. Later we shall see how the materialist tries to counter this prior presumption against his theory.

We shall now consider briefly the pros and cons of Cartesian dualism. Huxley's brand of dualism will be discussed later as an alternative to materialism.

Cartesian Dualism.   Why should anyone suppose that mental states are states of an immaterial substance that is distinct from the body? Well, if one is convinced by the considerations mentioned two paragraphs back, that conscious states are not physical in character, then the only remaining alternatives are bundle dualism and one-substance dualism. The Cartesian typically rejects the former because he holds that any state is a state of *some* underlying substance. And he typically rejects the latter because he feels that since states of consciousness are so different in character from bodily states, they could not both be states of one and the same substance. This then leaves two-substance dualism as the only alternative. These arguments are based on highly controversial metaphysical assumptions, which we will not be able to discuss here. The argument for two-substance dualism that is explicitly presented by Descartes in Reading 42 is rather different. When Descartes embarked on his program of systematic doubt, he found the one indubitable fact to be his own existence as a conscious subject. In Reading 42, he builds on this point the following argument for two-substance dualism. Since I was able to doubt that my body existed, while being unable to doubt that my mind existed, I "clearly and distinctly" apprehended the one apart from the other. But that shows that they are distinct things, at least in the sense that it is possible for the one to exist without the other. Descartes' contemporary, Arnauld, presents an ingenious objection to this argument (Reading 42).

In the last two centuries, the concept of an immaterial substance has lost favor, largely because it has remained a shadowy concept that is of little or no use in understanding human experience and behavior. By contrast, our knowledge of the brain and its relation to experience has grown by leaps and bounds. We know that we can stop pain by performing a certain operation on the hypothalmus; that destruction of a certain portion of the visual cortex impairs sight; that electric currents passing in various parts of the brain can cause enjoyment, fear, or anger. We know nothing comparable about the structure of the soul or its modes of operation. Its only function, it seems, is to be the substance of which conscious states are states. The concept also has remained undeveloped in another way; there are various basic questions about souls we have no idea how to answer. Does a person have one and only one soul throughout his lifetime, or several in succession? Could there be two different souls with exactly the same history of experiences? And if so, how would they be differentiated from each other?

In Descartes' own time, the main objection to his position was that it made causal interaction between mind and body unintelligible. It seemed inconceivable to many thinkers that a physical body should be set in motion except by impact from another physical body. But then if we construe a conscious decision as a nonphysical activity of a nonphysical substance, it would be inconceivable that a decision should cause the body to move. And, going in the reverse direction, it seemed equally inconceivable to many that physical processes could produce changes in an immaterial substance. How could the motions of material bodies affect anything other than the other material bodies they encounter? At the present time, philosophers are less bothered by these difficulties since, under the influence of Hume, they are much less ready to dogmatize about what can have a causal impact on what.

Classification Again.   At this point, it is necessary to introduce into our scheme a cross-classification based on the presence or absence of causal interaction between mind and body. We already have pointed out the apparent obviousness of such interaction, and we also have noted that many thinkers have held that on a dualist position such interaction would be inconceivable in either direction. In addition to that metaphysical argument, there are scientific reasons for denying that the dualist can handle causal influence from the mental to the nonmental. These reasons stem from the conviction that the human body, together with its physical environment, is a closed causal system; that everything that happens in the body, and all the physical behavior of the body, can be completely explained in terms of *physical* causes. It can hardly be claimed that science has "proven" this principle, but developments in physiology and physiological psychology have provided support for it. The more we learn about the physiology of the central nervous system and its influences on bodily behavior, the more plausible it becomes to regard behavior as strictly determined by physical happenings. But then, if, as dualism of any sort maintains, mental events are nonphysical in character, there is no room for them to play any causal role.

Thus, causal interaction is a severe problem for the dualist, and we must subdivide each form of dualism in terms of the position taken on the interaction issue. This is not the case, however, for either materialism or idealism. For these monistic positions, mind-body interaction is just a special case of interaction within the same basic metaphysical category, and hence poses no problem of principle. Materialists and idealists will all accept two-way interaction.

Putting all this together, we get the cross-classification scheme as seen in the figure that follows. (In the left-hand column the direction of the arrows indicates the direction of causal influence.)

We have scratched out those combinations that are not real possibilities,

Nature and Status of the Mental

	Materialism	Two-Substance Dualism	One-Substance Dualism	Bundle	Idealism
	Materialism	*Cartesianism*		*Hume (?)*	*Idealism*
Mental → Nonmental					
Mental → Nonmental			*Epiphenomenalism*		
Mental ← Nonmental					
Mental Nonmental (no causal influence either way)		*Parallelism*			

Causal Relations of Mental and Nonmental

and we have labelled only those boxes where the positions have had prominent exponents. No reasons have ever been provided for supposing that the mental affects the nonmental but not vice versa, and so that row has been deleted all across. When two-substance dualists have rejected interaction, it has been because of the inconceivability argument, which militates equally against interaction in both directions; one-way causal influence has no attraction for this position. Thus, the anti-interactionists among two-substance dualists have been *Parallelists,* such as the eighteenth century philosopher, Leibniz. He held, to put it in modern terminology, that the mind and the body have been "programmed" at their creation by God to run through their successive states so that they "match"; that is, so that their states are related to each other as they would be if there were causal connections between them.

As for bundle and one-substance dualism, it would seem that the "two-way" and the "neither-way" forms are real possibilities, but they have not been extensively developed. These views exist primarily in the form of epiphenomenalism, which asserts causal determination of mental states by bodily states, but no influence in the other direction. Epiphenomenalism is represented in our readings by Huxley (Reading 43). A good part of his essay is taken up with presenting evidence for the principle that physical behavior can be explained purely in terms of *physical* causes. One who accepts this principle and who, like Huxley, is convinced that conscious states are not physical in nature, is led to the view that a human being *as a causal system* is a purely physical mechanism, but that there also are mental "by-products" or "epiphenomena" that are "thrown off" by brain processes in the course of producing their physical effects, these mental "by-products" having no influence on the course of events. In the words of George Santayana, consciousness is a "lyric cry in the midst of business." An epiphenomenalist could be either a bundle dualist or a one-substance dualist. (Thus, in our diagram we have Epiphenomenalism straddling two boxes.) The epiphenomenalist can take conscious "epiphenomena" either to be nonphysical states of the embodied person (one-substance dualism) or to be events that do not "belong" to any substance (bundle dualism). Either view would be compatible with the position that conscious states are mere by-products without causal efficacy. As we have noted, Huxley does not make clear which alternative he has chosen.

Types of Materialism

Materialism maintains that a human being is a purely physical substance, completely describable in physical terms. What, then, is the materialist to say about mental states, which do not seem at first sight to be physical in character? There are two possible moves open: 1) The materialist may deny that there are any mental states. 2) He may admit the existence of mental states but maintain that they are physical in character after all. Despite the seeming absurdity of (1), it has been held, by psychologists such as B. F. Skinner and by philosophers such as W. V. Quine, that the entire mentalistic framework of concepts stems from a prescientific mode of explaining behavior, and that with the advance of science it will be junked in favor of neurophysiological concepts. According to this radical or "eliminative" materialism, the reality that we inadequately conceptualize as thoughts and feelings is adequately conceptualized only in neurophysiological terms.

IDENTITY THEORY

However, (2) is much more prevalent among materialists. According to this position, our mentalistic concepts really do apply to something; but neurophysiological terms apply to just the same things. One and the same event can be correctly termed a thought *and* a certain kind of physical process in the brain. This position is represented by J. J. C. Smart (Reading 44). It is sometimes called "the identity theory," since it maintains that every mental state is *identical* with some physical state of the brain.

This theory at first may seem obviously mistaken, and it has seemed this way to many philosophers. Suppose there is a state or occurrence that I (correctly) report by saying, "I feel remorse" or "The thought just occurred to me that I have an appointment at 2:00." Now, clearly, I was not reporting these facts in physical terms; "feel remorse" or "think that . . ." are not terms used in the physical sciences. And these examples are typical of how we report our mental states. But since the states and occurrences in question are *correctly* conceptualized in these nonphysical ways, they must be nonphysical in character, however closely they may be causally related to physical processes.

The identity theorist's reply is to point out the general possibility of one and the same thing's being conceptualized (identified) in quite different ways, in terms taken from quite different languages. For example, *a flash of lightning* is the same thing as a massive discharge of electricity in the clouds, despite the fact that only the second identification is in the language of electrical theory. Thus, my feelings of remorse could conceivably be the same thing as NP_1 (where "NP_1" is an abbreviation for some description of a brain state in neurophysiological terms), even though this one and the same thing is conceptualized in two quite different ways.

It is apparent from this reply that the identity asserted by the identity theorist is a "factual" or "contingent" identity, not a "logical" or "semantic" one. He is not asserting that "I feel remorse" *means the same* as "My brain is in state NP_1," or that the identity can be seen to hold just by reflecting on our psychological and physiological concepts. He maintains, rather, that *as a matter of fact,* mental states are physiological states of the brain. Similarly, the meteorologist holds that *as a matter of fact* lightning is a massive electrical discharge in the clouds. He does not suppose that people could have discovered this just by reflecting on what they meant by the term "lightning."

Reasons for the Identity Theory

Granted that the identity theory is not obviously false, what reason is there to think it true? Why should we suppose that every mental state is, as a matter of fact, identical with some physical state of the brain? The basic support for the materialist position comes from the development of science in modern times. There are several relevant aspects of this development.

First, there is the point, already mentioned in connection with the interaction issue, that progress has been made in finding purely physical determinants for the inner and outer behavior of the human organism. To the extent that this can be done, we are encouraged to think of man as a purely physical mechanism.

The second sort of advance concerns our understanding of the neural bases of conscious states and processes. We always have had some knowledge of the physiological conditions of perception and bodily sensation. Before the nineteenth century however, one was not contravening any empirical facts if he held that thought, imagination, and feeling were the activity of a nonmaterial substance that, in these functions, made use of no material organs at all. But in recent times our understanding of the physiological basis of the higher mental processes has greatly increased, even though our knowledge of the minute structure of brain processes is still rudimentary. Through observation of persons who have lost or suffered damage to parts of their brains, and through artificial stimulation of parts of the brain, we have been able to locate the brain regions responsible for such functions as memory, emotion, and abstract thought. It has been discovered that conscious sensations and imagery can be produced by the electrical stimulation of certain parts of the brain. More recently, investigators have discovered differences in patterns of brain activity in dreams and in dreamless sleep. As a result of these investigations, it is widely believed that every distinguishable conscious state has some neural state of (or process in) the brain as a necessary and sufficient condition. That is, it is believed that for any type of conscious state that one can specify (such as feeling a thrill of excitement), one can specify some type of brain state, B, such that it is a law of nature that one feels a thrill of excitement if and only if one's brain is in state B.[2] We are a long way from being able to spell out such "if and only if" laws in detail, but the results to date have encouraged people to think that there are such laws to be discovered.

Thirdly, the conception of mental processes as operations of a physical mechanism has received an additional boost from dramatic developments in computers that carry out, or simulate, various kinds of mental operations. Computers are best known for solving complicated mathematical problems, but they can also be designed to play chess, recognize objects, and store vast quantities of information. In Reading 46, A. M. Türing conducts a lively and witty defense of the proposition that automata could be produced that would be indistinguishable from human beings, so long as we go by their answers to questions and not by their physical appearance. But if it is possible to manufacture a computer that will think, perceive, and remember, does that not show that these mental functions are purely physical in character? We know that a computer is purely physical; we have *made* it without putting anything nonphysical into it. Two considerations cast doubt

2. This is a bit strong. A more realistic assumption would be that for each distinguishable type of conscious state, there are a number of different types of brain states, each of which is a sufficient condition for that conscious state; and that the disjunction of those brain states constitutes a necessary condition.

on the cogency of this argument. a) After all, the computer is only *like* a human being. Even if the psychological processes in a computer are purely physical, does that show that the analogous processes in a human being are purely physical? Couldn't the same functions be performed both by a physical mechanism and by an immaterial substance? b) If the behavior of the computer does warrant our ascribing mental states to it, doesn't that mean that the same old mind-body problem reappears there? Don't we have the same choice between dualism and materialism for the computer? For further discussion of these problems, see the bibliography at the end of this part.

As these questions suggest, the scientific developments that provide the strongest support for materialism have to do specifically with the scientific study of people—(1) and (2). However, even when we make the strongest possible extrapolations from these developments, they can be accommodated by epiphenomenalism as well as by materialism. Let us see how this works out for both (1) and (2).

Number (1) rules out any causal efficacy of the mental, conceived as nonphysical. But that simply leaves us with a choice of construing the mental as nonphysical and causally inefficacious (epiphenomenalism) or physical and efficacious (identity theory). As an example of what is claimed in (1), let's say that a particular voluntary movement, such as a student's raising his hand in class, is caused by muscular contractions, which in turn are caused by neural impulses in afferent nerves, which in turn are caused by neural processes in the brain. . . . No matter how far back we push the causal chain we find nothing but physical states and processes. Now what about the student's conscious decision to raise his hand, which common sense regards as the cause of the movement? We still have a choice between a) saying, with the epiphenomenalist, that the conscious decision is an event distinct from the brain processes but without any influence on what was happening, and b) saying, with the materialist, that the conscious decision is the same event as certain neural processes in the brain, and hence that the decision, as a kind of neural process, *was* among the causes of the bodily movement.

Number (2) also can be accommodated by both positions. Let M be *consciously intending to raise his hand* and P be some pattern of neuron firings connected with that intention by an "if and only if" law. This law implies that one cannot be in the one state without simultaneously being in the other. In the epiphenomenalist interpretation, this means that P invariably produces M as a "by-product." In the materialist interpretation, P and M are the *same* state under two descriptions, and that is why it is impossible to have one without the other.

If any possible scientific evidence, even that most favorable to materialism, also can be accommodated by epiphenomenalism, on what basis could we choose between them? For one thing, if one contender were disqualified on other grounds, that would leave the other in sole possession of the field. This is the line typically taken by the epiphenomenalist. He thinks it is obviously false that mental states are physical in nature; or else he considers materialism to fall victim to some of the difficulties we shall mention shortly. The other possibility is to recognize both positions as contenders but argue that one provides a *better way* of taking account of the scientific evidence. This is the line typically taken by identity theorists.

The respects in which materialism is most commonly alleged to be superior are the following:

1) Materialism permits a greater theoretical economy. It posits only one basic category of states and processes.

2) On the epiphenomenalist position, the mental side of biological evolution would be a mystery. According to epiphenomenalism, mental states and processes have no influence on bodily behavior and hence have no adaptive value; they in no way enable the organism to respond more effectively to environmental conditions. Nevertheless, in the course of evolution, organisms have developed these useless mental appanages. Materialism is not confronted with this dilemma, since it can recognize that mental states (as a special type of physical states) do have an influence on behavior.

3) In Reading 44, Smart points out that on a dualist position we are saddled with a queer sort of scientific law, one that relates enormously complicated neurophysiological states of the brain to simple conscious events. He argues that it is contrary to good scientific methodology to accept such laws as ultimate.

Objections to the Identity Theory

There are two main contemporary criticisms of materialism, both of which are represented in Malcolm's essay (Reading 45). First, it is argued that a mental state cannot be identical with any brain state, since certain things that are true of one are not (or even cannot be) true of the other. For example, it is alleged that whereas brain states have exact spatial location and brain processes are more or less swift, it makes no sense to speak of conscious feelings as having an exact spatial location and as having a certain velocity. Again, it is contended that whereas a feeling may be more or less intense and a thought more or less coherent, it makes no sense to characterize physical states or processes in these terms. (See Smart's reply to his "Objection 5" in Reading 44). The second criticism takes off from the point that the identity theorist does *not* assert that a given mental term, such as "feels lonely," has the same *meaning* as some neurophysiological term. But if in saying, "He feels lonely," we are not saying the same thing about him as we would be in attributing the correlated brain state to him, then it must be that we are ascribing different *properties* to him in the two statements. Even if feeling lonely and being in brain state of type B are the same concrete event, it is one feature (side, aspect) of this event that makes it a feeling of loneliness and a different feature (side, aspect) that makes it a case of a type B brain state. Hence, within this one-and-the-same event, we must distinguish a mental side as well as a physical side, the former of which cannot be described in physical terms. In other words, the price the materialist pays for "contingent" identity is that he is left with a nonphysical "aspect" of brain states and processes. In Malcolm's article, this criticism takes the form of claiming that thoughts typically presuppose social practices and rules, which themselves cannot be described in physical terms. (See Smart's reply to "Objection 3" in Reading 44.)

In our general introduction to this book, we stated that the observable facts available to science could not decide the mind-body problem. Now that we have reviewed the problem, you will see why we made that claim!

IMMORTALITY

Since most of us take a lively interest in the question of whether we survive the death of our bodies, it will be instructive to explore the implications of different positions on the mind-body problem for the issue of immortality. *Immortality,* in a strict sense, entails *never-ending* existence; we can confine ourselves to the question of whether a human person continues to exist for any significant period of time after death.

In discussing this issue, most philosophers have confined themselves to the question of whether one continues to exist after death as a disembodied conscious subject. Two-substance Dualism clearly allows for this possibility; according to that position, an embodied human being is a team of two "things"—an immaterial mind and a material body—each of which is intrinsically capable of existing apart from the other. On this position, it is at least possible for me to continue to exist as a conscious subject after my body has decayed. Whether this is actually the case is, of course, a further question. But it would seem that the other positions we were considering (excluding Idealism) do not even allow for the possibility. On those positions, conscious states and processes either belong to a material substance (One-substance dualism), or have the status of by-products of bodily activity (Epiphenomenalism), or are themselves bodily in character (Identity Theory). Without the body, they have no foothold in existence.

The discussions by Russell (Reading 47) and Broad (Reading 48) fit into this framework. Russell gives the standard argument against the possibility of a disembodied existence of a human person from an epiphenomenalist or one-substance dualist position. (Russell's exposition does not distinguish between these positions.) Since "habit and memory are both due to effects on the body," they cannot continue without the body. Broad, on the other hand, is prepared to consider a two-substance dualism (which he terms the "Instrumental Theory"), at least to the extent of considering whether paranormal psychic phenomena give empirical support to the hypothesis that the human mind survives the death of the body. He concludes that such phenomena do provide some reason for supposing that something survives, but something less than a complete mind. What survives, on this view, is a "psychic factor," which has to be combined with a "bodily factor" to make up a mind in the full sense.

It would be a mistake to confine the discussion of survival to *disembodied* survival. The belief in embodied survival is at least as common in religious and philosophical thought. The notion of "reincarnation," that one's soul is successively "incarnated" in numerous different bodies, is prevalent in the Orient. And the dominant conception in the Jewish and early Christian traditions is that of the miraculous resurrection of the body at the Last Judgment. (In the course of Christian history, this original idea has become merged with the belief in the disembodied existence of the soul, but only the resurrection of the body is affirmed in the classic Christian creeds.) In both these conceptions, a person is thought of as existing in bodily form after death, but in a *different* body. (Even when the Christian thinks of *his* body being resurrected, the resurrected body presumably will not pass the usual tests for being the *same* body as the one that died.)

The Identity Theory, Epiphenomenalism, and One-Substance Dualism clearly do not rule out these views in the way they rule out disembodied survival. These versions of immortality are quite compatible with the thesis that mental life is possible only in an embodied form, for they posit no disembodied mental life. The doctrine of reincarnation may seem to presuppose Two-Substance Dualism, for it is customarily formulated in terms of an immaterial *soul* that moves from one body to another; but the underlying idea that one and the same person "has" different bodies at different times does not require that assumption.

PERSONAL IDENTITY

In thinking about the possibility of "bodily transfer," we come up against a basic question that was just beneath the surface all along—viz., What does it take for X to be the same person as Y? If we suppose it conceivable that a person with a different body is the same person as I, we are pre-supposing that it is something other than sameness of body that constitutes sameness of person. The belief in disembodied existence makes the same assumption; it supposes that a being with no body at all could be the same person as I. But then what *is* required for personal identity?

A natural answer is that mental continuity constitutes sameness of person. So long as the mental life of a being has developed by a continuous process from my present mental life, in the same way my present mental life has developed from my past mental life, then that being is the same person as I, *is* I. Mental continuity involves a number of distinguishable aspects—thoughts, memories, feelings, attitudes, habits, personality charac-teristics, and so on. (Memory has been in the center of attention in much of the literature, but the classic treatments by Butler and Reid (see Suggested Readings) show that it cannot do the whole job.) This is the criterion of personal identity used by Russell (Reading 47), and by Hick (Reading 11) in his defense of the concept of resurrection.

It cannot be denied that we employ the criterion of mental continuity in settling questions of identity for embodied persons in everyday life. If a person of unfamiliar bodily appearance clearly remembers various incidents in the life of my old friend, Joe Krasnick, I will take him to be Joe Krasnick. But, as Russell points out, we also use the "same body" criterion. In fact, we often allow the latter to override the former; if Joe Krasnick suffers amnesia or some other radical break in mental continuity, it will still be Joe Krasnick, the same person, who suffered that break. What makes the person Joe Krasnick in this case is the sameness of body. Normally, the two criteria give the same result, but, as the above case indicates, there are occasions, even in everyday life, when they come into conflict.

The believer in survival is clearly taking the position that when, after my death, an embodied person (with a different body) exhibits mental continuity with me (to a sufficient degree) the *mental continuity* criterion should override the *same body* criterion, and we should judge that person to be me. Here, too, we have the problem of what to do when the criteria conflict. What is called for is a general theory of personal identity that could serve as a basis for judging particular cases.

The need for a general theory arises in other contexts as well. With further advances in bio-engineering, we may some day be in a position to exchange brains between different human bodies, to "copy" brains, or even copy complete bodies. If you and I have exchanged brains, and thereby exchanged memories, personality characteristics, and so on, which of the resulting organisms is me and which you? If I have been replicated in complete detail (including memories and other mental features), does my replica have as much right to be considered me as I do? These are not just questions for idle speculation. If such transformations become possible, serious legal and moral questions will hang on our answers.

None of our readings develop a fully general theory of personal identity, but some of them do present considerations that are relevant to the issues we have raised. Hick (Reading 11), in defending the legitimacy of the idea of resurrection, presents a series of cases of apparent bodily transfer; but he confines himself to claiming, in the case of each, that our intuitive judgment would be that it is the same person at both ends of the "transfer." Quinton in Reading 49 goes into the issues more generally and supports Hick's position by confronting squarely the general question of what to do about conflicts of bodily and mental criteria. Quinton does not contend that our everyday concept of a person is precise or complete enough to dictate any particular answer, but he does argue that "it would be the natural thing to extend our concept of a person, given the purposes for which it has been constructed, so as to identify anyone present to us now with whoever it was who used to have the same character and memories as he has." In other words, the mental criterion overrides the bodily criterion, so long as there is someone who satisfies the mental criterion. (Note that this last condition is *not* satisfied in the usual amnesia case; there no one has the previous memories of the amnesia victim.) Williams (Reading 50) carries out a searching and subtle examination of "bodily transfer" cases. He comes to no clear-cut conclusion, but the tendency of his discussion is to oppose the claims made by Hick and Quinton for the dominance of the *mental continuity* criterion.

42. René Descartes. With objections by Thomas Hobbes and Antoine Arnauld, and replies by Descartes.

René Descartes (1596–1650) was a key figure in the history
of mathematics and is generally regarded as the founder
of modern philosophy.
Thomas Hobbes (1588–1679) was one of the most important
philosophers of his time, largely because of his political
philosophy.
Antoine Arnauld (1612–1694), Jansenist theologian and
philosopher, is especially remembered for his controversies
with Descartes, Malebranche, and Leibniz.

Skepticism and Dualism

Meditation I: Of the Things Which May Be Brought within the Sphere of the Doubtful.

It is now some years since I detected how many were the false beliefs
that I had from my earliest youth admitted as true, and how doubtful
was everything I had since constructed on this basis; and from that time
I was convinced that I must once for all seriously undertake to rid myself of all the opinions which I had formerly accepted, and commence to
build anew from the foundation, if I wanted to establish any firm and
permanent structure in the sciences. But as this enterprise appeared to
be a very great one, I waited until I had attained an age so mature that

From René Descartes, *Meditations on First Philosophy*, 2nd ed., 1642, including
objections to the work collected from various eminent thinkers of the time and
answered by Descartes; in *The Philosophical Works of Descartes*, trans., E. S.
Haldane and G. R. T. Ross. Published by Cambridge University Press, Cambridge,
1931, and reprinted by their permission.

I could not hope that at any later date I should be better fitted to execute my design. This reason caused me to delay so long that I should feel that I was doing wrong were I to occupy in deliberation the time that yet remains to me for action. To-day, then, since very opportunely for the plan I have in view I have delivered my mind from every care [and am happily agitated by no passions] and since I have procured for myself an assured leisure in a peaceable retirement, I shall at last seriously and freely address myself to the general upheaval of all my former opinions.

Now for this object it is not necessary that I should show that all of these are false—I shall perhaps never arrive at this end. But inasmuch as reason already persuades me that I ought no less carefully to withhold my assent from matters which are not entirely certain and indubitable than from those which appear to me manifestly to be false, if I am able to find in each one some reason to doubt, this will suffice to justify my rejecting the whole. And for that end it will not be requisite that I should examine each in particular, which would be an endless undertaking; for owing to the fact that the destruction of the foundations of necessity brings with it the downfall of the rest of the edifice, I shall only in the first place attack those principles upon which all my former opinions rested.

All that up to the present time I have accepted as most true and certain I have learned either from the senses or through the senses; but it is sometimes proved to me that these senses are deceptive, and it is wiser not to trust entirely to any thing by which we have once been deceived.

But it may be that although the senses sometimes deceive us concerning things which are hardly perceptible, or very far away, there are yet many others to be met with as to which we cannot reasonably have any doubt, although we recognise them by their means. For example, there is the fact that I am here, seated by the fire, attired in a dressing gown, having this paper in my hands and other similar matters. And how could I deny that these hands and this body are mine, were it not perhaps that I compare myself to certain persons, devoid of sense, whose cerebella are so troubled and clouded by the violent vapours of black bile, that they constantly assure us that they think they are kings when they are really quite poor, or that they are clothed in purple when they are really without covering, or who imagine that they have an earthenware head or are nothing but pumpkins or are made of glass. But they are mad, and I should not be any the less insane were I to follow examples so extravagant.

At the same time I must remember that I am a man, and that consequently I am in the habit of sleeping, and in my dreams representing to myself the same things or sometimes even less probable things, than do those who are insane in their waking moments. How often has it happened to me that in the night I dreamt that I found myself in this particular place, that I was dressed and seated near the fire, whilst in reality I was lying undressed in bed! At this moment it does indeed seem to me that it is with eyes awake that I am looking at this paper; that this head which I move is not asleep, that it is deliberately and of set purpose that

I extend my hand and perceive it; what happens in sleep does not appear so clear nor so distinct as does all this. But in thinking over this I remind myself that on many occasions I have in sleep been deceived by similar illusions, and in dwelling carefully on this reflection I see so manifestly that there are no certain indications by which we may clearly distinguish wakefulness from sleep that I am lost in astonishment. And my astonishment is such that it is almost capable of persuading me that I now dream.

Now let us assume that we are asleep and that all these particulars, e.g. that we open our eyes, shake our head, extend our hands, and so on, are but false delusions; and let us reflect that possibly neither our hands nor our whole body are such as they appear to us to be. At the same time we must at least confess that the things which are represented to us in sleep are like painted representations which can only have been formed as the counterparts of something real and true, and that in this way those general things at least, i.e. eyes, a head, hands, and a whole body, are not imaginary things, but things really existent. For, as a matter of fact, painters, even when they study with the greatest skill to represent sirens and satyrs by forms the most strange and extraordinary, cannot give them natures which are entirely new, but merely make a certain medley of the members of different animals; or if their imagination is extravagant enough to invent something so novel that nothing similar has ever before been seen, and that their work represents a thing purely fictitious and absolutely false, it is certain all the same that the colours of which this is composed are necessarily real. And for the same reason, although these general things, to wit, [a body], eyes, a head, hands, and such like, may be imaginary, we are bound at the same time to confess that there are at least some other objects yet more simple and more universal, which are real and true; and of these just in the same way as with certain real colours, all these images of things which dwell in our thoughts, whether true and real or false and fantastic, are formed.

To such a class of things pertains corporeal nature in general, and its extension, the figure of extended things, their quantity or magnitude and number, as also the place in which they are, the time which measures their duration, and so on.

That is possibly why our reasoning is not unjust when we conclude from this that Physics, Astronomy, Medicine and all other sciences which have as their end the consideration of composite things, are very dubious and uncertain; but that Arithmetic, Geometry and other sciences of that kind which only treat of things that are very simple and very general, without taking great trouble to ascertain whether they are actually existent or not, contain some measure of certainty and an element of the indubitable. For whether I am awake or asleep, two and three together always form five, and the square can never have more than four sides, and it does not seem possible that truths so clear and apparent can be suspected of any falsity [or uncertainty].

Nevertheless I have long had fixed in my mind the belief that an all-powerful God existed by whom I have been created such as I am. But how do I know that He has not brought it to pass that there is no earth, no heaven, no extended body, no magnitude, no place, and that neverthe-less [I possess the perceptions of all these things and that] they seem to me to exist just exactly as I now see them? And, besides, as I some-times imagine that others deceive themselves in the things which they think they know best, how do I know that I am not deceived every time that I add two and three, or count the sides of a square, or judge of things yet simpler, if anything simpler can be imagined? But possibly God has not desired that I should be thus deceived, for He is said to be supremely good. If, however, it is contrary to His goodness to have made me such that I constantly deceive myself, it would also appear to be contrary to His goodness to permit me to be sometimes deceived, and nevertheless I cannot doubt that He does permit this.

There may indeed be those who would prefer to deny the existence of a God so powerful, rather than believe that all other things are uncer-tain. But let us not oppose them for the present, and grant that all that is here said of a God is a fable; nevertheless in whatever way they sup-pose that I have arrived at the state of being that I have reached—whether they attribute it to fate or to accident, or make out that it is by a continual succession of antecedents, or by some other method—since to err and deceive oneself is a defect, it is clear that the greater will be the probability of my being so imperfect as to deceive myself ever, as is the Author to whom they assign my origin the less powerful. To these reasons I have certainly nothing to reply, but at the end I feel con-strained to confess that there is nothing in all that I formerly believed to be true, of which I cannot in some measure doubt, and that not merely through want of thought or through levity, but for reasons which are very powerful and maturely considered; so that henceforth I ought not the less carefully to refrain from giving credence to these opinions than to that which is manifestly false, if I desire to arrive at any certainty [in the sciences].

But it is not sufficient to have made these remarks, we must also be careful to keep them in mind. For these ancient and commonly held opin-ions still revert frequently to my mind, long and familiar custom having given them the right to occupy my mind against my inclination and rendered them almost masters of my belief; nor will I ever lose the habit of deferring to them or of placing my confidence in them, so long as I consider them as they really are, i.e. opinions in some measure doubtful, as I have just shown, and at the same time highly probable, so that there is much more reason to believe in than to deny them. That is why I con-sider that I shall not be acting amiss, if, taking of set purpose a contrary belief, I allow myself to be deceived, and for a certain time pretend that all these opinions are entirely false and imaginary, until at last, having thus balanced my former prejudices with my latter [so that they cannot divert my opinions more to one side than to the other], my judgment will no longer be dominated by bad usage or turned away from the right knowledge of the truth. For I am assured that there can be neither peril nor error in this course, and that I cannot at present yield too much to distrust, since I am not considering the question of action, but only of knowledge.

I shall then suppose, not that God who is supremely good and the fountain of truth, but some evil genius not less powerful than deceitful, has employed his whole energies in deceiving me; I shall consider that the heavens, the earth, colours, figures, sound, and all other external things are nought but the illusions and dreams of which this genius has availed himself in order to lay traps for my credulity; I shall consider myself as having no hands, no eyes, no flesh, no blood, nor any senses, yet falsely believing myself to possess all these things; I shall remain obstinately attached to this idea, and if by this means it is not in my power to arrive at the knowledge of any truth, I may at least do what is in my power [i.e. suspend my judgment], and with firm purpose avoid giving credence to any false thing, or being imposed upon by this arch deceiver, however powerful and deceptive he may be. But this task is a laborious one, and insensibly a certain lassitude leads me into the course of my ordinary life. And just as a captive who in sleep enjoys an imaginary liberty, when he begins to suspect that his liberty is but a dream, fears to awaken, and conspires with these agreeable illusions that the deception may be prolonged, so insensibly of my own accord I fall back into my former opinions, and I dread awakening from this slumber, lest the laborious wakefulness which would follow the tranquillity of this repose should have to be spent not in daylight, but in the excessive darkness of the difficulties which have just been discussed.

Meditation II: Of the Nature of the Human Mind, and That It Is More Easily Known than the Body.

The Meditation of yesterday filled my mind with so many doubts that it is no longer in my power to forget them. And yet I do not see in what manner I can resolve them; and, just as if I had all of a sudden fallen into very deep water, I am so disconcerted that I can neither make certain of setting my feet on the bottom, nor can I swim and so support myself on the surface. I shall nevertheless make an effort and follow anew the same path as that on which I yesterday entered, i.e. I shall proceed by setting aside all that in which the least doubt could be supposed to exist, just as if I had discovered that it was absolutely false; and I shall ever follow in this road until I have met with something which is certain, or at least, if I can do nothing else, until I have learned for certain that there is nothing in the world that is certain. Archimedes, in order that he might draw the terrestrial globe out of its place, and transport it elsewhere, demanded only that one point should be fixed and immoveable; in the same way I shall have the right to conceive high hopes if I am happy enough to discover one thing only which is certain and indubitable.

I suppose, then, that all the things that I see are false; I persuade myself that nothing has ever existed of all that my fallacious memory represents to me. I consider that I possess no senses; I imagine that body, figure, extension, movement and place are but the fiction of my mind. What, then, can be esteemed as true? Perhaps nothing at all, unless that there is nothing in the world that is certain.

But how can I know there is not something different from those things that I have just considered, of which one cannot have the slightest doubt? Is there not some God, or some other being by whatever name we call it, who puts these reflections into my mind? That is not necessary, for is it not possible that I am capable of producing them myself? I myself, am I not at least something? But I have already denied that I had senses and body. Yet I hesitate, for what follows from that? Am I so dependent on body and senses that I cannot exist without these? But I was persuaded that there was nothing in all the world, that there was no heaven, no earth, that there were no minds, nor any bodies: was I not then likewise persuaded that I did not exist? Not at all; of a surety I myself did exist since I persuaded myself of something [or merely because I thought of something]. But there is some deceiver or other, very powerful and very cunning, who ever employs his ingenuity in deceiving me. Then without doubt I exist also if he deceives me, and let him deceive me as much as he will, he can never cause me to be nothing so long as I think that I am something. So that after having reflected well and carefully examined all things, we must come to the definite conclusion that this proposition: I am, I exist, is necessarily true each time that I pronounce it, or that I mentally conceive it.

But I do not yet know clearly enough what I am, I who am certain that I am; and hence I must be careful to see that I do not imprudently take some other object in place of myself, and thus that I do not go astray in respect of this knowledge that I hold to be the most certain and most evident of all that I have formerly learned. That is why I shall now consider anew what I believed myself to be before I embarked upon these last reflections; and of my former opinions I shall withdraw all that might even in a small degree be invalidated by the reasons which I have just brought forward, in order that there may be nothing at all left beyond what is absolutely certain and indubitable.

What then did I formerly believe myself to be? Undoubtedly I believed myself to be a man. But what is a man? Shall I say a reasonable animal? Certainly not; for then I should have to inquire what an animal is, and what is reasonable; and thus from a single question I should insensibly fall into an infinitude of others more difficult; and I should not wish to waste the little time and leisure remaining to me in trying to unravel subtleties like these. But I shall rather stop here to consider the thoughts which of themselves spring up in my mind, and which were not inspired by anything beyond my own nature alone when I applied myself to the consideration of my being. In the first place, then, I considered myself as having a face, hands, arms, and all that system of members composed of bones and flesh as seen in a corpse which I designated by the name of body. In addition to this I considered that I was nourished, that I walked, that I felt, and that I thought, and I referred all these actions to the soul: but I did not stop to consider what the soul was, or if I did stop, I imagined that it was something extremely rare and subtle like a wind, a flame, or an ether, which was spread throughout my grosser parts. As to body I had no manner of doubt about its nature, but thought I had a very clear knowledge of it; and if I had desired to explain it according to the notions that I had then formed of it, I should have described it thus: By the body I understand all that which can be defined by a certain figure: something which can be confined in a certain place, and which can fill a space in such a way that every other body will be excluded from it; which can be perceived either by touch, or by sight, or by hearing, or by taste, or by smell: which can be moved in many ways not, in truth, by itself but by something which is foreign to it, by which it is touched [and from which it receives impressions]: for to have the power of self-movement, as also of feeling or of thinking, I did not consider to appertain to the nature of body: on the contrary, I was rather astonished to find that faculties similar to them existed in some bodies.

But what am I, now that I suppose that there is a certain genius which is extremely powerful, and, if I may say so, malicious, who employs all his powers in deceiving me? Can I affirm that I possess the least of all those things which I have just said pertain to the nature of body? I pause to consider, I revolve all these things in my mind, and I find none of which I can say that it pertains to me. It would be tedious to stop to enumerate them. Let us pass to the attributes of soul and see if there is any one which is in me? What of nutrition or walking [the first mentioned]? But if it is so that I have no body it is also true that I can neither walk nor take nourishment. Another attribute is sensation. But one cannot feel without body, and besides I have thought I perceived many things during sleep that I recognised in my waking moments as not having been experienced at all. What of thinking? I find here that thought is an attribute that belongs to me; it alone cannot be separated from me. I am, I exist, that is certain. But how often? Just when I think; for it might possibly be the case if I ceased entirely to think, that I should likewise cease altogether to exist. I do not now admit anything which is not necessarily true: to speak accurately I am not more than a thing which thinks, that is to say a mind or a soul, or an understanding, or a reason, which are terms whose significance was formerly unknown to me. I am, however, a real thing and really exist; but what thing? I have answered: a thing which thinks.

And what more? I shall exercise my imagination [in order to see if I am not something more]. I am not a collection of members which we call the human body: I am not a subtle air distributed through these members, I am not a wind, a fire, a vapour, a breath, nor anything at all which I can imagine or conceive; because I have assumed that all these were nothing. Without changing that supposition I find that I only leave myself certain of the fact that I am somewhat. But perhaps it is true that these same things which I supposed were non-existent because they are unknown to me, are really not different from the self which I know. I am not sure about this, I shall not dispute about it now; I can only give judgment on things that are known to me. I know that I exist, and I inquire what I am, I whom I know to exist. But it is very certain that the knowledge of my existence taken in its precise significance does not depend on things whose existence is not yet known to me; consequently it does not depend on those which I can feign in imagination. And indeed the very term *feign* in imagination proves to me my error, for I really do this if I image myself a something, since to imagine is nothing else than to contemplate the figure or image of a corporeal thing. But I already know for certain that I am, and that it may be that all these images, and, speaking generally, all things that relate to the nature of body are nothing but dreams [and chimeras]. For this reason I see clearly that I have as little reason to say, 'I shall stimulate my imagination in order to know more distinctly what I am,' than if I were to say, 'I am now awake, and I perceive somewhat that is real and true: but because I do not yet perceive it distinctly enough, I shall go to sleep of express purpose, so that my dreams may represent the perception with greatest truth and evidence.' And, thus, I know for certain that nothing of all that I can understand by means of my imagination belongs to this knowledge which I have of myself, and that it is necessary to recall the mind from this mode of thought with the utmost diligence in order that it may be able to know its own nature with perfect distinctness.

But what then am I? A thing which thinks. What is a thing which thinks? It is a thing which doubts, understands, [conceives], affirms, denies, wills, refuses, which also imagines and feels.

Certainly it is no small matter if all these things pertain to my nature. But why should they not so pertain? Am I not that being who now doubts nearly everything, who nevertheless understands certain things, who affirms that one only is true, who denies all the others, who desires to know more, is averse from being deceived, who imagines many things, sometimes indeed despite his will, and who perceives many likewise, as by the intervention of the bodily organs? Is there nothing in all this which is as true as it is certain that I exist, even though I should always sleep and though he who has given me being employed all his ingenuity in deceiving me? Is there likewise any one of these attributes which can be distinguished from my thought, or which might be said to be separated from myself? For it is so evident of itself that it is I who doubts, who understands, and who desires, that there is no reason here to add anything to explain it. And I have certainly the power of imagining likewise; for although it may happen (as I formerly supposed) that none of the things which I imagine are true, nevertheless this power of imagining does not cease to be really in use, and it forms part of my thought. Finally, I am the same who feels, that is to say, who perceives certain things, as by the organs of sense, since in truth I see light, I hear noise, I feel heat. But it will be said that these phenomena are false and that I am dreaming. Let it be so; still it is at least quite certain that it seems to me that I see light, that I hear noise and that I feel heat. That cannot be false; properly speaking it is what is in me called feeling; and used in this precise sense that is no other thing than thinking.

. . . .

Meditation VI: Of the Existence of Material Things, and of the Real Distinction between the Soul and Body of Man.

. . . it is right that I should at the same time investigate the nature of sense perception, and that I should see if from the ideas which I apprehend by this mode of thought, which I call feeling, I cannot derive some certain proof of the existence of corporeal objects.

And first of all I shall recall to my memory those matters which I hitherto held to be true, as having perceived them through the senses, and the foundations on which my belief has rested; in the next place I shall examine the reasons which have since obliged me to place them in doubt; in the last place I shall consider which of them I must now believe.

First of all, then, I perceived that I had a head, hands, feet and all other members of which this body—which I considered as a part, or possibly even as the whole, of myself—is composed. Further I was sensible that this body was placed amidst many others, from which it was capable of being affected in many different ways, beneficial and hurtful, and I remarked that a certain feeling of pleasure accompanied those that were beneficial, and pain those which were harmful. And in addition to this pleasure and pain, I also experienced hunger, thirst, and other similar appetites, as also certain corporeal inclinations towards joy, sadness, anger, and other similar passions. And outside myself, in addition to extension, figure, and motions of bodies, I remarked in them hardness, heat, and all other tactile qualities, and, further, light and colour, and scents and sounds, the variety of which gave me the means of distinguishing the sky, the earth, the sea, and generally all the other bodies, one from the other. And certainly, considering the ideas of all these qualities which presented themselves to my mind, and which alone I perceived properly or immediately, it was not without reason that I believed myself to perceive objects quite different from my thought, to wit, bodies from which those ideas proceeded; for I found by experience that these ideas presented themselves to me without my consent being requisite, so that I could not perceive any object, however desirous I might be, unless it were present to the organs of sense; and it was not in my power not to perceive it, when it was present. And because the ideas which I received through the senses were much more lively, more clear, and even, in their own way, more distinct than any of those which I could of myself frame in meditation, or than those I found impressed on my memory, it appeared as though they could not have proceeded from my mind, so that they must necessarily have been produced in me by some other things. And having no knowledge of those objects excepting the knowledge which the ideas themselves gave me, nothing was more likely to occur to my mind than that the objects were similar to the ideas which were caused. And because I likewise remembered that I had formerly made use of my senses rather than my reason, and recognised that the ideas which I formed of myself were not so distinct as those which I perceived through the senses, and that they were most frequently even composed of portions of these last, I persuaded myself easily that I had no idea in my mind which had not formerly come to me through the senses. Nor was it without some reason that I believed that this body (which by a certain special right I call my own) belonged to me more properly and more strictly than any other; for in fact I could never be separated from it as from other bodies; I experienced in it and on account of it all my

505

appetites and affections, and finally I was touched by the feeling of pain and the titillation of pleasure in its parts, and not in the parts of other bodies which were separated from it. But when I inquired, why, from some, I know not what, painful sensations, there follows sadness of mind, and from the pleasurable sensation there arises joy, or why this mysterious pinching of the stomach which I call hunger causes me to desire to eat, and dryness of throat causes a desire to drink, and so on, I could give no reason excepting that nature taught me so; for there is certainly no affinity (that I at least can understand) between the craving of the stomach and the desire to eat, any more than between the perception of whatever causes pain and the thought of sadness which arises from this perception. And in the same way it appeared to me that I had learned from nature all the other judgments which I formed regarding the objects of my senses, since I remarked that these judgments were formed in me before I had the leisure to weigh and consider any reasons which might oblige me to make them.

But afterwards many experiences little by little destroyed all the faith which I had rested in my senses; for I from time to time observed that those towers which from afar appeared to me to be round, more closely observed seemed square, and that colossal statues raised on the summit of these towers, appeared as quite tiny statues when viewed from the bottom; and so in an infinitude of other cases I found error in judgments founded on the external senses. And not only in those founded on the external senses, but even in those founded on the internal as well; for is there anything more intimate or more internal than pain? And yet I have learned from some persons whose arms or legs have been cut off, that they sometimes seemed to feel pain in the part which had been amputated, which made me think that I could not be quite certain that it was a certain member which pained me, even although I felt pain in it. And to those grounds of doubt I have lately added two others, which are very general; the first is that I never have believed myself to feel anything in waking moments which I cannot also sometimes believe myself to feel when I sleep, and as I do not think that these things which I seem to feel in sleep, proceed from objects outside of me, I do not see any reason why I should have this belief regarding objects which I seem to perceive while awake. The other was that being still ignorant, or rather supposing myself to be ignorant, of the author of my being, I saw nothing to prevent me from having been so constituted by nature that I might be deceived even in matters which seemed to me to be most certain. And as to the grounds on which I was formerly persuaded of the truth of sensible objects, I had not much trouble in replying to them. For since nature seemed to cause me to lean towards many things from which reason repelled me, I did not believe that I should trust much to the teachings of nature. And although the ideas which I receive by the senses do not depend on my will, I did not think that one should for that reason conclude that they proceeded from things different from myself, since possibly some faculty might be discovered in me—though hitherto unknown to me—which produced them.

But now that I begin to know myself better, and to discover more clearly the author of my being, I do not in truth think that I should rashly admit all the matters which the senses seem to teach us, but, on the other hand, I do not think that I should doubt them all universally.

And first of all, because I know that all things which I apprehend clearly and distinctly can be created by God as I apprehend them, it suffices that I am able to apprehend one thing apart from another clearly and distinctly in order to be certain that the one is different from the other, since they may be made to exist in separation at least by the omnipotence of God; and it does not signify by what power this separation is made in order to compel me to judge them to be different: and, therefore, just because I know certainly that I exist, and that meanwhile I do not remark that any other thing necessarily pertains to my nature or essence, excepting that I am a thinking thing, I rightly conclude that my essence consists solely in the fact that I am a thinking thing [or a substance whose whole essence or nature is to think]. And although possibly (or rather certainly, as I shall say in a moment) I possess a body with which I am very intimately conjoined, yet because, on the one side, I have a clear and distinct idea of myself inasmuch as I am only a thinking and unextended thing, and as, on the other, I possess a distinct idea of body, inasmuch as it is only an extended and unthinking thing, it is certain that this I [that is to say, my soul by which I am what I am], is entirely and absolutely distinct from my body, and can exist without it.

I further find in myself faculties employing modes of thinking peculiar to themselves, to wit, the faculties of imagination and feeling, without which I can easily conceive myself clearly and distinctly as a complete being; while, on the other hand, they cannot be so conceived apart from me, that is without an intelligent substance in which they reside, for [in the notion we have of these faculties, or, to use the language of the Schools] in their formal concept, some kind of intellection is comprised, from which I infer that they are distinct from me as its modes are from a thing. I observe also in me some other faculties such as that of change of position, the assumption of different figures and such like, which cannot be conceived, any more than can the preceding, apart from some substance to which they are attached, and consequently cannot exist without it; but it is very clear that these faculties, if it be true that they exist, must be attached to some corporeal or extended substance, and not to an intelligent substance, since in the clear and distinct conception of these there is some sort of extension found to be present, but no intellection at all. There is certainly further in me a certain passive faculty of perception, that is, of receiving and recognising the ideas of sensible things, but this would be useless to me [and I could in no way avail myself of it], if there were not either in me or in some other thing another active faculty capable of forming and producing these ideas. But this active faculty cannot exist in me [inasmuch as I am a thing that thinks] seeing that it does not presuppose thought, and also that those ideas are often even against my will; it is thus necessarily the case that the faculty resides in some substance different from me in which all the reality which is objectively in the ideas that are produced by this faculty is formally or eminently contained, as I remarked before. And this substance is either a body, that is, a corporeal nature in which there is contained formally [and really] all that which is objectively [and by representation] in those ideas, or it is God Himself, or some other creature more noble than body in which that same is contained eminently. But, since God is no deceiver, it is very manifest that He does not communicate to me these ideas immediately and by Himself, nor yet by the intervention of some creature in which their reality is not formally, but only eminently, contained. For since He has given me no faculty to recognise that this is the case, but, on the other hand, a very great inclination to believe [that they are sent to me or] that they are conveyed to me by corporeal objects, I do not see how He could be defended from the accusation of deceit if these ideas were produced by causes other than corporeal objects. Hence we must allow that corporeal things exist. However, they are perhaps not exactly what we perceive by the senses, since this comprehension by the senses is in many instances very obscure and confused; but we must at least admit that all things which I conceive in them clearly and distinctly, that is to say, all things which, speaking generally, are comprehended in the object of pure mathematics, are truly to be recognised as external objects.

As to other things, however, which are either particular only, as, for example, that the sun is of such and such a figure, etc., or which are less clearly and distinctly conceived such as light, sound, pain and the like, it is certain that although they are very dubious and uncertain, yet on the sole ground that God is not a deceiver, and that consequently He has not permitted any falsity to exist in my opinion which He has not likewise given me the faculty of correcting, I may assuredly hope to conclude that I have within me the means of arriving at the truth even here. And first of all there is no doubt that in all things which nature teaches me there is some truth contained; for by nature, considered in general, I now understand no other thing than either God Himself or else the order and disposition which God has established in created things; and by my nature in particular I understand no other thing than the complexus of all the things which God has given me.

But there is nothing which this nature teaches me more expressly [nor more sensibly] than that I have a body which is adversely affected when I feel pain, which has need of food or drink when I experience the feelings of hunger and thirst, and so on; nor can I doubt there being some truth in all this.

Nature also teaches me by these sensations of pain, hunger, thirst, etc., that I am not only lodged in my body as a pilot in a vessel, but that I am very closely united to it, and so to speak so intermingled with it that I seem to compose with it one whole. For if that were not the case, when my body is hurt, I, who am merely a thinking thing, should not feel pain, for I should perceive this wound by the understanding only, just as the sailor perceives by sight when something is damaged in his vessel; and when my body has need of drink or food, I should clearly understand the fact without being warned of it by confused feelings of hunger and thirst. For all these sensations of hunger, thirst, pain, etc. are in truth none other than certain confused modes of thought which are produced by the union and apparent intermingling of mind and body.

. . . .

. . . in the first place, there is a great difference between mind and body, inasmuch as body is by nature always divisible, and the mind is entirely indivisible. For, as a matter of fact, when I consider the mind, that is to say, myself inasmuch as I am only a thinking thing, I cannot distinguish in myself any parts, but apprehend myself to be clearly one and entire; and although the whole mind seems to be united to the whole body, yet if a foot, or an arm, or some other part, is separated from my body, I am aware that nothing has been taken away from my mind. And the faculties of willing, feeling, conceiving, etc. cannot be properly speaking said to be its parts, for it is one and the same mind which employs itself in willing and in feeling and understanding. But it is quite otherwise with corporeal or extended objects, for there is not one of these imaginable by me which my mind cannot easily divide into parts, and which consequently I do not recognise as being divisible; this would be sufficient to teach me that the mind or soul of man is entirely different from the body, if I had not already learned it from other sources.

I further notice that the mind does not receive the impressions from all parts of the body immediately, but only from the brain, or perhaps even from one of its smallest parts, to wit, from that in which the common sense is said to reside, which, whenever it is disposed in the same particular way, conveys the same thing to the mind, although meanwhile the other portions of the body may be differently disposed, as is testified by innumerable experiments which it is unnecessary here to recount.

I notice, also, that the nature of body is such that none of its parts can be moved by another part a little way off which cannot also be moved in the same way by each one of the parts which are between the two, although this more remote part does not act at all. As, for example, in the cord *ABCD* [which is in tension] if we pull the last part *D*, the first part *A* will not be moved in any way differently from what would be the case if one of the intervening parts *B* or *C* were pulled, and the last part *D* were to remain unmoved. And in the same way, when I feel pain in my foot, my knowledge of physics teaches me that this sensation is communicated by means of nerves dispersed through the foot, which, being extended like cords from there to the brain, when they are contracted in the foot, at the same time contract the inmost portions of the brain which is their extremity and place of origin, and then excite a certain movement which nature has established in order to cause the mind to be affected by a sensation of pain represented as existing in the foot. But because these nerves must pass through the tibia, the thigh, the loins, the back and the neck, in order to reach from the leg to the brain, it may happen that although their extremities which are in the foot are not affected, but only certain ones of their intervening parts [which pass by the loins or the neck], this action will excite the same movement in the brain that might have been excited there by a hurt received in the foot, in consequence of which the mind will necessarily feel in the foot the same pain as if it had received a hurt. And the same holds good of all the other perceptions of our senses.

I notice finally that since each of the movements which are in the portion of the brain by which the mind is immediately affected brings about one particular sensation only, we cannot under the circumstances imagine anything more likely than that this movement, amongst all the sensations which it is capable of impressing on it, causes mind to be affected by that one which is best fitted and most generally useful for the conservation of the human body when it is in health. But experience makes us aware that all the feelings with which nature inspires us are such as I have just spoken of; and there is therefore nothing in them which does not give testimony to the power and goodness of the God [who has produced them]. Thus, for example, when the nerves which are in the feet are violently or more than usually moved, their movement, passing through the medulla of the spine to the inmost parts of the brain, gives a sign to the mind which makes it feel somewhat, to wit, pain, as though in the foot, by which the mind is excited to do its utmost to re-move the cause of the evil as dangerous and hurtful to the foot. It is true that God could have constituted the nature of man in such a way that this same movement in the brain would have conveyed something quite different to the mind; for example, it might have produced consciousness of itself either in so far as it is in the brain, or as it is in the foot, or as it is in some other place between the foot and the brain, or it might finally have produced consciousness of anything else whatsoever; but none of all this would have contributed so well to the conservation of the body. Similarly, when we desire to drink, a certain dryness of the throat is produced which moves its nerves, and by their means the internal portions of the brain; and this movement causes in the mind the sensa-tion of thirst, because in this case there is nothing more useful to us than to become aware that we have need to drink for the conservation of our health; and the same holds good in other instances.

From this it is quite clear that, notwithstanding the supreme good-ness of God, the nature of man, inasmuch as it is composed of mind and body, cannot be otherwise than sometimes a source of deception. For if there is any cause which excites, not in the foot but in some part of the nerves which are extended between the foot and the brain, or even in the brain itself, the same movement which usually is produced when the foot is detrimentally affected, pain will be experienced as though it were in the foot, and the sense will thus naturally be deceived; for since the same movement in the brain is capable of causing but one sensation in the mind, and this sensation is much more frequently excited by a cause which hurts the foot than by another existing in some other quar-ter, it is reasonable that it should convey to the mind pain in the foot rather than in any other part of the body. And although the parchedness of the throat does not always proceed, as it usually does, from the fact that drinking is necessary for the health of the body, but sometimes comes from quite a different cause, as is the case with dropsical patients, it is yet much better that it should mislead on this occasion than if, on the other hand, it were always to deceive us when the body is in good health; and so on in similar cases.

. . . .

Objection by Thomas Hobbes

I am a thing that thinks; *quite correct. From the fact that I think, or have an image, whether sleeping or waking, it is inferred that I am exercising thought, for* I think *and* I am exercising thought *mean the same thing. From the fact that I am exercising thought it follows that* I am, *since that which thinks is not nothing. But, where it is added,* this is the mind, the spirit, the understanding, the reason, *a doubt arises. For it does not seem to be good reasoning to say:* I am exercising thought, *hence* I am thought; *or* I am using my intellect, *hence* I am intellect. *For in the same way I might say,* I am walking; *hence* I am the walking. *It is hence an assumption on the part of M. Descartes that that which understands is the same as the exercise of understanding which is an act of that which understands, or, at least, that that which understands is the same as the understanding, which is a power possessed by that which thinks. Yet all Philosophers distinguish a subject from its faculties and activities, i.e. from its properties and essences; for the entity itself is one thing, its essence another. Hence it is possible for a thing that thinks to be the subject of the mind, reason, or understanding, and hence to be something corporeal; and the opposite of this has been assumed, not proved. Yet this inference is the basis of the conclusion that M. Descartes seems to wish to establish.*

. . . .

Reply by Descartes

Where I have said, *this is the mind, the spirit, the intellect, or the reason,* I understood by these names not merely faculties, but rather what is endowed with the faculty of thinking; and this sense the two former terms commonly, the latter frequently bear. But I used them in this sense so expressly and in so many places that I cannot see what occasion there was for any doubt about their meaning.

Further, there is here no parity between walking and thinking; for walking is usually held to refer only to that action itself, while thinking applies now to the action, now to the faculty of thinking, and again to that in which the faculty exists.

A thing that thinks, he says, may be something corporeal; and the opposite of this has been assumed; not proved. But really I did not assume the opposite, neither did I use it as a basis for my argument; I left it wholly undetermined until Meditation VI, in which its proof is given.

. . . .
    . . . it is certain that no thought can exist apart from a thing that thinks; no activity, no accident can be without a substance in which to

exist. Moreover, since we do not apprehend the substance itself immediately through itself, but by means only of the fact that it is the subject of certain activities, it is highly rational, and a requirement forced on us by custom, to give diverse names to those substances that we recognize to be the subjects of clearly diverse activities or accidents, and afterwards to inquire whether those diverse names refer to one and the same or to diverse things. But there are *certain* activities, which we call *corporeal*, e.g. magnitude, figure, motion, and all those that cannot be thought of apart from extension in space; and the substance in which they exist is called *body*. It cannot be pretended that the substance that is the subject of figure is different from that which is the subject of spatial motion, etc., since all these activities agree in presupposing extension. Further, there are other activities, which we call *thinking* activities, e.g. understanding, willing, imagining, feeling, etc., which agree in falling under the description of thought, perception, or consciousness. The substance in which they reside we call a *thinking thing* or *the mind*, or any other name we care, provided only we do not confound it with corporeal substance, since thinking activities have no affinity with corporeal activities, and thought, which is the common nature in which the former agree, is totally different from extension, the common term for describing the latter.

But after we have formed two distinct concepts of those two substances, it is easy, from what has been said in the Sixth Meditation, to determine whether they are one and the same or distinct.

Objection by Antoine Arnauld

. . . let us discover how we can demonstrate the fact that our mind is [distinct and] separate from our body.

I am able to doubt whether I have a body, nay, whether any body exists at all; yet I have no right to doubt whether I am, or exist, so long as I doubt or think.

Hence I, who doubt and think, am not a body; otherwise in entertaining doubt concerning body, I should doubt about myself.

Nay, even though I obstinately maintain that no body at all exists, the position taken up is unshaken: I am something, hence I am not a body.

This is really very acute, but someone could bring up the objection which our author urges against himself; the fact that I doubt about body or deny that body exists, does not bring it about that no body exists. Hence perhaps it happens that these very things which I suppose to be nothing, because they are unknown to me, yet do not in truth differ from that self which I do know. I know nothing about it, *he says,* I do not dispute this matter; [I can judge only about things that are known to me.] I know that I exist; I enquire who I, the known self, am; it is quite certain that the knowledge of this self thus precisely taken, does not depend on those things of the existence of which I am not yet acquainted.

But he admits in consonance with the argument laid down in the

Method, that the proof has proceeded only so far as to exclude from the nature of the human mind whatsoever is corporeal, not from the point of view of the ultimate truth, but relatively only to his consciousness (the meaning being that nothing at all was known to him to belong to his essential nature, beyond the fact that he was a thinking being). *Hence it is evident from this reply that the argument is exactly where it was, and that therefore the problem which he promises to solve remains entirely untouched. The problem is:* how it follows, from the fact that one is unaware that anything else [(except the fact of being a thinking thing)] belongs to one's essence, that nothing else really belongs to one's essence. *But, not to conceal my dullness, I have been unable to discover in the whole of Meditation II where he has shown this. Yet so far as I can conjecture, he attempts this proof in Meditation VI, because he believes that it is dependent on the possession of the clear knowledge of God to which in Meditation II he has not yet attained. Here is his proof:*

Because I know that all the things I clearly and distinctly understand can be created by God just as I conceive them to exist, it is sufficient for me to be able to comprehend one thing clearly and distinctly apart from another, in order to be sure that the one is diverse from the other, because at least God can isolate them; and it does not matter by what power that isolation is effected, in order that I may be obliged to think them different from one another. Hence because, on the one hand, I have a clear and distinct idea of myself in so far as I am a thinking being, and not extended, and on the other hand, a distinct idea of body, in so far as it is only an extended thing, not one that thinks, it is certain that I am in reality distinct from my body and can exist apart from it.

Here we must halt awhile; for on these few words the whole of the difficulty seems to hinge.

Firstly, in order to be true, the major premiss of that syllogism must be held to refer to the adequate notion of a thing (i.e., the notion which comprises everything which may be known of the thing), not to any notion, even a clear and distinct one.

. . . .

But, if anyone casts doubt on the (minor) premiss here assumed, and contends that it is merely that your conception is inadequate when you conceive yourself [(i.e. your mind)] as being a thinking but not an extended thing, and similarly when you conceive yourself [(i.e. your body)] as being an extended and not a thinking thing, we must look for its proof in the previous part of the argument. For I do not reckon a matter like this to be so clear as to warrant us in assuming it as an indemonstrable first principle and in dispensing with proof.

Now as to the first part of the statement, namely, that you completely understand what body is, merely by thinking that it is extended, has figure, can move, etc., and by denying of it everything which belongs to the nature of mind, *this is of little value. For one who contends that the human mind is corporeal does not on that account believe that every body is a mind. Hence body would be so related to mind as genus is to species. But the genus can be conceived without the species, even although one deny of it whatsoever is proper and peculiar to the species;*

whence comes the common dictum of Logicians, 'the negation of the species does not negate the genus.' Thus, I can conceive figure without conceiving any of the attributes proper to the circle. Therefore, we must prove over and above this that the mind can be completely and adequately conceived apart from the body.

*I can discover no passage in the whole work capable of effecting this proof, save the proposition laid down at the outset:—*I can deny that there is any body or that any extended thing exists, but yet it is certain that I exist, so long as I make this denial, or think; hence I am a thing that thinks and not a body, and the body does not pertain to the knowledge of myself.

But the only result that I can see to give, is that a certain knowledge of myself be obtained without a knowledge of the body. But it is not yet quite clear to me that this knowledge is complete and adequate, so as to make me sure that I am not in error in excluding the body from my essence. I shall explain by means of an example:

Let us assume that a certain man is quite sure that the angle in a semicircle is a right angle and that hence the triangle made by this angle and the diameter is right-angled; but suppose he questions and has not yet firmly apprehended, nay, let us imagine that, misled by some fallacy, he denies that the square on its base is equal to the squares on the sides of the right-angled triangle. Now, according to our author's reasoning, he will see himself confirmed in his false belief. For, *he will argue,* while I clearly and distinctly perceive that this triangle is right-angled, I yet doubt whether the square on its base is equal to the square on its sides. Hence the equality of the square on the base to those on the sides does not belong to its essence.

Further, even though I deny that the square on its base is equal to the squares on its sides, I yet remain certain that it is right-angled, and the knowledge that one of its angles is a right angle remains clear and distinct in my mind; and this remaining so, not God himself could cause it not to be right-angled.

Hence, that of which I doubt, or the removal of which leaves me with the idea still, cannot belong to its essence.

Besides, since I know that all things I clearly and distinctly understand can be created by God just as I conceive them to exist, it is sufficient for me, in order to be sure that one thing is distinct from another, to be able to comprehend the one clearly and distinctly apart from the other, because it can be isolated by God. *But I clearly and distinctly understand that this triangle is right-angled, without comprehending that the square on its base is equal to the squares on its sides. Hence God at least can create a right-angled triangle, the square on the base of which is not equal to the squares on its sides.*

I do not see what reply can here be made, except that the man in question does not perceive clearly that the triangle is right-angled. But whence do I obtain any perception of the nature of my mind clearer than that which he has of the nature of the triangle? He is as sure that the triangle in a semicircle has one right angle (which is the notion of a right-angled triangle) as I am in believing that I exist because I think.

514

Hence, just as a man errs in not believing that the equality of the square on its base to the squares on its sides belongs to the nature of that triangle, which he clearly and distinctly knows to be right-angled, so why am I not perhaps in the wrong in thinking that nothing else belongs to my nature, which I clearly and distinctly know to be something that thinks, except the fact that I am this thinking being? Perhaps it also belongs to my essence to be something extended.

. . . .

Reply by Descartes

But it can nowise be maintained that, in the words of M. Arnauld, *body is related to mind as genus is to species;* for although the genus can be apprehended apart from this or that specific difference, the species can by no means be thought apart from the genus.

For, to illustrate, we easily apprehend figure, without thinking at all of a circle (although that mental act is not distinct unless we refer to some specific figure, and it does not give us a complete thing, unless it embraces the nature of the body); but we are cognisant of no specific difference belonging to the circle, unless at the same time we think of figure.

But mind can be perceived clearly and distinctly, or sufficiently so to let it be considered to be a complete thing without any of those forms or attributes by which we recognize that body is a substance, as I think I have sufficiently shown in the Second Meditation; and body is understood distinctly and as a complete thing apart from the attributes attaching to the mind.

Nevertheless M. Arnauld here urges that *although a certain notion of myself can be obtained without a knowledge of the body, it yet does not thence result that this knowledge is complete and adequate, so as to make me sure that I am not in error in excluding the body from my essence.* He elucidates his meaning by taking as an illustration the triangle inscribed in a semicircle, which we can clearly and distinctly know to be right-angled, though we do not know, or even deny, that the square on its base is equal to the squares on its sides; and nevertheless we cannot thence infer that we can have a [right-angled] triangle, the square on the base of which is not equal to the squares on the sides.

But, as to this illustration, the example differs in many respects from the case in hand.

For firstly, although perhaps a triangle may be taken in the concrete as a substance possessing triangular shape, certainly the property of having the square on the base equal to the squares on the sides is not a substance; so too, neither can either of these two things be understood to be a complete thing in the sense in which *Mind and Body* are; indeed, they cannot be called *things* in the sense in which I used the word when I said *that I might comprehend one thing* (i.e. one complete thing) *apart from the other, etc.* as is evident from the succeeding words—*Besides, I discover in myself faculties, etc.* For I did not assert these faculties to be *things*, but distinguished them accurately from things or substances.

Secondly, although we can clearly and distinctly understand that the triangle in the semicircle is right-angled, without noting that the square on its base equals those on its sides, we yet cannot clearly apprehend a triangle in which the square on the base is equal to those on the sides, without at the same time perceiving that it is right-angled. But we do clearly and distinctly perceive mind without body and body without mind.

Thirdly, although our concept of the triangle inscribed in the semicircle may be such as not to comprise the equality between the square on its base and those on its sides, it cannot be such that no ratio between the square on the base and those on the sides is held to prevail in the triangle in question; and hence, so long as we remain ignorant of what the ratio is, nothing can be denied of the triangle other than what we clearly know not to belong to it: but to know this in the case of the equality of the ratio is entirely impossible. Now, on the other hand, there is nothing included in the concept of body that belongs to the mind; and nothing in that of mind that belongs to the body.

Therefore, though I said that *it was sufficient to be able to apprehend one thing clearly and distinctly apart from another, etc.*, we cannot go on to complete the argument thus:—*but I clearly and distinctly apprehend this triangle, etc.* Firstly, because the ratio between the square on the base and those on the sides is not a complete thing. Secondly, because that ratio is clearly understood only in the case of the right-angled triangle. Thirdly, because the triangle itself cannot be distinctly apprehended if the ratio between the square on the base and on the sides is denied.

But now I must explain how it is that, *from the mere fact that I apprehend one substance clearly and distinctly apart from another, I am sure that the one excludes the other.*

Really the notion of *substance* is just this—that which can exist by itself, without the aid of any substance. No one who perceives two substances by means of two diverse concepts ever doubts that they are really distinct.

Consequently, if I had not been in search of a certitude greater than the vulgar, I should have been satisfied with showing in the Second Meditation that *Mind* was apprehended as a thing that subsists, although nothing belonging to the body be ascribed to it, and conversely that *Body* was understood to be something subsistent without anything being attributed to it that pertains to the mind. And I should have added nothing more in order to prove that there was a real distinction between mind and body: because commonly we judge that all things stand to each other in respect to their actual relations in the same way as they are related in our consciousness. But, since one of those hyperbolical doubts adduced in the First Meditation went so far as to prevent me from being sure of this very fact (viz. that things are in their true nature exactly as we perceive them to be), so long as I supposed that I had no knowledge of the author of my being, all that I have said about God and about truth in the Third, Fourth and Fifth Meditations serves to further the conclusion as to the distinction between *mind* and *body*, which is finally completed in Meditation VI.

My opponent, however, says, *I apprehend the triangle inscribed in the semicircle without knowing that the square on its base is equal to the squares on the sides.* True, the triangle may indeed be apprehended although there is no thought of the ratio prevailing between the squares on the base and sides; but we can never think that this ratio must be denied. It is quite otherwise in the case of the mind where, not only do we understand that it exists apart from the body, but also that all the attributes of body may be denied of it; for reciprocal exclusion of one another belongs to the nature of substances.

43. T. H. Huxley

T. H. Huxley (1825–1895) was an English biologist who is best known to history for his effective defense of the Darwinian theory of evolution.

The Dependence of Consciousness on the Brain

But there remains a doctrine to which Descartes attached great weight, so that full acceptance of it became a sort of note of a thoroughgoing Cartesian, but which, nevertheless, is so opposed to ordinary prepossessions that it attained more general notoriety, and gave rise to more discussion, than almost any other Cartesian hypothesis. It is the doctrine that brute animals are mere machines or automata, devoid not only of reason, but of any kind of consciousness. . . .

Descartes' line of argument is perfectly clear. He starts from reflex action in man, from the unquestionable fact that, in ourselves, co-ordinate, purposive, actions may take place, without the intervention of consciousness or volition, or even contrary to the latter. As actions of a certain degree of complexity are brought about by mere mechanism, why may not actions of still greater complexity be the result of a more refined mechanism? What proof is there that brutes are other than a superior race of marionettes, which eat without pleasure, cry without pain, desire nothing, know nothing, and only simulate intelligence as a bee simulates a mathematician?

From the essay "On the Hypothesis That Animals Are Automata and Its History," first published in 1874 and reprinted in the collection of Huxley's essays, *Methods and Results*.

The Port Royalists adopted the hypothesis that brutes are machines, and are said to have carried its practical applications so far as to treat domestic animals with neglect, if not with actual cruelty. As late as the middle of the eighteenth century, the problem was discussed very fully and ably by Bouillier, in his "Essai philosophique sur l'Ame des Bêtes," while Condillac deals with it in his "Traité des Animaux"; but since then it has received little attention. Nevertheless, modern research has brought to light a great multitude of facts, which not only show that Descartes' view is defensible, but render it far more defensible than it was in his day.

It must be premised, that it is wholly impossible absolutely to prove the presence or absence of consciousness in anything but one's own brain, though, by analogy, we are justified in assuming its existence in other men. Now if, by some accident, a man's spinal cord is divided, his limbs are paralyzed, so far as his volition is concerned, below the point of injury; and he is incapable of experiencing all those states of consciousness which, in his uninjured state, would be excited by irritation of those nerves which come off below the injury. If the spinal cord is divided in the middle of the back, for example, the skin of the feet may be cut, or pinched, or burned, or wetted with vitriol, without any sensation of touch, or of pain, arising in consciousness. So far as the man is concerned, therefore, the part of the central nervous system which lies beyond the injury is cut off from consciousness. It must indeed be admitted, that, if any one think fit to maintain that the spinal cord below the injury is conscious, but that it is cut off from any means of making its consciousness known to the other consciousness in the brain, there is no means of driving him from his position by logic. But assuredly there is no way of proving it, and in the matter of consciousness, if in anything, we may hold by the rule, "De non apparentibus et de non existentibus eadem est ratio." However near the brain the spinal cord is injured, consciousness remains intact, except that the irritation of parts below the injury is no longer represented by sensation. On the other hand, pressure upon the anterior division of the brain, or extensive injuries to it, abolish consciousness. Hence, it is a highly probable conclusion, that consciousness in man depends upon the integrity of the anterior division of the brain, while the middle and hinder divisions of the brain,[1] and the rest of the nervous centres, have nothing to do with it. And it is further highly probable, that what is true for man is true for other vertebrated animals.

We may assume, then, that in a living vertebrated animal, any segment of the cerebro-spinal axis (or spinal cord and brain) separated from that anterior division of the brain which is the organ of consciousness, is as completely incapable of giving rise to consciousness as we know it to be incapable of carrying out volitions. Nevertheless, this separated segment of the spinal cord is not passive and inert. On the contrary, it is the seat of extremely remarkable powers. In our imaginary case of injury,

---

1. Not to be confounded with the anterior middle and hinder parts of the hemisphere of the cerebrum.

the man would, as we have seen, be devoid of sensation in his legs, and would not have the least power of moving them. But, if the soles of his feet were tickled, the legs would be drawn up just as vigorously as they would have been before the injury. We know exactly what happens when the soles of the feet are tickled; a molecular change takes place in the sensory nerves of the skin, and is propagated along them and through the posterior roots of the spinal nerves, which are constituted by them, to the grey matter of the spinal cord. Through that grey matter the molecular motion is reflected into the anterior roots of the same nerves, constituted by the filaments which supply the muscle of the legs, and, travelling along these motor filaments, reaches the muscles, which at once contract, and cause the limbs to be drawn up.

In order to move the legs in this way, a definite co-ordination of muscular contractions is necessary; the muscles must contract in a certain order and with duly proportioned force; and moreover, as the feet are drawn away from the source of irritation, it may be said that the action has a final cause, or is purposive.

Thus it follows, that the grey matter of the segment of the man's spinal cord, though it is devoid of consciousness, nevertheless responds to a simple stimulus by giving rise to a complex set of muscular contractions, co-ordinated towards a definite end, and serving an obvious purpose.

If the spinal cord of a frog is cut across, so as to provide us with a segment separated from the brain, we shall have a subject parallel to the injured man, on which experiments can be made without remorse; as we have a right to conclude that a frog's spinal cord is not likely to be conscious, when a man's is not.

Now the frog behaves just as the man did. The legs are utterly paralysed, so far as voluntary movement is concerned; but they are vigorously drawn up to the body when any irritant is applied to the foot. But let us study our frog a little farther. Touch the skin of the side of the body with a little acetic acid, which gives rise to all the signs of great pain in an uninjured frog. In this case, there can be no pain, because the application is made to a part of the skin supplied with nerves which come off the cord below the point of section; nevertheless, the frog lifts up the limb of the same side, and applies the foot to rub off the acetic acid; and, what is still more remarkable, if the limb be held so that the frog cannot use it, it will, by and by, move the limb of the other side, turn it across the body, and use it for the same rubbing process. It is impossible that the frog, if it were in its entirety and could reason, should perform actions more purposive than these: and yet we have most complete assurance that, in this case, the frog is not acting from purpose, has no consciousness, and is a mere insensible machine.

But now suppose that, instead of making a section of the cord in the middle of the body, it has been made in such a manner as to separate the hindermost division of the brain from the rest of the organ, and suppose the foremost two-thirds of the brain entirely taken away. The frog is then absolutely devoid of any spontaneity; it sits upright in the attitude which a frog habitually assumes; and it will not stir unless it is touched;

but it differs from the frog which I have just described in this, that, if it be thrown into the water, it begins to swim, and swims just as well as the perfect frog does. But swimming requires the combination and successive co-ordination of a great number of muscular actions. And as we are forced to conclude, that the impression made upon the sensory nerves of the skin of the frog by the contact with the water into which it is thrown, causes the transmission to the central nervous apparatus of an impulse which sets going a certain machinery by which all the muscles of swimming are brought into play in due co-ordination. If the frog be stimulated by some irritating body, it jumps or walks as well as the complete frog can do. The simple sensory impression, acting through the machinery of the cord, gives rise to these complex combined movements.

It is possible to go a step farther. Suppose that only the anterior division of the brain—so much of it as lies in front of the "optic lobes"—is removed. If that operation is performed quickly and skilfully, the frog may be kept in a state of full bodily vigour for months, or it may be for years; but it will sit unmoved. It sees nothing; it hears nothing. It will starve sooner than feed itself, although food put into its mouth is swallowed. On irritation, it jumps or walks; if thrown into the water it swims. If it be put on the hand, it sits there, crouched, perfectly quiet, and would sit there for ever. If the hand be inclined very gently and slowly, so that the frog would naturally tend to slip off, the creature's fore paws are shifted on to the edge of the hand, until he can just prevent himself from falling. If the turning of the hand be slowly continued, he mounts up with great care and deliberation, putting first one leg forward and then another, until he balances himself with perfect precision upon the edge; and if the turning of the hand is continued, he goes through the needful set of muscular operations, until he comes to be seated in security, upon the back of the hand. The doing of all this requires a delicacy of co-ordination, and a precision of adjustment of the muscular apparatus of the body, which are only comparable to those of a rope-dancer. To the ordinary influences of light, the frog, deprived of its cerebral hemispheres, appears to be blind. Nevertheless, if the animal be put upon a table, with a book at some little distance between it and the light, and the skin of the hinder parts of its body is then irritated, it will jump forward, avoiding the book by passing to the right or left of it. Therefore, although the frog appears to have no sensation of light, visible objects act through its brain upon the motor mechanism of its body.

It is obvious, that had Descartes been acquainted with these remarkable results of modern research, they would have furnished him with far more powerful arguments than he possessed in favour of his view of the automatism of brutes. The habits of a frog, leading its natural life, involve such simple adaptations to surrounding conditions, that the machinery which is competent to do so much without the intervention of consciousness, might well do all. And this argument is vastly strengthened by what has been learned in recent times of the marvellously complex operations which are performed mechanically, and to all appearance without consciousness, by men, when, in consequence of injury or disease, they are reduced to a condition more or less comparable to that of a frog, in which the anterior part of the brain has been removed. A case has recently been published by an eminent French physician, Dr. Mesnet, which illustrates this condition so remarkably, that I make no apology for dwelling upon it at considerable length.[2]

A sergeant of the French army, F———, twenty-seven years of age, was wounded during the battle of Bazeilles, by a ball which fractured his left parietal bone. He ran his bayonet through the Prussian soldier who wounded him, but almost immediately his right arm became paralysed; after walking about two hundred yards, his right leg became similarly affected, and he lost his senses. When he recovered them, three weeks afterwards, in hospital at Mayence, the right half of the body was completely paralysed, and remained in this condition for a year. At present, the only trace of the paralysis which remains is a slight weakness of the right half of the body. Three or four months after the wound was inflicted, periodical disturbances of the functions of the brain made their appearance, and have continued ever since. The disturbances last from fifteen to thirty hours; the intervals at which they occur being from fifteen to thirty days.

For four years, therefore, the life of this man has been divided into alternating phases—short abnormal states intervening between long normal states.

In the periods of normal life, the ex-sergeant's health is perfect; he is intelligent and kindly, and performs, satisfactorily, the duties of a hospital attendant. The commencement of the abnormal state is ushered in by uneasiness and a sense of weight about the forehead, which the patient compares to the constriction of a circle of iron; and, after its termination, he complains, for some hours, of dulness and heaviness of the head. But the transition from the normal to the abnormal state takes place in a few minutes, without convulsions or cries, and without anything to indicate the change to a bystander. His movements remain free and his expression calm, except for a contraction of the brow, an incessant movement of the eyeballs, and a chewing motion of the jaws. The eyes are wide open, and their pupils dilated. If the man happens to be in a place to which he is accustomed, he walks about as usual; but, if he is in a new place, or if obstacles are intentionally placed in his way, he stumbles gently against them, stops, and then, feeling over the objects with his hands, passes on one side of them. He offers no resistance to any change of direction which may be impressed upon him, or to the forcible acceleration or retardation of his movements. He eats, drinks, smokes, walks about, dresses and undresses himself, rises and goes to bed at the accustomed hours. Nevertheless, pins may be run into his body, or strong electric shocks sent through it, without causing the least indication of pain; no odorous substance, pleasant or unpleasant, makes the least impression; he eats and drinks with avidity whatever is offered, and takes

2. "De l'Automatisme de la Mémoire et du Souvenir, dans le Somnambulisme pathologique." Par le Dr. E. Mesnet, Médecin de l'Hôpital Saint-Antoine. *L'Union Médicale*, Juillet 21 et 23, 1874. My attention was first called to a summary of this remarkable case, which appeared in the *Journal des Débats* for the 7th of August, 1874, by my friend General Strachey, F.R.S.

asafoetida, or vinegar, or quinine, as readily as water; no noise affects him; and light influences him only under certain conditions. Dr. Mesnet remarks, that the sense of touch alone seems to persist, and indeed to be more acute and delicate than in the normal state; and it is by means of the nerves of touch, almost exclusively, that his organism is brought into relation with the external world. Here a difficulty arises. It is clear from the facts detailed, that the nervous apparatus by which, in the normal state, sensations of touch are excited, is that by which external influences determine the movements of the body, in the abnormal state. But does the state of consciousness, which we term a tactile sensation, accompany the operation of this nervous apparatus in the abnormal state? or is consciousness utterly absent, the man being reduced to an insensible mechanism?

It is impossible to obtain direct evidence in favour of the one conclusion or the other; all that can be said is, that the case of the frog shows that the man may be devoid of any kind of consciousness.

. . . .

The ex-sergeant has a good voice, and had, at one time, been employed as a singer at a café. In one of his abnormal states he was observed to begin humming a tune. He then went to his room, dressed himself carefully, and took up some parts of a periodical novel, which lay on his bed, as if he were trying to find something. Dr. Mesnet, suspecting that he was seeking his music, made up one of these into a roll and put it into his hand. He appeared satisfied, took his cane and went down stairs to the door. Here Dr. Mesnet turned him round, and he walked quite contentedly, in the opposite direction, towards the room of the concierge. The light of the sun shining through a window now happened to fall upon him, and seemed to suggest the footlights of the stage on which he was accustomed to make his appearance. He stopped, opened his roll of imaginary music, put himself into the attitude of a singer, and sang, with perfect execution, three songs, one after the other. After which he wiped his face with his handkerchief and drank, without a grimace, a tumbler of strong vinegar and water which was put into his hand.

An experiment which may be performed upon the frog deprived of the fore part of its brain, well known as Göltz's "Quak-versuch," affords a parallel to this performance. If the skin of a certain part of the back of such a frog is gently stroked with the finger, it immediately croaks. It never croaks unless it is so stroked, and the croak always follows the stroke, just as the sound of a repeater follows the touching of the spring. In the frog, this "song" is innate—so to speak à priori—and depends upon a mechanism in the brain governing the vocal apparatus, which is set at work by the molecular change set up in the sensory nerves of the skin of the back by the contact of a foreign body.

In man there is also a vocal mechanism, and the cry of an infant is in the same sense innate and à priori, inasmuch as it depends on an organic relation between its sensory nerves and the nervous mechanism which governs the vocal apparatus. Learning to speak, and learning to sing, are processes by which the vocal mechanism is set to new tunes. A song which has been learned has its molecular equivalent, which potentially represents it in the brain, just as a musical box, wound up, potentially represents an overture. Touch the stop and the overture begins; send a molecular impulse along the proper afferent nerve and the singer begins his song.

Again, the manner in which the frog, though apparently insensible to light, is yet, under some circumstances, influenced by visual images, finds a singular parallel in the case of the ex-sergeant.

Sitting at a table, in one of his abnormal states, he took up a pen, felt for paper and ink, and began to write a letter to his general, in which he recommended himself for a medal, on account of his good conduct and courage. It occurred to Dr. Mesnet to ascertain experimentally how far vision was concerned in this act of writing. He therefore interposed a screen between the man's eyes and his hands; under these circumstances he went on writing for a short time, but the words became illegible, and he finally stopped, without manifesting any discontent. On the withdrawal of the screen he began to write again where he had left off. The substitution of water for ink in the inkstand had a similar result. He stopped, looked at his pen, wiped it on his coat, dipped it in the water, and began again with the same effect.

On one occasion, he began to write upon the topmost of ten superimposed sheets of paper. After he had written a line or two, this sheet was suddenly drawn away. There was a slight expression of surprise, but he continued his letter on the second sheet exactly as if it had been the first. The operation was repeated five times, so that the fifth sheet contained nothing but the writer's signature at the bottom of the page. Nevertheless, when the signature was finished, his eyes turned to the top of the blank sheet, and he went through the form of reading over what he had written, a movement of the lips accompanying each word; moreover, with his pen, he put in such corrections as were needed, in that part of the blank page which corresponded with the position of the words which required correction, in the sheets which had been taken away. If the five sheets had been transparent, therefore, they would, when superposed, have formed a properly written and corrected letter.

Immediately after he had written his letter, F——— got up, walked down to the garden, made himself a cigarette, lighted and smoked it. He was about to prepare another, but sought in vain for his tobacco-pouch, which had been purposely taken away. The pouch was now thrust before his eyes and put under his nose, but he neither saw nor smelt it; yet, when it was placed in his hand, he at once seized it, made a fresh cigarette, and ignited a match to light the latter. The match was blown out, and another lighted match placed close before his eyes, but he made no attempt to take it; and, if his cigarette was lighted for him, he made no attempt to smoke. All this time the eyes were vacant, and neither winked, nor exhibited any contraction of the pupils. From these and other experiments, Dr. Mesnet draws the conclusion that his patient sees some things and not others; that the sense of sight is accessible to all things which are brought into relation with him by the sense of touch, and, on the contrary, insensible to things which lie outside this relation. He sees the match he holds and does not see any other.

Just so the frog "sees" the book which is in the way of his jump, at the same time that isolated visual impressions take no effect upon him.

As I have pointed out, it is impossible to prove that F——— is absolutely unconscious in his abnormal state, but it is no less impossible to prove the contrary; and the case of the frog goes a long way to justify the assumption that, in the abnormal state, the man is a mere insensible machine.

If such facts as these had come under the knowledge of Descartes, would they not have formed an apt commentary upon that remarkable passage in the "Traité de l'Homme," which I have quoted elsewhere, but which is worth repetition?

All the functions which I have attributed to this machine (the body), as the digestion of food, the pulsation of the heart and of the arteries; the nutrition and the growth of the limbs; respiration, wakefulness, and sleep; the reception of light, sounds, odours, flavours, heat, and such like qualities, in the organs of the external senses; the impression of the ideas of these in the organ of common sensation and in the imagination; the retention of the impression of these ideas on the memory; the internal movements of the appetites and the passions; and lastly the external movements of all the limbs, which follow so aptly, as well the action of the objects which are presented to the senses, as the impressions which meet in the memory, that they imitate as nearly as possible those of a real man; I desire, I say, that you should consider that these functions in the machine naturally proceed from the mere arrangement of its organs, neither more nor less than do the movements of a clock, or other automaton, from that of its weights and its wheels; so that, so far as these are concerned, it is not necessary to conceive any other vegetative or sensitive soul, nor any other principle of motion or of life, than the blood and the spirits agitated by the fire which burns continually in the heart, and which in no wise essentially differ from all the fires which exist in inanimate bodies.

And would Descartes not have been justified in asking why we need deny that animals are machines, when men, in a state of unconsciousness, perform, mechanically, actions as complicated and as seemingly rational as those of any animals?

But though I do not think that Descartes' hypothesis can be positively refuted, I am not disposed to accept it. The doctrine of continuity is too well established for it to be permissible to me to suppose that any complex natural phenomenon comes into existence suddenly, and without being preceded by simpler modifications; and very strong arguments would be needed to prove that such complex phenomena as those of consciousness, first make their appearance in man. We know, that, in the individual man, consciousness grows from a dim glimmer to its full light, whether we consider the infant advancing in years, or the adult emerging from slumber and swoon. We know, further, that the lower animals possess, though less developed, that part of the brain which we have every reason to believe to be the organ of consciousness in man; and as, in other cases, function and organ are proportional, so we have a right to conclude it is with the brain; and that the brutes, though they may not possess our intensity of consciousness, and though, from the absence of language, they can have no trains of thoughts, but only trains of feelings, yet have a consciousness which, more or less distinctly, foreshadows our own.

I confess that, in view of the struggle for existence which goes on in the animal world, and of the frightful quantity of pain with which it must be accompanied, I should be glad if the probabilities were in favour of Descartes' hypothesis; but, on the other hand, considering the terrible practical consequences to domestic animals which might ensue from any error on our part, it is as well to err on the right side, if we err at all, and deal with them as weaker brethren, who are bound, like the rest of us, to pay their toll for living, and suffer what is needful for the general good. As Hartley finely says, "We seem to be in the place of God to them"; and we may justly follow the precedents He sets in nature in our dealings with them.

But though we may see reason to disagree with Descartes' hypothesis that brutes are unconscious machines, it does not follow that he was wrong in regarding them as automata. They may be more or less conscious, sensitive, automata; and the view that they are such conscious machines is that which is implicitly, or explicitly, adopted by most persons. When we speak of the actions of the lower animals being guided by instinct and not by reason, what we really mean is that, though they feel as we do, yet their actions are the results of their physical organisation. We believe, in short, that they are machines, one part of which (the nervous system) not only sets the rest in motion, and co-ordinates its movements in relation with changes in surrounding bodies, but is provided with special apparatus, the function of which is the calling into existence of those states of consciousness which are termed sensations, emotions, and ideas. I believe that this generally accepted view is the best expression of the facts at present known.

It is experimentally demonstrable—any one who cares to run a pin into himself may perform a sufficient demonstration of the fact—that a mode of motion of the nervous system is the immediate antecedent of a state of consciousness. All but the adherents of "Occasionalism," or of the doctrine of "Pre-established Harmony" (if any such now exist), must admit that we have as much reason for regarding the mode of motion of the nervous system as the cause of the state of consciousness, as we have for regarding any event as the cause of another. How the one phenomenon causes the other we know, as much or as little, as in any other case of causation; but we have as much right to believe that the sensation is an effect of the molecular change, as we have to believe that motion is an effect of impact; and there is as much propriety in saying that the brain evolves sensation, as there is in saying that an iron rod, when hammered, evolves heat.

As I have endeavoured to show, we are justified in supposing that something analogous to what happens in ourselves takes place in the brutes, and that the affections of their sensory nerves give rise to molecular changes in the brain, which again give rise to, or evolve, the corresponding states of consciousness. Nor can there be any reasonable doubt that the emotion of brutes, and such ideas as they possess, are similarly dependent upon molecular brain changes. Each sensory impression leaves behind a record in the structure of the brain—an "ideagenous" molecule, so to speak, which is competent, under certain conditions, to reproduce, in a fainter condition, the state of consciousness which corresponds with that sensory impression; and it is these "ideagenous molecules" which are the physical basis of memory.

It may be assumed, then, that molecular changes in the brain are the causes of all the states of consciousness of brutes. Is there any evidence that these states of consciousness may, conversely, cause those molecular changes which give rise to muscular motion? I see no such evidence. The frog walks, hops, swims, and goes through his gymnastic performances quite as well without consciousness, and consequently without volition, as with it; and, if a frog, in his natural state, possesses anything corresponding with what we call volition, there is no reason to think that it is anything but a concomitant of the molecular changes in the brain which form part of the series involved in the production of motion.

The consciousness of brutes would appear to be related to the mechanism of their body simply as a collateral product of its working, and to be as completely without any power of modifying that working as the steam-whistle which accompanies the work of a locomotive engine is without influence upon its machinery. Their volition, if they have any, is an emotion indicative of physical changes, not a cause of such changes.

This conception of the relations of states of consciousness with molecular changes in the brain . . . does not prevent us from ascribing free will to brutes. For an agent is free when there is nothing to prevent him from doing that which he desires to do. If a greyhound chases a hare, he is a free agent, because his action is in entire accordance with his strong desire to catch the hare; while so long as he is held back by the leash he is not free, being prevented by external force from following his inclination. And the ascription of freedom to the greyhound under the former circumstances is by no means inconsistent with the other aspect of the facts of the case—that he is a machine impelled to the chase, and caused, at the same time, to have the desire to catch the game by the impression which the rays of light proceeding from the hare make upon his eyes, and through them upon his brain.

Much ingenious argument has at various times been bestowed upon the question: How is it possible to imagine that volition, which is a state of consciousness, and, as such, has not the slightest community of nature with matter in motion, can act upon the moving matter of which the body is composed, as it is assumed to do in voluntary acts? But if, as is here suggested, the voluntary acts of brutes—or, in other words, the acts which they desire to perform—are as purely mechanical as the rest of their actions, and are simply accompanied by the state of consciousness called volition, the inquiry, so far as they are concerned, becomes superfluous. Their volitions do not enter into the chain of causation of their actions at all.

The hypothesis that brutes are conscious automata is perfectly consistent with any view that may be held respecting the often discussed and curious question whether they have souls or not; and, if they have souls, whether those souls are immortal or not. It is obviously harmonious with the most literal adherence to the text of Scripture concerning "the beast that perisheth"; but it is not inconsistent with the amiable conviction ascribed by Pope to his "untutored savage," that when he passes to the happy hunting-grounds in the sky, "his faithful dog shall bear him company." If the brutes have consciousness and no souls, then it is clear that, in them, consciousness is a direct function of material changes; while, if they possess immaterial subjects of consciousness, or souls, then, as consciousness is brought into existence only as the consequence of molecular motion of the brain, it follows that it is an indirect product of material changes. The soul stands related to the body as the bell of a clock to the works, and consciousness answers to the sound which the bell gives out when it is struck.

Thus far I have strictly confined myself to the problem with which I proposed to deal at starting—the automatism of brutes. The question is, I believe, a perfectly open one, and I feel happy in running no risk of either Papal or Presbyterian condemnation for the views which I have ventured to put forward. And there are so very few interesting questions which one is, at present, allowed to think out scientifically—to go as far as reason leads, and stop where evidence comes to an end—without speedily being deafened by the tattoo of "the drum ecclesiastic"—that I have luxuriated in my rare freedom, and would now willingly bring this disquisition to an end if I could hope that other people would go no farther. Unfortunately, past experience debars me from entertaining any such hope, even if

> ". . . . that drum's discordant sound
> Parading round and round and round,"

were not, at present, as audible to me as it was to the mild poet who ventured to express his hatred of drums in general, in that well-known couplet.

It will be said, that I mean that the conclusions deduced from the study of the brutes are applicable to man, and that the logical consequences of such application are fatalism, materialism, and atheism—whereupon the drums will beat the *pas de charge*.

One does not do battle with drummers; but I venture to offer a few remarks for the calm consideration of thoughtful persons, untrammelled by foregone conclusions, unpledged to shore-up tottering dogmas, and anxious only to know the true bearings of the case.

It is quite true that, to the best of my judgment, the argumentation which applies to brutes holds equally good of men; and, therefore, that all states of consciousness in us, as in them, are immediately caused by molecular changes of the brain-substance. It seems to me that in men, as in brutes, there is no proof that any state of consciousness is the cause of change in the motion of the matter of the organism. If these positions are well based, it follows that our mental conditions are simply the symbols in consciousness of the changes which take place automatically in the organism; and that, to take an extreme illustration, the feeling we call volition is not the cause of a voluntary act, but the symbol of that state of the brain which is the immediate cause of that act. We are conscious automata, endowed with free will in the only intelligible sense of that much-abused term—inasmuch as in many respects we are able to do as we like—but none the less parts of the great series of causes and effects which, in unbroken continuity, composes that which is, and has been, and shall be—the sum of existence.

As to the logical consequences of this conviction of mine, I may be permitted to remark that logical consequences are the scarecrows of fools and the beacons of wise men. The only question which any wise man can ask himself, and which any honest man will ask himself, is whether a doctrine is true or false. Consequences will take care of themselves; at most their importance can only justify us in testing with extra care the reasoning process from which they result.

So that if the view I have taken did really and logically lead to fatalism, materialism, and atheism, I should profess myself a fatalist, materialist, and atheist; and I should look upon those who, while they believed in my honesty of purpose and intellectual competency, should raise a hue and cry against me, as people who by their own admission preferred lying to truth, and whose opinions therefore were unworthy of the smallest attention.

But, as I have endeavoured to explain on other occasions, I really have no claim to rank myself among fatalistic, materialistic, or atheistic philosophers. Not among fatalists, for I take the conception of necessity to have a logical, and not a physical foundation; not among materialists, for I am utterly incapable of conceiving the existence of matter if there is no mind in which to picture that existence; not among atheists, for the problem of the ultimate cause of existence is one which seems to me to be hopelessly out of reach of my poor powers. Of all the senseless babble I have ever had occasion to read, the demonstrations of these philosophers who undertake to tell us all about the nature of God would be the worst, if they were not surpassed by the still greater absurdities of the philosophers who try to prove that there is no God.

44. J. J. C. Smart

J. J. C. Smart is Professor of Philosophy at the University of Adelaide, Australia.

Sensations Are Brain Processes

. . . .

It seems to me that science is increasingly giving us a viewpoint whereby organisms are able to be seen as physico-chemical mechanisms: it seems that even the behavior of man himself will one day be explicable in mechanistic terms. There does seem to be, so far as science is concerned, nothing in the world but increasingly complex arrangements of physical constituents. All except for one place: in consciousness. That is, for a full description of what is going on in a man you would have to mention not only the physical processes in his tissue, glands, nervous system, and so forth, but also his states of consciousness: his visual, auditory, and tactual sensations, his aches and pains. That these should be *correlated* with brain processes does not help, for to say that they are *correlated* is to say that they are something "over and above." You cannot correlate something with itself. You correlate footprints with burglars, but not Bill Sikes the burglar with Bill Sikes the burglar. So sensations, states of consciousness, do seem to be the one sort of thing left outside the physicalist picture, and for various reasons I just cannot believe that this can be so. That everything should be explicable in terms of physics (together of course with descriptions of the ways in which the parts are put together—roughly, biology is to physics as radio-engineering is to electromagnetism) except the occurrence of sensations seems to be frankly

From "Sensations and Brain Processes," *Philosophical Review*, LXVIII (1959), pp. 141–156. Reprinted by permission of the author and the *Philosophical Review*.

unbelievable. Such sensations would be "nomological danglers," to use Feigl's expression. It is not often realized how odd would be the laws whereby these nomological danglers would dangle. It is sometimes asked, "Why can't there be psycho-physical laws which are of a novel sort, just as the laws of electricity and magnetism were novelties from the standpoint of Newtonian mechanics?" Certainly we are pretty sure in the future to come across new ultimate laws of a novel type, but I expect them to relate simple constituents: for example, whatever ultimate particles are then in vogue. I cannot believe that ultimate laws of nature could relate simple constituents to configurations consisting of perhaps billions of neurons (and goodness knows how many billion billions of ultimate particles) all put together for all the world as though their main purpose in life was to be a negative feedback mechanism of a complicated sort. Such ultimate laws would be like nothing so far known in science. They have a queer "smell" to them. I am just unable to believe in the nomological danglers themselves, or in the laws whereby they would dangle. If any philosophical arguments seemed to compel us to believe in such things, I would suspect a catch in the argument. In any case it is the object of this paper to show that there are no philosophical arguments which compel us to be dualists.

· ·

Why should not sensations just be brain processes of a certain sort? There are, of course, well-known (as well as lesser-known) philosophical objections to the view that reports of sensations are reports of brain-processes, but I shall try to argue that these arguments are by no means as cogent as is commonly thought to be the case.

Let me first try to state more accurately the thesis that sensations are brain processes. It is not the thesis that, for example, "after-image" or "ache" means the same as "brain process of sort X" (where "X" is replaced by a description of a certain sort of brain process). It is that, in so far as "after-image" or "ache" is a report of a process, it is a report of a process that *happens to be* a brain process. It follows that the thesis does not claim that sensation statements can be *translated* into statements about brain processes. Nor does it claim that the logic of a sensation statement is the same as that of a brain-process statement. All it claims is that in so far as a sensation statement is a report of something, that something is in fact a brain process. Sensations are nothing over and above brain processes. Nations are nothing "over and above" citizens, but this does not prevent the logic of nation statements being very different from the logic of citizen statements, nor does it insure the translatability of nation statements into citizen statements. (I do not, however, wish to assert that the relation of sensation statements to brain-process statements is very like that of nation statements to citizen statements. Nations do not just *happen to be* nothing over and above citizens, for example. I bring in the "nations" example merely to make a negative point: that the fact that the logic of A-statements is different from that of B-statements does not insure that A's are anything over and above B's.)

Remarks on identity. When I say that a sensation is a brain process or that lightning is an electric discharge, I am using "is" in the sense of strict identity. (Just as in the—in this case necessary—proposition "7 is identical with the smallest prime number greater than 5.") When I say that a sensation is a brain process or that lightning is an electric discharge I do not mean just that the sensation is somehow spatially or temporally continuous with the brain process or that the lightning is just spatially or temporally continuous with the discharge. When on the other hand I say that the successful general is the same person as the small boy who stole the apples I mean only that the successful general I see before me is a time slice of the same four-dimensional object of which the small boy stealing apples is an earlier time slice. However, the four-dimensional object which has the general-I-see-before-me for its late time slice is identical in the strict sense with the four-dimensional object which has the small-boy-stealing-apples for an early time slice. I distinguish these two senses of "is identical with" because I wish to make it clear that the brain-process doctrine asserts identity in the *strict* sense.

I shall now discuss various possible objections to the view that the processes reported in sensation statements are in fact processes in the brain. Most of us have met some of these objections in our first year as philosophy students. All the more reason to take a good look at them. Others of the objections will be more recondite and subtle.

Objection 1.   Any illiterate peasant can talk perfectly well about his after-images, or how things look or feel to him, or about his aches and pains, and yet he may know nothing whatever about neurophysiology. A man may, like Aristotle, believe that the brain is an organ for cooling the body without any impairment of his ability to make true statements about his sensations. Hence the things we are talking about when we describe our sensations cannot be processes in the brain.

Reply.   You might as well say that a nation of slug-abeds, who never saw the morning star or knew of its existence, or who had never thought of the expression "the Morning Star," but who used the expression "the Evening Star" perfectly well, could not use this expression to refer to the same entity as we refer to (and describe as) "the Morning Star."

You may object that the Morning Star is in a sense not the very same thing as the Evening Star, but only something spatio-temporally continuous with it. That is, you may say that the Morning Star is not the Evening Star in the strict sense of "identity" that I distinguished earlier.

There is, however, a more plausible example. Consider lightning. Modern physical science tells us that lightning is a certain kind of electrical discharge due to ionization of clouds of water-vapor in the atmosphere. This, it is now believed, is what the true nature of lightning is. Note that there are not two things: a flash of lightning and an electrical discharge. There is one thing, a flash of lightning, which is described scientifically as an electrical discharge to the earth from a cloud of ionized water-molecules. The case is not at all like that of explaining a footprint by reference to a burglar. We say that what lightning really is, what its true nature as revealed by science is, is an electric discharge. (It is not the true nature of a footprint to be a burglar.)

To forestall irrelevant objections, I should like to make it clear that by "lightning" I mean the publicly observable physical object, lightning, not a visual sense-datum of lightning. I say that the publicly observable physical object lightning is in fact the electric discharge, not just a correlate of it. The sense-datum, or at least the having of the sense-datum, the "look" of lightning, may well in my view be a correlate of the electric discharge. For in my view it is a brain state *caused* by the lightning. But we should no more confuse sensations of lightning with lightning than we confuse sensations of a table with the table.

In short, the reply to Objection 1 is that there can be contingent statements of the form "A is identical with B," and a person may well know that something is an A without knowing that it is a B. An illiterate peasant might well be able to talk about his sensations without knowing about his brain processes, just as he can talk about lightning though he knows nothing of electricity.

Objection 2. It is only a contingent fact (if it is a fact) that when we have a certain kind of sensation there is a certain kind of process in our brain. Indeed it is possible, though perhaps in the highest degree unlikely, that our present physiological theories will be as out of date as the ancient theory connecting mental processes with goings on in the heart. It follows that when we report a sensation we are not reporting a brain process.

Reply. The objection certainly proves that when we say "I have an after-image" we cannot *mean* something of the form "I have such and such a brain process." But this does not show that what we report (having an after-image) is not *in fact* a brain process. "I see lightning" does not *mean* "I see an electric discharge." Indeed, it is logically possible (though highly unlikely) that the electrical discharge account of lightning might one day be given up. Again, "I see the Evening Star" does not *mean* the same as "I see the Morning Star," and yet "the Evening Star and the Morning Star are one and the same thing" is a contingent proposition. Possibly Objection 2 derives some of its apparent strength from a "Fido" —Fido theory of meaning. If the meaning of an expression were what the expression named, then of course it *would* follow from the fact that "sensation" and "brain process" have different meanings that they cannot name one and the same thing.

Objection 3. Even if Objections 1 and 2 do not prove that sensations are something over and above brain processes, they do prove that the qualities of sensations are something over and above the qualities of brain processes. That is, it may be possible to get out of asserting the existence of irreducibly psychic processes, but not out of asserting the existence of irreducibly psychic *properties*. For suppose we identify the Morning Star with the Evening Star. Then there must be some properties which logically imply that of being the Morning Star, and quite distinct properties which entail that of being the Evening Star. Again, there must be some properties (for example, that of being a yellow flash) which are logically distinct from those in the physicalist story.

Now how do I get over the objection that a sensation can be identified with a brain process only if it has some phenomenal property, not possessed by brain processes, whereby one-half of the identification may be, so to speak, pinned down?

My suggestion is as follows. When a person says, "I see a yellowish-orange after-image," he is saying something like this: *"There is some-thing going on which is like what is going on when* I have my eyes open, am awake, and there is an orange illuminated in good light in front of me, that is, when I really see an orange." (And there is no reason why a person should not say the same thing when he is having a veridical sense-datum, so long as we construe "like" in the last sentence in such a sense that something can be like itself.) Notice that the italicized words, namely "there is something going on which is like what is going on when," are all quasi-logical or topic-neutral words. This explains why the ancient Greek peasant's reports about his sensations can be neutral be-tween dualistic metaphysics or my materialistic metaphysics. It explains how sensations can be brain-processes and yet how those who report them need know nothing about brain-processes. For he reports them only very abstractly as "something going on which is like what is going on when . . ." Similarly, a person may say "someone is in the room," thus reporting truly that the doctor is in the room, even though he has never heard of doctors. (There are not two people in the room: "someone" *and* the doctor.) This account of sensation statements also explains the singu-lar elusiveness of "raw feels"—why no one seems to be able to pin any properties on them. Raw feels, in my view, are colorless for the very same reason that *something* is colorless. This does not mean that sensations do not have properties, for if they are brain processes they certainly have properties. It only means that in speaking of them as being like or unlike one another we need not know or mention these properties.

This, then, is how I would reply to Objection 3. The strength of my reply depends on the possibility of our being able to report that one thing is like another without being able to state the respect in which it is like. I am not sure whether this is so or not, and that is why I regard Objection 3 as the strongest with which I have to deal.

Objection 4. The after-image is not in physical space. The brain process is. So the after-image is not a brain process.

Reply. This is an *ignoratio elenchi.* I am not arguing that the after-image is a brain process, but that the experience of having an after-image is a brain process. It is the *experience* which is reported in the introspec-tive report. Similarly, if it is objected that the after-image is yellowy-orange but that a surgeon looking into your brain would see nothing yellowy-orange, my reply is that it is the experience of seeing yellowy-orange that is being described, and this experience is not a yellowy-orange something. So to say that a brain process cannot be yellowy-orange is not to say that a brain process cannot in fact be the experience of having a yellowy-orange after-image. There is, in a sense, no such thing as an after-image or a sense-datum, though there is such a thing as the experience of having an image, and this experience is described indirectly in material object language, not in phenomenal language, for there is no such thing. We describe the experience by saying, in effect, that it is like the experi-ence we have when, for example, we really see a yellowy-orange patch on the wall. Trees and wallpaper can be green, but not the experience of see-ing or imagining a tree or wallpaper. (Or if they are described as green or yellow this can only be in a derived sense.)

Objection 5. It would make sense to say of a molecular movement in the brain that it is swift or slow, straight or circular, but it makes no sense to say this of the experience of seeing something yellow.

Reply. So far we have not given sense to talk of experiences as swift or slow, straight or circular. But I am not claiming that "experience" and "brain process" mean the same or even that they have the same logic. "Somebody" and "the doctor" do not have the same logic, but this does not lead us to suppose that talking about somebody telephoning is talking about someone over and above, say, the doctor. The ordinary man when he reports an experience is reporting that something is going on, but he leaves it open as to what sort of thing is going on, whether in a material solid medium, or perhaps in some sort of gaseous medium, or even perhaps in some sort of nonspatial medium (if this makes sense). All that I am saying is that "experience" and "brain process" may in fact refer to the same thing, and if so we may easily adopt a convention (which is not a change in our present rules for the use of experience words but an addition to them) whereby it would make sense to talk of an experience in terms appropriate to physical processes.

Objection 6. Sensations are private, brain processes are *public.* If I sincerely say, "I see a yellowish-orange after-image" and I am not making a verbal mistake, then I cannot be wrong. But I can be wrong about a brain process. The scientist looking into my brain might be having an illusion. Moreover, it makes sense to say that two or more people are observing the same brain process but not that two or more people are reporting the same inner experience.

Reply. This shows that the language of introspective reports has a different logic from the language of material processes. It is obvious that until the brain-process theory is much improved and widely accepted there will be no *criteria* for saying "Smith has an experience of such-and-such a sort" *except* Smith's introspective reports. So we have adopted a rule of language that (normally) what Smith says goes.

Objection 7. I can imagine myself turned to stone and yet having images, aches, pains, and so on.

Reply. I can imagine that the electrical theory of lightning is false, that lightning is some sort of purely optical phenomenon. I can imagine that lightning is not an electrical discharge. I can imagine that the Evening Star is not the Morning Star. But it is. All the objection shows is that "experience" and "brain process" do not have the same meaning. It does not show that an experience is not in fact a brain process.

I have now considered a number of objections to the brain-process thesis. I wish now to conclude by some remarks on the logical status of the thesis itself. U. T. Place seems to hold that it is a straight-out scientific hypothesis. If so, he is partly right and partly wrong. If the issue is between (say) a brain-process thesis and a heart thesis, or a liver thesis, or a kidney thesis, then the issue is a purely empirical one, and the verdict is overwhelmingly in favor of the brain. The right sorts of things don't go on in the heart, liver, or kidney, nor do these organs possess the right sort of complexity of structure. On the other hand, if the issue is between a brain-or-heart-or-liver-or-kidney thesis (that is, some form of materialism) on the one hand and epiphenomenalism on the other hand, then the issue is not an empirical one. For there is no conceivable experiment which could decide between materialism and epiphenomenalism. This latter issue is not like the average straight-out empirical issue in science, but like the issue between the nineteenth-century English naturalist Philip Gosse and the orthodox geologists and paleontologists of his day. According to Gosse, the earth was created about 4000 B.C. exactly as described in *Genesis*, with twisted rock strata, "evidence" of erosion, and so forth, and all sorts of fossils, all in their appropriate strata, just as if the usual evolutionist story had been true. Clearly this theory is in a sense irrefutable: no evidence can possibly tell against it. Let us ignore the theological setting in which Philip Gosse's hypothesis had been placed, thus ruling out objections of a theological kind, such as "what a queer God who would go to such elaborate lengths to deceive us." Let us suppose that it is held that the universe just *began* in 4004 B.C., with the initial conditions just everywhere as they were in 4004 B.C., and in particular that our own planet began with sediment in the rivers, eroded cliffs, fossils in the rocks, and so on. No scientist would ever entertain this as a serious hypothesis, consistent though it is with all possible evidence. The hypothesis offends against the principles of parsimony and simplicity. There would be far too many brute and inexplicable facts. Why are pterodactyl bones just as they are? No explanation in terms of the evolution of pterodactyls from earlier forms of life would any longer be possible. We would have millions of facts about the world as it was in 4004 B.C. that just have to be *accepted*.

The issue between the brain-process theory and epiphenomenalism seems to be of the above sort. (Assuming that a behavioristic reduction of introspective reports is not possible.) If it be agreed that there are no cogent philosophical arguments which force us into accepting dualism, and if the brain process theory and dualism are equally consistent with the facts, then the principles of parsimony and simplicity seem to me to decide overwhelmingly in favor of the brain-process theory. As I pointed out earlier, dualism involves a large number of irreducible psychophysical laws (whereby the "nomological danglers" dangle) of a queer sort, that just have to be taken on trust, and are just as difficult to swallow as the irreducible facts about the paleontology of the earth with which we are faced in Philip Gosse's theory.

45. Norman Malcolm

Norman Malcolm is Professor of Philosophy at Cornell
University.

A Critique of Materialism

I

My main topic will be, roughly speaking, the claim that mental events
or conscious experiences or inner experiences are brain processes. I
hasten to say, however, that I am not going to talk about "mental events"
or "conscious experiences" or "inner experiences." These expressions are
almost exclusively philosophers' terms, and I am not sure that I have got
the hang of any of them. Philosophers are not in agreement in their use
of these terms. One philosopher will say, for example, that a pain in the
foot is a mental event, whereas another will say that a pain *in the foot*
certainly is not a *mental* event.

I will avoid these expressions, and concentrate on the particular example of *sudden thoughts*. Suddenly remembering an engagement would
be an example of suddenly thinking of something. Suddenly realizing,
in a chess game, that moving this pawn would endanger one's queen,
would be another example of a sudden thought. Professor Smart says

From Norman Malcolm, "Scientific Materialism and the Identity Theory," *Dialogue*, Vol. 3 (1964), pp. 115–125 (with minor omissions). Reprinted by kind permission
of the author and the editor of *Dialogue*.

This paper was read at the Sixtieth Annual Meeting of the American Philosophical Association, Eastern Division. It is a reply to Professor J. J. C. Smart's essay,
"Materialism," published in *The Journal of Philosophy*, Vol. LX, No. 22: October,
1963.

that he wishes to "elucidate thought as an inner process,"[2] and he adds that he wants to identify "such inner processes with brain processes." He surely holds, therefore, that thinking and thoughts, including sudden thoughts, are brain processes. He holds also that conscious experiences, (pp. 656 and 657), illusions (p. 659), and aches and pains (p. 654) are brain processes, and that love (p. 652) is a brain state. I will restrict my discussion, however, to sudden thoughts.

My first inclination, when I began to think on this topic, was to believe that Smart's view is false—that a sudden thought certainly is not a brain process. But now I think that I do not know what it *means* to say that a sudden thought is a brain process. In saying this I imply, of course, that the proponents of this view also do not know what it means. This implication is risky for it might turn out, to my surprise and gratification, that Smart will explain his view with great clarity.

In trying to show that there is real difficulty in seeing what his view means, I will turn to Smart's article "Sensations and Brain Processes."[3] He says there that in holding that a sensation is a brain process he is "using 'is' in the sense of strict identity" (p. 163). "I wish to make it clear," he says, "that the brain process doctrine asserts identity in the *strict* sense" (p. 164). I assume that he wishes to say the same about the claimed identity of a thought with a brain process. Unfortunately he does not attempt to define this "strict sense of identity," and so we have to study his examples.

. . . .

Smart tells us that the sense in which the small boy who stole apples is the same person as the victorious general, is *not* the "strict" sense of "identity" (p. 164). He thinks there is a mere spatio-temporal continuity between the apple-stealing boy and the general who won the war. From this *non*-example of "strict identity" I think I obtain a clue as to what he means by it. Consider the following two sentences: "General De Gaulle is the tallest Frenchman"; "The victorious general is the small boy who stole apples." Each of these sentences might be said to express an identity: yet we can see a difference between the two cases. Even though the victorious general *is* the small boy who stole apples, it is possible for the victorious general to be in this room at a time when there is *no* small boy here. In contrast, if General De Gaulle *is* the tallest Frenchman, then General De Gaulle is not in this room unless the tallest Frenchman is here. It would be quite natural to say that this latter identity (if it holds) is a *strict* identity, and that the other one is not. I believe that Smart would say this. This suggests to me the following rule for his "strict identity": If something, x, is in a certain place at a certain time, then something, y, is strictly identical with x only if y is in that same place at that same time.

. . . .

Let us turn to what Smart calls his "more plausible" example of strict identity. It is this: Lightning is an electric discharge. Smart avows

2. Smart, *op. cit.*, p. 657.
3. J. J. C. Smart, "Sensations and Brain Processes," *The Philosophical Review*, April 1959; republished in *The Philosophy of Mind*, ed. V. C. Chappell, Prentice-Hall, 1962. Page references will be to the latter.

that this is truly a strict identity (p. 163 and pp. 164–165). This example provides additional evidence that he wants to follow the stated rule. If an electrical discharge occurred in one region of the sky and a flash of lightning occurred simultaneously in a different region of the sky, Smart would have no inclination to assert (I think) that the lightning was strictly identical with the electric discharge. Or if electrical discharges and corresponding lightning flashes occurred in the same region of the sky, but not at the same time, there normally being a perceptible interval of time between a discharge and a flash, then Smart (I believe) would not wish to hold that there was anything more strict than a systematic correlation (perhaps causal) between electric discharges and lightning.[4]

I proceed now to take up Smart's claim that a sudden thought is strictly identical with some brain process. It is clear that a brain process has spatial location. A brain process would be a mechanical, chemical or electrical process in the brain substance, or an electric discharge from the brain mass, or something of the sort. As Smart puts it, brain processes take place "inside our skulls."[5]

Let us consider an example of a sudden thought. Suppose that when I am in my house I hear the sound of a truck coming up the driveway and it suddenly occurs to me that I have not put out the milk bottles. Now is this sudden thought (which is also a sudden memory) literally inside my skull? I think that in our ordinary use of the terms "thought" and "thinking," we attach no meaning to the notion of determining the bodily location of a thought. We do not seriously debate whether someone's sudden thought occurred in his heart, or his throat, or his brain. Indeed, we should not know what the question meant. We should have no idea what to look for to settle this "question." We do say such a thing as "He can't get the thought out of his head"; but this is not taken as giving the location of a thought, any more than the remark "He still has that girl on the brain," is taken as giving the location of a girl.

It might be replied that *as things are* the bodily location of thoughts is not a meaningful notion; but if massive correlations were discovered between thoughts and brain processes then we might *begin* to locate thoughts in the head. To this I must answer that our philosophical problem *is* about how things are. It is a question about our *present* concepts of thinking and thought, not about some conjectured future concepts.

The difficulty I have in understanding Smart's identity theory is the following. Smart wants to use a concept of "strict identity." Since there are a multitude of uses of the word "is," from the mere fact that he tells us that he means "is" in the sense of "strict identity," it does not follow that he has explained which use of "is" he intends. From his examples

---

4. Mr. U. T. Place, in his article "Is Consciousness a Brain Process?" (*The Philosophy of Mind*, V. C. Chappell, ed., Prentice-Hall, 1962) also defends the identity theory. An example that he uses to illustrate the sense of identity in which, according to him, "consciousness" could turn out to be a brain process is this: "A cloud is a mass of water droplets or other particles in suspension" (*loc. cit.*, pp. 103 and 105). I believe that Place would not be ready to hold that this is a genuine identity, *as contrasted with* a systematic and/or causal correlation, if he did not assume that in the very same region of space occupied by a cloud there is, at the very same time, a mass of particles in suspension.

5. "Materialism," *loc. cit.*, p. 654.

and non-examples, I surmise that his so-called "strict identity" is governed by the necessary condition that if *x* occurs in a certain place at a certain time, then *y* is strictly identical with *x* only if *y* occurs in the same place at the same time. But if *x* is a brain process and *y* is a sudden thought, then this condition for strict identity is not (and cannot be) satisfied. Indeed, it does not even make sense to set up a test for it. Suppose we had determined, by means of some instrument, that a certain process occurred inside my skull at the exact moment I had the sudden thought about the milk bottles. How do we make the further test of whether my *thought* occurred inside my skull? For it would have to be a *further* test: it would have to be logically independent of the test for the presence of the brain process, because Smart's thesis is that the identity is *contingent*. But no one has any notion of what it would mean to test for the occurrence of the thought inside my skull *independently* of testing for a brain process. The idea of such a test is not intelligible. Smart's thesis, as I understand it, requires this unintelligible idea. For he is not satisfied with holding that there is a systematic correlation between sudden thoughts and certain brain processes. He wants to take the additional step of holding that there is a "strict identity." Now his concept of strict identity either embodies the necessary condition I stated previously, or it does not. If it does not, then I do not know what he means by "strict identity," over and above systematic correlation. If his concept of strict identity does embody that necessary condition, then his concept of strict identity cannot be meaningfully applied to the relationship between sudden thoughts and brain processes. My conclusion is what I said in the beginning: the identity theory has no clear meaning.

II

I turn now to a different consideration. A thought requires circumstances or, in Wittgenstein's word, "surroundings" (Umgebung). Putting a crown on a man's head is a coronation, only in certain circumstances.[6] The behavior of exclaiming, "Oh, I have not put out the milk bottles," or the behavior of suddenly jumping up, rushing to the kitchen, collecting the bottles and carrying them outside—such behavior expresses the thought that one has not put out the milk bottles, *only in certain circumstances*.

The circumstances necessary for this simple thought are complex. They include the existence of an organized community, of a practice of collecting and distributing milk, of a rule that empty bottles will not be collected unless placed outside the door, and so on. These practices, arrangements and rules could exist only if there was a common language; and this in turn would presuppose shared activities and agreement in the use of language. The thought about the milk bottles requires a background of mutual purpose, activity and understanding.

I assume that if a certain brain process were strictly identical with a certain thought, then the occurrence of that brain process would be an

6. *Investigations*, Sec. 584.

absolutely sufficient condition for the occurrence of that thought. If this assumption is incorrect, then my understanding of what Smart means by "strict identity" is even *less* than I have believed. In support of this assumption I will point out that Smart has never stated his identity theory in the following way: *In certain circumstances* a particular brain process is identical with a particular thought. His thesis has not carried such a qualification. I believe his thesis is the following: A particular brain process is, *without qualification*, strictly identical with a particular thought. If this thesis were true it would appear to follow that the occurrence of that brain process would be an absolutely sufficient condition for the occurrence of that thought.

I have remarked that a necessary condition for the occurrence of my sudden thought about the milk bottles is the previous existence of various practices, rules and agreements. If the identity theory were true, then the surroundings that are necessary for the existence of my sudden thought would also be necessary for the existence of the brain process with which it is identical.[7] That brain process would not have occurred unless, for example, there was or had been a practice of delivering milk.

This consequence creates a difficulty for those philosophers who, like Smart, hold both to the identity theory and also to the viewpoint that I shall call "scientific materialism." According to the latter viewpoint, the furniture of the world "in the last resort" consists of "the ultimate entities of physics."[8] Smart holds that everything in the world is "explicable in terms of physics."[9] It does not seem to me that this can be true. My sudden thought about the milk bottles was an occurrence in the world. That thought required a background of common practices, purposes and agreements. But a reference to a practice of (*e.g.*) delivering milk could not appear in a proposition of physics. The word "electron" is a term of physics, but the phrase "a practice of delivering milk" is not. There could not be an explanation of the occurrence of my thought (an explanation taking account of all the necessary circumstances) which was stated solely in terms of the entities and laws of physics.

My sudden thought about the milk bottles is not unique in requiring surroundings. The same holds for any other thought. No thought would be explicable wholly in the terms of physics (and/or biology) because the circumstances that form the "stage-setting" for a thought cannot be described in the terms of physics.

Now if I am right on this point, and if the identity theory were true, it would follow that none of those *brain processes* that are identical with thoughts could be given a purely physical explanation. A philosopher who holds both to the identity theory and to scientific materialism is forced,

---

7. It is easy to commit a fallacy here. The circumstances that I have mentioned are *conceptually* necessary for the occurrence of my thought. If the identity theory were true it would not follow that they were *conceptually* necessary for the occurrence of the brain process that is identical with that thought. But it would follow that those circumstances were necessary for the occurrence of the brain process *in the sense* that the brain process *would not* have occurred in the absence of those circumstances.

8. "Materialism," *loc. cit.*, p. 651.

9. "Sensations and Brain Processes," *loc. cit.*, p. 161

I think, into the self-defeating position of conceding that many brain processes are not explicable solely in terms of physics.[10] The position is self-defeating because such a philosopher regards a brain process as a *paradigm* of something wholly explicable in terms of physics.

A defender of these two positions might try to avoid this outcome by claiming that the circumstances required for the occurrence of a thought, do themselves consist of configurations of ultimate particles (or of their statistical properties, or something of the sort). I doubt, however, that anyone knows what it would mean to say, for example, that the *rule* that milk bottles will not be collected unless placed outside the door, is a configuration of ultimate particles. At the very least, this defence would have to assume a heavy burden of explanation.

III

There is a further point connected with the one just stated. At the foundation of Smart's monism there is, I believe, the desire for a homogeneous system of explanation. Everything in the world, he feels, should be capable of the same *kind* of explanation, namely, one in terms of the entities and laws of physics. He thinks we advance toward this goal when we see that sensations, thoughts, etc., are identical with brain processes.

Smart has rendered a service to the profession by warning us against a special type of fallacy. An illustration of this fallacy would be to argue that a sensation is not a brain process because a person can be talking about a sensation and yet not be talking about a brain process.[11] The verb "to talk about" might be called an "intentional" verb, and this fallacy committed with it might be called "the intentional fallacy." Other intentional verbs would be "to mean," "to intend," "to know," "to predict," "to describe," "to notice," and so on.

It is easy to commit the intentional fallacy, and I suspect that Smart himself has done so. The verb "to explain" is also an intentional verb and one must beware of using it to produce a fallacy. Suppose that the Prime Minister of Ireland is the ugliest Irishman. A man might argue that this cannot be so, because someone might be explaining the presence of the Irish Prime Minister in New York and yet not be explaining the presence in New York of the ugliest Irishman. It would be equally fallacious to argue that since the Irish Prime Minister and the ugliest Irishman *are* one and the same person, therefore, to explain the presence of the Prime Minister *is* to explain the presence of the ugliest Irishman.

I wonder if Smart has not reasoned fallaciously, somewhat as fol-

10. I believe this argument is pretty similar to a point made by J. T. Stevenson, in his "Sensations and Brain Processes: A Reply to J. J. C. Smart," *The Philosophical Review*, October 1960, p. 507. Smart's view, roughly speaking, is that unless sensations are identical with brain processes they are "nomological danglers." Stevenson's retort is that by insisting that sensations are identical with brain processes we have not got rid of any nomological danglers. He says: "Indeed, on Smart's thesis it turns out that brain processes are danglers, for now brain processes have all those properties that made sensations danglers."
11. Smart, "Sensations and Brain Processes," *loc. cit.*, p. 164.

lows: If a sudden thought *is* a certain brain process, then to *explain* the occurrence of the brain process *is* to explain the occurrence of the thought. Thus there will be just one kind of explanation for both thoughts and brain processes.

The intentional fallacy here is transparent. If a thought is identical with a brain process, it does not follow that to explain the occurrence of the brain process is to explain the occurrence of the thought. And in fact, an explanation of the one differs in *kind* from an explanation of the other. The explanation of why someone *thought* such and such, involves different assumptions and principles and is guided by different interests than is an explanation of why this or that process occurred in his brain. These explanations belong to different *systems* of explanation.

I conclude that even if Smart were right in holding that thoughts are strictly identical with brain processes (a claim that I do not yet find intelligible) he would not have established that there is one and the same explanation for the occurrence of the thoughts and for the occurrence of the brain processes. If he were to appreciate this fact then, I suspect, he would no longer have any *motive* for espousing the identity theory. For this theory, even if true, would not advance us one whit toward the single, homogeneous system of explanation that is the goal of Smart's materialism.

46. A. M. Türing

A. M. Türing (1912–1954) was an English mathematician who made important contributions to the design of computers.

Can Machines Think?

1. The Imitation Game

I propose to consider the question, 'Can machines think?' This should begin with definitions of the meaning of the terms 'machine' and 'think.' The definitions might be framed so as to reflect so far as possible the normal use of the words, but this attitude is dangerous. If the meaning of the words 'machine' and 'think' are to be found by examining how they are commonly used it is difficult to escape the conclusion that the meaning and the answer to the question, 'Can machines think?' is to be sought in a statistical survey such as a Gallup poll. But this is absurd. Instead of attempting such a definition I shall replace the question by another, which is closely related to it and is expressed in relatively unambiguous words.

The new form of the problem can be described in terms of a game which we call the 'imitation game.' It is played with three people, a man (A), a woman (B), and an interrogator (C) who may be of either sex. The interrogator stays in a room apart from the other two. The object of the game for the interrogator is to determine which of the other two is the man and which is the woman. He knows them by labels X

From "Computing Machinery and Intelligence," first published in *Mind*, Vol. LIX, No. 236, October, 1950. Pp. 433–460, *passim*. Reprinted by permission of the editor of *Mind*.

and Y, and at the end of the game he says either 'X is A and Y is B' or 'X is B and Y is A.' The interrogator is allowed to put questions to A and B thus:

C: Will X please tell me the length of his or her hair?

Now suppose X is actually A, then A must answer. It is A's object in the game to try and cause C to make the wrong identification. His answer might therefore be,

'My hair is shingled, and the longest strands are about nine inches long.'

In order that tones of voice may not help the interrogator the answers should be written, or better still, typewritten. The ideal arrangement is to have a teleprinter communicating between the two rooms. Alternatively the question and answers can be repeated by an intermediary. The object of the game for the third player (B) is to help the interrogator. The best strategy for her is probably to give truthful answers. She can add such things as 'I am the woman, don't listen to him!' to her answers, but it will avail nothing as the man can make similar remarks.

We now ask the question, 'What will happen when a machine takes the part of A in this game?' Will the interrogator decide wrongly as often when the game is played like this as he does when the game is played between a man and a woman? These questions replace our original, 'Can machines think?'

2. Critique of the New Problem

As well as asking, 'What is the answer to this new form of the question,' one may ask, 'Is this new question a worthy one to investigate?' This latter question we investigate without further ado, thereby cutting short an infinite regress.

The new problem has the advantage of drawing a fairly sharp line between the physical and the intellectual capacities of a man. No engineer or chemist claims to be able to produce a material which is indistinguishable from the human skin. It is possible that at some time this might be done, but even supposing this invention available we should feel there was little point in trying to make a 'thinking machine' more human by dressing it up in such artificial flesh. The form in which we have set the problem reflects this fact in the condition which prevents the interrogator from seeing or touching the other competitors, or hearing their voices. Some other advantages of the proposed criterion may be shown up by specimen questions and answers. Thus:

Q: Please write me a sonnet on the subject of the Forth Bridge.
A: Count me out on this one. I never could write poetry.

Q: Add 34957 to 70764.
A: (Pause about 30 seconds and then give answer as) 105621.

Q: Do you play chess?
A: Yes.

Q: I have K at my K1, and no other pieces. You have only K at K6 and R at R1. It is your move. What do you play?
A: (After a pause of 15 seconds) R–R8 mate.

The question and answer method seems to be suitable for introducing almost any one of the fields of human endeavour that we wish to include. We do not wish to penalise the machine for its inability to shine in beauty competitions, nor to penalise a man for losing in a race against an aeroplane. The conditions of our game make these disabilities irrelevant. The 'witnesses' can brag, if they consider it advisable, as much as they please about their charms, strength or heroism, but the interrogator cannot demand practical demonstrations.

. . . .

3. The Machines Concerned in the Game

The question which we put in §1 will not be quite definite until we have specified what we mean by the word 'machine.' It is natural that we should wish to permit every kind of engineering technique to be used in our machines. We also wish to allow the possibility that an engineer or team of engineers may construct a machine which works, but whose manner of operation cannot be satisfactorily described by its constructors because they have applied a method which is largely experimental. Finally, we wish to exclude from the machines men born in the usual manner. It is difficult to frame the definitions so as to satisfy those three conditions. One might for instance insist that the team of engineers should be all of one sex, but this would not really be satisfactory, for it is probably possible to rear a complex individual from a single cell of the skin (say) of a man. To do so would be a feat of biological technique deserving of the very highest praise, but we would not be inclined to regard it as a case of 'constructing a thinking machine.' This prompts us to abandon the requirement that every kind of technique should be permitted. We are the more ready to do so in view of the fact that the present interest in 'thinking machines' has been aroused by a particular kind of machine, usually called an 'electronic computer' or 'digital computer.' Following this suggestion we only permit digital computers to take part in our game.

This restriction appears at first sight to be a very drastic one. I shall attempt to show that it is not so in reality. To do this necessitates a short account of the nature and properties of these computers.

It may also be said that this identification of machines with digital computers, like our criterion for 'thinking,' will only be unsatisfactory if (contrary to my belief), it turns out that digital computers are unable to give a good showing in the game.

There are already a number of digital computers in working order, and it may be asked, 'Why not try the experiment straight away? It would be easy to satisfy the conditions of the game. A number of interrogators could be used, and statistics compiled to show how often the right identification was given.' The short answer is that we are not asking whether all digital computers would do well in the game nor whether the computers at present available would do well, but whether there are imaginable computers which would do well. But this is only the short answer. We shall see this question in a different light later.

4. Digital Computers

The idea behind digital computers may be explained by saying that these machines are intended to carry out any operations which could be done by a human computer. The human computer is supposed to be following fixed rules; he has no authority to deviate from them in any detail. We may suppose that these rules are supplied in a book, which is altered whenever he is put on to a new job. He has also an unlimited supply of paper on which he does his calculations. He may also do his multiplications and additions on a 'desk machine,' but this is not important.

If we use the above explanation as a definition we shall be in danger of circularity of argument. We avoid this by giving an outline of the means by which the desired effect is achieved. A digital computer can usually be regarded as consisting of three parts:

(i) Store.
(ii) Executive unit.
(iii) Control.

The store is a store of information, and corresponds to the human computer's paper, whether this is the paper on which he does his calculations or that on which his book of rules is printed. In so far as the human computer does calculations in his head a part of the store will correspond to his memory.

The executive unit is the part which carries out the various individual operations involved in a calculation. What these individual operations are will vary from machine to machine. Usually fairly lengthy operations can be done such as 'Multiply 3510675445 by 7076345687' but in some machines only very simple ones such as 'Write down 0' are possible.

We have mentioned that the 'book of rules' supplied to the computer is replaced in the machine by a part of the store. It is then called the 'table of instructions.' It is the duty of the control to see that these instructions are obeyed correctly and in the right order. The control is so constructed that this necessarily happens.

The information in the store is usually broken up into packets of moderately small size. In one machine, for instance, a packet might consist of ten decimal digits. Numbers are assigned to the parts of the store in which the various packets of information are stored, in some systematic manner. A typical instruction might say—

'Add the number stored in position 6809 to that in 4302 and put the result back into the latter storage position.'

Needless to say it would not occur in the machine expressed in English. It would more likely be coded in a form such as 6809430217. Here 17 says which of various possible operations is to be performed on the two numbers. In this case the operation is that described above, *viz.* 'Add the number. . . .' It will be noticed that the instruction takes up

10 digits and so forms one packet of information, very conveniently. The control will normally take the instructions to be obeyed in the order of the positions in which they are stored, but occasionally an instruction such as

'Now obey the instruction stored in position 5606, and continue from there' may be encountered, or again

'If position 4505 contains 0 obey next the instruction stored in 6707, otherwise continue straight on.'

Instructions of these latter types are very important because they make it possible for a sequence of operations to be repeated over and over again until some condition is fulfilled, but in doing so to obey, not fresh instructions on each repetition, but the same ones over and over again. To take a domestic analogy. Suppose Mother wants Tommy to call at the cobbler's every morning on his way to school to see if her shoes are done, she can ask him afresh every morning. Alternatively she can stick up a notice once and for all in the hall which he will see when he leaves for school and which tells him to call for the shoes, and also to destroy the notice when he comes back if he has the shoes with him.

The reader must accept it as a fact that digital computers can be constructed, and indeed have been constructed, according to the principles we have described, and that they can in fact mimic the actions of a human computer very closely.

The book of rules which we have described our human computer as using is of course a convenient fiction. Actual human computers really remember what they have got to do. If one wants to make a machine mimic the behaviour of the human computer in some complex operation one has to ask him how it is done, and then translate the answer into the form of an instruction table. Constructing instruction tables is usually described as 'programming.' To 'programme a machine to carry out the operation A' means to put the appropriate instruction table into the machine so that it will do A.

An interesting variant on the idea of a digital computer is a 'digital computer with a random element.' These have instructions involving the throwing of a die or some equivalent electronic process; one such instruction might for instance be, 'Throw the die and put the resulting number into store 1000.' Sometimes such a machine is described as having free will (though I would not use this phrase myself). It is not normally possible to determine from observing a machine whether it has a random element, for a similar effect can be produced by such devices as making the choices depend on the digits of the decimal for π.

Most actual digital computers have only a finite store. There is no theoretical difficulty in the idea of a computer with an unlimited store. Of course only a finite part can have been used at any one time. Likewise only a finite amount can have been constructed, but we can imagine more and more being added as required. Such computers have special theoretical interest and will be called infinitive capacity computers.

The idea of a digital computer is an old one. Charles Babbage, Lucasian Professor of Mathematics at Cambridge from 1828 to 1839, planned such a machine, called the Analytical Engine, but it was never completed. Although Babbage had all the essential ideas, his machine was not at that time such a very attractive prospect. The speed which would have been available would be definitely faster than a human computer but something like 100 times slower than the Manchester machine, itself one of the slower of the modern machines. The storage was to be purely mechanical, using wheels and cards.

The fact that Babbage's Analytical Engine was to be entirely mechanical will help us to rid ourselves of a superstition. Importance is often attributed to the fact that modern digital computers are electrical, and that the nervous system also is electrical. Since Babbage's machine was not electrical, and since all digital computers are in a sense equivalent, we see that this use of electricity cannot be of theoretical importance. Of course electricity usually comes in where fast signalling is concerned, so that it is not surprising that we find it in both these connections. In the nervous system chemical phenomena are at least as important as electrical. In certain computers the storage system is mainly acoustic. The feature of using electricity is thus seen to be only a very superficial similarity. If we wish to find such similarities we should look rather for mathematical analogies of function.

5. Universality of Digital Computers

The digital computers considered in the last section may be classified amongst the 'discrete-state machines.' These are the machines which move by sudden jumps or clicks from one quite definite state to another. These states are sufficiently different for the possibility of confusion between them to be ignored. Strictly speaking there are no such machines. Everything really moves continuously. But there are many kinds of machine which can profitably be *thought of* as being discrete-state machines. For instance in considering the switches for a lighting system it is a convenient fiction that each switch must be definitely on or definitely off. There must be intermediate positions, but for most purposes we can forget about them. As an example of a discrete-state machine we might consider a wheel which clicks round through 120° once a second, but may be stopped by a lever which can be operated from outside; in addition a lamp is to light in one of the positions of the wheel. This machine could be described abstractly as follows. The internal state of the machine (which is described by the position of the wheel) may be q_1, q_2 or q_3. There is an input signal i_0 or i_1 (position of lever). The internal state at any moment is determined by the last state and input signal according to the table.

Last State

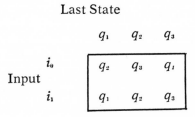

		q_1	q_2	q_3
Input	i_0	q_2	q_3	q_1
	i_1	q_1	q_2	q_3

The output signals, the only externally visible indication of the internal state (the light) are described by the table

State	q_1	q_2	q_3
Output	o_0	o_0	o_1

This example is typical of discrete-state machines. They can be described by such tables provided they have only a finite number of possible states.

It will seem that given the initial state of the machine and the input signals it is always possible to predict all future states. This is reminiscent of Laplace's view that from the complete state of the universe at one moment of time, as described by the positions and velocities of all particles, it should be possible to predict all future states. The prediction which we are considering is, however, rather nearer to practicability than that considered by Laplace. The system of the 'universe as a whole' is such that quite small errors in the initial conditions can have an overwhelming effect at a later time. The displacement of a single electron by a billionth of a centimetre at one moment might make the difference between a man being killed by an avalanche a year later, or escaping. It is an essential property of the mechanical systems which we have called 'discrete-state machines' that this phenomenon does not occur. Even when we consider the actual physical machines instead of the idealised machines, reasonably accurate knowledge of the state at one moment yields reasonably accurate knowledge any number of steps later.

As we have mentioned, digital computers fall within the class of discrete-state machines. But the number of states of which such a machine is capable is usually enormously large. For instance, the number for the machine now working at Manchester is about $2^{165,000}$, *i.e.* about $10^{50,000}$. Compare this with our example of the clicking wheel described above, which had three states. It is not difficult to see why the number of states should be so immense. The computer includes a store corresponding to the paper used by a human computer. It must be possible to write into the store any one of the combinations of symbols which might have been written on the paper. For simplicity suppose that only digits from 0 to 9 are used as symbols. Variations in handwriting are ignored. Suppose the computer is allowed 100 sheets of paper each containing 50 lines each with room for 30 digits. Then the number of states is $10^{100\times50\times30}$, *i.e.* $10^{150,000}$. This is about the number of states of three Manchester machines put together. The logarithm to the base two of the number of states is usually called the 'storage capacity' of the machine. Thus the Manchester machine has a storage capacity of about 165,000 and the wheel machine of our example about 1.6. If two machines are put together their capacities must be added to obtain the capacity of the resultant machine. This leads to the possibility of statements such as 'The Manchester machine contains 64 magnetic tracks each with a capacity of 2560, eight electronic tubes with a capacity of 1280. Miscellaneous storage amounts to about 300 making a total of 174,380.'

Given the table corresponding to a discrete-state machine it is possible to predict what it will do. There is no reason why this calculation should not be carried out by means of a digital computer. Provided it could be carried out sufficiently quickly the digital computer could mimic the behavior of any discrete-state machine. The imitation game could then be played with the machine in question (as B) and the mimicking digital computer (as A) and the interrogator would be unable to distinguish them. Of course the digital computer must have an adequate storage capacity as well as working sufficiently fast. Moreover, it must be programmed afresh for each new machine which it is desired to mimic.

This special property of digital computers, that they can mimic any discrete-state machine, is described by saying that they are *universal* machines. The existence of machines with this property has the important consequence that, considerations of speeds apart, it is unnecessary to design various new machines to do various computing processes. They can all be done with one digital computer, suitably programmed for each case. It will be seen that as a consequence of this all digital computers are in a sense equivalent.

We may now consider again the point raised at the end of §3. It was suggested tentatively that the question, 'Can machines think?' should be replaced by 'Are there imaginable digital computers which would do well in the imitation game?' If we wish we can make this superficially more general and ask 'Are there discrete-state machines which would do well?' But in view of the universality property we see that either of these questions is equivalent to this, 'Let us fix our attention on one particular digital computer C. Is it true that by modifying this computer to have an adequate storage, suitably increasing its speed of action, and providing it with an appropriate programme, C can be made to play satisfactorily the part of A in the imitation game, the part of B being taken by a man?'

6. Contrary Views on the Main Question

We may now consider the ground to have been cleared and we are ready to proceed to the debate on our question, 'Can machines think?' and the variant of it quoted at the end of the last section. We cannot altogether abandon the original form of the problem, for opinions will differ as to the appropriateness of the substitution and we must at least listen to what has to be said in this connexion.

It will simplify matters for the reader if I explain first my own beliefs in the matter. Consider first the more accurate form of the question. I believe that in about fifty years' time it will be possible to programme computers, with a store capacity of about 10^9, to make them play the imitation game so well that an average interrogator will not have more than 70 per cent chance of making the right identification after five minutes of questioning. The original question, 'Can machines think?' I believe to be too meaningless to deserve discussion. Nevertheless I believe that at the end of the century the use of words and general educated opinion will have altered so much that one will be able to speak of machines thinking without expecting to be contradicted. I believe further that no useful purpose is served by concealing these beliefs. The popular view that scientists proceed inexorably from well-established fact to well-established fact, never being influenced by any unproved conjecture, is quite mistaken. Provided it is made clear which are proved facts and which are conjectures, no harm can result. Conjectures are of great importance since they suggest useful lines of research.

I now proceed to consider opinions opposed to my own.

· ·

(4) *The Argument from Consciousness.* This argument is very well expressed in *Professor Jefferson's* Lister Oration for 1949, from which I quote. 'Not until a machine can write a sonnet or compose a concerto because of thoughts and emotions felt, and not by the chance fall of symbols, could we agree that machine equals brain—that is, not only write it but know that it had written it. No mechanism could feel (and not merely artificially signal, an easy contrivance) pleasure at its successes, grief when its valves fuse, be warmed by flattery, be made miserable by its mistakes, be charmed by sex, be angry or depressed when it cannot get what it wants.'

This argument appears to be a denial of the validity of our test. According to the most extreme form of this view the only way by which one could be sure that a machine thinks is to *be* the machine and to feel oneself thinking. One could then describe these feelings to the world, but of course no one would be justified in taking any notice. Likewise according to this view the only way to know that a *man* thinks is to be that particular man. It is in fact the solipsist point of view. It may be the most logical view to hold but it makes communication of ideas difficult. A is liable to believe 'A thinks but B does not' whilst B believes 'B thinks but A does not.' Instead of arguing continually over this point it is usual to have the polite convention that everyone thinks.

I am sure that Professor Jefferson does not wish to adopt the extreme and solipsist point of view. Probably he would be quite willing to accept the imitation game as a test. The game (with the player B omitted) is frequently used in practice under the name of *viva voce* to discover whether some one really understands something or has 'learnt it parrot fashion.' Let us listen in to a part of such a *viva voce:*

Interrogator: In the first line of your sonnet which reads 'Shall I compare thee to a summer's day,' would not 'a spring day' do as well or better?
Witness: It wouldn't scan.
Interrogator: How about 'a winter's day.' That would scan all right.
Witness: Yes, but nobody wants to be compared to a winter's day.
Interrogator: Would you say Mr. Pickwick reminded you of Christmas?
Witness: In a way.
Interrogator: Yet Christmas is a winter's day, and I do not think Mr. Pickwick would mind the comparison.
Witness: I don't think you're serious. By a winter's day one means a typical winter's day, rather than a special one like Christmas.

And so on. What would Professor Jefferson say if the sonnet-writing machine was able to answer like this in the *vive voce?* I do not know whether he would regard the machine as 'merely artificially signalling' these answers, but if the answers were as satisfactory and sustained as in the above passage I do not think he would describe it as 'an easy contrivance.' This phrase is, I think, intended to cover such devices as the inclusion in the machine of a record of someone reading a sonnet, with appropriate switching to turn it on from time to time.

In short then, I think that most of those who support the argument from consciousness could be persuaded to abandon it rather than be forced into the solipsist position. They will then probably be willing to accept our test.

I do not wish to give the impression that I think there is no mystery about consciousness. There is, for instance, something of a paradox connected with any attempt to localise it. But I do not think these mysteries necessarily need to be solved before we can answer the question with which we are concerned in this paper.

(5) *Arguments from Various Disabilities.* These arguments take the form, 'I grant you that you can make machines do all the things you have mentioned but you will never be able to make one to do X.' Numerous features X are suggested in this connexion. I offer a selection:

> Be kind, resourceful, beautiful, friendly (p. 554), have initiative, have a sense of humour, tell right from wrong, make mistakes (p. 554), fall in love, enjoy strawberries and cream (p. 554), make some one fall in love with it, learn from experience (pp. 558 f.), use words properly, be the subject of its own thought (p. 554), have as much diversity of behaviour as a man, do something really new (p. 555). (Some of these disabilities are given special consideration as indicated by the page numbers.)

No support is usually offered for these statements. I believe they are mostly founded on the principles of scientific induction. A man has seen thousands of machines in his lifetime. From what he sees of them he draws a number of general conclusions. They are ugly, each is designed for a very limited purpose, when required for a minutely different purpose they are useless, the variety of behaviour of any one of them is very small, etc., etc. Naturally he concludes that these are necessary properties of machines in general. Many of these limitations are associated with the very small storage capacity of most machines. (I am assuming that the idea of storage capacity is extended in some way to cover machines other than discrete-state machines. The exact definition does not matter as no mathematical accuracy is claimed in the present discussion.) A few years ago, when very little had been heard of digital computers, it was possible to elicit much incredulity concerning them, if one mentioned their properties without describing their construction. That was presumably due to a similar application of the principle of scientific induction. These applications of the principle are of course largely unconscious. When a burnt child fears the fire and shows that he fears it by avoiding it, I should say that he was applying scientific induction. (I could of course also describe his behaviour in many other ways.) The works and customs of mankind do not seem to be a very suitable material to which to apply scientific induction. A very large part of space-time must be investigated, if reliable results are to be obtained. Otherwise we may (as most English children do) decide that everybody speaks English, and that it is silly to learn French.

There are, however, special remarks to be made about many of the disabilities that have been mentioned. The inability to enjoy strawberries and cream may have struck the reader as frivolous. Possibly a machine might be made to enjoy this delicious dish, but any attempt to make one do so would be idiotic. What is important about this disability is that it contributes to some of the other disabilities, *e.g.* to the difficulty of the same kind of friendliness occurring between man and machine as between white man and white man, or between black man and black man.

The claim that 'machines cannot make mistakes' seems a curious one. One is tempted to retort, 'Are they any the worse for that?' But let us adopt a more sympathetic attitude, and try to see what is really meant. I think this criticism can be explained in terms of the imitation game. It is claimed that the interrogator could distinguish the machine from the man simply by setting them a number of problems in arithmetic. The machine would be unmasked because of its deadly accuracy. The reply to this is simple. The machine (programmed for playing the game) would not attempt to give the *right* answers to the arithmetic problems. It would deliberately introduce mistakes in a manner calculated to confuse the interrogator. A mechanical fault would probably show itself through an unsuitable decision as to what sort of a mistake to make in the arithmetic. Even this interpretation of the criticism is not sufficiently sympathetic. But we cannot afford the space to go into it much further. It seems to me that this criticism depends on a confusion between two kinds of mistake. We may call them 'errors of functioning' and 'errors of conclusion.' Errors of functioning are due to some mechanical or electrical fault which causes the machine to behave otherwise than it was designed to do. In philosophical discussions one likes to ignore the possibility of such errors; one is therefore discussing 'abstract machines.' These abstract machines are mathematical fictions rather than physical objects. By definition they are incapable of errors of functioning. In this sense we can truly say that 'machines can never make mistakes.' Errors of conclusion can only arise when some meaning is attached to the output signals from the machine. The machine might, for instance, type out mathematical equations, or sentences in English. When a false proposition is typed we say that the machine has committed an error of conclusion. There is clearly no reason at all for saying that a machine cannot make this kind of mistake. It might do nothing but type out repeatedly '10 = 1.' To take a less perverse example, it might have some method for drawing conclusions by scientific induction. We must expect such a method to lead occasionally to erroneous results.

The claim that a machine cannot be the subject of its own thought can of course only be answered if it can be shown that the machine has *some* thought with *some* subject matter. Nevertheless, 'the subject matter of a machine's operations' does seem to mean something, at least to the people who deal with it. If, for instance, the machine was trying to find a solution of the equation $x^2 - 40x - 1 = 0$ one would be tempted to describe this equation as part of the machine's subject matter at that moment. In this sort of sense a machine undoubtedly can be its own subject matter. It may be used to help in making up its own programmes, or to predict the effect of alterations in its own structure. By observing the results of its own behaviour it can modify its own programmes so as to achieve some purpose more effectively. These are possibilities of the near future, rather than Utopian dreams.

The criticism that a machine cannot have much diversity of behaviour is just a way of saying that it cannot have much storage capacity. Until fairly recently a storage capacity of even a thousand digits was very rare.

The criticisms that we are considering here are often disguised forms of the argument from consciousness. Usually if one maintains that a machine *can* do one of these things, and describes the kind of method that the machine could use, one will not make much of an impression. It is thought that the method (whatever it may be, for it must be mechanical) is really rather base. Compare the parenthesis in Jefferson's statement quoted on p. 552.

(6) *Lady Lovelace's Objection.* Our most detailed information of Babbage's Analytical Engine comes from a memoir by *Lady Lovelace.* In it she states, 'The Analytical Engine has no pretensions to *originate* anything. It can do *whatever we know how to order it* to perform' (her italics). This statement is quoted by *Hartree . . .* who adds: 'This does not imply that it may not be possible to construct electronic equipment which will "think for itself," or in which, in biological terms, one could set up a conditioned reflex, which would serve as a basis for "learning." Whether this is possible in principle or not is a stimulating and exciting question, suggested by some of these recent developments. But it did not seem that the machines constructed or projected at the time had this property.'

I am in thorough agreement with Hartree over this. It will be noticed that he does not assert that the machines in question had not got the property, but rather that the evidence available to Lady Lovelace did not encourage her to believe that they had it. It is quite possible that the machines in question had in a sense got this property. For suppose that some discrete-state machine has the property. The Analytical Engine was a universal digital computer, so that, if its storage capacity and speed were adequate, it could by suitable programming be made to mimic the machine in question. Probably this argument did not occur to the Countess or to Babbage. In any case there was no obligation on them to claim all that could be claimed.

This whole question will be considered again under the heading of learning machines.

A variant of Lady Lovelace's objection states that a machine can 'never do anything really new.' This may be parried for a moment with the saw, 'There is nothing new under the sun.' Who can be certain that 'original work' that he has done was not simply the growth of the seed planted in him by teaching, or the effect of following well-known general principles. A better variant of the objection says that a machine can never 'take us by surprise.' This statement is a more direct challenge and can be met directly. Machines take me by surprise with great frequency. This is largely because I do not do sufficient calculation to decide what to expect them to do, or rather because although I do a calculation, I do it in a hurried, slipshod fashion, taking risks. Perhaps I say to myself, 'I suppose the voltage here ought to be the same as there: anyway let's assume it is.' Naturally I am often wrong, and the result is a surprise for me for by the time the experiment is done these assumptions have been forgotten. These admissions lay me open to lectures on the subject of my vicious ways, but do not throw any doubt on my credibility when I testify to the surprises I experience.

I do not expect this reply to silence my critic. He will probably say that such surprises are due to some creative mental act on my part, and reflect no credit on the machine. This leads us back to the argument from consciousness, and far from the idea of surprise. It is a line of argument we must consider closed, but it is perhaps worth remarking that the appreciation of something as surprising requires as much of a 'creative mental act' whether the surprising event originates from a man, a book, a machine or anything else.

The view that machines cannot give rise to surprises is due, I believe, to a fallacy to which philosophers and mathematicians are particularly subject. This is the assumption that as soon as a fact is presented to a mind all consequences of that fact spring into the mind simultaneously with it. It is a very useful assumption under many circumstances, but one too easily forgets that it is false. A natural consequence of doing so is that one then assumes that there is no virtue in the mere working out of consequences from data and general principles.

(7) *Argument from Continuity in the Nervous System.* The nervous system is certainly not a discrete-state machine. A small error in the information about the size of a nervous impulse impinging on a neuron, may make a large difference to the size of the outgoing impulse. It may be argued that, this being so, one cannot expect to be able to mimic the behaviour of the nervous system with a discrete-state system.

It is true that a discrete-state machine must be different from a continuous machine. But if we adhere to the conditions of the imitation game, the interrogator will not be able to take any advantage of this difference. The situation can be made clearer if we consider some other simpler continuous machine. A differential analyser will do very well. (A differential analyser is a certain kind of machine not of the discrete-state type used for some kinds of calculation.) Some of these provide their answers in a typed form, and so are suitable for taking part in the game. It would not be possible for a digital computer to predict exactly what answers the differential analyser would give to a problem, but it would be quite capable of giving the right sort of answer. For instance, if asked to give the value of π (actually about $3 \cdot 1416$) it would be reasonable to choose at random between the values $3 \cdot 12$, $3 \cdot 13$, $3 \cdot 14$, $3 \cdot 15$, $3 \cdot 16$, with the probabilities of $0 \cdot 05$, $0 \cdot 15$, $0 \cdot 55$, $0 \cdot 19$, $0 \cdot 06$ (say). Under these circumstances it would be very difficult for the interrogator to distinguish the differential analyser from the digital computer.

(8) *The Argument from Informality of Behaviour.* It is not possible
to produce a set of rules purporting to describe what a man should do in
every conceivable set of circumstances. One might for instance have a
rule that one is to stop when one sees a red traffic light, and to go if one
sees a green one, but what if by some fault both appear together? One
may perhaps decide that it is safest to stop. But some further difficulty
may well arise from this decision later. To attempt to provide rules of
conduct to cover every eventuality, even those arising from traffic lights,
appears to be impossible. With all this I agree.

From this it is argued that we cannot be machines. I shall try to
reproduce the argument, but I fear I shall hardly do it justice. It seems
to run something like this. 'If each man had a definite set of rules of
conduct by which he regulated his life he would be no better than a
machine. But there are no such rules, so men cannot be machines.' The
undistributed middle is glaring. I do not think the argument is ever put
quite like this, but I believe this is the argument used nevertheless. There
may however be a certain confusion between 'rules of conduct' and 'laws
of behaviour' to cloud the issue. By 'rules of conduct' I mean precepts
such as 'Stop if you see red lights,' on which one can act, and of which
one can be conscious. By 'laws of behaviour' I mean laws of nature as
applied to a man's body such as 'if you pinch him he will squeak.' If we
substitute 'laws of behaviour which regulate his life' for 'laws of conduct
by which he regulates his life' in the argument quoted the undistributed
middle is no longer insuperable. For we believe that it is not only true
that being regulated by laws of behaviour implies being some sort of
machine (though not necessarily a discrete-state machine), but that conversely being such a machine implies being regulated by such laws. However, we cannot so easily convince ourselves of the absence of complete
laws of behaviour as of complete rules of conduct. The only way we know
of for finding such laws is scientific observation, and we certainly know
of no circumstances under which we would say, 'We have searched
enough. There are no such laws.'

We can demonstrate more forcibly that any such statement would
be unjustified. For suppose we could be sure of finding such laws if they
existed. Then given a discrete machine it should certainly be possible to
discover by observation sufficient about it to predict its future behaviour,
and this within a reasonable time, say a thousand years. But this does
not seem to be the case. I have set up on the Manchester computer a
small programme using only 1000 units of storage, whereby the machine
applied with one sixteen figure number replies with another within two
seconds. I would defy anyone to learn from these replies sufficient about
the programme to be able to predict any replies to untried values.

. . . .

7. Learning Machines

The reader will have anticipated that I have no very convincing arguments of a positive nature to support my views. If I had I should not

have taken such pains to point out the fallacies in contrary views. Such evidence as I have I shall now give.

The only really satisfactory support that can be given for the view expressed at the beginning of §6, will be that provided by waiting for the end of the century and then doing the experiment described. But what can we say in the meantime? What steps should be taken now if the experiment is to be successful?

As I have explained, the problem is mainly one of programming. Advances in engineering will have to be made too, but it seems unlikely that these will not be adequate for the requirements. Estimates of the storage capacity of the brain vary from 10^{10} to 10^{15} binary digits. I incline to the lower values and believe that only a very small fraction is used for the higher types of thinking. Most of it is probably used for the retention of visual impressions. I should be surprised if more than 10^9 was required for satisfactory playing of the imitation game, at any rate against a blind man. (Note—The capacity of the *Encyclopaedia Britannica*, 11th edition, is 2×10^9.) A storage capacity of 10^7 would be a very practicable possibility even by present techniques. It is probably not necessary to increase the speed of operations of the machines at all. Parts of modern machines which can be regarded as analogues of nerve cells work about a thousand times faster than the latter. This should provide a 'margin of safety' which could cover losses of speed arising in many ways. Our problem then is to find out how to programme these machines to play the game. At my present rate of working I produce about a thousand digits of programme a day, so that about sixty workers, working steadily through the fifty years might accomplish the job, if nothing went into the wastepaper basket. Some more expeditious method seems desirable.

In the process of trying to imitate an adult human mind we are bound to think a good deal about the process which has brought it to the state that it is in. We may notice three components,

(a) The initial state of the mind, say at birth,
(b) The education to which it has been subjected,
(c) Other experience, not to be described as education, to which it has been subjected.

Instead of trying to produce a programme to simulate the adult mind, why not rather try to produce one which simulates the child's? If this were then subjected to an appropriate course of education one would obtain the adult brain. Presumably the child-brain is something like a note-book as one buys it from the stationers. Rather little mechanisms, and lots of blank sheets. (Mechanism and writing are from our point of view almost synonymous.) Our hope is that there is so little mechanism in the child-brain that something like it can be easily programmed. The amount of work in the education we can assume, as a first approximation, to be much the same as for the human child.

We have thus divided our problem into two parts. The child-programme and the education process. These two remain very closely connected. We cannot expect to find a good child-machine at the first attempt. One must experiment with teaching one such machine and see how well it learns. One can then try another and see if it is better or worse. There is an obvious connection between this process and evolution, by the identifications

- Structure of the child machine = Hereditary material
- Changes   "   "   = Mutations
- Natural selection   = Judgment of the experimenter

One may hope, however, that this process will be more expeditious than evolution. The survival of the fittest is a slow method for measuring advantages. The experimenter, by the exercise of intelligence, should be able to speed it up. Equally important is the fact that he is not restricted to random mutations. If he can trace a cause for some weakness he can probably think of the kind of mutation which will improve it.

It will not be possible to apply exactly the same teaching process to the machine as to a normal child. It will not, for instance, be provided with legs, so that it could not be asked to go out and fill the coal scuttle. Possibly it might not have eyes. But however well these deficiencies might be overcome by clever engineering, one could not send the creature to school without the other children making excessive fun of it. It must be given some tuition. We need not be too concerned about the legs, eyes, etc. The example of Miss *Helen Keller* shows that education can take place provided that communication in both directions between teacher and pupil can take place by some means or other.

We normally associate punishments and rewards with the teaching process. Some simple child-machines can be constructed or programmed on this sort of principle. The machine has to be so constructed that events which shortly preceded the occurrence of a punishment-signal are unlikely to be repeated, whereas a reward-signal increased the probability of repetition of the events which led up to it. These definitions do not presuppose any feelings on the part of the machine. I have done some experiments with one such child-machine, and I succeeded in teaching it a few things, but the teaching method was too unorthodox for the experiment to be considered really successful.

The use of punishments and rewards can at best be a part of the teaching process. Roughly speaking, if the teacher has no other means of communicating to the pupil, the amount of information which can reach him does not exceed the total number of rewards and punishments applied. By the time a child has learnt to repeat 'Casabianca' he would probably feel very sore indeed, if the text could only be discovered by a 'Twenty Questions' technique, every 'NO' taking the form of a blow. It is necessary therefore to have some other 'unemotional' channels of communication. If these are available it is possible to teach a machine by punishments and rewards to obey orders given in some language, *e.g.* a symbolic language. These orders are to be transmitted through the 'unemotional' channels. The use of this language will diminish greatly the number of punishments and rewards required.

Opinions may vary as to the complexity which is suitable in the child-machine. One might try to make it as simple as possible consistent with the general principles. Alternatively one might have a complete system of logical inference 'built in.'[1] In the latter case the store would be largely occupied with definitions and propositions. The propositions would have various kinds of status, *e.g.* well-established facts, conjectures, mathematically proved theorems, statements given by an authority, expressions having the logical form of proposition but not belief-value. Certain propositions may be described as 'imperatives.' The machine should be so constructed that as soon as an imperative is classed as 'well-established' the appropriate action automatically takes place. To illustrate this, suppose the teacher says to the machine, 'Do your homework now.' This may cause 'Teacher says "Do your homework now" ' to be included amongst the well-established facts. Another such fact might be, 'Everything that teacher says is true.' Combining these may eventually lead to the imperative, 'Do your homework now,' being included amongst the well-established facts, and this, by the construction of the machine, will mean that homework actually gets started, but the effect is very satisfactory. The processes of inference used by the machine need not be such as would satisfy the most exacting logicians. There might for instance be no hierarchy of types. But this need not mean that type fallacies will occur, any more than we are bound to fall over unfenced cliffs. Suitable imperatives (expressed *within* the systems, not forming part of the rules *of* the system) such as 'Do not use a class unless it is a subclass of one which has been mentioned by teacher,' can have a similar effect to 'Do not go too near the edge.'

The imperatives that can be obeyed by a machine that has no limbs are bound to be of a rather intellectual character, as in the example (doing homework) given above. Important amongst such imperatives will be ones which regulate the order in which the rules of the logical system concerned are to be applied. For at each stage when one is using a logical system, there is a very large number of alternative steps, any of which one is permitted to apply, so far as obedience to the rules of the logical system is concerned. These choices make the difference between a brilliant and a footling reasoner, not the difference between a sound and a fallacious one. Propositions leading to imperatives of this kind might be 'When Socrates is mentioned, use the syllogism in Barbara' or 'If one method has been proved to be quicker than another, do not use the slower method.' Some of these may be 'given by authority,' but others may be produced by the machine itself, *e.g.* by scientific induction.

The idea of a learning machine may appear paradoxical to some readers. How can the rules of operation of the machine change? They should describe completely how the machine will react whatever its history might be, whatever changes it might undergo. The rules are thus quite time-invariant. This is quite true. The explanation of the paradox is that the rules which get changed in the learning process are of a rather less pretentious kind, claiming only an ephemeral validity. The reader may draw a parallel with the Constitution of the United States.

An important feature of a learning machine is that its teacher will often be very largely ignorant of quite what is going on inside, although

---

1. Or rather 'programmed in' for our child-machine will be programmed in a digital computer. But the logical system will not have to be learnt.

he may still be able to some extent to predict his pupil's behaviour. This should apply most strongly to the later education of a machine arising from a child-machine of well-tried design (or programme). This is in clear contrast with normal procedure when using a machine to do computations: one's object is then to have a clear mental picture of the state of the machine at each moment in the computation. This object can only be achieved with a struggle. The view that 'the machine can only do what we know how to order it to do,' appears strange in face of this. Most of the programmes which we can put into the machine will result in its doing something that we cannot make sense of at all, or which we regard as completely random behaviour. Intelligent behaviour presumably consists in a departure from the completely disciplined behaviour involved in computation, but a rather slight one, which does not give rise to random behaviour, or to pointless repetitive loops. Another important result of preparing our machine for its part in the imitation game by a process of teaching and learning is that 'human fallibility' is likely to be omitted in a rather natural way, *i.e.* without special 'coaching.' (The reader should reconcile this with the point of view on pp. 553–554.) Processes that are learnt do not produce a hundred per cent certainty of result; if they did they could not be unlearnt.

It is probably wise to include a random element in a learning machine . . . (see p. 551). A random element is rather useful when we are searching for a solution of some problem. Suppose for instance we wanted to find a number between 50 and 200 which was equal to the square of the sum of its digits, we might start at 51 and then try 52 and go on until we got a number that worked. Alternatively we might choose numbers at random until we got a good one. This method has the advantage that it is unnecessary to keep track of the values that have been tried, but the disadvantage that one may try the same one twice, but this is not very important if there are several solutions. The systematic method has the disadvantage that there may be an enormous block without any solutions in the region which has to be investigated first. Now the learning process may be regarded as a search for a form of behaviour which will satisfy the teacher (or some other criterion). Since there is probably a very large number of satisfactory solutions the random method seems to be better than the systematic. It should be noticed that it is used in the analogous process of evolution. But there the systematic method is not possible. How could one keep track of the different genetical combinations that had been tried, so as to avoid trying them again?

We may hope that machines will eventually compete with men in all purely intellectual fields. But which are the best ones to start with? Even this is a difficult decision. Many people think that a very abstract activity, like the playing of chess, would be best. It can also be maintained that it is best to provide the machine with the best sense organs that money can buy, and then teach it to understand and speak English. This process could follow the normal teaching of a child. Things would be pointed out and named, etc. Again I do not know what the right answer is, but I think both approaches should be tried.

We can only see a short distance ahead, but we can see plenty there that needs to be done.

47. Bertrand Russell

Bertrand Russell (1872–1970) was one of the most prominent
philosophers of the twentieth century, having left his mark
on virtually every branch of philosophy.

Science and Immortality

It remains to inquire what bearing modern doctrines as to physiology
and psychology have upon the credibility of the orthodox belief in immortality.

That the soul survives the death of the body is a doctrine which, as
we have seen, has been widely held, by Christians and non-Christians, by
civilized men and by barbarians. Among the Jews of the time of Christ,
the Pharisees believed in immortality, but the Sadducees, who adhered to
the older tradition, did not. In Christianity, the belief in the life everlasting has always held a very prominent place. Some enjoy felicity in
heaven—after a period of purifying suffering in purgatory, according to
Roman Catholic belief. Others endure unending torments in hell. In
modern times, liberal Christians often incline to the view that hell is not
eternal; this view has come to be held by many clergymen in the Church
of England since the Privy Council, in 1864, decided that it is not illegal
for them to do so. But until the middle of the nineteenth century very
few professing Christians doubted the reality of eternal punishment. The
fear of hell was—and to a lesser extent still is—a source of the deepest
anxiety, which much diminished the comfort to be derived from belief in
survival. The motive of saving others from hell was urged as a justifica-

Bertrand Russell, *Religion and Science* (1935). Reprinted by permission of the
Oxford University Press. From Chapter V, "Soul and Body."

tion of persecution; for if a heretic, by misleading others, could cause them to suffer damnation, no degree of earthly torture could be considered excessive if employed to prevent so terrible a result. For, whatever may now be thought, it was formerly believed, except by a small minority, that heresy was incompatible with salvation.

The decay of the belief in hell was not due to any new theological arguments, nor yet to the direct influence of science, but to the general diminution of ferocity which took place during the eighteenth and nineteenth centuries. It is part of the same movement which led, shortly before the French Revolution, to the abolition of judicial torture in many countries, and which, in the early nineteenth century, led to the reformation of the savage penal code by which England had been disgraced. In the present day, even among those who still believe in hell, the number of those who are condemned to suffer its torments is thought to be much smaller than was formerly held. Our fiercer passions, nowadays, take a political rather than a theological direction.

It is a curious fact that, as the belief in hell has grown less definite, belief in heaven has also lost vividness. Although heaven is still a recognized part of Christian orthodoxy, much less is said about it in modern discussions than about evidences of Divine purpose in evolution. Arguments in favour of religion now dwell more upon its influence in promoting a good life here on earth than on its connection with the life hereafter. The belief that this life is merely a preparation for another, which formerly influenced morals and conduct, has now ceased to have much influence even on those who have not consciously rejected it.

What science has to say on the subject of immortality is not very definite. There is, indeed, one line of argument in favour of survival after death, which is, at least in intention, completely scientific—I mean the line of argument associated with the phenomena investigated by psychical research. I have not myself sufficient knowledge on this subject to judge of the evidence already available, but it is clear that there could be evidence which would convince reasonable men. To this, however, certain provisos must be added. In the first place, the evidence, at the best, would only prove that we survive death, not that we survive for ever. In the second place, where strong desires are involved, it is very difficult to accept the testimony even of habitually accurate persons; of this there was much evidence during the War, and in all times of great excitement. In the third place, if, on other grounds, it seems unlikely that our personality does not die with the body, we shall require much stronger evidence of survival than we should if we thought the hypothesis antecedently probable. Not even the most ardent believer in spiritualism could pretend to have as much evidence of survival as historians can adduce to prove that witches did bodily homage to Satan, yet hardly anyone now regards the evidence of such occurrences as even worth examining.

The difficulty, for science, arises from the fact that there does not seem to be such an entity as the soul or self. As we saw, it is no longer possible to regard soul and body as two "substances," having that endurance through time which metaphysicians regarded as logically bound up with the notion of substance. Nor is there any reason, in psychology, to assume a "subject" which, in perception, is brought into contact with an "object." Until recently, it was thought that matter is immortal, but this is no longer assumed by the technique of physics. An atom is now merely a convenient way of grouping certain occurrences; it is convenient, up to a point, to think of the atom as a nucleus with attendant electrons, but the electrons at one time cannot be identified with those at another, and in any case no modern physicist thinks of them as "real." While there was still material substance which was supposed to be eternal, it was easy to argue that minds must be equally eternal; but this argument, which was never a very strong one, can now no longer be used. For sufficient reasons, physicists have reduced the atom to a series of events; for equally good reasons, psychologists find that a mind has not the identity of a single continuing "thing," but is a series of occurrences bound together by certain intimate relations. The question of immortality, therefore, has become the question whether these intimate relations exist between occurrences connected with a living body and other occurrences which take place after that body is dead.

We must first decide, before we can attempt to answer this question, what are the relations which bind certain events together in such a way as to make them the mental life of one person. Obviously the most important of these is memory: things that I can remember happened to *me*. And if I can remember a certain occasion, and on that occasion I could remember something else, then the something else also happened to me. It might be objected that two people may remember the same event, but that would be an error: no two people ever see exactly the same thing, because of differences in their positions. No more can they have precisely the same experiences of hearing or smelling or touching or tasting. My experience may closely resemble another person's, but always differs from it in a greater or less degree. Each person's experience is private to himself, and when one experience consists in recollecting another, the two are said to belong to the same "person."

There is another, less psychological, definition of personality, which derives it from the body. The definition of what makes the identity of a living body at different times would be complicated, but for the moment we will take it for granted. We will also take it for granted that every "mental" experience known to us is connected with some living body. We can then define a "person" as the series of mental occurrences connected with a given body. This is the legal definition. If John Smith's body committed a murder, and at a later time the police arrest John Smith's body, then the person inhabiting that body at the time of arrest is a murderer.

These two ways of defining a "person" conflict in cases of what is called dual personality. In such cases, what seems to outside observation to be one person is, subjectively, split into two; sometimes neither knows anything of the other, sometimes one knows the other, but not vice versa. In cases where neither knows anything of the other, there are two persons if memory is used as the definition, but only one if the body is used. There is a regular gradation to the extreme of dual personality, through absent-mindedness, hypnosis, and sleep-walking. This makes a difficulty in using memory as the definition of personality. But it appears that lost memories can be recovered by hypnotism or in the course of psycho-analysis; thus perhaps the difficulty is not insuperable.

In addition to actual recollection, various other elements, more or less analogous to memory, enter into personality—habits, for instance, which have been formed as a result of past experience. It is because, where there is life, events can form habits, that an "experience" differs from a mere occurrence. An animal, and still more a man, is formed by experiences in a way that dead matter is not. If an event is causally re-lated to another in that peculiar way that has to do with habit-formation, then the two events belong to the same "person." This is a wider defini-tion than that by memory alone, including all that the memory-definition included and a good deal more.

If we are to believe in the survival of a personality after the death of the body, we must suppose that there is continuity of memories or at least of habits, since otherwise there is no reason to suppose that the same person is continuing. But at this point physiology makes difficulties. Habit and memory are both due to effects on the body, especially the brain; the formation of a habit may be thought of as analogous to the formation of a water-course. Now the effects on the body, which give rise to habits and memories, are obliterated by death and decay, and it is difficult to see how, short of miracle, they can be transferred to a new body such as we may be supposed to inhabit in the next life. If we are to be disembodied spirits, the difficulty is only increased. Indeed I doubt whether, with modern views of matter, a disembodied spirit is logically possible. Matter is only a certain way of grouping events, and therefore where there are events there is matter. The continuity of a person throughout the life of his body, if, as I contend, it depends upon habit-formation, must also depend upon the continuity of the body. It would be as easy to transfer a water-course to heaven without loss of identity as it would be to transfer a person.

Personality is essentially a matter of organization. Certain events, grouped together by means of certain relations, form a person. The grouping is effected by means of causal laws—those connected with habit-formation, which includes memory—and the causal laws concerned de-pend upon the body. If this is true—and there are strong scientific grounds for thinking that it is—to expect a personality to survive the disintegration of the brain is like expecting a cricket club to survive when all its members are dead.

I do not pretend that this argument is conclusive. It is impossible to foresee the future of science, particularly of psychology, which is only just beginning to be scientific. It may be that psychological causation can be freed from its present dependence on the body. But in the present state of psychology and physiology, belief in immortality can, at any rate, claim no support from science, and such arguments as are possible on the subject point to the probable extinction of personality at death. We may regret the thought that we shall not survive, but it is a comfort to think that all the persecutors and Jewbaiters and humbugs will not con-tinue to exist for all eternity. We may be told that they would improve in time, but I doubt it.

48. C. D. Broad

C. D. Broad (1887–1971) was Professor of Philosophy at Cambridge University.

Paranormal Phenomena and Human Survival

The world then, as it presents itself to common-sense and everyday experience, offers no positive reasons for and no positive reasons against human survival. The only reason against it is the utter absence of all reasons for it; and we have seen that this is not a strong argument in the present case. Let us now enquire whether the more detailed investigations of science provide us with any grounds for deciding one way or the other.

Science on the whole does not reverse, but merely amplifies and elaborates, the views of common-sense on the connexion of body and mind. We already knew that body and mind were intimately connected, and that injury to the former may gravely modify or to all appearance destroy the latter. The additional information gained from science may be summed up as follows. (i) More detailed knowledge has been got of the correlation between injuries to particular regions of the brain and defects in certain departments of mental life. Connected with this is the knowledge that many mental processes, which seem to common-sense to be almost independent of the body, have bodily correlates. (ii) We have

From C. D. Broad, *The Mind and Its Place in Nature*, 1925. Published by Routledge & Kegan Paul Ltd., London, and Humanities Press, Inc., New York. Reprinted by permission of the publishers.

gained the surprising information that, in spite of the apparent interaction of body and mind, the body and its material surroundings form a closed energetic system from the point of view of the Conservation of Energy. (iii) We know more about the detailed structure and the general plan of the brain and nervous system. What bearing has all this on the probability of survival? We find bodies without minds; we never find minds without bodies. When we do find minds we always find a close correlation between their processes and those of their bodies. This, it is argued, strongly suggests that minds depend for their *existence* on bodies; in which case, though survival may still be abstractly possible, it is to the last degree unlikely. At death there takes place completely and permanently a process of bodily destruction which, when it occurs partially and temporarily, carries with it the destruction of part of our mental life. The inference seems only too obvious. I think it is fair to say that our ordinary scientific knowledge of the relation of body to mind most strongly suggests epiphenomenalism, though it does not necessitate it; and that epiphenomenalism is most unfavourable to the hypothesis of human survival.

It is, however, possible to put forward other theories about the mind and its relation to the body, which are consistent with ordinary experience and with scientific knowledge and are less unfavourable to survival then epiphenomenalism. I will call the first of these the "Instrumental Theory."

The Instrumental Theory. We must begin by drawing a distinction between the existence of a mind and its manifestation to other minds. On the Instrumental Theory the mind is a substance which is existentially independent of the body. It may have existed before the body began, and it may exist after the body is destroyed. For a time it is intimately connected with a certain body; and at such times it can get information about other things only by means of its body and can act on other things only by first moving its body. If the body be injured the mind may be cut off from certain sources of information about other things, and it may be prevented from expressing itself in certain ways; but otherwise it may be uninjured. It is certain that such a theory as this is consistent with a good many of the facts which are commonly held to prove the existential dependence of mind on body. Nevertheless, I think that, in this crude form, it cannot be maintained. Let us take the case of a man who is injured in a certain part of his brain, and for the time loses his power to remember certain events. It can hardly be maintained that, in any literal sense, he still remembers the events; and that all that has been damaged is his power of manifesting this knowledge to others by speech or writing. The latter case does sometimes arise, and it seems introspectively quite different from the former to the patient himself. Again, if the patient recovers these lost memories after a while, it seems to him that a change has taken place in the contents of his mind, and not merely a change in his ability to express to others what was going on in his mind before. We must suppose then that in such cases something more than the power to manifest one's knowledge to others has been injured. The only other alternative is to suppose that all such patients are lying and asserting that they cannot remember certain things which they actually are remembering. If we reject this very violent alternative we must hold that in some cases an injury to the brain does actually deprive the mind of the power to remember certain events which it formerly could remember. Could a supporter of the Instrumental Theory square the facts with this view? He might say that the general power of remembering is unchanged; and assert that all that has happened is that the injury to the body has prevented certain past events from being objects of memory, as blindfolding a man would prevent certain present objects from being perceived. But in that case the mind is reduced to something which has merely certain very general capacities, and any particular exercise of these powers seems to depend on the body.

Let us now take another example. We will suppose that a man is injured in the head; that before the injury he was of a cheerful and benevolent disposition; and that after the injury he is morose and liable to attacks of homicidal mania. Are we to say that the injury has made no difference to his mind; that this remains cheerful and benevolent; but that the change in his brain compels him to express his cheerfulness by scowling and his benevolence by attacking other people with carving-knives? This is scarcely plausible. And, if we accept it, we shall not be able to stop at this point. We shall have to conclude that it is impossible to tell what the character of anyone's mind really is. Lifelong philanthropists may be inwardly boiling with malice which some peculiar kink in their brains and nervous systems compels them to express by pensioning their poor relations and giving pennies to crossing-sweepers. Once more, the mind will be reduced to something with no definite traits of its own, such as benevolence or peevishness, but merely with certain very general powers to express itself in various ways according to the body with which it is provided. It seems to me that what is left of the mind when we try to square the Instrumental Theory with the known facts is so abstract and indefinite that it does not deserve to be called a "mind."

The Compound Theory. This suggests a modification of the Instrumental Theory, which I will call the "Compound Theory." Might not what we know as a "mind" be a compound of two factors, neither of which separately has the characteristic properties of a mind, just as salt is a compound of two substances, neither of which by itself has the characteristic properties of salt? Let us call one of these constituents the "psychic factor" and the other the "bodily factor." The psychic factor would be like some chemical element which has never been isolated; and the characteristics of a mind would depend jointly on those of the psychic factor and on those of the material organism with which it is united. This would allow of all the correlation between mind and body which could ever be discovered, and at the same time it is not open to the objections which I have pointed out in the ordinary form of the Instrumental Theory. Moreover, it is in accord with many facts which we know about other departments of nature. We know that chemical compounds have properties which cannot be deduced from those which their elements display in isolation or in other compounds. And yet the properties of these compounds are wholly dependent on those of their elements, in

568

the sense that, given such elements in such relations, a compound necessarily arises with such and such properties. These properties do not belong to either of the elements, but only to the compound as a whole. Now this does seem to accord fairly well with what we know about minds when we reflect upon them. On the one hand, it seems a mistake to ascribe perception, reasoning, anger, love, etc., to a mere body. On the other hand, as we have seen, it is almost equally difficult to ascribe them to what is left when the bodily factor is ignored. Thus the mind, as commonly conceived, does look as if it were a compound of two factors neither of which separately is a mind. And it does look as if specifically mental characteristics belonged only to this compound substance.

It would be unwise to press the analogy to chemical compounds too far. So far as we know, when two chemical elements are united to form a chemical compound no permanent change is produced in the properties of either. It would be rash to assume that this is also true when a psychic factor is united with a bodily organism so as to give a mind. Both factors may be permanently affected by this union; so that, if they become separated again and continue to exist, their properties are characteristically different from what they were when the two first became connected with each other. Of course many different views would be antecedently possible about the supposed psychic factor. At one extreme would be the view that there is only one psychic factor for all minds. Different minds would then be compounds of this one psychic factor with different brains and nervous systems. Such a view would bear some analogy to Green's theory of the one Eternal Consciousness and the many animal organisms. But the psychic factor on our view would have no claim to be called a "Consciousness"; it would not perform those feats of relating and unifying sense-data which Green ascribed to it; and there is no reason to suppose that it would deserve honorific titles like "eternal," or be an appropriate object for those religious emotions which Green felt towards it. At the opposite extreme would be the view that there is a different psychic factor for each different mind. Then the question could be raised whether some or all of them can exist out of combination with organisms; whether some one psychic factor can combine successively with a series of different organisms to give a series of different minds; and so on. (It may be remarked that the view that the psychic factor cannot exist out of combination with organisms, and yet that the same psychic factor can be combined with a series of successive organisms, has a pretty close analogy to certain chemical facts. There are groups, such as NH_4, CH_3, etc., which are incapable of more than the most transitory independent existence. Yet one such group may pass successively from one combination to another, and may impart certain characteristic properties to each of these compounds.) Finally, there is an intermediate possibility for which there might be a good deal to be said. It might be suggested that the marked individuality of human minds indicates that there is a different psychic factor as well as a different bodily organism to each coexisting human mind. On the other hand, it might be held that there is only one psychic factor for the whole species of earwigs; and that the very trivial differences between the mind of one earwig and another are due simply to differences in their bodily organisms. It is obvious that only empirical evidence of a very special kind could help us to decide between these alternatives, even if we accepted the Compound Theory in its main outlines.

Granted that the Compound Theory is consistent with all the facts which are commonly held to prove the existential dependence of mind on body, and granted that it is in better accord with the facts than the Instrumental Theory, is there any positive evidence for it? We have a set of facts which point to the dependence of mind on body. One explanation is that mind depends on nothing but body, *i.e.*, that mental events either *are* also bodily events, or that at any rate they are all *caused* wholly by bodily events and do not in turn affect either each other or the body. The present explanation is that the mind is a compound of the body and something else, and that mental events and mental characteristics belong to this compound substance and not to its separate constituents. Both explanations fit all the normal facts equally well. But the Compound Theory is more complex than the Epiphenomenal Theory, and it would be foolish to accept it unless there were some facts which it explains and which the Epiphenomenalist Theory does not. Now I do not think that there is anything in the normal phenomena which requires us to suppose that a mind depends for its existence and functioning on anything but the body and its processes. We must therefore turn to the abnormal phenomena.

Abnormal and Supernormal Phenomena

I think that it is very important to begin by drawing a distinction which is too commonly neglected, viz., the distinction between *Survival* and mere *Persistence*. It seems to me that a great many of the phenomena which are held to point to the survival of particular human minds point only to the persistence of some factor which was a constituent of a human mind. We are not justified in saying that the mind of John Jones has survived the death of his body unless we have reason to believe that there is still a continuous stream of conscious mental states which may be said to be "further experiences of John Jones." We must suppose that this contains conations as well as cognitions, that it puts ends before itself and tries to realise them, and that it feels elation or disappointment according to its success or failure in doing so. No doubt such a stream of consciousness would be impossible unless past experiences modified later experiences; and no doubt we should not say that John Jones had survived unless he were able to remember some events in his life in the body. But these mnemonic phenomena, though necessary to survival, are certainly not by themselves sufficient to constitute survival. If they occur alone, without the continuous stream of conscious cognitions, conations, and feelings, all that we have a right to say is that "some constituent of the mind of John Jones has persisted" and not that "John Jones has survived."

Now it seems to me that the vast majority of mediumistic phenomena which are taken to suggest survival really suggest only persist-ence. The additional notion of survival is read into them because in our ordinary experience we do not find memories without a pretty continuous stream of consciousness filling the gaps between the memory and the event remembered. The cases that I have in mind are these. A medium goes into a trance. He is then supposed either to be in contact with the spirit of some dead man, or in rarer cases to be directly possessed by such a spirit. In either case he sometimes mentions incidents in the past life of the supposed communicator which are unknown to the sitter and can afterwards be verified. And in the latter case he sometimes exhibits in a very remarkable way some of the mannerisms and even the verbal intonations of the supposed communicator. The evidence for such phe-nomena is, in my opinion, good enough to make them worth serious con-sideration by philosophers. Now the ordinary spiritualist interprets such phenomena in terms of the Instrumental Theory; he supposes that a human mind is existentially independent of its body and just uses it as an instrument; that it leaves its body at death, goes on living its own life, and from time to time uses a medium's body for purposes of communi-cation.

But it seems to me that, apart from the intrinsic difficulties of the Instrumental Theory, the Compound Theory fits these supernormal phe-nomena on the whole much better. One thing which is highly charac-teristic of the communications of alleged dead men is their singular reticence about their present life, occupations, and surroundings. Such observations as are made by entranced mediums on these subjects seem to me to be extraordinarily silly, and to have every appearance of being merely the crude beliefs about the spiritual world which are current in mediumistic circles. Yet this nonsense is at times mixed up with traits which are highly characteristic of the supposed communicator, and with bits of detailed information about his past life which can afterwards be verified. Now, on the Compound Theory, we can suppose that the psychic factor may persist for a time at least after the destruction of the organ-ism with which it was united to form the compound called "John Jones's mind." This psychic factor is not itself a mind, but it may carry modifi-cations due to experiences which happened to John Jones while he was alive. And it may become temporarily united with the organism of an entranced medium. If so, a little temporary "mind" (a "mindkin," if I may use that expression) will be formed. Since this mindkin will con-tain the same psychic factor as the mind of John Jones it will not be surprising if it displays some traits characteristic of John Jones, and some memories of events in his earthly life. Since the bodily factor of this mindkin is the medium's organism, which is adapted to the medium's psychic factor and not to John Jones's, it will not be surprising if it shows many traits which are characteristic of the medium. And the rea-son why we can get no information about the present life and experiences of John Jones is that no such mind is existing at all. When the medium is entranced the psychic factor which was a constituent of John Jones's mind forms with the medium's body a mindkin which lasts just as long as the medium remains in trance. At intermediate times, on this view, all that exists is this psychic factor; and this by itself is no more a mind than John Jones's corpse is a mind. To explain the positive part of the phenomena it is plausible to suppose that *something* has persisted, and that this something was an integral part of John Jones's mind. But it is an enormous jump from this to the conclusion that John Jones's mind has survived the death of his body. And the negative part of the phenomena strongly suggests that what has persisted is not a mind, but is at most something which in combination with a suitable organism is capable of producing a mind.

Some of the facts of multiple personality would also be neatly explained by the Compound Theory. Of course mediumistic phenomena are, in the first instance, cases of multiple personality. The peculiarity of them is that one of the personalities professes either to *be* a certain deceased human being, or more usually only to be in communication with one; and that, in some cases, there appear certain characteristic traits of this dead man, or knowledge is shown of some minute details in his past life. But ordinary multiple personality, such as that of the Beauchamp case, might be explained by supposing that the same organism can have two different psychic factors connected with it. We should then expect to find two minds having certain characteristic differences, and yet having a good deal more in common than two minds which differ in their organisms as well as in their psychic factors. Two personalities might be compared to two chemical compounds with one element in common, such as silver chloride and silver bromide; whilst two ordinary minds might be compared (say) to silver chloride and lead nitrate. I do not think, however, that ordinary multiple personality positively requires the Compound Theory for its explanation. We can never be sure that the organism is in precisely the same state when one personality is in control as it is when the other is in control. Hence it is possible that the facts could be explained on a purely epiphenomenalist theory. It is the apparent persistence of certain traces and dispositions after the destruction of the organism which seems to demand for its explanation something more than epiphenomenalism, and seems to suggest *at least* something like the Compound Theory.

We must now consider (*a*) whether there are any facts which require something *more* than the Compound Theory to explain them; and (*b*) whether the facts that I have already mentioned could be explained with something *less* than the Compound Theory. It seems to me that we should have grounds for postulating the *survival* of a *mind*, and not the mere persistence of a psychic factor, if and only if the communications showed traces of an intention which persisted between the experiments and deliberately modified and controlled each in the light of those which had preceded it. Now it is alleged that there are signs of this deliberate intention in the Cross-Correspondences which the Society for Psychical Research has been investigating for many years. If all or most of these came up to the ideal type of a Cross-Correspondence, I think we should have to admit that it looks as if a single intelligent being were deliberately trying in an extremely ingenious way to produce evidence of its continuous existence. The ideal Cross-Correspondence would be of the following form. Suppose three automatic writers in different places produce automatic scripts over a series of years. Suppose that they do not communicate with each other, but send their scripts from time to time to an impartial authority for comparison. Suppose that A, B, and C in their scripts get statements which, taken separately, are fragmentary and unintelligible to them; and suppose further that after such an unintelligible and fragmentary statement in A's script there comes an injunction to refer to what B and C are now writing or will shortly write or have written at some definite time in the past. Suppose that similar injunctions are found in B's and C's scripts after fragmentary and unintelligible passages in them. Suppose finally that when the impartial authority compares the scripts and follows the directions contained in them he finds that these separately unintelligible sentences combine to convey something which is highly characteristic of a certain deceased person who is alleged to be communicating. Then we should have a perfect instance of a Cross-Correspondence; and it would be difficult to resist the conviction that the phenomena are controlled intentionally by a single mind, which cannot be identified with the conscious part of the mind of any of the automatic writers.

Unfortunately it is not clear to me that most of the alleged Cross-Correspondences accurately exemplify this ideal type. I also cannot help feeling suspicious of the enormous amount of learning and ingenuity which the impartial authority has to exercise in order to find the key to the riddle which the scripts set. Would not the same amount of patience, learning, and ingenuity discover almost as good Cross-Correspondences between almost any set of manuscripts? I do not say that this is so; but I should need a good deal of negative evidence, *i.e.*, of failure to discover Cross-Correspondences between other manuscripts which were treated in the same way as these automatic scripts, before I was prepared to stake much on this argument for human survival. So far as I am aware, negative control experiments of this kind have not been tried. It is evident that they would be terribly laborious, and it is hardly to be expected that the same patience and ingenuity would be lavished on them as have been devoted to the interpretation of the automatic scripts in which positive results are hoped for.

. . . .

I pass now to the second question. Could the facts which we have been considering be explained by something *less* than the hypothesis of a persistent psychic factor? It will be remembered that the facts to be explained are the revelation of certain details in the past life of a certain dead man, which are unknown at the time to the sitter and can afterwards be verified; or the occurrence of certain characteristic tricks of voice and manner in the entranced medium. Now it must be admitted that it is very rare for a detail about a dead man's past life to be verifiable unless it is known or has been known to someone now living. It must therefore be admitted to be theoretically possible that these phenomena are due to telepathy from the unconscious parts of the minds of living men who are remote from the place at which the sitting is being held. But, although this is conceivable, I cannot regard it as very plausible. It is very difficult to see what can determine the medium to select just those pieces of information from distant minds which are relevant to the supposed communicator. It is true of course that the sitter has generally known the communicator; and we should have to suppose that the presence of a man who has known X causes the medium to select from other minds bits of information about X and to reject bits of information about other men. On any view some selective action on the part of the sitter must be postulated, since in the main those who are supposed to be communicating when a certain man has a sitting with a medium are people whom the sitter has known. In my own sittings with Mrs. Leonard, *e.g.*, the alleged communicator has from the first been one particular man who was described with considerable accuracy and named with approximate (though not complete) accuracy at the first sitting. On the Compound Theory we should have to suppose that the presence of a certain sitter "attracts" the psychic factors of certain dead men who were known to him. On the purely telepathic theory we should have to suppose that the presence of the sitter causes the medium to "select" from various minds scattered about the world certain bits of information which are relevant to someone whom the sitter has known.

Although this hypothesis is possible, there are, I think, two arguments which make slightly against it and slightly in favour of the Compound Theory. (1) On the purely telepathic theory it is difficult to see why mediumistic communications should not be as much or more concerned with one's living friends as with those who have died. This is not found to be so. On the Compound Theory this fact is explicable; for, on this hypothesis, the psychic factor of a living mind is already attached to a certain living organism, and this would presumably make it difficult or impossible for it to enter at the same time into the same relation with the organism of the entranced medium. I think that some weight must be attached to this argument, though it is not conclusive. The main interest and expectation of both sitter and medium is to get messages which purport to come from the dead and not from those who are still alive; and this might account for the fact that the medium "selects" bits of information about dead men, even on the purely telepathic theory.

(2) The second argument is due to Dr. Richard Hodgson. He used it against the hypothesis of telepathy from the sitter and in favour of the hypothesis that the messages are due to the disembodied spirits of dead men. I think that the argument can be adapted so that it can be used against the hypothesis of a more extended telepathy and in favour of the Compound Theory. The argument may be put as follows. Suppose that a number of sitters $S_1 \ldots S_n$ sit with a certain medium, and that a number of communicators $C_1 \ldots C_m$ profess to give messages through this medium. On the Compound Theory the adequacy or inadequacy of the communications which purport to come from a certain communicator C_r through a given medium would presumably depend mainly on two things; (*a*) on the complexity of the psychic factor, and (*b*) on its adaptation to the organism of the medium. There is no obvious reason why the number and accuracy of the messages which purport to come from a given communicator through the same medium should vary much from

one sitter to another; for the main function of the sitter, on this hypothesis, is simply to "attract" a certain psychic factor so that it enters into a temporary combination with the medium's organism. If this happens at all, the subsequent proceedings would seem to depend on the psychic factor and the medium rather than on the sitter. We should thus expect to find certain "communicators" who are good with most sitters, and others who are bad with most sitters; we should not expect to find certain sitters who are good with most "communicators" and others who are bad with most "communicators." On the telepathic hypothesis we should expect the opposite result. For, on this view, the sitter plays a much more active part. His thoughts and interests must determine the particular selection of information which the medium makes from a perfect rag-bag of living minds. And his power to do this would presumably depend on the peculiar endowments of his own mind and on its adaptation to the mind of the medium with whom he is sitting. On this hypothesis we should therefore expect that there would be some sitters who get good results from most alleged communicators through a given medium; and that there would be other sitters who get bad results from most alleged communicators through the same medium.

Now Dr. Hodgson had an enormous amount of experience of the results of sittings with Mrs. Piper extending over many years. And he carefully studied them and classified them from the above points of view. His conclusion was that certain alleged *communicators* gave copious and accurate information to *most sitters;* and that other alleged *communicators* gave fragmentary and incorrect information to *most sitters.* He did not find that certain *sitters* got copious and accurate information from *most communicators;* and that certain other *sitters* got feeble and fragmentary messages from *most communicators.* Thus, on the whole, the actual results are such as might be expected on the Compound Theory and are not such as might be expected on the theory of generalised telepathy from living minds. On the whole then I am inclined to think that there is slightly more to be said for the Compound Theory than for the other alternatives.

49. **Anthony Quinton**

Anthony Quinton is a fellow of New College, Oxford.

Mental and Bodily Criteria of Personal Identity

The Empirical Concept of the Soul

It will be admitted that among all the facts that involve a person there is a class that can be described as mental in some sense or other. Is it enough to define the soul as the temporally extended totality of mental states and events that belong to a person? It will not be enough to provide a concept of the soul as something logically distinct from the body if the idea of the series of a person's mental states involves some reference to the particular human body that he possesses. In the first place, therefore, a nonbodily criterion of personal identity must be produced. For if the soul were the series of mental states associated with a given body, in the sense of being publicly reported by it and being manifested by its behavior, two temporally separate mental states could belong to the history of the same soul only if they were in fact associated with one and the same human body. This notion of the soul could have no application to mental states that were not associated with bodies. The soul must, then, be a series of mental states that is identified through time in virtue of the properties and relations of these mental states themselves. Both the elements of the complex and the relations that make an identi-

From "The Soul," *Journal of Philosophy*, Vol. LIX (1962), pp. 393–409. Reprinted by permission of the author and the *Journal of Philosophy*.

fiable persisting thing out of them must be mental. To establish the possibility of such a mental criterion of identity will be the hardest part of the undertaking.

Locke's criterion of memory has been much criticized, and it is certainly untenable in some of the interpretations it has been given. It will not do to say that two mental states belong to the same soul if and only if whoever has the later one can recollect the earlier one if the possibility of recollection involved is factual and not formal. For people forget things, and the paradox of the gallant officer is generated in which he is revealed as identical with both his childish and his senile selves while these are not identical with each other. However, a more plausible criterion can be offered in terms of continuity of character and memory. Two soul-phases belong to the same soul, on this view, if they are connected by a continuous character and memory path. A soul-phase is a set of contemporaneous mental states belonging to the same momentary consciousness. Two soul-phases are directly continuous if they are temporally juxtaposed, if the character revealed by the constituents of each is closely similar, and if the later contains recollections of some elements of the earlier. Two soul-phases are indirectly continuous and connected by a continuous character and memory path if there is a series of soul-phases all of whose members are directly continuous with their immediate predecessors and successors in the series and if the original soul-phases are the two end points of the series. There is a clear analogy between this criterion and the one by means of which material objects, including human bodies, are identified. Two object-phases belong to the same object if they are connected by a continuous quality and position path. Direct continuity in this case obtains between two temporally juxtaposed object-phases which are closely similar in qualities and are in the same position or in closely neighboring positions. Indirect continuity is once again the ancestral of direct continuity. There is no limit to the amount of difference in position allowed by the criterion to two indirectly continuous object-phases, but in normal discourse a limit is set to the amount of qualitative difference allowed by the requirement that the two phases be of objects of the same kind. Character in the mental case corresponds to quality in the physical and memory to spatial position. The soul, then, can be defined empirically as a series of mental states connected by continuity of character and memory.

. . . .

Mental and Bodily Criteria of Identity

In recent philosophy there have been two apparently independent aspects to the view that the mind is logically dependent on the body. On the one hand, there are the doctrines that hold mental states either to be or necessarily to involve bodily states, whether bodily movement and dispositions thereto or neural events and configurations. With these doctrines, I have argued, the empirical concept of the soul can be reconciled. On the other hand, many philosophers have insisted that the basic and indispensable criterion of personal identity is bodily. Even mind-body dualists like Ayer, who have accepted the existence of a categorically clear-cut class of mental events, have sometimes taken this position. In his first treatment of the problem he appears at first to give a mental account of the concept of a person as being a series of experiences. But the relation that connects them in his theory involves an indispensable reference to a particular persisting human body. A person is made up of those total mental states which contain organic sensations belonging to one particular human body, presumably to be identified itself in terms of continuity of qualities and spatial position. Ayer draws the conclusion that properly follows from this and from any other account of personal identity that involves reference to a particular human body, namely that the notion of a person's disembodied existence is a self-contradictory one and, further, that even the association of a personality with different bodies at different times is inconceivable. These conclusions may well seem to constitute a reductio ad absurdum of the bodily criterion of personal identity rather than a disproof of the possibility of a person's survival of death. To explore them a little further will help to present the claims of mental as against bodily criteria in a clearer light.

At the outset it must be admitted that the theory of a bodily criterion has a number of virtues. It has, first, the theoretical attraction of simplicity, in that it requires only one mode of treatment for the identification through time of all enduring things, treating human beings as just one variety of concrete objects. Second, it has a practical appeal, in that its application yields uncontentiously correct answers in the very great majority of the actual cases of personal identification with which we are called upon to deal. Finally, it has the merit of realism, for it is, in fact, the procedure of identification that we do most commonly apply. Even where, for lack of relevant evidence, it is inapplicable, as in the case of the Tichborne claimant, it would not be supposed that the result of applying other criteria such as memory would conflict with what the bodily evidence would have shown if it had been forthcoming. Is there anything better to set against these powerful recommendations in favor of a bodily criterion than that it entails that things many people have wanted very deeply to say about the survival of death are inconsistent? A supporter of the bodily criterion might argue that it was so much the worse for them, that their inconsistent assertions arose from attempting to assert and deny at the same time that a person no longer existed.

It does seem strange, all the same, to say that all statements about disembodied or reincarnated persons are self-contradictory. Is it really at all plausible to say this about such familiar things as the simpler type of classical ghost story? It may be argued that there are plenty of stories which are really self-contradictory and yet which can be, in a way, understood and enjoyed, stories about time machines, for example. To try to settle the case we had better consider some concrete instances. Suppose I am walking on the beach with my friend A. He walks off a fair distance, treads on a large mine that someone has forgotten to remove, and is physically demolished in front of my eyes. Others, attracted by the noise, draw near and help to collect the scattered remains of A for burial. That night, alone in my room, I hear *A*'s voice and see a luminous but intangible object, of very much the shape and size of *A*, standing in the corner. The remarks that come from it are in *A*'s characteristic style and refer to matters that only *A* could have known about. Suspecting a hallucination, I photograph it and call in witnesses who hear and see what I do. The apparition returns afterwards and tells of where it has been and what it has seen. It would be very peculiar to insist, in these circumstances, that *A* no longer existed, even though his body no longer exists except as stains on the rocks and in a small box in the mortuary. It is not essential for the argument that the luminous object look like *A* or that it speak in *A*'s voice. If it were a featureless cylinder and spoke like a talking weighing machine we should simply take longer becoming convinced that it really was *A*. But if continuity of character and memory were manifested with normal amplitude, we surely should be convinced.

Consider a slightly different case. I know two men *B* and *C*. *B* is a dark, tall, thin, puritanical Scotsman of sardonic temperament with whom I have gone on bird-watching expeditions. *C* is a fair, short, plump, apolaustic Pole of indestructible enterprise and optimism with whom I have made a number of more urban outings. One day I come into a room where both appear to be, and the dark, tall, thin man suggests that he and I pursue tonight some acquaintances I made with *C*, though he says it was with him, a couple of nights ago. The short, fair, plump, cheerful-looking man reminds me in a strong Polish accent of a promise I had made to *B*, though he says it was to him, and which I had forgotten about, to go in search of owls on this very night. At first I suspect a conspiracy, but the thing continues far beyond any sort of joke, for good perhaps, and is accompanied by suitable amazement on their part at each other's appearance, their own reflections in the mirror, and so forth.

Now what would it be reasonable to say in these circumstances: that *B* and *C* have changed bodies (the consequence of a mental criterion), that they have switched character and memories (the consequence of a bodily criterion), or neither? It seems to me quite clear that we should not say that *B* and *C* had switched characters and memories. And if this is correct, it follows that bodily identity is not a logically complete criterion of personal identity; at best it could be a necessary condition of personal identity. Of the other alternatives, that of refusing to identify either of the psychophysical hybrids before us with *B* or *C* may seem the most scrupulous and proper. But the refusal might take a number of different forms. It might be a categorical denial that either of the hybrids is *B* or *C*. It might, more sophisticatedly be an assertion that the concept of personal identity had broken down and that there was no correct answer, affirmative or negative, to the question: which of these two is *B* and which *C*? It might, uninterestingly, be a state of amazed and inarticulate confusion.

What support is there for the conclusion required by the empirical concept of the soul, that *B* and *C* have substituted bodies? First of all, the rather weak evidence of imaginative literature. In F. Anstey's story *Vice Versa* the corpulent and repressive Mr. Bultitude and his athletic and impulsive schoolboy son are the victims of a similar rearrangement.

The author shows not the smallest trace of hesitation in calling the thing with the father's character and memories the father and the thing with the father's body the son. (Cf. also Conan Doyle's *Keinplatz Experiment*.) A solider support is to be found by reflecting on the probable attitude after the switch of those who are most concerned with our original pair, *B* and *C*, as persons, those who have the greatest interest in answering the question of their personal identity: their parents, their wives, their children, their closest friends. Would they say that *B* and *C* had ceased to exist, that they had exchanged characters and memories or that they had exchanged bodies? It is surely plain that if the character and memories of *B* and *C* really survived intact in their new bodily surroundings those closely concerned with them would say that the two had exchanged bodies, that the original persons were where the characters and memories were. For why, after all, do we bother to identify people so carefully? What is unique about individual people that is important enough for us to call them by individual proper names? In our general relations with other human beings their bodies are for the most part intrinsically unimportant. We use them as convenient recognition devices enabling us to locate without difficulty the persisting character and memory complexes in which we are interested, which we love or like. It would be upsetting if a complex with which we were emotionally involved came to have a monstrous or repulsive physical appearance, it would be socially embarrassing if it kept shifting from body to body while most such complexes stayed put, and it would be confusing and tiresome if such shifting around were generally widespread, for it would be a laborious business finding out where one's friends and family were. But that our concern and affection would follow the character and memory complex and not its original bodily associate is surely clear. In the case of general shifting about we should be in the position of people trying to find their intimates in the dark. If the shifts were both frequent and spatially radical we should no doubt give up the attempt to identify individual people, the whole character of relations between people would change, and human life would be like an unending sequence of shortish ocean trips. But, as long as the transfers did not involve large movements in space, the character and memory complexes we are concerned with could be kept track of through their audible identification of themselves. And there is no reason to doubt that the victim of such a bodily transfer would regard himself as the person whom he seems to remember himself as being. I conclude, then, that although, as things stand, our concept of a person is not called upon to withstand these strains and, therefore, that in the face of a psychophysical transfer we might at first not know what to say, we should not identify the people in question as those who now have the bodies they used to have and that it would be the natural thing to extend our concept of a person, given the purposes for which it has been constructed, so as to identify anyone present to us now with whoever it was who used to have the same character and memories as he has. In other words the soul, defined as a series of mental states connected by continuity of character and memory, is the essential constituent of personality. The soul, therefore, is not only logically distinct from any particular human body with which it is associated; it is also what a person fundamentally is.

It may be objected to the extension of the concept of personal identity that I have argued for that it rests on an incorrect and even sentimental view of the nature of personal relations. There are, it may be said, personal relationships which are of an exclusively bodily character and which would not survive a change of body but which would perfectly well survive a change of soul. Relations of a rather unmitigatedly sexual type might be instanced and also those where the first party to the relationship has violent racial feelings. It can easily be shown that these objections are without substance. In the first place, even the most tired of entrepreneurs is going to take some note of the character and memories of the companion of his later nights at work. He will want her to be docile and quiet, perhaps, and to remember that he takes two parts of water to one of scotch, and no ice. If she ceases to be plump and redheaded and vigorous he may lose interest in and abandon her, but he would have done so anyway in response to the analogous effects of the aging process. If he has any idea of her as a person at all, it will be as a unique cluster of character traits and recollections. As a body, she is simply an instrument of a particular type, no more and no less interesting to him than a physically identical twin. In the case of a purely sexual relationship no particular human body is required, only one of a more or less precisely demarcated kind. Where concern with the soul is wholly absent there is no interest in individual identity at all, only in identity of type. It may be said that this argument cuts both ways: that parents and children are concerned only that they should have round them children and parents with the same sort of character and memories as the children and parents they were with yesterday. But this is doubly incorrect. First, the memories of individual persons cannot be exactly similar, since even the closest of identical twins must see things from slightly different angles; they cannot be in the same place at the same time. More seriously, if more contingently, individual memories, even of identical twins, are seldom, if ever, closely similar. To put the point crudely, the people I want to be with are the people who remember me and the experiences we have shared, not those who remember someone more or less like me with whom they have shared more or less similar experiences. The relevant complexity of the memories of an individual person is of an altogether different order of magnitude from that of the bodily properties of an entrepreneur's lady friend. The lady friend's bodily type is simply enough defined for it to have a large number of instances. It is barely conceivable that two individual memories should be similar enough to be emotionally adequate substitutes for each other. There is the case of the absolutely identical twins who go everywhere together, side by side, and always have done so. Our tendency here would be to treat the pair as a physically dual single person. There would be no point in distinguishing one from the other. As soon as their ways parted sufficiently for the question of which was which to arise, the condition of different memories required for individuation would be satisfied.

It may be felt that the absolutely identical twins present a certain

difficulty for the empirical concept of the soul. For suppose their characters and memories to be totally indistinguishable and their thoughts
and feelings to have been precisely the same since the first dawning of
consciousness in them. Won't the later phases of one of the twins be as
continuous in respect of character and memory with the earlier phases
of the other as they are with his own earlier phases? Should we even say
that there are two persons there at all? The positional difference of the
two bodies provides an answer to the second question. Although they
are always excited and gloomy together, the thrills and pangs are manifested in distinct bodies and are conceivable as existing separately. We
might ignore the duality of their mental states, but we should be able
in principle to assert it. As to the matter of continuity, the environment
of the two will be inevitably asymmetrical, each will at various times be
nearer something than the other, each will block some things from the
other's field of vision or touch; so there will always be some, perhaps
trivial, difference in the memories of the two. But even if trivial, the
difference will be enough to allow the application in this special case of
a criterion that normally relies on radical and serious differences. However alike the character and memories of twin no. 1 on Tuesday and
twin no. 2 on Wednesday, they will inevitably be less continuous than
those of twin no. 2 on the two days.

. . . .

The Problem of Disembodiment

Nothing that I have said so far has any direct bearing on the question whether the soul can exist in an entirely disembodied state. All I
have tried to show is that there is no necessary connection between the
soul as a series of mental states linked by character and memory and
any particular continuing human body. The question now arises: must
the soul be associated with some human body? The apparent intelligibility of my crude ghost story might seem to suggest that not even a body
is required, let alone a human one. And the same point appears to be
made by the intelligibility of stories in which trees, toadstools, pieces of
furniture, and so on are endowed with personal characteristics. But a
good deal of caution is needed here. In the first place, even where these
personal characteristics are not associated with any sort of body in the
physiological sense, they are associated with a body in the epistemological sense; in other words, it is an essential part of the story that the
soul in question have physical manifestations. Only in our own case does
it seem that strictly disembodied existence is conceivable, in the sense
that we can conceive circumstances in which there would be some good
reason to claim that a soul existed in a disembodied state. Now how
tenuous and nonhuman could these physical manifestations be? To take
a fairly mild example, discussed by Professor Malcolm, could we regard
a tree as another person? He maintains with great firmness that we
could not, on the rather flimsy ground that trees haven't got mouths and,
therefore, could not be said to speak or communicate with us or make

memory claims. But if a knothole in a tree trunk physically emitted sounds in the form of speech, why should we not call it a mouth? We may presume that ventriloquism, hidden record-players and microphones, dwarfs concealed in the foliage, and so forth have all been ruled out. If the remarks of the tree were coherent and appropriate to its situation and exhibited the type of continuity that the remarks of persons normally do exhibit, why shouldn't we regard the tree as a person? The point is that we might, by a serious conceptual effort, allow this in the case of one tree or even several trees or even a great many nonhuman physical things. But the sense of our attribution of personality to them would be logically parasitic on our attributions of personality to ordinary human bodies. It is from their utterances and behavior that we derive our concept of personality, and this concept would be applicable to nonhuman things only by more or less far-fetched analogy. That trees should be personal presupposes, then, the personality of human beings. The same considerations hold in the extreme case of absolutely minimal embodiment, as when a recurrent and localized voice of a recognizable tone is heard to make publicly audible remarks. The voice might give evidence of qualitative and positional continuity sufficient to treat it as an identifiable body, even if of an excessively diaphanous kind. The possibility of this procedure, however, is contingent on there being persons in the standard, humanly embodied sense to provide a clear basis for the acquisition of the concept that is being more or less speculatively applied to the voice.

Whatever the logic of the matter, it might be argued, the causal facts of the situation make the whole inquiry into the possibility of a soul's humanly or totally disembodied existence an entirely fantastic one. That people have the memories and characters that they do, that they have memories and characters at all, has as its causally necessary condition the relatively undisturbed persistence of a particular bit of physiological apparatus. One can admit this without concluding that the inquiry is altogether without practical point. For the bit of physiological apparatus in question is not the human body as a whole, but the brain. Certainly lavish changes in the noncerebral parts of the human body often affect the character and perhaps even to some extent the memories of the person whose body it is. But there is no strict relationship here. Now it is sometimes said that the last bit of the body to wear out is the brain, that the brain takes the first and lion's share of the body's nourishment, and that the brains of people who have starved to death are often found in perfectly good structural order. It is already possible to graft bits of one human body on to another, corneas, fingers, and, even, I believe, legs. Might it not be possible to remove the brain from an otherwise worn-out human body and replace it either in a manufactured human body or in a cerebrally untenanted one? In this case we should have a causally conceivable analogue of reincarnation. If this were to become possible and if the resultant creatures appeared in a coherent way to exhibit the character and memories previously associated with the brain that had been fitted into them, we could say that the original person was still in existence even though only a relatively minute part of its original mass and volume was present in the new physical whole. Yet if strict bodily identity is a necessary condition of personal identity, such a description of the outcome would be ruled out as self-contradictory. I conclude, therefore, not only that a logically adequate concept of the soul is constructible but that the construction has some possible utility even in the light of our knowledge of the causal conditions of human life.

50. Bernard Williams

Bernard Williams is Knightbridge Professor of Philosophy
at the University of Cambridge, England.

How Do I Decide Which One
I Am?

Suppose that there were some process to which two persons, *A* and *B*,
could be subjected as a result of which they might be said—question-
beggingly—to have *exchanged bodies*. That is to say—less question-beg-
gingly—there is a certain human body which is such that when previously
we were confronted with it, we were confronted with person *A*, certain
utterances coming from it were expressive of memories of the past
experiences of *A*, certain movements of it partly constituted the actions
of *A* and were taken as expressive of the character of *A*, and so forth; but
now, after the process is completed, utterances coming from this body
are expressive of what seem to be just those memories which previously
we identified as memories of the past experiences of *B*, its movements
partly constitute actions expressive of the character of *B*, and so forth;
and conversely with the other body.

. . . .

It would seem a necessary condition of so doing that the utterances
coming from that body be taken as genuinely expressive of memories of
B's past. But memory is a causal notion; and as we actually use it, it
seems a necessary condition on *x*'s present knowledge of *x*'s earlier ex-

From "The Self and the Future," *Philosophical Review*, Vol. LXXIX (1970), pp.
161–180. Reprinted by permission of the author and the *Philosophical Review*. This
paper also appears in Bernard Williams, *Problems of the Self* (Cambridge: Cambridge University Press, 1973).

periences constituting memory of those experiences that the causal chain linking the experiences and the knowledge should not run outside x's body. Hence if utterances coming from a given body are to be taken as expressive of memories of the experiences of B, there should be some suitable causal link between the appropriate state of that body and the original happening of those experiences to B. One radical way of securing that condition in the imagined exchange case is to suppose, with Shoemaker,[1] that the brains of A and of B are transposed. We may not need so radical a condition. Thus suppose it were possible to extract information from a man's brain and store it in a device while his brain was repaired, or even renewed, the information then being replaced: it would seem exaggerated to insist that the resultant man could not possibly have the memories he had before the operation. With regard to our knowledge of our own past, we draw distinctions between merely recalling, being reminded, and learning again, and those distinctions correspond (roughly) to distinctions between no new input, partial new input, and total new input with regard to the information in question; and it seems clear that the information-parking case just imagined would not count as new input in the sense necessary and sufficient for "learning again." Hence we can imagine the case we are concerned with in terms of information extracted into such devices from A's and B's brains and replaced in the other brain; this is the sort of model which, I think not unfairly for the present argument, I shall have in mind.

We imagine the following. The process considered above exists; two persons can enter some machine, let us say, and emerge changed in the appropriate ways. If A and B are the persons who enter, let us call the persons who emerge the *A-body-person* and the *B-body-person:* the A-body-person is that person (whoever it is) with whom I am confronted when, after the experiment, I am confronted with that body which previously was A's body—that is to say, that person who would naturally be taken for A by someone who just saw this person, was familiar with A's appearance before the experiment, and did not know about the happening of the experiment. A non-question-begging description of the experiment will leave it open which (if either) of the persons A and B the A-body-person is; the description of the experiment as "persons changing bodies" of course implies that the A-body-person is actually B.

We take two persons A and B who are going to have the process carried out on them. (We can suppose, rather hazily, that they are willing for this to happen; to investigate at all closely at this stage why they might be willing or unwilling, what they would fear, and so forth, would anticipate some later issues.) We further announce that one of the two resultant persons, the A-body-person and the B-body-person, is going after the experiment to be given $100,000, while the other is going to be tortured. We then ask each A and B to choose which treatment should be dealt out to which of the persons who will emerge from the experiment, the choice to be made (if it can be) on selfish grounds.

Suppose that A chooses that the B-body-person should get the pleasant treatment and the A-body-person the unpleasant treatment; and B

1. *Self-Knowledge and Self-Identity* (Ithaca, N.Y., 1963), p. 23 f.

chooses conversely (this might indicate that they thought that "changing bodies" was indeed a good description of the outcome). The experimenter cannot act in accordance with both these sets of preferences, those expressed by *A* and those expressed by *B*. Hence there is one clear sense in which *A* and *B* cannot both get what they want: namely, that if the experimenter, before the experiment, announces to *A* and *B* that he intends to carry out the alternative (for example), of treating the *B*-body-person unpleasantly and the *A*-body-person pleasantly—then *A* can say rightly, "That's not the outcome I chose to happen," and *B* can say rightly, "That's just the outcome I chose to happen." So, evidently, *A* and *B* before the experiment can each come to know either that the outcome he chose will be that which will happen, or that the one he chose will not happen, and in that sense they can get or fail to get what they wanted. But is it also true that when the experimenter proceeds *after* the experiment to act in accordance with one of the preferences and not the other, then one of *A* and *B* will have got what he wanted, and the other not?

There seems very good ground for saying so. For suppose the experimenter, having elicited *A*'s and *B*'s preference, says nothing to *A* and *B* about what he will do; conducts the experiment; and then, for example, gives the unpleasant treatment to the *B*-body-person and the pleasant treatment to the *A*-body-person. Then the *B*-body-person will not only complain of the unpleasant treatment as such, but will complain (since he has *A*'s memories) that that was not the outcome he chose, since he chose that the *B*-body-person should be well treated; and since *A* made his choice in selfish spirit, he may add that he precisely chose in that way because he did not want the unpleasant things to happen to *him*. The *A*-body-person meanwhile will express satisfaction both at the receipt of the $100,000, and also at the fact that the experimenter has chosen to act in the way that he, *B*, so wisely chose. These facts make a strong case for saying that the experimenter has brought it about that *B* did in the outcome get what he wanted and *A* did not. It is therefore a strong case for saying that the *B*-body-person really is *A*, and the *A*-body-person really is *B*; and therefore for saying that the process of the experiment really is that of changing bodies. For the same reasons it would seem that *A* and *B* in our example really did choose wisely, and that it was *A*'s bad luck that the choice he correctly made was not carried out, *B*'s good luck that the choice he correctly made was carried out. This seems to show that to care about what happens to me in the future is not necessarily to care about what happens to *this* body (the one I now have); and this in turn might be taken to show that in some sense of Descartes's obscure phrase, I and my body are "really distinct" (though, of course, nothing in these considerations could support the idea that I could exist without a body at all).

. . . .

Let us now consider the question, not of *A* and *B* choosing certain outcomes to take place after the experiment, but of their willingness to engage in the experiment at all. If they were initially inclined to accept the description of the experiment as "changing bodies" then one thing that would interest them would be the character of the other person's body. In this respect also what would happen after the experiment would seem to suggest that "changing bodies" was a good description of the experiment. If *A* and *B* agreed to the experiment, being each not displeased with the appearance, physique, and so forth of the other person's body; after the experiment the *B*-body-person might well be found saying such things as: "When I agreed to this experiment, I thought that *B*'s face was quite attractive, but now I look at it in the mirror, I am not so sure"; or the *A*-body-person might say "When I agreed to this experiment I did not know that *A* had a wooden leg; but now, after it is over, I find that I have this wooden leg, and I want the experiment reversed." It is possible that he might say further that he finds the leg very uncomfortable, and that the *B*-body-person should say, for instance, that he recalls that he found it very uncomfortable at first, but one gets used to it: but perhaps one would need to know more than at least I do about the physiology of habituation to artificial limbs to know whether the *A*-body-person would find the leg uncomfortable: that body, after all, has had the leg on it for some time. But apart from this sort of detail, the general line of the outcome regarded from this point of view seems to confirm our previous conclusions about the experiment.

Now let us suppose that when the experiment is proposed (in non-question-begging terms) *A* and *B* think rather of their psychological advantages and disadvantages. *A*'s thoughts turn primarily to certain sorts of anxiety to which he is very prone, while *B* is concerned with the frightful memories he has of past experiences which still distress him. They each hope that the experiment will in some way result in their being able to get away from these things. They may even have been impressed by philosophical arguments to the effect that bodily continuity is at least a necessary condition of personal identity: *A*, for example, reasons that, granted the experiment comes off, then the person who is bodily continuous with him will not have this anxiety, while the other person will no doubt have some anxiety—perhaps in some sense his anxiety—and at least that person will not be he. The experiment is performed and the experimenter (to whom *A* and *B* previously revealed privately their several difficulties and hopes) asks the *A*-body-person whether he has gotten rid of his anxiety. This person presumably replies that he does not know what the man is talking about; he never had such anxiety, but he did have some very disagreeable memories, and recalls engaging in the experiment to get rid of them, and is disappointed to discover that he still has them. The *B*-body-person will react in a similar way to questions about his painful memories, pointing out that he still has his anxiety. These results seem to confirm still further the description of the experiment as "changing bodies." And all the results suggest that the only rational thing to do, confronted with such an experiment, would be to identify oneself with one's memories, and so forth, and not with one's body. The philosophical arguments designed to show that bodily continuity was at least a necessary condition of personal identity would seem to be just mistaken.

Let us now consider something apparently different. Someone in whose power I am tells me that I am going to be tortured tomorrow. I am frightened, and look forward to tomorrow in great apprehension. He adds that when the time comes, I shall not remember being told that this was going to happen to me, since shortly before the torture something else will be done to me which will make me forget the announcement. This certainly will not cheer me up, since I know perfectly well that I can forget things, and that there is such a thing as indeed being tortured unexpectedly because I had forgotten or been made to forget a prediction of the torture: that will still be a torture which, so long as I do know about the prediction, I look forward to in fear. He then adds that my forgetting the announcement will be only part of a larger process: when the moment of torture comes, I shall not remember any of the things I am now in a position to remember. This does not cheer me up, either, since I can readily conceive of being involved in an accident, for instance, as a result of which I wake up in a completely amnesiac state and also in great pain; that could certainly happen to me, I should not like it to happen to me, nor to know that it was going to happen to me. He now further adds that at the moment of torture I shall not only not remember the things I am now in a position to remember, but will have a different set of impressions of my past, quite different from the memories I now have. I do not think that this would cheer me up, either. For I can at least conceive the possibility, if not the concrete reality, of going completely mad, and thinking perhaps that I am George IV or somebody; and being told that something like that was going to happen to me would have no tendency to reduce the terror of being told authoritatively that I was going to be tortured, but would merely compound the horror. Nor do I see why I should be put into any better frame of mind by the person in charge adding lastly that the impressions of my past with which I shall be equipped on the eve of torture will exactly fit the past of another person now living, and that indeed I shall acquire these impressions by (for instance) information now in his brain being copied into mine. Fear, surely, would still be the proper reaction: and not because one did not know what was going to happen, but because in one vital respect at least one did know what was going to happen—torture, which one can indeed expect to happen to oneself, and to be preceded by certain mental derangements as well.

If this is right, the whole question seems now to be totally mysterious. For what we have just been through is of course merely one side, differently represented, of the transaction which we considered before; and it represents it as a perfectly hateful prospect, while the previous considerations represented it as something one should rationally, perhaps even cheerfully, choose out of the options there presented. It is differently presented, of course, and in two notable respects; but when we look at these two differences of presentation, can we really convince ourselves that the second presentation is wrong or misleading, thus leaving the road open to the first version which at the time seemed so convincing? Surely not.

The first difference is that in the second version the torture is throughout represented as going to happen to *me:* "you," the man in charge persistently says. Thus he is not very neutral. But should he have been neutral? Or, to put it another way, does his use of the second person have a merely emotional and rhetorical effect on me, making me afraid when further reflection would have shown that I had no reason to be? It is certainly not obviously so. The problem just is that through every step of his predictions I seem to be able to follow him successfully. And if I reflect on whether what he has said gives me grounds for fearing that I shall be tortured, I could consider that behind my fears lies some principle such as this: that my undergoing physical pain in the future is not excluded by any psychological state I may be in at the time, with the platitudinous exception of those psychological states which in themselves exclude experiencing pain, notably (if it is a psychological state) unconsciousness. In particular, what impressions I have about the past will not have any effect on whether I undergo the pain or not. This principle seems sound enough.

· ·

I said that there were two notable differences between the second presentation of our situation and the first. The first difference, which we have just said something about, was that the man predicted the torture for *me*, a psychologically very changed "me." We have yet to find a reason for saying that he should not have done this, or that I really should be unable to follow him if he does; I seem to be able to follow him only too well. The second difference is that in this presentation he does not mention the other man, except in the somewhat incidental role of being the provenance of the impressions of the past I end up with. He does not mention him at all as someone who will end up with impressions of the past derived from me (and, incidentally, with $100,000 as well—a consideration which, in the frame of mind appropriate to this version, will merely make me jealous).

But why *should* he mention this man and what is going to happen to him? My selfish concern is to be told what is going to happen to me, and now I know: torture, preceded by changes of character, brain operations, changes in impressions of the past. The knowledge that one other person, or none, or many will be similarly mistreated may affect me in other ways, of sympathy, greater horror at the power of this tyrant, and so forth; but surely it cannot affect my expectations of torture? But— someone will say—this is to leave out exactly the feature which, as the first presentation of the case showed, makes all the difference: for it is to leave out the person who, as the first presentation showed, will be you. It is to leave out not merely a feature which should fundamentally affect your fears, it is to leave out the very person for whom you are fearful. So of course, the objector will say, this makes all the difference.

But can it? Consider the following series of cases. In each case we are to suppose that after what is described, A is, as before, to be tortured; we are also to suppose the person A is informed beforehand that just these things followed by the torture will happen to him:

(*i*) A is subjected to an operation which produces total amnesia;
(*ii*) amnesia is produced in A, and other interference leads to certain changes in his character;
(*iii*) changes in his character are produced, and at the same time certain

590

illusory "memory" beliefs are induced in him; these are of a quite fictitious kind and do not fit the life of any actual person;

(*iv*) the same as (*iii*), except that both the character traits and the "memory" impressions are designed to be appropriate to another actual person, *B;*

(*v*) the same as (*iv*), except that the result is produced by putting the information into *A* from the brain of *B*, by a method which leaves *B* the same as he was before;

(*vi*) the same happens to *A* as in (*v*), but *B* is not left the same, since a similar operation is conducted in the reverse direction.

I take it that no one is going to dispute that *A* has reasons, and fairly straightforward reasons, for fear of pain when the prospect is that of situation (*i*); there seems no conceivable reason why this should not extend to situation (*ii*), and the situation (*iii*) can surely introduce no difference of principle—it just seems a situation which for more than one reason we should have grounds for fearing, as suggested above. Situation (*iv*) at least introduces the person *B*, who was the focus of the objection we are now discussing. But it does not seem to introduce him in any way which makes a material difference; if I can expect pain through a transformation which involves new "memory"-impressions, it would seem a purely external fact, relative to that, that the "memory"-impressions had a model. Nor, in (*iv*), do we satisfy a causal condition which I mentioned at the beginning for the "memories" actually being memories; though notice that if the job were done thoroughly, I might well be able to elicit from the *A*-body-person the kinds of remarks about his previous expectations of the experiment—remarks appropriate to the original *B*—which so impressed us in the first version of the story. I shall have a similar assurance of this being so in situation (*v*), where, moreover, a plausible application of the causal condition is available.

But two things are to be noticed about this situation. First, if we concentrate on *A* and the *A*-body-person, we do not seem to have added anything which from the point of view of his fears makes any material difference; just as, in the move from (*iii*) to (*iv*), it made no relevant difference that the new "memory"-impressions which precede the pain had, as it happened, a model, so in the move from (*iv*) to (*v*) all we have added is that they have a model which is also their cause: and it is still difficult to see why that, to him looking forward, could possibly make the difference between expecting pain and not expecting pain. To illustrate that point from the case of character: if *A* is capable of expecting pain, he is capable of expecting pain preceded by a change in his dispositions —and to that expectation it can make no difference, whether that change in his dispositions is modeled on, or indeed indirectly caused by, the dispositions of some other person. If his fears can, as it were, reach through the change, it seems a mere trimming how the change is in fact induced. The second point about situation (*v*) is that if the crucial question for *A*'s fears with regard to what befalls the *A*-body-person is whether the *A*-body-person is or is not the person *B*,[2] then that condition

2. This of course does not have to be the crucial question, but it seems one fair way of taking up the present objection.

has not yet been satisfied in situation (v): for there we have an undisputed B in addition to the A-body-person, and certainly those two are not the same person.

But in situation (vi), we seemed to think, that is finally what he is. But if A's original fears could reach through the expected changes in (v), as they did in (iv) and (iii), then certainly they can reach through in (vi). Indeed, from the point of view of A's expectations and fears, there is less difference between (vi) and (v) than there is between (v) and (iv) or between (iv) and (iii). In those transitions, there were at least differences—though we could not see that they were really relevant differences—in the content and cause of what happened to him; in the present case there is absolutely no difference at all in what happens to him, the only difference being in what happens to someone else. If he can fear pain when (v) is predicted, why should he cease to when (vi) is?

I can see only one way of relevantly laying great weight on the transition from (v) to (vi); and this involves a considerable difficulty. This is to deny that, as I put it, the transition from (v) to (vi) involves merely the addition of something happening to *somebody else;* what rather it does, it will be said, is to involve the reintroduction of A himself, as the B-body-person; since he has reappeared in this form, it is for this person, and not for the unfortunate A-body-person, that A will have his expectations. This is to reassert, in effect, the viewpoint emphasized in our first presentation of the experiment. But this surely has the consequence that A should not have fears for the A-body-person who appeared in situation (v). For by the present argument, the A-body-person in (vi) is not A; the B-body-person is. But the A-body-person in (v) is, in character, history, everything, exactly the same as the A-body-person in (vi); so if the latter is not A, then neither is the former. (It is this point, no doubt, that encourages one to speak of the difference that goes with [vi] as being, on the present view, the *reintroduction of A.*) But no one else in (v) has any better claim to be A. So in (v), it seems, A just does not exist. This would certainly explain why A should have no fears for the state of things in (v)—though he might well have fears for the path to it. But it rather looked earlier as though he could well have fears for the state of things in (v). Let us grant, however, that that was an illusion, and that A really does not exist in (v); then does he exist in (iv), (iii), (ii), or (i)? It seems very difficult to deny it for (i) and (ii); are we perhaps to draw the line between (iii) and (iv)?

Here someone will say: you must not insist on drawing a line—borderline cases are borderline cases, and you must not push our concepts beyond their limits. But this well-known piece of advice, sensible as it is in many cases, seems in the present case to involve an extraordinary difficulty. It may intellectually comfort observers of A's situation; but what is A supposed to make of it? To be told that a future situation is a borderline one for its being myself that is hurt, that it is conceptually undecidable whether it will be me or not, is something which, it seems, I can do nothing with; because, in particular, it seems to have no comprehensible representation in my expectations and the emotions that go with them.

If I expect that a certain situation, S, will come about in the future, there is of course a wide range of emotions and concerns, directed on S, which I may experience now in relation to my expectation. Unless I am exceptionally egoistic, it is not a condition on my being concerned in relation to this expectation, that I myself will be involved in S—where my being "involved" in S means that I figure in S as someone doing something at that time or having something done to me, or, again, that S will have consequences affecting me at that or some subsequent time. There are some emotions, however, which I will feel only if I will be involved in S, and fear is an obvious example.

Now the description of S under which it figures in my expectations will necessarily be, in various ways, indeterminate; and one way in which it may be indeterminate is that it leave open whether I shall be involved in S or not. Thus I may have good reason to expect that one out of us five is going to get hurt, but no reason to expect it to be me rather than one of the others. My present emotions will be correspondingly affected by this indeterminacy. Thus, sticking to the egoistic concern involved in fear, I shall presumably be somewhat more cheerful than if I knew it was going to be me, somewhat less cheerful than if I had been left out altogether.

. . . .

There are other ways in which indeterminate expectations can be related to fear. Thus I may expect (perhaps neurotically) that something nasty is going to happen to me, indeed expect that when it happens it will take some determinate form, but have no range, or no closed range, of candidates for the determinate form to rehearse in my present thought. Different from this would be the fear of something radically indeterminate—the fear (one might say) of a nameless horror. If somebody had such a fear, one could even say that he had, in a sense, a perfectly determinate expectation: if what he expects indeed comes about, there will be nothing more determinate to be said about it after the event than was said in the expectation. Both these cases of course are cases of *fear* because one thing that is fixed amid the indeterminacy is the belief that it is to me to which the things will happen.

. . . .

Suppose now that there is an S with regard to which it is for conceptual reasons undecidable whether it involves me or not, as is proposed for the experimental situation by the line we are discussing. It is important that the expectation of S is not *indeterminate* in any of the ways we have just been considering. It is not like the nameless horror, since the fixed point of that case was that it was going to happen to the subject, and that made his state unequivocally fear. Nor is it like the expectation of the man who expects one of the five to be hurt; his fear was indeed equivocal, but its focus, and that of the expectation, was that when S came about, it would certainly come about in one way or the other. In the present case, fear (of the torture, that is to say, not of the initial experiment) seems neither appropriate, nor inappropriate, nor appropriately equivocal. Relatedly, the subject has an incurable difficulty about how he may think about *S*. If he engages in projective imaginative thinking (about how it will be for him), he implicitly answers the necessarily unanswerable question; if he thinks that he cannot engage in such thinking, it looks very much as if he also answers it, though in the opposite direction. Perhaps he must just refrain from such thinking; but is he just refraining from it, if it is incurably undecidable whether he can or cannot engage in it?

· ·

The bafflement seems, moreover, to turn to plain absurdity if we move from conceptual undecidability to its close friend and neighbor, conventionalist decision. This comes out if we consider another description, overtly conventionalist, of the series of cases which occasioned the present discussion. This description would reject a point I relied on in an earlier argument—namely, that if we deny that the *A*-body-person in (*vi*) is *A* (because the *B*-body-person is), then we must deny that the *A*-body-person in (*v*) is *A*, since they are exactly the same. "No," it may be said, "this is just to assume that we say the same in different sorts of situation. No doubt when we have the very good candidate for being *A* —namely, the *B*-body-person—we call him *A;* but this does not mean that we should not call the *A*-body-person *A* in that other situation when we have no better candidate around. Different situations call for different descriptions." This line of talk is the sort of thing indeed appropriate to lawyers deciding the ownership of some property which has undergone some bewildering set of transformations; they just have to decide, and in each situation, let us suppose, it has got to go to somebody, on as reasonable grounds as the facts and the law admit. But as a line to deal with a person's fears or expectations about his own future, it seems to have no sense at all. If *A*'s fears can extend to what will happen to the *A*-body-person in (*v*), I do not see how they can be rationally diverted from the fate of the exactly similar person in (*vi*) by his being told that someone would have a reason in the latter situation which he would not have in the former for deciding to call another person *A*.

Thus, to sum up, it looks as though there are two presentations of the imagined experiment and the choice associated with it, each of which carries conviction, and which lead to contrary conclusions. The idea, moreover, that the situation after the experiment is conceptually undecidable in the relevant respect seems not to assist, but rather to increase, the puzzlement; while the idea (so often appealed to in these matters) that it is conventionally decidable is even worse. Following from all that, I am not in the least clear which option it would be wise to take if one were presented with them before the experiment. I find that rather disturbing.

Whatever the puzzlement, there is one feature of the arguments which have led to it which is worth picking out, since it runs counter to something which is, I think, often rather vaguely supposed. It is often recognized that there are "first-personal" and "third-personal" aspects of questions about persons, and that there are difficulties about the relations between them. It is also recognized that "mentalistic" considerations (as we may vaguely call them) and considerations of bodily continuity are involved in questions of personal identity (which is not to say that there are mentalistic and bodily criteria of personal identity). It is tempting to think that the two distinctions run in parallel: roughly, that a first-personal approach concentrates attention on mentalistic considerations, while a third-personal approach emphasizes considerations of bodily continuity. The present discussion is an illustration of exactly the opposite. The first argument, which led to the "mentalistic" conclusion that *A* and *B* would change bodies and that each person should identify himself with the destination of his memories and character, was an argument entirely conducted in third-personal terms. The second argument, which suggested the bodily continuity identification, concerned itself with the first-personal issue of what *A* could expect. That this is so seems to me (though I will not discuss it further here) of some significance.

I will end by suggesting one rather shaky way in which one might approach a resolution of the problem, using only the limited materials already available.

The apparently decisive arguments of the first presentation, which suggested that *A* should identify himself with the *B*-body-person, turned on the extreme neatness of the situation in satisfying, if any could, the description of "changing bodies." But this neatness is basically artificial; it is the product of the will of the experimenter to produce a situation which would naturally elicit, with minimum hesitation, that description. By the sorts of methods he employed, he could easily have left off earlier or gone on further. He could have stopped at situation (*v*), leaving *B* as he was; or he could have gone on and produced two persons each with *A*-like character and memories, as well as one or two with *B*-like characteristics. If he had done either of those, we should have been in yet greater difficulty about what to say; he just chose to make it as easy as possible for us to find something to say. Now if we had some model of ghostly persons in bodies, which were in some sense actually moved around by certain procedures, we could regard the neat experiment just as the *effective* experiment: the one method that really did result in the ghostly persons' changing places without being destroyed, dispersed, or whatever. But we cannot seriously use such a model. The experimenter has not in the sense of that model *induced* a change of bodies; he has rather produced the one situation out of a range of equally possible situations which we should be most disposed to call a change of bodies. As against this, the principle that one's fears can extend to future pain whatever psychological changes precede it seems positively straightforward. Perhaps, indeed, it is not; but we need to be shown what is wrong with it. Until we are shown what is wrong with it, we should perhaps decide that if we were the person *A* then, if we were to decide selfishly, we should pass the pain to the *B*-body-person. It would be risky: that there is room for the notion of a *risk* here is itself a major feature of the problem.

SUGGESTED READINGS

Mind and Body

Collections of Writings on the Philosophy of Mind

Borst, C. V. (ed.). *The Mind/Brain Identity Theory.* New York: St. Martin's
Press, 1970.

Chappell, V. C. (ed.). *The Philosophy of Mind.* Englewood Cliffs, N.J.:
Prentice-Hall, Inc., 1962.

Flew, Antony (ed.). *Body, Mind and Death.* New York: Macmillan, 1964.

Glover, J. (ed.). *The Philosophy of Mind.* New York.: Oxford University
Press, 1976.

Gustafson, D. F. (ed.). *Essays in Philosophical Psychology.* Garden City,
N.Y.: Doubleday, 1964.

Hampshire, Stuart (ed.). *Philosophy of Mind.* New York: Harper & Row, 1966.

O'Connor, J. (ed.). *Modern Materialism: Readings on Mind-Body Identity.*
New York: Harcourt, Brace, & World, Inc., 1969.

Rosenthal, D. M. (ed.). *Materialism and the Mind-Body Problem.* Englewood
Cliffs, N.J.: Prentice-Hall, 1971.

Vesey, G. N. A. (ed.). *Body and Mind.* London: George Allen & Unwin, 1964.

General Discussions of the Mind-Body Problem

Armstrong. D. M. *A Materialist Theory of the Mind.* New York: Humanities
Press, 1968.

Beardsley, M. C. and E. L. *Philosophical Thinking.* New York: Harcourt, 1965.
Chap. 11.

Broad, C. D. *The Mind and Its Place in Nature.* London: Routledge & Kegan
Paul, 1925. Chaps. 3, 14 [partly in Edwards-Pap, Feinberg, Margolis].

Ducasse, C. J. *Nature, Mind and Death.* LaSalle, Ill.: Open Court, 1951
[partly in Alston, Edwards-Pap].

Feigl, Herbert, "The 'Mental' and the 'Physical,' " in H. Feigl et al. (eds.).
Minnesota Studies in the Philosophy of Science. Minneapolis: University
of Minnesota Press, 1958.

Hook, Sidney (ed.). *Dimensions of Mind.* New York: New York University
Press, 1960. Part I.

Kneale, William. *On Having a Mind.* Cambridge: Cambridge University Press,
1962.

Pap, Arthur. *Elements of Analytical Philosophy.* New York: Macmillan,
1949. Chap. 12.

Pratt, J. B. *Matter and Spirit.* New York: Macmillan, 1926 [partly in
Mandelbaum-Gramlich-Anderson].

Shaffer, J. A. *Philosophy of Mind.* Englewood Cliffs, N.J.: Prentice-Hall,
Inc., 1968.

Taylor, Richard. *Metaphysics.* Englewood Cliffs, N.J.: Prentice-Hall, Inc.,
1963. Chaps. 1, 2.

Wisdom, John. *Problems of Mind and Matter.* London: Cambridge University
Press, 1934. Part I.

Dualism

Ducasse, C. J. *Nature, Mind, and Death.* LaSalle, Ill.: Open Court, 1951. Chap. 18.

Malcolm, N. "Descartes' Proof That His Essence Is Thinking," *Philosophical Review,* Vol. 74 (1965).

McDougall, William. *Body and Mind.* London: Methuen, 1911.

Plato. *Phaedo.*

Shaffer, J. "Persons and Their Bodies," *Philosophical Review,* Vol. 74 (1965).

Parallelism

Clifford, W. K. "Body and Mind," "Things-in-Themselves," in *Lectures and Essays.* London: Macmillan, 1879. Vol. II.

Fechner, G. T. *Religion of a Scientist,* ed. W. Lowrie. New York: Pantheon, 1946.

Hoffding, Harold. *The Problems of Philosophy.* New York: Macmillan, 1905.

Leibniz, G. W. *Exposition and Defence of the New System.*

Behaviorism

Carnap, Rudolf. "Psychology in Physical Language," in A. J. Ayer (ed.), *Logical Positivism.* Glencoe, Ill.: Free Press, 1959.

Farrell, B. A. "Experience," *Mind,* Vol. 59 (1950).

Hempel, C. G. "The Logical Analysis of Psychology" [in Feigl and Sellars].

Ryle, Gilbert. *The Concept of Mind.* London: Hutchinson, 1949.

Skinner, B. F. "Behaviorism at Fifty," in T. W. Wann (ed.), *Behaviorism and Phenomenology.* Chicago: University of Chicago Press, 1964.

——————. *Science and Human Behavior.* New York: The Macmillan Co., 1953.

Tolman, E. C. "Operational Behaviorism and Current Trends in Psychology," in M. H. Marx (ed.), *Psychological Theory.* New York: Macmillan, 1951, pp. 87–102.

Watson, J. B. *Behaviorism.* New York: Norton, 1924.

Ziff, P. "About Behaviorism," *Analysis* (1958) [in Chappell].

Criticisms of Behaviorism

Ewing, A. C. "Professor Ryle's Attack on Dualism," *Proceedings of the Aristotelian Society,* Vol. 53 (1952).

Fodor, J. A. *Psychological Explanation.* New York: Random House, 1968, Ch. 2.

Lewis, C. I. "Some Logical Considerations Concerning the Mental," *Journal of Philosophy,* Vol. 38 (1941) [in Feigl-Sellars, Vesey].

Putnam, H. "Brains and Behavior," in R. Butler (ed.), *Analytical Philosophy Second Series.* Oxford: Blackwell's, 1963.

Russell, Bertrand, *Philosophy.* New York: Norton, 1927. Part III.

Scriven, Michael. "A Study of Radical Behaviorism," in *Minnesota Studies in the Philosophy of Science,* Vol. I, Minneapolis: University of Minnesota Press, 1956.
Whiteley, C. H. "Behaviorism," *Mind,* Vol. 70 (1961).

Materialism

Armstrong, D. M. *A Materialistic Theory of the Mind.* New York: Humanities Press, 1968.
Brandt, R. B., and Kim, J. "The Logic of the Identity Theory," *Journal of Philosophy,* Vol. 64 (1967) [in O'Connor].
Buchner, Ludwig. *Force and Matter.* London: Asher, 1884.
Elliot, Hugh. *Modern Science and Materialism.* London: Longmans, Green, 1919 [partly in Randall-Buchler-Shirk].
Feyerabend, Paul. "Materialism and the Mind Body Problem," *Review of Metaphysics,* Vol. 17 (1963) [in O'Connor, Borst].
Fodor, J. A. *Psychological Explanation.* New York: Random House, 1968, Chap. 3 [in Rosenthal].
Hobbes, Thomas. *De Corpore.* [partly in R. S. Peters (ed.), *Body, Man, and Citizen*]. New York: Collier Books, 1962.
Kim, J. "On The Psycho-Physical Identity Theory," *American Philosophical Quarterly,* III (1966) [in Rosenthal].
Lucretius. *On the Nature of Things.* Book III.
Nagel, T. "Physicalism," *Philosophical Review,* Vol. 74 (1965) [in Borst, O'Connor].
Rorty, R. "Mind-Body Identity, Privacy, and Categories," *Review of Metaphysics,* Vol. 19 (1965) [in Borst, O'Connor, Hampshire].

Criticisms of Materialism

Baier, K. "Smart on Sensations," *Australasian Journal of Philosophy,* Vol. 40 (1962) [in Borst].
Shaffer, Jerome. "Could Mental States Be Brain Processes?" *Journal of Philosophy,* Vol. 58 (1961) [in Vesey, Borst].

Minds and Machines

Anderson, A. R. (ed.). *Minds and Machines.* Englewood Cliffs, N.J.: Prentice-Hall, 1964.
Hook, Sidney (ed.). *Dimensions of Mind.* New York: New York University Press, 1960. Part II.
Sluckin, W. *Minds and Machines.* London: Pelican Books, 1954.

One's Knowledge of Other Minds

Ayer, A. J. *The Problem of Knowledge.* London: Penguin Books, 1956. Chap. 5.
Broad, C. D. *The Mind and Its Place in Nature.* London: Routledge & Kegan Paul, 1925. Chap. 7.

Malcolm, Norman. "Knowledge of Other Minds," in *Knowledge and Certainty.* Englewood Cliffs, N.J.: Prentice-Hall, 1963 [in Chappell, Gustafson, Margolis, Tillman-Berofsky-O'Connor].
——————. "Wittgenstein's Philosophical Investigations," *ibid.* [in Chappell].
Mill, J. S. *An Examination of Sir William Hamilton's Philosophy.* London: Longmans, Green, 1872. Chap. 12.
Strawson, P. F. *Individuals.* London: Methuen, 1959. Chap. 3.
Wisdom, John. *Other Minds.* Oxford: Basil Blackwell, 1952.
Wisdom, John, Austin, J. L., and Ayer, A. J. "Other Minds," *Aristotelian Society,* Supplementary Vol. 20 (1946).

Personal Identity

Ayer, A. J. *The Problem of Knowledge,* London: Penguin Books, 1956. Chap. 5.
Broad, C. D. *The Mind and Its Place in Nature.* London: Routledge & Kegan Paul, 1925. Chap. 13.
Butler, Joseph. "Dissertation of Personal Identity" [in Flew].
Grice, H. P. "Personal Identity," *Mind,* Vol. 50 (1941).
Hume, David. *Treatise of Human Nature,* Book I, Part IV, Secs. 5, 6, and Appendix [partly in Bierman-Gould, Edwards-Pap, Flew, Margolis, Tillman-Berofsky-O'Connor].
James, William. *Psychology.* New York: Holt, 1893. Chap. 12.
Locke, John. *An Essay Concerning Human Understanding,* Book II, Ch. 27.
Penelhum, Terence. "Hume on Personal Identity," *Philosophical Review,* Vol. 64 (1955).
——————. "Personal Identity, Memory, and Survival," *Journal of Philosophy,* Vol. 56 (1959).
Reid, Thomas. *Essays on the Intellectual Powers of Man.* Essay III, Ch. 3.
Shoemaker, Sidney. "Personal Identity and Memory," *ibid.,* Vol. 56 (1959).
——————. *Self-Knowledge and Self-Identity.* Ithaca, N.Y.: Cornell University Press, 1963.
Williams, B. A. O. *Problems of the Self.* London: Cambridge University Press, 1973.

General Treatments of Immortality

Ducasse, C. J. *A Critical Examination of the Belief in a Life After Death.* Springfield, Ill.: C. C. Thomas, 1961.
Seth, Andrew Pringle-Pattison. *The Idea of Immortality.* London: Oxford University Press, 1922 [partly in Abernethy-Langford, Bronstein-Schulweis].
Tsanoff, Radoslav. *The Problem of Immortality.* New York: Macmillan, 1924.

Arguments in Support of Immortality

Butler, Joseph. *The Analogy of Religion,* 1736, Chap. 1 [partly in Smart].
James, W. *Human Immortality; Two Supposed Objections to the Doctrine.* Cambridge, Mass.: Harvard University Press, 1899.

Maritain, Jacques. "The Immortality of the Soul," in *The Range of Reason*. New York: Scribner's, 1952 [in Alston].

McTaggart, J. M. E. *Some Dogmas of Religion*. London: Arnold, 1906. Chaps. 3, 4.

Plato. *Phaedo* [partly in Bronstein-Schulweis, Hick, Smart].

Royce, Josiah. *The Conception of Immortality*. Boston: Houghton Mifflin, 1900.

St. Augustine. "On the Immortality of the Soul," in W. J. Oates (ed.), *Basic Writings*. New York: Random House, 1948.

Taylor, A. E. *The Christian Hope of Immortality*. New York: Macmillan, 1947 [partly in Bronstein-Schulweis, Abernethy-Langford].

Tennant, F. R. *Philosophical Theology*. London: Cambridge Univ. Press, 1928. Vol. II, Appendix, Note E [in Abernethy-Langford, Bronstein-Krikorian-Weiner, 3rd ed.].

Arguments Against Immortality

Flew, Antony (ed.). *Body, Mind, and Death*. New York: Macmillan, 1964. Introduction.

Hume, David. "Of the Immortality of the Soul," 1756 [in Edwards-Pap].

Lamont, Corliss. *The Illusion of Immortality*. New York: Putnam, 1935.

Lucretius. *On the Nature of Things,* Book III.

Martin, C. B. *Religious Belief*. Ithaca, N.Y.: Cornell Univ. Press, 1959. Chap. 6.

Russell, Bertrand. *Why I Am Not a Christian and Other Essays*. New York: Simon and Schuster, 1957.

Sellars, R. W. *The Next Step in Religion*. New York: Macmillan, 1918. Chap. 11 [partly in Alston].

The Bearing of Psychical Research on the Problem of Immortality

Broad, C. D. *Lectures on Psychical Research*. London: Routledge & Kegan Paul, 1962.

Ducasse, C. J. *Nature, Mind, and Death*. LaSalle, Ill.: Open Court, 1951. Chaps. 20, 21.

Flew, Antony. *A New Approach to Psychical Research*. London: C. A. Watts, 1953, esp. Chap. 7 [partly in Alston].

Murphy, Gardner. "An Outline of Survival Evidence," *Journal of the American Society of Psychical Research*, 1945.

PART VI

The Structure of Knowledge

601

Introduction

Philosophy, we urged in our general introductory comments, is an attempt to arrive at rigorously reasoned answers to important questions that are not within the scope of the sciences. One of these important questions, indeed, one that has some claim to be considered prior to any of the rest, is *when any belief is reasonable, well-supported, or well-justified.*

We think that many beliefs are well-justified: the beliefs that Kepler's laws are approximately true of the movements of the planets, that the President of the United States resigned in 1974, and so on. Other beliefs, some of them shared by many people, we think are *not* reasonable or justified by the evidence: for instance, that one can predict a person's future life by considering the position of the heavenly bodies at the time of his birth. This contrast presents a challenge: can we show that members of our first set of beliefs can be given a reasonable defense whereas ones such as the latter cannot? What does it take to justify a belief? And under what conditions is a belief *adequately* justified?

In the present section, we tackle this difficult matter—but with a restriction. The restriction is that we shall consider only *factual* beliefs, as contrasted with beliefs about *values* (about what is right or wrong to do, about what is worthwhile or good, or about what is beautiful). It may be that there is no significant difference between beliefs about facts and beliefs about values, as far as justification is concerned. But the matter is controversial, and we confine ourselves here to the question when beliefs about fact are well-supported—using as examples the affirmations of the empirical sciences such as physics, and of the "pure" sciences such as mathematics.

SKEPTICISM

One very simple answer to our question as to when a belief is well-justified is just that it *never* is. According to this view, one is as little justified in relying on the news stories of the *New York Times* as one is in relying on the "horoscope for today." Reliance on neither can be rationally justified.

603

We label a person a "moderate" skeptic if he thinks that only beliefs about certain topics are never justified by the evidence; for example, beliefs about theology or ethics or the parts of science that deal with unobservable entities such as electrons. Less moderate skeptics, but still "moderate" by this definition, believe that no beliefs in general laws, or predictions about the future (for example, that my dog will not vanish into thin air in the next moment) are well-justified. The most radical skeptics, the "extreme" ones, deny that one is ever better justified in believing *any* proposition than its contradiction—perhaps even the skeptical thesis itself! Skeptics, both extreme and moderate, form a tradition going right back to ancient Greece.

In the first chapter of the *Meditations* (Reading 42), which should be read at this point, Descartes plays devil's advocate and temporarily takes the part of the extreme skeptic, although at the end he concedes that at least he is justified in believing that he doubts and hence that he exists. (In the second chapter, he goes on to affirm many other theses.) The reasons he gives for his initial skepticism are not untypical.

You may be inclined to dismiss extreme skepticism, and perhaps all the weaker forms of skepticism as well, as simply silly. But if it is silly, presumably we can explain *why* it is silly. The existence of skepticism is an invitation to lay out, step by step, the reasons we have, such as they are, for the beliefs we regard as well-justified. By doing that, we shall come to see in detail what kind of reasons we have for the beliefs we hold and what kind we do not have; and then, if we decide against skepticism, we shall do so in full awareness of what we are doing. Bertrand Russell once declared that *extreme* skepticism cannot be refuted but may be ignored. He wrote:

No arguments are logically possible either for or against complete skepticism, which must be admitted to be one among possible philosophies. It is, however, too short and simple to be interesting. I shall, therefore, without more ado, develop the opposite hypothesis, according to which beliefs caused by perception are to be accepted unless there are positive grounds for rejecting them.

Do we want to dismiss skepticism simply by saying it is too short and simple to be interesting? Is it true that no arguments (presumably, no *good* ones) are possible, either for or against extreme skepticism?

Descartes purports to offer some arguments for the skeptical view. You will want to consider whether they are good ones. For instance, he considers how often we make mistakes about matters such as "There's a tower," and asks us whether any similar judgment we are currently making also may not turn out to be mistaken. The argument, of course, *assumes* that he knows we have made mistakes. Is it, then, an argument a skeptic can offer consistently? Again, he sometimes appeals to a logical possibility: God *could* have made us with "memories" of events that never happened, or made us so that arguments that strike us as sound ones actually are not. And what reason have we for thinking that He actually didn't? To this, a critic might reply that one can impugn our right to believe only by appeal to what is reasonably believed to be true, not by appeal to a mere logical possibility. Is that a good reply? Or is Russell perhaps right in his suggestion that if a person starts out by questioning the reliability of reasoning itself, nothing can ever be proved either way?

AN ANSWER TO SKEPTICISM: THE PYRAMID THEORY

The answer that philosophers traditionally have made to the skeptic has not been just an attack on the skeptic's own arguments, but rather a detailed exposition of the kind of justification that can be given for beliefs of various types. As such, it hopefully provides the means for showing that there is a difference between the status of justified and unjustified beliefs, and what that difference is. The types of justification that have been given are quite different, and we cannot represent them all. We have chosen to concentrate on the dominant type of justification offered in Western thought for at least the past four hundred years. Other theorists (e.g., the "coherence theorists" and the "contextualists") have had hard words for it, but it is the Establishment, and one does not know what the guerrilla snipers are shooting at unless one knows what it is. Of course, in the end you may wish to join the guerrillas!

What is this theory? The central idea is twofold: 1) that some beliefs are justified because they are logically supported (inductively or deductively —see below) by other beliefs already justified, and 2) that some beliefs are justified *independently* of logical support by already justified beliefs. We may call these latter beliefs *independently credible.* Thus, the theory is that knowledge is like a pyramid, with foundations; the latter beliefs comprise the base, with the former beliefs constituting the upper tiers, which rest on the foundation.

Should one accept this central idea? No one will doubt that there are some beliefs that we are justified in holding, if we are, only because of logical support by other already justified beliefs. For instance, if someone asks, "Why do you think there are small invisible particles with negative charge?" one might reply, "Some experimental data with cathode tubes can be explained in no other way." Evidently the belief in electrons is justified, among other things, by the logical support given them by justified beliefs about experiments with cathode tubes. But how could we show there are *independently credible* beliefs, which can serve as foundations for the rest of the structure of knowledge? One thing we might do is produce an example. (This is part of what Lewis is doing in Reading 51.) But we also can give an argument. The argument runs like this: "Not *every* belief we hold can be justified only by its logical relations with other beliefs, for a belief *B* is justified by pointing out its logical relation to belief *B′* only if one is already justified in believing *B′*. Now, if *B′* were questioned, one could, of course, go on to show that believing it is justified because of its logical relation to *B″*. But somewhere this chain has got to stop. You cannot justify beliefs by pointing to their logical relations to other beliefs unless there are *some* beliefs one is justified in holding *independently* of their logical relations to other beliefs."

Of course, a showing that the central idea of the Pyramid Theory is plausible is only the beginning of a reply to the skeptic. For one thing, one must go on to identify types of independently credible premises—and about this there is much room for debate. (Lewis takes them to be judgments, sometimes certain, about experience, in Reading 51; Carnap, Reading 58, apparently is taking a somewhat different view.) After that, there may be debate about which kinds of logical relation to already justified premises constitute "logical support" for a "theorem." Thus, we want to know how to identify the self-evident (independently credible) premises having to do with cathode tubes; we also want to know by what kind of logical warrant we proceed from there to justified beliefs about electrons, a matter discussed in Readings 55 to 58. It is clear that a complete answer to the skeptic, or, in other words, a complete account of our justification for believing mathematics and the major outlines of empirical science, is going to be a complicated piece of work.

THE BASIC EMPIRICAL PREMISES

Philosophers who accept the Pyramid Theory believe that the premises of our corpus of justified beliefs are of two kinds: *empirical premises,* about what is in some sense observed, and "truths of reason." Let us begin with the identity and status of empirical premises. This is what Lewis's discussion is mainly about.

The Lewis piece is a difficult one; it is included because the topic is important and no other discussion of it is as good. Since it is difficult, it may be helpful if we outline its main points here.

Lewis does not use the term "independently credible belief" in the case of judgments about experience one is having at a given time or the memories (see the very last paragraph of his article) of earlier experience. He does, however, think such beliefs are independently credible; in fact, he thinks they are *certain.* At any given time, Lewis thinks, just as Descartes thought one could be certain one exists because one is certain of one's doubting, so one is certain of the character of the experience one is having —of the sounds one is hearing, of the visual experiences one is having, of the feel of one's body, and so on. He also thinks one is certain that one seems to remember a certain thing (if one is seeming to recollect something). Lewis thinks these certain beliefs are the justification for the other beliefs we have.

Lewis distinguishes two other kinds of belief one may be having at any time, one of them simpler (the terminating beliefs), the other more complex (the nonterminating beliefs or beliefs about the objective world). Terminating beliefs are, roughly, what experiences one will have next if one acts, or rather seems to act, in a certain way. That is, given the experience one is having now, then, if one seems to do a certain thing, one will have a further experience of a certain kind. That is a terminating belief. If the anticipated experience occurs when the apparent action has been taken, the belief turns out to be true, or is confirmed. Nonterminating beliefs are rather like the first, only more complex. For instance, I might be thinking that I am looking at a piece of white paper. This is a nonterminating belief. Lewis thinks that, given what it is for there to be a piece of white paper before me, this belief implies an indefinitely large number of predictions of what will happen next if I do so-and-so, or seem to do so-and-so. For instance, if it is paper before me, if I put pressure on it, it will tear. Both kinds of beliefs are roughly expectations, either simple or complex, about what will happen, or rather, be experienced, in the future given certain events (e.g., actions of mine) occur.

For Lewis, then, the problem of justifying our beliefs is that of showing that it is reasonable to place confidence in both terminating and nonterminating judgments of specific kinds, given our *evidence* at the moment—the certain beliefs about how things look now, and the certain seeming recollections I have about what experiences occurred in the past.

Lewis inclines to classify all the alleged knowledge of science, however complex, as nonterminating judgments. You may think this is too simple. But he is trying to work with simple examples: he thinks that if we can show how I am justified in believing that there is a piece of white paper before me, we shall have gone a long way toward showing the justification of the most recondite pieces of "scientific knowledge."

The main problems facing Lewis, if you grant him his certain premises about experience and memories, are two: how we are justified in extrapolating from knowledge of past sequences to future sequences of the same sort (the problem of induction, with which we shall deal shortly); and how we are justified in moving from awareness of the fact that we *seem* to remember certain occurrences or sequences in the past, to a justified belief that those occurrences really did happen. (This second problem, of the reliability of memory, is not discussed in this book.)

You may think Lewis is too restrictive about what belongs among the premises of knowledge. Why not include facts that go beyond the content of my experience, as that I am now sitting before a typewriter, that I am wearing trousers, and so on? Are these not matters of "experience"? You probably will feel more convinced by Lewis's view after you have read Section VII and have considered the reasons for distinguishing between material things and "sense-data." Lewis also might argue that his restriction has the advantage of *economy*. Since he thinks that if one starts with the narrower set of premises one can still derive the other beliefs as theorems, then why not start with the more restricted set?

Toward the end of his article, Lewis emphasizes what is true and important—that a person's beliefs about his own experiences are independently credible only *for him.* People sometimes are justified in thinking that *other* people have certain experiences, but for this they need inference, from the testimony of those who had the experience and from data justifying the belief that their testimony is apt to be reliable.

What Lewis really does, in reply to Descartes, is to argue that a somewhat wider group of beliefs—beliefs about present experiences, including introspective beliefs about one's feelings, etc., and about one's seeming to remember various experiences in the past—is secure against sceptical attack, and to sketch a *program.* The program, not here worked out, consists of justifying reliance on one's own memory and reliance on the principles of deductive and inductive logic. With these things done, Lewis thinks, we can go on from the basic premises about experiences to the upper tiers of knowledge—to show, roughly in the way Euclid derived his theorems from his axioms, that the premises of knowledge give appropriate support to other beliefs, beliefs about ordinary objects like chairs, other persons, and unobservable entities in physics such as electrons.

If this program can be carried out, it may give us something we would like to have: a basis for differentiating reasonable from unreasonable beliefs, a means of showing that whereas one is justified in believing the principles of physics, one is not justified in taking seriously one's "horoscope today."

TRUTHS OF REASON

Let us now leave the question of the place of "empirical premises" in the pyramid of knowledge and look at the status of "truths of reason": for example, if a plane figure is square, it is not circular, or $2 + 2 = 4$. Writers on this topic have largely ignored Descartes' doubts, and we shall follow them in that, leaving reflections on the problem to the reader.

In order to make clear the controversies about truths of reason, we now must explain two technical terms frequently found in the literature: "a posteriori" and "a priori." When we come to know something on the basis of experience we are said to know it *a posteriori,* and the truth known may be called an *a posteriori* truth (or proposition). When our knowledge of something is not based on experience, we are said to know it *a priori* (and the truth or proposition may be spoken of as *a priori*). Thus, in order to know (or be justified in believing) that animals with cloven hooves chew their cud, one must examine a number of individual cloven-hoofed animals and discover by observation, in each case, that it chews its cud. (Or else one must learn this truth from someone else who has made the observations.) This is a proposition that can be known only *a posteriori*. By contrast, in order to know that a square has four sides of equal length, no observations are necessary. (Perhaps we have to have had some experience of the world in order to understand the geometrical concepts of a square, a side, and so on; but that is another matter. The issue we are presently concerned with is what is required to justify our acceptance of a proposition, once we have understood what proposition is in question.) We do not have to examine a number of squares, one by one, to determine by observation, in the case of each, whether it has four sides and whether all the sides are of equal length. All we need do, in order to assure ourselves of the truth of this proposition, is to understand it. This is a proposition that can be known *a priori*.

We can now define a "truth of reason" as a "truth knowable *a priori*."

There has been much discussion as to just what truths of reason there are and as to precisely how they are known. The following selections from Kant, Mill, and Ayer are all concerned with this subject. It is useful to distinguish two topics about which controversy has raged.

1) Are Only Analytic Statements Known *A Priori?*—The Empiricist-Rationalist Controversy

In our discussion above, we suggested that some truths of reason are legitimate premises for inference, but we did not explain how to identify one; we only stated that there are some, and mentioned some examples. But which statements are truths of reason? What is to prevent a person from claiming that almost any proposition he believes, and for which he can produce no observational support, is a "truth of reason"? In fact, a great many propositions have been claimed to be truths of reason: not only the principles of logic and arithmetic, but Archimedes' principle of the lever, the impossibility of perpetual motion, the conservation of energy and of matter, some of the inverse square laws (e.g., of gravitational attraction), and the basic principles of ethics.

Many philosophers have felt that the whole concept of truths of reason is a dangerous one, and that, unless its use is severely restricted, there is an open invitation to claim as a truth of reason any statement for which there is no evidence of observation but which one very much wants to believe. They have thought, however, that there is one clear line that can be drawn, and that one type of statement can fairly be claimed to be knowable by reflection without observation, and that none other can be. More specifically, they have held that *analytic* statements, and only these, are knowable *a priori*. Such philosophers are called *empiricists*. *Rationalist* philosophers, by definition of "rationalist," deny this in one way or another.

What exactly, however, is an *analytic* statement? If we look to our readings, we find that Kant explains "analytic" as follows. Consider the statement, "All bodies are extended," which he says is analytic, and contrast it with "All bodies are heavy," which he says is synthetic. In the case of the former, he says that the predicate "is [covertly] contained" in the concept of the subject. The statement adds nothing, in the predicate, to the concept of the subject, but merely breaks it up "into those constituent concepts that have all along been thought in it, although confusedly. . . ." When these features are present, a statement is analytic, according to Kant. Thus, if the concept of a *body* is made up of the concepts of *substance* and *extended* (i.e., if what we mean by "body" is "extended substance"), then in the judgment "All bodies are extended," the predicate merely makes explicit part of the content of the subject. The denial of an analytic statement, in this sense of the term, would be self-contradictory. For if the concept of a body *is* the concept of an extended substance, then to deny that all bodies are extended is to say that something that *is extended* (among other features) *is not extended*.

Kant's definition, as Ayer points out, leads to awkwardness. First, it is applicable only to subject-predicate statements, whereas we want to say, for instance, that "If a man is mortal he is not immortal" is analytic. Second, the idea of one concept "being contained" in another is vague, and liable to misuse. Thus, Kant himself denies that arithmetical statements such as "$7 + 5 = 12$" are analytic, on the ground that the concept of 12 is not "contained in" the concept of $7 + 5$. But it is not clear how we go about determining whether it is or not. Ayer provides a clearer and more convenient definition, which we shall employ. He says, essentially, that a statement is analytic if and only if its truth (or falsity) can be determined from information about the meanings (or rules of use) of the words in the sentence, and from these alone. Obviously, this is true for both "All bodies are extended" and "$7 + 5 = 12$" as well as for many other statements.

If a statement is meaningful but is not *analytic,* we shall call it *synthetic.*

609

(Here we must be careful to avoid Ayer's definition of "synthetic" as meaning "when its validity is determined by the facts of experience"—a proposal that makes the thesis of empiricism an analytic truth!)

It may be a useful exercise for the reader to consider whether, according to the above definition, the following statements are analytic: "The sun always rises in the east"; "A person always ought to do his duty."

Given these definitions of "analytic" and "synthetic," then, we now may ask ourselves whether the thesis of empiricism is true. That is, are all statements knowable to be true or false *a priori* analytic? Or are some of them synthetic?

As a typical example of controversies over these matters, consider the following: It is sometimes contended that according to our definitions the statement, "Nothing red all over is green all over," which we seem to know to be true *a priori,* is a synthetic statement—contrary to the thesis of empiricism. For one cannot show this statement to be true by reference to the *definitions* of "red" and "green"; these terms, in their most important use, are so simple that they *do not have any definitions*. To this objection some empiricists reply that the meaning of a word is properly explained not merely by giving a verbal definition relating it to other words (as "bachelor" can be defined as "unmarried adult male"), but also by showing examples (as we can do for "green") which make clear in which circumstances the term is to be used and when not. And, the rejoinder goes, if we allow ourselves to take this kind of information about meanings rather broadly into account, we can treat the above statement about red and green to be an analytic statement by our definition of "analytic" after all.

Among our readings, Ayer takes the empiricist position; he affirms that only analytic statements can be known to be true (or false) *a priori.* In contrast, Kant adopts the rationalist position; he affirms that synthetic propositions can be known *a priori*—including, according to him, all the propositions of pure mathematics, "Every event has a cause," and "The quantity of matter in the universe must remain unchanged."

Some philosophers today think that the whole analytic-synthetic distinction is fundamentally obscure, and hence the whole controversy misguided. Readings on that topic are listed at the end of this section.

2) The Status of Mathematics

Are the propositions of mathematics truths of reason (knowable *a priori*), or not? If they are, are they synthetic or analytic? Controversy about the status of mathematics is in part just a local engagement in the general war between empiricists and rationalists. As such, it may not seem very important. However, the prestige of mathematics is such that the issue of its status is of great interest. This is a case of the "camel's nose in the tent"; if we were to admit that such a well-developed and prestigious area of knowledge includes synthetic *a priori* knowledge, we would be asked: Why not more? Why not ethical propositions? In fact, the essay by W. D. Ross (Reading 23) does claim that mathematical and ethical propositions have the same status, of being cases of synthetic *a priori* knowledge. But the status of mathematics has an importance that goes beyond the issue between empiricists and rationalists. It is a significant part of the general attempt to understand the logic of the various sciences. Are the propositions of arithmetic or geometry defensible in just the same way as the propositions of physics or psychology, and if not, exactly what kind of reasoning can provide justification for believing in them? This is one of the most basic questions of the philosophy of mathematics.

Among our readings, J. S. Mill represents one form of an empiricist position on this issue. He holds that geometry, arithmetic, and even logic are in the end dependent on observations; the axioms of these subjects are generalizations of what we find in experience, just like those of physics or psychology. It is logically possible for there to be a world in which the true principles of arithmetic, geometry, and logic are different. In contrast, Kant, while agreeing with Mill that the axioms of these subjects are synthetic, regards them as knowable *a priori;* we can know the principles of Euclid to be true just by taking thought. Ayer agrees with Kant, against Mill, in urging that the axioms of these subjects can be known *a priori,* and that observation is entirely irrelevant to knowledge of their truth. But he maintains his empiricism (which he shares with Mill) by affirming that these statements are one and all analytic.

The reader will have to decide who is right in this controversy. We shall, however, mention one possibility: that Ayer is right about arithmetic and logic, but Mill about geometry. At least, one might say that what is known *a priori,* and is analytic, in geometry is just that the theorems do follow from the axioms; whereas the truth of the axioms, e.g., that two straight lines cannot enclose a space, is a matter of observation.

Justified Modes of Inference: Laws and Theories in Science

We now have explained some views of philosophers about observational premises and "truths of reason." But these are only the *foundation* of knowledge. In order to appraise the beliefs we really want to appraise (such as the statements of astronomy as compared with those of astrology), we have to move by inference from these premises to further statements. Or, to use the metaphor of the pyramid, we have to move from the foundations to the upper levels, and we have to get clear about the justification for doing this. In doing so, we are still engaged in replying to the skeptic; for if we are well-justified in accepting certain premises, we are well-justified in accepting any derivative statements to which we may move, from these premises, by a valid mode of inference.

Which, however, are legitimate modes of inference, and how may we show that they are legitimate? These questions are not easy. The next four readings, beginning with Russell, attempt to give a partial answer to them.

Inferences generally are classified into two major types: *deductive* and *inductive.* In explaining this difference, it is best to proceed by explaining the somewhat more restricted notions of a *valid deductive inference* and a *valid inductive inference* (where the *general* notion of validity is, roughly, *doing its job properly;* a valid inference is one that does what it is supposed to do).

1) Valid Deductive Inference. In a valid deductive inference, the premises "guarantee" the conclusion, in the sense that it is impossible for the premises to be true without the conclusion being true. If we attempted to affirm the premises while denying the conclusion we would be contradicting ourselves; we would be taking back something we had already implicitly committed ourselves to. Consider a very simple example of deductive inference, Aristotle's favorite example of a syllogistic argument: "All men are mortal; Socrates is a man; therefore Socrates is mortal." This is deductively valid, for if one assents to the premises, he may not deny the conclusion; the acceptance of the premises already commits him to the conclusion. Having admitted both that Socrates falls within the class of men and that everything in that class is mortal, he has already, in effect, admitted that Socrates is mortal. To deny that Socrates is mortal would be to take back what is already contained (implicitly) in the premises.

Having explained what a valid deductive inference is, we can very simply define the more general notion of a *deductive inference* as an *inference that is put forward as a valid deductive argument* (that "claims" to be a valid deductive argument).

A valid deductive argument is valid by virtue of its form, rather than because of the particular subject matter with which it deals. Thus, the above argument is of the form: "All *A*'s are *B; x* is an *A; therefore x* is *B.*" Whenever a deductive argument is of that form, it is valid; it does not matter which terms replace the variables *"A," "B,"* and *"x"* (so long as, in a single argument, we replace a particular letter with the *same* term each time it occurs). Thus, consider the following argument, which is of the same form: "All dogs are carnivorous; Fido is a dog; therefore Fido is carnivorous." This is also valid, and for exactly the same reasons as the argument with which we started. (The reader would find it useful to apply to this argument our comments about the first one.) The shift in subject matter from men to dogs has absolutely no bearing on the question of validity.

There is no real controversy among philosophers about the point that we can know *a priori* whether an argument of a certain form is deductively valid. When, two paragraphs back, we were showing that the argument about Socrates is deductively valid, we did not appeal to any observations, or to any empirical evidence of any kind. We simply reflected on what one is asserting when he asserts the premises and conclusion. Of course, that is an extremely simple example of a deductive argument, and for many sorts of deductive arguments, it is not such a simple matter to tell whether they are valid. (That is why logic is such an extremely technical subject.) However, whatever the complexity of the argument, the basic point remains that the determination of its validity is a matter for reflection on the content of what is said, rather than a matter for empirical investigation.

2) *Valid Inductive Inference.* The term "inductive" is used in wider and narrower senses. In the very wide sense in which we shall use it here, a valid inductive inference is one in which the premises give some support to the conclusion (i.e., provide some reason for accepting the conclusion), but not the conclusive support provided in a deductive argument. In other words, the relation between premises and conclusion in an inductive argument is less "tight" than in a deductive argument, so that there is no contradiction involved in asserting the premises and denying the conclusion. There are many different types of inductive arguments. In our readings we are concerned with only two.

2a) *Enumerative (extrapolative) inductive inference.* This is an inference from the character of one or more examined cases to the character of one or more unexamined cases (or, more ambitiously, to a general principle concerning all such cases). Thus, after examining various pieces of copper and discovering that they all conduct heat rapidly, we infer that the next piece of copper we encounter will conduct heat rapidly (or, more ambitiously, that all pieces of copper will conduct heat rapidly). It is obvious that inferences of this sort play an enormous role both in everyday life and in science. All learning from experience involves forming expectations for the future on the basis of past experience. As an individual grows up in the world, he learns that fire is hot, that the ground will support his weight while the air will not, and so on. Each such piece of learning involves an inference from experienced cases to a generalization about all such cases (or at least an extrapolation to some not-yet-experienced cases). In science, low-level generalizations (for example, that copper is a good conductor of heat) are arrived at by such inferences; and these generalizations are the foundations on which the whole edifice of science rests.

We cannot make as sharp differentiations between forms of inductive arguments as we can with deductive arguments. Enumerative inductive arguments vary to an almost indefinite extent with respect to the number and variety of the observed cases, and with respect to the strength of the conclusion. (On the last point, consider the difference between the conclusions, "All pieces of copper conduct heat rapidly," "A certain (75%?) proportion of pieces of copper conduct heat rapidly," and "There is a strong probability that any given piece of copper will conduct heat rapidly.") One of the main problems in this area is working out these details. Just how great a quantity and variety of observed cases do we need to support how strong a conclusion? And what other factors affect the strength of the inference in a particular case? However, there are also more basic, less detailed questions concerning induction. In particular, there is an enormous philosophical literature devoted to the very basic question as to whether any sort of enumerative induction can be shown to have any validity. That is, does the citation of observed instance ever give *any* reason for beliefs about all or some unobserved instances?

It is to this last question that our selections are devoted. The essay by Russell is a classical statement of the problem; his point is, especially, that since it is not *inconsistent* to admit that observed instances of copper conduct heat but deny that this is true generally of copper, one may, until and unless some as yet unproduced argument is forthcoming, reasonably remain skeptical about the extrapolation. It is an idiosyncrasy of human psychology that we naturally draw such inferences, but no one has shown that they are justified. Edwards, in contrast, urges that Russell's doubts rest on a confusion. He concedes Russell's premise that there is no inconsistency in refusing to extrapolate (if there were, inductive inference would be deductive!). But he rejects Russell's inference, on the ground that Russell misunderstood what it is to be "reasonable." Indeed, he thinks that, once we see how "reasonable" or "justifiable" is used in English, we can see that it is an *analytic* truth that it is reasonable to subscribe to a rule of induction. Edward's solution of the "problem," then, is a semantical one: it relies on a thesis about the use of certain words in English. Reichenbach, whose theory is stated and criticized by Lenz in Reading 57, takes a very different line. He also agrees with Russell that there is no inconsistency in rejecting a rule of induction. But he thinks we have a *pragmatic* reason for adopting and follow- ing it, even though we cannot know that the guidance of the rule will lead to true beliefs. What is this pragmatic reason? It is, essentially, that there *may be* general laws of nature. If there are, believing in them will be very helpful for the guidance of life; if there are not, then we cannot guide our actions intelligently anyway. But, wherever there is such a law, following a principle of induction eventually will lead us to believe it. Contrariwise, if we follow no such rule (or follow, say, the opposite of the inductive rule), observation of instances conforming to a law will not lead us to believe in the law, even when there is one. So we do best to take our chances with following a principle of induction.

2b) Hypothetical inductve inference.   Hypothetical inductive inferences are different. Roughly, they are inferences from certain facts to propositions which, if true, would constitute the *best explanation* of these facts. For in- stance, Sherlock Holmes once told a man, much to his astonishment, that he had done much manual work, probably as a carpenter. Holmes inferred this from the observation that the man's right hand was larger than his left, along with some general principles he could justify by enumerative induction. Roughly, Holmes argued that the fact that the right hand was larger was best explained by supposing that the man had done labor primarily with his right hand (which would be the case were he a right-handed carpenter), and therefore asserted that the man had in fact done manual labor. More specifically, we can take Holmes to argue in the following way: Suppose we assume that the man has done manual labor, primarily with his right hand. Then it follows from the principle (known by enumerative induction) that muscles get larger when exercised, that his right hand will be larger. Thus the supposition explains the fact that his right hand is larger. But is this the *best* explanation? Well, we can look around for other possibilities. We might just suggest that the man was born that way. But we happen to know (again by enumerative induction) that people are rarely born with one hand de- cidedly larger than the other. So this assumption is initially implausible, as compared with the assumption that the man had done manual labor, say, as a carpenter. Holmes, on reflection, could not think of any assumption initially as plausible as the one that the man had worked with his right hand, which would lead us to expect, by principles themselves supportable by inductive reasoning, that the man's right hand would be larger. So he inferred that the man must have been employed in the way suggested.

The above account is very rough, but the student who has worked in the sciences will recognize at once that hypothetical inductive inference is of the highest importance in science. The whole of atomic physics, for in- stance, is based on it. The most substantial argument for the existence of God—the teleological argument—has the form of an hypothetical inference.

The reading from Carnap is primarily devoted to identifying this form of inference, particularly as it occurs in the advanced sciences. (There are some differences between its use in advanced science and Holmes's use of it, which are connected with the necessity of what Carnap calls "correspondence rules.") Carnap shows that this kind of reasoning is required for parts of science where enumerative inductive inference will clearly not take us, but where we want to go.

There is, of course, a problem of the justification for using this mode of inference, just as Hume pointed out there is for the case of enumerative inductive inference—there is no contradiction in accepting the premises of the inference, but denying the conclusion. Carnap does not say very much about this matter in the reading. Some philosophers would disagree with his suggestion that the value of the theories to which hypothetical reasoning leads in advanced science is in their fertility in predicting new empirical laws, and not in their capacity to provide a simpler total theory of things. The question, however, is one about which we ought to think, although it seems unlikely that anyone will really refuse to make use of hypothetical inductive inferences.

INFERENCES TO CONCLUSIONS ABOUT THE STATES OF MIND OF OTHER PERSONS

We turn now to a concrete problem that has great intrinsic interest, which it is useful to consider at the present juncture because it will enable us to sharpen our conception of various types of inductive inference, through seeing where a given type of inference will lead and where it will not lead. Hopefully, an examination of rules of inductive inference in this context will give some perspective on them, and raise questions in our minds that ought to trouble us.

Let us begin with a statement of the problem. Everybody in fact has strong beliefs, on occasion, about the states of mind of other persons. For instance, suppose an athlete has twisted his knee, and a physician is manipulating the leg to try to find out just what has gone wrong. The athlete is wincing; his face is pale; the perspiration is dripping; he says the manipulation is *very* painful. In these circumstances we should not doubt that he actually is feeling pain. But we cannot *observe* his pain in the way in which we can observe our own pain, or can observe his body. Evidently if we are justified in believing that he is in pain, it is because we can properly *infer* that he is, from something that we can observe. But exactly how? Will enumerative induction do the job?

Some philosophers have been skeptics about the mental states of other persons; they have denied that we are ever justified in believing statements about the mental states of others, and some have even denied that such statements have meaning. Behavioristic psychologists have taken this position, at least some of the time, and also some economists. The reader may be familiar with the "problem of interpersonal comparisons." This "problem" arises because of the difficulty of determining that the enjoyment or desire of one person is greater than that of another—for instance, that Jimmy, ecstatic at a big-league ball game, enjoyed the episode more than his bored sister. Indeed, the whole subject of "welfare economics" was produced by economists, in order to see how far there is a rational basis for economic policies if we assume that we cannot make any comparisons between the satisfaction which, say, a rich man might get out of ten dollars, and that which a poor or even starving man might get from that amount of money. Skepticism about other minds is evidently not purely a philosopher's puzzle!

In Reading 59, John Stuart Mill claims that inferences to the mental states of others are roughly examples of valid extrapolative induction. For example, I have had many experiences in which an insult has led to my feeling anger, which in turn has led to my responding with a cutting remark. Generalizing from these cases, I infer that this kind of sequence is typical of men generally. Thus, when I see another person respond to an insult with a cutting remark, I infer that a feeling of anger mediated between stimulus and response, even though, of course, I do not experience any such feeling in this case.

The validity of such argumentation has often been questioned, usually on the grounds that if my observation of the entire sequence is restricted to only one human being (myself), that is a very weak basis for a generalization to human beings generally.

In the other selection on this topic, Reading 60, H. H. Price emphasizes speech as a basis for the inference. When I hear sounds that I can construe as a statement coming from another body, and furthermore this statement conveys information to me, I am justified in supposing that certain kinds of mental acts (of perception and thought) were behind this sound-production. At first, Price presents his argument as having the same form as Mill's. (He calls this form of argument "analogical," but it seems to be roughly what Mill was calling a "generalization.") However, Price also suggests that his argument might be construed as a case of hypothetical inductive reasoning. On this latter interpretation it is an argument to the effect that in situations of the sort Price describes the sounds are best explained on the hypothesis that a mind has produced these sounds in an act of spontaneous thinking. This can serve as an example of hypothetical inference in everyday life.

51. Clarence Irving Lewis

Clarence Irving Lewis (1884–1964) was for many years
professor of philosophy at Harvard University.

The Justification of Empirical Beliefs

Empirical truth cannot be known except, finally, through presentations
of sense. . . . Our empirical knowledge rises as a structure of enormous
complexity, most parts of which are stabilized in measure by their
mutual support, but all of which rest, at bottom, on direct findings of
sense. Unless there should be some statements, or rather something
apprehensible and statable, whose truth is determined by given experience and is not determinable in any other way, there would be no
non-analytic affirmation whose truth could be determined at all, and no
such thing as empirical knowledge.

It is not, of course, intended to deny here that one objective statement can be confirmed by others; or to maintain that all corroborations
of belief are by direct reference to immediate experience. Some objective
beliefs are deductively derivable from others; and many—or even most
—objective beliefs are inductively supported by other, and perhaps better substantiated, objective beliefs. It is only contended that in such
cases where one objective belief is corroborated or supported by another,
(1) such confirmation is only provisional or hypothetical, and (2) it
must have reference *eventually* to confirmations by direct experience,
which alone is capable of being decisive and providing any sure foundation. If one objective statement, '*Q*,' is supported by another objective
statement, '*P*,' the assurance of the truth of '*Q*' is so far, only as good as
the evidence for '*P*.' Eventually such evidence must go back to something
which is certain—or, as we have said, go round in a circle and so fail
of any genuine basis whatever. Two propositions which have some
antecedent probability may, under certain circumstances, become more
credible because of their congruence with one another. But objective

Reprinted from *An Analysis of Knowledge and Valuation* by Clarence Irving Lewis
by permission of The Open Court Publishing Co., La Salle, Illinois. *An Analysis of
Knowledge and Valuation* by Clarence Irving Lewis. Copyright 1946 THE OPEN
COURT PUBLISHING COMPANY.

judgments, *none* of which could acquire probability by direct confirmations in experience, would gain no support by leaning up against one another in the fashion of the 'coherence theory of truth.' No empirical statement can become credible without a reference to experience.

Let us turn to the simplest kind of empirical cognition; knowledge by direct perception. . . .

I am descending the steps of Emerson Hall, and using my eyes to guide my feet. This is a habitual and ordinarily automatic action. But for this occasion, and in order that it may clearly constitute an instance of perceptual cognition instead of unconsidered behavior, I put enough attention on the process to bring the major features of it to clear consciousness. There is a certain visual pattern presented to me, a feeling of pressure on the soles of my feet, and certain muscle-sensations and feelings of balance and motion. And these items mentioned are fused together with others in one moving whole of presentation, within which they can be genuinely elicited but in which they do not exist as separate. Much of this presented content, I should find it difficult to put in words. . . . I know by my feelings when I am walking erect—or I think I do. And you, by putting yourself in my place, know how I feel—or think you do. That is all that is necessary, because we are here speaking of direct experience. You will follow me through the example by using your imagination, and understand what I mean—or what *you* would mean by the same language—in terms of your own experience. . . .

This given presentation—what looks like a flight of granite steps before me—leads to a prediction: "If I step forward and down, I shall come safely to rest on the step below." Ordinarily this prediction is unexpressed and would not even be explicitly thought. When so formulated, it is altogether too pedantic and portentous to fit the simple forward-looking quality of my conscious attitude. But unless I were prepared to assent to it, in case my attention were drawn to the matter, I should not now proceed as I do. . . . As I stand momentarily poised and looking before me, the presented visual pattern leads me to predict that acting in a certain manner—stepping forward and down—will be followed by a further empirical content, equally specific and recognizable but equally difficult to express without suggesting more than I now mean—the felt experience of coming to balance on the step below.

I adopt the mode of action envisaged; and the expected empirical sequent actually follows. My prediction is verified. The cognitive significance of the visual presentation which operated as cue, is found valid. This functioning of it was a genuine case of perceptual knowledge.

Let us take another and different example; different not in any important character of the situation involved, but different in the manner in which we shall consider it.

I believe there is a piece of white paper now before me. The reason that I believe this is that I see it: a certain visual presentation is given. By my belief includes the expectation that so long as I continue to look in the same direction, this presentation, with its qualitative character essentially unchanged, will persist; that if I move my eyes right, it will be displaced to the left in the visual field; that if I close them, it will disappear; and so on. If any of these predictions should, upon trial, be disproved, I should abandon my present belief in a real piece of paper before me, in favor of belief in some extraordinary after-image or some puzzling reflection or some disconcerting hallucination.

I do look in the same direction for a time; then turn my eyes; and after that try closing them: all with the expected results. My belief is so far corroborated. And these corroborations give me even greater assurance in any further predictions based upon it. But theoretically and ideally it is not completely verified, because the belief in a real piece of white paper now before me has further implications not yet tested: that what I see could be folded without cracking, as a piece of celluloid could not; that it would tear easily, as architect's drawing-cloth would not; that this experience will not be followed by waking in quite different surroundings; and others too numerous to mention. If it is a real piece of paper before me now, then I shall expect to find it here tomorrow with the number I just put on the corner: its reality and the real character I attribute in my belief imply innumerable possible verifications, or partial verifications, tomorrow and later on.

But looking back over what I have just written, I observe that I have succumbed to precisely those difficulties of formulation which have been mentioned. I have here spoken of predictable results of further tests I am not now making; of folding the paper and trying to tear it, and so on. Finding these predictions borne out would, in each case, be only a partial test, theoretically, of my belief in a real piece of paper. But it was my intention to mention predictions which, though only partial verification of the objective fact I believe in, could themselves be decisively tested. And there I have failed. That the paper, upon trial, would really be torn, will no more be evidenced with perfect certainty than is the presence of real paper before me now. It—provided it take place—will be a real objective event about which, theoretically, my momentary experience could deceive me. What I meant to speak of was certain expected experiences—of the *appearance and feeling* of paper being folded; of its *seeming* to be torn. These predictions of *experience*, would be decisively and indubitably borne out or disproved if I make trial of them. But on this point, the reader will most likely have caught my intent and improved upon my statement as made.

Let us return to the point we were discussing. We had just noted that even if the mentioned tests of the empirical belief about the paper should have been made, the result would not be a theoretically complete verification of it because there would be further and similar implications of the belief which would still not have been tested. In the case of an important piece of paper like a deed or a will, or an important issue like the question whether "Midsummer Night's Dream" was written by Shakespeare or by Bacon, such implications might be subject to test years or even centuries afterward. And a negative result might then rationally lead to doubt that a particular piece of paper lay on a certain desk at a certain time. My present example is no different except in importance: what I now believe has consequences which will be deter-minable indefinitely in the future.

. . . .

If now we ask ourselves how extensive such implied consequences of the belief are, it seems clear that in so simple a case as the white paper supposedly now before me, the number of them is inexhaustible. . . .

Let us now give attention to our two examples, and especially to the different manner in which the two have been considered. Both represent cases of knowledge by perception. And in both, while the sensory cues to this knowledge are provided by the given presentation, the cognitive significance is seen to lie not in the mere givenness of these sensory cues but in prediction based upon them. In both cases, it is such prediction the verification of which would mark the judgment made as true or as false.

In the first case, of using my eyes to guide me down the steps, the prediction made was a single one. Or if more than one was made, the others would presumably be like the one considered and this was taken as exemplary. This judgment is of the form, "If I act in manner A, the empirical eventuation will include E." We found difficulty in expressing, in language which would not say more than was intended, the content of the presentation which functioned as sensory cue. We encountered the same difficulty in expressing the mode of action, A, as we envisaged it in terms of our own felt experience and as we should recognize it, when performed, as the act we intended. And again this difficulty at-tended our attempt to express that expected presentational eventuality, E, the accrual of which was anticipated in our prediction. . . .

. . . .

This use of language to formulate a directly presented or presentable content of experience, may be called its *expressive* use. This is in con-trast to that more common intent of language, exemplified by, "I see (what in fact *is*) a flight of granite steps before me," which may be called its *objective* use. The distinctive character of expressive language, or the expressive use of language, is that such language signifies *appear-ances*. And in thus referring to appearances, or affirming what appears, such expressive language *neither asserts any objective reality of what appears nor denies any*. It is confined to description of the content of presentation itself.

In such expressive language, the cognitive judgment, "If I act in manner A, the empirical eventuality will include E," is one which can be verified by putting it to the test—supposing I can in fact put it to the test; can act in manner A. When the hypothesis of this hypothetical judg-ment is made true by my volition, the consequent is found true or found false by what follows; and this verification is decisive and complete, because nothing beyond the content of this passage of experience was implied in the judgment.

In the second example, as we considered it, what was judged was an *objective fact*: "A piece of white paper is now before me." This judgment will be false if the presentation is illusory; it will be false if what I see is not really paper; false if it is not really white but only looks white. This objective judgment also is one capable of corroboration. As in the other example, so here too, any test of the judgment would pretty surely involve some way of acting—*making* the test, as by continuing to look, or turning my eyes, or grasping to tear, etc.—and would be determined by finding or failing to find some expected result in experience. But in this example, if the result of any single test is as expected, it constitutes a partial verification of the judgment only; never one which is absolutely decisive and theoretically complete. This is so because, while the judgment, so far as it is significant, contains nothing which could not be tested, still it has a significance which outruns what any single test, or any limited set of tests, could exhaust. No matter how fully I may have investigated this objective fact, there will remain some theoretical possibility of mistake; there will be further consequences which must be thus and so if the judgment is true, and not all of these will have been determined. The possibility that such further tests, if made, might have a negative result, cannot be altogether precluded; and this possibility marks the judgment as, at the time in question, not fully verified and less than absolutely certain. To quibble about such possible doubts will not, in most cases, be common sense. But we are not trying to weigh the degree of theoretical dubiety which common-sense practicality should take account of, but to arrive at an accurate analysis of knowledge. This character of being further testable and less than theoretically certain characterizes every judgment of objective fact at all times; every judgment that such and such a real thing exists or has a certain objectively factual property, or that a certain objective event actually occurs, or that any objective state of affairs actually is the case.

A judgment of the type of the first example—prediction of a particular passage of experience, describable in expressive language—may be called *terminating*. It admits of decisive and complete verification or falsification. One of the type of the second example—judgment of objective fact which is always further verifiable and never completely verified —may be called *non-terminating*.

The conception is thus that there are three classes of empirical statements. First, there are formulations of what is presently given in experience. Only infrequently are such statements of the given actually made: there is seldom need to formulate what is directly and indubitably presented. They are also difficult or—it might plausibly be said—impossible to state in ordinary language, which, as usually understood, carries implications of something more and further verifiable which *ipso facto* is not given. But this difficulty of formulating precisely and only a given content of experience, is a relatively inessential consideration for the analysis of knowledge. That which we should thus attempt to formulate plays the same role whether it is expressed, or could be precisely expressed, or not. Without such apprehensions of direct and indubitable content of experience, there could be no basis for any empirical judgment, and no verification of one.

· ·

Second, there are terminating judgments, and statements of them. These represent some prediction of further possible experience. They find their cue in what is given: but what they state is something taken to be verifiable by some test which involves a way of acting. Thus terminating judgments are, in general, of the form, "If *A* then *E*," or "*S* being given, if *A* then *E*," where '*A*' represents some mode of action taken to be possible, '*E*' some expected consequent in experience, and '*S*' the sensory cue. The hypothesis '*A*' must here express something which, if made true by adopted action, will be *indubitably* true, and not, like a condition of my musculature in relation to the environment, an objective state of affairs only partially verified and not completely certain at the time. And the consequent '*E*' represents an eventuality of *experience*, directly and certainly recognizable in case it accrues; not a resultant objective event, whose factuality could have, and would call for, further verification. Thus both antecedent and consequent of this judgment, "If *A* then *E*," require to be formulated in expressive language; though we shall not call it an expressive statement, reserving that phrase for formulations of the given. . . .

Third, there are non-terminating judgments which assert objective reality; some state of affairs as actual. These are so named because, while there is nothing in the import of such objective statements which is intrinsically unverifiable, and hence nothing included in them which is not expressible by some terminating judgment, nevertheless no limited set of particular predictions of empirical eventualities can completely exhaust the significance of such an objective statement. This is true of the simplest and most trivial, as much as of the most important. The statement that something is blue, for example, or is square—as contrasted with merely looking blue or appearing to be square—has, always, implications of further possible experience, beyond what should, at any particular time, have been found true. Theoretically complete and absolute verification of any objective judgment would be a never-ending task: any actual verification of them is no more than partial; and our assurance of them is always, theoretically, less than certain.

Non-terminating judgments represents an enormous class; they include, in fact, pretty much all the empirical statements we habitually make. They range in type from the simplest assertion of perceived fact —"There is a piece of white paper now before me"—to the most impressive of scientific generalizations—"The universe is expanding." In general, the more important an assertion of empirical objective fact, the more remote it is from its eventual grounds. The laws of science, for example, are arrived at by induction from inductions from inductions - - -. But objective judgments are all alike in being non-terminating, and in having no other eventual foundation than data of given experience.

We turn now to matters affecting the justification of [terminating and non-terminating judgments]. . . .

It is obvious that, in general, the important ground of empirical belief is past experience of like cases. Whatever the problems which attend upon this commonplace conception that empirical knowledge depends on generalization from past experience, it is sufficiently evident that there is no plausible alternative to it. The issue remains, broadly speaking, that which Hume posed: either such generalization validly supports belief about the future or the presently unobserved, or empirical beliefs have no validity. Whatever it might be that we feel called upon to think about under the head of 'validity of knowledge,' it will remain a fact that the human attitudes called cognitive are taken in the light of past experience; and this being so, any 'validity of empirical knowledge' must require and turn upon the validity of thus extending to the future what past experience has taught. No amount of epistemological ingenuity could displace that commonplace understanding of the issue. . . .

Apprehension of an object, or of an objective property even, presumes these more primitive generalizations and, further, presumes validity of them. And the same is true for the apprehension of objective size, shape, color, or any other objective property. The apprehension of objects, objective events, and properties, is built upon and presumes as valid antecedent generalizations, in terms of direct experience, which are the only conceivable basis of our terminating judgments. When we generalize in terms of objective things and events, we are adding another story to our structure of knowledge, but built on the same foundation. And if in turn, we utilize such general facts about objects as premises of further induction; and conclusions so reached, perhaps, as basis for still higher generalization; our whole edifice still rests at bottom on these primitive generalizations which we make in terms of direct experience.

The extreme complexity, the many-storied character, of our cognition of those items we are most likely to recite if called on for examples of empirical knowledge, should receive at least some passing attention. Ordinarily this escapes our notice because, if challenged as to the validity of what we say we know, we usually satisfy ourselves by adducing proximate premises which validate it; and though these premises are themselves items of empirical knowledge, which in turn must have their justification, we do not feel called upon to pursue the matter to any final and incontestable grounds. Hence the remoteness of our everyday knowledge from its ultimate basis in actual experience, may easily pass unremarked. Yet however staggering by its mere complexity the business of going back to such initial premises might be, it is obvious that only in the light of such eventual grounding in actual experiences has anything the character of empirical knowledge; and only as the entire regress of such grounds should be valid throughout, could what we say we know be valid empirical knowledge.

However, if in view of such considerations, the structure of our knowledge begins to look like the task of erecting an Empire State Building out of toothpicks, we may remark in passing that the whole complexity of such construction is frequently inessential for the use we make of our knowledge. . . .

There are also two further considerations, equally obvious and inescapable, which contribute to the complexities and difficulties to be met in justification of our knowledge: the only experience which finally we can appeal to is our own; and the validity of memory is involved.

Ordinarily in citing the bases of what we say we know, we not only let ourselves off with mention of proximate premises, taken for granted, but also we avail ourselves of any handy and pertinent information, whether from our own experience or from other sources. And the extent to which we learn from others, is a distinctive feature marking the superiority of the human mentality. But obviously, what we thus learn must, in becoming knowledge for us, be credited; and credited by reference to grounds which are, eventually, those of first-person experience. It can have such credibility only by reference to our own past experience of receiving such reports and our subsequent experience of finding true or finding false what was reported. Receiving information from others and observing their behavior is—so experience has taught us—a relatively painless and a particularly fruitful mode of acquiring knowledge. But it is merely a complex way of learning from certain experiences of our own. And apart from a certain complexity which characterizes the interpretation of verbal signals, it is not particularly different from other ways of being advised of objective fact—not particularly different, for example, from learning by the reading of recording instruments. All knowledge is knowledge of someone; and ultimately no one can have any ground for his beliefs which does not lie within his own experience.

This consideration accentuates the importance of questions concerning the validity of memory. Because when we say that the ground of empirical judgment is past experience, it cannot escape us that past experience as such cannot be literally repossessed. And there is here the particular difficulty that such evidence as we have for crediting what is remembered, includes evidence that memory is not universally reliable; and that therefore to remember a thing is not to be certain of it but at best to have a warrant for crediting it as probable. Past experience on the basis of which we say that we generalize is not an ultimate datum for generalization from experience. It is only the memory of such past experience which is the actually given datum. And when this fact is taken into account, it may seem that, in order actually to validate the kind of beliefs we commonly hold and express, we are required not only to build an Empire State Building out of toothpicks but to build it out of toothpicks most of which we haven't got and cannot be given.

52. Immanuel Kant

Immanuel Kant (1724–1804) was a professor at the University
of Königsberg. His work has probably elicited more
discussion than that of any other philosopher of modern
times.

The Concept of Synthetic A Priori *Knowledge, and the* *Nature of Mathematics*

I. The Distinction between Pure and Empirical Knowledge

There can be no doubt that all our knowledge begins with experience.
For how should our faculty of knowledge be awakened into action did
not objects affecting our senses partly of themselves produce representations, partly arouse the activity of our understanding to compare these
representations, and, by combining or separating them, work up the raw
material of the sensible impressions into that knowledge of objects which
is entitled experience? In the order of time, therefore, we have no knowledge antecedent to experience, and with experience all our knowledge
begins.

But though all our knowledge begins with experience, it does not

This selection is drawn from his *Critique of Pure Reason*, first published in 1781,
translated 1956 by Norman Kemp Smith, published by St. Martin's Press, New York,
and Macmillan & Co., Ltd., London. Reprinted by permission of Macmillan London
and Basingstoke, and St. Martin's Press.

follow that it all arises out of experience. For it may well be that even our empirical knowledge is made up of what we receive through impressions and of what our own faculty of knowledge (sensible impressions serving merely as the occasion) supplies from itself. If our faculty of knowledge makes any such addition, it may be that we are not in a position to distinguish it from the raw material, until with long practice of attention we have become skilled in separating it.

This, then, is a question which at least calls for closer examination, and does not allow of any off-hand answer:—whether there is any knowledge that is thus independent of experience and even of all impressions of the senses. Such knowledge is entitled *a priori*, and distinguished from the *empirical*, which has its sources *a posteriori*, that is, in experience.

The expression '*a priori*' does not, however, indicate with sufficient precision the full meaning of our question. For it has been customary to say, even of much knowledge that is derived from empirical sources, that we have it or are capable of having it *a priori*, meaning thereby that we do not derive it immediately from experience, but from a universal rule—a rule which is itself, however, borrowed by us from experience. Thus we would say of a man who undermined the foundations of his house, that he might have known *a priori* that it would fall, that is, that he need not have waited for the experience of its actual falling. But still he could not know this completely *a priori*. For he had first to learn through experience that bodies are heavy, and therefore fall when their supports are withdrawn.

In what follows, therefore, we shall understand by *a priori* knowledge, not knowledge independent of this or that experience, but knowledge absolutely independent of all experience. Opposed to it is empirical knowledge, which is knowledge possible only *a posteriori*, that is, through experience. *A priori* modes of knowledge are entitled pure when there is no admixture of anything empirical. Thus, for instance, the proposition, 'every alteration has its cause,' while an *a priori* proposition, is not a pure proposition, because alteration is a concept which can be derived only from experience.

II. We are in Possession of Certain Modes of <u>A Priori</u> Knowledge, and Even the Common Understanding Is Never without Them

What we here require is a criterion by which to distinguish with certainty between pure and empirical knowledge. Experience teaches us that a thing is so and so, but not that it cannot be otherwise. First, then, if we have a proposition which in being thought is thought as *necessary*, it is an *a priori* judgment; and if, besides, it is not derived from any proposition except one which also has the validity of a necessary judgment, it is an absolutely *a priori* judgment. Secondly, experience never confers on its judgments true or strict, but only assumed and comparative *universality*, through induction. We can properly only say, therefore, that, so far as we have hitherto observed, there is no exception to this or that rule. If, then, a judgment is thought with strict universality, that is, in such manner that no exception is allowed as possible, it is not derived from experience, but is valid absolutely *a priori*. Empirical universality is only an arbitrary extension of a validity holding in most cases to one which holds in all, for instance, in the proposition, 'all bodies are heavy.' When, on the other hand, strict universality is essential to a judgment, this indicates a special source of knowledge, namely, a faculty of *a priori* knowledge. Necessity and strict universality are thus sure criteria of *a priori* knowledge, and are inseparable from one another. But since in the employment of these criteria the contingency of judgments is sometimes more easily shown than their empirical limitation, or, as sometimes also happens, their unlimited universality can be more convincingly proved than their necessity, it is advisable to use the two criteria separately, each by itself being infallible.

Now it is easy to show that there actually are in human knowledge judgments which are necessary and in the strictest sense universal, and which are therefore pure *a priori* judgments. If an example from the sciences be desired, we have only to look to any of the propositions of mathematics; if we seek an example from the understanding in its quite ordinary employment, the proposition, 'every alteration must have a cause,' will serve our purpose. In the latter case, indeed, the very concept of a cause so manifestly contains the concept of a necessity of connection with an effect and of the strict universality of the rule, that the concept would be altogether lost if we attempted to derive it, as Hume has done, from a repeated association of that which happens with that which precedes, and from a custom of connecting representations, a custom originating in this repeated association, and constituting therefore a merely subjective necessity. Even without appealing to such examples, it is possible to show that pure *a priori* principles are indispensable for the possibility of experience, and so to prove their existence *a priori*. For whence could experience derive its certainty, if all the rules, according to which it proceeds, were always themselves empirical, and therefore contingent? Such rules could hardly be regarded as first principles. At present, however, we may be content to have established the fact that our faculty of knowledge does have a pure employment, and to have shown what are the criteria of such an employment.

Such *a priori* origin is manifest in certain concepts, no less than in judgments. If we remove from our empirical concept of a body, one by one, every feature in it which is [merely] empirical, the colour, the hardness or softness, the weight, even the impenetrability, there still remains the space which the body (now entirely vanished) occupied, and this cannot be removed. Again, if we remove from our empirical concept of any object, corporeal or incorporeal, all properties which experience has taught us, we yet cannot take away that property through which the object is thought as substance or as inhering in a substance (although this concept of substance is more determinate than that of an object in general). Owing, therefore, to the necessity, with which this concept of substance forces itself upon us, we have no option save to admit that it has its seat in our faculty of *a priori* knowledge.

III. Philosophy Stands in Need of a Science Which Shall Determine the Possibility, the Principles, and the Extent of all <u>A Priori</u> Knowledge

But what is still more extraordinary than all the preceding is this, that certain modes of knowledge leave the field of all possible experiences and have the appearance of extending the scope of our judgments beyond all limits of experience, and this by means of concepts to which no corresponding object can ever be given in experience.

It is precisely by means of the latter modes of knowledge, in a realm beyond the world of the senses, where experience can yield neither guidance nor correction, that our reason carries on those enquiries which owing to their importance we consider to be far more excellent, and in their purpose far more lofty, than all that the understanding can learn in the field of appearances. Indeed we prefer to run every risk of error rather than desist from such urgent enquiries, on the ground of their dubious character, or from disdain and indifference. These unavoidable problems set by pure reason itself are *God, freedom*, and *immortality*. The science which, with all its preparations, is in its final intention directed solely to their solution is metaphysics; and its procedure is at first dogmatic, that is, it confidently sets itself to this task without any previous examination of the capacity or incapacity of reason for so great an undertaking.

Now it does indeed seem natural that, as soon as we have left the ground of experience, we should, through careful enquiries, assure ourselves as to the foundations of any building that we propose to erect, not making use of any knowledge that we possess without first determining whence it has come, and not trusting to principles without knowing their origin. It is natural, that is to say, that the question should first be considered, how the understanding can arrive at all this knowledge *a priori*, and what extent, validity, and worth it may have. Nothing, indeed, could be more natural, if by the term 'natural' we signify what fittingly and reasonably ought to happen. But if we mean by 'natural' what ordinarily happens, then on the contrary nothing is more natural and more intelligible than the fact that this enquiry has been so long neglected. For one part of this knowledge, the mathematical, has long been of established reliability, and so gives rise to a favourable presumption as regards the other part, which may yet be of quite different nature. Besides, once we are outside the circle of experience, we can be sure of not being *contradicted* by experience. The charm of extending our knowledge is so great that nothing short of encountering a direct contradiction can suffice to arrest us in our course; and this can be avoided, if we are careful in our fabrications—which none the less will still remain fabrications. Mathematics gives us a shining example of how far, independently of experience, we can progress in *a priori* knowledge. It does, indeed, occupy itself with objects and with knowledge solely in so far as they allow of being exhibited in intuition. But this circumstance is easily overlooked, since this intuition can itself be given *a priori*, and is therefore hardly to be distinguished from a bare and pure concept. Misled by

628

such a proof of the power of reason, the demand for the extension of knowledge recognises no limits. The light dove, cleaving the air in her free flight, and feeling its resistance, might imagine that its flight would be still easier in empty space. It was thus that Plato left the world of the senses, as setting too narrow limits to the understanding, and ventured out beyond it on the wings of the ideas, in the empty space of the pure understanding. He did not observe that with all his efforts he made no advance—meeting no resistance that might, as it were, serve as a support upon which he could take a stand, to which he could apply his powers, and so set his understanding in motion. It is, indeed, the common fate of human reason to complete its speculative structures as speedily as may be, and only afterwards to enquire whether the foundations are reliable. All sorts of excuses will then be appealed to, in order to reassure us of their solidity, or rather indeed to enable us to dispense altogether with so late and so dangerous an enquiry. But what keeps us, during the actual building, free from all apprehension and suspicion, and flatters us with a seeming thoroughness, is this other circumstance, namely, that a great, perhaps the greatest, part of the business of our reason consists in analysis of the concepts which we already have of objects. This analysis supplies us with a considerable body of knowledge, which, while nothing but explanation or elucidation of what has already been thought in our concepts, though in a confused manner, is yet prized as being, at least as regards its form, new insight. But so far as the matter or content is concerned, there has been no extension of our previously possessed concepts, but only an analysis of them. Since this procedure yields real knowledge *a priori*, which progresses in an assured and useful fashion, reason is so far misled as surreptitiously to introduce, without itself being aware of so doing, assertions of an entirely different order, in which it attaches to given concepts others completely foreign to them, and moreover attaches them *a priori*. And yet it is not known how reason can be in position to do this. Such a question is never so much as thought of. I shall therefore at once proceed to deal with the difference between these two kinds of knowledge.

IV. The Distinction between Analytic and Synthetic Judgments

In all judgments in which the relation of a subject to the predicate is thought (I take into consideration affirmative judgments only, the subsequent application to negative judgments being easily made), this relation is possible in two different ways. Either the predicate B belongs to the subject A, as something which is (covertly) contained in this concept A; or B lies outside the concept A, although it does indeed stand in connection with it. In the one case I entitle the judgment analytic, in the other synthetic. Analytic judgments (affirmative) are therefore those in which the connection of the predicate with the subject is thought through identity; those in which this connection is thought without identity should be entitled synthetic. The former, as adding nothing through the predicate to the concept of the subject, but merely breaking it up into

629

those constituent concepts that have all along been thought in it, although confusedly, can also be entitled explicative. The latter, on the other hand, add to the concept of the subject a predicate which has not been in any wise thought in it, and which no analysis could possibly extract from it; and they may therefore be entitled ampliative. If I say, for instance, 'All bodies are extended,' this is an analytic judgment. For I do not require to go beyond the concept which I connect with 'body' in order to find extension as bound up with it. To meet with this predicate, I have merely to analyse the concept, that is, to become conscious to myself of the manifold which I always think in that concept. The judgment is therefore analytic. But when I say, 'All bodies are heavy,' the predicate is something quite different from anything that I think in the mere concept of body in general; and the addition of such a predicate therefore yields a synthetic judgment.

Judgments of experience, as such, are one and all synthetic. For it would be absurd to found an analytic judgment on experience. Since, in framing the judgment, I must not go outside my concept, there is no need to appeal to the testimony of experience in its support. That a body is extended is a proposition that holds *a priori* and is not empirical. For, before appealing to experience, I have already in the concept of body all the conditions required for my judgment. I have only to extract from it, in accordance with the principle of contradiction, the required predicate, and in so doing can at the same time become conscious of the necessity of the judgment—and that is what experience could never have taught me. On the other hand, though I do not include in the concept of a body in general the predicate 'weight,' none the less this concept indicates an object of experience through one of its parts, and I can add to that part other parts of this same experience, as in this way belonging together with the concept. From the start I can apprehend the concept of body analytically through the characters of extension, impenetrability, figure, etc., all of which are thought in the concept. Now, however, looking back on the experience from which I have derived this concept of body, and finding weight to be invariably connected with the above characters, I attach it as a predicate to the concept; and in doing so I attach it synthetically, and am therefore extending my knowledge. The possibility of the synthesis of the predicate 'weight' with the concept of 'body' thus rests upon experience. While the one concept is not contained in the other, they yet belong to one another, though only contingently, as parts of a whole, namely, of an experience which is itself a synthetic combination of intuitions.

But in *a priori* synthetic judgments this help is entirely lacking. [I do not here have the advantage of looking around in the field of experience.] Upon what, then, am I to rely, when I seek to go beyond the concept A, and to know that another concept B is connected with it? Through what is the synthesis made possible? Let us take the proposition, 'Everything which happens has its cause.' In the concept of 'something which happens,' I do indeed think an existence which is preceded by a time, etc., and from this concept analytic judgments may be obtained. But the concept of a 'cause' lies entirely outside the other concept, and signifies something different from 'that which happens,' and is not therefore in any way contained in this latter representation. How come I then to predicate of that which happens something quite different, and to apprehend that the concept of cause, though not contained in it, yet belongs, and indeed necessarily belongs, to it? What is here the unknown = X which gives support to the understanding when it believes that it can discover outside the concept A a predicate B foreign to this concept, which it yet at the same time considers to be connected with it? It cannot be experience, because the suggested principle has connected the second representation with the first, not only with greater universality, but also with the character of necessity, and therefore completely *a priori* and on the basis of mere concepts. Upon such synthetic, that is, ampliative principles, all our *a priori* speculative knowledge must ultimately rest; analytic judgments are very important, and indeed necessary, but only for obtaining that clearness in the concepts which is requisite for such a sure and wide synthesis as will lead to a genuinely new addition to all previous knowledge.

V. In All Theoretical Sciences of Reason Synthetic <u>A Priori</u> Judgments Are Contained as Principles

1. *All mathematical judgments, without exception, are synthetic.* This fact, though incontestably certain and in its consequences very important, has hitherto escaped the notice of those who are engaged in the analysis of human reason, and is, indeed, directly opposed to all their conjectures. For as it was found that all mathematical inferences proceed in accordance with the principle of contradiction (which the nature of all apodeictic certainty requires), it was supposed that the fundamental propositions of the science can themselves be known to be true through that principle. This is an erroneous view. For though a synthetic proposition can indeed be discerned in accordance with the principle of contradiction, this can only be if another synthetic proposition is presupposed, and if it can then be apprehended as following from this other proposition; it can never be so discerned in and by itself.

First of all, it has to be noted that mathematical propositions, strictly so called, are always judgments *a priori*, not empirical; because they carry with them necessity, which cannot be derived from experience. If this be demurred to, I am willing to limit my statement to *pure* mathematics, the very concept of which implies that it does not contain empirical, but only pure *a priori* knowledge.

We might, indeed, at first suppose that the proposition $7 + 5 = 12$ is a merely analytic proposition, and follows by the principle of contradiction from the concept of a sum of 7 and 5. But if we look more closely we find that the concept of the sum of 7 and 5 contains nothing save the union of the two numbers into one, and in this no thought is being taken as to what that single number may be which combines both. The concept of 12 is by no means already thought in merely thinking this union of 7 and 5; and I may analyse my concept of such a possible sum as long as I please, still I shall never find the 12 in it. We have to go outside these concepts, and call in the aid of the intuition which corresponds to one of them, our five fingers, for instance, or, as Segner does in his *Arithmetic*, five points, adding to the concept of 7, unit by unit, the five given in intuition. For starting with the number 7, and for the concept of 5 calling in the aid of the fingers of my hand as intuition, I now add one by one to the number 7 the units which I previously took together to form the number 5, and with the aid of that figure [the hand] see the number 12 come into being. That 5 should be added to 7, I have indeed already thought in the concept of a sum $= 7 + 5$, but not that this sum is equivalent to the number 12. Arithmetical propositions are therefore always synthetic. This is still more evident if we take larger numbers. For it is then obvious that, however we might turn and twist our concepts, we could never, by the mere analysis of them, and without the aid of intuition, discover what [the number is that] is the sum.

Just as little is any fundamental proposition of pure geometry analytic. That the straight line between two points is the shortest, is a synthetic proposition. For my concept of *straight* contains nothing of quantity, but only of quality. The concept of the shortest is wholly an addition, and cannot be derived, through any process of analysis, from the concept of the straight line. Intuition, therefore, must here be called in; only by its aid is the synthesis possible. What here causes us commonly to believe that the predicate of such apodeictic judgments is already contained in our concept, and that the judgment is therefore analytic, is merely the ambiguous character of the terms used. We are required to join in thought a certain predicate to a given concept, and this necessity is inherent in the concepts themselves. But the question is not what we *ought* to join in thought to the given concept, but what we *actually* think in it, even if only obscurely; and it is then manifest that, while the predicate is indeed attached necessarily to the concept, it is so in virtue of an intuition which must be added to the concept, not as thought in the concept itself.

Some few fundamental propositions, presupposed by the geometrician, are, indeed, really analytic, and rest on the principle of contradiction. But, as identical propositions, they serve only as links in the chain of method and not as principles; for instance, $a = a$; the whole is equal to itself; or $(a + b) > a$, that is, the whole is greater than its part. And even these propositions, though they are valid according to pure concepts, are only admitted in mathematics because they can be exhibited in intuition.

2. *Natural science (physics) contains* a priori *synthetic judgments as principles.* I need cite only two such judgments: that in all changes of the material world the quantity of matter remains unchanged; and that in all communication of motion, action and reaction must always be equal. Both propositions, it is evident, are not only necessary, and therefore in their origin a priori, but also synthetic. For in the concept of matter I do not think its permanence, but only its presence in the space which it occupies. I go outside and beyond the concept of matter, joining to it *a priori* in thought something which I have not thought *in* it. The

proposition is not, therefore, analytic, but synthetic, and yet is thought *a priori;* and so likewise are the other propositions of the pure part of natural science.

3. *Metaphysics,* even if we look upon it as having hitherto failed in all its endeavours, is yet, owing to the nature of human reason, a quite indispensable science, and *ought to contain* a priori *synthetic knowledge.* For its business is not merely to analyse concepts which we make for ourselves *a priori* of things, and thereby to clarify them analytically, but to extend our *a priori* knowledge. And for this purpose we must employ principles which add to the given concept something that was not contained in it, and through *a priori* synthetic judgments venture out so far that experience is quite unable to follow us, as, for instance, in the proposition, that the world must have a first beginning, and such like. Thus metaphysics consists, at least *in intention,* entirely of *a priori* synthetic propositions.

VI. The General Problem of Pure Reason

Much is already gained if we can bring a number of investigations under the formula of a single problem. For we not only lighten our own task, by defining it accurately, but make it easier for others, who would test our results, to judge whether or not we have succeeded in what we set out to do. Now the proper problem of pure reason is contained in the question: How are *a priori* synthetic judgments possible?

That metaphysics has hitherto remained in so vacillating a state of uncertainty and contradiction, is entirely due to the fact that this problem, and perhaps even the distinction between analytic and synthetic judgments, has never previously been considered. Upon the solution of this problem, or upon a sufficient proof that the possibility which it desires to have explained does in fact not exist at all, depends the success or failure of metaphysics. Among philosophers, David Hume came nearest to envisaging this problem, but still was very far from conceiving it with sufficient definiteness and universality. He occupied himself exclusively with the synthetic proposition regarding the connection of an effect with its cause (*principium causalitatis*), and he believed himself to have shown that such an *a priori* proposition is entirely impossible. If we accept his conclusions, then all that we call metaphysics is a mere delusion whereby we fancy ourselves to have rational insight into what, in actual fact, is borrowed solely from experience, and under the influence of custom has taken the illusory semblance of necessity. If he had envisaged our problem in all its universality, he would never have been guilty of this statement, so destructive of all pure philosophy. For he would then have recognised that, according to his own argument, pure mathematics, as certainly containing *a priori* synthetic propositions, would also not be possible; and from such an assertion his good sense would have saved him.

In the solution of the above problem, we are at the same time deciding as to the possibility of the employment of pure reason in establishing and developing all those sciences which contain a theoretical *a priori* knowledge of objects, and have therefore to answer the questions:

· How is pure mathematics possible?
· How is pure science of nature possible?

Since these sciences actually exist, it is quite proper to ask *how* they are possible; for that they must be possible is proved by the fact that they exist. But the poor progress which has hitherto been made in metaphysics, and the fact that no system yet propounded can, in view of the essential purpose of metaphysics, be said really to exist, leaves everyone sufficient ground for doubting as to its possibility.

Yet, in a certain sense, this *kind of knowledge* is to be looked upon as given; that is to say, metaphysics actually exists, if not as a science, yet still as natural disposition (*metaphysica naturalis*). For human reason, without being moved merely by the idle desire for extent and variety of knowledge, proceeds impetuously, driven on by an inward need, to questions such as cannot be answered by any empirical employment of reason, or by principles thence derived. Thus in all men, as soon as their reason has become ripe for speculation, there has always existed and will always continue to exist some kind of metaphysics. And so we have the question:

How is metaphysics, as natural disposition, possible?

that is, how from the nature of universal human reason do those questions arise which pure reason propounds to itself, and which it is impelled by its own need to answer as best it can?

But since all attempts which have hitherto been made to answer these natural questions—for instance, whether the world has a beginning or is from eternity—have always met with unavoidable contradictions, we cannot rest satisfied with the mere natural disposition to metaphysics, that is, with the pure faculty of reason itself, from which, indeed, some sort of metaphysics (be it what it may) always arises. It must be possible for reason to attain to certainty whether we know or do not know the objects of metaphysics, that is, to come to a decision either in regard to the objects of its enquiries or in regard to the capacity or incapacity of reason to pass any judgment upon them, so that we may either with confidence extend our pure reason or set to it sure and determinate limits. This last question, which arises out of the previous general problem, may, rightly stated, take the form:

How is metaphysics, as science, possible?

Thus the critique of reason, in the end, necessarily leads to scientific knowledge; while its dogmatic employment, on the other hand, lands us in dogmatic assertions to which other assertions, equally specious, can always be opposed—that is, in *scepticism.*

This science cannot be of any very formidable prolixity, since it has to deal not with the objects of reason, the variety of which is inexhaustible, but only with itself and the problems which arise entirely from within itself, and which are imposed upon it by its own nature, not by the nature of things which are distinct from it. When once reason has learnt completely to understand its own power in respect of objects which can be presented to it in experience, it should easily be able to determine, with completeness and certainty, the extent and the limits of its attempted employment beyond the bounds of all experience.

We may, then, and indeed we must, regard as abortive all attempts, hitherto made, to establish a metaphysic *dogmatically*. For the analytic part in any such attempted system, namely, the mere analysis of the concepts that inhere in our reason *a priori*, is by no means the aim of, but only a preparation for, metaphysics proper, that is, the extension of its *a priori* synthetic knowledge. For such a purpose, the analysis of concepts is useless, since it merely shows what is contained in these concepts, not how we arrive at them *a priori*. A solution of this latter problem is required, that we may be able to determine the valid employment of such concepts in regard to the objects of all knowledge in general. Nor is much self-denial needed to give up these claims, seeing that the undeniable, and in the dogmatic procedure of reason also unavoidable, contradictions of reason with itself have long since undermined the authority of every metaphysical system yet propounded. Greater firmness will be required if we are not to be deterred by inward difficulties and outward opposition from endeavouring, through application of a method entirely different from any hitherto employed, at last to bring to a prosperous and fruitful growth a science indispensable to human reason—a science whose every branch may be cut away but whose root cannot be destroyed.

53. John Stuart Mill

Logic and Mathematics Based on Observation

The Theorems of Geometry Are Necessarily True Only in the Sense of Following from the Axioms

§ 1. If, as laid down in the two preceding chapters, the foundation of all sciences, even deductive or demonstrative sciences, is Induction; if every step in the ratiocinations even of geometry is an act of induction; and if a train of reasoning is but bringing many inductions to bear upon the same subject of inquiry, and drawing a case within one induction by means of another; wherein lies the peculiar certainty always ascribed to the sciences which are entirely, or almost entirely, deductive? Why are they called the Exact Sciences? Why are mathematical certainty, and the evidence of demonstration, common phrases to express the very highest degree of assurance attainable by reason? Why are mathematics by almost all philosophers, and (by some) even those branches of natural philosophy which, through the medium of mathematics, have been converted into deductive sciences, considered to be independent of the evidence of experience and observation, and characterized as systems of Necessary Truth?

The answer I conceive to be, that this character of necessity, ascribed to the truths of mathematics and even (with some reservations to be hereafter made) the peculiar certainty attributed to them, is an illusion; in order to sustain which, it is necessary to suppose that those truths relate to, and express the properties of purely imaginary objects. It is

From John Stuart Mill, *System of Logic*, Book II, Chapters 5, 6, and 7.

acknowledged that the conclusions of geometry are deduced, partly at least, from the so-called Definitions, and that those definitions are assumed to be correct representations, as far as they go, of the objects with which geometry is conversant. Now we have pointed out that, from a definition as such, no proposition, unless it be one concerning the meaning of a word, can ever follow; and that what apparently follows from a definition, follows in reality from an implied assumption that there exists a real thing conformable thereto. This assumption in the case of the definitions of geometry, is not strictly true: there exist no real things exactly conformable to the definitions. There exist no points without magnitude; no lines without breadth, nor perfectly straight; no circles with all their radii exactly equal, nor squares with all their angles perfectly right. It will perhaps be said that the assumption does not extend to the actual, but only to the possible, existence of such things. I answer that, according to any test we have of possibility, they are not even possible. Their existence, so far as we can form any judgment, would seem to be inconsistent with the physical constitution of our planet at least, if not of the universe. To get rid of this difficulty, and at the same time to save the credit of the supposed system of necessary truth, it is customary to say that the points, lines, circles, and squares which are the subject of geometry, exist in our conceptions merely, and are part of our minds; which minds, by working on their own materials, construct an *à priori* science, the evidence of which is purely mental, and has nothing whatever to do with outward experience. By howsoever high authorities this doctrine may have been sanctioned, it appears to me psychologically incorrect. The points, lines, circles, and squares which any one has in his mind, are (I apprehend) simply copies of the points, lines, circles, and squares which he has known in his experience. Our idea of a point, I apprehend to be simply our idea of the *minimum visible*, the smallest portion of surface which we can see. A line as defined by geometers is wholly inconceivable. We can reason about a line as if it had no breadth; because we have a power, which is the foundation of all the control we can exercise over the operations of our minds; the power, when a perception is present to our senses or a conception to our intellects, of *attending* to a part only of that perception or conception, instead of the whole. But we cannot *conceive* a line without breadth; we can form no mental picture of such a line: all the lines which we have in our minds are lines possessing breadth. If any one doubts this, we may refer him to his own experience. I much question if any one who fancies that he can conceive what is called a mathematical line, thinks so from the evidence of his consciousness: I suspect it is rather because he supposes that unless such a conception were possible, mathematics could not exist as a science: a supposition which there will be no difficulty in showing to be entirely groundless.

Since, then, neither in nature, nor in the human mind, do there exist any objects exactly corresponding to the definitions of geometry, while yet that science cannot be supposed to be conversant about non-entities; nothing remains but to consider geometry as conversant with such lines, angles, and figures, as really exist; and the definitions, as they are called, must be regarded as some of our first and most obvious generalizations concerning those natural objects. The correctness of those generalizations, *as* generalizations, is without a flaw: the equality of all the radii of a circle is true of all circles, so far as it is true of any one: but it is not exactly true of any circle; it is only nearly true; so nearly that no error of any importance in practice will be incurred by feigning it to be exactly true. When we have occasion to extend these inductions, or their consequences, to cases in which the error would be appreciable—to lines of perceptible breadth or thickness, parallels which deviate sensibly from equidistance, and the like—we correct our conclusions, by combining with them a fresh set of propositions relating to the aberration; just as we also take in propositions relating to the physical or chemical properties of the material, if those properties happen to introduce any modification into the result; which they easily may, even with respect to figure and magnitude, as in the case, for instance, of expansion by heat. So long, however, as there exists no practical necessity for attending to any of the properties of the object except its geometrical properties, or to any of the natural irregularities in those, it is convenient to neglect the consideration of the other properties and of the irregularities, and to reason as if these did not exist: accordingly, we formally announce in the definitions, that we intend to proceed on this plan. But it is an error to suppose, because we resolve to confine our attention to a certain number of the properties of an object, that we therefore conceive, or have an idea of, the object denuded of its other properties. We are thinking, all the time, of precisely such objects as we have seen and touched, and with all the properties which naturally belong to them; but for scientific convenience, we feign them to be divested of all properties, except those which are material to our purpose, and in regard to which we design to consider them.

The peculiar accuracy, supposed to be characteristic of the first principles of geometry, thus appears to be fictitious. The assertions on which the reasonings of the science are founded, do not, any more than in other sciences, exactly correspond with the fact; but we suppose that they do so, for the sake of tracing the consequences which follow from the supposition. The opinion of Dugald Stewart respecting the foundations of geometry, is, I conceive, substantially correct; that it is built on hypotheses; that it owes to this alone the peculiar certainty supposed to distinguish it; and that in any science whatever, by reasoning from a set of hypotheses, we may obtain a body of conclusions as certain as those of geometry, that is, as strictly in accordance with the hypotheses, and as irresistibly compelling assent, *on condition* that those hypotheses are true.

When, therefore, it is affirmed that the conclusions of geometry are necessary truths, the necessity consists in reality only in this, that they correctly follow from the suppositions from which they are deduced. Those suppositions are so far from being necessary, that they are not even true; they purposely depart, more or less widely, from the truth. The only sense in which necessity can be ascribed to the conclusions of any scientific investigation, is that of legitimately following from some assumption, which, by the conditions of the inquiry, is not to be questioned. In this relation, of course, the derivative truths of every deductive science must stand to the inductions, or assumptions, on which the science is founded, and which, whether true or untrue, certain or doubtful in themselves, are always supposed certain for the purposes of the particular science. And therefore the conclusions of all deductive sciences were said by the ancients to be necessary propositions. We have observed already that to be predicated necessarily was characteristic of the predictable Proprium, and that a proprium was any property of a thing which could be deduced from its essence, that is, from the properties included in its definition.

. . . .

The Axioms of Geometry Are Generalizations of Observations

§ 4. It remains to inquire, what is the ground of our belief in axioms—what is the evidence on which they rest? I answer, they are experimental truths; generalizations from observation. The proposition, Two straight lines cannot inclose a space—or in other words, two straight lines which have once met do not meet again, but continue to diverge—is an induction from the evidence of our senses.

. . . .

It is not necessary to show that the truths which we call axioms are originally *suggested* by observation, and that we should never have known that two straight lines cannot inclose a space if we had never seen a straight line: thus much being admitted by Dr. Whewell, and by all, in recent times, who have taken his view of the subject. But they contend, that it is not experience which *proves* the axiom; but that its truth is perceived *à priori*, by the constitution of the mind itself, from the first moment when the meaning of the proposition is apprehended; and without any necessity for verifying it by repeated trials, as is requisite in the case of truths really ascertained by observation.

They cannot, however, but allow that the truth of the axiom, Two straight lines cannot inclose a space, even if evident independently of experience, is also evident from experience. Whether the axiom needs confirmation or not, it receives confirmation in almost every instant of our lives; since we cannot look at any two straight lines which intersect one another, without seeing that from that point they continue to diverge more and more. Experimental proof crowds in upon us in such endless profusion, and without one instance in which there can be even a suspicion of an exception to the rule, that we should soon have stronger ground for believing the axiom, even as an experimental truth, than we have for almost any of the general truths which we confessedly learn from the evidence of our senses. Independently of *à priori* evidence we should certainly believe it with an intensity of conviction far greater than we accord to any ordinary physical truth: and this too at a time of life much earlier than that from which we date almost any part of our acquired knowledge, and much too early to admit of our retaining any recollection of the history of our intellectual operations at that period. Where then is the necessity for assuming that our recognition of these truths has a different origin from the rest of our knowledge, when its existence is perfectly accounted for by supposing its origin to be the same? when the causes which produce belief in all other instances, exist in this instance, and in a degree of strength as much superior to what exists in other cases, as the intensity of the belief itself is superior? The burden of proof lies on the advocates of the contrary opinion: it is for them to point out some fact inconsistent with the supposition that this part of our knowledge of nature is derived from the same sources as every other part.

This, for instance, they would be able to do, if they could prove chronologically that we had the conviction (at least practically) so early in infancy as to be anterior to those impressions on the senses, upon which, on the other theory, the conviction is founded. This, however, cannot be proved: the point being too far back to be within the reach of memory, and too obscure for external observation. The advocates of the *à priori* theory are obliged to have recourse to other arguments. These are reducible to two, which I shall endeavour to state as clearly and as forcibly as possible.

§ 5. In the first place it is said, that if our assent to the proposition that two straight lines cannot inclose a space, were derived from the senses, we could only be convinced of its truth by actual trial, that is, by seeing or feeling the straight lines; whereas in fact it is seen to be true by merely thinking of them. That a stone thrown into water goes to the bottom, may be perceived by our senses, but mere thinking of a stone thrown into the water would never have led us to that conclusion: not so, however, with the axioms relating to straight lines: if I could be made to conceive what a straight line is, without having seen one, I should at once recognise that two such lines cannot inclose a space. Intuition is "imaginary looking"; but experience must be real looking: if we see a property of straight lines to be true by merely fancying ourselves to be looking at them, the ground of our belief cannot be the senses, or experience; it must be something mental.

To this argument it might be added in the case of this particular axiom, (for the assertion would not be true of all axioms,) that the evidence of it from actual ocular inspection is not only unnecessary but unattainable. What says the axiom? That two straight lines *cannot* inclose a space; that after having once intersected, if they are prolonged to infinity they do not meet, but continue to diverge from one another. How can this, in any single case, be proved by actual observation? We may follow the lines to any distance we please; but we cannot follow them to infinity: for aught our senses can testify, they may, immediately beyond the farthest point to which we have traced them, begin to approach, and at last meet. Unless, therefore, we had some other proof of the impossibility than observation affords us, we should have no grounds for believing the axiom at all.

To these arguments, which I trust I cannot be accused of understating, a satisfactory answer will, I conceive, be found, if we advert to one of the characteristic properties of geometrical forms—their capacity of being painted in the imagination with a distinctness equal to reality: in other words, the exact resemblance of our ideas of form to the sensations which suggest them. This, in the first place, enables us to make (at least with a little practice) mental pictures of all possible combinations of lines and angles, which resemble the realities quite as well as any which we could make on paper; and in the next place, make those pictures just as fit subjects of geometrical experimentation as the realities themselves; inasmuch as pictures, if sufficiently accurate, exhibit of course all the properties which would be manifested by the realities at one given instant, and on simple inspection: and in geometry we are concerned only with such properties, and not with that which pictures could not exhibit, the mutual action of bodies one upon another. The foundations of geometry would therefore be laid in direct experience, even if the experiments (which in this case consist merely in attentive contemplation) were practised solely upon what we call our ideas, that is, upon the diagrams in our minds, and not upon outward objects. For in all systems of experimentation we take some objects to serve as representatives of all which resemble them; and in the present case the conditions which qualify a real object to be the representative of its class, are completely fulfilled by an object existing only in our fancy. Without denying, therefore, the possibility of satisfying ourselves that two straight lines cannot inclose a space, by merely thinking of straight lines without actually looking at them; I contend that we do not believe this truth on the ground of the imaginary intuition simply, but because we know that the imaginary lines exactly resemble real ones, and that we may conclude from them to real ones with quite as much certainty as we could conclude from one real line to another. The conclusion, therefore, is still an induction from observation.

. . . .

The Truths of Arithmetic Not Verbal Tautologies but, Like the Axioms of Geometry, Generalizations of Observed Facts in Nature

What we have now asserted, however, cannot be received as universally true of Deductive or Demonstrative Sciences, until verified by being applied to the most remarkable of all those sciences, that of Numbers; the theory of the Calculus; Arithmetic and Algebra. It is harder to believe of the doctrines of this science than of any other, either that they are not truths *à priori*, but experimental truths, or that their peculiar certainty is owing to their being not absolute but only conditional truths. This, therefore, is a case which merits examination apart; and the more so, because on this subject we have a double set of doctrines to contend with; that of the *à priori* philosophers on one side; and on the other, a theory the most opposite to theirs, which was at one time very generally received, and is still far from being altogether exploded, among metaphysicians.

§ 2. This theory attempts to solve the difficulty apparently inherent in the case, by representing the propositions of the science of numbers as merely verbal, and it processes as simple transformations of language, substitutions of one expression for another. The proposition, Two and one is equal to three, according to these writers, is not a truth, is not the assertion of a really existing fact, but a definition of the word three; a statement that mankind have agreed to use the name three as a sign exactly equivalent to two and one; to call by the former name whatever is called by the other more clumsy phrase. According to this doctrine the longest process in algebra is but a succession of changes in terminology, by which equivalent expressions are substituted one for another; a series of translations of the same fact, from one into another language; though how, after such a series of translations, the fact itself comes out changed (as when we demonstrate a new geometrical theorem by algebra), they have not explained; and it is a difficulty which is fatal to their theory.

It must be acknowledged that there are peculiarities in the processes of arithmetic and algebra which render the theory in question very plausible, and have not unnaturally made those sciences the stronghold of Nominalism. The doctrine that we can discover facts, detect the hidden processes of nature, by an artful manipulation of language, is so contrary to common sense, that a person must have made some advances in philosophy to believe it; men fly to so paradoxical a belief to avoid, as they think, some even greater difficulty, which the vulgar do not see. What has led many to believe that reasoning is a mere verbal process, is, that no other theory seemed reconcileable with the nature of the Science of Numbers. For we do not carry any ideas along with us when we use the symbols of arithmetic or of algebra. In a geometrical demonstration we have a mental diagram, if not one on paper; AB, AC, are present to our imagination as lines, intersecting other lines, forming an angle with one another, and the like; but not so *a* and *b*. The ideas which, on the particular occasion, they happen to represent, are banished from the mind during every intermediate part of the process, between the beginning, when the premises are translated from things into signs, and the end, when the conclusion is translated back from signs into things. Nothing, then, being in the reasoner's mind but the symbols, what can seem more inadmissible than to contend that the reasoning process has to do with anything more? We seem to have come to one of Bacon's Prerogative Instances; an *experimentum crucis* on the nature of reasoning itself.

Nevertheless, it will appear on consideration, that this apparently so decisive instance is no instance at all; that there is in every step of an arithmetical or algebraical calculation a real induction, a real inference of facts from facts; and that what disguises the induction is simply its comprehensive nature and the consequent extreme generality of the language. All numbers must be numbers of something; there are no such things as numbers in the abstract. *Ten* must mean ten bodies, or ten sounds, or ten beatings of the pulse. But though numbers must be numbers of something, they may be numbers of anything. Propositions, therefore, concerning numbers, have the remarkable peculiarity that they are propositions concerning all things whatever; all objects, all existences of every kind, known to our experience. All things possess quantity; consist of parts which can be numbered; and in that character possess all the properties which are called properties of numbers. That half of four is two, must be true whatever the word four represents, whether four hours, four miles, or four pounds weight. We need only conceive a thing divided into four equal parts (and all things may be conceived as so divided), to be able to predicate of it every property of the number four, that is, every arithmetical proposition in which the number four stands on one side of the equation. Algebra extends the generalization still farther: every number represents that particular number of all things without distinction, but every algebraical symbol does more, it represents all numbers without distinction.

There is another circumstance, which, still more than that which we have now mentioned, gives plausibility to the notion that the propositions of arithmetic and algebra are merely verbal. That is, that when considered as propositions respecting Things, they all have the appearance of being identical propositions. The assertion, Two and one is equal to three, considered as an assertion respecting objects, as for instance "Two pebbles and one pebble are equal to three pebbles," does not affirm equality between two collections of pebbles, but absolute identity. It affirms that if we put one pebble to two pebbles, those very pebbles are three. The objects, therefore, being the very same, and the mere assertion that "objects are themselves" being insignificant, it seems but natural to consider the proposition Two and one is equal to three, as asserting mere identity of signification between the two names.

This, however, though it looks so plausible, will not bear examination. The expression "two pebbles and one pebble," and the expression, "three pebbles," stand indeed for the same aggregation of objects, but they by no means stand for the same physical fact. They are names of the same objects, but of those objects in two different states: though they *de*note the same things, their *con*notation is different. Three pebbles in two separate parcels, and three pebbles in one parcel, do not make the same impression on our senses; and the assertion that the very same pebbles may by an alteration of place and arrangement be made to produce either the one set of sensations or the other, though a very familiar proposition, is not an identical one. It is a truth known to us by early and constant experience: an inductive truth; and such truths are the foundation of the science of Number. The fundamental truths of that science all rest on the evidence of sense; they are proved by showing to our eyes and our fingers that any given number of objects, ten balls for example, may by separation and re-arrangement exhibit to our senses all the different sets of numbers the sum of which is equal to ten. All the improved methods of teaching arithmetic to children proceed on a knowledge of this fact. All who wish to carry the child's *mind* along with them in learning arithmetic; all who wish to teach numbers, and not mere ciphers—now teach it through the evidence of the senses, in the manner we have described.

We may, if we please, call the proposition, "Three is two and one," a definition of the number three, and assert that arithmetic, as it has been asserted that geometry, is a science founded on definitions. But they are definitions in the geometrical sense, not the logical; asserting not the meaning of a term only, but along with it an observed matter of fact. The proposition, "A circle is a figure bounded by a line which has all its points equally distant from a point within it," is called the definition of a circle; but the proposition from which so many consequences follow, and which is really a first principle in geometry, is, that figures answering to this description exist. And thus we may call "Three is two and one" a definition of three; but the calculations which depend on that proposition do not follow from the definition itself, but from an arithmetical theorem presupposed in it, namely, that collections of objects exist, which while they impress the senses thus, ˙·˙, may be separated into two parts, thus, ... This proposition being granted, we term all such parcels Threes, after which the enunciation of the above mentioned physical fact will serve also for a definition of the word Three.

The Science of Numbers is thus no exception to the conclusion we previously arrived at, that the processes even of deductive sciences are altogether inductive, and that their first principles are generalizations from experience.

The Status of the Basic Principles of Logic

. . . Sir William Hamilton is . . . a firm believer in the à priori charac-ter of many axioms, and of the sciences deduced from them; and is so far from considering those axioms to rest on the evidence of experience, that he declares certain of them to be true even of Noumena—of the Uncon-ditioned—of which it is one of the principal aims of his philosophy to prove that the nature of our faculties debars us from having any knowl-edge. The axioms to which he attributes this exceptional emancipation from the limits which confine all our other possibilities of knowledge; the chinks through which, as he represents, one ray of light finds its way to us from behind the curtain which veils from us the mysterious world of Things in themselves,—are the two principles, which he terms, after the schoolmen, the Principle of Contradiction, and the Principle of Ex-cluded Middle: the first, that two contradictory propositions cannot both be true; the second, that they cannot both be false.

As I have hitherto said nothing of the two axioms in question, those of Contradiction and of Excluded Middle, it is not unseasonable to con-sider them here. The former asserts that an affirmative proposition and the corresponding negative proposition cannot both be true; which has generally been held to be intuitively evident. Sir William Hamilton and the Germans consider it to be the statement in words of a form or law of our thinking faculty. Other philosophers, not less deserving of con-sideration, deem it to be an identical proposition, an assertion involved in the meaning of the terms; a mode of defining Negation, and the word Not.

I am able to go one step with these last. An affirmative assertion and its negative are not two independent assertions, connected with each other only as mutually incompatible. That if the negative be true, the affirmative must be false, really is a mere identical proposition; for the negative proposition asserts nothing but the falsity of the affirmative, and has no other sense or meaning whatever. The Principium Contradictionis should therefore put off the ambitious phraseology which gives it the air of a fundamental antithesis pervading nature, and should be enunciated in the simpler form, that the same proposition cannot at the same time be false and true. But I can go no farther with the Nominalists; for I cannot look upon this last as a merely verbal proposition. I consider it to be, like other axioms, one of our first and most familiar generalizations from experience. The original foundation of it I take to be, that Belief and Disbelief are two different mental states, excluding one another. This we know by the simplest observation of our own minds. And if we carry our observation outwards, we also find that light and darkness, sound and silence, motion and quiescence, equality and inequality, preceding and following, succession and simultaneousness, any positive phenomenon whatever and its negative, are distinct phenomena, pointedly contrasted, and the one always absent where the other is present. I consider the maxim in question to be a generalization from all these facts.

In like manner as the Principle of Contradiction (that one of two contradictories must be false) means that an assertion cannot be *both* true and false, so the Principle of Excluded Middle, or that one of two contradictories must be true, means that an assertion must be *either* true or false: either the affirmative is true, or otherwise the negative is true, which means that the affirmative is false. I cannot help thinking this principle a surprising specimen of a so-called necessity of Thought, since it is not even true, unless with a large qualification. A proposition must be either true or false, *provided* that the predicate be one which can in any intelligible sense be attributed to the subject; (and as this is always assumed to be the case in treatises on logic, the axiom is always laid down there as of absolute truth). "Abracadabra is a second intention" is neither true nor false. Between the true and the false there is a third possibility, the Unmeaning: and this alternative is fatal to Sir William Hamilton's extension of the maxim to Noumena. That Matter must either have a minimum of divisibility or be infinitely divisible, is more than we can ever know. For in the first place, Matter, in any other than the phenomenal sense of the term, may not exist: and it will scarcely be said that a non-entity must be either infinitely or finitely divisible. In the second place, though matter, considered as the occult cause of our sensations, do really exist, yet what we call divisibility may be an attribute only of our sensations of sight and touch, and not of their uncognizable cause. Divisibility may not be predictable at all, in any intelligible sense, of Things in themselves, nor therefore of Matter in itself; and the assumed necessity of being either infinitely or finitely divisible, may be an inapplicable alternative.

54. Alfred Jules Ayer

Only Analytic Statements Are Knowable A Priori

Having admitted that we are empiricists, we must now deal with the objection that is commonly brought against all forms of empiricism; the objection, namely, that it is impossible on empiricist principles to account for our knowledge of necessary truths. For, as Hume conclusively showed, no general proposition whose validity is subject to the test of actual experience can ever be logically certain. No matter how often it is verified in practice, there still remains the possibility that it will be confuted on some future occasion. The fact that a law has been substantiated in $n-1$ cases affords no logical guarantee that it will be substantiated in the nth case also, no matter how large we take n to be. And this means that no general proposition referring to a matter of fact can ever be shown to be necessarily and universally true. It can at best be a probable hypothesis. And this, we shall find, applies not only to general propositions, but to all propositions which have a factual content. They can none of them ever become logically certain. This conclusion, which we shall elaborate later on, is one which must be accepted by every consistent empiricist. It is often thought to involve him in complete scepticism; but this is not the case. For the fact that the validity of a proposition cannot be logically guaranteed in no way entails that it is irrational for us to believe it. On the contrary, what is irrational is to look for a guarantee where none can be forthcoming; to demand certainty where

From A. J. Ayer, *Language, Truth, and Logic,* first published in 1936 by Dover Publications, Inc., New York, and by Victor Gollancz, Ltd., London. Reprinted by permission of the publishers.

probability is all that is obtainable. We have already remarked upon this, in referring to the work of Hume. And we shall make the point clearer when we come to treat of probability, in explaining the use which we make of empirical propositions. We shall discover that there is nothing perverse or paradoxical about the view that all the "truths" of science and common sense are hypotheses; and consequently that the fact that it involves this view constitutes no objection to the empiricist thesis.

Where the empiricist does encounter difficulty is in connection with the truths of formal logic and mathematics. For whereas a scientific generalization is readily admitted to be fallible, the truths of mathematics and logic appear to everyone to be necessary and certain. But if empiricism is correct no proposition which has a factual content can be necessary or certain. Accordingly the empiricist must deal with the truths of logic and mathematics in one of the two following ways: he must say either that they are not necessary truths, in which case he must account for the universal conviction that they are; or he must say that they have no factual content, and then he must explain how a proposition which is empty of all factual content can be true and useful and surprising.

If neither of these courses proves satisfactory, we shall be obliged to give way to rationalism. We shall be obliged to admit that there are some truths about the world which we can know independently of experience; that there are some properties which we can ascribe to all objects, even though we cannot conceivably observe that all objects have them. And we shall have to accept it as a mysterious inexplicable fact that our thought has this power to reveal to us authoritatively the nature of objects which we have never observed. Or else we must accept the Kantian explanation which, apart from the epistemological difficulties which we have already touched on, only pushes the mystery a stage further back.

It is clear that any such concession to rationalism would upset the main argument of this book. For the admission that there were some facts about the world which could be known independently of experience would be incompatible with our fundamental contention that a sentence says nothing unless it is empirically verifiable. And thus the whole force of our attacks on metaphysics would be destroyed. It is vital, therefore, for us to be able to show that one or other of the empiricist accounts of the propositions of logic and mathematics is correct. If we are successful in this, we shall have destroyed the foundations of rationalism. For the fundamental tenet of rationalism is that thought is an independent source of knowledge, and is moreover a more trustworthy source of knowledge than experience; indeed some rationalists have gone so far as to say that thought is the only source of knowledge. And the ground for this view is simply that the only necessary truths about the world which are known to us are known through thought and not through experience. So that if we can show either that the truths in question are not necessary or that they are not "truths about the world," we shall be taking away the support on which rationalism rests. We shall be making good the empiricist contention that there are no "truths of reason" which refer to matters of fact.

The course of maintaining that the truths of logic and mathematics are not necessary or certain was adopted by Mill. He maintained that these propositions were inductive generalizations based on an extremely large number of instances. The fact that the number of supporting instances was so very large accounted, in his view, for our believing these generalizations to be necessarily and universally true. The evidence in their favour was so strong that it seemed incredible to us that a contrary instance should ever arise. Nevertheless it was in principle possible for such generalizations to be confuted. They were highly probable, but, being inductive generalizations, they were not certain. The difference between them and the hypotheses of natural science was a difference in degree and not in kind. Experience gave us very good reason to suppose that a "truth" of mathematics or logic was true universally; but we were not possessed of a guarantee. For these "truths" were only empirical hypotheses which had worked particularly well in the past; and, like all empirical hypotheses, they were theoretically fallible.

I do not think that this solution of the empiricist's difficulty with regard to the propositions of logic and mathematics is acceptable. In discussing it, it is necessary to make a distinction which is perhaps already enshrined in Kant's famous dictum that, although there can be no doubt that all our knowledge begins with experience, it does not follow that it all arises out of experience.[1] When we say that the truths of logic are known independently of experience, we are not of course saying that they are innate, in the sense that we are born knowing them. It is obvious that mathematics and logic have to be learned in the same way as chemistry and history have to be learned. Nor are we denying that the first person to discover a given logical or mathematical truth was led to it by an inductive procedure. It is very probable, for example, that the principle of the syllogism was formulated not before but after the validity of syllogistic reasoning had been observed in a number of particular cases. What we are discussing, however, when we say that logical and mathematical truths are known independently of experience, is not a historical question concerning the way in which these truths were originally discovered, nor a psychological question concerning the way in which each of us comes to learn them, but an epistemological question. The contention of Mill's which we reject is that the propositions of logic and mathematics have the same status as empirical hypotheses; that their validity is determined in the same way. We maintain that they are independent of experience in the sense that they do not owe their validity to empirical verification. We may come to discover them through an inductive process; but once we have apprehended them we see that they are necessarily true, that they hold good for every conceivable instance. And this serves to distinguish them from empirical generalizations. For we know that a proposition whose validity depends upon experience cannot be seen to be necessarily and universally true.

In rejecting Mill's theory, we are obliged to be somewhat dogmatic. We can do no more than state the issue clearly and then trust that his

1. *Critique of Pure Reason*, 2nd ed., Introduction, section i.

contention will be seen to be discrepant with the relevant logical facts. The following considerations may serve to show that of the two ways of dealing with logic and mathematics which are open to the empiricist, the one which Mill adopted is not the one which is correct.

The best way to substantiate our assertion that the truths of formal logic and pure mathematics are necessarily true is to examine cases in which they might seem to be confuted. It might easily happen, for example, that when I came to count what I had taken to be five pairs of objects, I found that they amounted only to nine. And if I wished to mislead people I might say that on this occasion twice five was not ten. But in that case I should not be using the complex sign "$2 \times 5 = 10$" in the way in which it is ordinarily used. I should be taking it not as the expression of a purely mathematical proposition, but as the expression of an empirical generalization, to the effect that whenever I counted what appeared to me to be five pairs of objects I discovered that they were ten in number. This generalization may very well be false. But if it proved false in a given case, one would not say that the mathematical proposition "$2 \times 5 = 10$" had been confuted. One would say that I was wrong in supposing that there were five pairs of objects to start with, or that one of the objects had been taken away while I was counting, or that two of them had coalesced, or that I had counted wrongly. One would adopt as an explanation whatever empirical hypothesis fitted in best with the accredited facts. The whole explanation which would in no circumstances be adopted is that ten is not always the product of two and five.

To take another example: if what appears to be a Euclidean triangle is found by measurement not to have angles totalling 180 degrees, we do not say that we have met with an instance which invalidates the mathematical proposition that the sum of the three angles of a Euclidean triangle is 180 degrees. We say that we have measured wrongly, or, more probably, that the triangle we have been measuring is not Euclidean. And this is our procedure in every case in which a mathematical truth might appear to be confuted. We always preserve its validity by adopting some other explanation of the occurrence.

The same thing applies to the principles of formal logic. We may take an example relating to the so-called law of excluded middle, which states that a proposition must be either true or false, or, in other words, that it is impossible that a proposition and its contradictory should neither of them be true. One might suppose that a proposition of the form "x has stopped doing y" would in certain cases constitute an exception to this law. For instance, if my friend has never yet written to me, it seems fair to say that it is neither true nor false that he has stopped writing to me. But in fact one would refuse to accept such an instance as an invalidation of the law of excluded middle. One would point out that the proposition "My friend has stopped writing to me" is not a simple proposition, but the conjunction of the two propositions "My friend wrote to me in the past" and "My friend does not write to me now": and, furthermore, that the proposition "My friend has not stopped writing to me" is not, as it appears to be, contradictory to "My friend has stopped writing to me," but only contrary to it. For it means "My friend wrote to me in the past, and he still writes to me." When, therefore, we say that such a proposition as "My friend has stopped writing to me" is sometimes neither true nor false, we are speaking inaccurately. For we seem to be saying that neither it nor its contradictory is true. Whereas what we mean, or anyhow should mean, is that neither it nor its apparent contradictory is true. And its apparent contradictory is really only its contrary. Thus we preserve the law of excluded middle by showing that the negating of a sentence does not always yield the contradictory of the proposition originally expressed.

There is no need to give further examples. Whatever instance we care to take, we shall always find that the situations in which a logical or mathematical principle might appear to be confuted are accounted for in such a way as to leave the principle unassailed. And this indicates that Mill was wrong in supposing that a situation could arise which would overthrow a mathematical truth. The principles of logic and mathematics are true universally simply because we never allow them to be anything else. And the reason for this is that we cannot abandon them without contradicting ourselves, without sinning against the rules which govern the use of language, and so making our utterances self-stultifying. In other words, the truths of logic and mathematics are analytic propositions or tautologies. In saying this we are making what will be held to be an extremely controversial statement, and we must now proceed to make its implications clear.

The most familiar definition of an analytic proposition, or judgement, as he called it, is that given by Kant. He said[2] that an analytic judgement was one in which the predicate B belonged to the subject A as something which was covertly contained in the concept of A. He contrasted analytic with synthetic judgements, in which the predicate B lay outside the subject A, although it did stand in connection with it. Analytic judgements, he explains, "add nothing through the predicate to the concept of the subject, but merely break it up into those constituent concepts that have all along been thought in it, although confusedly." Synthetic judgements, on the other hand, "add to the concept of the subject a predicate which has not been in any wise thought in it, and which no analysis could possibly extract from it." Kant gives "all bodies are extended" as an example of an analytic judgement, on the ground that the required predicate can be extracted from the concept of "body," "in accordance with the principle of contradiction"; as an example of a synthetic judgement, he gives "all bodies are heavy." He refers also to "$7 + 5 = 12$" as a synthetic judgement, on the ground that the concept of twelve is by no means already thought in merely thinking of the union of seven and five. And he appears to regard this as tantamount to saying that the judgement does not rest on the principle of contradiction alone. He holds, also, that through analytic judgements our knowledge is not extended as it is through synthetic judgements. For in analytic judgements "the concept which I already have is merely set forth and made intelligible to me."

2. *Ibid.*, Introduction, sections iv and v.

I think that this is a fair summary of Kant's account of the distinction between analytic and synthetic propositions, but I do not think that it succeeds in making the distinction clear. For even if we pass over the difficulties which arise out of the use of the vague term "concept," and the unwarranted assumption that every judgement, as well as every German or English sentence, can be said to have a subject and a predicate, there remains still this crucial defect. Kant does not give one straightforward criterion for distinguishing between analytic and synthetic propositions; he gives two distinct criteria, which are by no means equivalent. Thus his ground for holding that the proposition "$7 + 5 = 12$" is synthetic is, as we have seen, that the subjective intension of "$7 + 5$" does not comprise the subjective intension of "12"; whereas his ground for holding that "all bodies are extended" is an analytic proposition is that it rests on the principle of contradiction alone. That is, he employs a psychological criterion in the first of these examples, and a logical criterion in the second, and takes their equivalence for granted. But, in fact, a proposition which is synthetic according to the former criterion may very well be analytic according to the latter. For, as we have already pointed out, it is possible for symbols to be synonymous without having the same intensional meaning for anyone: and accordingly from the fact that one can think of the sum of seven and five without necessarily thinking of twelve, it by no means follows that the proposition "$7 + 5 = 12$" can be denied without self-contradiction. From the rest of his argument, it is clear that it is this logical proposition, and not any psychological proposition, that Kant is really anxious to establish. His use of the psychological criterion leads him to think that he has established it, when he has not.

I think that we can preserve the logical import of Kant's distinction between analytic and synthetic propositions, while avoiding the confusions which mar his actual account of it, if we say that a proposition is analytic when its validity depends solely on the definitions of the symbols it contains, and synthetic when its validity is determined by the facts of experience. Thus, the proposition "There are ants which have established a system of slavery" is a synthetic proposition. For we cannot tell whether it is true or false merely by considering the definitions of the symbols which constitute it. We have to resort to actual observation of the behaviour of ants. On the other hand, the proposition "Either some ants are parasitic or none are" is an analytic proposition. For one need not resort to observation to discover that there either are or are not ants which are parasitic. If one knows what is the function of the words "either," "or," and "not," then one can see that any proposition of the form "Either p is true or p is not true" is valid, independently of experience. Accordingly, all such propositions are analytic.

It is to be noticed that the proposition "Either some ants are parasitic or none are" provides no information whatsoever about the behaviour of ants, or, indeed, about any matter of fact. And this applies to all analytic propositions. They none of them provide any information about any matter of fact. In other words, they are entirely devoid of factual content. And it is for this reason that no experience can confute them.

When we say that analytic propositions are devoid of factual content, and consequently that they say nothing, we are not suggesting that they are senseless in the way that metaphysical utterances are senseless. For, although they give us no information about any empirical situation, they do enlighten us by illustrating the way in which we use certain symbols. Thus if I say, "Nothing can be coloured in different ways at the same time with respect to the same part of itself," I am not saying anything about the properties of any actual thing; but I am not talking nonsense. I am expressing an analytic proposition, which records our determination to call a colour expanse which differs in quality from a neighboring colour expanse a different part of a given thing. In other words, I am simply calling attention to the implications of a certain linguistic usage. Similarly, in saying that if all Bretons are Frenchmen, and all Frenchmen Europeans, then all Bretons are Europeans, I am not describing any matter of fact. But I am showing that in the statement that all Bretons are Frenchmen, and all Frenchmen Europeans, the further statement that all Bretons are Europeans is implicitly contained. And I am thereby indicating the convention which governs our usage of the words "if" and "all."

We see, then, that there is a sense in which analytic propositions do give us new knowledge. They call attention to linguistic usages, of which we might otherwise not be conscious, and they reveal unsuspected implications in our assertions and beliefs. But we can see also that there is a sense in which they may be said to add nothing to our knowledge. For they tell us only what we may be said to know already. Thus, if I know that the existence of May Queens is a relic of tree-worship, and I discover that May Queens still exist in England, I can employ the tautology "If p implies q, and p is true, q is true" to show that there still exists a relic of tree-worship in England. But in saying that there are still May Queens in England, and that the existence of May Queens is a relic of tree-worship, I have already asserted the existence in England of a relic of tree-worship. The use of the tautology does, indeed, enable me to make this concealed assertion explicit. But it does not provide me with any new knowledge, in the sense in which empirical evidence that the election of May Queens had been forbidden by law would provide me with new knowledge. If one had to set forth all the information one possessed, with regard to matters of fact, one would not write down any analytic propositions. But one would make use of analytic propositions in compiling one's encyclopaedia, and would thus come to include propositions which one would otherwise have overlooked. And, besides enabling one to make one's list of information complete, the formulation of analytic propositions would enable one to make sure that the synthetic propositions of which the list was composed formed a self-consistent system. By showing which ways of combining propositions resulted in contradictions, they would prevent one from including incompatible propositions and so making the list self-stultifying. But in so far as we had actually used such words as "all" and "or" and "not" without falling into self-contradiction, we might be said already to know what was revealed in the formulation of analytic propositions illustrating the rules which govern our usage of these logical particles. So that here again we are justified in saying that analytic proposi-tions do not increase our knowledge.

The analytic character of the truths of formal logic was obscured in the traditional logic through its being insufficiently formalized. For in speaking always of judgements, instead of propositions, and introducing irrelevant psychological questions, the traditional logic gave the impres-sion of being concerned in some specially intimate way with the workings of thought. What it was actually concerned with was the formal relation-ship of classes, as is shown by the fact that all its principles of inference are subsumed in the Boolean class-calculus, which is subsumed in its turn in the propositional calculus of Russell and Whitehead. Their sys-tem, expounded in *Principia Mathematica*, makes it clear that formal logic is not concerned with the properties of men's minds, much less with the properties of material objects, but simply with the possibility of com-bining propositions by means of logical particles into analytic proposi-tions, and with studying the formal relationship of these analytic propositions, in virtue of which one is deductible from another. Their procedure is to exhibit the propositions of formal logic as a deductive system, based on five primitive propositions, subsequently reduced in number to one. Hereby the distinction between logical truths and prin-ciples of inference, which was maintained in the Aristotelian logic, very properly disappears. Every principle of inference is put forward as a logical truth and every logical truth can serve as a principle of inference. The three Aristotelian "laws of thought," the law of identity, the law of excluded middle, and the law of noncontradiction, are incorporated in the system, but they are not considered more important than the other analytic propositions. They are not reckoned among the premises of the system. And the system of Russell and Whitehead itself is probably only one among many possible logics, each of which is composed of tautolo-gies as interesting to the logician as the arbitrarily selected Aristotelian "laws of thought."

A point which is not sufficiently brought out by Russell, if indeed it is recognised by him at all, is that every logical proposition is valid in its own right. Its validity does not depend on its being incorporated in a sys-tem, and deduced from certain propositions which are taken as self-evident. The construction of systems of logic is useful as a means of discovering and certifying analytic propositions, but it is not in principle essential even for this purpose. For it is possible to conceive of a sym-bolism in which every analytic proposition could be seen to be analytic in virtue of its form alone.

The fact that the validity of an analytic proposition in no way de-pends on its being deductible from other analytic propositions is our justification for disregarding the question whether the propositions of mathematics are reducible to propositions of formal logic, in the way that Russell supposed.[3] For even if it is the case that the definition of a cardinal number as a class of classes similar to a given class is circular,

3. Vide, *Introduction to Mathematical Philosophy*, Chapter ii.

and it is not possible to reduce mathematical notions to purely logical notions, it will still remain true that the propositions of mathematics are analytic propositions. They will form a special class of analytic propositions, containing special terms, but they will be none the less analytic for that. For the criterion of an analytic proposition is that its validity should follow simply from the definition of the terms contained in it, and this condition is fulfilled by the propositions of pure mathematics.

The mathematical propositions which one might most pardonably suppose to be synthetic are the propositions of geometry. For it is natural for us to think, as Kant thought, that geometry is the study of the properties of physical space, and consequently that its propositions have factual content. And if we believe this, and also recognise that the truths of geometry are necessary and certain, then we may be inclined to accept Kant's hypothesis that space is the form of intuition of our outer sense, a form imposed by us on the matter of sensation, as the only possible explanation of our *a priori* knowledge of these synthetic propositions. But while the view that pure geometry is concerned with physical space was plausible enough in Kant's day, when the geometry of Euclid was the only geometry known, the subsequent invention of non-Euclidean geometries has shown it to be mistaken. We see now that the axioms of a geometry are simply definitions, and that the theorems of a geometry are simply the logical consequences of these definitions.[4] A geometry is not in itself about physical space; in itself it cannot be said to be "about" anything. But we can use a geometry to reason about physical space. That is to say, once we have given the axioms a physical interpretation, we can proceed to apply the theorems to the objects which satisfy the axioms. Whether a geometry can be applied to the actual physical world or not, is an empirical question which falls outside the scope of the geometry itself. There is no sense, therefore, in asking which of the various geometries known to us are false and which are true. In so far as they are all free from contradiction, they are all true. What one can ask is which of them is the most useful on any given occasion, which of them can be applied most easily and most fruitfully to an actual empirical situation. But the proposition which states that a certain application of a geometry is possible is not itself a proposition of that geometry. All that the geometry itself tells us is that if anything can be brought under the definitions, it will also satisfy the theorems. It is therefore a purely logical system, and its propositions are purely analytic propositions.

It might be objected that the use made of diagrams in geometrical treatises shows that geometrical reasoning is not purely abstract and logical, but depends on our intuition of the properties of figures. In fact, however, the use of diagrams is not essential to completely rigorous geometry. The diagrams are introduced as an aid to our reason. They provide us with a particular application of the geometry, and so assist us to perceive the more general truth that the axioms of the geometry involve certain consequences. But the fact that most of us need the help

---

4. Cf. H. Poincaré, *La Science et l'Hypothèse*, Part II, Chapter iii.

of an example to make us aware of those consequences does not show that the relation between them and the axioms is not a purely logical relation. It shows merely that our intellects are unequal to the task of carrying out very abstract processes of reasoning without the assistance of intuition. In other words, it has no bearing on the nature of geometrical propositions, but is simply an empirical fact about ourselves. Moreover, the appeal to intuition, though generally of psychological value, is also a source of danger to the geometer. He is tempted to make assumptions which are accidentally true of the particular figure he is taking as an illustration, but do not follow from his axioms. It has, indeed, been shown that Euclid himself was guilty of this, and consequently that the presence of the figure is essential to some of his proofs.[5] This shows that his system is not, as he presents it, completely rigorous, although of course it can be made so. It does not show that the presence of the figure is essential to a truly rigorous geometrical proof. To suppose that it did would be to take as a necessary feature of all geometries what is really only an incidental defect in one particular geometrical system.

We conclude, then, that the propositions of pure geometry are analytic. And this leads us to reject Kant's hypothesis that geometry deals with the form of intuition of our outer sense. For the ground for this hypothesis was that it alone explained how the propositions of geometry could be both true *a priori* and synthetic: and we have seen that they are not synthetic. Similarly our view that the propositions of arithmetic are not synthetic but analytic leads us to reject the Kantian hypothesis[6] that arithmetic is concerned with our pure intuition of time, the form of our inner sense. And thus we are able to dismiss Kant's transcendental aesthetic without having to bring forward the epistemological difficulties which it is commonly said to involve. For the only argument which can be brought in favour of Kant's theory is that it alone explains certain "facts." And now we have found that the "facts" which it purports to explain are not facts at all. For while it is true that we have *a priori* knowledge of necessary propositions, it is not true, as Kant supposed, that any of these propositions are synthetic. They are without exception analytic propositions, or, in other words, tautologies.

We have already explained how it is that these analytic propositions are necessary and certain. We saw that the reason why they cannot be confuted in experience is that they do not make any assertion about the empirical world. They simply record our determination to use words in a certain fashion. We cannot deny them without infringing the conventions which are presupposed by our very denial, and so falling into self-contradiction. And this is the sole ground of their necessity. As Wittgenstein puts it, our justification for holding that the world could not conceivably disobey the laws of logic is simply that we could not say of an unlogical world how it would look.[7] And just as the validity of an analytic proposi-

5. Cf. M. Black, *The Nature of Mathematics*, p. 154.
6. This hypothesis is not mentioned in the *Critique of Pure Reason*, but was maintained by Kant at an earlier date.
7. *Tractatus Logico-Philosophicus*, 3.031.

tion is independent of the nature of the external world, so it is independent of the nature of our minds. It is perfectly conceivable that we should have employed different linguistic conventions from those which we actually do employ. But whatever these conventions might be, the tautologies in which we recorded them would always be necessary. For any denial of them would be self-stultifying.

We see, then, that there is nothing mysterious about the apodeictic certainty of logic and mathematics. Our knowledge that no observation can ever refute the proposition "$7 + 5 = 12$" depends simply on the fact that the symbolic expression "$7 + 5$" is synonymous with "12," just as our knowledge that every oculist is an eye-doctor depends on the fact that the symbol "eye-doctor" is synonymous with "oculist." And the same explanation holds good for every other *a priori* truth.

What is mysterious at first sight is that these tautologies should on occasion be so surprising, that there should be in mathematics and logic the possibility of invention and discovery. As Poincaré says: "If all the assertions which mathematics puts forward can be derived from one another by formal logic, mathematics cannot amount to anything more than an immense tautology. Logical inference can teach us nothing essentially new, and if everything is to proceed from the principle of identity, everything must be reducible to it. But can we really allow that these theorems which fill so many books serve no other purpose than to say in a round-about fashion 'A = A'?"[8] Poincaré finds this incredible. His own theory is that the sense of invention and discovery in mathematics belongs to it in virtue of mathematical induction, the principle that what is true for the number 1, and true for $n + 1$ when it is true for n, is true for all numbers. And he claims that this is a synthetic *a priori* principle. It is, in fact, *a priori*, but it is not synthetic. It is a defining principle of the natural numbers, serving to distinguish them from such numbers as the infinite cardinal numbers, to which it cannot be applied.[9] Moreover, we must remember that discoveries can be made, not only in arithmetic, but also in geometry and formal logic, where no use is made of mathematical induction. So that even if Poincaré were right about mathematical induction, he would not have provided a satisfactory explanation of the paradox that a mere body of tautologies can be so interesting and so surprising.

The true explanation is very simple. The power of logic and mathematics to surprise us depends, like their usefulness, on the limitations of our reason. A being whose intellect was infinitely powerful would take no interest in logic and mathematics. For he would be able to see at a glance everything that his definitions implied, and, accordingly, could never learn anything from logical inference which he was not fully conscious of already. But our intellects are not of this order. It is only a minute proportion of the consequences of our definitions that we are able to detect at a glance. Even so simple a tautology as "$91 \times 79 = 7189$" is beyond the scope of our immediate apprehension. To assure ourselves that "7189" is

8. *La Science et l'Hypothèse*, Part I, Chapter i.
9. Cf. B. Russell's *Introduction to Mathematical Philosophy*, Chapter iii, p. 27.

synonymous with "91 × 79" we have to resort to calculation, which is simply a process of tautological transformation—that is, a process by which we change the form of expressions without altering their significance. The multiplication tables are rules for carrying out this process in arithmetic, just as the laws of logic are rules for the tautological transformation of sentences expressed in logical symbolism or in ordinary language. As the process of calculation is carried out more or less mechanically, it is easy for us to make a slip and so unwittingly contradict ourselves. And this accounts for the existence of logical and mathematical "falsehoods," which otherwise might appear paradoxical. Clearly the risk of error in logical reasoning is proportionate to the length and the complexity of the process of calculation. And in the same way, the more complex an analytic proposition is, the more chance it has of interesting and surprising us.

It is easy to see that the danger of error in logical reasoning can be minimized by the introduction of symbolic devices, which enable us to express highly complex tautologies in a conveniently simple form. And this gives us an opportunity for the exercise of invention in the pursuit of logical enquiries. For a well-chosen definition will call our attention to analytic truths, which would otherwise have escaped us. And the framing of definitions which are useful and fruitful may well be regarded as a creative act.

Having thus shown that there is no inexplicable paradox involved in the view that the truths of logic and mathematics are all of them analytic, we may safely adopt it as the only satisfactory explanation of their *a priori* necessity. And in adopting it we vindicate the empiricist claim that there can be no *a priori* knowledge of reality. For we show that the truths of pure reason, the propositions which we know to be valid independently of all experience, are so only in virtue of their lack of factual content. To say that a proposition is true *a priori* is to say that it is a tautology. And tautologies, though they may serve to guide us in our empirical search for knowledge, do not in themselves contain any information about any matter of fact.

55. Bertrand Russell

Bertrand Russell (1872–1970) was for many years Fellow of
Trinity College, Cambridge, and Lecturer in Philosophy
at Cambridge University. He was awarded the Nobel Prize
for Literature.

The Problem of Induction

In almost all our previous discussions we have been concerned in the
attempt to get clear as to our data in the way of knowledge of existence.
What things are there in the universe whose existence is known to us
owing to our being acquainted with them? So far, our answer has been
that we are acquainted with our sense-data, and, probably, with ourselves. These we know to exist. And past sense-data which are remembered are known to have existed in the past. This knowledge supplies our
data.

But if we are to be able to draw inferences from these data—if we are
to know of the existence of matter, of other people, of the past before our
individual memory begins, or of the future, we must know general principles of some kind by means of which such inferences can be drawn. It
must be known to us that the existence of some one sort of thing, A, is a
sign of the existence of some other sort of thing, B, either at the same
time as A or at some earlier or later time, as, for example, thunder is a
sign of the earlier existence of lightning. If this were not known to us,
we could never extend our knowledge beyond the sphere of our private
experience; and this sphere, as we have seen, is exceedingly limited. The
question we have now to consider is whether such an extension is possible, and if so, how it is effected.

From Bertrand Russell, *The Problems of Philosophy*, 1912. Chapter 6. Reprinted
by permission of the Oxford University Press.

Let us take as an illustration a matter about which none of us, in fact, feel the slightest doubt. We are all convinced that the sun will rise to-morrow. Why? Is this belief a mere blind outcome of past experience, or can it be justified as a reasonable belief? It is not easy to find a test by which to judge whether a belief of this kind is reasonable or not, but we can at least ascertain what sort of general beliefs would suffice, if true, to justify the judgement that the sun will rise to-morrow, and the many other similar judgements upon which our actions are based.

It is obvious that if we asked why we believe that the sun will rise to-morrow, we shall naturally answer, "Because it always has risen every day." We have a firm belief that it will rise in the future, because it has risen in the past. If we are challenged as to why we believe that it will continue to rise as heretofore, we may appeal to the laws of motion: the earth, we shall say, is a freely rotating body, and such bodies do not cease to rotate unless something interferes from outside, and there is nothing outside to interfere with the earth between now and to-morrow. Of course it might be doubted whether we are quite certain that there is nothing outside to interfere, but this is not the interesting doubt. The interesting doubt is as to whether the laws of motion will remain in operation until to-morrow. If this doubt is raised, we find ourselves in the same position as when the doubt about the sunrise was first raised.

The *only* reason for believing that the laws of motion will remain in operation is that they have operated hitherto, so far as our knowledge of the past enables us to judge. It is true that we have a greater body of evidence from the past in favour of the laws of motion than we have in favour of the sunrise, because the sunrise is merely a particular case of fulfilment of the laws of motion, and there are countless other particular cases. But the real question is: Do *any* number of cases of a law being fulfilled in the past afford evidence that it will be fulfilled in the future? If not, it becomes plain that we have no ground whatever for expecting the sun to rise to-morrow, or for expecting the bread we shall eat at our next meal not to poison us, or for any of the other scarcely conscious expectations that control our daily lives. It is to be observed that all such expectations are only *probable*; thus we have not to seek for a proof that they *must* be fulfilled, but only for some reason in favour of the view that they are *likely* to be fulfilled.

Now in dealing with this question we must, to begin with, make an important distinction, without which we should soon become involved in hopeless confusions. Experience has shown us that, hitherto, the frequent repetition of some uniform succession or coexistence has been a *cause* of our expecting the same succession or coexistence on the next occasion. Food that has a certain appearance generally has a certain taste, and it is a severe shock to our expectations when the familiar appearance is found to be associated with an unusual taste. Things which we see become associated, by habit, with certain tactile sensations which we expect if we touch them; one of the horrors of a ghost (in many ghost-stories) is that it fails to give us any sensations of touch. Uneducated people who go abroad for the first time are so surprised as to be incredulous when they find their native language not understood.

And this kind of association is not confined to men; in animals also it is very strong. A horse which has been often driven along a certain road resists the attempt to drive him in a different direction. Domestic animals expect food when they see the person who usually feeds them. We know that all these rather crude expectations of uniformity are liable to be misleading. The man who has fed the chicken every day throughout its life at last wrings its neck instead, showing that more refined views as to the uniformity of nature would have been useful to the chicken.

But in spite of the misleadingness of such expectations, they never-theless exist. The mere fact that something has happened a certain num-ber of times causes animals and men to expect that it will happen again. Thus our instincts certainly cause us to believe that the sun will rise to-morrow, but we may be in no better a position than the chicken which unexpectedly has its neck wrung. We have therefore to distinguish the fact that past uniformities *cause* expectations as to the future, from the question whether there is any reasonable ground for giving weight to such expectations after the question of their validity had been raised.

The problem we have to discuss is whether there is any reason for believing in what is called "the uniformity of nature." The belief in the uniformity of nature is the belief that everything that has happened or will happen is an instance of some general law to which there are *no* exceptions. The crude expectations which we have been considering are all subject to exceptions, and therefore liable to disappoint those who entertain them. But science habitually assumes, at least as a working hypothesis, that general rules which have exceptions can be replaced by general rules which have no exceptions. "Unsupported bodies in the air fall" is a general rule to which balloons and aeroplanes are exceptions. But the laws of motion and the law of gravitation, which account for the fact that most bodies fall, also account for the fact that balloons and aeroplanes can rise; thus the laws of motion and the law of gravitation are not subject to these exceptions.

The belief that the sun will rise to-morrow might be falsified if the earth came suddenly into contact with a large body which destroyed its rotation; but the laws of motion and the law of gravitation would not be infringed by such an event. The business of science is to find uniformi-ties, such as the laws of motion and the law of gravitation, to which, so far as our experience extends, there are no exceptions. In this search science has been remarkably successful, and it may be conceded that such uniformities have held hitherto. This brings us back to the question: Have we any reason, assuming that they have always held in the past, to suppose that they will hold in the future?

It has been argued that we have reason to know that the future will resemble the past, because what was the future has constantly become the past, and has always been found to resemble the past, so that we really have experience of the future, namely of times which were for-merly future, which we may call past futures. But such an argument really begs the very question at issue. We have experience of past futures, but not of future futures, and the question is: Will future futures resem-ble past futures? This question is not to be answered by an argument which starts from past futures alone. We have therefore still to seek for some principle which shall enable us to know that the future will follow the same laws as the past.

The reference to the future in this question is not essential. The same question arises when we apply the laws that work in our experience to past things of which we have no experience—as, for example, in geology, or in theories as to the origin of the Solar System. The question we really have to ask is: "When two things have been found to be often associated, and no instance is known of the one occurring without the other, does the occurrence of one of the two, in a fresh instance, give any good ground for expecting the other?" On our answer to this question must depend the validity of the whole of our expectations as to the future, the whole of the results obtained by induction, and in fact practically all the beliefs upon which our daily life is based.

It must be conceded, to begin with, that the fact that two things have been found often together and never apart does not, by itself, suffice to *prove* demonstratively that they will be found together in the next case we examine. The most we can hope is that the oftener things are found together, the more probable it becomes that they will be found together another time, and that, if they have been found together often enough, the probability will amount *almost* to certainty. It can never quite reach certainty, because we know that in spite of frequent repetitions there sometimes is a failure at the last, as in the case of the chicken whose neck is wrung. Thus probability is all we ought to seek.

It might be urged, as against the view we are advocating, that we know all natural phenomena to be subject to the reign of law, and that sometimes, on the basis of observation, we can see that only one law can possibly fit the facts of the case. Now to this view there are two answers. The first is that, even if *some* law which has no exceptions applies to our case, we can never, in practice, be sure that we have discovered that law and not one to which there are exceptions. The second is that the reign of law would seem to be itself only probable, and that our belief that it will hold in the future, or in unexamined cases in the past, is itself based upon the very principle we are examining.

The principle we are examining may be called the *principle of induction*, and its two parts may be stated as follows:

(*a*) When a thing of a certain sort A has been found to be associated with a thing of a certain other sort B, and has never been found dissociated from a thing of the sort B, the greater the number of cases in which A and B have been associated, the greater is the probability that they will be associated in a fresh case in which one of them is known to be present;

(*b*) Under the same circumstances, a sufficient number of cases of association will make the probability of a fresh association nearly a certainty, and will make it approach certainty without limit.

As just stated, the principle applies only to the verification of our expectation in a single fresh instance. But we want also to know that there is a probability in favour of the general law that things of the sort A are *always* associated with things of the sort B, provided a sufficient number of cases of association are known, and no cases of failure of association are known. The probability of the general law is obviously less than the probability of the particular case, since if the general law is true, the particular case must also be true, whereas the particular case may be true without the general law being true. Nevertheless the probability of the general law is increased by repetitions, just as the probability of the particular case is. We may therefore repeat the two parts of our principle as regards the general law, thus:

(a) The greater the number of cases in which a thing of the sort A has been found associated with a thing of the sort B, the more probable it is (if no cases of failure of association are known) that A is always associated with B;

(b) Under the same circumstances, a sufficient number of cases of the association of A with B will make it nearly certain that A is always associated with B, and will make this general law approach certainty without limit.

It should be noted that probability is always relative to certain data. In our case, the data are merely the known cases of coexistence of A and B. There may be other data, which *might* be taken into account, which would gravely alter the probability. For example, a man who had seen a great many white swans might argue, by our principle, that on the data it was *probable* that all swans were white, and this might be a perfectly sound argument. The argument is not disproved by the fact that some swans are black, because a thing may very well happen in spite of the fact that data render it improbable. In the case of the swans, a man might know that color is a very variable characteristic in many species of animals, and that, therefore, an induction as to color is peculiarly liable to error. But this knowledge would be a fresh datum, by no means proving that the probability relative to our previous data had been wrongly estimated. The fact, therefore, that things often fail to fulfill our expectations is no evidence that our expectations will not *probably* be fulfilled in a given case or a given class of cases. Thus our inductive principle is at any rate not capable of being *disproved* by an appeal to experience.

The inductive principle, however, is equally incapable of being *proved* by an appeal to experience. Experience might conceivably confirm the inductive principle as regards the cases that have been already examined; but as regards unexamined cases, it is the inductive principle alone that can justify any inference from what has been examined to what has not been examined. All arguments which, on the basis of experience, argue as to the future or the unexperienced parts of the past or present, assume the inductive principle; hence we can never use experience to prove the inductive principle without begging the question. Thus we must either accept the inductive principle on the ground of its intrinsic evidence, or forego all justification of our expectations about the future. If the principle is unsound, we have no reason to expect the sun to rise to-morrow, to expect bread to be more nourishing than a stone, or to expect that if we throw ourselves off the roof we shall fall. When we see what looks like our best friend approaching us, we shall have no reason to suppose that his body is not inhabited by the mind of our worst enemy or of some total stranger. All our conduct is based upon associations which have worked in the past, and which we therefore regard as likely to work in the future; and this likelihood is dependent for its validity upon the inductive principle.

The general principles of science, such as the belief in the reign of law, and the belief that every event must have a cause, are as completely dependent upon the inductive principle as are the beliefs of daily life. All such general principles are believed because mankind have found innumerable instances of their truth and no instances of their falsehood. But this accords no evidence for their truth in the future, unless the inductive principle is assumed.

Thus all knowledge which, on the basis of experience tells us something about what is not experienced, is based upon a belief which experience can neither confirm nor confute, yet which, at least in its more concrete applications, appears to be as firmly rooted in us as many of the facts of experience. The existence and justification of such beliefs—for the inductive principle, as we shall see, is not the only example—raises some of the most difficult and most debated problems of philosophy.

56. Paul Edwards

Paul Edwards is Professor of Philosophy in the City
University of New York.

Bertrand Russell's Doubts about Induction

I

A. In the celebrated chapter on induction in his *Problems of Philosophy*,
Bertrand Russell asks the question: 'Have we any reason, assuming that
they (laws like the law of gravitation) have always held in the past, to
suppose that these laws will hold in the future?' (p. 660).[1] Earlier in the
same chapter he raises the more specific question: 'Do *any* number of
cases of a law being fulfilled in the past afford evidence that it will be
fulfilled in the future?' (p. 659). We may reformulate these questions in
a way which lends itself more easily to critical discussion as follows:

(1) Assuming that we possess n positive instances of a phenomenon, observed in extensively varied circumstances, and that we have not
observed a single negative instance (where n is a large number), have
we any reason to suppose that the $n + 1$st instance will also be positive?

(2) Is there any number n of observed positive instances of a phenomenon which affords evidence that the $n + 1$st instance will also
be positive?

From Paul Edwards, "Bertrand Russell's Doubts about Induction," A. G. N. Flew
(ed.), *Logic and Language*, 1951, published by Basil Blackwell, Oxford. First published
in *Mind*, 1949. Reprinted by kind permission of the author and of the Editor of *Mind*.

1. The references are to Chapter 6 of *The Problems of Philosophy*, with the pages
listed corresponding to those of the preceding reading in this anthology. [Eds.]

It is clear that Russell uses 'reason' synonymously with 'good reason' and 'evidence' with 'sufficient evidence.' I shall follow the same procedure throughout this article.

Russell asserts that unless we appeal to a non-empirical principle which he calls the 'principle of induction,' both of his questions must be answered in the negative. . . . 'We must either accept the inductive principle on the ground of its intrinsic evidence or forego all justification of our expectations about the future' (*Problems of Philosophy*, p. 662; also *Outline of Philosophy*, p. 286).

In conjunction with the inductive principle, on the other hand, question (1) at least, he contends, can be answered in the affirmative. 'Whether inferences from past to future are valid depends wholly, if our discussion has been sound, upon the inductive principle: if it is true, such inferences are valid' (*External World*, p. 226). Unfortunately Russell does not make it clear whether in his opinion the same is true about question (2).

As against Russell, I shall try to show in this article that question (1) can be answered in the affirmative without in any way appealing to a non-empirical principle. . . .

It will be well to conduct our discussion in terms of a concrete example. Supposing a man jumps from a window on the fiftieth floor of the Empire State Building. Is there any reason to suppose that his body will move in the direction of the street rather than say in the direction of the sky or in a flat plane? There can be no doubt that any ordinary person and any philosophically unsophisticated scientist, would answer this question in the affirmative without in any way appealing to a non-empirical principle. He would say that there is an excellent reason to suppose that the man's body will move towards the street. This excellent reason, he would say, consists in the fact that whenever in the past a human being jumped out of a window of the Empire State Building his body moved in a downward direction; that whenever any human being anywhere jumped out of a house he moved in the direction of the ground; that, more generally, whenever a human body jumped or was thrown off an elevated locality in the neighbourhood of the earth, it moved downwards and not either upwards or at an angle of 180°; that the only objects which have been observed to be capable of moving upwards by themselves possess certain special characteristics which human beings lack; and finally in all the other observed confirmations of the theory of gravitation.

B. The philosophers who reject common-sense answers like the one just described, have relied mainly on three arguments. Russell himself explicitly employs two of them and some of his remarks make it clear that he also approves of the third. These three arguments are as follows: (*a*) Defenders of common sense point to the fact that many inferences to unobserved events were subsequently, by means of direct observation, found to have resulted in true conclusions. However, any such appeal to observed results of inductive inferences is irrelevant. For the question at stake is: Have we ever a reason, assuming that all the large number of observed instances of a phenomenon are positive, to suppose that an instance which is still unobserved is also positive? The question is not:

Have we ever a reason for supposing that instances which have by now been observed but were at one time unobserved are positive? In Russell's own words: 'We have experience of past futures, but not of future futures, and the question is: Will future futures resemble past futures? This question is not to be answered by an argument which starts from past futures alone' (*Problems of Philosophy*, p. 660).

(*b*) Cases are known where at a certain time a large number of positive instances and not a single negative instance had been observed and where the next instance nevertheless turned out to be negative. 'We know that in spite of frequent repetitions there sometimes is a failure at the last' (*Problems of Philosophy*, p. 661). The man, for instance, 'who has fed the chicken every day throughout its life at last wrings its neck instead' (*Problems of Philosophy*, p. 660). Even in the case of the human being who is jumping out of the Empire State Building, 'we may be in no better position than the chicken which unexpectedly has its neck wrung' (*Problems of Philosophy*, p. 660).

(*c*) The number of positive and negative necessary conditions for the occurrence of any event is infinite or at any rate too large to be directly observed by a human being or indeed by all human beings put together. None of us, for example, has explored every corner of the universe to make sure that there nowhere exists a malicious but powerful individual who controls the movements of the sun by means of wires which are too fine to be detected by any of our microscopes. None of us can be sure that there is no such Controller who, in order to play a joke with the human race, will prevent the sun from rising to-morrow. Equally, none of us can be sure that there is nowhere a powerful individual who can, if he wishes, regulate the movement of human bodies by means of ropes which are too thin to be detected by any of our present instruments. None of us therefore can be sure that when a man jumps out of the Empire State Building he will not be drawn skyward by the Controller of Motion. Hence we have no reason to suppose that the man's body will move in the direction of the street and not in the direction of the sky.

In connection with the last of these three arguments attention ought to be drawn to a distinction which Russell makes between what he calls the 'interesting' and the 'uninteresting' doubt about induction (*Problems of Philosophy*, p. 659). The uninteresting doubt is doubt about the occurrence of a given event on the ground that not all the conditions which are known to be necessary are in fact known to be present. What Russell calls the interesting doubt is the doubt whether an event will take place although all the conditions known to be necessary are known to obtain. . . .

II

As I indicated above, it is my object in this article to defend the common-sense answers to both of Russell's questions. I propose to show, in other words, that, without in any way calling upon a non-empirical principle for assistance, we often have a reason for supposing that a generalization will be confirmed in the future as it has been confirmed in the past. I also propose to show that numbers 'of cases of a law being fulfilled in the past' do often afford evidence that it will be fulfilled in the future.

However, what I have to say in support of these answers is so exceedingly simple that I am afraid it will not impress the philosophers who are looking for elaborate and complicated theories to answer these questions. But I think I can make my case appear plausible even in the eyes of some of these philosophers if I describe at some length the general method of resolving philosophical puzzles which I shall apply to the problem of induction.

Let us consider a simple statement like 'there are several thousand physicians in New York.' We may call this a statement of common-sense, meaning thereby no more than that anybody above a certain very moderate level of instruction and intelligence would confidently give his assent to it.

The word 'physician,' as ordinarily used, is not entirely free from ambiguity. At times it simply means 'person who possesses a medical degree from a recognized academic institution.' At other times, though less often, it means the same as 'person who possesses what is by ordinary standards a considerable skill in curing diseases.' On yet other occasions when people say about somebody that he is a physician they mean both that he has a medical degree and that he possesses a skill in curing diseases which considerably exceeds that of the average layman.

Let us suppose that in the common-sense statement 'there are several thousand physicians in New York' the word 'physician' is used exclusively in the last-mentioned sense. This assumption will simplify our discussion, but it is not at all essential to any of the points I am about to make. It is essential, however, to realize that when somebody asserts in ordinary life that there are several thousand physicians in New York, he is using the word 'physician' in one or other of the ordinary senses just listed. By 'physician' he does not mean for example 'person who can speedily repair bicycles' or 'person who can cure any conceivable illness in less than two minutes.'

Now, supposing somebody were to say 'Really, there are no physicians at all in New York,' in the belief that he was contradicting and refuting common-sense. Supposing that on investigation it turns out that by 'physician' he does not mean 'person who has a medical degree and who has considerably more skill in curing disease than the average layman.' It turns out that by 'physician' he means 'person who has a medical degree and who can cure any conceivable illness in less than two minutes.'

What would be an adequate reply to such an 'enemy of common-sense'? Clearly it would be along the following lines: 'What you say is true. There are no physicians in New York—in *your* sense of the word. There are no persons in New York who can cure any conceivable disease in less than two minutes. But this in no way contradicts the common-sense view expressed by "there are several thousand physicians in New York." For the latter asserts no more than that there are several thousand people in New York who have a medical degree and who possess a skill in curing disease which considerably exceeds that of the average layman. You are guilty of *ignoratio elenchi* since the proposition you refute is different from the proposition you set out to refute.'

Our discussion from here on will be greatly simplified by introducing a few technical terms. Let us, firstly, call '*ignoratio elenchi* by *redefinition*' any instance of *ignoratio elenchi* in which (i) the same sentence expresses both the proposition which ought to be proved and the proposition which is confused with it and where (ii) in the latter employment of the sentence one or more of its parts are used in a sense which is different from their ordinary sense or senses. Secondly, let us refer to any redefinition of a word which includes all that the ordinary definition of the word includes but which includes something else as well as a '*high* redefinition'; and to the sense which is defined by a high redefinition we shall refer as a high sense of the word. Thus 'person who has a medical degree and who is capable of curing any conceivable disease in less than two minutes' is a high redefinition of 'physician' and anybody using the word in that fashion is using it in a high sense. Thirdly, we shall refer to a redefinition of a word which includes something but not all of what the ordinary definition includes and which includes nothing else as a '*low* redefinition'; and the sense which is defined by a low redefinition we shall call a low sense of the word. 'Person capable of giving first aid' or 'person who knows means of alleviating pain' would be low redefinitions of 'physician.' Finally, it will be convenient to call a statement in which a word is used in a high or in a low sense a *redefinitional statement*. If the word is used in a high sense we shall speak of a high-definitional statement; if it is used in a low sense we shall speak of a low-definitional statement.

A short while ago, I pointed out that the man who says 'there are no physicians in New York,' meaning that there are no people in New York who have a medical degree and who can cure any conceivable illness in less than two minutes, is not really contradicting the common-sense view that there are physicians in New York. I pointed out that he would be guilty of what in our technical language is called an *ignoratio elenchi* by redefinition. Now, it seems to me that the relation between the assertion of various philosophers that past experience never constitutes a reason for prediction or generalization except perhaps in conjunction with a non-empirical principle and the common-sense view that past experience does often by itself constitute a reason for inferences to unobserved events has some striking resemblances to the relation between the redefinitional statement about physicians in New York and the common-sense view which this redefinitional statement fails to refute. And more generally, it strongly seems to me that almost all the bizarre pronouncements of philosophers—their 'paradoxes,' their 'silly' theories—are in certain respects strikingly like the statement that there are no physicians in New York, made by one who means to assert that there are no people in New York who have medical degrees and who are capable of curing any conceivable disease in less than two minutes.

In making the last statement I do not mean to deny that there are also important differences between philosophical paradoxes and the high-definitional statement about physicians. There are three differences in particular which have to be mentioned if my subsequent remarks are not to be seriously misleading. Firstly, many of the philosophical paradoxes are not without some point; they do often draw attention to likenesses and differences which ordinary usage obscures. Secondly, the redefinitions which are implicit in philosophical paradoxes do quite often, though by no means always, receive a certain backing from ordinary usage. Frequently, that is to say, there is a secondary sense or trend in ordinary usage which corresponds to the philosophical redefinition, the 'real' sense of the word.[2] Thirdly, philosophical paradoxes are invariably ambiguous in a sense in which the high-definitional statement about the physicians is not ambiguous.[3]

Now, while fully admitting all these (and other) differences, I wish to insist on the great likenesses between philosophical paradoxes and the redefinitional statement about the physicians. And in this article I am mainly concerned with the likenesses, not with the differences. My main object, of course, is to point out the likenesses between the high-definitional statement 'there are no physicians in New York' and the statement that past experience never by itself affords a reason for making inferences to unobserved events. . . .

III

A. Supposing a man, let us call him M, said to us 'I have not yet found any physicians in New York.' Suppose we take him to Park Avenue and introduce him to Brown, a man who has a medical degree and who has cured many people suffering from diseases of the ear. Brown admits, however, that he has not been able to cure *all* the patients who ever consulted him. He also admits that many of his cures took a long time, some as long as eight years. On hearing this, M says 'Brown certainly isn't a physician.'

Supposing we next take M to meet Black who has a medical degree and who can prove to M's and to our satisfaction that he has cured every patient who ever consulted him. Moreover, none of Black's cures took more than three years. However, on hearing that some of Black's cures took as long as two years and ten months, M says 'Black certainly isn't a physician either.'

Finally we introduce M to White who has a medical degree and who has cured every one of his patients in less than six months. When M hears that some of White's cures took as long as five and a half months, he is adamant and exclaims 'White—what a ridiculous error to call him a physician!'

2. Prominent instances of this phenomenon are 'real certainty,' 'real knowledge,' 'real sameness,' 'real freedom,' and 'really contemporaneous events.'
3. The last of these points seems to me to be of enormous importance for understanding the phenomenon of philosophical paradoxes.

At this stage, if not much sooner, all of us would impatiently ask M: What on earth do you mean by 'physician'? And we would plainly be justified in adding: Whatever you may mean by 'physician,' in any sense in which we ever use the word, Black and Brown and White are physicians and very excellent ones at that.

Let us return now to Russell's doubt about the sun's rising tomorrow or about what would happen to a man who jumps out of the Empire State Building. Let us consider what Russell would say in reply to the following question: Supposing that the observed confirmatory instances for the theory of gravitation were a million or ten million times as extensive as they now are and that they were drawn from a very much wider field; would we then have a reason to suppose that the man will fall into the street and not move up into the sky? It is obvious that Russell and anybody taking his view would say 'No.' He would reply that though our *expectation* that the man's body will move in the direction of the street would be even stronger then than it is at present, we would still be without a *reason*.

Next, let us imagine ourselves to be putting the following question to Russell: Supposing the world were such that no accumulation of more than five hundred observed positive instances of a phenomenon has ever been found to be followed by a negative instance; supposing, for instance, that all the chickens who have ever been fed by the same man for 501 days in succession or more are still alive and that all the men too are still alive feeding the chickens every day—would the observed confirmations of the law of gravity in that case be a reason to suppose that the man jumping out of the Empire State Building will move in the direction of the street and not in the direction of the sky? I am not quite sure what Russell would say in reply to this question. Let us assume he would once again answer 'No—past experience would not even then ever be a *reason*.'

Thirdly and finally, we have to consider what Russell would say to the following question: Supposing we had explored every corner of the universe with instruments millions of times as fine and accurate as any we now possess and that we had yet failed to discover any Controller of the movements of human bodies—would we then in our predictions about the man jumping out of the Empire State Building be in a better position than the chicken is in predicting its meals? Would our past observations then be a reason for our prediction? Whatever Russell would in fact say to this, it is clear that his remarks concerning the 'interesting' doubt about induction require him to answer our question in the negative. He would have to say something like this: 'Our *expectation* that the man's body will move in a downward direction will be even stronger than it is now. However, without invoking a non-empirical principle, we shall not *really* be in a better position than the chicken. We should still fail to possess a *reason*.'

As in the case of the man who refused to say that Brown, Black, and White were doctors, our natural response to all this will be to turn to Russell and say: What do you mean by 'being in a better position'? What on earth do you mean by 'a reason'? And, furthermore, why should anybody be interested in a reason in your sense of the word?

Russell's remarks about the need for a general principle like his principle of induction to serve as major premiss in every inductive argument make it clear what he means by a reason: like the Rationalists and Hume (in most places), he means by 'reason' a *logically conclusive* reason and by 'evidence' *deductively conclusive* evidence. When 'reason' is used in this sense, it must be admitted that past observations can never by themselves be a reason for any prediction whatsoever. But 'reason' is not used in this sense when, in science or in ordinary life, people claim to have a reason for a prediction.

So far as I can see, there are three different trends in the ordinary usage of 'reason for an inductive conclusion' and according to none of them does the word mean 'logically conclusive reason.' Among the three trends one is much more prominent than the others. It may fitly be called the main sense of the word. According to this main sense, what we mean when we claim that we have a reason for a prediction is that the past observations of this phenomenon or of analogical phenomena are of a certain kind: they are exclusively or predominantly positive, the number of the positive observations is at least fairly large, and they come from extensively varied sets of circumstances. This is, of course, a very crude formulation. But for the purposes of this article it is, I think, sufficient.[4]

Next, there is a number of trends according to which we mean very much less than this. Occasionally, for instance, we simply mean that it is *Reasonable* to infer the inductive conclusion. And clearly it may be reasonable to infer an inductive conclusion for which we have no reason in the main sense. Thus let us suppose I know that Parker will meet Schroeder in a game in the near future and that it is imperative for me not to suspend my judgement but to come to a conclusion as to who will win. Supposing I know nothing about their present form and nothing also about the type of court on which the match is to be played. All I know is that Parker and Schroeder have in the previous two seasons met six times, Parker scoring four victories to Schroeder's two. In these circumstances it would be reasonable for me to predict that Parker will win and unreasonable to predict that Schroeder will win. Clearly, however, in the main sense of the word I have no reason for either prediction.

Again there is a trend according to which any positive instance of a phenomenon is *a* reason for concluding that the next instance of the phenomenon will be positive. Thus in the circumstances described in the preceding paragraph, it would be quite proper to say we have *more reason* for supposing that Parker will win than for predicting Schroeder's victory. It would be quite proper also to say that we have *some reason* for supposing that Schroeder will win. It would be proper to say this even if Schroeder had won only one of the six matches. To all these and similar trends in the ordinary usage of 'reason for an inductive conclusion' I shall from now on refer as the second ordinary sense of the word.

There can be no doubt that in both these ordinary senses of the word, we frequently have a reason for an inductive conclusion. In these senses

---

4. I have so far left out one important element in the main sense of 'reason for an inductive conclusion.' I shall come to that in Section IV. In the meantime this omission will not affect any of my points.

we have an excellent reason for supposing that the man jumping out of the Empire State Building will move in the direction of the street, that the sun will rise to-morrow and that Stalin will die before the year 2000. The answer to question (I) is therefore a firm and clear 'Yes': in many domains we have a multitude of exclusively positive instances coming from extensively different circumstances. . . .

It should now be clear that, when Russell says that observed instances are never by themselves a reason for an inductive conclusion, he is guilty of an *ignoratio elenchi* by redefinition. His assertion that the premisses of an inductive argument never by themselves constitute a *logically conclusive* reason for an inductive conclusion in no way contradicts the common-sense assertion that they frequently constitute a reason *in the ordinary sense of the word*. Russell's definition of 'reason' is indeed in one respect not a redefinition since in certain contexts we do use 'reason' to mean 'deductively conclusive reason.' However, it is a redefinition in that we never in ordinary life use 'reason' in Russell's sense when we are talking about inductive arguments.

Moreover, if 'reason' means 'deductively conclusive reason,' Russell's questions are no more genuinely questions than e.g. the sentence 'Is a father a female parent?' For, since part of the definition of 'inductive inference' is inference from something observed to something unobserved, it is a *contradiction* to say that an inference is both inductive and at the same time in the same respect deductively conclusive. Russell's 'interesting' doubt, then, is no more sensible or interesting than the 'doubt' whether we shall ever see something invisible or find an object which is a father and also female or an object which is a man but not a human being. . . .

IV

A few words must now be said about the claim, made by Russell, Ewing and others, that empiricism cannot provide a justification of induction since any inductive or empirical justification of induction would necessarily beg the question. If the principle of induction 'is not true,' to use Russell's words, 'every attempt to arrive at general scientific laws from particular observations is fallacious, and Hume's scepticism is inescapable for an empiricist.' But 'the principle itself cannot, without circularity, be inferred from observed uniformities, since it is required to justify any such inference' (*History of Western Philosophy*, p. 699).

In the light of our remarks about redefinitions it is easy to see that all claims of this nature are either mistaken or else cases of *ignoratio elenchi* by redefinition. Before showing this, it will be well to restate the principle of induction in a form which is less confusing than that which Russell uses. Let us try the following formulation:

'The greater the number of positive instances of a phenomenon which have been observed, assuming that no or none except easily explicable negative instances have been found, *and* the greater the number of kinds from which the positive instances are drawn, the less often does it happen that a new instance of the phenomenon turns out to be negative.'[5]

I admit that this statement is rather vague and I also admit that, unless one qualifies it so as to deprive it of all factual significance, one can find exceptions to it.

At the same time, it seems plain that the principle as here stated is very much closer to the truth than its contrary. Furthermore, whether or not it would be correct to regard the inductive principle as a *premiss* of all inductive arguments, it does seem to me part of the *reason* for every inductive conclusion. I mean by this that we would not apply 'reason' to a large number of positive and widely varied instances if the contrary of the inductive principle were true or nearer the truth than the inductive principle. Supposing, for example, it had been found in all domains that after 10,000 instances had been observed, all of them positive and gathered from very varied circumstances, chaos was found among the rest. After the 10,000th instance, in other words, predictions always became thoroughly unreliable. Supposing that in these circumstances we discover a new species of animal—let us call them grats. We want to find how long it takes the grats to solve a certain puzzle and find that all our first 10,000 subjects can solve it in less than an hour. Would we say, knowing what happened in all the many observed domains after the 10,000th instance, we had a reason for supposing that the 10,001st grat would also solve the puzzle in less than an hour? It seems clear that most of us would refuse to say this.

It is now apparent that my analysis in Section III of the main sense and also of the second ordinary sense of 'reason for an inductive conclusion' was incomplete. It will be sufficient here to indicate how my analysis requires to be supplemented in the case of the main sense. To say that p is a reason for an inductive conclusion, in the main sense of 'reason,' is to say firstly that part of p asserts what I earlier claimed the whole of p to assert *and* secondly that the rest of p asserts the inductive principle. Part of p asserts the inductive principle at least in the sense of asserting that it is much closer to the truth than its contrary. . . .

And I want to show now that my admission that the inductive principle is part of the reason for every inductive conclusion implies nothing against common-sense or against empiricism. For this purpose it is necessary to distinguish two possible senses of any statement of the form 'All S are P.' Such a statement may either mean 'All *observed* S are P'; or it may mean 'All S *whatsoever* are P.' I propose to refer to statements of the first class as 'universal premisses' and to statements of the second class as 'universal conclusions.' Now, the charge of *petitio principii* could be sustained only if the inductive principle were meant as a universal *conclusion* when forming part of the evidence of inductive conclusions. But it is clear that when it forms part of the evidence of inductive conclusions, the inductive principle is or requires to be meant only as a universal *premiss*. We would refuse to regard a large collection of ex-

5. Cf. Ernest Nagel, *Principles of the Theory of Probability*, p. 72.

clusively positive and widely varied instances of a phenomenon as a good reason for predicting that the next instance will also be positive if in all or most previous cases large collections of exclusively positive and widely varied instances turned out to be a thoroughly unreliable basis for prediction. However, given a large collection of exclusively positive and widely varied instances of a phenomenon, it would be sufficient for a correct application of 'reason' that in all or most *observed* cases large collections of exclusively positive and widely varied instances turned out to be a reliable basis for prediction. Any opinion to the contrary rests on the belief, exploded in the previous section, that according to ordinary usage 'reason for an inductive conclusion' means 'deductively conclusive reason for the inductive conclusion.'

57. John W. Lenz

John W. Lenz is Professor of Philosophy at Brown University.

A Pragmatic Justification of Inductive Policy?

The purpose of this paper is to examine critically Reichenbach's pragmatic justification of induction. I shall, first, explain his formulation of the rule of induction; second, explain his pragmatic justification of this rule; and, third, assess the significance of his defense. Nowhere in this paper shall I discuss the much larger question whether induction needs some kind of justification, though, in my opinion, the answer is yes. And though I shall be highly critical of Reichenbach's pragmatic vindication, I shall leave aside the residual question of how induction should be justified.

1. *Reichenbach's rule of induction.* The rule of induction has been formulated in many ways, some of which are none too precise: "When predicting, assume that the future will be like the past," "make one's predictions on the assumption that nature is uniform," etc. To understand Reichenbach's justification, we must first see what specific formulation of the inductive rule he is defending.

This paper, "Reichenbach's Defense of Induction," is reprinted by permission of the author. It is a slightly revised version of his "The Pragmatic Justification of Induction," contained in *The Structure of Scientific Thought*, ed. E. H. Madden, Boston, 1960, pp. 299–303. For Reichenbach's formulation of his justification of induction, see his *Theory of Probability*, Berkeley, 1949, pp. 429–82 and *Experience and Prediction*, Chicago, 1938, pp. 339–363. The present paper appeared previously in Marguerite H. Foster and Michael L. Martin, eds., *Probability, Confirmation, and Simplicity*, The Odyssey Press, Inc., New York, 1966.

Reichenbach's rule of induction can be illustrated by the following simple application of it. Suppose that we have tossed a coin 200 times, and that it has turned up heads 98 times. Suppose, that is, that in an initial segment of a series of coin tosses the relative frequency with which heads has turned up is 98/200. Reichenbach's rule of induction tells us to predict that, if the coin is tossed long enough, the relative frequency with which heads occurs remains approximately 98/200. More exactly and more generally, his rule is: If in an initial segment of a series of events the relative frequency with which A's have been B's is m/n (where n is the number of A's and m is the number of A's that are B's), predict that in the long run, that is, as the number of A's gets larger and larger, the relative frequency will after some point continue to be approximately m/n. Those who are familiar with Reichenbach's frequency interpretation of probability will see that his rule of induction tells us to predict that the limit of the relative frequency in an infinite series of events is identical with, or close to, the relative frequency in the initial segment of the series.[1]

It is necessary to always keep in mind that it is *this* rule of induction alone which Reichenbach tries to justify. Certainly there are many other formulations of the rule of induction to which his pragmatic justification is irrelevant. We must note too that while in one sense Reichenbach's formulation of the rule of induction is fairly broad, in another sense it is extremely narrow. It is broad in the sense that the usual inductive rule: "When all observed A's have been B's, predict that all A's will continue to be B's" is simply a particular case of Reichenbach's more general rule. It is a particular case in that here the observed relative frequency with which A's have been B's is 1. Reichenbach's rule has the virtue of allowing us to make not only universal generalizations but statistical generalizations as well.

On the other hand, Reichenbach's rule of induction is narrow in at least two ways. It is narrow, first of all, in that it is only one among many inductive rules that are actually employed in science and everyday life. For example, it is also a rule of science and of common sense that we should not make predictions on the basis of small samples. Reichenbach's reply here, however, would be that all other such rules can be established by using his inductive rule.[2] The conclusion that we should "avoid predicting on the basis of small samples" is itself inductively inferred from our having observed that in the past such predictions have been very unreliable. Whether Reichenbach's general claim here is valid is a complex question into which I cannot enter in this paper.

In any case, Reichenbach's rule of induction is narrow in a more crucial sense. It is narrow in that the predictions it advises concern only what will happen in the long run (for example, that, as the coin is tossed

1. Here as elsewhere in this paper I am trying to avoid technicalities. Reichenbach's exact formulation is: "If an initial section of n elements of a sequence x_i is given, resulting in the frequency f^n, and if, furthermore, nothing is known about the probability of the second level for the occurrence of a certain limit p, we posit that the frequency f^i $(i > n)$ will approach a limit p within $f^n \pm \delta$ when the sequence is continued." *Theory of Probability*, 446.

2. *Theory of Probability*, 442–444.

more and more, the relative frequency with which heads occurs will after some point remain approximately 98/200). His rule of induction does not enable us to predict what will happen in the short run (for example, to predict that in the next 100 tosses of the coin, the frequency with which heads occurs is 98/200). This means that even if Reichenbach succeeds in justifying his rule of induction it does not follow that he will have succeeded in justifying a rule of induction enabling us to predict what happens in the short run.

2. *Reichenbach's justification of induction.* The traditional problem of induction is easily formulated. In any inductive inference employing Reichenbach's rule, the conclusion asserts more than the evidence upon which it is based. The problem of induction is simply to justify such inferences in which "the conclusion goes beyond the premises," or more exactly, to justify the rule which such inferences employ.

Reichenbach points out that obviously the conclusion of an inductive inference does not logically follow from a statement of the evidence; it is not contradictory to affirm the evidence and deny the conclusion. Hence, he concludes that it is not possible to justify induction "logically" in the sense of demonstrating that all, or even some, inductive conclusions are correct. He insists, moreover, that one cannot inductively justify the rule of induction, that is, infer that because it has been successful it will continue to be successful. Such a justification, Reichenbach insists, would be circular. In denying that one can give such *a priori* or *a posteriori* justifications of induction Reichenbach follows Hume completely.

Nonetheless Reichenbach assures us that we need not despair, for another kind of justification is possible. It can best be explained in terms of the simple example we used in explaining his rule of induction. Suppose, again, that we have tossed a coin 200 times, and that it has turned up heads 98 times. Reichenbach's rule, we will remember, tells us to predict that in the long run the relative frequency with which heads occurs will remain 98/200. Reichenbach admits that no guarantee can be given that this particular prediction is correct. It might be that as the coin is tossed more and more the frequency with which heads occurs remains 1/4. Reichenbach admits, furthermore, that we cannot guarantee that even the repeated use of his rule of induction will ever lead to a successful prediction. Suppose, that is, that as we toss the coin more and more we use the "latest" observed relative frequency with which heads occurs in making our predictions of the relative frequency in the long run. Reichenbach admits that no guarantee can be given that a single one of these predictions is correct. It might be the case that as the coin is tossed more and more the relative frequency with which heads occurs continues to oscillate considerably.

Reichenbach's justification of induction rests upon a different claim. Reichenbach shows that if it is the case that, as the coin is tossed more and more, there is some point after which the relative frequency with which heads occurs remains more or less constant, then the *repeated* use of the rule of induction will discover that relative frequency. One can easily generalize his claim here: If, as the number of *A*'s gets larger and larger, there is some point after which the relative frequency with which A's are B's remains fairly constant, then the repeated use of his rule of induction will lead to correct predictions of that relative frequency. This, Reichenbach shows, is demonstrably true.

Several points are important here. First, Reichenbach's claim is hypothetical in form. It says that *if success is possible* (where success is interpreted narrowly to mean correctly predicting long-run relative frequencies) then the repeated use of the inductive method will bring success. Second, Reichenbach does not defend any particular use of the rule of induction but only its *repeated* use. The rule of induction is self-corrective in the precise sense that its repeated use will eventually lead to success, if success is possible. Thirdly, Reichenbach admits that one cannot know *at what point* the repeated use of the inductive method will bring success, if success is possible. Fourthly, Reichenbach shows that we can *know*, prior to any inductive evidence, that the rule of induction is self-corrective in the above sense.

So far Reichenbach's defense consists simply in stating certain properties which his rule of induction has. We must now turn to Reichenbach's further claim that, in comparison with other methods of predicting, the rule of induction is the *best* means we have of attaining our end of successful prediction.

At times Reichenbach makes the very misleading statement that the method of induction is a necessary condition of successful prediction. This is surely misleading in that it suggests that only the inductive method will lead to successful prediction. This cannot be Reichenbach's claim, for he agrees that other methods, for example, that of the clairvoyant, could be successful. Reichenbach agrees, even, that other methods, for example, that of the soothsayer, might be successful more quickly than the inductive method. Reichenbach's claim is, first, that if any other method of prediction is successful then the repeated use of the inductive method will eventually lead to success. In other words, the eventual success of the repeated use of the inductive method is a necessary condition of any successful prediction. His claim is, second, that only the inductive method can be known in advance, and without any prior inductive inference, to lead to success if success is possible. This is enough, Reichenbach claims, to justify our use of the inductive method.

3. *Criticism.* To deny that Reichenbach has justified induction would be, I think, to enter into a somewhat fruitless quarrel concerning the word "justify."[3] However, a clear understanding of Reichenbach's pragmatic justification of induction will show how very weak it is. In this section I shall simply underline the insignificance of Reichenbach's defense.

First, it must never be forgotten that since his rule of induction speaks only about relative frequencies in the long run, his justification leaves entirely aside the problem of justifying predictions of short-run relative frequencies. And surely in science and everyday life we are most concerned with the latter. An insurance company does not care to know

3. One could, perhaps, charge Reichenbach with using words like "justify," "success," "self-corrective," etc. in an unusual and, therefore, potentially misleading way. Cf. Max Black, *Problems of Analysis*, Ithaca, N.Y. 1954, 187.

the long-run relative frequency with which American males of age 32 die before reaching 60. The company is, very likely, concerned only with the next 50 years or so. Of course, if one could assume that the short-run relative frequencies will approximate those of the long run, Reichenbach's justification would be helpful. But of the truth of this assumption Reichenbach gives us no assurance. As we shall see, this problem is further complicated by the last difficulty I shall mention.

Second, it must always be remembered that Reichenbach in his pragmatic justification of induction gives us no assurance that any of the predictions one actually makes using his rule of induction are correct or even probably correct. He does show, it is true, that the repeated use of the inductive rule will lead to success (in his narrow sense of success) if success is possible. However, as he readily admits, there is no reason to believe that success will come.

Third, even if success does come, it may do so too late. It hardly helps to be assured that the repeated use of the inductive method will eventually lead to success, when that eventuality may come too late not only for one man but also for every member of the human race. This is all the more disconcerting in view of Reichenbach's admission that methods other than induction could well lead to success earlier.

It is true that Reichenbach tries to mitigate the force of this objection by putting at times his justification of induction in terms of a practical limit, that is, a limit of a series whose convergence is rapid enough to be discovered in practice. But Reichenbach gives us no more assurance that such a limit exists than he does that there is a limit of any kind.

Fourth, even if success is achieved by using his rule of induction, one will never *know* it on the strength of Reichenbach's justification. As Reichenbach admits, we do not know how many tries with the inductive method we must make before we shall correctly predict the limit of a relative frequency. We can safely say, therefore, that the epistemic significance of Reichenbach's justification of induction is slight.

My last point is one that cannot be easily explained, but since it is an extremely crucial one, I shall outline it here. Actually, one can show that there are other inductive methods which are known to be self-corrective in Reichenbach's sense. Reichenbach not only "justifies" his rule of induction but also a whole class of inductive rules. It is true that the predictions made on the basis of any of these rules converge towards the limit of the relative frequency in an infinite series of events, if there is such a limit. That is, as the evidence gets larger and larger the predictions these rules lead to vary less and less. But before this happens, the predictions we make will vary tremendously depending upon which rule is used. Since we have, on Reichenbach's own terms, no decisive reason for choosing between these rules, our predictions will accordingly be almost entirely arbitrary. We simply shall not know what predictions to make.

One of these rules may lead to the best predictions, as a simple illustration will show. Suppose that the long-run relative frequency with which A's are B's is 3/5. Suppose further that the observed relative frequency with which A's have been B's is 40/60. There exists an inductive rule, justified in Reichenbach's sense, which would predict, on the basis of this evidence, that the long-run relative frequency is 3/5. This rule, if used in this case, would, therefore, actually be superior to Reichenbach's own rule of induction, which would predict that the long-run relative frequency was 2/3. It would be superior to Reichenbach's rule of induction in that by using it, we would achieve success earlier. The trouble is, of course, that we do not know in advance what the actual long-run relative frequency is, and accordingly we do not know which rule to use, which predictions to make.

This difficulty is relevant to the first problem I mentioned, that of justifying predictions of short-run relative frequencies. Presumably, any attempt on Reichenbach's part to solve this latter problem would have taken the form of showing that we can "work back" from long-run to short-run relative frequencies. The fact that there are an infinity of inductive rules, all equally justified in Reichenbach's sense, would, however, make it impossible to "work back" in any but an arbitrary way. That is, there would be an infinity of ways of working back, each giving different values to the short-run relative frequency, among which we would have no reason to choose.

4. *Conclusion.* In conclusion I want to make just two points. First, nowhere in this paper have I denied that Reichenbach has done valuable service in clarifying the logical properties of his rule of induction. Pragmatic considerations aside, it is worthwhile having shown that his rule of induction is "self-corrective" in at least one precise sense. Second, I want to suggest why any such "justification" as Reichenbach's must remain pragmatically insignificant. When one understands Reichenbach's principle of induction one sees that all it asserts is that there is a limit to a given relative frequency in an infinite series of events. Reichenbach's justification of this principle is that it is true, if there is such a limit. Thus his justification of the principle of induction reduces to the bare tautology that if there is a limit, there is a limit. In his formulation of the problem of induction, Hume pointed out that no tautology can by itself lead to "useful" conclusions, and the one upon which Reichenbach bases his justification of inductive inference is no exception.

Rudolf Carnap was one of the founders and leading spirits
of the Vienna Circle and of the "logical positivist" movement;
he taught at several universities, both in Germany and
in the United States, most recently before his death at
the University of California in Los Angeles.

The Nature and Justification of Hypothetical Reasoning

Theories and Nonobservables

One of the most important distinctions between two types of laws in
science is the distinction between what may be called (there is no generally accepted terminology for them) empirical laws and theoretical
laws. Empirical laws are laws that can be confirmed directly by empirical
observations. The term "observable" is often used for any phenomenon
that can be directly observed, so it can be said that empirical laws are
laws about observables.

Here, a warning must be issued. Philosophers and scientists have
quite different ways of using the terms "observable" and "nonobservable." To a philosopher, "observable" has a very narrow meaning. It applies to such properties as "blue," "hard," "hot." These are properties
directly perceived by the senses. To the physicist, the word has a much
broader meaning. It includes any quantitative magnitude that can be

From *Philosophical Foundations of Physics:* An Introduction to the Philosophy of
Science, by Rudolf Carnap, edited by Martin Gardner, pp. 225-235, © 1966 by Basic
Books, Inc., Publishers, New York.

measured in a relatively simple, direct way. A philosopher would not consider a temperature of, perhaps, 80 degrees centigrade, or a weight of 93½ pounds, an observable because there is no direct sensory perception of such magnitudes. To a physicist, both are observables because they can be measured in an extremely simple way. The object to be weighed is placed on a balance scale. The temperature is measured with a thermometer. The physicist would not say that the mass of a molecule, let alone the mass of an electron, is something observable, because here the procedures of measurement are much more complicated and indirect. But magnitudes that can be established by relatively simple procedures —length with a ruler, time with a clock, or frequency of light waves with a spectrometer—are called observables.

A philosopher might object that the intensity of an electric current is not really observed. Only a pointer position was observed. An ammeter was attached to the circuit and it was noted that the pointer pointed to a mark labeled 5.3. Certainly the current's intensity was not observed. It was *inferred* from what was observed.

The physicist would reply that this was true enough, but the inference was not very complicated. The procedure of measurement is so simple, so well established, that it could not be doubted that the ammeter would give an accurate measurement of current intensity. Therefore, it is included among what are called observables.

There is no question here of who is using the term "observable" in a right or proper way. There is a continuum which starts with direct sensory observations and proceeds to enormously complex, indirect methods of observation. Obviously no sharp line can be drawn across this continuum; it is a matter of degree. A philosopher is sure that the sound of his wife's voice, coming from across the room, is an observable. But suppose he listens to her on the telephone. Is her voice an observable or isn't it? A physicist would certainly say that when he looks at something through an ordinary microscope, he is observing it directly. Is this also the case when he looks into an electron microscope? Does he observe the path of a particle when he sees the track it makes in a bubble chamber? In general, the physicist speaks of observables in a very wide sense compared with the narrow sense of the philosopher, but, in both cases, the line separating observable from nonobservable is highly arbitrary. It is well to keep this in mind whenever these terms are encountered in a book by a philosopher or scientist. Individual authors will draw the line where it is most convenient, depending on their points of view, and there is no reason why they should not have this privilege.

Empirical laws, in my terminology, are laws containing terms either directly observable by the senses or measurable by relatively simple techniques. Sometimes such laws are called empirical generalizations, as a reminder that they have been obtained by generalizing results found by observations and measurements. They include not only simple qualitative laws (such as, "All ravens are black") but also quantitative laws that arise from simple measurements. The laws relating pressure, volume, and temperature of gases are of this type. Ohm's law, connecting the electric potential difference, resistance, and intensity of current, is another familiar example. The scientist makes repeated measurements, finds certain regularities, and expresses them in a law. These are the empirical laws. As indicated in earlier chapters, they are used for explaining observed facts and for predicting future observable events.

There is no commonly accepted term for the second kind of laws, which I call *theoretical laws*. Sometimes they are called abstract or hypothetical laws. "Hypothetical" is perhaps not suitable because it suggests that the distinction between the two types of laws is based on the degree to which the laws are confirmed. But an empirical law, if it is a tentative hypothesis, confirmed only to a low degree, would still be an empirical law although it might be said that it was rather hypothetical. A theoretical law is not to be distinguished from an empirical law by the fact that it is not well established, but by the fact that it contains terms of a different kind. The terms of a theoretical law do not refer to observables even when the physicist's wide meaning for what can be observed is adopted. They are laws about such entities as molecules, atoms, electrons, protons, electromagnetic fields, and others that cannot be measured in simple, direct ways.

If there is a static field of large dimensions, which does not vary from point to point, physicists call it an observable field because it can be measured with a simple apparatus. But if the field changes from point to point in very small distances, or varies very quickly in time, perhaps changing billions of times each second, then it cannot be directly measured by simple techniques. Physicists would not call such a field an observable. Sometimes a physicist will distinguish between observables and nonobservables in just this way. If the magnitude remains the same within large enough spatial distances, or large enough time intervals, so that an apparatus can be applied for a direct measurement of the magnitude, it is called a *macroevent*. If the magnitude changes within such extremely small intervals of space and time that it cannot be directly measured by simple apparatus, it is a *microevent*. (Earlier authors used the terms "microscopic" and "macroscopic," but today many authors have shortened these terms to "micro" and "macro.")

A microprocess is simply a process involving extremely small intervals of space and time. For example, the oscillation of an electromagnetic wave of invisible light is a microprocess. No instrument can directly measure how its intensity varies. The distinction between macro- and microconcepts is sometimes taken to be parallel to observable and nonobservable. It is not exactly the same, but it is roughly so. Theoretical laws concern nonobservables, and very often these are microprocesses. If so, the laws are sometimes called microlaws. I use the term "theoretical laws" in a wider sense than this, to include all those laws that contain nonobservables, regardless of whether they are microconcepts or macroconcepts.

It is true, as shown earlier, that the concepts "observable" and "nonobservable" cannot be sharply defined because they lie on a continuum. In actual practice, however, the difference is usually great enough so there is not likely to be debate. All physicists would agree that the laws relating pressure, volume, and temperature of a gas, for example, are empirical laws. Here the amount of gas is large enough so that the magnitudes to be measured remain constant over a sufficiently large volume of space and period of time to permit direct, simple measurements which can then be generalized into laws. All physicists would agree that laws about the behavior of single molecules are theoretical. Such laws concern a microprocess about which generalizations cannot be based on simple, direct measurements.

Theoretical laws are, of course, more general than empirical laws. It is important to understand, however, that theoretical laws cannot be arrived at simply by taking the empirical laws, then generalizing a few steps further. How does a physicist arrive at an empirical law? He observes certain events in nature. He notices a certain regularity. He describes this regularity by making an inductive generalization. It might be supposed that he could now put together a group of empirical laws, observe some sort of pattern, make a wider inductive generalization, and arrive at a theoretical law. Such is not the case.

To make this clear, suppose it has been observed that a certain iron bar expands when heated. After the experiment has been repeated many times, always with the same result, the regularity is generalized by saying that this bar expands when heated. An empirical law has been stated, even though it has a narrow range and applies only to one particular iron bar. Now further tests are made of other iron objects with the ensuing discovery that every time an iron object is heated it expands. This permits a more general law to be formulated, namely that all bodies of iron expand when heated. In similar fashion, the still more general laws "All metals . . . ," then "All solid bodies . . . ," are developed. These are all simple generalizations, each a bit more general than the previous one, but they are all empirical laws. Why? Because in each case, the objects dealt with are observable (iron, copper, metal, solid bodies); in each case the increases in temperature and length are measurable by simple, direct techniques.

In contrast, a theoretical law relating to this process would refer to the behavior of molecules in the iron bar. In what way is the behavior of the molecules connected with the expansion of the bar when heated? You see at once that we are now speaking of nonobservables. We must introduce a theory—the atomic theory of matter—and we are quickly plunged into atomic laws involving concepts radically different from those we had before. It is true that these theoretical concepts differ from concepts of length and temperature only in the degree to which they are directly or indirectly observable, but the difference is so great that there is no debate about the radically different nature of the laws that must be formulated.

Theoretical laws are related to empirical laws in a way somewhat analogous to the way empirical laws are related to single facts. An empirical law helps to explain a fact that has been observed and to predict a fact not yet observed. In similar fashion, the theoretical law helps to explain empirical laws already formulated, and to permit the derivation of new empirical laws. Just as the single, separate facts fall into place in an orderly pattern when they are generalized in an empirical law, the single and separate empirical laws fit into the orderly pattern of a theoretical law. This raises one of the main problems in the methodology of science. How can the kind of knowledge that will justify the assertion of a theoretical law be obtained? An empirical law may be justified by making observations of single facts. But to justify a theoretical law, comparable observations cannot be made because the entities referred to in theoretical laws are nonobservables.

Before taking up this problem, some remarks made in an earlier chapter, about the use of the word "fact," should be repeated. It is important in the present context to be extremely careful in the use of this word because some authors, especially scientists, use "fact" or "empirical fact" for some propositions which I would call empirical laws. For example, many physicists will refer to the "fact" that the specific heat of copper is .090. I would call this a law because in its full formulation it is seen to be a universal conditional statement: "For any x, and any time t, if x is a solid body of copper, then the specific heat of x at t is .090." Some physicists may even speak of the law of thermal expansion, Ohm's law, and others, as facts. Of course, they can then say that theoretical laws help explain such facts. This sounds like my statement that empirical laws explain facts, but the word "fact" is being used here in two different ways. I restrict the word to particular, concrete facts that can be spatio-temporally specified, not thermal expansion in general, but *the* expansion of this iron bar observed this morning at ten o'clock when it was heated. It is important to bear in mind the restricted way in which I speak of facts. If the word "fact" is used in an ambiguous manner, the important difference between the ways in which empirical and theoretical laws serve for explanation will be entirely blurred.

How can theoretical laws be discovered? We cannot say: "Let's just collect more and more data, then generalize beyond the empirical laws until we reach theoretical ones." No theoretical law was ever found that way. We observe stones and trees and flowers, noting various regularities and describing them by empirical laws. But no matter how long or how carefully we observe such things, we never reach a point at which we observe a molecule. The term "molecule" never arises as a result of observations. For this reason, no amount of generalization from observations will ever produce a theory of molecular processes. Such a theory must arise in another way. It is stated not as a generalization of facts but as a hypothesis. The hypothesis is then tested in a manner analogous in certain ways to the testing of an empirical law. From the hypothesis, certain empirical laws are derived, and these empirical laws are tested in turn by observation of facts. Perhaps the empirical laws derived from the theory are already known and well confirmed. (Such laws may even have motivated the formulation of the theoretical law.) Regardless of whether the derived empirical laws are known and confirmed, or whether they are new laws confirmed by new observations, the confirmation of such derived laws provides indirect confirmation of the theoretical law.

The point to be made clear is this. A scientist does not start with one empirical law, perhaps Boyle's law for gases, and then seek a theory about molecules from which this law can be derived. The scientist tries to formulate a much more general theory from which a variety of empirical laws can be derived. The more such laws, the greater their variety and apparent lack of connection with one another, the stronger will be the theory that explains them. Some of these derived laws may have been known before, but the theory may also make it possible to derive new empirical laws which can be confirmed by new tests. If this is the case, it can be said that the theory made it possible to predict new empirical laws. The prediction is understood in a hypothetical way. If the theory holds, certain empirical laws will also hold. The predicted empirical law speaks about relations between observables, so it is now possible to make experiments to see if the empirical law holds. If the empirical law is confirmed, it provides indirect confirmation of the theory. Every confirmation of a law, empirical or theoretical, is, of course, only partial, never complete and absolute. But in the case of empirical laws, it is a more direct confirmation. The confirmation of a theoretical law is indirect, because it takes place only through the confirmation of empirical laws derived from the theory.

The supreme value of a new theory is its power to predict new empirical laws. It is true that it also has value in explaining known empirical laws, but this is a minor value. If a scientist proposes a new theoretical system, from which no new laws can be derived, then it is logically equivalent to the set of all known empirical laws. The theory may have a certain elegance, and it may simplify to some degree the set of all known laws, although it is not likely that there would be an essential simplification. On the other hand, every new theory in physics that has led to a great leap forward has been a theory from which new empirical laws could be derived. If Einstein had done no more than propose his theory of relativity as an elegant new theory that would embrace certain known laws—perhaps also simplify them to a certain degree— then his theory would not have had such a revolutionary effect.

Of course it was quite otherwise. The theory of relativity led to new empirical laws which explained for the first time such phenomena as the movement of the perihelion of Mercury, and the bending of light rays in the neighborhood of the sun. These predictions showed that relativity theory was more than just a new way of expressing the old laws. Indeed, it was a theory of great predictive power. The consequences that can be derived from Einstein's theory are far from being exhausted. These are consequences that could not have been derived from earlier theories. Usually a theory of such power does have an elegance, and a unifying effect on known laws. It is simpler than the total collection of known laws. But the great value of the theory lies in its power to suggest new laws that can be confirmed by empirical means.

Correspondence Rules

An important qualification must now be added to the discussion of theoretical laws and terms given in the last chapter. The statement that empirical laws are derived from theoretical laws is an oversimplification. It is not possible to derive them directly because a theoretical law contains theoretical terms, whereas an empirical law contains only observable terms. This prevents any direct deduction of an empirical law from a theoretical one.

To understand this, imagine that we are back in the nineteenth century, preparing to state for the first time some theoretical laws about molecules in a gas. These laws are to describe the number of molecules per unit volume of the gas, the molecular velocities, and so forth. To simplify matters, we assume that all the molecules have the same velocity. (This was indeed the original assumption; later it was abandoned in favor of a certain probability distribution of velocities.) Further assumptions must be made about what happens when molecules collide. We do not know the exact shape of molecules, so let us suppose that they are tiny spheres. How do spheres collide? There are laws about colliding spheres, but they concern large bodies. Since we cannot directly observe molecules, we assume their collisions are analogous to those of large bodies; perhaps they behave like perfect billiard balls on a frictionless table. These are, of course, only assumptions; guesses suggested by analogies with known macrolaws.

But now we come up against a difficult problem. Our theoretical laws deal exclusively with the behavior of molecules, which cannot be seen. How, therefore, can we deduce from such laws a law about observable properties such as the pressure or temperature of a gas or properties of sound waves that pass through the gas? The theoretical laws contain only theoretical terms. What we seek are empirical laws containing observable terms. Obviously, such laws cannot be derived without having something else given in addition to the theoretical laws.

The something else that must be given is this: a set of rules connecting the theoretical terms with the observable terms. Scientists and philosophers of science have long recognized the need for such a set of rules, and their nature has been often discussed. An example of such a rule is: "If there is an electromagnetic oscillation of a specified frequency, then there is a visible greenish-blue color of a certain hue." Here something observable is connected with a nonobservable microprocess.

Another example is: "The temperature (measured by a thermometer and, therefore, an observable in the wider sense explained earlier) of a gas is proportional to the mean kinetic energy of its molecules." This rule connects a nonobservable in molecular theory, the kinetic energy of molecules, with an observable, the temperature of the gas. If statements of this kind did not exist, there would be no way of deriving empirical laws about observables from theoretical laws about nonobservables.

Different writers have different names for these rules. I call them "correspondence rules." . . .

There is a temptation at times to think that the set of rules provides a means for defining theoretical terms, whereas just the opposite is really true. A theoretical term can never be explicitly defined on the basis of observable terms, although sometimes an observable can be defined in theoretical terms. For example, "iron" can be defined as a substance consisting of small crystalline parts, each having a certain arrangement of atoms and each atom being a configuration of particles of a certain type. In theoretical terms then, it is possible to express what is meant by the observable term "iron," but the reverse is not true.

There is no answer to the question: "Exactly what is an electron?" Later we shall come back to this question, because it is the kind that philosophers are always asking scientists. They want the physicist to tell them just what he means by "electricity," "magnetism," "gravity," "a molecule." If the physicist explains them in theoretical terms, the philosopher may be disappointed. "That is not what I meant at all," he will say. "I want you to tell me, in ordinary language, what those terms mean." Sometimes the philosopher writes a book in which he talks about the great mysteries of nature. "No one," he writes, "has been able so far, and perhaps no one ever will be able, to give us a straight-forward answer to the question: 'What is electricity?' And so electricity remains forever one of the great, unfathomable mysteries of the universe."

There is no special mystery here. There is only an improperly phrased question. Definitions that cannot, in the nature of the case, be given, should not be demanded. If a child does not know what an elephant is, we can tell him it is a huge animal with big ears and a long trunk. We can show him a picture of an elephant. It serves admirably to define an elephant in observable terms that a child can understand. By analogy, there is a temptation to believe that, when a scientist introduces theoretical terms, he should also be able to define them in familiar terms. But this is not possible. There is no way a physicist can show us a picture of electricity in the way he can show his child a picture of an elephant. Even the cell of an organism, although it cannot be seen with the unaided eye, can be represented by a picture because the cell can be seen when it is viewed through a microscope. But we do not possess a picture of the electron. We cannot say how it looks or how it feels, because it cannot be seen or touched. The best we can do is to say that it is an extremely small body that behaves in a certain manner. This may seem to be analogous to our description of an elephant. We can describe an elephant as a large animal that behaves in a certain manner. Why not do the same with an electron?

The answer is that a physicist can describe the behavior of an electron only by stating theoretical laws, and these laws contain only theoretical terms. They describe the field produced by an electron, the reaction of an electron to a field, and so on. If an electron is in an electrostatic field, its velocity will accelerate in a certain way. Unfortunately, the electron's acceleration is an unobservable. It is not like the acceleration of a billiard ball, which can be studied by direct observation. There is no way that a theoretical concept can be defined in terms of observables. We must, therefore, resign ourselves to the fact that definitions of the kind that can be supplied for observable terms cannot be formulated for theoretical terms. . . .

59. John Stuart Mill

John Stuart Mill (1806–73) not only wrote widely on ethics and political philosophy, but also on logic, metaphysics, the theory of knowledge, and even economics.

Extrapolative Induction Can Justify Beliefs about the Mental States of Other Persons

By what evidence do I know, or by what considerations am I led to believe, that there exist other sentient creatures; that the walking and speaking figures which I see and hear, have sensations and thoughts, or, in other words, possess Minds? The most strenuous Intuitionist does not include this among the things that I know by direct intuition. I conclude it from certain things, which my experience of my own states of feeling proves to me to be marks of it. These marks are of two kinds, antecedent and subsequent; the previous conditions requisite for feeling, and the effects or consequences of it. I conclude that other human beings have feelings like me, because, first, they have bodies like me, which I know, in my own case, to be the antecedent condition of feelings; and because, secondly, they exhibit the acts, and other outward signs, which in my own case I know by experience to be caused by feelings. I am conscious in myself of a series of facts connected by a uniform sequence, of which the beginning is modifications of my body, the middle is feelings, the end

From *An Examination of Sir William Hamilton's Philosophy.* 1865, Chap. 12.

is outward demeanor. In the case of other human beings I have the evidence of my senses for the first and last links of the series, but not for the intermediate link. I find, however, that the sequence between the first and last is as regular and constant in those other cases as it is in mine. In my own case I know that the first link produces the last through the intermediate link, and could not produce it without. Experience, therefore, obliges me to conclude that there must be an intermediate link; which must either be the same in others as in myself, or a different one: I must either believe them to be alive, or to be automatons: and by believing them to be alive, that is, by supposing the link to be of the same nature as in the case of which I have experience, and which is in all other respects similar, I bring other human beings, as phænomena, under the same generalizations which I know by experience to be the true theory of my own existence. And in doing so I conform to the legitimate rules of experimental inquiry. The process is exactly parallel to that by which Newton proved that the force which keeps the planets in their orbits is identical with that by which an apple falls to the ground. It was not incumbent on Newton to prove the impossibility of its being any other force; he was thought to have made out his point when he had simply shown, that no other force need be supposed. We know the existence of other beings by generalization from the knowledge of our own; the generalization merely postulates that what experience shows to be a mark of the existence of something within the sphere of our consciousness, may be concluded to be a mark of the same thing beyond that sphere.

60. Henry Habberley Price

H. H. Price was Professor of Philosophy at Oxford University.

An Application of Hypothetical Reasoning: The Conscious States of Other Persons

I

In ordinary life everyone assumes that he has a great deal of knowledge about other minds or persons. This assumption has naturally aroused the curiosity of philosophers; though perhaps they have not been as curious about it as they ought to have been, for they have devoted many volumes to our consciousness of the material world, but very few to our consciousness of one another. It was thought at one time that each of us derives his knowledge of other minds from the observation of other human organisms. I observe (it was said) that there are a number of bodies which resemble my own fairly closely in their shape, size, and manner of movement; I conclude by analogy that each of these bodies is animated by a mind more or less like myself. It was admitted that this argument was not demonstrative. At the best it would only provide evidence for the existence of other minds, not proof; and one's alleged knowledge of

Taken from H. H. Price, "Our Evidence for the Existence of Other Minds," *Philosophy*, Vol. 13 (1938). Reprinted by kind permission of the author and of the editors of *Philosophy*.

other minds would only be, at the most, well-grounded opinion. It was further admitted, by some philosophers, that our belief in the existence of other minds was probably not *reached* by an argument of this sort, indeed was not reached by an argument at all, but was an uncritical and unquestioning taking-for-granted, a mere piece of primitive credulity; but, it was claimed, the belief can only be justified by an argument of this sort.

This theory, which may be called the Analogical Theory, has come in for a good deal of criticism, and has now been generally abandoned. Perhaps it has sometimes been abandoned for the wrong reasons; for some of its critics (not all) seem to have overlooked the distinction between the genesis of a belief and its justification. However this may be, I shall not discuss the theory any further at present. My aim in this paper is to consider certain other theories which have been or might be suggested in its place, and to develop one of them at some length.

II

The suggestion I wish to examine is that one's evidence for the existence of other minds is derived primarily from the understanding of language. I shall use the word "language" in a wide sense, to include not only speech and writing, but also signals such as waving a red flag, and gestures such as beckoning and pointing. One might say, the suggestion is that one's evidence for the existence of other minds comes from *communication* situations. But this would be question-begging. For communication is by definition a relation between two or more minds. Thus if I have reason to believe that a communication is occurring, I must already have reason to believe that a mind other than my own exists. However, it would be true, according to the theory which I am about to consider, that the study of communication is of fundamental importance. For according to it one's most important evidence for the existence of another mind is always also evidence for the occurrence of communication between that mind and oneself. Even so, the word "communication" has to be taken in a wide sense, as the word "language" has to be. Utterances which I am not intended to hear, and writings or signals which I am not intended to see, will have to be counted as communications, provided I do in fact observe and understand them. In other words, we shall have to allow that there is such a thing as involuntary communication.

Let us consider some instances. Suppose I hear a foreign body[1] utter the noises "Look! there is the bus." I understand these noises. That is to say, they have for me a *symbolic* character, and on hearing them I find myself entertaining a certain proposition, or if you like entertaining a certain thought. (It does not matter how they came to have this symbolic character for me. The point is that they do have it now, however they got it.) As yet I only *entertain* what they symbolize, with perhaps some slight inclination towards belief; for as yet I have no decisive ground for either belief or disbelief. However, I now proceed to look round; and sure

1. I use a phrase "a foreign body" to mean "a body other than my own." As we shall see, it need not be a *human* body.

enough there is the bus, which I had not seen before, and perhaps was not expecting yet. This simple occurrence, of hearing an utterance, understanding it and then verifying it for oneself, provides some evidence that the foreign body which uttered the noises is animated by a mind like one's own. And at the same time it provides evidence that the mind in question is or recently has been in a determinate state. Either it has been itself observing the bus, or it has been observing some other physical object or event from which the advent of the bus could be inferred.

Now suppose that I frequently have experiences of this sort in connection with this particular foreign body. Suppose I am often in its neighbourhood, and it repeatedly produces utterances which I can understand, and which I then proceed to verify for myself. And suppose that this happens in many different kinds of situations. I think that my evidence for believing that this body is animated by a mind like my own would then become very strong. It is true that it will never amount to demonstration. But in the sphere of matters of fact it is a mistake to expect demonstration. We may expect it in the spheres of Pure Mathematics and Formal Logic, but not elsewhere. So much at least we may learn from Hume. If I have no direct extrospective acquaintance with other minds, the most that can be demanded is adequate *evidence* for their existence. If anyone demands *proof* of it his demand is nonsensical, at least if the word "proof" is used in the strict sense which it bears in Pure Mathematics. It is not that the demand unfortunately cannot be fulfilled, owing to the limitations of human knowledge. It is that it cannot really be made at all. The words which purport to formulate it do not really formulate anything.

To return to our argument: the evidence will be strongest where the utterance I hear gives me new information; that is to say, where it symbolizes something which I do *not* already believe, but which I subsequently manage to verify for myself. For if I did already believe it at the time of hearing, I cannot exclude the possibility that it was my own believing which caused the foreign body to utter it. And this might happen even if my own believing were, as we say, "unconscious"; as when I have been believing for many hours that today is Saturday, though until this moment I have not thought about the matter. I know by experience that my believings can cause my own body to utter symbolic noises; and for all I can tell they may sometimes cause a foreign body to do the same. Indeed, there is some empirical evidence in favour of this suggestion. The utterances of an entranced medium at a spiritualistic séance do sometimes seem to be caused by the unspoken beliefs of the sitters. That one mind—my own—can animate two or more bodies at the same time is therefore not an absurd hypothesis, but only a queer one. It cannot be ruled out of court *a priori*, but must be refuted by specific empirical evidence. . . .

IV

In the situations hitherto mentioned the noises which I hear and understand are uttered by a foreign organism which I observe. And the foreign organism is more or less similar to my own. But of course I need not actually observe it. It suffices if I hear an intelligible and informative utterance proceeding from a megaphone or a telephone, from the next room or from behind my back. It may, however, be thought that such a foreign organism must be in principle observable if I am to have evidence of the existence of another mind, and further that it must be more or less similar to my own organism. But I believe that both of these opinions are mistaken, as I shall now try to show by examples.

There is a passage in the Old Testament which reads, "Thou shalt hear a voice behind thee saying, 'This is the way, walk ye in it.'" Now suppose that something like this did actually occur. For instance, I am lost on a mountaintop, and I hear a voice saying that on the other side of such-and-such a rock there is a sheep-track which leads down the mountain. After the best search that I can make, I can find no organism from which the voice could have proceeded. However, I go to the rock in question, and I do find a sheep-track which leads me down safely into the valley. Is it not clear that I should then have good evidence of the existence of another mind? The fact that so far as I can discover there was no organism, human or other, from which the voice proceeded makes no difference, provided I hear the noises, understand them, and verify the information which they convey. Now suppose I go up the mountain many times, and each time I hear an intelligible set of noises, conveying information which is new to me and subsequently verified; but I never find an organism from which they could have proceeded, search as I may. I should then have reason for concluding that the place was "haunted" by an unembodied mind. Such things do not happen, no doubt. But still there is no contradiction whatever in supposing them. The point is that if they did happen they would provide perfectly good evidence for the existence of another mind. And this is sufficient to show that the presence of an observable organism is not essential; *a fortiori*, the presence of an observable organism more or less resembling my own is not essential. . . .

It appears then that I could conceivably get strong evidence of the existence of another mind even if there was no observable organism with which such a mind could be connected. This incidentally is a new and fatal argument against the old Analogical Theory which was referred to at the beginning of this paper. For that theory maintained that one's evidence of the existence of other minds could *only* come from observing foreign bodies which resemble one's own. It is also clear that even when I do observe a foreign body producing the relevant utterances, that body need not be in the least like my own. There is no logical absurdity in the hypothesis of a rational parrot or a rational caterpillar. And if there was such a creature, I could have as good evidence of its rationality as I have in the case of my human neighbours; better evidence indeed than I can have in the case of a human idiot. There is no *a priori* reason why even vegetable organisms should not give evidence of being animated by rational minds, though as it happens they never do. If the rustlings of the leaves of an oak formed intelligible words conveying new information to me, and if gorse-bushes made intelligible gestures, I should have evidence that the oak or the gorse-bush was animated by an intelligence like my own. . . .

VI

We may now return to the main argument. We have described a number of situations in which the perceiving and understanding of symbols gives one evidence of the existence of another mind. But how exactly do they provide evidence for this conclusion? Let us confine ourselves for simplicity to the cases in which the evidence comes from the hearing of sounds. Two conditions, we have seen, must be fulfilled. The first, and most important, is that they must have a symbolic character. And they must be symbolic *for me*. It is obvious that the characteristic of being symbolic is a relational character. An entity S is only a symbol in so far as it stands for some object—whatever the right analysis of "standing for" may be. It is no less obvious, though sometimes forgotten, that the relation is not a simple two-term relation. It involves at least three terms: the entity S, the object O, and in addition a mind or minds. S symbolizes O *to someone*. The relation is more like "to the right of" than it is like "larger than." A is to the right of B from somewhere, from a certain limited set of places. From other places it is not to the right of B, but to the left of it, or in front of it or behind it.

But if the hearing or seeing of S, or its presentation to me in the form of an image, is to provide me with evidence of the existence of another mind, it is not sufficient that S should symbolize some object to someone. It must symbolize some object *to me*. I myself must understand it. Otherwise all I know about it is that it is a noise or black mark having such-and-such sensible qualities. It is true that if I heard sounds uttered in the Arabic language, which I do not understand, I could reasonably conclude to the existence of another mind. But only by analogy. The sounds have some similarity to others which *are* symbolic to me; I therefore assume that they, too, might come to be symbolic to me if I took the trouble.

Secondly, it is essential, I think, that the sounds should symbolize to me something *true or false*. They must propound *propositions* to me. It is not, however, necessary that they should have the grammatical form of a statement. A single word may propound a proposition. Thus the word "snake" may be equivalent to "there is a snake in the immediate neighbourhood." Again, the phrase "the bus" may be equivalent to "the bus is now approaching." Must the proposition propounded be such that I can *test* it, whether in fact I do test it or not? It must certainly be such that I know what the world would be like if it were true. Otherwise I have not understood the symbols: for me they are not symbols at all. But it is not necessary that I should be able to discover by direct observation that the world is in fact like that, or is not. Otherwise I could not understand statements about the remote past, whereas actually I can understand them perfectly well.

The third condition is the one which we have already emphasized.

The noises must not only be symbolic to me; they must give me information. The proposition which they propound must be new to me. That is, it must be new to me as a whole, though of course its constituents and their mode of combination must be familiar to me; otherwise I do not understand the utterance. If it is not new (i.e. new as a whole) the noises do still give evidence of the occurrence of a mental act other than the present act which understands them, and even of a mental act which is in a sense "foreign." But as we have seen, it might conceivably be an unconscious mental act of my own. And this greatly diminishes the evidential value of the utterance.

Now suppose these conditions are fulfilled. I hear noises which are symbolic to me; they propound to me something true or false; and what they propound is new to me. For instance, I hear the noises "here is a black cat" at a time when I do not myself see the cat and was not expecting it to appear. How exactly does this situation provide me with evidence of the existence of another mind? (It is well to insist once again that evidence, not proof, is all that can be demanded.) . . .

VII

We must now raise certain general questions about this argument for the existence of other minds. Though very different in detail from the one used by the old Analogical Theory, it is clearly an argument from analogy. The form of the argument is: situations a and b resemble each other in respect of a characteristic C_1; situation a also has the characteristic C_2; therefore situation b probably has the characteristic C_2 likewise. The noises I am now aware of closely resemble certain ones which I have been aware of before (in technical phraseology, they are *tokens* of the same *type*), and the resemblance covers both their qualities and their manner of combination. Those which I was aware of before functioned as symbols in acts of spontaneous thinking. Therefore these present ones probably resemble them in that respect too; they too probably function as instruments to an act of spontaneous thinking, which in this case is not my own.

But the argument is not only analogical. The hypothesis which it seeks to establish may also be considered in another way. It provides a simple *explanation* of an otherwise mysterious set of occurrences. It explains the curious fact that certain noises not originated by me nevertheless have for me a symbolic character, and moreover are combined in complexes which are symbolic for me as wholes (i.e. propound propositions). Many varieties of sounds occur in the world, and of these only a relatively small proportion are symbolic for me. Those which are symbolic for me can occur in a variety of combinations, and the number of mathematically possible combinations of them is very large; of these combinations only a small proportion "make sense," that is, result in noise-complexes which are symbolic for me *as wholes*. But if there is another mind which uses the same symbols as I do and combines them according to the same principles, and if this mind has produced these noises in the course of an act of spontaneous thinking: then I can account for the occurrence of these noises, and for the fact that they are combined in one of these mathematically-improbable combinations. When I say that these facts are "explained" or "accounted for" by our hypothesis, I mean that if the hypothesis is true these facts are instances of a rule which is already known to hold good in a large number of instances. The rule is, that symbolically-functioning noises combined in symbolically-functioning combinations are produced in the course of acts of spontaneous thinking; and the instances in which it is already known to hold good have been presented to me by introspection.

SUGGESTED READINGS

The Structure of Knowledge

Useful General Discussions

Ayer, A. J. *The Problem of Knowledge.* New York: St. Martin's Press, 1956.
Chisholm, R. M. *Theory of Knowledge,* Englewood Cliffs, N.J.: Prentice-Hall, Inc., 1956.
Hamlyn, D. W. *The Theory of Knowledge.* London: Macmillan. 1970.

Readings in the Theory of Knowledge

Canfield, J. V., and Donnell, Franklin H. (eds.). *Readings in the Theory of Knowledge.* New York: Appleton-Century-Crofts, 1964.
Chisholm, R. M., and Swartz, R. J. (eds.). *Empirical Knowledge: Readings from Contemporary Sources.* Englewood Cliffs, N.J.: Prentice-Hall, Inc., 1973.
Nagel, E., and Brandt, R. *Meaning and Knowledge.* New York: Harcourt, Brace & World, 1965.

Skepticism and the Problem of a Foundation

Cornman, J. W., and Lehrer, K. *Philosophical Problems and Arguments.* New York: Macmillan, 1974.
Hamlyn, D. W. *The Theory of Knowledge.* London: Macmillan. 1970.
Pollock, J. L. *Knowledge and Justification.* Princeton: Princeton University Press, 1974.
Quine, W. V. *Ontological Relativity and Other Essays,* Chap. 3. New York: Columbia University Press, 1969.
Quinton, A. M. *The Nature of Things,* Chaps. 5 and 8. London: Routledge and Kegan Paul, 1973.
Unger, P. "A Defense of Scepticism," *Philosophical Review,* 80 (1971), 198–219.

The Concept of an Analytic Statement

Carnap, R. "Meaning and Synonymy in Natural Languages," *Philosophical Studies,* VI (1955). [Excerpted in Nagel and Brandt.]
Grice, H. P., and Strawson, P. F. "In Defense of a Dogma," *Philosophical Review,* 65 (1956). [Excerpted in Nagel and Brandt.]
Pap, A. *Semantics and Necessary Truth.* New Haven: Yale University Press, 1958.
Putnam, H. *Mind, Matter and Reality,* Chap. 2. Cambridge: Cambridge University Press, 1975.
Quine, W. V. "Two Dogmas of Empiricism, in *From a Logical Point of View.* Cambridge, Mass.: Harvard University Press, 1953. [Excerpted in Nagel and Brandt.]
White, M. "The Analytic and the Synthetic: An Untenable Dualism," in S. Hook, (ed.), *John Dewey: Philosopher of Science and Freedom.*

Logical and Mathematical Truth

Barker, S. F. *Philosophy of Mathematics.* Englewood Cliffs, N.J.: Prentice-Hall, Inc., 1964.

Benacerraf, P, and Putnam, H. (eds.), *Philosophy of Mathematics.* Englewood Cliffs, N.J.: Prentice-Hall, Inc. 1964.

Bradley, R. D. "Geometry and Necessary Truth," *Philosophical Review,* 73 (1964), 59–75. [Reprinted in Bobbs-Merrill Reprint Series.]

Britton, K., Urmson, J. O., and Kneale, W. Symposium: "Are Necessary Truths True by Convention?" Supplementary Vol. 20, Aristotelian Society, London, 1947.

Butchvarov, P. *The Concept of Knowledge,* Pt. 2. Evanston: Northwestern University Press, 1970.

Carnap, R. *Foundations of Logic and Mathematics.* International Encyclopedia of Unified Science, Vol. I, No. 3. Chicago: University of Chicago Press, 1939.

Chisholm, R. M. "Reasons and the A Priori," in R. M. Chisholm, *et al., Philosophy.* Englewood Cliffs, N.J.: Prentice-Hall, Inc., 1964.
——————*Theory of Knowledge.* Chap. 5.

Dewey, J. *The Quest for Certainty.* New York: Minton, Balch & Company, 1929.

Hempel, C. G. "Geometry and Empirical Science," *American Mathematical Monthly,* 52 (1945) and "On the Nature of Mathematical Truth," *American Mathematical Monthly,* 52 (1945), both reprinted in H. Feigl and W. Sellars, (eds.), *Readings in Philosophical Analysis.* New York: Appleton-Century-Crofts, Inc., 1949.

Lewis, C. I. *An Analysis of Knowledge and Valuation.* LaSalle, Ill.: Open Court, 1946.

Malcolm, N. "The Nature of Entailment," and "Are Necessary Propositions Really Verbal?" *Mind,* 49 (1940).

Nagel, E. "Logic Without Ontology," in Y. H. Krikorian, (ed.), *Naturalism and the Human Spirit.* New York: Columbia University Press, 1944.

Putnam, H. *Mathematics, Matter, and Method,* Chaps. 1–4. Cambridge: Cambridge University Press, 1975.

Quine, W. V. *The Ways of Paradox.* New York: Random House, 1966.

Reichenbach, H. *The Rise of Scientific Philosophy.* Berkeley: University of California Press, 1951.

Russell, B. *The Problems of Philosophy.* New York: Henry Holt & Co., 1912. Chap. 7.

Ryle, G., Lewy, C., and Popper, K. R. Symposium: "Why Are the Calculuses of Logic and Arithmetic Applicable to Reality?" Supplementary Vol. 20, Aristotelian Society, London, 1946.

Strawson, P. F. *Introduction to Logical Theory.* New York: John Wiley & Sons, Inc., 1952. Chap. 1.

Waissman, F. "Are There Alternative Logics?" *Proceedings,* The Aristotelian Society (1945–46).

Is There Synthetic A Priori Knowledge?

Ewing, A. C. *Fundamental Questions of Philosophy.* London: Routledge & Kegan Paul Ltd., 1951, pp. 26–36. [Reprinted in Feinberg, also Tillman, Berofsky, and O'Connor.]

Kant, I. *Prolegomena to Any Future Metaphysics.* L. W. Beck, trans. New York: Liberal Arts Press, 1951. [Excerpted in Nagel and Brandt.]

——————————. *Critique of Pure Reason.* N. K. Smith, trans. London: Macmillan & Co., Ltd., 1929. [Excerpted in A. Pap and P. Edwards, (eds.), *A Modern Introduction to Philosophy.* New York: The Free Press, 1965.]

Langford, C. H. "A Proof That Synthetic A Priori Propositions Exist," *Journal of Philosophy,* 46 (1949).

Leibniz, G. W. *Letter to Queen Sophie Charlotte,* 1702. [Excerpted in Pap and Edwards, 608–611.]

Chisholm, R. M. *Theory of Knowledge,* Englewood Cliffs, N.J.: Prentice-Hall, Inc., 87–90, and in R. M. Chisholm, *et al., Philosophy.* Englewood Cliffs, N.J.: Prentice-Hall, Inc., 1964, 304–311.

Pap, A. "Are All Necessary Propositions Analytic?" *Philosophical Review,* 58 (1949).

——————————. *Semantics and Necessary Truth.* New Haven: Yale University Press, 1958.

Pears, D. F. "Incompatibilities of Color," in A. G. N. Flew, *Logic and Language,* Second Series. Oxford: Basil Blackwell.

Schlick, M. "Is There a Factual A Priori?" in Feigl-Sellars, *Readings in Philosophical Analysis,* 277–294.

Stout. G. F. "Self-Evidence," *Philosophy,* Vol. 9 (1934).

The Problem of Induction

Barker, S. F. *Induction and Hypothesis.* Ithaca, N.Y.: Cornell University Press, 1957.

Black, M. *Language and Philosophy.* Ithaca, N.Y.: Cornell University Press, 1949. Chap. 3.

——————————. *Problems of Analysis.* Ithaca, N.Y.: Cornell University Press, 1954, 157–225.

Braithwaite, R. B. *Scientific Explanation.* Cambridge: Cambridge University Press, 1953.

Burks, A. "On the Presuppositions of Induction," *Review of Metaphysics,* VIII, 1955.

Carnap, R. "The Aim of Inductive Logic," in E. Nagel, P. Suppes, and A. Tarski, (eds.), *Logic, Methodology and Philosophy of Science.* Stanford, Calif.: Stanford University Press, 1962.

Edwards, P. "Bertrand Russell's Doubts About Induction," in A. G. N. Flew, *Logic and Language,* First series. Oxford: Basil Blackwell, 1951.

Goodman, N. *Fact, Fiction, and Forecast.* Cambridge, Mass.: Harvard University Press, 1955. Chap. 3.

Kneale, W. *Probability and Induction.* Oxford: Clarendon Press, 1949, 234–237.

Mill, J. S. *A System of Logic,* 1843. Chaps. III, XXI.

Salmon, W. "Should We Attempt to Justify Induction?" *Philosophical Studies,* 8 (1957). [Excerpted in Nagel and Brandt.]

——————————. "The Vindication of Induction," in H. Feigl and C. Maxwell, (eds.), *Current Issues in the Philosophy of Science.* New York: Holt, Rinehart and Winston, 1961.

Williams, D. *The Ground of Induction.* Cambridge, Mass.: Harvard University Press, 1947. Chaps. 4, 6.

Hypothetical Inference, Explanation, and Transcendent Theories

Barker, S. F. *Induction and Hypothesis*. Ithaca, N.Y.: Cornell University Press, 1957, 106–200.

Beck, L. W. "Constructions and Inferred Entities," *Philosophy of Science,* 17 (1950). [Reprinted in H. Feigl and M. Brodeck, (eds.), *Readings in the Philosophy of Science*. New York: Appleton-Century-Crofts, Inc., 1953.]

Hempel, C. G. "A Theoretician's Dilemma," *University of Minnesota Studies in the Philosophy of Science*. Minneapolis: University of Minnesota Press, II, 1958, 37–87.

——————————. *Philosophy of Natural Science*. Englewood Cliffs, N.J.: Prentice-Hall, Inc., 1966.

Kneale, William. *Probability and Induction*. Oxford: Clarendon Press, 1949. Sects. 19–21, 46, 47.

Nagel, E. *The Structure of Science*. New York: Harcourt, Brace & World, 1961.

Popper, K. R. "Three Views Concerning Human Knowledge," in H. D. Lewis, (ed.), *Contemporary British Philosophy*. New York: The Macmillan Company, 1956.

Putnam, H. "What Theories Are Not," in E. Nagel, P. Suppes, and A. Tarski, (eds.), *Logic, Methodology and Philosophy of Science*. Stanford, Calif.: Stanford University Press, 1962.

Smart, J. J. C. *Philosophy and Scientific Realism*. New York: Humanities Press, 1963. Chap. 2.

Toulmin, S. *Philosophy of Science*. London: Hutchinson's University Library, 1953. Chaps. 2, 4.

Inferences to the Conscious States of Other Persons

Alexander, Peter. "Other People's Experience," *Proceedings,* The Aristotelian Society, Vol. 51 (1950–51).

Aune, Bruce. "On Thought and Feeling," *Philosophical Quarterly*, 13 (1963).

Ayer, A. J. *The Problem of Knowledge*. London: Macmillan & Co. Ltd., 1956, 116–254.

——————————. "Our Knowledge of Other Minds" in *Philosophical Essays*. London: Macmillan, 1954.

Eaton, R. M. *General Logic*. New York: Scribner's, 1931, 550–566.

Hampshire, Stuart. "The Analogy of Feeling," *Mind,* 61 (1952).

Hempel, C. G. "The Logical Analysis of Psychology," in H. Feigl and W. Sellars, (eds.), *Readings in Philosophical Analysis*. New York: Appleton-Century-Crofts, 1949.

Malcolm, Norman. "Knowledge of Other Minds," *The Journal of Philosophy,* 56 (1959). [Reprinted in Nagel and Brandt.]

Plantinga, Alvin. "Induction and Other Minds," *Review of Metaphysics*, 19 (1966). [Reprinted in Bobbs-Merrill Reprint Series.]

Thomson, James. "The Argument from Analogy and Our Knowledge of Other Minds," *Mind,* 60 (1951).

Whiteley, C. A. "Behaviorism," *Mind,* 70 (1961).

PART VII

Perceiving the Material World

Introduction

Perceiving (e.g., seeing or hearing something) has been a major preoccupation of philosophers, especially in the present century. Why should this be? Basically because certain complexities in our perceptual commerce with the world introduce some fundamental questions about the foundations of empirical knowledge and about the nature of physical objects. Let us first make explicit these complexities and then spell out the philosophical questions to which they give rise.

The most important complexity is simply the fact that often things cannot really be just as they appear to our senses. We are forced to recognize a distinction between what the object is like (in itself) and the way it sounds or looks to us.

Take, for example, the whistle of a train. If you are standing by the track, the whistle goes up in pitch as the train approaches, and goes down after it has passed; but to the engineer, or to someone standing a distance away, its pitch seems to be steady. It is clear that the sound cannot be both varying and unvarying in pitch at the same time; it cannot be that the sound is what it seems to *everybody*. Furthermore, we know that a whistle blows when the steam issues from the whistle; but from a mile away a sound is heard only some seconds after we have seen the steam. Moreover, how loud a whistle sounds depends on how far away the listener is, and on how good his hearing is—the integrity of various mechanisms in his ear, and of the relevant part of his nervous system. And sometimes you may hear sounds of a whistle when there is no whistle—if you are dreaming, or have suffered from a stroke and are liable to auditory hallucinations.

What is the implication of facts like these? We seem to be forced to distinguish three things: first, something of which you are directly aware, which could occur even if no real whistle were blowing, and such that if it does not occur you do not *hear* the whistle even if it blows loudly near you (perhaps because you are deaf). Let us call this an "auditory sense-datum." Then, there is the physical process which is the real whistle blowing—a complicated event which sets in motion the air in the immediate vicinity. (Of course, a bell can ring in a complete vacuum, in which case nobody hears anything.) Third, there is a complex process leading from the physical event at the whistle to our ears, and eventually to the auditory sense-datum —some sort of causal process.

There is a close parallel to all this, for vision and for the other senses. Things often do not *look* the way they really are, and all the differences between how things are and how they sound can be duplicated for the case of vision. How an object looks obviously depends on things other than the object itself—in particular, on the kind of light which the object is reflecting and the kind of medium it traverses on the way to the eye. For example, the page of a telephone book will look very different to a man over fifty, when he has his glasses on, from how it will look to his naked eye. The presence of mirrors has a similar effect. How an object looks, then, depends on the kind of pattern of light rays which enters the lens of the eye; what a person sees is a function of this and not of the characteristics of the object, except as they influence this. Indeed, an object may not exist at all but still be seen if a typical pattern of light rays enters the eye; for instance, a distant star may have blown up and ceased to be luminous a hundred years ago, but we still see it up to the point when light rays from it cease to arrive. But neither is how things look a function just of the pattern of light rays which enters the eye. If the optic nerve is damaged, we see nothing at all; or if the retinal cortex is damaged, we may see only part of the object we are looking at. How things look is further influenced by cortical processes which we know little about. For instance, the moon appears much larger at the horizon than overhead; whether an object looks white or gray depends on the *relative* amount of light being received from it as contrasted with the environment. Moreover, we have visual experiences in dreams and hallucinations even if our eyes are shut and there is virtually no pattern of light stimulus from the external world at all. How things look is apparently a function of the kind of process going on in the visual area of the brain.

So in the case of vision, too, we are led to distinguish what we are directly aware of (the visual appearance, the *"visual sense-datum"*) from the external object seen, and to suppose that there is some complex causal relation between the two when we see the thing.

The first of our readings in this section, by Broad, is concerned with making clear the necessity for these distinctions, and with clarifying the notion of a sense-datum.

The "sense-datum view," as we may term this two-layer picture of perception, conflicts with a relatively unreflective "common sense" view of perception, sometimes called "naïve realism," according to which physical objects just disclose themselves to our perceptual awareness just as they are. I open my eyes and see a green filing cabinet in front of me. There it is. What is the problem? (So this theory goes.) Well, the considerations adduced in the last few paragraphs show what the problems are. However, "common sense" is by no means totally and inflexibly "naïve realist" about perception. The common man often holds, perhaps as a consequence of knowing about television or because of something learned in school, a very different view of perception (or sometimes an amalgam of naïve realism and this other view) —as being something like television reception. In this second "common sense" view, what I really see when I look at the filing cabinet is a kind of picture on my "mental screen." This picture is produced by my "receiving" and "amplifying" equipment, when this is stimulated by light waves from the filing cabinet. Clearly *this* common-sense view is a crude version of the sense-datum theory.

Since perception is our basic means of access to the physical world (and, hence, to whatever we get to know through the physical world, such as the mental states of other people), it is to be expected that complexities in our concept of perception will give rise to (epistemological) problems about empirical knowledge and (metaphysical) problems about our conception of physical objects. Let us see what those problems are.

As for the epistemological problems, let us recall the introduction to Part VI. There we pointed out that according to the pyramid conception of knowledge, our empirical knowledge of the physical world rests on basic premises supplied by sense perception. Each of these premises embodies something we know to be true, not because we infer it from something else we know, but because it formulates what we are directly aware of in sense-perception. But what is it that we are directly aware of in a case of sense-perception? What is it that we can know without inference in perception? Clearly, the sense-datum view of perception implies that what one gets to know about *directly* in perception is one's private sense-data; any knowledge we get of independently existing physical objects must come by inference from premises about sense-data. When I look at the filing cabinet, what I can claim to know directly is that a greenish visual sense-datum of a certain shape is in my visual field. If I am to find out anything about "public" filing cabinets I will have to make inferences from directly known facts about my sense-data. It will be noted that this consequence of the sense-datum theory is identical with the conclusion reached by C. I. Lewis in Reading 51—that our basic premises are about private experiences rather than about public physical objects.

But if this is so, it raises serious problems as to how one makes the inference from facts about his private sense-data to facts about physical objects. This is a stage in the construction of the pyramid of knowledge that was not explicitly discussed by the selections in Part VI. These selections had to do with the identification of the ultimate premises of knowledge, with generalizations from observations of individual situations to further situations of the same kind or to all situations of the same kind, and with postulations of unobserved objects or events when this was called for by the "best explanation" of the premises. But just how one moves from ultimate premises to conclusions about particular physical objects was not discussed. Does the belief that there are physical objects with certain qualities require some different mode of inference from the basic premises, or can it be justified by the kinds of inference already discussed? This question is discussed in the present Part.

This epistemological problem is intimately related to the metaphysical question of the nature of physical objects. What it takes to infer the existence of a filing cabinet from the existence of one or more sense-data is obviously dependent on what the existence of a filing cabinet amounts to. As we shall see in the selections to follow, some philosophers, partly out of despair at showing how physical objects as common-sensically conceived, can be validly inferred from sense-data, were motivated to construe the nature of the physical world in ways far removed from common sense.

Readings 62, 63, and 64, by Locke, Berkeley, and Whiteley, represent ways of dealing with these problems. All of them start from a sense-datum account of the nature of perception (though Locke and Berkeley use the term "idea" rather than "sense-datum"), but they fan out from this starting point in different directions.

Locke has a somewhat common-sense view of what material objects are like. They do *not* have, e.g., color or warmth—qualities in our experience which are produced by bodies, but do not resemble the qualities of material things. But bodies do have "primary qualities" like shape, size, position, and velocity; indeed, Locke assigns to bodies more or less the properties that modern physics assigns to them. Bodies do also *in a sense* have qualities like color or warmth; by virtue of their primary qualities they have the power to produce sensations like those of color or warmth in a normal human observer. Locke terms these powers "secondary qualities." Locke thinks that when an object is being perceived there is a complex process involving it, the medium, and one's body, as a result of which sense-data get produced. The sense-data represent the material objects to us; indeed, the representation is so close that for practical purposes we need not distinguish between the sense-data and the objects—we can take the visual sense-data as being the actual surfaces of the objects which produce them. According to Locke, of course, material objects are not themselves open to direct inspection; it is only their representatives that are directly observed. He was therefore conscious of the objection that perhaps there are no such objects at all, or at least that we are not in a position to have any reliable information as to their nature. Locke's answer, stated in the concluding pages of the reading, is not fully worked out; the main idea is that his account of the existence and nature of the physical world is the best explanation of the detailed order of our sense experiences. We directly observe only our sense-data, but our beliefs about the material world can be justified by hypothetical inductive inference.

Berkeley agrees with Locke that we are directly aware only of our sense-data; he also agrees that our sense-data are caused by something outside ourselves. But he rejects altogether Locke's conception of an independently existing world of material substance with "primary" qualities. The selection from Berkeley contains many attacks on this whole conception, and on Locke's reasons for espousing it—many of them obviously ineffective, but some of them carrying force. But Berkeley's distinctiveness lies in his radically novel suggestion as to what "material things" are. Berkeley fastens on a fact which Locke would concede—that when a material object such as a filing cabinet is in the presence of a normal person, there is an orderly set of sense experiences which he may have under varying conditions: various visual data when the object is looked at from various angles and distances; various tactual data he can obtain by touching various parts of it; olfactory data in case he sniffs it, and so on. Let us call the whole set of experiences a person *could* have if there were a filing cabinet of a certain kind in his presence a "family" of sense-data for that filing cabinet. Now Berkeley's stroke of genius was to have suggested that *all it is for there to be a filing cabinet* in a person's presence is for there to be (in some sense) a certain family of sense-data—for it to be the case that the person *would* have certain kinds of sense-data under certain conditions (e.g., a trapezoidal green patch if he were looking from a certain angle, etc.). So a physical object is not something distinct from our sensory experience; it is a collection of sense-data. But neither did he hold that sense-data are somehow independently real, sitting around waiting for someone to become aware of them. They are mind-dependent; they exist only when they are objects of sensory awareness. As stated above, he believed that all *our* sense-data are *caused* by something outside of us. Caused by what? There is no independent material world to cause them. You might suggest: perhaps they are caused by other (earlier) sense-data. But Berkeley thinks sense experiences cannot cause anything, for reasons good or bad as you may judge. Neither does he think that you yourself cause your own sense-data, although Berkeley thinks you do cause some experiences—your daydreams, your thoughts, and so on. But you do not cause the sense-data you receive in perception; if you did, you'd make them better ones—perhaps you would adopt the sense-data of a South Sea island rather than of a winter in Michigan! Then what does cause them? Berkeley completes his proposal by urging that they are caused by an infinitely powerful mind, essentially like our minds except for its greater intelligence and power: God. God produces each and every sense-datum. He also brings it about that they come to us in families; God produces such order in our sense experiences that it is possible for us to organize our experience in terms of physical-object concepts. (That is, instead of speaking of individual sense-data, we can think of a great variety of sense-data as all being experiences "of" a single object, the filing cabinet.) We therefore can say that God is the creator and preserver of the material universe, even though in a sense there is no material universe at all in addition to finite minds with their sense experiences, and God. Minds are the whole furniture of heaven and earth.

Berkeley's view may be called a "mentalist" or "idealist" view of the material world and its relation to sense experiences, in contrast with Locke's view which may be called a "causal realist" or a "representative realist" type of theory.

The next reading, by C. H. Whiteley, both presents and criticizes a view called "phenomenalism." We shall not speculate on its historical origins. Some have claimed it was held by philosophers in India over two thousand years ago. In some form it was espoused by David Hume, Immanuel Kant, and J. S. Mill. It has been widely held in the present century by "logical positivists." What is the phenomenalist view? In essence, the phenomenalist accepts Berkeley's concept of physical objects as families of sense-data but *without* the part about causation by God; the theory of a Supreme Mind does not enter the phenomenalist's view of the material world. Instead—and this is the phenomenalist's stroke of genius—the phenomenalist returns to the Lockean view that sense-data are caused by objects, but he says they are *caused by specific objects as the phenomenalist understands these.* The phenomenalist urges that what it is for one event *A* to cause another event *B* is for *A* and *B* both to occur and for it to be a rule (a law of nature) that *anything* (at any time) exactly like *A* is followed by something exactly like *B*. And, of course, an object on the phenomenalist view is a family of sense-data. Suppose that *B* is a sense-datum. Then, to say that *B* is caused by the event *A* (of a green filing cabinet being before your open eyes, at a certain distance and angle, when the light is on, when there is no intervening screen, and when your nervous system is in good order) is to say that event (situation) *A* occurred, followed by *B,* and that situations like *A* are generally followed by an occurrence like *B*—and the facts constitutive of *A* are themselves *construed as families of sense-data,* or, in other words, construed as the fact that certain sense-data, corresponding to the objects or circumstances mentioned, *would* be obtained by normal observers in certain conditions. This proposal is certainly not a common-sense one, and it is very puzzling, but it has some attraction after you have thought about it a bit.

It is clear that the phenomenalist can claim that in a sense his view is much more economical than that of either Locke or Berkeley; he does not have to justify belief in an independently existing but unobserved world of material things, or a belief in an infinitely powerful mind. He asserts no facts which Berkeley and Locke would not both also admit (that certain sense-data occur in certain circumstances). He can justify everything he asserts, in his talk about "physical objects," by simple enumerative (extrapolative) inference from past experiences—which can tell us which "families" of sense-data there are, and what regularities there are in their sequence. He avoids the hypothetical inductive inference Locke requires for his inference to unobserved material substances; and he avoids some allegedly self-evident principles Berkeley uses in his argument to God. The theory does not require us to talk of anything which is not accessible to direct observation.

It is no wonder that the phenomenalist position has attracted many philosophers in the past century and a half. It has been the staple view of contemporary "radical empiricism" or "logical positivism," which characterizes the views of Locke and Berkeley as "meaningless" affirmations of a metaphysical kind. The theory may seem to be out of line with modern physics, which appears to assert the independent existence of numerous unseen small particles; but the phenomenalist thinks that he can interpret those assertions as claims that certain sensory experiences (e.g., of cloud-chamber pictures, etc.) would occur in certain conditions. Phenomenalism thus looks like a hard-headed nonmetaphysical view suitable for a scientific age. And this is what its proponents have claimed for it.

Is there anything wrong with phenomenalism? The objections to it which at once come to mind, that it does not seem to allow for the distinction between appearance and reality, or for the permanence of things, or for the causal activity of material things (including their causation of sense-data), are considered by Whiteley and dismissed as being a result of misunderstandings. Whiteley is himself, however, not wholly convinced by phenomenalism, and at the end he lists three "paradoxes" for the phenomenalist. Of these three, the first two would strike contemporary phenomenalists as just *not* very paradoxical (e.g., they would say, in reply to the first, that while it is true that we think objects exist now, when we do not see them, they exist only in the phenomenalist sense, that *if* there were an observer there, he *could* have certain sense experiences); and some would say in reply to the third "paradox" that their phenomenalism does not commit them to any view about the mental states of other persons. Probably the objection to phenomenalism most influential today is one stated clearly only in recent years, by R. M. Chisholm. Essentially, the objection is that you cannot identify any set of possible experiences as the "family" with which the object can be identified. The trouble is that the sense-data that do or would occur in certain circumstances are *not a function only of the object;* they are a function also of the character of the intervening medium and of the perceiver's sense organs and brain. For instance, suppose a door knob is directly in front of me. The phenomenalist holds that this is, among other things, for it to be true that if I reach out and touch I shall have a certain sort of tactual datum. But that cannot be right, for in case my hand is anesthetized it will be false that I shall receive that tactual datum under those circumstances—even if there is a door knob in front of me. Or, if a red object is in front of me, you cannot say that if I look I shall have a red sense-datum, for if the light is blue I shall have a black sense-datum. So it looks as if, given that there is an object of a certain kind in my presence, this fact does not by itself make it true that there is any special kind of sense-datum that I shall have, and given that I am having a certain kind of sense-datum (or finite sequence of sense-data), you cannot infer that there is any special kind of object in my presence. If this is correct, then it looks as if Berkeley's basic assumption (which we suggested a Lockean might also readily grant), that there is a special kind of family of sense-data associated with the existence of a kind of physical object, is mistaken. And if that is mistaken, then phenomenalism appears untenable. Now some phenomenalists are unmoved by this objection, but it appears that if phenomenalism can be restated at all to meet the objection, it will become a much less simple theory.

61.   Charlie Dunbar Broad

C. D. Broad (1887–1971) was Professor of Philosophy at Cambridge University.

The Concept of Sense-Data

The Traditional Notion of a Bit of Matter. When we ask what is meant by a bit of Matter the question is itself ambiguous. In one sense a complete answer to it would be a complete theory of Matter, and this could only be made, if at all, at the very end of our discussion. This, however, is not the sense in which I am asking the question here. All that I am asking is: "What is the irreducible minimum of properties which practically every-body would agree that an object must possess if it is to be called a bit of Matter?" I think that science and common-sense would agree that at least the following conditions must be fulfilled: (i) Its existence and properties must be independent of the minds that happen to observe it, and it must be capable of being observed by many minds. This character-istic may be summed up by saying that Matter is neutral as between various observers, or is "public"—to use a convenient word of Mr. Rus-sell's. This distinguishes Matter sharply from any ordinary conscious state of mind. . . .

(ii) A bit of Matter is supposed to be neutral, not only between dif-ferent observers, but also to be in a certain way neutral as between several senses of the same observer. We are said to see, hear, and feel a bell. This sort of neutrality is not supposed to be complete. The shape and size of the bell are indeed supposed to be in some way common to

From C. D. Broad, *Scientific Thought*, 1923. Published by Routledge & Kegan Paul Ltd., London, and Humanities Press Inc., New Jersey. Reprinted by permission of the publishers.

sight and touch. As regards its sensible qualities the view of common-sense is that any bit of Matter combines a number of these, and that different senses are needed to reveal different sensible qualities. Thus sight, and it alone, makes us aware of the colours of bodies; touch, and it alone, makes us aware of their temperatures; and so on. But it is part of the ordinary view of a piece of Matter that all these various sensible qualities co-exist in it, whether the requisite senses be in action to reveal them all or not. If we first only look at a body, and then shut our eyes and go up to it and feel it, it is not supposed that it had no temperature on the first occasion and no colour on the second.

(iii) These two properties of publicity, as between different observers, and neutrality, as between the various senses of a single observer, are closely connected with a third feature which is held to be characteristic of Matter. Bits of Matter are supposed to persist with very little change, whether anyone happens to observe them or not, and to pursue their own affairs and interact with each other, regardless of our presence and absence.

(iv) This brings us to the fourth characteristic of Matter. It is commonly held to be part of what we mean by a bit of Matter that it shall have a more or less permanent shape and size, and that it shall have a position in Space, and be capable of moving from one position to another. It is admitted that bits of Matter are constantly changing their shapes, sizes, and positions; but it is held that they do this through their interactions with each other and not through any change in our acts of observation, and that in all their changes they continue to have *some* shape, size and position. If it could be shown that nothing in the world actually has such properties as these, it would commonly be held that the existence of Matter had been disproved, even though there were public, independent, and persistent objects. . . .

The Notion of Sensible Appearance. I have now tried to point out what is the irreducible minimum of properties which ordinary people consider must be possessed by anything if it is to count as a piece of Matter.

. . . It is necessary to distinguish between things as they are and things as they seem to us, or between physical reality and sensible appearance. Difficulties always arise when two sets of properties apparently belong to the same object, and yet are apparently incompatible with each other. Now the difficulty here is to reconcile the supposed neutrality, persistence, and independence of a physical object with the obvious differences between its various sensible appearances to different observers at the same moment, and to the same observer at different moments between which it is held not to have undergone any physical change. We know, *e.g.*, that when we lay a penny down on a table and view it from different positions it generally looks more or less elliptical in shape. The eccentricity of these various appearances varies as we move about, and so does the direction of their major axes. Now we hold that the penny, at which we say we were looking all the time, has not changed; and that it is round, and not elliptical in shape. This is, of course, only one example out of millions. It would be easy to offer much wilder ones; but it is simple and obvious, and involves no complications about a transmitting medium; so we will start with it as a typical case to discuss.

Now there is nothing in the mere ellipticity or the mere variation, taken by itself, to worry us. The difficulty arises because of the incompatibility between the apparent shapes and the supposed real shape, and between the change in the appearances and the supposed constancy of the physical object. We need not at present ask *why* we believe that there is a single physical object with these characteristics, which appears to us in all these different ways. It is a fact that we do believe in. It is an equally certain fact that the penny does look different as we move about. The difficulty is to reconcile the different appearances with the supposed constancy of the penny, and the ellipticity of most of the appearances with the supposed roundness of the penny. It is probable that at first sight the reader will not see much difficulty in this. He will be inclined to say that we can explain these various visual appearances by the laws of perspective, and so on. This is not a relevant answer. It is quite true that we can *predict what particular appearance* an object will present to an observer, when we know the shape of the object and its position with respect to the observer. But this is not the question that is troubling us at present. Our question is as to the compatibiliy of these changing elliptical appearances, however they may be correlated with other facts in the world, with the supposed constancy and roundness of the physical object.

Now what I call *Sensible Appearance* is just a general name for such facts as I have been describing. It is important, here as always, to state the *facts* in a form to which everyone will agree, before attempting any particular *analysis* of them, with which it is certain that many people will violently disagree. The fundamental fact is that we constantly make such judgments as: "This *seems to me* elliptical, or red, or hot," as the case may be, and that about the truth of these judgments we do not feel the least doubt. We may, however, at the same time doubt or positively disbelieve that this *is* elliptical, or red, or hot. I may be perfectly certain at one and the same time that I have the peculiar experience expressed by the judgment: "This looks elliptical to me," and that in fact the object is not elliptical but is round.

I do not suppose that anyone, on reflection, will quarrel with this statement of fact. The next question is as to the right way to analyse such facts; and it is most important not to confuse the facts themselves with any particular theory as to how they ought to be analysed. We may start with a negative remark, which seems to me to be true, and is certainly of the utmost importance if it be true. Appearance is *not* merely mistaken *judgment* about physical objects. When I judge that a penny looks elliptical I am not mistakenly ascribing elliptical shape to what is in fact round. Sensible appearances *may* lead me to make a mistaken judgment about physical objects, but they *need* not, and, so far as we know, commonly do not. My certainty that the penny looks elliptical exists comfortably alongside of my conviction that it is round. But a mistaken judgment that the penny *is* elliptical would not continue to exist after I knew that the penny was really round. The plain fact is then that "looking elliptical to me" stands for a peculiar experience, which, whatever the right analysis of it may be, is not just a mistaken judgment about the shape of the penny.

Appearance then cannot be described as mistaken judgment about the properties of some physical object. How are we to describe it, and can we analyse it? Two different types of theory seem to be possible, which I will call respectively the *Multiple Relation Theory*, and the *Object Theory* of sensible appearance. The Multiple Relation Theory takes the view that "appearing to be so and so" is a unique kind of relation between an object, a mind, and a characteristic. (This is a rough statement, but it will suffice for the present.) On this type of theory to say that the penny looks elliptical to me is to say that a unique and not further analysable relation of "appearing" holds between the penny, my mind, and the general characteristic of ellipticity. The essential point for us to notice at present about theories of this kind is that they do not imply that we are aware of *anything* that *really is* elliptical when we have the experience which we express by saying that the penny looks elliptical to us. Theories of this type have been suggested lately by Professor Dawes Hicks and by Dr. G. E. Moore. So far, they have not been worked out in any great detail, but they undoubtedly deserve careful attention.

Theories of the Object type are quite different. They do not involve a unique and unanalysable multiple relation of "appear*ing*," but a peculiar kind of object— an "appear*ance*." Such objects, it is held, actually *do have* the characteristics which the physical object *seems to have*. Thus the Object Theory analyses the statement that the penny looks to me elliptical into a statement which involves the actual existence of an elliptical object, which stands in a certain cognitive relation to me on the one hand, and in another relation, yet to be determined, to the round penny. This type of theory, though it has been much mixed up with irrelevant matter, and has never been clearly stated and worked out till our own day, is of respectable antiquity. The doctrine of "representative ideas" is the traditional and highly muddled form of it. It lies at the basis of such works as Russell's *Lowell Lectures on the External World*. In this book I shall deliberately confine myself to this type of theory, and shall try to state it clearly, and work it out in detail.

The Theory of Sensa

I propose now to state more fully the theory that appearances are a peculiar kind of objects, and to consider what sort of objects they must be. The reader will bear in mind throughout the whole of the long story which follows that there is a totally different view of sensible appearance, viz., the Multiple Relation Theory, and that this may quite possibly be true. In this book I shall leave it wholly aside. On the theory that we are now going to discuss, whenever a penny looks to me elliptical, what really happens is that I am aware of an object which is, in fact, elliptical. This object is connected in some specially intimate way with the round physical penny, and for this reason is called an appearance *of* the penny. It really is elliptical, and for this reason the penny is said to look *elliptical*. We may generalise this theory of sensible appearance as follows: Whenever I truly judge that x appears to me to have the sensible quality q, what happens is that I am directly aware of a certain object y, which (*a*) really does have the quality q, and (*b*) stands in some peculiarly intimate relation, yet to be determined, to x. (At the present stage, for all that we know, y might sometimes be identical with x, or might be literally a part of x.) Such objects as y I am going to to call *Sensa*. Thus, when I look at a penny from the side, what happens, on the present theory, is at least this: I have a sensation, whose object is an elliptical, brown sensum; and this sensum is related in some specially intimate way to a certain round physical object, viz., the penny.

Now I think it must at least be admitted that the sensum theory is highly plausible. When I look at a penny from the side I am certainly aware of *something;* and it is certainly plausible to hold that this something is elliptical in the same plain sense in which a suitably bent piece of wire, looked at from straight above, is elliptical. If, in fact, nothing elliptical is before my mind, it is very hard to understand why the penny should seem *elliptical* rather than of any other shape. I do not now regard this argument as absolutely conclusive, because I am inclined to think that the Multiple Relation theory can explain these facts also. But it is at least a good enough argument to make the sensum theory well worth further consideration.

Assuming that when I look at a penny from the side I am directly aware of something which is in fact elliptical, it is clear that this something cannot be identified with the penny, if the latter really has the characteristics that it is commonly supposed to have. The penny is supposed to be round, whilst the sensum is elliptical. Again, the penny is supposed to keep the same shape and size as we move about, whilst the sensa alter in shape and size. Now one and the same thing cannot, at the same time and in the same sense, be round and elliptical. Nor can one and the same thing at once change its shape and keep its shape unaltered, if "shape" be used in the same sense in both statements. Thus it is certain that, if there be sensa, they cannot in general be identified with the physical objects of which they are the appearances, if these literally have the properties commonly assigned to them. On the other hand, all that I ever come to know about physical objects and their qualities seems to be based upon the qualities of the sensa that I become aware of in sense-perception. If the visual sensa were not elliptical and did not vary in certain ways as I move about, I should not judge that I was seeing a round penny.

The distinction between sensum and physical object can perhaps be made still clearer by taking some wilder examples. Consider, *e.g.*, the case of looking at a stick which is half in water and half in air. We say that it looks bent. And we certainly do not mean by this that we mistakenly judge it to be bent; we generally make no such mistake. We are aware of an object which is very much like what we should be aware of if we were looking at a stick with a physical kink in it, immersed wholly in air. The most obvious analysis of the facts is that, when we judge that a straight stick *looks* bent, we are aware of an object which really *is* bent, and which is related in a peculiarly intimate way to the physically straight stick. The relation cannot be that of identity; since the same thing cannot at once be bent and straight, in the same sense of these words. If there be *nothing* with a kink in it before our minds at the moment, why should we think then of kinks at all, as we do when we say that the stick looks bent? No doubt we can quite well mistakenly *believe* a property to be present which is really absent, when we are dealing with something that is only known to us indirectly, like Julius Caesar or the North Pole. But in our example we are dealing with a concrete visible object, which is bodily present to our senses; and it is very hard to understand how we could seem to ourselves to *see* the property of bentness exhibited in a concrete instance, if in fact *nothing* was present to our minds that possessed that property.

As I want to make the grounds for the sensum theory as clear as possible, I will take one more example. Scientists often assert that physical objects are not "really" red or hot. We are not at present concerned with the truth or falsehood of this strange opinion, but only with its application to our present problem. Let us suppose then, for the sake of argument, that it is true. When a scientist looks at a penny stamp or burns his mouth with a potato he has exactly the same sort of experience as men of baser clay, who know nothing of the scientific theories of light and heat. The visual experience seems to be adequately described by saying that each of them is aware of a red patch of approximately square shape. If such patches be not in fact red, and if people be not in fact aware of such patches, where could the notion of red or of any other colour have come from? The scientific theory of colour would have nothing to explain, unless people really are aware of patches under various circumstances which really do have different colours. The scientists would be in the position of Mr. Munro's duchess, who congratulated herself that unbelief had become impossible, as the Liberal Theologians had left us nothing to disbelieve in. Thus we seem forced to the view that there are at least hot and coloured sensa; and, if we accept the scientific view that physical objects are neither hot nor coloured, it will follow that sensa cannot be identified with physical objects.

The reader may be inclined to say, "After all, these sensa are not real; they are mere appearances, so why trouble about them?" The answer is that you do not get rid of anything by labelling it "appearance." Appearances are as real in their own way as anything else. If an appearance were nothing at all, nothing would appear, and if nothing appeared, there would be nothing for scientific theories to account for. To put the matter in another way: Words like *real* and *reality* are ambiguous. A round penny and an elliptical visual sensum are not real in precisely the same sense. But both are real in the most general sense that a complete inventory of the universe must mention the one as much as the other. No doubt the kind of reality which is to be ascribed to appearances will vary with the particular type of theory as to the nature of sensible appearance that we adopt. On the present theory an appearance is a sensum, and a sensum is a particular existent, though it may be a short-lived one. On the Multiple Relation theory appearances have a very different type of reality. But *all* possible theories have to admit the reality, *in some sense*, of appearances; and therefore it is no objection to any particular theory that it ascribes a sort of reality to appearances.

I hope that I have now made fairly clear the grounds on which the sensum theory of sensible appearance has been put forward. Closely connected with it is a theory about the perception of physical objects, and we may sum up the whole view under discussion as follows: Under certain conditions I have states of mind called sensations. These sensations have objects, which are always concrete particular existents, like coloured or hot patches, noises, smells, etc. Such objects are called sensa. Sensa have properties, such as shape, size, hardness, colour, loudness, coldness, and so on. The existence of such sensa, and their presence to our minds in sensation, lead us to judge that a physical object exists and is present to our senses. To this physical object we ascribe various properties. These properties are not in general identical with those of the sensum which is before our minds at the moment. For instance, the elliptical sensum makes us believe in the existence of a *round* physical penny. Nevertheless, all the properties that we do ascribe to physical objects are based upon and correlated with the properties that actually characterise our sensa. The sensa that are connected with a physical object x in a certain specially intimate way are called the appearances of that object to those observers who sense these sensa. The properties which x is said to *appear* to have are the properties which those sensa that are x's appearances *really do* have. Of course, the two properties may happen to be the same, *e.g.*, when I look straight down on a penny, both the physical object and the visual appearance are round. Generally, however, there is only a correlation between the two.

It follows from this theory that sensa cannot appear to have properties which they do not really have, though there is no reason why they should not have more properties than we do or can notice in them. This point perhaps needs a little more elaboration, since a good deal of nonsense has been talked by opponents of the sensum theory in this connexion. We must distinguish between failing to notice what is present in an object and "noticing" what is not present in an object. The former presents no special difficulty. There may well be in any object much which is too minute and obscure for us to recognise distinctly. Again, it is obvious that we may sense an object without necessarily being aware of all its relations even to another object that we sense at the same time. Still more certain is it that we may sense an object without being aware of all its relations to some other object which we are not sensing at the time. Consequently, there is no difficulty whatever in supposing that sensa may be much more differentiated than we think them to be, and that two sensa may really differ in quality when we think that they are exactly alike. Arguments such as Stumpf's render it practically certain that the latter possibility is in fact realised.

The real difficulty is when we seem to be directly aware of some property in an object, and this property is not really present and is perhaps incompatible with others which are present. This is the kind of difficulty that the sensum theory is put forward to meet. We seem to recognise elliptical shape in the penny, when the penny really has the incompatible quality of roundness. The solution which the sensum theory offers is to "change the subject." *Something*, it admits, is elliptical, and something is round; but they are not the same something. What is round is the penny, what is elliptical is the sensum. Now, clearly, this would be no solution, if the same sort of difficulty were to break out in sensa themselves. In that case we should need to postulate appearances of appearances, and so on indefinitely.

We must hold, as regards positive sensible qualities which characterise a sensum as a whole and do not involve relations to other sensa, that a sensum is at least all that it appears to be. Now, so far as I know, there is no evidence to the contrary. Some people have thought that arguments like Stumpf's raised this difficulty; but that is simply a mistake. Stumpf's argument deals merely with the relation of qualitative likeness and difference between different sensa, and shows that we may think that two of them are exactly alike when there is really a slight qualitative or quantitative difference between them. This has no tendency to prove that we ever find a positive non-relational quality in a sensum, which is not really there.

Next, we must remember that attributes which involve a negative factor often have positive names. A man might quite well think, on inspecting one of his sensa, that it was exactly round and uniformly red. And he might well be mistaken. But then, "exactly round" means "with no variation of curvature," and "uniformly red" means "with no variation of shade from one part to another." Now universal negative judgments like these can never be guaranteed by mere inspection; and so, in such cases, the man is not "seeing properties that are not there" in the sense in which he would be doing so if a round sensum appeared to him to be elliptical. To sum up, it is no objection to the sensum theory that a sensum may seem to be *less* differentiated than it is; it would be a fatal objection if a sensum ever seemed *more* differentiated than it is; but we have no evidence that the latter ever happens.

Before going further we must remove a baseless prejudice which is sometimes felt against the sensum theory. It is often objected that we are not aware of sensa and their properties, as a rule, unless we specially look for them. It is a fact that it often needs a good deal of persuasion to make a man believe that, when he looks at a penny from the side, it seems elliptical to him. And I am afraid that very often, when he is persuaded, it is not by his own direct inspection (which is the only relevant evidence in such a matter); but by some absurd and irrelevant argument that the area of his retina affected by the light from the penny, is an oblique projection of a circle, and is therefore an ellipse. Accordingly, it is argued that we have no right to believe that such a man is directly sensing an object which is, in fact, elliptical. To this objection a partial answer has already been given, by implication. It is only when we are looking at a penny almost normally that any doubt is felt of the ellipticity of the sensum; and, in that case, the sensum is, in fact, very nearly round.

Now we have seen that it is no objection to our theory that a sensum which is not quite round should be thought to be exactly round, though it would be an objection if an exactly round sensum seemed to be elliptical. The reason, of course, is that an ellipse, with its variable curvature, is a more differentiated figure than a circle, with its uniform curvature. There is no difficulty in the fact that we overlook minute differentiations that are really present in our sensa; difficulties would only arise if we seemed to notice distinctions that are not really present.

Apart, however, from this special answer, a more general reply can be made to the type of objection under discussion. The whole argument rests on a misunderstanding of the view about perception which the sensum theory holds. If the theory were that, in perceiving a penny, a man first becomes aware of a sensum, then notices that it is elliptical, and then infers from this fact and the laws of perspective that he is looking at a round physical object, the argument would be fatal to the theory. But this is quite obviously not what happens. Perceptual judgments are indeed *based upon* sensa and their properties to this extent, that if we were not aware of a sensum we should not now judge that any physical object is present to our senses, and that if this sensum had different properties we should ascribe different properties to the physical object. But the relation between the sensum and its properties, on the one hand, and the perceptual judgment about the physical object, on the other, is not that of *inference*. The best analogy that we can offer to the relation between our sensing of a sensum and our perceiving a physical object, is to be found in the case of reading a book in a familiar language. What interests us as a rule is the meaning of the printed words, and not the peculiarities of the print. We do not explicitly notice the latter, unless there be something markedly wrong with it, such as a letter upside down. Nevertheless, if there were no print we should cognise no meaning, and if the print were different in certain specific ways we should cognise a different meaning. We *can* attend to the print itself if we choose, as in proof-reading. In exactly the same way, we are not as a rule interested in sensa, as such, but only in what we think they can tell us about physical objects, which alone can help or hurt us. Sensa themselves "cut no ice." We therefore pass automatically from the sensum and its properties to judgments about the physical object and its properties. If it should happen that the sensum is queer, as when we see double, we notice the sensum, as we notice an inverted letter. And, even in normal cases, we generally can detect the properties of sensa, and contrast them with those which they are leading us to ascribe to the physical object, provided that we make a special effort of attention.

From what has just been said, it will not appear strange that, even though there be sensa, they should have been overlooked by most plain men and by many philosophers. Of course, everyone is constantly sensing them, and, in specially abnormal cases, has noted the difference between them and physical objects. But sensa have never been objects of special interest, and therefore have never been given a name in common speech. A result of this is that all words like "seeing," "hearing," etc., are ambiguous. They stand sometimes for acts of sensing, whose objects are of

721

course sensa, and sometimes for acts of perceiving, whose objects are supposed to be bits of matter and their sensible qualities. This is especially clear about hearing. We talk of "hearing a noise" and of "hearing a bell." In the first case we mean that we are sensing an auditory sensum, with certain attributes of pitch, loudness, quality, etc. In the second case we mean that, in consequence of sensing such a sensum, we judge that a certain physical object exists and is present to our senses. Here the word "hearing" stands for an act of perceiving. Exactly the same remarks apply to sight. In one sense we see a penny; in a somewhat stricter sense we see only one side of the penny; in another sense we see only a brown elliptical sensum. The first two uses refer to acts of perceiving, the last to an act of sensing. It is best on the whole to confine words like "seeing" and "hearing" to acts of perceiving. This is, of course, their ordinary use. I shall therefore talk of seeing a penny, but not of seeing a brown elliptical sensum. I shall speak of the latter kind of cognition as "visually sensing," or merely as "sensing," when no misunderstanding is to be feared by dropping the adjective. This distinction will be found important when we come to deal with illusory perceptions.

62. John Locke

John Locke (1632–1706), an English philosopher, wrote the
first comprehensive treatise on the theory of knowledge.

Sense Experiences Caused by Objects

7. Ideas in the Mind, Qualities in Bodies. To discover the nature of our
ideas the better, and to discourse of them intelligibly, it will be convenient to distinguish them as they are ideas or perceptions in our minds,
and as they are modifications of matter in the bodies that cause such
perceptions in us, that so we may not think (as perhaps usually is done)
that they are exactly the images and resemblances of something inherent
in the subject; most of those of sensation being in the mind no more the
likeness of something existing without us, than the names that stand for
them are the likeness of our ideas, which yet upon hearing they are apt
to excite in us.

8. Whatsoever the mind perceives in itself, or is the immediate object of perception, thought, or understanding, that I call idea; and the
power to produce any idea in our mind, I call quality of the subject
wherein that power is. Thus a snowball having the power to produce in
us the ideas of white, cold, and round, the power to produce those ideas
in us, as they are in the snowball, I call qualities; and as they are sensations or perceptions in our understandings, I call them ideas; which
ideas, if I speak of sometimes as in the things themselves, I would be

From John Locke, *An Essay Concerning Human Understanding*, Book II, Chapters 8 and 9, and Book IV, Chapter 11, first published in 1690.

understood to mean those qualities in the objects which produce them in us.

9. *Primary Qualities.* Qualities thus considered in bodies are, first, such as are utterly inseparable from the body, in what state soever it be; such as in all the alterations and changes it suffers, all the force can be used upon it, it constantly keeps; and such as sense constantly finds in every particle of matter which has bulk enough to be perceived and the mind finds inseparable from every particle of matter, though less than to make itself singly be perceived by our senses, v.g., take a grain of wheat, divide it into two parts, each part has still solidity, extension, figure, and mobility; divide it again, and it retains still the same qualities; and so divide it on till the parts become insensible, they must retain still each of them all those qualities. For division (which is all that a mill, or pestle, or any other body, does upon another, in reducing it to insensible parts) can never take away either solidity, extension, figure, or mobility from any body, but only makes two or more distinct separate masses of matter, of that which was but one before; all which distinct masses, reckoned as so many distinct bodies, after division, make a certain number. These I call original or primary qualities of body, which I think we may observe to produce simple ideas in us, viz., solidity, extension, figure, motion or rest, and number.

10. *Secondary Qualities.* Secondly, such qualities which in truth are nothing in the objects themselves, but powers to produce various sensations in us by their primary qualities, i.e., by the bulk, figure, texture, and motion of their insensible parts, as colours, sounds, tastes, &c., these I call secondary qualities. To these might be added a third sort, which are allowed to be barely powers, though they are as much real qualities in the subject, as those which I, to comply with the common way of speaking, call qualities, but for distinction, secondary qualities. For the power in fire to produce a new colour or consistency in wax or clay, by its primary qualities, is as much a quality in fire as the power it has to produce in me a new idea or sensation of warmth or burning, which I felt not before, by the same primary qualities, viz., the bulk, texture, and motion of its insensible parts.

11. *How primary Qualities produce their Ideas.* The next thing to be considered is, how bodies produce ideas in us; and that is manifestly by impulse, the only way which we can conceive bodies to operate in.

12. If then external objects be not united to our minds when they produce ideas therein, and yet we perceive these original qualities in such of them as singly fall under our senses, it is evident that some motion must be thence continued by our nerves or animal spirits, by some parts of our bodies, to the brain, or the seat of sensation, there to produce in our minds the particular ideas we have of them. And since the extension, figure, number, and motion of bodies of an observable bigness, may be perceived at a distance by the sight, it is evident some singly imperceptible bodies must come from them to the eyes, and thereby convey to the brain some motion, which produces these ideas which we have of them in us.

13. *How secondary.* After the same manner that the ideas of these

original qualities are produced in us, we may conceive that the ideas of secondary qualities are also produced, viz., by the operations of insensible particles on our senses. For it being manifest that there are bodies and good store of bodies, each whereof are so small, that we cannot by any of our senses discover either their bulk, figure, or motion, as is evident in the particles of the air and water, and others extremely smaller than those, perhaps as much smaller than the particles of air and water, as the particles of air and water are smaller than peas or hail-stones; let us suppose that the different motions and figures, bulk and number, of such particles, affecting the several organs of our senses, produce in us those different sensations which we have from the colours and smells of bodies; v.g., that a violet, by the impulse of such insensible particles of matter of peculiar figures and bulks, and in different degrees and modifications of their motions, causes the ideas of the blue colour and sweet scent of that flower to be produced in our minds; it being no more impossible to conceive that God should annex such ideas to such motions, with which they have no similitude, than that he should annex the idea of pain to the motion of a piece of steel dividing our flesh, with which that idea hath no resemblance.

14. What I have said concerning colours and smells may be understood also of tastes and sounds, and other the like sensible qualities; which, whatever reality we by mistake attribute to them, are in truth nothing in the objects themselves, but powers to produce various sensations in us, and depend on those primary qualities, viz., bulk, figure, texture, and motion of parts, as I have said.

15. *Ideas of primary Qualities are Resemblances; of secondary, not.* From whence I think it easy to draw this observation, that the ideas of primary qualities of bodies are resemblances of them, and their patterns do really exist in the bodies themselves; but the ideas produced in us by these secondary qualities have no resemblance of them at all. There is nothing like our ideas existing in the bodies themselves. They are in the bodies we denominate from them, only a power to produce those sensations in us; and what is sweet, blue, or warm in idea, is but the certain bulk, figure, and motion of the insensible parts in the bodies themselves, which we call so.

16. Flame is denominated hot and light; snow, white and cold; and manna, white and sweet, from the ideas they produce in us; which qualities are commonly thought to be the same in those bodies that those ideas are in us, the one the perfect resemblance of the other, as they are in a mirror; and it would by most men be judged very extravagant if one should say otherwise. And yet he that will consider that the same fire that at one distance produces in us the sensation of warmth, which was produced in him by the fire, is actually in the fire; and his idea of pain, which the same fire produced in him the same way, is not in the fire. Why are whiteness and coldness in snow, and pain not, when it produces the one and the other idea in us; and can do neither, but by the bulk, figure, number, and motion of its solid parts?

17. The particular bulk, number, figure, and motion of the parts of fire or snow are really in them, whether any one's senses perceive them

or not, and therefore they may be called real qualities, because they really exist in those bodies; but light, heat, whiteness, or coldness, are no more really in them than sickness or pain is in manna. Take away the sensation of them; let not the eyes see light or colours, nor the ears hear sounds; let the palate not taste, nor the nose smell; and the colours, tastes, odours, and sounds, as they are such particular ideas, vanish and cease, and are reduced to their causes, i.e., bulk, figure, and motion of parts.

18. A piece of manna of a sensible bulk is able to produce in us the idea of a round or square figure; and by being removed from one place to another, the idea of motion. This idea of motion represents it as it really is in the manna moving: a circle or square are the same, whether in idea or existence, in the mind or in the manna; and this both motion and figure are really in the manna, whether we take notice of them or no: this everybody is ready to agree to. Besides, manna, by the bulk, figure, texture, and motion of its parts, has a power to produce the sensations of sickness, and sometimes of acute pains or gripings in us. That these ideas of sickness and pain are not in the manna, but effects of its operations on us, and are nowhere when we feel them not, this also every one readily agrees to. And yet men are hardly to be brought to think that sweetness and whiteness are not really in manna, which are but the effects of the operations of manna, by the motion, size, and figure of its particles on the eyes and palate; as the pain and sickness caused by manna are confessedly nothing but the effects of its operations on the stomach and guts, by the size, motion, and figure of its insensible parts, (for by nothing else can a body operate, as has been proved); as if it could not operate on the eyes and palate, and thereby produce in the mind particular distinct ideas, which in itself it has not, as well as we allow it can operate on the guts and stomach, and thereby produce distinct ideas, which in itself it has not. These ideas being all effects of the operations of manna on several parts of our bodies, by the size, figure, number, and motion of its parts; why those produced by the eyes and palate should rather be thought to be really in the manna, than those produced by the stomach and guts; or why the pain and sickness, ideas that are the effect of manna, should be thought to be nowhere when they are not felt; and yet the sweetness and whiteness, effects of the same manna on other parts of the body, by ways equally as unknown, should be thought to exist in the manna, when they are not seen or tasted, would need some reason to explain.

19. *Ideas of primary Qualities are Resemblances; of secondary, not.* Let us consider the red and white colours in porphyry: hinder light from striking on it, and its colours vanish, it no longer produces any such ideas in us; upon the return of light it produces these appearances on us again. Can any one think any real alterations are made in the porphyry by the presence or absence of light, and that those ideas of whiteness and redness are really in porphyry in the light, when it is plain it has no colour in the dark? It has, indeed, such a configuration of particles, both night and day, as are apt, by the rays of light rebounding from some parts of that hard stone, to produce in us the idea of redness, and from

others the idea of whiteness; but whiteness or redness are not in it at any time, but such a texture that hath the power to produce such a sensation in us.

20. Pound an almond, and the clear white colour will be altered into a dirty one, and the sweet taste into an oily one. What real alteration can the beating of the pestle make in any body, but an alteration of the texture of it?

21. Ideas being thus distinguished and understood, we may be able to give an account how the same water, at the same time, may produce the idea of cold by one hand and of heat by the other; whereas it is impossible that the same water, if those ideas were really in it, should at the same time be both hot and cold; for if we imagine warmth, as it is in our hands, to be nothing but a certain sort and degree of motion in the minute particles of our nerves or animal spirits, we may understand how it is possible that the same water may, at the same time, produce the sensations of heat in one hand and cold in the other; which yet figure never does, that never producing the idea of a square by one hand which has produced the idea of a globe by another. But if the sensation of heat and cold be nothing but the increase of diminution of the motion of the minute parts of our bodies, caused by the corpuscles of any other body, it is easy to be understood, that if that motion be greater in one hand than in the other, if a body be applied to the two hands, which has in its minute particles a greater motion than in those of one of the hands, and a less than in those of the other, it will increase the motion of the one hand and lessen it in the other, and so cause the different sensations of heat and cold that depend thereon.

22. I have in what just goes before been engaged in physical inquiries a little further than perhaps I intended; but it being necessary to make the nature of sensation a little understood, and to make the difference between the qualities in bodies, and the ideas produced by them in the mind, to be distinctly conceived, without which it were impossible to discourse intelligibly of them, I hope I shall be pardoned this little excursion into natural philosophy, it being necessary in our present inquiry to distinguish the primary and real qualities of bodies which are always in them, (viz., solidity, extension, figure, number, and motion, or rest, and are sometimes perceived by us, viz., when the bodies they are in are big enough singly to be discerned,) from those secondary and imputed qualities which are but the powers of several combinations of those primary ones, when they operate without being distinctly discerned; whereby we may also come to know what ideas are, and what are not, resemblances of something really existing in the bodies we denominate from them.

23. *Three Sorts of Qualities in Bodies.* The qualities, then, that are in bodies, rightly considered, are of three sorts.

First, the bulk, figure, number, situation, and motion or rest of their solid parts; those are in them, whether we perceive them or not; and when they are of that size that we can discover them, we have by these an idea of the thing as it is in itself, as is plain in artificial things. These I call primary qualities.

Secondly, the power that is in any body, by reason of its insensible primary qualities, to operate after a peculiar manner on any of our senses, and thereby produce in us the different ideas of several colours, sounds, smells, tastes, &c. These are usually called sensible qualities.

Thirdly, the power that is in any body, by reason of the particular constitution of its primary qualities, to make such a change in the bulk, figure, texture, and motion of another body, as to make it operate on our senses differently from what it did before. Thus the sun has a power to make wax white, and fire to make lead fluid. These are usually called powers.

The first of these, as has been said, I think may be properly called real, original, or primary qualities, because they are in the things themselves, whether they are perceived or not; and upon their different modifications it is that the secondary qualities depend.

The other two are only powers to act differently upon other things, which powers result from the different modifications of those primary qualities.

24. *The first are Resemblances; the second thought Resemblances, but are not; the third neither are, nor are thought so.* But though the two latter sorts of qualities are powers barely, and nothing but powers, relating to several other bodies, and resulting from the different modifications of the original qualities, yet they are generally otherwise thought of; for the second sort, viz., the powers to produce several ideas in us by our senses, are looked upon as real qualities in the things thus affecting us; but the third sort are called and esteemed barely powers; v.g., the idea of heat or light, which we receive by our eyes or touch from the sun, are commonly thought real qualities existing in the sun, and something more than mere powers in it. But when we consider the sun in reference to wax, which it melts or blanches, we look on the whiteness and softness produced in the wax, not as qualities in the sun, but effects produced by powers in it; whereas, if rightly considered, these qualities of light and warmth, which are perceptions in me when I am warmed or enlightened by the sun, are no otherwise in the sun, when the changes made in the wax, when it is blanched, or melted, are in the sun. They are all of them equally powers in the sun, depending on its primary qualities, whereby it is able, in the one case, so to alter the bulk, figure, texture, or motion of some of the insensible parts of my eyes or hands, as thereby to produce in me the idea of light or heat; and in the other, it is able so to alter the bulk, figure, texture, or motion of the insensible parts of the wax, as to make them fit to produce in me the distinct ideas of white and fluid.

25. The reason why the one are ordinarily taken for real qualities, and the other only for bare powers, seems to be, because the ideas we have of distinct colours, sound, &c., containing nothing at all in them of bulk, figure, or motion, we are not apt to think them the effects of these primary qualities, which appear not, to our senses, to operate in their production, and with which they have not any apparent congruity or conceivable connexion. Hence it is that we are so forward to imagine that those ideas are the resemblances of something really existing in the objects themselves; since sensation discovers nothing of bulk, figure, or

motion of parts in their production; nor can reason show how bodies, by their bulk, figure, and motion, should produce in the mind the ideas of blue or yellow, &c. But in the other case, in the operations of bodies, changing the qualities one of another, we plainly discover that the quality produced hath commonly no resemblance with anything in the thing producing it; wherefore we look on it as a bare effect of power. For though receiving the idea of heat or light from the sun, we are apt to think it is a perception and resemblance of such a quality in the sun; yet when we see wax, or a fair face, receive change of colour from the sun, we cannot imagine that to be the reception or resemblance of anything in the sun, because we find not those different colours in the sun itself. For our senses being able to observe a likeness or unlikeness of sensible qualities in two different external objects, we forwardly enough conclude the production of any sensible quality in any subject to be an effect of bare power, and not the communication of any quality, which was really in the efficient, when we find no such sensible quality in the thing that produced it; but our senses not being able to discover any unlikeness between the idea produced in us, and the quality of the object producing it, we are apt to imagine that our ideas are resemblances of something in the objects, and not the effects of certain powers placed in the modification of their primary qualities, with which primary qualities the ideas produced in us have no resemblance.

26. *Secondary Qualities twofold; first, immediately perceivable; secondly, mediately perceivable.* To conclude, beside those before-mentioned primary qualities in bodies, viz., bulk, figure, extension, number, and motion of their solid parts, all the rest whereby we take notice of bodies, and distinguish them one from another, are nothing else but several powers in them depending on those primary qualities, whereby they are fitted, either by immediately operating on our bodies, to produce several different ideas in us, or else, by operating on other bodies, so to change their primary qualities as to render them capable of producing ideas in us different from what before they did. The former of these, I think, may be called secondary qualities, immediately perceivable; the latter, secondary qualities, mediately perceivable.

Of Perception

1. *Perception the first simple Idea of Reflection.* Perception, as it is the first faculty of the mind exercised about her ideas, so it is the first and simplest idea we have from reflection, and is by some called thinking in general: though thinking, in the propriety of the English tongue, signifies that sort of operation in the mind about its ideas, wherein the mind is active; where it, with some degree of voluntary attention, considers anything. For in bare naked perception, the mind is, for the most part, only passive; and what it perceives, it cannot avoid perceiving.

2. *Is only when the Mind receives the Impression.* What perception is, every one will know better by reflecting on what he does himself, what he sees, hears, feels, &c., or thinks, than by any discourse of mine.

Whoever reflects on what passes in his own mind cannot miss it; and if he does not reflect, all the words in the world cannot make him have any notion of it.

3. This is certain, that whatever alterations are made in the body, if they reach not the mind, whatever impressions are made on the outward parts, if they are not taken notice of within, there is no perception. Fire may burn our bodies with no other effect than it does a billet, unless the motion be continued to the brain, and there the sense of heat, or idea of pain, be produced in the mind, wherein consists actual perception.

4. How often may a man observe in himself, that whilst his mind is intently employed in the contemplation of some objects, and curiously surveying some ideas that are there, it takes no notice of impressions of sounding bodies made upon the organ of hearing, with the same alteration that uses to be for the producing the idea of sound! A sufficient impulse there may be on the organ; but if not reaching the observation of the mind, there follows no perception; and though the motion that uses to produce the idea of sound be made in the ear, yet no sound is heard. Want of sensation, in this case, is not through any defect in the organ, or that the man's ears are less affected than at other times when he does hear: but that which uses to produce the idea, though conveyed in by the usual organ, not being taken notice of in the understanding, and so imprinting no idea in the mind, there follows no sensation. So that wherever there is sense or perception, there some idea is actually produced, and present, in the understanding.

. . . .

8. *Ideas of Sensation often changed by the Judgment.* We are further to consider concerning perception, that the ideas we receive by sensation are often in grown people altered by the judgment, without our taking notice of it. When we set before our eyes a round globe of any uniform colour, v.g., gold, alabaster, or jet, it is certain that the idea thereby imprinted on our mind is of a flat circle variously shadowed, with several degrees of light and brightness coming to our eyes. But we have by use been accustomed to perceive what kind of appearance convex bodies are wont to make in us, what alterations are made in the reflections of light by the difference on the sensible figures of bodies, the judgment presently, by an habitual custom, alters the appearances into their causes, so that from that which is truly variety of shadow or colour, collecting the figure, it makes it pass for a mark of figure, and frames to itself the perception of a convex figure and an uniform colour, when the idea we receive from thence is only a plane variously coloured, as is evident in painting. To which purpose I shall here insert a problem of that very ingenious and studious promoter of real knowledge, the learned and worthy Mr. Molineux, which he was pleased to send me in a letter some months since; and it is this: "Suppose a man born blind, and now adult, and taught by his touch to distinguish between a cube and a sphere of the same metal, and nighly of the same bigness, so as to tell, when he felt one and the other, which is the cube, which the sphere. Suppose, then, the cube and sphere placed on a table, and the blind man be made to see: quaere, whether by his sight, before he touched them, he could

now distinguish and tell which is the globe, which the cube?" To which the acute and judicious proposer answers, "Not. For though he has obtained the experience of how a globe, how a cube affects his touch, yet he has not yet obtained the experience, that what affects his touch so or so, must affect his sight so or so; or that a protuberant angle in the cube, that pressed his hand unequally, shall appear to his eye as it does in the cube." I agree with this thinking gentleman, whom I am proud to call my friend, in his answer to this problem; and am of opinion that the blind man, at first sight, would not be able with certainty to say which was the globe, which the cube, whilst he only saw them; though he could unerringly name them by his touch, and certainly distinguish them by the difference of their figures felt. This I have set down, and leave with my reader, as an occasion for him to consider how much he may be beholden to experience, improvement, and acquired notions, where he thinks he had not the least use of, or help from them; and the rather, because this observing gentleman further adds, that having, upon the occasion of my book, proposed this to divers very ingenious men, he hardly ever met with one that at first gave the answer to it which he thinks true, till by hearing his reasons they were convinced.

9. But this is not, I think, usual in any of our ideas, but those received by sight; because sight, the most comprehensive of all our senses, conveying to our minds the ideas of light and colours, which are peculiar only to that sense; and also the far different ideas of space, figure, and motion, the several varieties whereof change the appearances of its proper object, viz., light and colours; we bring ourselves by use to judge of the one by the other. This, in many cases, by a settled habit, in things whereof we have frequent experience, is performed so constantly and so quick, that we take that for the perception of our sensation, which is an idea formed by our judgment; so that one, viz., that of sensation, serves only to excite the other, and is scarce taken notice of itself; as a man who reads or hears with attention and understanding, takes little notice of the characters or sounds, but of the ideas that are excited in him by them.

10. Nor need we wonder that this is done with so little notice, if we consider how very quick the actions of the mind are performed; for as itself is thought to take up no space, to have no extension, so its actions seem to require no time, but many of them seem to be crowded into an instant. I speak this in comparison to the actions of the body. Any one may easily observe this in his own thoughts, who will take the pains to reflect on them. How, as it were in an instant do our minds with one glance see all the parts of a demonstration, which may very well be called a long one, if we consider the time it will require to put it into words, and step by step show it another? Secondly, we shall not be so much surprised that this is done in us with so little notice, if we consider how the facility which we get of doing things by a custom of doing, makes them often pass in us without our notice. Habits, especially such as are begun very early, come at last to produce actions in us, which often escape our observation. How frequently do we, in a day, cover our eyes with our eyelids, without perceiving that we are at all in the dark! Men

that by custom have got the use of a by-word, do almost in every sentence pronounce sounds which, though taken notice of by others, they them- selves neither hear nor observe. And therefore it is not so strange that our mind should often change the idea of its sensation into that of its judgment, and make one serve only to excite the other, without our taking notice of it.

. . . .

Of Our Knowledge of the Existence of Other Things

1. *It is to be had only by sensation.* The knowledge of our own being we have by intuition. The existence of a God reason clearly makes known to us, as has been shown.

The knowledge of the existence of any other thing we can have only by sensation: for there being no necessary connexion of real existence with any idea a man hath in his memory; nor of any other existence but that of God with the existence of any particular man: no particular man can know the existence of any other being, but only when, by actual operating upon him, it makes itself perceived by him. For the having the idea of anything in our mind no more proves the existence of that thing than the picture of a man evidences his being in the world, or the visions of a dream make thereby a true history.

2. It is therefore the actual receiving of ideas from without that gives us notice of the existence of other things, and makes us know that some- thing doth exist at that time without us which causes that idea in us, though perhaps we neither know nor consider how it does it. For it takes not from the certainty of our senses, and the ideas we receive by them, that we know not the manner wherein they are produced: v.g., whilst I write this, I have, by the paper affecting my eyes, that idea produced in my mind, which whatever object causes, I call white; by which I know that the quality or accident (i.e., whose appearance before my eyes al- ways causes that idea) doth really exist, and hath a being without me. And of this, the greatest assurance I can possibly have, and to which my faculties can attain, is the testimony of my eyes, which are the proper and sole judges of this thing; whose testimony I have reason to rely on as so certain, that I can no more doubt, whilst I write this, that I see white and black, and that something really exists that causes that sen- sation in me, than that I write or move my hand; which is a certainty as great as human nature is capable of, concerning the existence of anything but a man's self alone, and of God.

3. *This, though not so certain as demonstration, yet may be called knowledge, and proves the existence of things without us.* The notice we have by our senses of the existing of things without us, though it be not altogether so certain as our intuitive knowledge, or the deductions of our reason employed about the clear abstract ideas of our own minds; yet it is an assurance that deserves the name of *knowledge.* If we persuade ourselves that our faculties act and inform us right concerning the existence of those objects that affect them, it cannot pass for an ill-

grounded confidence: for I think nobody can, in earnest, be so sceptical as to be uncertain of the existence of those things which he sees and feels. At least, he that can doubt so far (whatever he may have with his own thoughts) will never have any controversy with me; since he can never be sure I say anything contrary to his opinion. As to myself, I think God has given me assurance enough of the existence of things without me; since by their different application I can produce in myself both pleasure and pain, which is one great concernment of my present state. This is certain, the confidence that our faculties do not herein deceive us is the greatest assurance we are capable of concerning the existence of material beings. For we cannot act anything but by our faculties, nor talk of knowledge itself, but by the help of those faculties which are fitted to apprehend even what knowledge is. But besides the assurance we have from our senses themselves, that they do not err in the information they give us of the existence of things without us, when they are affected by them, we are farther confirmed in this assurance by other concurrent reasons.

4. *Because we cannot have them but by the inlet of the senses.* First, it is plain those perceptions are produced in us by exterior causes affect-ing our senses, because those that want the organs of any sense never can have the ideas belonging to that sense produced in their minds. The organs, themselves, it is plain, do not produce them; for then the eyes of a man in the dark would produce colours, and his nose smell roses in the winter: but we see nobody gets the relish of a pineapple till he goes to the Indies where it is, and tastes it.

5. *Because an idea from actual sensation and another from memory are very distinct perceptions.* Secondly, Because sometimes I find that I cannot avoid the having those ideas produced in my mind. For though when my eyes are shut, or windows fast, I can at pleasure recall to my mind the ideas of light or the sun, which former sensations had lodged in my memory; so I can at pleasure lay by that idea, and take into my view that of the smell of a rose, or taste of sugar. But if I turn my eyes at noon towards the sun, I cannot avoid the ideas which the light or sun then produces in me. So that there is a manifest difference between the ideas laid up in my memory, and those which force themselves upon me, and I cannot avoid having. And therefore it must needs be some exterior cause, and the brisk acting of some objects without me, whose efficacy I cannot resist, that produces those ideas in my mind, whether I will or no. Besides, there is nobody who doth not perceive the difference in him-self between contemplating the sun as he hath the idea of it in his memory, and actually looking upon it: of which two, his perception is so distinct, that few of his ideas are more distinguishable one from another. And therefore he hath certain knowledge that they are not both memory, or the actions of his mind, and fancies only within him; but that actual seeing hath a cause without.

. . . .

7. *Our senses assist one another's testimony of the existence of out-ward things.* Fourthly, Our senses, in many cases, bear witness to the truth of each other's report concerning the existence of sensible things

without us. He that sees a fire may, if he doubt whether it be anything more than a bare fancy, feel it too, and be convinced by putting his hand in it; which certainly could never be put into such exquisite pain by a bare idea or phantom, unless that the pain be a fancy too; which yet he cannot, when the burn is well, by raising the idea of it, bring upon himself again.

Thus I see, whilst I write this, I can change the appearance of the paper; and by designing the letters, tell beforehand what new idea it shall exhibit the very next moment, barely by drawing my pen over it: which will neither appear (let me fancy as much as I will) if my hand stand still, or though I move my pen, if my eyes be shut: nor, when those characters are once made on the paper, can I choose afterwards but see them as they are; that is, have the ideas of such letters as I have made. Whence it is manifest that they are not barely the sport and play of my own imagination, when I find that the characters that were made at the pleasure of my own thoughts do not obey them; nor yet cease to be, whenever I shall fancy it, but continue to affect my senses constantly and regularly, according to the figures I made them. To which if we will add, that the sight of those shall, from another man, draw such sounds as I beforehand design they shall stand for, there will be little reason left to doubt that those words I write do really exist without me, when they cause a long series of regular sounds to affect my ears, which could not be the effect of my imagination, nor could my memory retain them in that order.

8. *This certainty is as great as our condition needs.* But yet, if after all this any one will be so sceptical as to distrust his senses, and to affirm that all we see and hear, feel and taste, think and do, during our whole being, is but the series and deluding appearances of a long dream whereof there is no reality; and therefore will question the existence of all things or our knowledge of anything; I must desire him to consider, that if all be a dream, then he doth but dream that he makes the question; and so it is not much matter that a waking man should answer him. But yet, if he pleases, he may dream that I make him this answer, that the certainty of things existing *in rerum natura* when we have the testimony of our senses for it, is not only as great as our frame can attain to, but as our condition needs. For our faculties being suited not to the full extent of being, nor to a perfect, clear, comprehensive knowledge of things free from all doubt and scruple; but to the preservation of us, in whom they are; and accommodated to the use of life: they serve to our purpose well enough, if they will but give us certain notice of those things which are convenient or inconvenient to us. For he that sees a candle burning, and hath experimented the force of its flame by putting his finger in it, will little doubt that this is something existing without him, which does him harm and puts him to great pain. And if our dreamer pleases to try whether the glowing heat of a glass furnace be barely a wandering imagination in a drowsy man's fancy, by putting his hand into it, he may perhaps be awakened into a certainty, greater than he could wish, that it is something more than bare imagination. So that this evidence is as great as we can desire, being as certain to us as our pleasure or pain, i.e.,

happiness or misery; beyond which we have no concernment, either of knowing or being. Such an assurance of the existence of things without us is sufficient to direct us in the attaining the good and avoiding the evil which is caused by them, which is the important concernment we have of being made acquainted with them.

63. George Berkeley

George Berkeley (1685–1753), Bishop of Cloyne, wrote various important philosophical works.

Material Things Are Experiences of Men or God

1. It is evident to any one who takes a survey of the *objects of human knowledge*, that they are either *ideas* actually imprinted on the senses; or else such as are perceived by attending to the passions and operations of the mind; or lastly, *ideas* formed by help of memory and imagination —either compounding, dividing, or barely representing those originally perceived in the aforesaid ways. By sight I have the ideas of light and colours, with their several degrees and variations. By touch I perceive hard and soft, heat and cold, motion and resistance; and of all these more and less either as to quantity or degree. Smelling furnishes me with odours; the palate with tastes; and hearing conveys sounds to the mind in all their variety of tone and composition.

And as several of these are observed to accompany each other, they come to be marked by one name, and so to be reputed as one *thing*. Thus, for example, a certain colour, taste, smell, figure and consistence having been observed to go together, are accounted one distinct thing, signified by the name apple; other collections of ideas constitute a stone, a tree, a book, and the like sensible things; which as they are pleasing or disagreeable excite the passions of love, hatred, joy, grief, and so forth.

From George Berkeley, *A Treatise Concerning the Principles of Human Knowledge*, first published in 1710. Sentences in brackets were added by Berkeley after the first edition.

2. But, besides all that endless variety of ideas or objects of knowledge, there is likewise Something which knows or perceives them; and exercises divers operations, as willing, imagining, remembering, about them. This perceiving, active being is what I call *mind, spirit, soul,* or *myself.* By which words I do not denote any one of my ideas, but a thing entirely distinct from them, wherein they exist, or, which is the same thing, whereby they are perceived; for the existence of an idea consists in being perceived.

3. That neither our thoughts, nor passions, nor ideas formed by the imagination exist without the mind is what everybody will allow. And to me it seems no less evident that the various sensations or ideas imprinted on the Sense, however blended or combined together (that is, whatever objects they compose), cannot exist otherwise than in a mind perceiving them. I think an intuitive knowledge may be obtained of this, by any one that shall attend to what is meant by the term *exist* when applied to sensible things. The table I write on I say exists; that is, I see and feel it: and if I were out of my study I should say it existed; meaning thereby that if I was in my study I might perceive it, or that some other spirit actually does perceive it. There was an odour, that is, it was smelt; there was a sound, that is, it was heard; a colour or figure, and it was perceived by sight or touch. This is all that I can understand by these and the like expressions. For as to what is said of the *absolute* existence of unthinking things, without any relation to their being perceived, that is to me perfectly unintelligible. Their *esse* is *percipi*; nor is it possible they should have any existence out of the minds or thinking things which perceive them.

4. It is indeed an opinion strangely prevailing amongst men, that houses, mountains, rivers, and in a world all sensible objects, have an existence, natural or real, distinct from their being perceived by the understanding. But, with how great an assurance and acquiescence soever this Principle may be entertained in the world, yet whoever shall find in his heart to call it in question may, if I mistake not, perceive it to involve a manifest contradiction. For, what are the forementioned objects but the things we perceive by sense? and what do we perceive besides our own ideas or sensations? and is it not plainly repugnant that any one of these, or any combination of them, should exist unperceived?

5. If we thoroughly examine this tenet it will, perhaps, be found at bottom to depend on the doctrine of *abstract ideas.* For can there be a nicer strain of abstraction than to distinguish the existence of sensible objects from their being perceived, so as to conceive them existing unperceived? Light and colours, heat and cold, extension and figures—in a word the things we see and feel—what are they but so many sensations, notions, ideas, or impressions on the sense? and is it possible to separate, even in thought, any of these from perception? For my part, I might as easily divide a thing from itself. I may, indeed, divide in my thoughts, or conceive apart from each other, those things which perhaps I never perceived by sense so divided. Thus, I imagine the trunk of a human body without the limbs, or conceive the smell of a rose without thinking on the rose itself. So far, I will not deny, I can abstract; if that may properly

be called *abstraction* which extends only to the conceiving separately such objects as it is possible may really exist or be actually perceived asunder. But my conceiving or imagining power does not extend beyond the possibility of real existence or perception. Hence, as it is impossible for me to see or feel anything without an actual sensation of that thing, so it is impossible for me to conceive in my thoughts any sensible thing or object distinct from the sensation or perception of it. [In truth, the object and the sensation are the same things, and cannot therefore be abstracted from each other.]

6. Some truths there are so near and obvious to the mind that a man need only open his eyes to see them. Such I take this important one to be, viz. that all the choir of heaven and furniture of the earth, in a word all those bodies which compose the mighty frame of the world, have not any subsistence without a mind; that their *being* is to be perceived or known; that consequently so long as they are not actually perceived by me, or do not exist in my mind, or that of any other created spirit, they must either have no existence at all, or else subsist in the mind of some Eternal Spirit: it being perfectly unintelligible, and involving all the absurdity of abstraction, to attribute to any single part of them an existence independent to a spirit. [To be convinced of which, the reader need only reflect, and try to separate in his own thoughts the *being* of a sensible thing from its *being perceived*.]

7. From what has been said it is evident there is not any other Substance than *Spirit*, or that which perceives. But, for the fuller proof of this point, let it be considered the sensible qualities are colour, figure, motion, smell, taste, and such like, that is, the ideas perceived by sense. Now, for an idea to exist in an unperceiving thing is a manifest contradiction; for to have an idea is all one as to perceive: that therefore wherein colour, figure, and the like qualities exist must perceive them. Hence it is clear there can be no unthinking substance or *substratum* of those ideas.

8. But, say you, though the ideas themselves do not exist without the mind, yet there may be things like them, whereof they are copies or resemblances; which things exist without the mind, in an unthinking substance. I answer, an idea can be like nothing but an idea; a colour or figure can be like nothing but another colour or figure. If we look but never so little into our thoughts, we shall find it impossible for us to conceive a likeness except only between our ideas. Again, I ask whether those supposed *originals*, or external things, of which our ideas are the pictures or representations, be themselves perceivable or no? If they are, then *they* are ideas, and we have gained our point: but if you say they are not, I appeal to any one whether it be sense to assert a colour is like something which is invisible; hard or soft, like something which is intangible; and so of the rest.

9. Some there are who make a distinction betwixt *primary* and *secondary* qualities. By the former they mean extension, figure, motion, rest, solidity or impenetrability, and number; by the latter they denote all other sensible qualities, as colours, sounds, tastes, and so forth. The ideas we have of these last they acknowledge not to be the resemblances of anything existing without the mind, or unperceived; but they will have

our ideas of the *primary qualities* to be patterns or images of things which exist without the mind, in an unthinking substance which they call Matter. By Matter, therefore, we are to understand an inert, senseless substance, in which extension, figure, and motion do actually subsist. But it is evident, from what we have already shewn, that extension, figure, and motion are only ideas existing in the mind, and that an idea can be like nothing but another idea; and that consequently neither they nor their archetypes can exist in an unperceiving substance. Hence, it is plain that the very notion of what is called *Matter* or *corporeal substance*, involves a contradiction in it. [Insomuch that I should not think it necessary to spend more time in exposing its absurdity. But, because the tenet of the existence of Matter seems to have taken so deep a root in the minds of philosophers, and draws after it so many ill consequences, I choose rather to be thought prolix and tedious than omit anything that might conduce to the full discovery and extirpation of that prejudice.]

10. They who assert that figure, motion, and the rest of the primary or original qualities do exist without the mind, in unthinking substances, do at the same time acknowledge that colours, sounds, heat, cold, and suchlike secondary qualities, do not; which they tell us are sensations, existing in the mind alone, that depend on and are occasioned by the different size, texture, and motion of the minute particles of matter. This they take for an undoubted truth, which they can demonstrate beyond all exception. Now, if it be certain that those *original* qualities are inseparably united with the other sensible qualities, and not, even in thought, capable of being abstracted from them, it plainly follows that *they* exist only in the mind. But I desire any one to reflect, and try whether he can, by any abstraction of thought, conceive the extension and motion of a body without all other sensible qualities. For my own part, I see evidently that it is not in my power to frame an idea of a body extended and moving, but I must withal give it some colour or other sensible quality, which is acknowledged to exist only in the mind. In short, extension, figure, and motion, abstracted from all other qualities, are inconceivable. Where therefore the other sensible qualities are, there must these be also, to wit, in the mind and nowhere else.

. . . .

14. I shall farther add, that, after the same manner as modern philosophers prove certain sensible qualities to have no existence in Matter, or without the mind, the same thing may be likewise proved of all other sensible qualities whatsoever. Thus, for instance, it is said that heat and cold are affections only of the mind, and not at all patterns of real beings, existing in the corporeal substances which excite them; for that the same body which appears cold to one hand seems warm to another. Now, why may we not as well argue that figure and extension are not patterns or resemblances of qualities existing in Matter; because to the same eye at different stations, or eyes of a different texture at the same station, they appear various, and cannot therefore be the images of anything settled and determinate without the mind? Again, it is proved that sweetness is not really in the sapid thing; because the thing remaining unaltered the sweetness is changed into bitter, as in case of a

fever or otherwise vitiated palate. Is it not as reasonable to say that motion is not without the mind; since if the succession of ideas in the mind become swifter, the motion, it is acknowledged, shall appear slower, without any alteration in any external object?

15. In short, let any one consider those arguments which are thought manifestly to prove that colours and tastes exist only in the mind, and he shall find they may with equal force be brought to prove the same thing of extension, figure, and motion. Though it must be confessed this method of arguing does not so much prove that there is no extension or colour in an outward object, as that we do not know by sense which is the true extension or colour of the object. But the arguments foregoing plainly shew it to be impossible that any colour or extension at all, or other sensible quality whatsoever, should exist in an unthinking subject without the mind, or in truth that there should be any such thing as an outward object.

16. But let us examine a little the received opinion. It is said extension is a *mode* or *accident* of Matter, and that Matter is the *substratum* that supports it. Now I desire that you would explain to me what is meant by Matter's *supporting* extension. Say you, I have no idea of Matter; and therefore cannot explain it. I answer, though you have no positive, yet, if you have any meaning at all, you must at least have a relative idea of Matter; though you know not what it is, yet you must be supposed to know what relation it bears to accidents, and what is meant by its supporting them. It is evident *support* cannot here be taken in its usual or literal sense, as when we say that pillars support a building. In what sense therefore must it be taken? [For my part, I am not able to discover any sense at all that can be applicable to it.]

17. If we inquire into what the most accurate philosophers declare themselves to mean by *material substance,* we shall find them acknowledge they have no other meaning annexed to those sounds but the idea of Being in general, together with the relative notion of its supporting accidents. The general idea of Being appeareth to me the most abstract and incomprehensible of all other; and as for its supporting accidents, this, as we have just now observed, cannot be understood in the common sense of those words: it must therefore be taken in some other sense, but what that is they do not explain. So that when I consider the two parts or branches which make the signification of the words *material substance,* I am convinced there is no distinct meaning annexed to them. But why should we trouble ourselves any farther, in discussing this material *substratum* or support of figure and motion and other sensible qualities? Does it not suppose they have an existence without the mind? And is not this a direct repugnancy, and altogether inconceivable?

18. But, though it were possible that solid, figured, moveable substances may exist without the mind, corresponding to the ideas we have of bodies, yet how is it possible for us to know this? Either we must know it by Sense or by Reason. As for our senses, by them we have the knowledge only of our sensations, ideas, or those things that are immediately perceived by sense, call them what you will: but they do not inform us that things exist without the mind, or unperceived, like to those which

are perceived. This the materialists themselves acknowledge.—It remains therefore that if we have any knowledge at all of external things, it must be by reason inferring their existence from what is immediately perceived by sense. But (I do not see) what reason can induce us to believe the existence of bodies without the mind, from what we perceive, since the very patrons of Matter themselves do not pretend there is any necessary connexion betwixt them and our ideas? I say it is granted on all hands (and what happens in dreams, frensies, and the like, puts it beyond dispute) that it is possible we might be affected with all the ideas we have now, though no bodies existed without resembling them. Hence it is evident the supposition of external bodies is not necessary for the producing our ideas; since it is granted they are produced sometimes, and might possibly be produced always, in the same order we see them in at present, without their concurrence.

19. But, though we might possibly have all our sensations without them, yet perhaps it may be thought easier to conceive and explain the manner of their production, by supposing external bodies in their likeness rather than otherwise; and so it might be at least probable there are such things as bodies that excite their ideas in our minds. But neither can this be said. For, though we give the materialists their external bodies, they by their own confession are never the nearer knowing how our ideas are produced; since they own themselves unable to comprehend in what manner body can act upon spirit, or how it is possible it should imprint any idea in the mind. Hence it is evident the production of ideas or sensations in our minds, can be no reason why we should suppose Matter or corporeal substances; since that is acknowledged to remain equally inexplicable with or without this supposition. If therefore it were possible for bodies to exist without the mind, yet to hold they do so must needs be a very precarious opinion: since it is to suppose, without any reason at all, that God has created innumerable beings that are entirely useless, and serve to no manner of purpose.

. . . .

22. I am afraid I have given cause to think I am needlessly prolix in handling this subject. For, to what purpose is it to dilate on that which may be demonstrated with the utmost evidence in a line or two, to any one that is capable of the least reflexion? It is but looking into your own thoughts, and so trying whether you can conceive it possible for a sound, or figure, or motion, or colour to exist without the mind or unperceived. This easy trial may perhaps make you see that what you contend for is a downright contradiction. Insomuch that I am content to put the whole upon this issue:—If you can but conceive it possible for one extended moveable substance, or in general for any one idea, or anything like an idea, to exist otherwise than in a mind perceiving it, I shall readily give up the cause. And, as for all that compages of external bodies you contend for, I shall grant you its existence, though you cannot either give me any reason why you believe it exists, or assign any use to it when it is supposed to exist. I say, the bare possibility of your opinions being true shall pass for an argument that it is so.

23. But, say you, surely there is nothing easier than for me to imagine

trees, for instance, in a park, or books existing in a closet, and nobody by to perceive them. I answer, you may so, there is no difficulty in it. But what is all this, I beseech you, more than framing in your mind certain ideas which you call *books* and *trees*, and at the same time omitting to frame the idea of any one that may perceive them? But do not you yourself perceive or think of them all the while? This therefore is nothing to the purpose: it only shews you have the power of imagining, or forming ideas in your mind; but it does not shew that you can conceive it possible the objects of your thought may exist without the mind. To make out this, it is necessary that you conceive them existing unconceived or unthought of; which is a manifest repugnancy. When we do our utmost to conceive the existence of external bodies, we are all the while only contemplating our own ideas. But the mind, taking no notice of itself, is deluded to think it can and does conceive bodies existing unthought of, or without the mind, though at the same time they are apprehended by, or exist in, itself. A little attention will discover to any one the truth and evidence of what is here said, and make it unnecessary to insist on any other proofs against the existence of *material substance*.

. . . .

25. All our ideas, sensations, notions, or the things which we perceive, by whatsoever names they may be distinguished, are visibly inactive: there is nothing of power or agency included in them. So that one idea or object of thought cannot produce or make any alteration in another. To be satisfied of the truth of this, there is nothing else requisite but a bare observation of our ideas. For, since they and every part of them exist only in the mind, it follows that there is nothing in them but what is perceived: but whoever shall attend to his ideas, whether of sense or reflexion, will not perceive in them any power or activity; there is, therefore, no such thing contained in them. A little attention will discover to us that the very being of an idea implies passiveness and inertness in it; insomuch that it is impossible for an idea to do anything, or, strictly speaking, to be the cause of anything: neither can it be the resemblance or pattern of any active being, as is evident from sect. 8. Whence it plainly follows that extension, figure, and motion cannot be the cause of our sensations. To say, therefore, that these are the effects of powers resulting from the configuration, number, motion, and size of corpuscles, must certainly be false.

26. We perceive a continual succession of ideas; some are anew excited, others are changed or totally disappear. There is therefore *some* cause of these ideas, whereon they depend, and which produces and changes them. That this cause cannot be any quality or idea or combination of *ideas*, is clear from the preceding section. It must therefore be a *substance;* but it has been shewn that there is no corporeal or material substance: it remains therefore that the cause of ideas is an incorporeal active substance or Spirit.

27. A Spirit is one simple, undivided, active being—as it perceives ideas it is called the *understanding,* and as it produces or otherwise operates about them it is called the *will.* Hence there can be no *idea* formed of a soul or spirit; for all ideas whatever, being passive and inert

742

(vid. sect. 25), they cannot represent unto us, by way of image or likeness, that which acts. A little attention will make it plain to any one, that to have an idea which shall be *like* that active Principle of motion and change of ideas is absolutely impossible. Such is the nature of Spirit, or that which acts, that it cannot be of itself perceived, but only by the effects which it produceth. If any man shall doubt of the truth of what is here delivered, let him but reflect and try if he can frame the idea of any power or active being; and whether he has ideas of two principal powers, marked by the names *will* and *understanding*, distinct from each other, as well as from a third idea of Substance or Being in general, with a relative notion of its supporting or being the subject of the aforesaid powers—which is signified by the name *soul* or *spirit*. This is what some hold; but, so far as I can see, the words *will*, [*understanding, mind*,] *soul*, *spirit*, do not stand for different ideas, or, in truth, for any idea at all, but for something which is very different from ideas, and which, being an agent, cannot be like unto, or represented by, any idea whatsoever. [Though it must be owned at the same time that we have some *notion* of soul, spirit, and the operations of the mind, such as willing, loving, hating —inasmuch as we know or understand the meaning of these words.]

28. I find I can excite ideas in my mind at pleasure, and vary and shift the scene as oft as I think fit. It is no more than *willing*, and straightway this or that idea arises in my fancy; and by the same power it is obliterated and makes way for another. This making and unmaking of ideas doth very properly denominate the mind active. Thus much is certain and grounded on experience: but when we talk of unthinking agents, or of exciting ideas exclusive of volition, we only amuse ourselves with words.

29. But, whatever power I may have over my thoughts, I find the ideas actually perceived by Sense have not a like dependence on *my* will. When in broad daylight I open my eyes, it is not in my power to choose whether I shall see or no, or to determine what particular objects shall present themselves to my view: and so likewise as to the hearing and other senses; the ideas imprinted on them are not creatures of *my* will. There is therefore some other Will or Spirit that produces them.

30. The ideas of Sense are more strong, lively, and distinct than those of the Imagination; they have likewise a steadiness, order, and coherence, and are not excited at random, as those which are the effects of human wills often are, but in a regular train or series—the admirable connexion whereof sufficiently testifies the wisdom and benevolence of its Author. Now the set rules, or established methods, wherein the Mind we depend on excites in us the ideas of Sense, are called *the laws of nature;* and these we learn by experience, which teaches us that such and such ideas are attended with such and such other ideas, in the ordinary course of things.

31. This gives us a sort of foresight, which enables us to regulate our actions for the benefit of life. And without this we should be eternally at a loss: we could not know how to act anything that might procure us the least pleasure, or remove the least pain of sense. That food nourishes, sleep refreshes, and fire warms us; that to sow in the seedtime is the

way to reap in the harvest; and in general that to obtain such or such ends, such or such means are conducive—all this we know, not by dis-covering any *necessary connexion* between our ideas, but only by the observation of the *settled laws* of nature; without which we should be all in uncertainty and confusion, and a grown man no more know how to manage himself in the affairs of life than an infant just born.

32. And yet this consistent uniform working, which so evidently dis-plays the Goodness and Wisdom of that Governing Spirit whose Will constitutes the laws of nature, in so far from leading our thoughts to Him, that it rather sends them wandering after second causes. For, when we perceive certain ideas of Sense constantly followed by other ideas, and we know this is not of our own doing, we forthwith attribute power and agency to the ideas themselves, and make one the cause of another, than which nothing can be more absurd and unintelligible. Thus, for example, having observed that when we perceive by sight a certain round luminous figure, we at the same time perceive by touch the idea or sensation called heat, we do from thence conclude the sun to be the *cause* of heat. And in like manner perceiving the motion and collision of bodies to be attended with sound, we are inclined to think the latter the *effect* of the former.

33. The ideas imprinted on the Senses by the Author of nature are called *real things:* and those excited in the imagination, being less regular, vivid, and constant, are more properly termed *ideas* or *images* of things, which they copy and represent. But then our *sensations*, be they never so vivid and distinct, are nevertheless ideas: that is, they exist in the mind, or are perceived by it, as truly as the ideas of its own framing. The ideas of Sense are allowed to have more reality in them, that is, to be more strong, orderly, and coherent than the creatures of the mind; but this is no argument that they exist without the mind. They are also less dependent on the spirit or thinking substance which perceives them, in that they are excited by the will of another and more powerful Spirit: yet still they are *ideas:* and certainly no idea, whether faint or strong, can exist otherwise than in a mind perceiving it.

. . . .

57. But why they should suppose the ideas of sense to be excited in us by things in their likeness, and not rather have recourse to *Spirit*, which alone can act, may be accounted for. First, because they were not aware of the repugnancy there is, as well in supposing things like unto our ideas existing without, as in attributing to them power or activity. Secondly, because the Supreme Spirit which excites those ideas in our minds, is not marked out and limited to our view by any particular finite collection of sensible ideas, as human agents are by their size, com-plexion, limbs, and motions. And thirdly, because His operations are regular and uniform. Whenever the course of nature is interrupted by a miracle, men are ready to own the presence of a Superior Agent. But, when we see things go on in the ordinary course, they do not excite in us any reflexion; their order and concatenation, though it be an argument of the greatest wisdom, power, and goodness in their Creator, is yet so constant and familiar to us, that we do not think them the immediate

effects of a *Free Spirit;* especially since inconsistency and mutability in acting, though it be an imperfection, is looked on as a mark of *freedom.*

. . . .

139. But it will be objected that, if there is no *idea* signified by the terms *soul, spirit,* and *substance,* they are wholly insignificant, or have no meaning in them. I answer, those words do mean or signify a real thing; which is neither an idea, nor like an idea, but that which perceives ideas, and wills, and reasons about them. What I am *myself,* that which I denote by the term *I,* is the same with what is meant by *soul,* or *spiritual substance.* [But if I should say that *I* was nothing, or that *I* was an *idea* or *notion,* nothing could be more evidently absurd than either of these propositions.] If it be said that this is only quarrelling at a word, and that, since the immediate significations of other names are by common consent called *ideas,* no reason can be assigned why that which is signified by the name *spirit* or *soul* may not partake in the same appellation. I answer, all the unthinking objects of the mind agree in that they are entirely passive, and their existence consists only in being perceived: whereas a *soul* or *spirit* is an active being, whose existence consists, not in being perceived, but in perceiving ideas and thinking. It is therefore necessary, in order to prevent equivocation and confounding natures perfectly disagreeing and unlike, that we distinguish between *spirit* and *idea.*

. . . .

145. From what hath been said, it is plain that we cannot know the existence of *other spirits* otherwise than by their operations, or the ideas by them, excited in us. I perceive several motions, changes, and combinations of ideas, that inform me there are certain particular agents, like myself, which accompany them, and concur in their production. Hence, the knowledge I have of other spirits is not immediate, as is the knowledge of my ideas; but depending on the intervention of ideas, by me referred to agents or spirits distinct from myself, as effects or concomitant signs.

146. But, though there be some things which convince us human agents are concerned in producing them, yet it is evident to everyone that those things which are called the Works of Nature, that is, the far greater part of the ideas or sensations perceived by us, are *not* produced by, or dependent on, the wills of *men.* There is therefore some other Spirit that causes them; since it is repugnant that they should subsist by themselves. . . . . But, if we attentively consider the constant regularity, order, and concatenation of natural things, the surprising magnificence, beauty and perfection of the larger, and the exquisite contrivance of the smaller parts of the creation, together with the exact harmony and correspondence of the whole, but above all the never-enough-admired laws of pain and pleasure, and the instincts of natural inclinations, appetites, and passions of animals;—I say if we consider all these things, and at the same time attend to the meaning and import of the attributes One, Eternal, Infinitely Wise, Good, and Perfect, we shall clearly perceive that they belong to the aforesaid Spirit, 'who works all in all' and 'by whom all things consist.'

147. Hence, it is evident that God is known as certainly and immedi-

ately as any other mind or spirit whatsoever, distinct from ourselves. We may even assert that the existence of God is far more evidently perceived than the existence of men; because the effects of Nature are infinitely more numerous and considerable than those ascribed to human agents. There is not any one mark that denotes a man, or affect produced by him, which does not more strongly evince the being of that Spirit who is the Author of Nature. For it is evident that, in affecting other persons, the will of man hath no other object than barely the motion of the limbs of his body; but that such a motion should be attended by, or excite any idea in the mind of another, depends wholly on the will of the Creator. He alone it is who, 'upholding all things by the word of His power,' maintains that intercourse between spirits whereby they are able to perceive the existence of each other. And yet this pure and clear Light which enlightens every one is itself invisible [to the greatest part of mankind.]

64. C. H. Whiteley

C. H. Whiteley is Professor of Philosophy at the University of Birmingham.

Phenomenalism: Its Grounds and Difficulties

48. The Non-Existence of Matter

From such arguments as these, Berkeley draws the conclusion that Matter does not exist, or at least there is no good reason for believing that it does. This seems a most alarming conclusion. But he assures us that there is no cause for alarm, if we are careful to understand exactly what he is saying. He is denying that there is any such thing as material substance as the materialist philosophers define it; that is, a substance apart from and independent of all awareness, permanent, public, the cause of our sensations, having shape, size, position, motion. He is not denying that there are such things as tables and chairs and clouds and apples and cats, or that we know quite a lot about them and often make true statements concerning them. It is true that there is a table in this room, that it is 3 feet long, etc. It is true that grass is green and snow is white. It is true that water is a compound of oxygen and hydrogen, and malaria is caused by the bite of a mosquito. These statements are false if they are interpreted as referring to some unobservable "material" thing which is outside all experience. But there is another way of interpreting them in which they may well be true. That is to take them as descrip-

From C. H. Whiteley, *An Introduction to Metaphysics*, Methuen & Co. Ltd., London. 1950. Reprinted by permission of Methuen & Co. Ltd.

tions, not of a mysterious unexperienceable Matter, but of sense-experiences which people have or might have.

49. The Meaning of Words

And this seems a reasonable way of interpreting our statements when we consider how it is that we come to understand and make use of language. When I am teaching a child the meaning of the word "table," I point to the table, so that he sees it; I put his hand to it, so that he feels it; that is, I cause him to sense certain sense-data. Surely it is with these sense-data that he thereupon associates the sound "table"; when he sees and feels similar sense-data, he repeats "table." It is by the differences in what they look like and feel like that he distinguishes tables from chairs and apples and half-crowns. It is natural to conclude that when he uses the word "table" or "apple," he is using it to describe what he sees, feels, tastes, etc., rather than to propound some theory about an invisible and intangible material substance.

The word "table" *means* a certain visible squareness and brownness, a certain tangible hardness; i.e., it means a certain type of sense-experience. When I say "There is a table in this room" I am describing the sense-data which I am now sensing, and if I do not sense such sense-data, then, being a truthful person, I do not say that there is a table in the room. If someone else says that there is, I test his statement by looking and feeling, i.e., by finding out whether the appropriate sense-data are available; if they are not, I dismiss his statement as false. If I say "Socrates drank his companions under the table," I am not describing any sense-experiences which I have now, but I am describing sense-experiences which I suppose Socrates and his companions to have had at another time and place.

We cannot, of course, identify "the table" with any one single sense-datum; an experience which was entirely unique and did not recur would not be worth naming. The function of words is not to name everything we see or hear, but to pick out the recurrent patterns in our experience. They identify our present sense-data as being of the same group or type as others which we have sensed before. A word, then, describes, not a single experience, but a group or type of experiences; the word "table" describes all the various sense-data which we normally refer to as appearances or sensations "of" the table. So a material thing is not indeed identical with any sense-datum; but neither is it something different in kind from sense-data. It is a group, or class, or system of sense-data; and nothing but sense-data goes to constitute it. So this doctrine may be expressed by saying that every statement we make about a material thing is equivalent to another statement about sense-data.

50. Phenomenalism

This analysis of the notion of a material thing is called Phenomenalism, since it makes of a material thing a group of phenomena, appearances, instead of a transcendent reality distinct from appearances. It is a widespread view, and has been accepted by many philosophers who do not call themselves Idealists and are far from accepting Berkeley's view that the fundamental reality is Mind. The term "idealism" itself, however, though it has shifted in meaning since, does properly denote just this part of Berkeley's theory, that the material world—"the whole choir of heaven and furniture of the earth" says Berkeley—consists of what he calls "ideas" and I have been calling "sense-data." The word in this sense has nothing to do with ideals, and the theory would have been called "ideaism" but for considerations of pronunciation.

Phenomenalism, then, is the doctrine that all statements about material objects can be completely analysed into statements about sense-data. The analysis of any such statement must be very complex; and the value of the "material-object language" is that it enables us to refer in one word, such as "table," to a vast number of sense-data differing very much among themselves. The group of sense-data constituting the table includes all the different views I can obtain at different distances, from different angles, in different lights, no two of them exactly alike, but all of them variations on one central pattern; it includes sense-data of touch, and those of sound (though these last seem somewhat more loosely connected with the main visuo-tactual group); and with other kinds of material things, such as apples, sense-data of taste and smell form important constituents of the thing.

51. Its Advantages

This type of theory has certain clear advantages. On the representative theory, the very existence of a material world or of any given material object must always be in principle doubtful. I am directly aware of my sense-data, and so can be certain of their existence and character: but "material objects" are quite different—their existence and character can be known only by an inference, which cannot give the complete certainty which comes from observation. Descartes, for example, accepts this consequence of the theory, and will not allow himself to believe that there is a material world at all, until he has convinced himself that there exists an omnipotent and benevolent God who would never have led him to believe in the material world if it had not been real. But if Descartes really succeeded in keeping up this attitude of doubt for more than a moment, few men have been able to imitate him. We *cannot* believe that the existence of the table is in any way subject to doubt.

The phenomenalist theory, by making the existence of the table *the same thing* as the occurrence of certain sense-data, removes that doubt; for the system of sense-data constituting the table has beyond doubt come under my observation.

The theory not only removes the doubt, but makes it clear why we cannot seriously entertain it. The Plain Man was right after all: material things are seen and touched, are objects of direct awareness, and it is by seeing and touching that we know that they exist, though no material thing is straightforwardly identical with what I am seeing and touching *at this particular moment.*

So, by accepting the phenomenalist analysis, we escape being involved in any reference to an unobservable Matter. We can preserve our empiricism inviolate, and talk about the things we see and hear and smell and touch, and not about other hypothetical things beyond the reach of our observation. Science, the knowledge of nature, on this view becomes the recording, ordering and forecasting of human experiences. Therein lies its interest for us. If the physical world lay outside our experience, why should we be concerned with it?

52. Criticisms of Phenomenalism

But these advantages of phenomenalism are purchased at a cost. Along several different lines the phenomenalist interpretation of our statements about material things seem to conflict with our usual beliefs, and produces paradoxes not very easy to accept.

"Appearance and Reality"

(1) In ordinary speech we are accustomed to draw a distinction between "appearance" and "reality," and to allow that a thing may appear to be what it is not, as Descartes' stick half under water may appear bent although it is really straight. Hence we reckon some of our perceptions as "real" or "true" or "genuine," and others as "illusions." The representative theory of perception is in accordance with this way of thinking; for on that theory our sense-data are in some respects copies of material things; some are accurate copies, and so are genuine and true, others are inaccurate copies, and so false and illusory. The representative theory differs from common sense mainly in holding that the discrepancies between the sense-datum and the material object which it represents are greater than we realise.

But what is the phenomenalist to make of this distinction? He can admit no essential difference between appearance and reality; for on his view the appearances *are* the reality. Material things consist of appearances—sense-data—and of nothing else. And these sense-data all actually occur and so are equally real. Moreover, they are what they appear to be; their reality consists in appearing, and the suggestion that they might "really" have qualities which they do not appear to have is without meaning. Thus the phenomenalist has no justification for classifying them into "real" and "unreal," or "genuine" and "counterfeit." The various sense-data which go to constitute a material object, such as my table, are of many different shapes and colours. All of them are equally real, and none of them can be *the* "real shape" or "real colour" of the table. Evidently tables are more versatile objects than we thought, and may have as many different shapes and colours as there are occasions of observing them. Why then should we come by the idea that there is only one "real shape," and the rest are mere appearances?

The phenomenalist solution of this difficulty is to allow that in a strict philosophical sense of the word "real," the distinction between reality and appearance cannot be drawn. But the purpose of the common-sense distinction between appearance and reality is not to pry into the ultimacies of metaphysics, but to enable us to deal with the experiences we encounter. What causes us to condemn an experience as an "illusion" is that it leads us astray. A mirage is an illusion because it causes us to make a mistake. But what kind of mistake? Surely, not the mistake of thinking that we now see trees and water, but the mistake of expecting that we shall soon be able to have a drink and sit in the shade. The mistake consists in the false expectation of certain other sense-data. Thus the illusoriness is not in the sense-datum itself, but in the expectation which we form when we sense it.

Error of this sort is possible because sense-data are not chaotic, but in the main are arranged in orderly series. Normally, when the visual sense-data belonging to water are obtainable, so are the gustatory sense-data of drinking water and relieving one's thirst. The mirage deceives us because, abnormally, we get the visual sense-data without the gustatory ones. Mirror-images may deceive us because the things seen in a mirror cannot be observed from the back and cannot be touched. Thus a "real" table consists of a complete set of sense-data of different senses related to one another in certain systematic ways (e.g., visual sense-data become continuously smaller and auditory ones continuously fainter as we move away from a certain region of space). When, as in the case of a table seen in a mirror, you have some members of the set but not others, you say that what is seen in the mirror is not a "real" table, or is not "really" there.

Again, the stick in water may lead us into error because sticks that "look bent" usually "feel bent" as well; and so we are surprised to find that it "feels straight," and say that though it "looks bent" it is not "really bent."

The precise interpretation of the word "real" is different in different contexts. But in general, say phenomenalists, it will be found that what we call the "real world" is not a world different from that of appearances; it is a selection from the world of appearances, a collection of appearances which are normal, systematic, and so reliable. The "unreal" consists of eccentric appearances which in one way or another fail to fit in with the normal type of sets of sense-data, and therefore cause us to form false expectations.

53. The Permanence of Material Things

(2) Sensations come and go. Few of them last for very long, and none of them lasts for ever. If we add up all the occasions in my life on which I have been looking at this table, we get a very short period indeed. And, like the rest of my species, I frequently go to sleep, and cease to perceive any material object whatsoever. That is to say, if a material thing consists of sense-data, its existence must be intermittent. Sense-data belonging to

the thing exist only now and again, and most of the time they do not exist at all. But material objects such as tables are normally supposed to be permanent things, which endure uninterruptedly for very long periods. How can a permanent object be made out of momentary sense-data?

If I am alone in the room and close my eyes, there are then no sense-data belonging to the table; are we to suppose that I can annihilate so substantial a material object simply by shutting my eyes? It seems as though the phenomenalist must deny that any such statement as "There is a table in the room" can be true unless there is someone there seeing or touching it; and he must also deny that any such statement as "The table has been here for twenty years" can be true, unless (what seems most improbable) gangs of watchers have been observing it in relays for the whole of that time.

54. Phenomenalist Analysis of Permanence

The phenomenalist answer to these difficulties involves a radical re-interpretation of the whole notion of a permanent material thing. That the existence of the table should be permanent in the way in which my waking experience is uninterrupted, that the table should last for twenty years in the way that my hearing a performance of a symphony can last for three-quarters of an hour, is of course impossible on a phenomenalist view. Whatever kind of permanence is attributed to the table must be understood in another sense.

Clearly, when I say that there is a table in the now uninhabited attic, I am not describing the sense-data of anyone. But, though the statement cannot be a description of *actual* sense-data, it can be a description of *possible* sense-data; and this is what it is according to phenomenalists. To say that there is a table there now is to say that *if* there were anyone in the room he *would be* having the kind of experience which we call seeing a table. "There is a table" means "Go and look and you will see a table." And to say that it has been there twenty years means that if at any time during those years anyone had been in the room, he could have seen or touched a table.

So we must modify our original account of the nature of a material thing. It consists not merely of actual sense-data, but also of possible sense-data; or more precisely, of the fact that under certain conditions sense-data are obtainable. What is permanent is then not any sense-datum or group of sense-data, but the possibility of obtaining sense-data of a certain kind. Hence J. S. Mill defined matter as "the permanent possibility of sensation."

I think this much at least must be admitted: if it is true that there is a table in the attic, it is also true that if anyone with the use of normal eyes in a good light were to be in the attic now, he would have the experience of seeing the table; if it is true that the table has been there for twenty years, it is also true that if anyone has been there under those conditions at any time during those twenty years, he would have had the experience of seeing the table. That is to say, the statement about sense-data is involved in or implied by the statement about the table. According to the phenomenalist, such statements about possible sense-data constitute the whole of what the statement about the table means. All statements about material objects are equivalent to statements about what people have experienced, or would have experienced if circumstances had been different.

He points out that if we try to imagine the presence of the table in the attic, what we do is to imagine what it would look like and feel like. If we want to test the statement that it is there, we go and look. Statements which are not, in the final analysis, about actual or possible experiences, cannot be tested at all, and are therefore without meaning for us.

55. Berkeley's Account of Permanence

Berkeley himself gives another explanation of the permanence of material things. According to his theory, God is eternally perceiving everything, and therefore, at times when neither I nor any other human being or animal is perceiving the table, God is still perceiving it. But whether or not this is really the case, it is obviously not a correct interpretation of what we mean when we attribute continuous existence in time to the table. For if it were, we should not believe in permanent material things at all unless we believed, not only in God, but in an omnisentient God such as Berkeley believed in.

56. Causal Activity

(3) According to our ordinary notions of them, material objects are causally active: they do things. The table supports the tablecloth, the fire warms the room. Material objects exercise force, have influences on one another and incidentally on ourselves, causing, among other things, our sensations of them. This continually active causal interplay makes up the system of nature, which it is the business of science to study and reduce to laws. Does not science explain what happens by referring events to their causes, which in the material realm at least are material things, exercising physical force? Surely, the room cannot be warmed by my visual sense-datum of a fire! Still less can it be warmed by the possibility of a visual sense-datum of a fire during my absence, when I am not looking at the fire but the room gets warmed all the same. When we all sit round the table and sense sense-data very similar in shape, size and colour, what is the explanation of this fact, if not that there is an independent table which is the common cause of all our similar sense-data? Berkeley himself admits, or rather insists, that an "idea" is "inert," and can *do* nothing.

57. Phenomenalist Analysis of Causation

To deal with this problem, we need a fresh analysis and re-interpretation of the notion of cause, parallel to the phenomenalist re-interpretation of the notion of "substance" or "thing." Such an analysis was given in David Hume's *Treatise of Human Nature* (1739), and modern phenomenalists in the main follow his line of thought. Hume's aim is to interpret statements about cause and effect in such a way that the relation between a cause and its effect shall be an observable fact, and shall contain nothing mysterious or occult. For unless the words "cause and effect" described something we could observe, they would not, according to Hume, be intelligible to us.

What, then, do I observe in cases in which I should naturally use causal language? I am watching a game of billiards. I observe the event which I might naturally describe by saying that one ball A moved across the table and made or caused another ball B to roll into a pocket. What do I actually *see:* I see a certain sequence of events: first the movement of A, then the touching of A and B, then the movement of B. This temporal sequence of movements, the one which I call the effect following on the one I call the cause, seems to be all the visible relation there is between them.

But obviously, mere temporal sequence is not the same thing as causation; *post hoc* is not the same as *propter hoc;* plenty of other things preceded the movement of my billiard ball in time which were not causes of it. Yet nothing seems to be observable but temporal sequence—first one event, then the other. Whence do I get this notion of the ball being made or caused or forced to move?

If I were pushing the ball myself, I should be aware of myself making a certain muscular effort, *trying* to make it move; and, when I observe the collision of the two balls and the ensuing movement of B, I may perhaps have a vague image of a similar kind of pushing going on between the balls. But if I do, it is clear that this feeling of musclar effort is not observed in the situation presented to my senses, but is a "projection" of my own past feelings in similar situations. For billiard balls do not have muscles, or make efforts, and even if they did, I could not observe what efforts they were making, I could only observe their movements.

Certainly when I see the collision, I expect that the second ball will move—there is a "felt tendency of the mind" to pass from the "cause" to the "effect"; but this is a psychological fact about me, not a physical fact about the balls. There seems nothing in the observed situation corresponding to the words "cause," "power," "force," which I am inclined to apply to it; only the observed sequence of one event on the other. But how, then, do I distinguish between those temporal antecedents of an event which are its causes, and those which are not? How do I establish the difference between *post hoc* and *propter hoc?*

The answer is plain enough; I repeat the experiment, and if the same sequence of events recurs, I conclude that it was a causal and not an accidental sequence. The reason I believe that the movement of the ball was caused by the impact of the other ball, and not by somebody lighting a cigarette at the same time, is that I know by long experience that balls always move when they are struck by other balls moving fairly quickly, whereas they do not usually move when men light cigarettes in their neighbourhood. When medical men inquire into the cause of cancer, what they are looking for is something which always happens to a man before he becomes ill with cancer, just as, when they say that malaria is caused by the bite of a mosquito, they mean that a man has always been bitten by a mosquito before developing malaria. The observable fact which leads us to say that C is the cause of E is the fact that events of the kind C are followed by events of the kind E, not once or sometimes, but whenever they occur.

Causality, as a fact about the world, is then, according to Hume, a relation of invariable sequence. What is required to convert *post hoc* into *propter hoc* is regular repetition. To say that every event has a cause is to say that for any event E there is another event (or complex of "conditions") C such that whenever an event of the kind C occurs, an event of the kind E follows. It is to say that the sequence of phenomena is patterned, systematic; that there are in nature discoverable regularities.

But these regularities are discoverable among the observed phenomena themselves, and not between phenomena and something transcending phenomena. Causation, thus interpreted, is a relation between sense-data. The causes, that is to say, the invariable antecedents, of sense-experiences, are other sense-experiences.

Of course, not all causes are actually observed phenomena. In the analysis of cause, as in the analysis of substance, we must sometimes refer to possible sense-data which are not actual. But to say, for example, that a burst pipe was caused by the formation of a lump of ice which I have not seen, is not to desert the realm of sense-data; it is only to refer to sense-data which were not actually observed, but which might, in principle, have been observed; if I had been in a position to look at the interior of the pipe, I should have seen a lump of ice there.

Thus Hume and his followers do not deny that the relation of cause and effect is a real feature of the world; but they interpret it as a relation between sense-data, actual or possible. So the principle of causality does not carry us beyond the sphere of the observed and the observable, or compel us to admit the existence of "material substance" over and above systems of sense-data.

Thus, on this theory, the material world consists of sets of sense-experiences, together with the fact that an indefinitely large number of other similar sense-experiences might be had under certain specified conditions. Its "substances" are orderly groups of sense-data; and its causal relations are relations of regular sequence between sense-data of specified kinds. The main business of science is to discover causal laws, i.e., to reveal the patterns in that complex of experiences we call Nature. Science tells us what experiences to expect as the sequel to the experiences we are now having, and so renders our knowledge of the world systematic.

Phenomenalism Examined

We thus have, arising out of this discussion, two questions to answer. (1) Is phenomenalism true, that is, can we take the series of sense-data as complete in itself and self-explanatory, or must we postulate some other kind of reality to be its source? (2) Is idealism true, that is, if we assume some other kind of reality to exist, ought we to assume that it is mental?

61. The Relation between Sense-Data and Material Things

As to the first question, there is one point on which the argument seems to me quite conclusive. Our sense-data are not identical with physical objects, whether these are defined as the plain man, or as the physicist, or even as the phenomenalist define them. They are not identical with the physical objects of the plain man or of the physicist, for both these persons require a physical object to remain unchanged in circumstances in which the sense-data certainly change. Both hold that the table does not change its shape when I change the position from which I look at it, whereas the sense-datum *is* changed. Unless these comparatively stable physical objects are assumed, the scientific explanation of sensation itself falls to pieces. As for the phenomenalist, even on his view no sense-datum is identical with a physical object, for the physical object is a system of possibilities, only a few of which can ever be actualised in any one experience. "This is a table" is never a mere record of what I am now observing, but involves the assertion that I and other people will be able to make further observations of a specific kind; and this possibility of further observations, which is part of what I mean when I say "This is a table," is not a matter of direct observation. So in any case our acquaintance with physical objects is not direct but mediate (to call it "inferential" would suggest a much more deliberate, self-consciously logical process than usually takes place). The properties of the sense-datum are not those of the material thing.

Yet—here is a paradox to be resolved—if I set out to describe a material thing, it seems that I invariably find myself describing sense-data. The table is square, brown, hard . . . all these, and all the other things I can say about the table, are expressed in terms of what is observed through the senses. Three alternatives are open to us here. (*a*) We can say that there is after all a real table which has some of the properties of our sense-data, though not all of them (Locke's theory). (*b*) We can say that the table consists of a set of actual and possible sense-data, which between them possess the properties which we commonly assign to "the table" (phenomenalism). (*c*) We can say that a statement like "The table is brown" is more complex than it looks. It must be understood to mean, not that anything in the world is both a table (a material object) and brown, but that there is some material object in existence such that, when it comes into a certain causal relation with a normal percipient under certain conditions, there will be a brown sense-datum in that percipient's experience.

Now for alternative (*a*) I cannot see any good reason. Once it is granted that we do not know the properties of the table directly, I cannot see any convincing reason for holding that it has any of the properties of the sense-datum. It cannot have them all; any arguments which can be brought against its having one of them are equally valid against the others; and we cannot produce any evidence of its having any of them except the observation of the sense-data themselves. We cannot, then, permit ourselves to assign to the material object any property of a sense-datum just because it belongs to that sense-datum. We are not entitled, from the square look of the sense-datum of the table, to infer that the material object is square. We are left with the other two alternatives.

62. The Paradoxes of Phenomenalism

If we take the phenomenalist alternative, let us not do so without being clearly and fully aware of what it involves. (1) It involves the denial that physical objects are permanent, or exist unperceived. It must be granted to the phenomenalists that when I say "There is a table upstairs," I am at least implying that if you were to go upstairs and look (given normal eyesight, normal lighting, etc.) you would have certain visual sense-data. But it seems quite clear to me that this is not the whole nor the essential part of what I am asserting. For when I say that the table is there, I am stating something about what exists or happens *in fact, now;* my statement is about the actual present, and not, as the phenomenalists make it, about the possible future. And if the phenomenalist account is to be accepted, we must say that this statement is a mistake. There is nothing at all in the attic now; there is no attic now at all; for there is nobody perceiving it.

(2) We must very seriously revise our opinions about the nature of causality. As a rule, we are in the habit of believing that a cause is something which actually exists or occurs, and that something which does not actually exist or occur can have no effects. This opinion must be given up if we accept the phenomenalist view. For on that view, to say that the bursting of pipes is caused by the formation of ice in them is to say that whenever one observes or could observe sense-data of the set constituting a burst pipe, one either has or could have previously observed sense-data of the set constituting a lump of ice inside that pipe. But quite clearly, in practically every instance of this rule, nobody does actually observe the ice; the sense-data of the ice are possible, not actual. That is to say, causality in such a case is a relation between something and nothing, between an actually observed burst, and a hypothetical proposition to the effect that if something had happened which did not happen and in practice could not have happened, then something else would have happened which also did not happen. This interpretation flouts our usual assumption that what might have happened but did not happen can have no effects. The actual material agents of physics and common sense must be replaced by a set of hypothetical facts relating to unfulfilled conditions. If this is so, it is difficult to see why we should suppose that these hypothetical propositions are true. If I leave a fire in my room, I expect it to be warm on my return; but is this not because I believe that the fire is still now burning, a real present fire exercising

an influence on a real present atmosphere? I cannot see what reason can be given for expecting the room to be warmed, independently of my reasons for supposing that the fire *is* burning *now* (and not that, *if* I went and looked, I should see flame). I can see reason for believing in regularities in nature holding between one event and another; but no reason at all for believing in regularities holding between one event which happened and another which might have happened but did not.

(3) A similar paradox arises with regard to other persons. According to the phenomenalist theory, all the statements I make about the consciousness of other people must be interpreted in terms of actual or possible observations of my own. A statement like "Jones is bored but he is not giving any sign of it" is a contradiction in terms, for on this theory the boredom *is* the sign. The only experiences I can intelligibly talk about or think about are my own, and whatever is not expressible in terms of actual or possible observations of mine is not intelligible to me. That is, there is no good argument for phenomenalism which is not an equally good argument for solipsism—the doctrine that the only experience in the world is my experience, and the only person existing in the universe is myself.

These paradoxical conclusions have been accepted by able philosophers, and one cannot therefore say that they are beyond belief. But they are markedly at variance with the ordinary assumptions, not only of common sense, but also of scientific investigation (for, whatever some scientists may manage to persuade themselves, they are not concerned only with the cataloguing and ordering of phenomena, but believe themselves to be dealing with permanent and independent objects). Hence we must demand very strong reasons indeed for accepting them.

SUGGESTED READINGS

Perceiving the Material World

Anthologies

Hirst, R. J. (ed.). *Perception and the External World.* New York: The Macmillan Company, 1965.

Nagel, E., and Brandt, R. (eds.). *Meaning and Knowledge.* New York: Harcourt, Brace & World, 1965.

Swartz, R. J. (ed.). *Perceiving, Sensing, and Knowing.* Garden City, N.Y.: Doubleday & Company, Inc., 1965.

Warnock, G. J. *The Philosophy of Perception.* Oxford: Oxford University Press, 1967.

Valuable Single-Author Books

Armstrong, D. M. *Perception and the Physical World.* London: Routledge and Kegan Paul, 1961.

Austin, J. L. *Sense and Sensibilia.* Oxford: Clarendon Press, 1962.

Ayer, A. J. *The Foundations of Empirical Knowledge.* New York: St. Martin's Press, 1956.

Chisholm, R. M. *Perceiving: A Philosophical Study.* Ithaca, N.Y.: Cornell University Press, 1957.

Dretske, F. I. *Seeing and Knowing.* Chicago: The University of Chicago Press, 1969.

Locke, Don. *Perception and our Knowledge of the External World.* London: George Allen & Unwin Ltd., 1967.

Lovejoy, A. O. *The Revolt Against Dualism.* Wilmette, Ill.: Open Court, 1930.

Mandelbaum, M. *Philosophy, Science, and Sense Perception.* Baltimore: Johns Hopkins Press, 1964.

Price, H. H. *Perception.* London: Methuen & Co., 1933.

Is the Concept of Sensory Appearances Confused?

Austin, J. L. *Sense and Sensibilia,* 1962, 20–32, 44–54.

Ayer, A. J. *Metaphysics and Common Sense.* London: Macmillan and Company, Ltd., 1969. Chap. 9. [A reply to Austin.]

Barnes, W. H. F. "On Seeing and Hearing," in H. D. Lewis, (ed.), *Contemporary British Philosophy,* 1956.

——————. "The Myth of Sense-Data," *Proceedings.* The Aristotelian Society, 45 (1944–45).

Black, M., and Firth, R. Symposium: "Phenomenalism," American Philosophical Association, Eastern Division, I (1952). Philadelphia: University of Pennsylvania Press.

Broad, C. D. *Scientific Thought.* New York: Harcourt, Brace & World, 1927. Chaps. 7, 8. [Reprinted, in more complete form than the present text, in Swartz.]

Chisholm, R. M. "The Theory of Appearing," in M. Black, (ed.), *Philosophical Analysis*. Ithaca, N.Y.: Cornell University Press, 1950. [Reprinted in Swartz.]

Firth, R. "Sense Data and the Percept Theory," *Mind,* 48 (1949) and 49 (1950). [Reprinted in Swartz.]

Moore, G. E. *Philosophical Studies*. London: Routledge and Kegan Paul, Ltd., 1922. Chap. 5.

Paul, G. A. "Is There a Problem About Sense Data?" London: The Aristotelian Society, Supplementary Vol. 15, 1946. [Reprinted in Swartz.]

Price, H. H. "Appearing and Appearances," *American Philosophical Quarterly,* 1, 3–19.

——————————. *Perception,* 1933. Chap. 1.

Quinton, A. M. "The Problem of Perception," *Mind,* 64 (1955). [Reprinted in Swartz.]

Ryle, G. "Sensation," in H. D. Lewis, (ed.), *Contemporary British Philosophy*. New York: Macmillan, 1956. [Reprinted in Swartz.]

——————————. *The Concept of Mind*. London: Hutchinson's University Library, 1949, 213–220. [Reprinted in Hirst.]

What Is Proved by the Fact of Illusion?

Armstrong, D. M. "Berkeley's Puzzle About the Water That Seems both Hot and Cold," *Analysis,* 15, 1955.

Austin, J. L. *Sense and Sensibilia,* 1962, 20–32.

Ayer, A. J. *Foundations of Empirical Knowledge,* 1956. Chap. 1. [Excerpted in Hirst.]

——————————. *The Central Questions of Philosophy*. London: Weidenfeld and Nicholson, 1973. Chap. 4.

Butchvarov, P. *The Concept of Knowledge*. Evanston: Northwestern University Press, 1970. Part 3.

Firth, R. "Austin and the Argument from Illusion," *Philosophical Review,* 73 (1964).

Lovejoy, A. O. *The Revolt Against Dualism,* 1930. Chap. 1. [Excerpted in Hirst.]

Myers, G. "Perception and the Time-lag Argument," *Analysis,* 17 (1957).

Price, H. H. *Perception,* 1933. Chap. 2.

——————————. "The Argument from Illusion," in H. D. Lewis, (ed.), *Contemporary British Philosophy*. New York: Macmillan, 1956.

Quinton, A. M. *The Nature of Things*. London: Routledge and Kegan Paul, 1973. Chap. 7.

Taylor, R., and Duggan, T. "On Seeing Double," *Philosophical Quarterly,* 8 (1958).

Phenomenalism

Armstrong, D. M. *Perception and the Physical World*. London: Routledge and Kegan Paul, 1961, 47–80.

Ayer, A. J. *Foundations of Empirical Knowledge,* 1956. Chap. 5. [Excerpted in Nagel and Brandt.]

Berlin, I. "Empirical Propositions and Hypothetical Statements," *Mind,* 59 (1950).

Chisholm, R. M. "The Problem of Empiricism," *Journal of Philosophy,* 45 (1948). [Reprinted in Swartz.]

Firth, R. "Radical Empiricism and Perceptual Relativity," *Philosophical Review,* 59 (1950).

Hardie, W. F. R. "The Paradox of Phenomenalism," *Proceedings,* The Aristotelian Society, 46 (1945–46).

Lewis, C. I. *An Analysis of Knowledge and Valuation.* LaSalle, Ill.: Open Court, 1946. Chap. 8. [Reprinted in Swartz.]

——————————. "Professor Chisholm and Empiricism," *Journal of Philosophy,* 45 (1948). [Reprinted in Swartz.]

Mill, J. S. *An Examination of Sir William Hamilton's Philosophy,* 1865. Chap. 11. [Reprinted in Feinberg.]

Price, H. H. *Hume's Theory of the External World.* Oxford: Clarendon Press, 1940, 177–192.

——————————. "Mill's View of the External World," *Proceedings,* The Aristotelian Society, 27 (1926–27).

Sellars, W. *Science, Perception, and Reality.* New York: Humanities Press, 1963. Chap. 3.

Stace, W. T. "The Refutation of Realism," *Mind,* 43 (1934). [Reprinted in A. Pap and P. Edwards, *A Modern Introduction to Philosophy.* New York: The Free Press, 1965.]

The Causal Theory

Broad, C. D. *The Mind and Its Place in Nature.* New York: Harcourt, Brace & World, 1927.

Grice, H. P. "The Causal Theory of Perception," The Aristotelian Society, London. Supplementary Vol. 35, 1961. [Reprinted in Swartz, excerpted in Nagel and Brandt.]

Mandelbaum, M. *Philosophy, Science, and Sense Perception.* Baltimore: Johns Hopkins Press, 1964. Chaps. 1, 4.

Critics of the Causal Theory

Armstrong, D. M. *Perception and the Physical World.* London: Routledge and Kegan Paul, 1961. Chap. 9.

Ayer, A. J. *The Central Questions of Philosophy.* London: Weidenfeld and Nicholson, 1973. Chaps. 4 and 5.

——————————. *Foundations of Empirical Knowledge, 1947.* Chap. 4.

Mundle, C. W. "Common Sense vs. Hirst's Theory of Perception," *Proceedings,* The Aristotelian Society, 60 (1959–60).

Price, H. H. *Perception,* 1933. Chap. 4.

Quinton, A. M. *The Nature of Things.* London: Routledge and Kegan Paul, 1973. Chap. 7.

Russell, B. *The Analysis of Matter.* New York: Dover Publications, Inc., 1927. Chap. 20. [Excerpted in Hirst.]

Sellars, R. W. "A Statement of Critical Realism," *Revue Internationale de Philosophie* I, 1938–39. [Excerpted in Hirst.]

Whiteley, C. H. "Physical Objects," *Philosophy,* 34 (1959). [Reprinted in Nagel and Brandt.]

Index